UNIDENTIFIED FLYING OBJECTS

Fact or Fiction?

By
Lillian Crowner Desguin

ISBN: 0-89412–188–X (soft cover)

ISBN: 0-89412–189-8 (library bound)

AEGEAN PARK PRESS
P.O. Box 2837
Laguna Hills, California 92654

(714) 586-8811

Manufactured in The United States of America

ACKNOWLEDGMENTS

I would like to express
my sincere appreciation to my friends and family,
who have helped me in so many ways.

In addition, a special thank you goes to
The Weekly World News,
The National Examiner,
and
The Sun.
for the right to reprint their
excellent articles
which are included in this book.

Lillian Crowner Desguin, 1992

About the Cover

On the cover is a photograph of a painting by a local artist, painted under the direction of Jimmy Flynn, from his description of the UFO he watched in the Florida swamps some 25 years ago. The craft was a tarnished metal color, cone-shaped, and about 36 ft. high. *See Chapter Two.*

CONTENTS

Chapter One	Early Sightings — UFO Scuttlebutt My Opinions in the Fifties and Sixties	1
Chapter Two	Early Sightings — Hypnosis Early Columns in the Public Opinion	25
Chapter Three	More Speakers — Space Probes — UFO Invasion UFOs and Crystals	57
Chapter Four	Time Travel — Cross-breeding — Astrology and Charts Noah's Ark — Reincarnation — Bigfoot And Much, Much More	78
Chapter Five	Reincarnation — Dreams — Possession	129
Chapter Six	UFO Kidnappings — World Abductions	149
Chapter Seven	Space Probes from Heaven	179
Chapter Eight	The Faces Found in Space — The Three Faces of Mars, Venus and the Moon — Bigfoot	187
Chapter Nine	Healings and Rescues — The Devil's Triangle Time Travel — Atlantis	211
Chapter Ten	Personal Opinions After 40 Years — Epilogue Special Sightings	227
	References	241
	Alphabetical Index	243

CHAPTER ONE

Early Sightings — UFO Scuttlebutt

My Introduction to UFOs . . . 2
Bruce Stevenson Learns about "Flying Saucers" . . . 2
A Visit with Rev. M.J. Miller . . . 3
Meeting Edna . . . 3
Jack and George . . . 4
We Entertain Desmond Leslie . . . 5
The Reeves Come to Columbus . . . 5
The Mexican and the Spaceman . . . 5
Mark Probert and the "Inner Circle" . . . 6
Pattern of Rebirth Shown . . . 7
November, 1896 Sightings — *Public Opinion* . . . 8
U.S. Invaded by UFOs 100 Years Ago — *National Examiner* . . . 8
The 1950 Ohio State–Michigan Game . . . 9
Aliens Who Can Go Through Walls . . . 10
George Van Tassel and the Spaceman . . . 10
The Andreason Affair . . . 10
Writer Believes She Saw Her First Saucer — *Public Opinion* . . . 11
UFOs are Bugging My Brain — *Sun* . . . 11
Two UFOs and a Headache . . . 12
Mr. X and the Captain of a Spaceship . . . 12
The Truman Bethurum Story . . . 13
Jack W. Grant and "The Saucers" . . . 13
Dan Fry's Two-Way Trip to N.Y. . . . 14
One Way Trip? . . . 14

My Opinions in the Fifties and Sixties

NICAP . . . 15
In Defense of George . . . 16
Peter Hurkos and the UFO . . . 17
The Grain Buyer from California . . . 18
What Happened to Dr. Hynek? . . . 19
UFOs and Dr. M.K. Jessup . . . 19
Moon Craters and the Moon Bridge . . . 20
Astronomy and the Intergalactic Looking Society . . . 20
Kentucky's Little Green Men . . . 20
Six Oaks and the UFOs . . . 21
You be the Judge . . . 22
UFO Scuttlebutt . . . 22
UFOs — Poem . . . 24

MY INTRODUCTION TO UFOs

It happened about the time that George Adamski's book hit the market. A couple I knew needed a babysitter so they could go out and celebrate New Year's Eve.

That's how No. 1 son got his first babysitting job. It was a long night and Jon looked around for something to do. He picked up a copy of Adamski's *Flying Saucers Have Landed*. It was co-authored by Desmond Leslie, who was a cousin of Winston Churchill and had a few things to say on this subject.

The next morning Jon told me he had read the book and thought it might be something worth checking. I called my acquaintance and asked where this book could be found. Frank said he had borrowed it from a friend but had to return it the following day; however, if I wanted it for the day, I might pick it up. That's how I spent New Year's Day. By evening I had decided to go look for other evidence to support such a tale.

It wasn't long before I found Cedric Allingham's book, *Flying Saucers From Mars*. The most impressive thing in this book came from the sons of a dentist in England. His boys had taken their camera and gone for a walk. When they came home they told of seeing a "flying craft." They had been able to take several pictures and when developed, they matched those taken by George Adamski but from a different angle. By complicated restructuring, the pictures were found to be identical even though they had been taken several thousand miles apart.

I made up my mind: never again would I look into this subject unless I could find something that was within my own locality. I thought I was safe but not so, it wasn't long before a local lawyer told me his secretary was a friend of a family near Circleville, Ohio. The girl's father has had an impressive sighting. It happened on February 1, 1948, and had been kept hidden for a couple of years.

BRUCE STEVENSON LEARNS ABOUT "FLYING SAUCERS"

Bruce Stevenson was in the barber shop listening to two men arguing whether there was such a thing as a "flying saucer." He couldn't keep quiet any longer. Bruce had everything one looks for when it's necessary to be impressive. If President Bush had chosen him for one of those Washington jobs, even Congress couldn't have found something to complain about! Though it was a couple of years later, the story was carried in the Columbus, Ohio papers.

I couldn't resist a short afternoon trip to Circleville. My husband and I met the Stevensons at their home just west of town. It was a large farm with much acreage and numerous buildings.

Bruce went to the kitchen, pulled out a plate, and placing it upside down, put a soup bowl on top of it. "Now it was something like this," he said. We walked into the backyard where he stood hanging onto the clothesline.

It was 2 a.m. on February 1, 1948. He had just been in the house for a coffee break after spending time in the farrowing house with his prize pigs. Five sows had chosen to produce at 2 degrees below zero. He couldn't risk anything happening to them — they were too valuable to lose. This building was a 100 ft. quonset hut with several openings in its top for ventilation. These were opened enough to show blue germicidal lights shining through from below. Between this building and the house were two other structures. One was a shed that held all the heating units for the farrowing house, the other was a farm building running horizontal to the quonset hut.

As Bruce stood there, he said, "I knew if there was a fire it would have started in the heating shed. It wasn't there; it was right above the farrowing house." He went on, "It was a large orange object that stood on edge as if someone were standing looking into those vents. I ran into the yard and held onto this clothesline. Just then, it turned to a flat position and floated towards me." He thought it would take the top off the chimney of the farm building in front of him. This building was 18 ft. high and 100 ft. long. The object stopped about 65 ft. away from him. It dimmed in color while it was in this position. It was approximately 60 feet across and 10 to 12 ft. high. The rim of the ship seemed to be surrounded with a spot of light which circled it. All he could think of was "light induction." Bruce said he knew that all his previous thoughts about UFOs would have to be chucked.

The yard where we stood was separated from this building by a fence, a dirt road, and a few yards of grass which was deeply covered with snow. Bruce wanted to go nearer but received the impression it wasn't wise. He was "told" they would be back again someday. This caused him to do a lot of thinking; he decided he has had a good life but "IF" they ever came back he would go without question. The ship turned a deeper orange, made a right-hand turn, and disappeared so quickly he couldn't be sure what happened to it. There was a long farm building on his left that blocked his view.

I never saw the Stevensons again but I met his sister and brother-in-law who were English professors at Ohio State University. Later I met the professor's brother who was a science and math teacher in Mansfield, Ohio. Dan Haber believed that anything Bruce Stevenson said was good enough to convince him. Dan spent the rest of his life trying to find the truth about "flying saucers." He remained my very close friend and we both did research in many of the same areas.

A VISIT WITH REV. M.J. MILLER

It was along about this time I began to wonder what truth could be found in such a report. I thought I wanted to know the truth, but that was before I realized that it might differ from what I wanted to believe. I worried about this for several weeks and finally made up my mind to drop in to Rev. Millard J. Miller's office in the United Brethren Church in Westerville, Ohio. After all my concern it didn't bother him a bit! He just said, "If you can keep your cool, and want to look into this subject, I don't see why you shouldn't." (Or something like that.)

Long before this, my friend Ila Grindell had told me quite seriously that she wouldn't be surprised to find that we weren't alone. Ila was a much respected scholar and one whose opinion I valued highly.

The following comments date back to 1945 but the following information is a full-page advertisement in *The Weekly World News,* August 29, 1989. "UFOs and The Space Brothers Want You To Survive."

It's the same old story — pretty soon now — anytime now — all hell is going to break loose! And if you've got the right vibes — the space brothers will pick you up and take you somewhere. Nobody knows whether it's going to be a global war, a polar shift, or some other form of utter chaos, but many psychics, spiritual leaders, and even scientists are convinced something will happen....

Some of those who have contributed to this advertised material include "new agers" Brad and Francie Stieger, "space channel" Robert Short, the spiritual group Mark Age, UFO communicator Jane Allyson, parapsychologist Warren Freiberg, and the space-being known as Ashtar.

The one that bothers me is "Ashtar." Ashtar was the captain of a spaceship who contacted an old lady who lived in Massachusetts in 1945. According to his message, "they" wanted to see how my friend would react to that abnormal sighting over downtown Columbus, Ohio. Just how that woman was able to know the name and address of Edna, who wasn't about to let her own family know that she had been seeing "impossible things," is beyond me. It's no wonder she hid the letter in the bottom of a trunk.

Is it possible that Ashtar contacted a lot of other people and gave all of them information about spaceships which are supposed to come to our aid in a time of catastrophe? Or rescue those that need to go somewhere? I'm never sure whether it's our bodies or souls that are going to be saved, but perhaps we'll find out in due time.

MEETING EDNA

From that time on I seemed to meet people who had some knowledge about this subject. I met Edna Kaehele, who had written a book about *Living with Cancer.* It was printed in *Reader's Digest* and gave quite an interesting account of her fight to overcome what seemed to be a hopeless brush with death. She managed to pull through and stretched her life out another twenty years.

It was at this time she told me of her encounter with a UFO. Edna had three children and lived north of Broad Street in Columbus, Ohio. In 1945, she was packing to move to Denver. One evening, as she was carrying cartons from a storage shed, she looked up in amazement.

There, over what appeared to be the center of Columbus, was a large cigar-shaped ship. She saw a ramp coming out its side. It had lighted windows with people moving inside.

Edna lived with two sisters and knew better than to tell such a tale. She headed straight for the bathroom where she sat and prayed that it would go away. After ten minutes she went back to look again, sure enough it was gone!

The next morning she hurried to the porch for the morning paper. She wanted to see what the news would have to report. She was thankful she hadn't said a word. There was no one to share her thoughts and frustration. No one had reported this sighting.

Edna moved to Denver and after several weeks found it necessary to go for a medical check-up. A grim-faced doctor told her to start packing again. She had advanced cancer and not more than six months to live. By Christmas she was at Columbus, in Grant Hospital. She was there to die. Even hospitals don't want guests for Christmas, so they released her so she might have one more holiday with her family. The doctors didn't know the power of a determined woman. Edna had a sister who decided she wasn't going to allow her to die and she didn't. Day by day she nursed her back to health. Edna wrote a couple of books, and began enjoying life again.

Kenneth Arnold reported his sighting in 1947, Bruce Stevenson in 1948, but Edna's tale dates back to 1945, which makes it a very early and unusual experience. Nearly two years after returning to Columbus, she received a letter from an old lady who lived in Boston, Mass. The woman told her she lived with a dentist's family. Edna knew no one in Massachusetts and had never been there.

This person told her she had been instructed to give her a message from Ashtar, who was the captain of a spaceship. He said she had been chosen for her sighting to see how she would react. She certainly reacted: she hid that letter in the bottom of a trunk in the attic.

Years later, when Major Donald Keyhoe came to Columbus, Edna heard a man in the audience describe what he and his son had seen back at the same time she had her sighting. It helped — that's probably why she gathered up the nerve to tell me her story.

One evening years later, Edna was driving from Columbus to my home north of Worthington. She had her second and only other sighting. She saw a large spool-like object in the sky. On each end it had a lighted section with what appeared to be portholes. The portion on each end was spinning in opposite directions.

As she was looking at it, the word "Shekinah" came into her mind. She felt she had known it before. Not knowing the word or how to spell it she didn't know what to do. A couple of months later she came across the Hebrew word, "Shekinah" and noted its definition. (Manifestation of God, altar of God, and dwelling place of God.) There are a number of spool-shaped sightings.

JACK AND GEORGE

The '50s were exciting times. George Adamski was in Columbus. I read the notice in the news and noted that he was the guest of Jack Grant, on E. Wilson Bridge Rd. That did it, I thought, the thing to do was to go hunting. After all, he wasn't more than two miles away; I didn't know Jack Grant, but it was worth a try.

It was a Saturday afternoon and it wasn't long before I found the doorway. From the doorstep there was a good view through a large adjacent window. There was George, comfortably stretched out, and it became obvious he intended to stay that way.

After a few trials with a gonging bell, I decided no one wanted to see me. I walked about fifty feet towards my car and thought to myself, "Why should I give up this easily; perhaps a faint heart never won a fair lady." With that I turned around, went back to the door and let the boys really have it. It appeared I was on the losing side, I retraced my steps again for seventy-five feet. With that I stopped and said out loud, "The heck with them, they can just answer that door," and that's just what they did! It was obvious I was going to wear out the bell, it would be easier to just say, "Go away."

Jack opened the door and George changed his position. I let him know I had read his book and would like a chance to visit with him. We made a deal: if I'd come back tomorrow at 2 p.m., I would be allowed a little special attention. That's how I met Jack, and George, and I've always been glad that I kept ringing that bell!

Sunday afternoon I took my husband and dutifully appeared at the proper time. A half dozen others did too; there were several who wanted to know if this man was really on the level. By the end of the visit I'm not sure I was any more convinced, but at least I had to admit George was a likeable and interesting man.

It wasn't long before I learned that I shouldn't accept or reject what I heard or read, but rather to put it on a mental shelf and shove it from one end to the other according to how impressed I was with each case. What a shelf! It's become a very big one. Sightings have been shoved first one way and then back again not because of the tales that were told but rather my own experience caused me to change my view of what was on the shelf. I felt a little like the young man who left home for several years. When he returned he was surprised how much more intelligent his father seemed to be.

WE ENTERTAIN DESMOND LESLIE

Eventually Desmond Leslie arrived from England to make his pitch for *Flying Saucers Have Landed*. After all, he was a co-author and equally interested in its success. The lecture was to be given in the new Veteran's Memorial Auditorium in Columbus, Ohio on October 26, 1956.

The day of the program I received a call asking if I would help sell tickets that evening. I've never learned to say no, so that's what I did.

During the day I threw together a batch of chop suey, put a pile of plates on the table, and thought maybe someone would come home with me. They did; we had about fourteen people, including Desmond Leslie, Bryant and Helen Reeve (who wrote *Flying Saucer Pilgrimage*), Monroe Courtright, editor of the *Westerville Public Opinion*, and Roy Metz, a local lawyer.

Desmond did quite a bit of playing around on the Steinway and there was a lot of just plain getting acquainted with the person nearest to you. I'm not sure I knew anyone except Monroe and Roy.

Most of us wanted to believe there was something true in this book. It was a lot like grabbing at straws. Many things about it caused me to push it pretty far back on my mental shelf.

THE REEVES COME TO COLUMBUS

Bryant and Helen became my very close friends for the rest of their lives. The Reeves wrote *Flying Saucer Pilgrimage*, and also *The Advent of the Cosmic Viewpoint*. They made a 23,000-mile trip out west and took George Adamski with them where he was to lecture in Mexico City. Their trip was in January 1955.

Bryant also attempted to give his own lecture. He had recently retired from American Motors. He was a graduate from Yale University and the Massachusetts Institute of Technology. He hoped to educate his audience to the reality that we are all "space people" since we all live in space. The translator asked the audience, "How many of you have seen a spaceman?"

His technique backfired. After a very long pause a man in the back row held up his hand. That ended Bryant's lecture. Someone dragged a Mexican chauffeur to the front of the room. His name was Salvadór Villanueva Medina. He had a wife and seven children and a job. That's what worried him. He was afraid to tell of his contact for fear of losing his job.

THE MEXICAN AND THE SPACEMAN

Salvador had little choice, his audience wanted to know about that spaceman. It was hard not to believe him.

The next day he took the Reeves and their friends many miles to the place of his contact and convinced them he had really talked to a spaceman and in Spanish!

In 1953 he had picked up a couple of Americans who wanted their car driven to Laredo. During the afternoon the car developed trouble. They were forced to leave Salvador, while they went for help.

While he was waiting, Salvador crawled under the car in hopes he could repair what was wrong. He heard a noise and glanced out to see a pair of unusual feet and legs. He crawled out and couldn't believe his eyes! The man was about 4 ft. tall with a very white face. He wore a thick blue belt with holes in it. It was as if there were electric lights in them. (One evening at a banquet I sat next to a woman minister who described a similar belted alien.) Salvador noticed that these little lights flashed on and off. He was too frightened to talk. Finally he asked if he were an aviator. The man pointed to a mound where he had landed. Then he said he came from a place at much space. (quote)

Later that night, he came back with another person like himself. They sat and talked until nearly morning. They said they were from a place where there was not much room between people.

Their roads were made of metal and their vehicles took power directly from the road. There were no intersections. Their streets were on different levels, and their sidewalks were like conveyor belts. They produced all the food they needed and each house had its own garden and water. They did not have tall trees or tall buildings. Their buildings were continuous. He asked about their power, and was told energy was generated in productive centers which took advantage of inexhaustible solar rays. (This all sounded very far out in 1953. Today, we know space beings make people understand, regardless of any particular language).

Salvador was told they were men just like he was, but had lived through this experience years ago. It was their job to report all data from our planet.

He walked toward the craft with them. While he was getting muddy they were floating above the ground. The aliens offered to show him their ship. This frightened him; he ran back to the car and watched them take off over the trees. His wife told him he must never tell this story for fear of losing his job.

MARK PROBERT AND THE "INNER CIRCLE"

On their return trip from Mexico the Reeves took an apartment in California, where they could be near the "sensitive" or medium, Mark Probert. They were able to make many tapes of the various controls who took over his body. They brought through much knowledge and wisdom which captivated those who listened. It was there they met Dr. Meade Layne, who also was aware of Mark's abilities and made many tapes of his own. Some of these are concerning spacecraft and other kinds of life in space. Much of this was made in 1950 and 1951; a number have been put into printed form. Seven of these sessions have been published by W.L. Moore at Burbank, CA and are on the market at the present time.

Mark and Irene also published some of their own meetings. Their book was written under the name "The Magic Bag" and indicated that life in our present state is much like the outside of that bag. When the bag is turned inside out we see life on its other side. The idea being that it's all one and the same thing. The bag is consciousness, and the bag is all.

When the Reeves came to live in Columbus they brought many tapes from all their travels. This included numerous contact cases. Besides these tapes, many of these people came to talk to local groups. Not knowing enough to say no helped me to acquire the title of "The Jr Hostess with the Mostest." It meant that I took care of our guests, found a place for them to speak, and gave them a place to sleep, as well as enough food to keep them alive. People who spoke on any of these subjects were not doing it for money. If they made it to the next meeting with the cash they acquired by passing a hat they were lucky.

The Proberts came as my guests several times. We had dinner meetings, library meetings, and whatever meetings. The whatever meetings were best, and generally contained higher quality vibrations. Of course, if you don't know about vibrations you're in trouble. I guess I'd have to think about the way people feel when they're walking through a department store at Christmas. The music radiating from every section doesn't allow a negative feeling in the place. It amazes me to find how apropos the material they gave pertains to information we are given today.

We had quite a group of people who thought they wanted to know — just what they wanted to know was questionable.

Besides the Proberts, we had tapes of George Van Tassel, Dan Fry, George Adamski, Dr. George Hunt Williamson, Neva Dell Hunter, Orfeo Angeluci and many other guests. This was before our government had everyone convinced there wasn't any such thing as a "flying saucer." As for little bug-eyed aliens, forget it — we were assured this was all poppycock, they had investigated and found all such cases were hoaxes.

No one could have been much higher on our list than Mark Probert. How a former bellhop, jockey, and dancer could become a trans-medium, and bring through all those people, "who were out of this world," was hard to imagine. He did and we listened and we understand how Shirley Maclaine found an entity who is influencing her life.

After Mark and Irene were married she found he was talking in his sleep. She couldn't understand what he said, it wasn't in English. He was unaware of what was happening. She insisted he see a psychiatrist.

The doctor assured her she was imagining all this nonsense and told her to forget it. She told him to imagine he was being paid because he wouldn't be! The next doctor to see him was Dr. Meade Layne. He recognized him as a trans-medium and found him speaking in at least seven foreign languages as well as a couple they couldn't identify. Mark didn't know any foreign languages and all of this seemed unbelievable.

The Yada Di Shiite (translated honored chief of the Shiite Clans) lived in the civilization of Yu, located in the Himalayan Mountains, 500,000 years ago. Yada was the main and most influential member of the group; however, all these personalities were interesting. They included Professor Alfred Luntz, a clergyman of the High Episcopal Church of England. This personality is a very knowledgeable and interesting man. He is often in control of Mark's body. Then there is a Dr. Sukuto Nikkioi and also a Holy man, Arakashi, whose teachings were Buddhistic. Ramond Natalli was an astronomer in Rome, Italy. Lo Sunyat was no doubt responsible for one of those foreign languages. Kay Ting, another member of what is called "The Inner Circle," a term used to describe the group of beings who made themselves known through Mark's mediumship. Ali Ben Casi, Maharaja Natcha Tramalaki, Martin Lattimore Lingford and Lao-Tse are all personalities who have given scientific lectures through this man. Even a Catholic nun comes through. Mark's body becomes that of a female in tone, action, and words. The controls told us that all things and places have an etheric counterpart which is what brings our material world into being. The "flying discs" or spacecrafts that were being seen came mostly from the etheric civilization and could exist in space itself even though we weren't aware of them.

The controls always made it clear they were only giving their views and that we should always search for truth, wherever we might find it. The personalities had different accents and occasionally conflicting opinions.

Most people were looking for something that had a little more solidity. We were told that life existed in all kinds of descriptions and included beings that looked a lot like us to those who didn't look a bit like us. As time went on many more would be seen. There were abductions, but as a rule these discs were more concerned with checking us out and weren't harmful as long as we didn't get too inquisitive. Capt. Thomas Mantell was an example of one who became too inquisitive; his remains were disintegrated when he tried to chase a craft near Godman Base, Kentucky, on January 7, 1948.

The "Etherians" were known as the "Guardians." Since they lived in another dimension they didn't have to operate in the same manner as we do. They can make themselves visible to us and as solid as they choose to be.

Many people wanted to contact them; they soon found if there was any contacting to be done it would have to come from the visitors themselves.

The controls told us that people went to an astral zone after death where they were thrown back into physical life again or progressed to a higher plane. This might go on for an unlimited time until that person decided this kind of life was not what he wanted.

PATTERN OF REBIRTH SHOWN

A friend of mine told me that his wife came to him in a dream after her death. He shared several outstanding experiences.

At one time she showed him a huge room that looked like a basement. He saw people marching in one door and out the other. (I'm sure it never occurred to him that this could have symbolized the low astral and referred to those who marched back and forth into the pattern of rebirth again and again.) Then he saw an elevator in which she was taken far above this place. It opened into a City of Gold which was bathed in light and beauty. He knew this was where she would be.

Back in 1890, Mary Baker Eddy published her book *Science and Health.* In the preface she says, "The time for thinkers has come." Truth, independent of doctrines and time-honored systems, knocks at the portal of humanity. Contentment with the past, and the cold conventionality of materialism, are crumbling away. "Ignorance of God" is no longer the stepping stone to faith.

Again on page 264 Mrs. Eddy says, "As mortals gain more correct views of God and man, multitudinous objects of creation, which before were invisible, will become visible."

These statements are just as true today as they were then. The multitudinous objects Mrs. Eddy talks about sound very much like the Etheric discs Mark Probert's controls are describing. When our government decides to take us into its confidence this will need to be considered.

The following article, one I wrote years ago, shows that "Flying Saucers," "Flying Discs," "Spacecraft," "the Indians," "Flying Canoes," "Flying Machines," "Sky Vehicles," and UFOs are all related phenomena.

NOVEMBER 19, 1896 SIGHTING

***Public Opinion,* March 2, 1961**

It is said that on November 19, 1896, astonished citizens up and down the Sacramento Valley of California were favored with a manifestation of scientific achievement the like of which has never been forgotten. A flying machine, whose origin is still in dispute maneuvered from Oroville to San Francisco from Oakland to Sacramento.

"The San Francisco Call", ran a full front page on Nov. 19 on the sightings. A couple or rival papers tried to question the veracity of these tales but were so overrun by reports From their own subscribers that they soon thought better of it.

This sky vehicle was able to move straight up and down with the greatest of ease and without any noticeable noise. It swooped and soared over the roof tops of San Francisco and glided over the mining shacks of Cherokee in Butte County.

In all pictures it is shown to be wingless, and apparently operated a huge spotlight that far surpassed light which was produced at that time. The ship came down through rain swept skies and startled hundreds of people.

Mayor Sutro of San Francisco witnessed the slow approach of the object as it sailed toward the Golden Gate from somewhere above the Pacific Ocean. Both his family and servants shared a viewing of this sky monster. Mayor Davies of Oakland also saw this craft and watched its maneuvers.

One of Camptonville' s leading citizens reported a landing made just outside of town and five of the strongest and bravest young men ventured to investigate. They claimed there was no hostility. Only one crew member they saw, failed to be able to understand them and vice versa.

It was at the time the Spanish American war was brewing. This in itself was enough to create wonder as to what new gadget had been cooked up by the enemy. Both the railroad and the government investigated and found plenty of eye-witnesses but no evidence.

The saucer-like drawings which were made at that time are not too unlike present day drawings and descriptions. The chances are that this phenomenon was closely related to the ones of today."●

☐ *When I started to write this book my main idea was to show how saucer stories of the '50s relate to those of today.*

October 10, 1989, the *National Examiner* carried a column by Julia Spain. Don't ever fail to remember that this is not a new subject but one which has been forever with us waiting for man to mature sufficiently to understand more about the Creator's creation.

U.S. WAS INVADED BY UFOs — NEARLY 100 YEARS AGO!

***National Examiner,* October, 1989**

by Julia Spain

Flying saucers invaded the U.S — nearly a century ago! They were spotted in September, 1896, by California astronomers, who first thought the mysterious lights in the sky were new stars or comets.

But by October they had come frighteningly close, and observers discovered them to be six lights in a triangular pattern, with six more in an oval grouping directly behind them.

On December 20, the strange lights appeared closer still, and public concern started to grow.

A prospector named Harry Lutz discovered three scorch marks totaling 100 feet in circumference on a hillside near Sacramento, and experts took soil samples of the area.

Amazingly, a strange, white, ash-like substance collected at the scene seemed to emit a continual warmth as if it were radioactive.

Shortly after that, a local farm boy named Jackie Hooper became sick, stricken with a strange rash and a high temperature.

In his troubled sleep he babbled about a bizarre green-faced creature with silver rings on his fingers.

A few days later, the youngster died.

Klaus Arndt, the owner of a lumber factory told authorities he saw one of the unusual craft circle Sacramento, almost striking a brewery tower.

He also claimed to see lights within the craft, and strange figures working what appeared to be controls.

Other citizens also reported strange lights and mysterious cigar-shaped objects in the California sky.

Several days later, similar sightings were reported throughout the nation- then the lights and flying saucers suddenly disappeared as quickly as they had arrived.

A panicked public demanded and the newspapers turned to scientist Thomas Edison.

His conclusion: "Airships they are not. Spacecraft they could be, but we don't know and perhaps never will.●

I have been digging into my mildewed scrapbooks to see if there aren't some tales which will be worth repeating again. Many of these are ones I wrote for the *Public Opinion* in Westerville, Ohio. You may remember some of them.

The following is an article which was published ten years after it took place, that was nearly forty years ago. It's as much up to date as when I heard it from Dr. Grace Jordan of Columbus, Ohio. One of her patients told her what happened to him. She allowed me to read his experiences for which I am very grateful.

THE 1950 OHIO STATE–MICHIGAN GAME

It was the day after Thanksgiving, the year of the big snow — the Friday night before the Ohio State–Michigan game back in 1950. That was the time when traffic became so stalled that Ohio fans had to desert their cars for several days. That snow didn't know when to stop!

It is a date well remembered by a man who lived in that neighborhood. He has never had nerve enough to give out his story with his name attached; at least he wrote down his experience and it reached a friend of mine.

If this were the only story of its kind it might be easily dismissed, but it is not. Time after time people claim to have had experiences which are equally incredible. Mr. "X" states that when he came home from work all was as usual except he had the uncanny feeling of another presence within his premises. After searching the place he settled down for a nice quiet evening; it was a good night for hibernation.

After a few hours of TV and reading, which seemed necessary to overcome this strange feeling, Mr. X gave up and retired. The next thing he knew he was being awakened by a magnificent creature who beckoned him to arise and come into the living room. There was no fear involved and he found himself following the orders that were given. When the light was turned on he saw a man so perfect, the only fitting description was that of an angel. The door was still locked and the visitor gave an illustration of how he had entered. He raised one hand and the door slowly opened.

This made Mr. X very nervous; he soon realized that his guest was not of earthly origin. Even as the visitor admitted this was so, he also insisted he was of real flesh, body, and soul, and had come to invite Mr. X to take a trip in his craft to his planet as an ambassador of peace and friendship.

Mr. X had a background of science, particularly of astronomy, so it didn't take him long to tell this fellow off. He didn't believe in "flying saucers" and he had no intention of changing his mind. Nevertheless he went. He wrote quite a lengthy tale describing what happened.

When they returned he found banks of snow ranging up to three feet deep. Apparently this was no trouble to a spaceman. The ray gun which he was able to use melted a path in front of them and Mr. X was taken right back through his locked door.

When morning came Mr. X went out to view the snow; in amazement he noted all the stalled cars. He inquired as to where they came from and was told that this happened during Saturday's football game. Mr. X caught his breath and said, "What day is this?" The response was, "Tuesday."

It was bad enough to figure out what happened to Saturday, Sunday, and Monday, but when Mr. X went to check that melted path made by his outerspace visitor he had had it. For, just as he remembered it, a burrow of melted snow ran from his doorway to where he had left the spaceship.

The experience of Mr. X doesn't bother me. If he's still living it shouldn't bother him. There are too many others who have been awakened and taken somewhere for something. Mr. X was very fortunate to have such an attractive companion. If he had been hypnotized later—Lord knows what he might have seen. Aliens who wake people at night are pretty well able to control what is seen and how their subject will react.

ALIENS WHO CAN GO THROUGH WALLS

Back in 1958 a boy who was in specialized Air Force training in Texas came home on leave. His grandmother said, "Buddy, are there really such things as 'Flying Saucers'?" He told her he couldn't talk about it but said, "Grandma, would you believe there really are people who can walk through walls?" Floating or gliding aliens as well as ones who get through walls are old stuff anymore!

George Van Tassel knows how it feels to find a space visitor standing beside his bed. The Van Tassels are from Giant Rock, California. In November 1958 he came to Toledo, Ohio to lecture in the YMCA building. I still believe he had an experience of some kind. The following is a small part of what we were told.

GEORGE VAN TASSEL AND THE SPACEMAN

The Van Tassels sleep out-of-doors in their desert home at least six months of the year. He was awakened one night to find a man standing within a few feet of his bed. This had happened before and usually indicated a stranger out of gas, or in trouble. The visitor asked him if he would like to see his craft. George claims he decided to go after pinching his wife three times and finding he couldn't awaken her. He described his experience in a tale that would make a book instead of a column, so you'll have to do your own reading.

He claims to have been told the men in this ship were beings like us, but only a few of them speak our language. Among themselves only telepathy is used.

These men carried an apparatus which they could use to bend light rays about them and make themselves invisible to us. One man allowed George to place a hand on his shoulder while he made himself disappear to sight but not to touch. Mr. Van Tassel says he was told that our planet has been changing its position enough to cause ice to melt in some regions and to form in other areas at the poles. If this becomes top heavy it can cause another ice age, or water age, or something, and will tend to wipe off a lot of the excess population we've been worrying about. If and when such an event happens these people claim they have thousands of ships which will rescue people temporarily, so that we won't have to start civilization all over again.

It's a long complicated story, very interesting, and sometimes quite impressive. One of the best pieces of evidence to show that he knows what's going on is a receipt to show he wrote the Pentagon to let them know the exact date they were going to be buzzed by saucers two days before the Washington National sightings. Naturally this was ignored, that is, until after the buzzing. From then on he received all the attention desired, and even a little more. We were told that the government has been well informed on this subject, but that they do not feel it wise to give out information. Now, I can't tell you whether the Van Tassel story is true, but I can tell you I have every reason to be sure "flying saucers" do exist.

THE ANDREASON AFFAIR

In 1979 Raymond Fowler wrote *The Andreason Affair*. This was ten years after the event took place. Under hypnosis Betty Andreason told how she had seen a group of entities enter her house. "They came right through the door, right through the wood, one right after the other." Is this what was being taught technicians in Air Force Schools?

Whitley Streiber would be most sympathetic to these experiences. His own memories in *Communion* and *Transformation* would ring lots of bells. Many early contacts were discredited; people need to know that forty years later there are numerous cases which are compatible.

If you're going to ask others to share their sightings and experiences it's only fair to give a couple of your own. Here's one of mine.

WRITER BELIEVES SHE SAW HER FIRST SAUCER

***Public Opinion*, October 30, 1958**

Last Friday about 5 pm. my son David and I were going from Flint, to Westerville when we noticed a silvery looking sphere high in the sky north of town. I laughed and said, "We'd better take a good look, maybe it's a flying saucer." After a minute or so it disappeared just as if a light switch had been turned off.

When I came home my next door neighbor said, "We just saw something that looked like a flying saucer." I thought I was being funny so I said, "We did too, north of Westerville at 5 pm." This really dampened the conversation as he's a non-believer about such things. It just happened he had been on the County Line Road east of Westerville and had watched a high object until they had driven under it and was no longer in view.

It seemed to be a stationary sphere but had a tail-like exhaust. Neither of us were much impressed but decided to listen to see if "Chet Long" had received reports. Sure enough he had. He called the military and had been assured that Northsiders were seeing kites. This may have satisfied Chet, but it was still more ridiculous than the flying object.

Saturday morning's *Ohio State Journal* carried a report from Mr. and M.H. Harvey, Jr. of Tremont Road. Mrs. Harvey told me the following story.

Friday evening somewhere between 5:15 and 5:45 her son came running in and said, "Mother come and look at these queer things in the sky!" Mother, father, friends, neighbors, and children all gathered and brought their binoculars with them. Two spheres bounced around and made themselves a bit hard to follow. One side of the sphere appeared fiery red and orange striped. The other side was dark. The possibility that this was caused by the sun can not be dismissed.

Quickly they called the *Columbus Dispatch* to ask if they were receiving any reports of UFOs. The answer was a bang of the receiver. Then they called Lockbourne Air Base. By this time the objects left for parts unknown. Within five minutes planes arrived from Lockbourne. They were flying far below the area where the sightings had taken place. Lockbourne officials took the trouble to come out and interview the observers and didn't bother to suggest that they were seeing kites.

Saturday's reports also brought a story from Russ Canto, of WBNS, about a motorist who had been driving near Youngstown when he saw two objects fall from the sky. They were two pieces of warm metal. He rescued them and took them to a nearby university to be analyzed and the following report was given.

If the motorist was telling the truth this material may well have come from a space craft. It could not be identified.●

UFOs ARE BUGGING MY BRAIN

***Sun*, November 7, 1989**

by Ted Holiday

The author of the best-selling book about his many abductions by UFO aliens says the strange creatures planted super-sophisticated tracking devices inside his brain! "Scans taken last year show I have two anomalous, bright-metallic objects in my brain," says Whitley Strieber, 44.

"One is lodged in the left temporal lobe, the other in the right parietal lobe.

"The proof of what I'm telling you is right there on the brain scans for any interested observer to see."

Whitley, who described his eerie encounters in the best-selling book *Communion*, that has now been made into a movie, says his nightmare began on December 26, 1985.

He was asleep in his isolated cabin in upstate New York with his wife Anne and son Andrew.

Whitley awoke suddenly with the feeling that something was wrong — and looked up to see a small figure with a rounded hat inching towards his bed.

He was taken to the woods behind his house and lifted above the trees to a tiny room where small beings hovered over him.

"The beings showed me a tiny gray box with a sliding lid," he recalls. "When they opened it, I saw a shiny needle. I realized that it was going to be inserted in my brain. I became crazy with terror and I began screaming.

"There was a bang and a flash and I realized they performed the operation on my head. I felt like weeping and I remember sinking into a cradle of tiny arms."

He awoke the next morning remembering only that he'd had a restless night — and then fell into a very deep depression that left him unable to work.

When the problem persisted and he was haunted by hazy recollections of his frightening ordeal, Whitley sought psychiatric help.

Under hypnosis, he vividly recalled several abductions by UFO aliens.

When Whitley first went public with his amazing tale, some people said he was crazy.

But experts like Dr. Donald Klein of the New York State Psychiatric Institute and Columbia University vouched for his sanity.

"I see no evidence that he is hallucinating, suffering from psychosis or experiencing any mood or personality disorder," says Klein.

Whitley says that *Communion* has turned out to be much more than a commercial success.

"It is helping many people who had imagined their half-buried memories of alien intrusions might be a symptom of madness," says Whitley.

"I get thousands of letters a year from readers who say they've been contacted and experimented on throughout their lives."

The movie *Communion*, which is patterned after Whitley Strieber's best seller, reminds many people of their own experiences. "They often believe they have been marked by aliens so they can be located and possibly controlled by these beings. Aliens observe us much like we observe animals."●

☐ *On a basis of 1–10, this deserves the full 10. No researcher I know would question it.*

TWO UFOs AND A HEADACHE

My number two story makes me squirm a bit. I've kept it pretty well tucked under the covers. What's the use telling a tale that no one will believe? I've wondered what the odds are that this could occur.

My husband's French background gave me access to different ways of cooking. I learned to create a mean casserole of rabbit layered with prunes and onions. If you don't go for the prunes and onions you can always pitch them. It does wonders for the rabbit.

The Jean Shea cooking program on WOSU was asking for people who had recipes to share. I called and was told to bring mine and come in the next morning for an interview. I chose a lemon cream pie and some yummy chocolates to go with the rabbit casserole and looked forward to a new experience.

Having gone to bed at about 10:00 p.m., I hoped for a good night's rest. I might as well have drunk four cups of coffee. I tossed and turned and went for a drink of water followed by a trip to the bathroom — nothing worked, I just couldn't sleep. My mind was flooded with thoughts concerning UFOs. I was tired and wanted so badly to go to sleep. This went on and on — I wasn't able to take my mind off the subject. I looked at the clock, it was nearly 1 a.m. I felt desperate. I sat up, raised both arms with clinched fists and struck the bed two hard blows and said, "Leave me alone!"

Fifteen minutes later the phone rang. How many calls do you get 1:15 a.m.? Especially from a bachelor who you've only met a short time ago. Perhaps Jack was evening up scores for that time I forced him and George Adamski to open the door for me!

Jack Grant worked for a company that sold radio and television towers or something like that. He was on the road and out of town a good bit. He told me he had just driven in from Indiana and noticed a couple of UFOs which appeared to be over my house. (We both lived near the same railroad track.) It was relatively easy to judge my locality; we aren't more than one and a half miles apart. Jack said, "They told me to tell you they were there!"

I'm not sure I remember my response. I do remember the splitting headache I had the following morning when I went in for my interview. Mrs. Shea did accept all of my recipes, they turned out to be quite successful.

MR. X AND THE CAPTAIN OF A SPACESHIP

I finally told what happened to me to a friend of mine and hoped he wouldn't be too critical. He just smiled and said, "Now I'll tell you the one I can't tell anyone!"

He had gone to the San Diego Airport to bid his daughter a fond goodbye as she left for a vacation. Looking for a place to sit where he might observe the door she'd be using, he chose a curved stairway which was lined with seats. Finally he found an empty area which gave him a good view. There was a vacant seat on each side of him. Two seats to his right there was a man who probably was waiting for someone or something.

After a couple of minutes the gentleman turned and said, "I understand you're interested in UFOs." My friend, (we'll call him Mr. X) said. "Yes. How did you know?" The reply was, "You are writing a paper. You have four errors in it." My friend said. "That's true but I have had them corrected; I don't believe I know you, who are you?" The response was jarring. "Would you believe the Captain of a spaceship?"

Mr. X knew the answer to that one; he said, "No, I wouldn't." The Captain reached down picked up his briefcase and brought out a sheaf of material related to the inner workings of a spaceship. My friend picked up his own briefcase and showed him the work he'd been doing.

It was time for his daughter to arrive — he explained why he was there and asked the Captain if he would wait while he made a quick trip to the door to say good-by. It was agreed and Mr. X hurried back to his seat as quickly as possible. He had so many things he wanted to show the Captain. Again he asked if he might go to the car to bring some other papers to show him.

The Captain agreed and a lengthy conversation ensued. Mr. X had a problem — he had an important appointment. At last he said. "How can I reach you again? I don't want to lose contact." I knew the answer to that one. He said, "You can't, I can only reach you." That was the only answer. There are times it's best to let the other person worry about the appointment.

After Mr. X left, he remembered a woman who sat facing him across the curve on the stairway. Her expression was one of "I don't believe what I'm seeing!" This may have been the answer, much as Mr. X hates to admit it — it's a possibility that jars the daylights out of him! There are many cases that fit into this category, too numerous to mention. It is more than possible Mr. X is the only one who saw or heard the Captain of a spaceship.

THE TRUMAN BETHURUM STORY

After I found George Adamski relaxing on Jack Grant's davenport, we became pretty good friends. Eventually he told me about the time George asked him to take his place at a banquet which was given in Los Angeles.

George Adamski and Truman Bethurum were to be the featured guests but George had heard that Major Edward Ruppelt was also invited. He didn't think he could cope with the Major and that's how Jack ended up at the head table with Bethurum at his side. (After all that concern, the Major didn't show.) Anyway, Truman turned to Jack with tears in his eyes and said, "Please believe me, I am telling the truth."

If you can get though Bethurum's experience and still go on to another, you may survive the subject of UFOs. When Truman met Aura Rhanes (the captain of a spaceship) one wonders, but when she shows up in a local restaurant and at a bus stop, everybody wonders!

Truman claimed to have nearly a dozen and a half meetings with the captain and her crew. I'm not betting any money on this case — by now I know anything is possible when you're dealing with UFOs.

JACK W. GRANT AND "THE SAUCERS"

(Reprinted with permission from the *Columbus Dispatch,* February 23, 1954.)

Do you remember what the front page headlines looked like in 1954? I have a copy of the *Columbus Evening Dispatch,* Feb. 23, 1954 — 34 pages, 5 cents.

Besides a couple of robbery suspects there's a 4 x 4-1/2 in. picture of Jack W. Grant addressing the Kiwanis Club at the Neil House. Then there's another foot-long double headline that says "Ex-FBI Informant calls Army Code Handler Red" — right down below "McCARTHY SAYS BRASS KNEW FACTS."

That was about the time the government had an FBI agent behind every pole. "Flying Saucers" were serious business, we didn't dare let the Russians find out more than we did!

Under Jack's picture are a couple more features. "BEINGS FROM OUTER SPACE — Says AF to admit saucers exist" — Jack is shown holding a couple of plates to illustrate what these objects look like.

Anybody who sets a time when there's going to be an announcement concerning this subject is plumb full of wishful thinking. Senator Goldwater comes the closest. He says, "Anytime there's a sighting so BIG there is no longer anyway to deny it — that's when you'll be told about UFOs!" He says he believes this topic is so highly classified it can't be released. It is quoted as being so "secret," it is even more-so than the hydrogen bomb.

Jack had traveled all over the country checking flying saucer stories for several years. That's why he happened to know George Adamski, Truman Bethurum, George Hunt Williamson, and other contact cases. Plastering your picture on the front page of the *Dispatch,* holding a make-believe flying saucer, was a great way to make sure all your phones would be bugged. Probably you were going to get plenty of attention. Adamski was also being watched and checked. While Jack was being checked out too, he had been asked to help the FBI make sure that Adamski wasn't up to "something" that the government needed to know.

Of course, there were others. Jack had met a questionable character who wanted to be flown around over some "places" to take pictures. Fortunately Jack's plane had a problem at the moment and that took care of that. Nobody trusted this fellow; the FBI was watching him, Jack had been asked to keep an eye on him, even Adamski didn't want anything to do with him.

Jack has a collection of private letters from George. I have read them. They would help you understand Adamski's thinking and comments.

At the present time Jack Grant is vice president for Columbus Galvanizing Plant, at 100

Buckeye Park Rd. When he retires in a couple of years he's thinking of printing a collection of these letters. Perhaps we'll have another book.

DAN FRY'S TWO-WAY TRIP TO N.Y.

Do people ever disappear after meeting with a flying saucer? It's a dead cinch they do disappear. Now and then there are reports of near-by UFOs. Then again there are those who claim to have gone for a ride and have been delivered back to the same place.

Dan Fry, an engineering technician from New Mexico's proving ground, is one of the persons who claims to have stepped into a ship which in a half-hour returned him within a few feet of the same spot.

If his footsteps hadn't ended so abruptly and then reappeared going the opposite direction, probably he would have headed for a mental institution. Footprints in the sand are hard to explain away.

It was in 1950, the evening of July 4. Dan found himself stranded in camp and had gone for a walk in search of a breeze. While watching what appeared to be a star, he found it was moving straight toward him and actually landed within seventy feet. It was an oblate spheroid with a metallic surface. Walking around it he found no evidence of an opening and finally decided to reach out and touch it. As he did so he heard a voice saying, "Don't do that, buddy — it's hot."

His surprise caused him to take several quick steps backwards which landed him in a briar patch. Hearing laughter he felt that at least whoever was near must have a sense of humor.

As he picked himself up he heard the same voice invite him to go for a ride. Dan agreed but said he saw no door. Instantly a portion of the ship slid back and it was his turn to proceed. When he entered, the door went back into place and a very scared man found himself inside a shell which contained no one. He was told this object was remotely controlled and picked up air samples which were hauled back to a larger base out in space. It was decided that he should be shown New York City twenty miles from above.

This round trip was made in a half-hour. A beam was directed to the ship's metal-like surface, and was instantly transformed into a substance which could be seen through just like glass. (Notice how many times you'll hear this, 40 years later.)

During the trip his mental questions were answered and he was shown various working parts of the craft. There was no feeling of speed — the earth appeared to fall away from the ship rather than otherwise. When Dan complained about this he was given an illustration of how it would feel to be in freefall. He was told this ship created its own force field and did not operate like our aircraft.

When he was delivered back to White Sands he found himself within six or eight feet of the place where he had made his entrance.

By morning Dan felt he had either dreamed this or he was insane. Sure enough, when he went back to this deserted area, he found his footprints plus those made by the ship.

ONE WAY TRIP?

One wonders whether some of our missing persons could have gone for a one-way trip. According to an article in *Coronet* magazine in September, 1955, two British airmen have long puzzled those who searched in vain.

On July 24, 1924, Flight Lt. W.T. Day and Pilot Officer D.R. Stewart were flying over the Iraq desert on a routine reconnaissance flight. At that time it was not hostile Arab territory. Whatever caused them to land, no one has ever been able to reason.

When searchers found their plane it was in good condition and showed no evidence of any kind of an attack. The gas tank was half full and is not likely to have been a problem.

The two men had climbed out of the plane, walked side by side for forty yards and then suddenly left no further trail. There were no other tracks of any kind and no sign of a struggle. Searchers combed the desert for a hundred miles in all directions. Rewards were offered in hopes that some other evidence would be brought to light. Tribal patrols checked every village and oasis.

The British army is still at a loss to explain why these men should have landed and what could possibly have happened to them. The Arabs have lived peaceably with the English for many years. No information has come forth to indicate the slightest clue to solve the mystery.

Whether UFOs have ever been considered as a suspect in this case, I really don't know. Many times these ships have been seen to hover a few inches above ground and it would have been possible that no tracks would be made in the sand. If the airmen had sighted such a foreign-looking object, curiosity might have led them to land in hopes of solving the illusive UFO.

MY OPINIONS IN THE FIFTIES AND SIXTIES

The *Public Opinion*

I've been waiting for a "Scout Ship" to land in the rose garden at the White House. That will be the time when the sightings of the '50s take on value which they haven't had for years. Sighting after sighting agreed, though the ship's walls seemed to be made of metal, something opened so contactees were able to see through them. If you look for evidence of similar value between today's UFO experiences and those of the '50s you will increase your knowledge of UFOs.

George King came all the way from London, England to tell what he thought he knew. He claims to be in contact with space people and his messages are not too different from many others who feel they receive mental impressions from outer space. How these people manage to bring in enough money for expenses is beyond me. They say the space people promise to help them and this may be so....

Then we had a letter from Major Wayne S. Aho, who wished to visit us and talk about "The Spacecraft, A Sign of the Latter Days."

Wayne Aho is a former Major who had been contacting Washington representatives and senators in hopes that he would inspire them to do a little searching on their own. In some cases he created a definite interest while in others he couldn't get to first base.

George Van Tassel came from Giant Rock, California to tell us about a large dome spaced structure. This is to be a rejuvenation center made almost without metal and he claims that it will be a way of keeping youthful, like some of the space people whom he has contacted. As I understand it, if such a structure could be placed over the occupants who were in a severe accident their various parts would tend to go back in place in spite of their condition.

Since Van Tassel doesn't have the equipment ready to produce it at present, there can't be much discussion on the subject—so any time he gets this machine working, I think he'll have the world under his thumb.●

NICAP

(My notes show this is how I felt about NICAP in 1961. I find my opinion has changed very little.)

Researchers such as the National Investigation Committee on Aerial Phenomena have concentrated on calling attention to the possibility that there is life on other planets and there is no doubt as to the existence of the UFO. However, they have carefully turned their backs on any attempt to find out about the contents of these ships.

It has been said by those who visited NICAP that their files were full of claimed contact cases. If only one in 100 of these is true, surely there is no excuse for not attempting to solve this problem. If, on the other hand, NICAP feels that solving this part of the picture would defeat the purpose of the organization, perhaps it can be forgiven.

For a number of years Major Donald E. Keyhoe spent much time trying to persuade Congress that "Flying Saucers" deserve Congressional investigation. He has been able to convince a number of senators and representatives of the existence of these objects but somewhere beyond his reach he finds a block which prevents this topic from reaching the floor. This subject is "Top Secret" and regardless of the desire of the individual, is not apt to be put in a position where information will be revealed. A hearing by our lawmakers would bring out so much evidence that it is hard to imagine the length of time that such an investigation would require.

I wonder if Congress wouldn't find itself in much the same position as the time it held a congressional investigation on Spiritualism. Hearings in the House of Representatives determined Spiritualism to be in a realm beyond legislation.

An article by Richard E. Saunders recalls the date in 1926 when Representative Sol Bloom from New York City, prompted by the stage magician Harry Houdini, decided that tighter controls should be placed on mediums and fortunetellers in the District of Columbia.

For three months Bloom and Houdini fought to force this legislation into existence; they were met with rebuffs strong enough that eventually they went down to defeat.

Mrs. Duncan Fletcher, wife of the senior senator from Florida, was one of the witnesses who testified in favor of the spiritualist cause. She assured the congressmen that some of the most prominent people in Washington had attended seances in her home.

She declined to give their names but told the sub-committee they would be surprised if they knew who some of these people were. She said they were ministers, doctors, officials, and world-renowned writers.

Mrs. Fletcher went on to reveal how her father had been left in charge of a valuable violin which was to be given to the son of a certain man. The boy at this time was only eight years old. Soon after, his family disappeared and was not able to be traced.

Forty-five years later, and long after the death of her father, he was able to give a message through a medium which contained enough information for her to locate this man and return his rightful possession.

Mrs. Fletcher said she could see no reason for legislation which would prevent information of this kind being given and it was her purpose to see that it was not prohibited. Presumably the congressmen felt that enough of their colleagues might be involved that it would be well for them to keep out of such debatable areas, thus it was decided that "Spiritualism is a realm beyond legislation."

IN DEFENSE OF GEORGE

The first I ever read about UFOs was *Flying Saucers Have Landed* by George Adamski. At its best it was a very questionable experience. However, I was fortunate in being able to interview him and I must say I do believe he will be high on the list in the annals of UFO history. Since his death, "flying saucers" have become much more recognized and respectable than they used to be. Until his story hit the market it hadn't become popular to write about such things. When you are a "first" it isn't so easy to conjure up a story out of nothingness. Mr. Adamski had studied this subject as well as other philosophical material for a number of years before his eventful trip into the desert. He was aware of the art of projection, which would have allowed him to be at home in his chair while his mind wandered off into the universe. How much of his repertoire came from such experiences is anyone's guess, but the important point to me is — what did he accomplish by such actions? Here are some of the outstanding statements which are in relative agreement with today's research on UFOs. His description of large cigar-shaped ships, which he called motherships, is so accurate that it is as good today as the day it was written. A minister's wife in Marysville told me that personnel from Wright-Patterson Field brought large map-like pictures of air ships to show in her school classroom. When they reached one of George Adamski's cigar-shaped ships all the room cried out, "That's the one!" Her entire class had seen this craft during a recess period and had gathered a spider web-like material which floated down from it.

Mr. Adamski also called the saucer-shaped ships "scout ships," and said that they were carried here on the large motherships. This is still recognized as true by most all those who delve into the subject. Another description is of small disc-like objects which have been seen many places. During the war they were called "Foo fighters" and accompanied many of our planes and those of the enemy. George said these were like television eyes and were unmanned craft. This statement is also good today.

In his book *Inside the Space Ships*, he described space as he viewed it from a spacecraft window. "It was beautiful, like millions of little colored fireflies." One of our astronauts came back and used almost his identical words. I don't know how Adamski came up with the idea that faulty pieces of alien equipment were destroyed, apparently from an observing craft rather than allow it to be captured. There is some evidence that this is true.

After reading numerous letters from George Adamski to Jack Grant, I couldn't help begging permission to make some quotes from one of them concerning the authenticity of Frank Scully's book, *Behind The Flying Saucers*.

The following excerpts have been taken from several different paragraphs in Jack's letter. It shows how convinced Adamski was of Scully's experience and why it was that Scully's book had to be discredited. The following letter was written on September 9, 1952.

> Now as to Frank Scully's book, *Behind The Flying Saucers*. What I have previously stated in letters to you still stands. And if my information is correct, by the time Newton and Scully get through with *True*, there might not be any such magazine. The Dr. Gee spoken of in this magazine is not the man written of in Frank's book, I will assure you, for I have met the man. As far as Frank Scully's home is concerned, I don't believe anybody would find a finer nor more orderly home than his. I have been there many times. Theirs is as nice a family as anyone could wish to have.

It is more than odd that the *True* edition did not investigate the facts, but accepted the story hook, line and sinker — (the story which the *Chronicle* did not accept).... What I can't understand is that a magazine supposed to give the public nothing but the truth would come out with such a false story after two years of Scully's book being on the market. Besides, I received a letter from a friend in New York who is now in Aztec, New Mexico — the spot is still visible where one of the saucers mentioned in Scully's book landed and was dismantled. A letter from another friend, an engineer in one of the aircraft plants near Los Angeles, states that he has official information that Scully's book is not only true, but it contains only half of the truth that could have been written. Which means that some sort of organization or something, whatever it may be, is trying to keep the truth from the public, even though slander has to be used, since they have no other means by which to do it.

☐ *How many times have I told you this is the way the UFO problem was handled?! Timothy Green Beckley in his book,* MJ-12 and the Riddle of Hangar 18, *tells us that flying saucer researchers have almost unanimously agreed Scully was telling the truth and that goes back to the original incident! Adamski says in spite of mistakes that were made in Scully's book, he feels it was his intention to give the truth of other worlds' people visiting man on Earth!*

There were many more comments which were too accurate to discount. For this reason I shan't pile any more debris on George's head because I do believe he has offered "something," no matter how he went about doing it!

PETER HURKOS AND THE UFO

It used to be that psychics were satisfied to predict a UFO landing which would take place in a cow pasture 34 miles from nowhere, providing there weren't more than two witnesses and the creek didn't rise, but nowadays it's different.

A while back a couple of reporters managed to get an appointment with the world-renowned psychic, Peter Hurkos. They were to bring articles concerning UFOs and he was to try to come up with all the right answers. It's not easy to round up such material, especially when you have someone else make up sealed envelopes so that even you won't know what's in them.

When Mr. Hurkos saw the stack of material he went into one of his tizzies and complained that they had brought him two days' work, etc. etc. After he calmed down it was suggested he choose as many of the envelopes as he wished. This seemed satisfactory and without opening them, he proved to be 100% accurate on all material which could be verified and gave most intriguing solutions for the rest.

He also predicted that there would be a number of UFO landings in the southwest sometime after Election Day but before the earthquake which would hit California this fall. I don't know anything about his number of failures but his successes would have been too good for me to visit my California relatives at that particular time.

For example, a number of years ago the Virginia police brought Hurkos over from Europe to help solve a tough murder case. The chief met him at the airport and while they were driving the chief was told that he would become the father of a baby girl July 24, or some such date, one year in the future.

The chief wasn't much impressed, since he hadn't had any children in 18 years. The following year on July 24, he sent Peter a telegram confirming the prediction along with his new daughter's name.

So much for the power of suggestion, but the thing that bothers me is how he was able to tell the chief that his wife was driving ahead of them and they would be able to catch up with her if he stepped on the gas a little. By the way, with Hurkos' help the police found the murderer.

THE GRAIN BUYER FROM CALIFORNIA

The 1958 Yearbook of the *American People's Encyclopedia* gives a well-known contact story which is found under the listing "Flying Saucers" on page 123. I too have interviewed this man and his story. Though utterly fantastic, it left me with a feeling that here was a man who felt he was telling the truth. No doubt it is possible to lie and not know you are doing so; if his story is untrue at least I feel he doesn't know it.

Mr. Reinhold Schmidt was a grain buyer for a multi-million dollar firm in California. His job was to cover large producing areas in several states. On November 5, 1957, he was touring the outskirts of Kearney, Nebraska, when he saw what looked like a large silver balloon fall from the sky. He drove in the general direction until his motor refused to work. Getting out of the car, he started walking through the brush and soon came upon a 100-foot-long ship which was shaped something like a weiner bun. Either he became petrified with fright or a ray had been shone upon him, but he found it impossible to move. Two men came towards him and after searching for weapons allowed him to enter the craft. He was told they would have to be there awhile and he might look around as long as he didn't touch anything.

Outside of some knobs with roman numerals on them there was nothing unusual on the control board, except in the ends of the ship which he supposed contained machinery. *He could see through the metal walls as if they were glass.* Four men and two women seemed to be the complete crew. They spoke high German among themselves and broken English to him. Their clothes and appearance were in no way unusual. When he asked where they were from they just smiled and said, "You'll know before too long." Smitty says he figured he had had it. It didn't seem possible that he would be allowed to leave and carry back such information. However, a half-hour later he was taken outside and asked to stand to one side while the ship made its take-off. At about 150 feet it changed to a dark color and just disappeared into nothingness.

Sufficient imprints and greasy stains were left and he felt someone should be notified. The battery which had gone dead started as if nothing had happened. Mr. Schmidt claims to have had no former interest in or knowledge of "flying saucers," and only felt he was fulfilling an obligation by reporting it.

For the first few hours he was quite a hero but this ended when the Air Force arrived. His reputation had to be discredited. It wasn't hard to do. During the Depression he had been a produce buyer. He was allowed to write checks for this firm, signed with his own name. The company folded and left him responsible for several checks. In a few days every state knew that an ex-convict had reported contact with a strange craft.

Immediately he was taken to a mental institution. He went against his will and that of his family. He sued the city of Kearney. How long such a case can be postponed will be interesting. The whole world knew this man was thrown into an institution, but few knew he passed all tests so perfectly that the city of Kearney could be in for a bit of trouble itself.

Finally the California firm for whom he worked came to his rescue. An official asked for evidence against his employee and finding none, gave notice to expect a full crew of lawyers the following morning. Smitty was dismissed in a matter of minutes and told not to wait to sign any papers. The hospital knew when it was licked.

Fourteen hours later, a twelve-year-old boy reported a similar incident in Tennessee. Don't bother to ask me for explanations. All I can do is to assure you "flying saucers" do exist.

WHAT HAPPENED TO DR. HYNEK?

In December 1958 a couple of hundred people braved snow and slippery streets to hear Dr. Allen J. Hynek speak on "Man's Satellites: Doorway to the Stars." It was given in Cowan Hall in Westerville, Ohio and was presented as one of a series chosen by the Concert Association.

The Satellite program was sponsored by the national government. It didn't prove to be overly successful but it put out a lot of data to show where your money would be spent.

At that time it was Dr. Hynek's duty to belittle anything that looked like a UFO. He could always get a laugh by describing a little old lady who called him about seeing Venus and was sure she had located a genuine UFO.

Years later I reminded him of his comments. This happened when he was new on the job. It took some time before he realized that he too was being used. Hynek said at last there was a Naval sighting so good he had to inform the government. Officers and the crew had told him about it. They had watched a UFO circle their ship and dive in and out of the water. Hynek was delighted; he wrote it up to let the government know it should be investigated.

On his next trip to Wright-Patterson's "Blue Book" he took it to the office and waited for a pat on the back.

In due time he got it. It was to the effect, "Mind your own business, forget it!" This was when he knew what he'd been hired to do! It was to under-estimate any sighting that was given too much publicity. For instance, if someone sees one land in the lot next door, he might have said, "Possibly." The idea being his job was to softpedal all sightings. Hynek said he bent over backward to minimize what was seen, always his evaluation was lowered.

Dr. Hynek said he was making such good money he decided to stick it out and find out as much as he could. Eventually he hoped to make up for the damage he had done. As soon as he retired he formed "The Center for UFO Studies." He spent the rest of his life trying to let people know flying saucers exist.

UFOs AND DR. M.K. JESSUP

Dr. Hynek wasn't the only astronomer who investigated UFOs. In the '50s Dr. M.K. Jessup from the University of Michigan did his share in this field. He wrote numerous books on the subject: *The Case for the UFO*, *UFO and the Bible*, and *The UFO Annuals.*

Dr. Jessup spent many years in this field and has written over 100 pages on selenology. In his recent book *The Expanding Case for the UFO,* he discusses the possibility that the moon may be a base for explorers who have reached there before us. Dr. Jessup says the moon has shown many changes in the past two centuries and quotes astronomers' names and dates which go way back. Even Otterbein College is mentioned in the following quote.

In the *Sidereal Messenger*, (Volume III, 1884, page 252) Haywood of Otterbein College, Westerville, Ohio stated that on September 16 from 3:30 to 4:00 a.m. he found a bright glow covering the dark part of the moon. Professor Haywood considered it an electrical manifestation because it was too bright for earth shine and it obscured the features of the moon's surface. The professor said. "This latter fact is puzzling and unsatisfactory."

Sorry to say, Dr. Jessup's life didn't have a happy ending. At the time I was visiting my friends Bryant and Helen Reeve, they received a letter from Dr. Jessup saying he was very despondent and planned to take his own life. Though they called immediately, it was an hour too late. There's more to the field of UFOs than meets the eye.

MOON CRATERS AND THE MOON BRIDGE

It seems records are chockfull of puzzling things concerning the moon. Several years ago the English astronomer H.P. Wilkins shook his colleagues and others in a BBC radio interview by describing what appeared to be a gigantic bridge nearly twenty miles long. It goes across a mountain gap in the Mare Crisium. Dr. Wilkins judged the structure to be nearly 5000 feet high, 1-1/2 or 2 miles wide at the ends, and tapering in at the center. He said its features are so regular it looks almost like an engineering job, and when the sun is low the light can be seen shining beneath it. The most unusual part of this story is why it has taken all these years for it to be noticed. Where had it been hiding?

During the past 200 years many dome-shaped structures have appeared to spring up in various moon craters. Then again they seem to leave the area and may appear elsewhere. What appears at one viewing to be a recession may take on the opposite appearance a few days later. This causes a good astronomer to become frustrated.

Another disturbing element has been unexplainable lights which have been seen on the moon over a long period of years. These have been seen more in certain craters than others. Unknown objects have been seen crossing the moon's surface between the moon and the observer. Most such sightings have been tossed aside as incorrect statements made by the fellers away back.

ASTRONOMY AND THE INTERGALACTIC LOOKING SOCIETY

Every UFO group should have a good telescope and we did! I was the director, my husband did the brain work, and our boys had the job of laying up 500 "bull-nosed" cement blocks. I found a company with an oversupply who agreed to sell them for 5 cents apiece. That was the delivered price. The man who brought them was flabbergasted. "What in the hell are you going to do with 500 bull-nosed blocks?" I showed him how I intended to make a circle with them and create an observatory.

No. 1 son laid the blocks, while No. 2 son mixed the mortar. They were my slave labor and had to produce 22 blocks per day. My brother Charlie was the overseer — he dropped in every few hours to check on the slave labor and undo anything which had been too badly botched.

I took a month-long job at the florist's and made enough money to buy a 14-inch mirror for the project. My husband Gene was in charge of building an apparatus that would support the mirror and a timing gear that would follow the moon and stars across the sky. We hauled a dome from the west side of Columbus. (It was the original model of the Astro Dome. This was a twenty-mile stretch with Charlie's tractor and a haywagon. Thank heaven for slave labor!)

We had lots of company for several years. We learned to watch for the satellites when they flew over and to recognize the big stars that roamed around the skies. Gene saw several objects which he felt had to be UFOs — particularly one that made a 90-degree turn at full speed. Most of our group were interested in the stars as well as UFOs.

The State had a road project in progress. One of our members came up with a large round tube used to make cement forms under the bridges. That's the way you build things when you have lots of ambition but not very much cash. It worked beautifully!

We managed to round up a collection of eyepieces all the way up to 500 power. This was powerful enough to bring a very large moon rock into view. However, in order to use that 500 power, the atmosphere had to be perfect. That only happened twice when Gene was watching, and it was just a couple of seconds viewing time. Oh well, it was a good excuse for staying up all night! We never did see that moon bridge, but we could locate a lot of interesting areas.

KENTUCKY'S LITTLE GREEN MEN

Once you're convinced that flying saucers exist, the $64,000 question is, "What kind of people or things are in them?" Here are a few descriptions which have been duplicated by many.

The most popular occupants have been those who have beautiful, kind faces, shoulder-length hair, and are often dressed in ski suit uniforms. This type apparel persists even when the occupant's hair style is a shorter one. The height of the people generally ranges from five feet four inches to around seven feet. It is interesting to note that these reports come from all countries.

Almost equally described are various small beings who range from three to four feet and who appear more or less human. Often a description of large bulging eyes is given. More often than not, they may be enveloped in a diver's suit with a helmet over the head.

Years ago, Cincinnati papers carried drawings describing what fourteen people in a cabin near Hopkinsville, Ky., had seen. Within less than twenty-four hours the same description was repeated by other observers in various states. Little green men or boys, three and a half feet tall, with bulging eyes, pointed ears, web-like feet, short capes, scaly bodies, etc. were seen by several teenagers, a high school principal, a science teacher, and a doctor's wife. Two young men in Europe gave descriptions of jelly-like grey creatures who tried to pull them near a space craft.

A popular story from South America describes animal-like beings with a structure so hard that a steel knife slid off their bodies just as if it had been a brick wall. The "Kentucky green men" also seemed able to withstand a barrage of shots, only being rolled over by them. Robot-like creatures have been seen, as well as other queer-looking bodies.

Jack Grant went to Hopkinsville. He saw both the police and the people who had this experience. The police said, "No one could have been that scared, unless they were telling the truth." The contactees to whom Jack talked convinced him beyond a shadow of a doubt there had been alien intruders.

These people believed that Federal agents came to their cabin pretending to sell aluminum ware. Their only interest was in asking questions about the sighting and weren't concerned about the products they were selling.

It seems to me it was in 1954 the little green men landed on the Sutton property near Hopkinsville, Ky. Somebody went out for a bucket of water and saw a landed saucer and several little aliens. The monkey-like creatures climbed upon the roof and in the near-by trees. The family (nearly a dozen of them) were very frightened. The men shot at them but it only knocked them down. When they left, the family piled into cars and headed for the police station.

SIX OAKS AND THE UFOs

Back in the '50s we had a nearby night club a mile or so north of Worthington, Ohio. Six Oaks had a lot of customers from near and far. The owner's name was Flo. She probably had another, but that's what everybody called her. She phoned to say she had a piece of gray wool and wanted me to make her a suit. No one ever told me to say "no," so I wouldn't have to keep proving I could do something I couldn't. I made the suit and Flo came to try it on a time or so. She had heard I was writing a UFO column for a local newspaper and thought I might be interested in a conversation she had overheard at the bar.

Two men from Wright-Patterson Air Base were enjoying a night out. By 2 a.m. they became more talkative than the law allowed. They told their companions about little dead frozen aliens they had seen at the base. They weren't the only ones to spread that story from far and near.

An engineer friend told me one of his neighbors hinted at such a tale. I went to see him. I had a little problem getting him to talk very much. He finally said he knew he'd been under observation. He found his phone had been tapped and he'd received some threatening calls.

A military man can't afford to lose his pension. Since he'd been cleared for "top security work" he was allowed to do some mechanical jobs on equipment in a security room at Wright-Patterson. He also saw a disc that was about 49 feet across which was balanced in the air between the floor and the ceiling. He was able to move it with his hand. He had seen questionable deliveries made at a Columbus airport.

None of these stories by themselves tend to be impressive — after hearing several of them, one begins to wonder.

I used to pick up the gossip sheet tabloids at the local pharmacy. The young man at the cash register noticed I bought them every week. I explained that it was my way of keeping up on all UFO-related material. The next time I came in he told me that when he had been a driver for Ryder Trucks, he had been given an assignment to pick up a special load at a Columbus airport, to be taken to Wright-Patterson Air Base. His van was locked and sealed before he was given the key. Instructions were to proceed to Wright-Patterson with no stops for anything — no food, no pit stops, no emergencies, and no accidents! Any variation and he'd be in trouble with the FBI. He made it but always wondered what was in that van.

YOU BE THE JUDGE

When I insist our government has been covering up the UFO story for over forty years, the response is, "How could our government keep a secret about anything? Why would they want to keep such a secret? If someone knows why don't they tell?"

In the forties, the only thing that was known was that unidentified flying objects were coming from somewhere. They didn't appear to be doing any harm; it seemed just as well to postpone talking about a subject when you don't have the answer.

In 1947, when the government recovered a craft and several week-old dead bodies in New Mexico, it seemed better to investigate and not throw too many people into a tizzy. The people who knew about the crash were sworn to secrecy, those who were in military units were threatened with 10 years in jail, a $10,000 fine, and the possible loss of their pensions forever. In many cases they told their friends and relatives so the truth would not die with them. Some are seen in documentaries in which they tell what happened and why they didn't talk.

Those who did talk found themselves in a position where it was wise to have a change of mind. The astronaut Gordon Cooper was so convinced of his space sightings, he took the trouble to inform the United Nations he had seen these ships and believed they and their crews were coming from outer space. Later he revoked his decision and said he'd changed his mind.

Senator Barry Goldwater was told so many tales, he became determined to get to the National Archives and prove to the world we were being fed lies. After heckling his friend Major General Curtis LeMay for permission to see some of these official documents, he finally decided to give up. The General had told him, "Hell no, and don't ask me again!"

I'm sure that was for the record, but off the record — I'll bet the Senator knew good and well why he wasn't allowed to see those documents.

For instance, a friend of mine was assigned the task of interviewing General Curtis LeMay for a magazine article. This was when LeMay was commandant at Lockbourne Air Base.

Being in a very friendly mood, the General smiled and said, "You may ask me anything you want." The question he was asked was, "Is there anything to this UFO talk and are they real?"

General LeMay thought a moment and said, "Is this for the record, or off the record?"

Since he didn't have to use it for his interview, it seemed the wise response was, "It can be off the record." If you were given the following response, what would you think?

"If you read or hear of a crashed disc being found and the next day the *News* tells you it was a weather balloon, don't believe it!"

Don't you think that Major General Curtis LeMay probably gave Major General Barry Goldwater an off-the-record reply that was more explicit than, "Hell no, and don't ask me again!"

UFO SCUTTLEBUTT

Dr. Bruce S. Maccabee, a Navy Laser Physicist, compiled about sixty pages of information which came from the National Archives files through the Freedom of Information Act as well as other helpful sources. Dr. Stanton Friedman, a nuclear physicist, Bill Moore, Jaime Shandera and others procured helpful data which was given to them. The object was to take all this material and tie it together so the world would know we have had a "crashed saucer with occupants" since the summer of 1947. To do the report, it had to be taken in bits and pieces and fitted together to show the true story.

And so we come across a "Top Secret Research and Development Operation," responsible only to the President. Among the goodies is a memorandum for the Secretary of Defense, Secretary Forrestal. It states that from this time on "September 24, 1947, this matter shall be referred to only as 'Operation Majestic Twelve'." Any future discussions will be only with Dr. Bush and the Director of Central Intelligence (Adm. Roscoe H. Hillenkotter). This was labeled "TOP SECRET, EYES ONLY," The White House, Washington. It is signed by "Harry Truman;" his signature has been checked for authenticity.

The group became known as Operation Majestic-12 or MJ-12. These were the twelve members — Adm. Roscoe H. Hillenkotter, Dr. Vannevar Bush, Secretary James V. Forrestal, Gen. Nathan F. Twining, Gen. Hoyt S. Vandenburg, Dr. Detlew Bronk, Dr. Jerome Hunsaker, Mr. Sidney W. Souers, Mr. Gordon Gray, Dr. Donald Menzel, Gen. Robert M. Montague, Dr. Lloyd V. Berkner.

After his death, Secretary Forrestal was replaced by Gen. Walter B. Smith. I wonder who has replaced the rest of those men by now?

The following information was taken from MJ-12's Preliminary Briefing for President-elect Eisenhower. It was prepared November 18, 1952, and the briefing officer was Adm. Roscoe H. Hillenkotter. This briefing was related to UFOs. I am giving you some of the material which is known as the "Roswell Incident."

A local rancher, Brazel, reported a crashed disc in a remote region of New Mexico, approximately 75 miles northwest of Roswell Army Air Base (now known as Walder Field). On July 7, 1947, a secret operation was begun to recover the wreckage of the object for scientific study. Apparently four small human-like beings had ejected just before it exploded. They were found about two miles east of the craft and all were badly decomposed due to predators and a week's exposure. A special team took charge and the wreckage was removed to several different locations. Civilian and military witnesses were debriefed and the effective cover story that the object was a misguided weather research balloon was given to the news reporters.

Gen. Twining and Dr. Bush acted upon direct orders from President Truman. Their preliminary consensus was (Sept. 19, 1947) that the disc was most likely a short range reconnaissance craft.

The analysis of the four dead occupants was arranged by Dr. Bronk. The tentative conclusion was that although these creatures were human-like in appearance, the biological and evolutionary processes responsible for their development was apparently quite different from those observed or postulated in homo sapiens. Dr. Bronk's team suggested the term "Extra-terrestrial Biological Entities" until a standard term of reference could be agreed upon.

Since it was not known where they originated, Dr. Donald Menzel considered it likely that they were dealing with beings from another solar system.

For years, Dr. Menzel gave out information which even I knew was incorrect. I thought he didn't know any better. Apparently he, too, was one more person who was paid to do a job.

General Twining convinced Assistant Chief of Intelligence (General Shulgen) he should interview witnesses to verify what UFO cases were worth investigating. He told him UFOs were REAL but NOT that they had procured any hard evidence. After all, General Shulgen was not a member of MJ-12. Too many people would have had access to that statement.

Most of these people were sworn to secrecy and even though a few talked, they didn't dare to admit their story publicly.

Major Jessie Marcel, who died in 1968, was an Intelligence Officer who was one of the first at the scene of the UFO accident. Both he and the farmer described the material as being as lightweight metal foil with small light-weight bars like balsa wood. These had many odd shaped script-like figures on them.

The son of Jessie Marcel was interviewed by Mr. Lee Graham (Oct. 21, 1981). He was in training as a Flight Surgeon. His description fits what already has been given. Dr. Marcel also gave Mr. Graham his father's address.

Much of this material was mailed to Jaime Shandera in December, 1984. It was on undeveloped film and was sent in a plain brown wrapper. Moore, Friedman, and Shandera have spent nearly seven years doing their best to verify all information. They have found little to indicate that it could have been a hoax.

It is being quoted that UFOs are the most highly kept secret of our government, even beyond the Hydrogen Bomb!

☐ *Pretend you have the responsibility for educating the people of the United States as to the existence of UFOs. The decision would be the same as that of President Truman, all the way down to President Bush. You have the advantage of knowing that UFOs exist, but the disadvantage of not knowing other things about UFOs on which all presidents are briefed. What would you do? I believe that we the people are fed both true and false information at the same time. I see it as a way to educate the public. By this process we have a chance to know, or protection against knowing, if the truth hurts too much. I think the government deserves somewhere between a B and an A- for the way this subject has been handled. That's pretty good for dealing with a tough job.*

UFOs

I wrote a book about UFOs,
But what good will it do —
Unless someone reads this stuff,
I might as well yell, "Boo"!

I told them that these crafts are here,
And pictured those that fly them —
Unless you're going to read this stuff,
Convincing you — is pretty tough!

I'm grateful to the Weekly World
And also other tabloids —
Their contribution to this cause
In no way can be flawed.

I think our government feeds them this,
And hopes that they will print it —
They may not prove the picture they paint,
I doubt that you can prove it ain't!

I wrote a friend in Africa,
And asked her to check a tabloid,
She checked out an article or two,
And decided they would do for you.

Notice how schools teach drugs and sex?
Now that should tell you something.
Day after day they repeat drugs don't pay —
And sex will cause problems, if you play!

Educating people about UFOs,
Has to be done in a similar manner.
Repeat over and over for a few more years,
Perhaps if you're lucky, someone will hear.

CHAPTER TWO

Early Sightings — Hypnosis
Early Columns in the *Public Opinion*

Angelhair at Marysville . . . 26
Only the Pentagon Knows . . . 26
The Army Chaplin . . . 27
1956 Sighting on Sunbury Road — *Public Opinion* . . . 27
The Pilot of a Spaceship — 1958 . . . 28
Hypnosis . . . 28
Cross-Breeding . . . 29
The Anglican Priest From New Guinea . . . 29
Olan Moore — Leta Koon . . . 29
Another Local Sighting in the '50s . . . 30
UFO at Lockbourne Airbase? . . . 31
Unidentified Flying Objects . . . 31
The Children at Johnstown . . . 32
John and the UFO . . . 33
The Dublin Episode . . . 34
Uncanny Happenings . . . 34
Unusual Life Forms . . . 35
Space Creatures Seen on Earth — *Weekly World* . . . 36
New Galaxy Shaped Like Fetus — *Weekly World* . . . 36
Detailed Account of Sighting . . . 37
The Condon Report . . . 38
The UFO and the Computer . . . 39
The Little People . . . 39
Chased by a UFO . . . 40
The Lunatic Fringe . . . 40
The Mundo UFO Report . . . 41
UFOs in Time of Catastrophe . . . 41
The Betty and Barney Hill Movie . . . 42
A 1962 Sighting in Columbus, Ohio . . . 43
My Views in 1962 . . . 43
Religion . . . 44
The Message From Bala Krishnan . . . 44
Thanks to W. Raymond Drake . . . 45
Chariots of the Gods . . . 45
Travis Walton and the Woodcutters . . . 46
The Missing Professor . . . 46
Those Trinidad UFO Pictures . . . 47
The Bumblebee Can Fly . . . 47
The Alien at Saranac Lake . . . 48
Documentaries such as *Outer Space Connection* and *Chariots of the Gods* . . . 48
The Jimmy Flynn Story . . . 49
UFO Contact from the Pleiades . . . 51
UFO Flies Out of the Ocean — *Weekly World* . . . 51
Hynek and His Debunking Service . . . 52
Aliens From Space . . . 52
Major Ruppelt — "Blue Book" and the Scoutmaster . . . 53
Frank Edwards and the News . . . 53
Space Music Draws UFOs — *National Examiner* . . . 55
Looking Back — Poem . . . 56

ANGELHAIR AT MARYSVILLE

One of the sightings you don't hear much about has to do with children outside a school near Marysville, Ohio. At a later date I had Mrs. George Dittman, the children's teacher, as a guest. Mrs. Dittman was a minister's wife; she wasn't looking for publicity, but there was no way to avoid it.

Mrs. D's students were outside for a play period. During this time the children discovered a cigar-shaped ship floating quietly high above them. They knew this was something different, and one child ran to notify the principal. The observers realized they'd been discovered.

By the time the principal appeared the ship had turned its nose upward in a 45-degree angle and took off at a tremendous speed. It disappeared quickly leaving a long white cloud.

This should have been the end of the story but it's just the beginning. It wasn't long until the air was filled with fine white webs. It floated down from everywhere. It looked much like spider webs or cotton candy.

The kids had a new game, "Let's catch the white stuff!" They gathered it in gobs. No matter how much they had, it dissolved into small tiny balls and soon disintegrated.

When the bell rang a bunch of little green aliens marched into class, their hands and faces covered with green stains. Mrs. D. sent them all to the washroom to scrub thoroughly. She was worried this "green stain" might be something dangerous, but water easily washed it away.

For several miles around, the trees, wires, fences, and car antennas were well decorated. The next morning much of it still remained waving in the wind.

As soon as Mrs. D. arrived at school, she gave a couple of her students a jar so they could gather some of it. The boys used sticks to pick it up. It was labeled Marysville, and sent to Wright-Patterson in Dayton, Ohio.

It didn't take long to have company from the Air Base. They brought along some large folding maps which were flipped over for students to observe. When the officers came to one that looked like Adamski's cigar-shaped mothership in unison they cried, "That's the one!"

They were each asked to draw what they'd seen, and they were interviewed separately to make sure of careful evaluation.

Everyone wanted to know about the webby stuff and what was that ship they'd seen? They were told they'd be notified after the webs had been examined.

They waited and waited and waited. Apparently Wright-Pat. forgot to tell them.

When questioned, officers admitted not knowing what happened to that jar of webs.

☐ *The way I heard it — a friend of mine was working for a large research organization in Columbus, Ohio. He told me this story. J.P. had a friend in another department where there was a jar of webby white stuff. It was labeled Marysville. He was allowed to look at it under a microscope. Each thread seemed to consist of 4 or 5 threads.*

His friend told him they were unable to identify it. It was nothing they'd seen before. Some years later I read an article which said that the product, which is sometimes called "angelhair," is thought to be made by certain gases which under extreme pressure solidify but disintegrate very easily. I don't know whether that's true but it sounded reasonable. These large ships have often been seen spewing forth some of this webby material. Just sounds like a byproduct to me.

ONLY THE PENTAGON KNOWS

About the end of the fifties I had a former neighbor who stopped by for a visit on his way home from the Philippines. I told him I was writing a column on UFOs for a local newspaper. He did a lot of shifting around — finally he said, "You can't quote me on this because the penalties are too high and I'd have to deny it.... I can't resist telling you what happened to me! I was with a party of six men who were sent into the jungle to look for anything that resembled a crash. It took three days to reach the area. Before we got back to the base we had lost two of the three jeeps.... The word UFO was never used! One person out of the six was sent with us to make sure we didn't do any talking. We didn't know which one not to trust."

The forest was very wet. Eventually they reached a place with a large burned-out circle.

There in the center was a piece of round fused metal, 1 ft. thick and 6 ft. wide. It was so hard that it couldn't be scratched. Two men were able to lift it onto a jeep. All six men knew this wasn't any metal they'd ever seen.

When they returned to the base six plainclothes men were there to relieve them of their burden. Not a word was spoken but my friend said, "I'd bet my eyeteeth it was on a plane and flown out of there within ten minutes."

The six men never knew any more about their mission. The six men at the gate would know nothing about their work except it was their job to take it to a plane. The pilot would know nothing about this delivery except that it would be picked up by someone. Rest assured, back in the Pentagon someone knew all the answers from the time the object was seen to crash.

THE ARMY CHAPLAIN

Writing a column for the *Public Opinion* helped me to get stories that otherwise never would have been reached. One day when I happened to meet Col. Lloyd B. Mignerey, he said, "I've been reading your columns, and it seems to me you may be right about those 'flying discs'.

"When I was a chaplain, I was called in for a special meeting, behind locked doors. An officer with a briefcase came in to talk to us. We weren't given anything; he just read this notice to us. We were told these flying discs do exist and that the government takes them very seriously. Anytime we had anything to report, it was to go to the Pentagon and NOWHERE ELSE."

Now that he had retired, he heard the government saying there aren't any such things, and they aren't interested in the subject. He knew they had either lied to him or they were lying to us.

1956 SIGHTING ON SUNBURY ROAD

Public Opinion

In February 1956 an interesting sighting took place north of Sunbury, Ohio on Route 37. When I interviewed this farmer and his wife I found them not too anxious to be ridiculed, but permission was given to use their names. Remember in most of these incidents, people are concerned, fearing no one will believe them.

About 10:30 p.m. Mrs. Carl F. Loar had taken their dog out the back door for his final airing. Two buildings and a farm pond backed by a stand of trees made a setting for this unusual experience in which distances could be measured. Back of the pond and in front of the trees a long well-lighted object appeared. This couldn't have been more than 500 yards away as whatever it was appeared to be within inches of the ground — if not resting upon it. A long row of well-lighted windows gave the appearance of a pullman car which had suddenly settled down in the wrong location. The differing feature was that the light from these windows was an eerie blue or fluorescent glare which in no way resembled anything she had seen before.

Keep in mind that all this took place within a second of time. Even though it was moonlight there was a limit to what she was able to notice during a flash picture. Perhaps under hypnosis a still better description could be given. The subconscious registers our experiences more fully.

While I was unable to see how reflections of any kind could have taken place in this location I am sure that Professor Menzell of Harvard would have been able to explain this away easily — therefore I am glad to be able to give more substantial evidence.

Together with the sighting, a cracking report ran through the kitchen light wires. Mrs. Loar was terrified. Lightning in winter on a clear moonlight night is not normal. Had she seen this object and heard nothing she would have been disturbed. The combination of seeing and hearing was too much. As soon as she could recover sufficiently she ran to the bedroom to tell what had happened. In a moment's time her husband was out of bed and ready for action. Taking his flashlight and a piece of firewood as a weapon, he spent the next hour covering areas for possible intruders. No evidence was found either that night or the next day. It is hard to tell these people that all this was imagination. You will find they don't believe it.

I understand that a strong electromagnetic field in this vicinity could have caused this reaction in the nearby wiring. Over and over again the suggestion of a magnetic field is brought up in connection with flying saucers. Could this have been a power which as yet we do not understand? Note that here again is a case of instantaneous disappearance.●

THE PILOT OF A SPACESHIP (WRITTEN IN 1958)

Even dreams seem to support the existence of "flying saucers." It is in this area that one finds another dimension poking its head into the picture. Wherever I go someone comes to me and asserts, "I believe in flying saucers and this is why." A few months ago I found myself in a conversation with a well-known, brilliant young man who said, "I haven't read much about saucers but I'm sure they exist."

Since the age of five or six he had dreamed of piloting a dish-like ship through space. Always in color, always approximately the same — the dream would recur several times a week. Twenty-five years of the same dream puts a lot of reality into the unreasonable. At the time this began such stories had not become fashionable.

Feeling sure that it was he himself he was seeing, it was hard to figure why the man in his dream was so different in appearance. He had Mongolian features, hair to his shoulders, wore a uniform like a ski-suit with straps across his chest, and boot-like shoes. Sailing into a sea of darkness he would find groups of people whose confused faces filled him with a feeling of compassion. A section of his "upside-down dish" would open and people would file in, much like filling an elevator. Then the door would close, he would adjust the controls, and in a short time his carload would be landed on an orange planet. Everything but the buildings seemed to be this color.

When the ship arrived his passengers filed out, never to be seen again. Each load had different faces. During all these trips not one word was spoken by anyone. His only feeling was that of compassion — theirs, of confusion.

Occasionally he would enter a very modern building, the doors of which opened as he walked toward them. Often he went down a long corridor—only to awaken, never knowing where this led. One point seemed very certain to him. He had seen cities in space. It doesn't sound like firm footing but perhaps in another dimension that too, wasn't necessary. I couldn't help smiling at the similarity to other tales which are told.

My answer was this: I can't explain your dream but I can tell you several possibilities which could cause such an experience.

If your subconscious mind accepts any of these as being the explanation you are seeking, your dream will probably come to a screeching halt. I don't know whether my theories were right but it was interesting to find that twenty-five years of a recurring dream have ended.

☐ *At one time I did some work interpreting dreams. The above experience came from a thirty-year-old man whose father-in-law was our County Engineer. We've been led to believe everyone wants to sell himself for money. Not so, most wish to avoid all notoriety of this kind. This dream was the kind of experience which should have taken advantage of hypnotism. It is a much under-used science.*

HYPNOSIS

Hypnosis may not have all the answers but it certainly helps to eliminate the desire to exaggerate. In close contact cases it's a necessity. Many of these people have been programmed not to remember what has happened. The hypnotist gives instructions that these details will be remembered when he is awakened. Very few earlier contacts ever considered being hypnotized or a reason for such an action.

I often think of a case which happened in Columbus, Ohio many years ago. A 72-year-old mental patient from over on the "Hilltop" developed a brain tumor. His physical condition was so poor that it was too dangerous to give him an anesthetic. A hypnotist from Pennsylvania was called in to work with him and find out whether he would respond to hypnosis. After several days it was decided that he met the requirements and a large staff stood by in case of an emergency.

This was a five-hour operation. It normally would have been a very bloody one and the staff was ready for business. In amazement they all stood through the entire operation while the hypnotist was in complete control. By suggestion, the blood flow was so controlled that it left almost nothing to be done except the surgery. When the operation was finished the hypnotist told his patient he might sit up and ask for a chair and to be taken back to his room. Only one "no-no" was mentioned. His head was not to be touched at any time.

The horrified staff was dumbfounded; the instructions continued. When the man reached his room he might ask to be wheeled to the window and given a newspaper to read if he wished; apparently he wished, for this is what he did! He needed no blood transfusions or intravenous feedings and recovered quickly and successfully. A psychiatrist I knew was one of the observers. Just remember, not all people make good subjects. Some of the more recent UFO contacts are followed up by hypnosis. The agreement among these cases is overwhelming. No matter what the country, what age, what sex, or what have you — the people involved tell similar tales. When hypnotized, the subject may tell you he has been contacted several times; often these experiences took place when the person was a child or teenager. One of the first memories is of a cut being made in the back of the leg. Another is of an implant or something being inserted high in one nostril. Men describe sperm being taken against their will. Women, many very young, tell of an operation which indicates they had been contacted at a time when an egg could be removed from them. These are only the beginning of the intrusions being told. There are so many of them that it would be foolish not to take them seriously.

The recently published books by Budd Hopkins and Whitley Streiber will make the reader well aware of this subject. They aren't good places for a neophyte to cut his eyeteeth.

CROSS-BREEDING

This is another dream which demands the aid of hypnosis. Back in the Sixties a friend of mine from Canada came down to the States to visit her daughter and a new son-in-law whom she had never met. During the evening the subject of UFOs came up in the conversation. The young man went into a complete tailspin. He said "Don't ever mention that word in my house!" Being a somewhat aggressive mother-in-law she followed him into another room and demanded an explanation. She felt there must be a reason for such an outburst. Eventually, he calmed down and told this story. He had been taking night classes at a nearby university. On his way home one night he found himself pulled over in the ditch. When he came to, his clothes looked as if he'd been out working all day. He didn't know what happened. He did know it had to do with a UFO. He also knew he didn't want to know!

This is not an unusual case. Often contactees are programmed not to remember.

Most all these abductees are given physical examinations. Many of the men have sperm taken from them to be used in cross-breeding experiments. The men involved are never very happy about the event.

THE ANGLICAN PRIEST FROM NEW GUINEA

One of the most verified sightings of 1959 was the Rev. Father William Gill who was an Anglican Priest of the Boiannai Mission in New Guinea. His fifteen-page report was signed and verified by 27 of the 38 witnesses who agreed with his description. These saucer-like ships were seen from January 21st for nearly a week; at times they were close enough that those watching were able to wave a greeting which also was returned to them. This information is so well known, you will find it in most any serious research.

OLAN MOORE — LETA KOON

One of the most common complaints concerning UFOs is the lack of material evidence to prove their existence. This certainly is a touchy subject. I am forced to admit one really must dig to uncover very much. However, circumstantial evidence is not without some value and this can be found if fair investigations are made.

In 1958, within a two-week period, two well-known cases took place near Painesville, Ohio. The story of Olan Moore is a well known tale. He observed an unusual object which landed along the road where he was driving. After parking his car and waiting several minutes he decided to go for help before examining whatever this might be. In the meantime the UFO left, but the next morning's investigation showed prints in the ground surrounded by an area of high radio-activity. This gave credence to his truthfulness.

By estimating the decrease in radioactivity it was felt that Mr. Moore might well have lost his life had he approached for a nearer view of the UFO. Other witnesses indicated they too had seen what was felt to be the same object.

When this story was investigated, Mr. Moore disappeared for a couple of days — even his wife not knowing his whereabouts. He finally admitted being taken to Washington but stated he was unable to talk about anything else. Mrs. Moore said she'd been able to pry from her husband that he felt this craft came from outer space. Markings on a car parked nearby indicated possible radiation damage. Approximately two weeks later a woman watched a large object which hovered near her garage for twenty minutes or more. This 100– to 150-foot disc which appeared not more than 100 feet above the ground gave off a brilliant glow which also left its after-effect. Within a day's time she broke out with a red rash, also radiation burns to her eyes which caused severe damage.

Mrs. Koon had a nearby dog kennel. At least two of the female dogs were pregnant. Both of them produced badly damaged pups. All the animals were very frightened by the presence of the UFO. I believe Mrs. Koon lost some of her dogs too. There are many cases where dogs have died within a day or so from similar near-contacts. A number of hospitalized cases where the person who viewed certain UFOs too closely, have indicated that rashes and eye damage are a common experience. Under hypnosis she felt as if she were both inside and outside the UFO. Her experience was interesting — you will find other cases with a similar reaction.

Does it occur to you that a person planning a hoax is very foolish indeed to so endanger himself? If these stories are hoaxes, at least every country reports similar imaginary experiences.

If our government admits that it is aware of such goings-on and cannot explain all the other questions which follow, what will be the reaction of the general public? It isn't that this should be — the subject is merely so big, and so beyond our present range that it will require time to slowly educate people to new concepts which eventually must be faced.

ANOTHER LOCAL SIGHTING IN THE 50s

Once in awhile there is a coincidence where a sighting takes place at an appropriate moment. This is true in the story told by Fred Cave of Colonial Hills. Years ago he lived at 451 Colonial Avenue; his business was real estate and he was also a member of the Worthington Board of Public Affairs.

A night or so before seeing this UFO Fred had just finished reading *Flying Saucers Have Landed.* As per usual, he too was all ready to stretch out his hand to the first Venusian who might appear out of the bushes. Almost anyone who read this book was bound to keep his head turned upward for at least a week and Fred was no exception. This September evening at about 9:30 he and his nine-year-old son John were in their back yard. The Graceland Shopping area was new — and at that time a large revolving light was being used to draw the crowds. The light was still turned on but was stationary and directed at an angle somewhat to the south.

John must have read his father's mind for he said: "Dad, are there really 'flying saucers'?" Without much thought he answered, "Why yes, John, they're really there, but we don't always see them. You're more apt to see them than I for you're younger and your eyes are better than mine." At that moment he noticed a band of light which appeared high over the beam originating at the shopping center. As he watched, it rolled directly toward him and came to a standstill over his next-door neighbor's house. This appeared as a trail of light made up of strips of orange light and darkness much like the stripes in our flag. The bands appeared to be several feet wide and looked almost the same in the distance as when they were close. In other words the trail didn't appear to converge with distance. The trail divided into four sections and at various times seemed to have more bands of light. As it approached him there was a few seconds pause and there above him he saw a dark sphere about the size of a house with a tube of light surrounding it. This was much like a neon tube and gave off a sound like corn being popped. By the time it reached his neighbor's house, he felt it was less than fifty feet high. It seemed as if it absorbed the light rays just ahead of it. Suddenly another set of bands shot up at about a 65-degree angle. The UFO followed this path at high speed causing a slight breeze and blotting out the light as it went.

Both father and son claim to have seen the same thing. The entire sighting took place within less than 15 seconds and it was quite a long time before Fred met a couple of witnesses who had seen the orange stripes and wondered at its peculiar appearance. It is no wonder the term "Unidentified Flying Objects" has come into being.

This man also claimed to have seen a piece of unknown metal at a Columbus research organization. The description sounded like the metal which has been found at UFO crashes that was too hard to cut.

UFO AT LOCKBOURNE AIR BASE?

Radar controls have become as practical as a pocket on a shirt and almost as common. It is difficult to drive a 10-mile stretch without being reminded that we are usually in view of the law. Where the use of radar really shines is in the air above us. Intruders are supposed to have a rough time if they expect to fly here and find us napping. A radar beam is sent out to cover a designated area and does not show a signal or blip without first bouncing off a good solid object. A radar specialist soon learns to recognize a solid object from a light inversion and similar freak phenomena. UFO books are full of stories which indicate that "flying saucers" can be a real headache to radar technicians. Numerous cases have been reported where a plane and a UFO have "met up" in mid-air and only one object seen to leave the screen. The one leaving was not the plane, and not a hide or hair of the planes involved could be found.

On July 19, 1952, UFOs made life miserable for Pentagon officials by flying over the White House where no one was permitted.

At one time a UFO was seen over Andrews Radio Range station by three different radarscopes. The tower operators looked up to see a huge fiery orange sphere. As all three compared notes, the UFO disappeared simultaneously from their scopes.

According to a tale I heard from Lockbourne Air Base, they too have had experiences with UFOs. It seems the radar tower managed to spot one of these objects, when to their amazement, it landed down at the end of one of the runways. A squadron was sent there, guided by radar.

When the men reached the area, they were directed within a few feet of the object and told: "There it is — right in front of you." The way I heard it, there was nothing to see in the spot, which had to contain something.

This account was told to me by a guard at the gate. He told me he was on duty when it happened. I wrote my article the last part of 1961, so I'm not sure when it happened.

UNIDENTIFIED FLYING OBJECTS

The story printed in the *Plain Dealer* so nearly matches mine, I decided to use theirs. To think this woman's story a hoax is ridiculous! That's what it's meant to be — if you feel comforted with such as explanation from the Air Force, relax and enjoy it.

After reading Lt. Col. Tacker's book *Flying Saucers and the U.S. Air Force* it seems only fair to give you an example of the sort of work being done by the Air Force. This sighting took place September 21, 1958 at approximately 3 a.m. The story was covered by Allen Ashbolt of the *Cleveland Plain Dealer* on September 22. Quoting from his article: "Terrified and shaken by their experience, a Sheffield Lake housewife and her 10-year-old stepson related a weird account of a 3 a.m. visit by a 'flying saucer'.

This is how sightings are solved. Would you report to the Air Force if you saw a 'flying saucer'?

Cleveland Plain Dealer
September 22, 1958

Mrs. Wm. H. Fitzgerald, 934 East Drive, said she watched the object for more than five minutes at close range after a brilliant light roused her from her bed. Tears filled her eyes, still reddened from crying until dawn following the experience. Blinded at first, she hid her head under the pillow until the light subsided. Then she stood on her bed, looked through the window and watched the 'saucer' glide over her driveway.

"It hovered a foot above a neighbor's lawn, suddenly glowed and discharged a cloud of heavy pinkish-grayish-purplish smoke from the saucer's back and sides," she said. It then swept in a curve onto her front lawn and rose to about seven feet above the ground. After it completed two short maneuvers she lost sight of it. Then it sped straight up into the sky over the top of her home.

Mrs. Fitzgerald described this object as the most horrible thing she had ever seen. When I talked to her the Air Force had not yet arrived. I assured her they would — and it would be well to do her talking beforehand. I had no trouble reaching her by phone. Now I find her phone no longer listed. It is my opinion that from now on she'll be harder to reach.

The Air Force investigation revealed that a railroad track ran near the home of the witness. Contact with railroad officials revealed that a train passed the home of the witness at approximately the hour and date of the sighting.

This train has an oscillating headlight and this light could have been seen by the witness. Contact was also made with the local Coast Guard Station and the Officer in Charge reported that he was using his spotlight on the Coast Guard Cutter to attract the attention of another ship. His light was directed toward shore in the general direction of the witness' home.

Time and date of this incident was coincident with those reported by the witness. The weather at the time of the sighting, as determined from the Coast Guard log, was intermittent mist and rain with haze and smoke. The Air Force conclusion is that a combination of lights, coupled with the prevailing weather, was responsible for the illusion experienced by this witness.●

THE CHILDREN AT JOHNSTOWN

When and if we ever have an official announcement which confirms the existence of UFOs, there will always be those who don't believe. There is no truer statement than the one that says: "A man convinced against his will is of the same opinion still." It can't be helped and it shouldn't be: a mental block is a protective device of great value. Do you remember years ago when TV programs would bring on some poor soul who vowed we didn't send our astronauts to the moon? Of course one was an old man of 102, who had every reason to put up a good fight. The younger ones were convinced that all this took place in Hollywood and generally it seemed to be their religious convictions which made them so cocksure they'd been lied to. I can remember when my husband assured me we would never send anyone to the moon because there were just too many problems to overcome. And a scientist friend of mine told me all about those poisonous belts between here and there and that they were a natural barrier which was going to make it impossible for man to leave this planet. I think they've both forgotten all about their predictions.

I've been trying to think of ways to discuss the fourth dimension and flying saucers. It's a tough subject — it isn't that I don't recognize this aspect, but it's only apparent in some of the cases. Sightings are so varied that I wonder how many different explanations are going to have to be presented to explain these phenomena. A few years ago I went to Johnstown to talk to several children who had seen a snapping, popping, spherical object hovering above a tree in the yard next door. It seemed to be translucent and of many colors. They watched it take a diagonal path across the street where it appeared to land at the rear side of a large building. What bothered the children was — where did it go? It just disappeared. It's much like looking at a beautiful soap bubble — no one questions its reality, suddenly it's gone and the residue is so small that it seems like a miracle. The object that the children saw changed form and its residue couldn't be found. Not for one minute did I question the sincerity of the children. They just couldn't believe that something that appeared so real to them could get away without their knowledge.

The first person I ever interviewed concerning a sighting was Bud Stevenson, who lives near Circleville, Ohio. In no way have I ever questioned the reality of the event or the sincerity or integrity of the man. He was watching a 60-ft. object which was only 75 feet away from him. It seemed to be a solid metallic craft. The thing that most confused him was — right while he was trying to watch it, the thing disappeared and he couldn't figure out where it had gone. The UFO researcher Brad Steiger, in one of his many articles, tells of a salesman who was driving home when he noticed a UFO hovering over a pond about 100 yards from the highway. It was a clear day with good visibility, so he pulled to the side of the road and rolled down his window for a better view. The object appeared transparent and he could see two beings whom he thought were working on some equipment. They were turned away from him and didn't seem to know he was watching them. One happened to turn around and noticed him; this seemed to give them great concern. They quickly finished their task. One nodded his head and the other reached to pull two levers. Instantly they were gone. Just like the soap bubble — now you see it, now you don't.

Notice that the children said they had seen a snapping, popping, spherical object. A few pages earlier, Fred Cave said it gave off a sound like corn being popped. Then the case of Mrs. Carl Loar on Sunbury Road said, "A cracking report ran through the kitchen light wires." Notice, Mrs. Loar tries to find a place with which to attach the sound.

Not all sightings turn out to be sugar and spice and everything nice. Far from it, there are those that have a threatening element related to them. An investigator never knew whether to blame the UFO, CIA or FBI. Perhaps it was a little of all of them.

John Keel met up with some of these cases. From the first time I met him in West Virginia on the "Mothman sighting," I felt I was seeing the best of research being done. His recent book, *Disneyland of the Gods*, shows to what extent he has dug into this subject.

Linda Howe, author of *The Alien Harvest,* presents much to show the negative element connected with UFOs. The fact that we have good and bad people in our world makes it reasonable to assume we may find the same problem elsewhere.

JOHN AND THE UFO

A student from Otterbein College had an experience with a UFO sighting. During his summer vacation he was a night watchman for a country club in Dayton, Ohio. About 5 a.m. one morning he saw an eerie blue light out on the golf course. He took his five-cell flashlight and walked in its direction. As he approached there was a deep ravine between him and the lighted object. Instead of going nearer, he flashed his light towards it.

Instantly it was gone. (Does that sound familiar?) John said it was a sphere which had a translucent appearance; it was like looking through glass blocks of a *Dairy Queen* shop. The light coming through was an eerie blue. The dogs on the adjoining property either died of fright, radiation, or barked their heads off.

John took down all the details. The next day he notified Wright-Patterson Air Base. After a few days with no response he called again. This time he received papers to fill out, followed by a notice to appear at the main gate on a certain day and time. He was met by a car and two men. He felt they were there to keep an eye on him. He was taken to a specific building on the base. It's the one you read about that has no windows and limited access.

He was taken through five locked doors before reaching his goal. This is where he met Major Friend. Major Friend is now retired Col. Friend and has been seen on recent UFO documentaries.

After talking awhile, John said: "Major, there's one thing I want to know: What did I see?" The answer from Major Friend was: "Well, John, there are certain things we cannot tell you, there are other things we will not tell you, yours lies within these categories." When John arrived home he was alone. Five minutes later the doorbell rang. He opened it to find an oriental-looking man with a briefcase. He allowed him to come in. John said he had a stern fatherly look, slightly graying hair, and was well dressed. He was there to give John advice. He told him he had had a "UFO sighting," but was to forget about it. This was for his own welfare. John felt as if he might be being hypnotized. He remembers what may have been a tie pin. This was the kind of a lecture no one could forget.

John's house had those small 4 x 8 door windows which you can peep through so conveniently. He waited long enough for the man to take a few steps and then peeked out to see where he went. There wasn't anyone there: no man, no car, no nothing. He ran out the door, looked behind the trees and bushes, there was no place for the man to hide. John came very near to having a nervous breakdown during the next couple of years. He had been badly threatened and he didn't know by whom! Do you know? No wonder some people will think the military was responsible — but they don't disappear that easily. Others will blame the CIA, the FBI, and other organizations.

It's the disappearing act that causes all the problem. UFOs can disappear with the snap of a finger, but why would they threaten someone? Why? Why? Why?

I suppose it would have been possible for a hypnotist to have given John the suggestion that he would not be able to see him after he left the house. I wonder if John ever thought of that?

THE DUBLIN EPISODE

Another case which I first saw printed was in the NICAP Journal. Since it wasn't more than ten or fifteen miles I thought I'd check it out.

A boy near Dublin, Ohio, had seen something land in a nearby field. He decided to go see what it was. This happened at about 9:30 p.m. He was curious and went closer and closer. There was a landed craft with balls which were suspended around it in the air. As the boy watched he accidentally stepped on a twig and the occupants were alerted. He turned to run but was captured. He had a cut on the back of his neck. The aliens dragged him back toward the craft. The leader told them to let him go. The balls were taken from the air, and the craft left quickly.

At school the next day a teacher noticed the cut on his neck. She asked what happened. He didn't want to tell. Finally he described the sighting and life became more interesting. Twice he was chased off the road by a big black car. He told his teacher he was afraid to walk home. She told him she'd take him home; she was chased off the road by the same black car.

She had moved to another town when I talked to her. She felt the boy was telling the truth. He didn't want to talk about it. There were several frightening episodes. Cuts on the neck are very common in UFO abductions. I felt this sighting was a 100% undesirable experience.

UNCANNY HAPPENINGS

UFOs have been blamed for almost anything that can't be explained in a normal way. Every writer seems to want to take a turn at comments concerning the "Devil's Triangle" and I suppose that gives me leeway to express my opinion. The area bounded by Bermuda, Miami, and Puerto Rico for years has been known as a real problem zone for planes and ships. Something happens to all electrical and mechanical equipment, radios go dead, compasses spin, and all navigational aids stop working. Many planes and ships disappear and are never heard of again. UFOs have been reported in these areas at this time. That could mean that they have more control over magnetic forces than we do and are not affected by them. Lindbergh, Godfrey, and many other pilots tell of their experiences when being caught in the edge of this zone, as well as mechanical failures; military pilots have radioed back that they seemed to be caught in a strange atmosphere of milky white clouds and were unable to recognize up from down. Contact was lost immediately and in one instance, five planes were lost due to these abnormalities.

In this locality, our weather satellites are reported as having behaved irrationally since 1972. An electromagnetic force is so powerful that it blacks out pictures on the magnetic tapes where they are stored for resending to earth. This only happens over the triangle and indicates an enormous electromagnetic field in order to affect a satellite 800 miles above the earth's surface (according to Dr. Meshejian, professor of physics at Longwood College in Farmville, Va.)

There are a number of such areas and they seem to run straight through the earth and bedevil people on the other side of the globe. When our scientists get to the place where they understand the workings of the universe better no doubt we will be able to cope with these problems. Until then, "flying saucers" and other questionable explanations will probably get credit for what is a long way from the truth.

Occasionally reporters become convinced that UFOs deserve recognition. Arthur Shuttlewood, a chief reporter and feature writer of the *Warminster Journal*, told *Sagas* writer Timothy Beckley about UFOs in their small town of Warminster, England. Everything about this report smacks of the fourth dimension. It is not easy to discard the material because it has become too common.

Warminster is a small town of 14,000 and is surrounded by prehistoric relics, stone monoliths, and ritualistic circles. It is near Stonehenge, a gigantic complex of rocks built by an unknown society. One theory claims that it was built as an astronomical observatory centuries ago. The Druids, who were an almost extinct religious sect, used these stone pillars hundreds of years later for equinoctial religious gatherings, but scholars tell us their true origin dates back thousands of years. Avebury, to the north, has a similar history and consists of a series of stones which supposedly had a mathematical purpose. Shuttlewood claims that he personally has had more than 800 sightings in nine years, including coming into close contact with some of the occupants of these eerie objects.

The first uncanny happening began on Christmas morning in 1964, when a middle-aged woman was thrown to the ground by an invisible shock wave that originated a short distance above her. She was pinned down to the ground by fingers of sound that left her so weak that she had great difficulty in recovering enough strength to continue her way to church.

Disturbing sounds filled the air and there have been many unexplained deaths of small animals and birds, apparently from these shock waves. Strange solid-looking craft that dematerialize while in plain sight were very confusing to witnesses. UFO observers have found that objects belonging to them would disappear and reappear in strange ways.

Numerous people saw or heard ghostly walkers and most were glad that their contacts were not any closer. The UFOs which are seen in Warminster take on various shapes and come in many colors. They have been seen as glowing spheres, luminous teardrops, ovoid jewels that range from blood red rubies, twinkling diamonds of flashing light, fiery green emeralds, and in the daytime have been described as lustrous gray pearl. Every shape and size which has been reported anywhere seems to show up in this vicinity. Those who investigate these sightings wonder if this location has created a vortex for these phenomena.

UNUSUAL LIFE FORMS

The problem with most people who advocate full disclosure of knowledge concerning UFOs is that they don't have a full knowledge of the phenomena. The idea that some UFOs may be living biological organisms which sail through the air much as fish swim in the sea is too far out from life as we know it.

As early as April 27, 1948, the Air Force stated in an official release that, "The possible existence of some sort of strange extraterrestrial animals had also been remotely considered. Many of the objects acted more like animals than anything else...."

USAF aircraft are said to have carried infrared homing rockets in order to photograph this phenomenon above the Mojave Desert.

Dr. Carl Sagan is quoted as saying, "A bona fide example of extraterrestrial life, even in a very simple form, would revolutionize biology.... It would be truly immense."

Such life is more apt to be seen at high altitudes. In 1935 mountain climber Frank Smythe felt that he had witnessed such an oddity when climbing Mt. Everest. While he was about 200 ft. above Camp VI he saw two objects floating in the sky, resembling kite balloons in shape. One appeared to have squat, underdeveloped wings and the other something which was suggestive of a beak. They were a dark color and seemed to pulsate slowly, slower than his own heartbeat.

He was an electrical engineer, a former Royal Air Force officer, and a Lt. Col. in the British Army as well as a long list of other accomplishments. Smythe had observed with extreme care and did everything he could to eliminate the suspicion of hallucination.

In 1957 Trevor Constable and Dr. James Woods teamed up to explore the invisible realm which these strange creatures inhabit. They used a 35mm camera, infrared film and various filters as well as a Bolex movie camera. These creatures or "critters," as they called them, were amoeba-like life forms existing in the plasma state. They are living heat substance. Normally they are hidden from us because they are in the infrared range of the electromagnetic spectrum; occasionally they emerge into the visible portion, pulsating with a reddish to orange glow. Sometimes their blinding intensity causes them to be identified as UFOs but they are not craft, they are living organisms.

They are considered an elemental branch of evolution with a low intelligence such as a fish. They grow from the size of a dime up to half-mile in diameter. Most of them have a diaphanous, milk-like construction, usually disc-shaped or spherical, but capable of changing form like amoebas. They give a solid radar return when seen by the naked eye. Trevor and James have published numerous pictures which show the peculiar forms of their "critters."

I can't resist following the scientific work of Constable and Woods with a 1985 *Weekly World News* article. These serious scientists certainly lend credence to the Argentina sighting.

SPACE CREATURES SEEN ON EARTH

Weekly World News, **October 1, 1985**

A herd of space animals, the size and shape of the Goodyear blimp, grazed for three hours on cattle pastures near the remote Argentine ranching settlement of Villa Iruya.

The alien animals, appearing semitransparent and resembling "gigantic bags of gas" according to several witnesses, soared into the sky and slowly vanished from sight when they had finished their browsing.

The bizarre sighting was reported in a news dispatch from Buenos Aires and quoted scientific speculation that the creatures are drifting across the cosmos, moving from planet to planet like a herd of gargantuan cows.

"Their life span must be incredible to cross such vast distances of space at what amounts to a snail's pace," one scientist said. "To all intents and purposes, these cows must be immortal."

Skeptics at first laughed off the reported sightings as merely a "natural aberration" created by fog or low-lying clouds illuminated by the moon.

But that off-the-cuff theory was quickly discounted when it was learned that the space animals had not made their Earth visit at night — they had been seen under clear blue skies in the bright light of day!

"The creatures were colossal...like nothing I have seen before," said 55-year-old ranch foreman Louis Pedroza. They made no sound, but their bodies seemed to quiver and roll slowly from side to side as they rested on the grass. "If I alone had seen them, I would have told no one. They would have thought me mad.

"But I was not alone. Several of my workers were there with me and they say they saw cow-like animals that looked like gigantic bags of gas, resting on the cooling grass of the pampas."

Pedroza said the animals—an even dozen in all—had no apparent features to indicate they were living creatures. But he said he and his workers could sense that they were looking at a strange life-form from another world.

"I have not the words or wisdom to explain what we felt," Pedroza said. "But it was as though we could feel the surging of life in those transparent bodies. It was like when I feel the presence of God when I am in church."

Pedroza and the other witnesses said the space animals gave no indication of being hostile and none made a menacing move toward them.

The workers said they watched the grazing space herd for about three hours. Then, shortly after 2 o'clock, one of them began to drift upward and the rest followed. They rose into the sky until they vanished from sight.

"We all knew we were witness to a sight no man on Earth has ever seen before," Pedroza said. "We just sat there, watching them...and praying."●

NEW GALAXY SHAPED LIKE FETUS

Weekly World News, **May 15, 1990**

by Nelson Mann

Astronomers who discovered a new galaxy at the edge of the Milky Way say the cluster of stars, dust and gas is shaped like a human fetus — and may be alive!

Dr. William Radinski says the galaxy is located forty thousand light years from Earth and measures millions of miles across.

He could not explain why scientists haven't spotted the galaxy before. He did say that the star system appears to be growing and emits radio waves in short bursts that amazingly sound like a human heartbeat.

"We've never seen anything like it," said Radinski, whose studies of galaxies and black holes have earned him a global reputation. "The galaxy is unusually bright and definitely resembles a human fetus. It has a large head, torso, arms, feet and hands.

"There is even the suggestion of an umbilical cord protruding from the belly. We don't know exactly what to make of it at this point.

"But the sheer intensity of radio waves and radiation coming from the galaxy indicate that it is growing rapidly and is unusually active.

"I don't think it's going too far to say that we might be witnessing the birth of a new life-form."

Dr. Radinski and a research team discovered the galaxy while performing a routine telescopic survey of the heavens from a base in Kenya on March 24.

The scientists initially thought that its human shape was caused by moisture or dust in their equipment. But computer-enhanced satellite photos obtained from the Soviet Union and United States clearly show the galaxy to be human in shape.

Further study revealed that radio waves are coming from the galaxy in heartbeat-like bursts that indicate the star system may be alive.

"It could be a coincidence — but I doubt it," said Dr. Radinski.

"When we plot the bursts on a graph they look exactly like an EKG.

"If that thing is alive we're definitely going to hear more from it. Sometimes I look at the galaxy and expect to hear it scream."

Other astronomers studying the new galaxy agree that its human form is unusual but are reluctant to suggest that it might be alive.

One U.S. astronomer says the heartbeat-like radio pulses "may not mean anything at all."

"The pulses are definitely unique but that doesn't mean the galaxy is a living creature," said the expert. "I'm not ruling anything out. We simply need to study this further.

Said Dr. Radinski: "We'll know much more in the months and years to come.

"If the galaxy grows and develops along human lines there will then be no doubt that it is indeed alive. Even if it's not, we've still made an exciting discovery.

"Every new star and galaxy we discover brings us that much closer to finding out how our entire universe was born."●

☐ *I feel forced to carry the above article. I am sure it will be ignored by the majority of people who see it. The preceding material which dates back in the '50s and '60s borders on this kind of information. This present article seems to be a continuation of thought in the same direction. We have so much to learn—you'd better not throw this FETUS out with the bath water! 9.5 for a new galaxy that appears to be alive.*

DETAILED ACCOUNT OF SIGHTING

Some of the best research on flying saucers has been by the APRO group which has been headed by Coral and Jim Lorenzen. The November 1962 issue of Ray Palmer's magazine *Flying Saucers* carries an article by Lorenzen which begs a missing soldier to please make contact with them in order to clear up one of the weird cases on their records.

Pvt. Gerry Irwin possessed a good record until his first sighting of a UFO February 28, 1959. Since that time his actions have kept him in hot water to the extent that finally, after being AWOL for a month, he was listed as a deserter on August 30, 1959.

Gerry was stationed at Ft. Bliss, El Paso, Texas and was returning by car to duty via Cedar City, Utah. He was southeast of town on Rt. 14, a shortcut between two main routes. Suddenly he was aware of a glowing object of an indefinite shape which glided across his path. For a moment the surrounding landscape was lighted and his first thought was that an airliner must have crashed.

He drove to the area nearest where he had seen the object and then left a note inside the car to tell where he had gone and why. On the outside of the car he printed a big stop sign with his shoe polish dauber.

A half hour later a game inspector found the car and went back to Cedar City for help. When volunteers arrived for the search they found Pvt. Irwin face down in the mud and unconscious. He was taken to the nearest hospital where his condition was checked and found to be normal with the exception that he could not be awakened.

For over 23 hours he tossed and mumbled before he finally opened his eyes. In his unconscious state he had jabbered "jacket on the bus," but no one had found a jacket, so this was ignored.

The first thing Pvt. Irwin said when he came to was, "Were there any survivors?" He was told there was no crash and that he was wearing an overcoat with no jacket. Because of the cold, Pvt. Irwin said he had worn a jacket and put his overcoat on top.

He supposed someone had stolen his jacket; his memory seemed to have lapsed from the time he left the car. The doctor claimed his amnesia probably came from hysteria which no doubt brought on the fainting spell. Up to this time, Gerry had no record of blackouts.

The Army sent the general's plane to bring Pvt. Irwin back to Ft. Bliss, to Ward 30 (known by the boys as the psycho ward), where for four days he was placed under observation and then given a clean bill of health.

A few days later he was walking near his barracks when he fell over in a dead faint. He recovered quickly and seemed to have no ill effects.

On Sunday, March 15 at 10 p.m., Pvt. Irwin was walking down the street in El Paso when again he fainted dead away. He was taken to the Southwest General Hospital for emergency treatment and found to be in normal condition except that he could not be awakened. At 2 a.m. Monday he finally opened his eyes, looked around the room, and said, "Were there any survivors?"

This time an ambulance arrived from Ft. Bliss to cart him back to the psycho ward where he was kept for 32 more days. All tests indicated that he was normal and cooperative. Even the drug sodium amytal was used in order to probe his mind. He was told this was unsuccessful; however, he had no way of knowing whether this was true.

Pvt. Irwin was discharged from hospital on April 17, 1959. The next morning he felt an urge to return to the location of his original experience in Utah. His car's engine block had been frozen during his hospitalization in Utah, so he had no way to make the trip except by bus. What made him go AWOL to travel back to this lonely spot no one knows. Only he knows why he went to the place where some weeks ago he had removed his jacket and left it on a bush.

There was a paper wrapped around a pencil sticking through his buttonhole. He carefully burned the paper and threw the jacket down and then observed what he had done. With difficulty he found his way back to the road. This time he was told that he was not only AWOL but was goldbricking and responsible for his actions.

Pvt. Irwin went to the inspector general, who apparently turned a sympathetic ear. He was scheduled to go back in the Army hospital on July 10. On May 30 the Lorenzens entertained Pvt. Irwin for the weekend. He promised faithfully to keep in touch with them; this case was similar to several others in their files. No one knows what happened to Pvt. Gerry Irwin—for some reason he just seemed to have disappeared.

☐ *This research is the kind that can be compared to contacts and abductions in the future. The Lorenzens will certainly go down in history as one of the benefactors for the sacrifices they've made.*

THE CONDON REPORT

In 1953, Dr. H.P. Robertson, a Cal Tech physicist now deceased, was chosen to head a seven-member group, officially known as the Scientific Advisory Panel on Unidentified Flying Objects. Because of military regulations some of these men's names have never been revealed but the ones that were are clear at the top of the ladder. Among suggestions made by these scientists were that "the national security agencies take steps to strip the Unidentified Flying Objects of the special status they have been given and the air of mystery they have acquired," and that "the national security agencies institute policies designed to prepare the country to recognize promptly and to react effectively to true indications of hostile intent or action."

Only a few days were spent in making these decisions. Since that time we have been blessed with various programs and projects that should eventually bring about a recognition of UFOs, hopefully in an unemotional matter-of-fact manner.

The "Condon Committee's Report on UFOs" was an officially inspired project which gave people a good chance to be bored by most of its contents. Part of its members were bent on giving people a true picture of flying phenomena. This was not necessarily so with those in charge of the investigation. Two scientists were dismissed from the project after the following letter was taken from the office files and given to the news media. This 1966 memorandum was to James Archer and Thurston E. Manning from Robert Low, assistant dean of the University of Colorado's Graduate School who became project coordinator. This material was made public by Dr. David Saunders and R. Rogers Harkins. Dr. Saunders did much field work for the Condon Report and disapproved of the way in which the affair was handled. Do read the following memo and decide whether you would have wanted this man in charge of an investigation for you:

> Branscomb is very much against it. Gordon Little thinks it would be a disaster. George Benton likewise is negative. Their arguments, combined, run like this: In order to undertake such a project, one has to approach it objectively. That is, one has to admit the possibility that such things as UFOs exist. It is not respectable to give serious consideration to such a possibility. Believers, in other words, remain outcasts. ... The analogy with ESP, Rhine, and Duke is only partially valid. The Duke study was done by believers who, after they had finished, convinced almost no one. Our study would be conducted almost exclusively by non-believers who, although they couldn't possibly prove a negative result, could and probably would add an impressive body of evidence that there is no reality to the observations. The trick would be, I think, to describe the project so that to the public it would appear a totally objective study but to the scientific community would present the image of a group of non-believers trying their best to be objective but having an almost zero expectation of finding a saucer. One way to do this would be to stress investigation, not of the physical phenomena, but rather of the people who do the observing — the psychology and sociology of persons and groups who report seeing UFOs. If the emphasis were put here, rather than on examination of the old question of the physical reality of the saucer, I think the scientific community would quickly get the message.... It is premature to have much of an opinion, but I'm inclined to feel at this early stage that, if we set up the thing right and take pains to get the proper people involved and have success in presenting the image we want to present to the scientific community, we could carry the job off to our benefit.

The Elmira *Star Gazette* of January 26, 1967 quoted Dr. Condon as saying, "It is my inclination right now to recommend that the government get out of this business. My attitude right now is that there's nothing to it." Reporter Olive then asserted that Dr. Condon added, with a smile, "But I'm not supposed to reach a conclusion for another year." This was less than three months after the project was formed and three months before the methodology had been chosen.

THE UFO AND THE COMPUTER

Twenty-five years ago it was easy to solve all cases where contact was claimed with the occupants of UFOs. This was true with the whole field of investigations. Some were ready to admit foreign craft were coming into our skies, but not that they were making contact with anyone. They were quickly solved by plastering the word "hoax" across every story that dared to mention the beings who were responsible for the new-fangled "flying disks." A computer might soon show that the time has come for a better approach. As years have gone by, many of these wronged individuals have been put under hypnosis and also given truth serums. When under these drugs their stories bring out many similar details to confirm the experiences of other contactees. For instance, under hypnosis quite a number of people have described being taken into a craft by a ray of light. A number of people have told that a cigarette lighter was taken from them. Many people mention the occupants as making a buzzing sound with lips that do not move. Many mention robot-like occupants who seem to have radio operated sounds coming from their middle section. These beings are credited with using mind control to a greater degree than we are able to understand. People were given post-hypnotic suggestions which are on a level that our doctors and scientists cannot reach. After examining these patients, men of research frankly admit that it appears that some people have actually been through unbelievable episodes which they describe. Scientists including Dr. Allen J. Hynek have long ago stopped laughing at such weird tales. They well know that it's too easy to throw out the baby with the bathwater.

It is my belief that every reported contact case on record should be followed up with a full investigation of this kind — no matter what the date of the case may be. Not that I believe that everything that comes forth would be the whole truth and nothing but the truth, but rather that fed into a computer, a number of very definite facts would be resolved.

THE LITTLE PEOPLE

After I finished reading the paperback edition of *The Unidentified*, by Jerome Clark and Loren Coleman, UFOs were high on the list of the unidentified, but there are many other topics that are uncovered by this subject.

For instance, have you heard of the little people who were seen in Europe for hundreds of years? These include fairies, gnomes, elves, etc. Two little girls took photographs of fairies that specialists were never able to disprove. The persons who saw them were just as sincere as those who insist they are seeing UFOs and their occupants today.

We keep reading about the Abominable Snowman who just can't be caught. He is a very real thing to those who stumble onto his tracks. He leaves plenty of physical evidence behind but somehow we can't seem to capture one. The visions of Joan of Arc and also of Joseph Smith (founder of the Mormon religion) are experiences that we tend to ignore because we haven't any legitimate answer as to how these things can happen.

The airship sightings in the 1890's are too numerous to mention. Newspapers from many states carried stories that are just as impressive as the ones we read about today. There are bound to be hoaxes and always will be, the problem is what to do about the ones that aren't. These include certified copies by men of unquestionable reputation. Indian tribes have been aware of "sky canoes" for hundreds of years. "Ubigiawa" claim to have made contact with these beings and are expecting the coming of the true White Brother. Contactees have found it is not a very wise choice to depend upon the help and the appearance of these craft beings — they may show, or they may not.

In their book, Clark and Coleman attempt to analyze the contacts of George Adamski. This isn't any easy job—at least it makes very interesting reading. The authors present cases from way back when, and compare them to sightings right up to the minute. It is well-written and a very intriguing book and will give you much to think about. Dr. Carl Jung is quoted liberally as well as other well-known scientists. It is going to be hard to convince people who have lived through these experiences that they are dealing with a form of life that has a limited solidity. That's about what the author has in mind. No good investigator really questions the sincerity of the contactees. The question is, just what has he contacted? It doesn't look as if the subject of UFOs is apt to desert us in the near future. Why don't you read it for yourself?

CHASED BY A UFO

One of the closest sightings which I have checked is that of Charlotte Nipper, a Georgia girl who lived just off route I-75 at the Barneyville Rd. exit. The first time I tried to find her, even the service stations wouldn't help me. It took several attempts to locate the right exit. The first man said, "Government men have been here and it's classified." I assumed the man thought that the Air Force had been checking their secret equipment a quarter of a mile off I-75 at 5:30 a.m.... Then I found a boy who had been in high school with Charlotte and eked out a little more information. Finally I got close enough that the next man said, "I don't know how you know about all this, but no government man is going to tell me I can't talk." And that's how I found the right exit and directions to her house. No one was home so there was nothing to do but wait a few years and try again.

Next time I found her father and sister. Charlotte had married and moved to a nearby town. Someone had written a lengthy report of her experience. She had had no further contact with UFOs. Her story goes like this:

Miss Nipper had just finished high school. She was a telephone operator in Valdosta, Georgia. She was due at the office on the early morning shift and had left for work about 5:00 a.m. When she was less than a half mile from I-75 she noticed what she thought must be a load of hay stalled in the middle of the road. It had red lights all around it and the girl supposed some farmer had a breakdown. Since it covered the entire road she drove over in the flat sandy ditch to go around it and suddenly realized it belonged in the category of UFOs.

Her new car was able to reach Route 75 only a moment before the UFO. Her goal was to try to reach the next exit where a service station would be open. She was aware of this UFO being close above the car while she was holding the gas pedal at 95 miles per hour.

Suddenly a large truck appeared from the opposite side of the road. Apparently the UFO was frightened away and disappeared in a few seconds. Charlotte made it to the nearest exit and called home for help. Her father said it took her five attempts to say Mamma.

The truck driver headed for the nearest exit. During his breakfast he described the exit of the UFO. When Charlotte's story hit the news the restaurant owner was able to confirm it. This craft had parked directly under a power line which went diagonally across the road. There are many sightings where UFOs have been seen tapping into such lines.

☐ *How many tales of this kind would you investigate before you'd stop calling them all "plasmas" and hoaxes? Many cars and occupants have been picked up with a beam of light. Charlotte felt this might happen to her.*

THE LUNATIC FRINGE

What is meant by the lunatic fringe? This is one of the expressions often used to describe people interested in UFOs. As near as I can tell it means some one who doesn't believe the same things that you do. Generally speaking, they have had some type of UFO sighting or experience which causes them to become curious in the workings of the universe.

It appears that some people see objects and hear things that other people doubt. Usually they aren't locked up, but their sanity is often a subject for discussion. I must say that I haven't seen much or heard much but have tried to figure what happens to the other fellow.

It does seem to me that ego is the greatest deterrent to spiritual growth. When you go off in the wilds and start looking for objects in the sky someone starts to wonder about you. Particularly if you think you are seeing strange lights and conversing with beings who purport to be from Venus, Mars, or only the Lord knows where.

There is an advantage of being with such people. You don't have to know them to feel safe in their presence. You may leave your car unlocked, throw your purse and sweater on the handiest tree stump, and take off for a walk in the woods. Their food supplies are left unguarded and a money box is open and available.

Strange people — it's obvious they must come from some other planet. They sing the same songs and say the same prayers, but they believe they are guided by unseen beings who lead them in the paths of righteousness.

Some of these entities or guides are thought to inhabit space craft which may come from space itself, comparable to the way we live on our planet. Being of another dimension of life, they aren't generally visible. Presbyterians, United Methodists, and members of other religions who claim to hear voices attribute this source to God. These people think God is sending space brothers to guide them into a higher state of consciousness. Who can say?

☐ *In our own group we depended on speakers who might have different ideas and experiences which were presented in informal lectures. These lectures covered related subjects that were interesting enough to warrant our time. Reincarnation, psychic phenomena, research on Uri Geller, the Power of Prayer on Plants, etc., are all examples of subjects we found worth evaluating.*

For twenty years we spent a summer weekend in Pennsylvania with the Warren Light Center and their members. There we found a mixture of everything. They presented material regardless of whether it was their own choice or what came their way. We heard speakers who were so good they should have been on national TV and others that didn't fit into our way of thinking. It was a way of being aware of many topics.

THE MUNDO UFO REPORT

In 1957, Laura Mundo of Inkster, Mich. presented Desmond Leslie on a lecture tour in the U.S. She had brought George Adamski to Detroit in 1954, and many other well-known contactees.

Leslie was a co-author of *Flying Saucers Have Landed.* Desmond, a cousin of Winston Churchill, was acquainted with Prince Philip, Lord Dowding, and family members. These people were aware of UFOs and took them very seriously.

In 1982 Laura wrote *The Mundo UFO Report*, published by Vantage Press. Much of the information presented comes from mental contacts who give advice and comments on the subject of space, spacecraft, and their occupants. It's chockfull of words that are hard to understand so you'd better have a good background in metaphysics. Only time will tell how much value has been received. She is one of the many who had threatening calls from what became known as the "Men in Black" or the MIB's. (These were very common but no one was certain as to the culprits who were behind them. The CIA probably was at the top of the suspected list).

After returning from a UFO convention, Laura had a 2 a.m. phone call telling her to get out of flying saucer research. The voice was threatening; he told her she had come too close to the truth. She was told her phone had been bugged. I believe my own experience may have been similar. I ran into two other cases which followed the same pattern.

Mrs. Mundo believes the flying saucers are sent to salvage a part of our people in case of a catastrophe. If you don't have the right vibes you won't get picked up.

One story she repeated is a wingding. Many people believe Elvis is still alive. That makes news and sells papers. Ten years before his death, Elvis had seen a UFO flying low, back and forth, over his house. After that he was a believer.

The September 10, 1978 issue of *People* magazine says that thirteen saucers flew over his grave in Memphis in the spring of 1978. Several times they have been seen hovering over his tomb. They come in the wee small hours and hover within a few yards of the grave. A guard said the craft made a strange noise like electrical popping. That's when he got my attention! It's identical to cases I've investigated. The guard was too scared to do anything; he didn't dare give his name or he'd be fired.

Some local teenage girls took a late-night tour of Graceland and saw a saucer dart over the grave and fly away. When they told a guard what happened he told them to get out and not to tell anyone or he'd tell the police they were on pot.

UFOs IN TIME OF CATASTROPHE

Whenever and wherever I find material which relates in anyway to flying saucers I try to give it a fair evaluation. It is only in this way that I have any assurance that the true answers finally may be covered.

In reading *The Brotherhood of the Seven Rays* I was interested in a chapter titled "Master Kuthuni." Presumably the author has acted as a medium or channel for the material given.

He makes this statement:

> The space people are beings. Three dimensional like ourselves. They are not spooks. There are beings of other dimensions that are working with the Space Confederation but they are not coming into your living rooms.
>
> They are the mentors to the Space Brothers coming in physical form. Those operating in space ships above your world that you can see, feel, and touch are the same as you — three dimensional. The reason you see space ships is because people on other worlds still need them in order to travel.

It is said that both good and evil forces will come to us in the garb of angels of light. Many will be fooled, for it is very difficult to recognize one from the other. Master Kuthuni indicates that all life has a spark of divinity in it or it would not exist, and that since this is so, all individuals must continue an upward path.

This would be to say that all in existence is of God. Since this is so, then apparently all that appears to be either good or evil is a part of God. Even the forces of darkness which seem evil are merely a part of God which is in the process of evolving to a higher understanding.

The important thing is to be able to choose that force with which we wish to associate. The master suggests that we can recognize a false prophet by the fact that he is the first to throw stones. By doing this he draws attention away from himself and causes observers to look in another direction.

He also says flying saucers will be seen more in the future and will come to the aid of our civilization in times of great catastrophe.

The occupants in the saucers are pictured as beings whose job it would be to rescue souls and take them to appropriate places.

☐ *By the time you were rescued, I'm not sure whether you would be dead or alive — apparently it would be hard to know the difference. Whatever happens it is suggested that you no longer would be seen visibly, yet everything sounds like a new heaven on earth.*

THE BETTY AND BARNEY HILL MOVIE

It is my understanding from various articles which I have read that the movie premiere *The UFO Incident,* was a part of a government-inspired series. It was shown at 9 p.m. on Monday, October 20, 1975 on NBC. The idea was said to be to see how people would react to such information. If it appeared that the reaction was not too serious, the complete information concerning UfOs would be released to the public by July 4, 1976.

I took my own little "Gallup poll" to see what I felt the reaction to such an announcement would be. Frankly, it's not good. I do not believe that people are ready for such an announcement. You can't lie for such a long period and then retract your statements. It's like telling children to write to Santa Claus and then saying, "Cut it, kids, you're too old to believe that stuff." The kids don't want to stop believing. Many people don't want to give up their security blankets. The assurance that UFOs are imaginary has lulled many into a state in which they don't seem to think for themselves. Even though Uncle Sam has shown them his information was false and that this was done for a purpose, there are those who close their eyes because they don't want to see.

The UFO Incident is a souped-up story of the true experience of Barney and Betty Hill. The fact that it was experienced by a white woman and a black man was sufficient to turn off less than a quarter of its viewers, but turn them off it certainly did. Then the garb that was used to impersonate a spaceman took care of another small percentage. Goodness knows what would have happened if they had succeeded in constructing something that did look like the creatures.

NBC's *Tomorrow* show with Tom Snyder did a follow-up by interviewing Betty Hill and Stan Friedman (a nuclear physicist and UFO investigator). This was ten times more interesting, convincing, and spectacular than the show itself. Friedman is lecturing at universities all over the country and finds little problem in reaching the minds of the younger generation. He has statistics to uphold his information and plenty of scientists to agree with him.

Under hypnosis, Betty Hill was able to produce a star map which at the time it was drawn was unknown to astronomers. Its view shows these stars from the position of space to earth and was displayed on the wall of the spacecraft. In the stars which she drew, all fifteen are thought likely to produce life. Scientists and astronomers say that the odds of Betty Hill being able to draw such a map are astronomical or virtually impossible.

☐ *Much as I hate to admit it, I believe that a release of all government information would result in one third of our population being jarred, another third flabbergasted or dumbfounded, and the rest in a state which would be unpredictable. It's the "unpredictable" that gives me concern. This article was written in 1975, and I find it not too far off line.*

A 1962 SIGHTING IN COLUMBUS, OHIO

Who's kidding whom? Last week's explanations of UFO sightings are typical examples of what may be expected from Government, Air Force, and news media officials. Many reporters avoid the term "UFO" and state that a meteor or several meteorites have been reported.

You will find Wright-Patterson Field as well as Lockbourne a poor place to inquire about unidentified flying objects. Official reports generally assure you that nothing has been seen, or at least it's a balloon or a meteor.

Wednesday, January 3, from 5:30–9:30 p.m., reports were sent to radio stations, police headquarters, the Weather Bureau, and Lockbourne AFB, describing what appeared to be UFOs.

By the next day news flashes were being sent out so people would understand about these things. That day's issue of the Columbus *Citizen-Journal* carried Wednesday evening's story.

The last paragraph mentions a little of what was seen by a North High School boy. This is the story as told to me by Phil Bougher, 1112 E. Cooke Rd.

Mr. Bougher had gone down to a nearby store about 8:30 p.m. He found a man looking up at something, so he looked too. It wasn't just ordinary, so he called Phil's mother so they could look through their 152-power telescope. They opened a window and Phil's mother watched this blue white light while Phil managed to set up the scope.

Phil feels he could see only a portion of the UFO at a time. It looked to him like a metallic craft shaped something like a coffee can resting on an upside down plate. A continuous band of window panes seemed to encircle the craft.

Inside these windows were a group of four square-looking soft yellow lights. Up and down the outside of the craft were electrical impulses which were blue but shifted to red whenever the craft decided to move.

When the boy took his first look he immediately felt that this was an object from outer-space.

Of course meteors are from outer-space. The Pentagon has seen to it that people are well aware that many of these meteors may be seen right now. How would you like to see a meteor with windows and lights? Who's kidding whom?

MY VIEWS IN 1962

I find myself in constant trouble when I try to find words and expressions to describe information which needs to be presented. There is a dictionary of mysticism which attempts to define words of this kind but I don't own one and if I did I'm not sure people would know what is being said.

Only the other day I found myself in trouble because I use the term "dimensional" so loosely. Anytime I am dealing with life which doesn't act and behave in a normal fashion, I toss it over in this category. I realize that this isn't strictly correct but I don't know what other word to use.

Life is life, and is real to itself, no matter where you find it. To think life as we see it is all there is, is ridiculous. Our life is merely adapted to the planet on which we live.

Life on Venus or Mars is not apt to bear much resemblance to us. On the other hand, there are thousands of other locations that have conditions so similar that no doubt development has gone through a similar evolution.

Life in space, however, is just as real and of necessity must vary from us to such an extent as to be fantastic. We are only starting our journey into space and each time we investigate the outer regions we find ourselves being observed by unknown things.

Whether these are mechanical devices that accompany our missiles and space rockets certainly hasn't been proved. But something is there. How can you expect our government to explain objects to you which they themselves haven't figured out? Of course, if they had, I doubt that this would be shared with the public.

For me to say I think all the phenomena which reaches us is from another planet seems just as absurd as to say that all of it comes from space. Anything which I give you must be just an opinion which I have arrived at by reading a great many books and by contacting many people with various thoughts on such subjects.

From my own investigations it would appear that the phenomena which we see in our skies is just as apt to originate from space itself as from any particular planet.

However, this doesn't mean that it's not coming from other planets! The objects which appear are of many varieties and probably are apt to be as good and as bad as the best and the worst of us.

Just because life comes from elsewhere doesn't indicate that it needs to be on a higher plane or a lower one. We are probably being visited by beings far beyond us in our growth and spiritual development. On the other hand, some of these phenomena probably should be avoided.

Generally we are attracted or repelled by that which is wise for us. If I were to contact such an object I would sincerely hope that extra sensory perception is as possible as Dr. B. Rhine indicates in his many detailed books.

☐ *I see little reason for changing my comments in 1990! Remember, I published this in 1962....*

RELIGION

How many times have you heard someone say, "You must keep religion out of the UFO subject"? You can't keep religion out of politics, how on earth do you expect to keep it out of space? Whether you like it or not the borderline is close.

For years, comments from space-beings seem to have softpedaled the information concerning religion. The only comment I've heard is they believe in a "universal God." I guess that spreads God around a good bit. He must need quite a few helpers.

Whether he had delivered Jesus via a UFO is occasionally discussed. There are a number of books written on the UFO and the Bible. UFOs have been with us since the beginning of time. I feel most churches are aware of these craft; whether they think they are angels or devils probably depends upon the brand of religion.

☐ *When we were having so many speakers back in 1962, the following article was from a report given by a man who was sent to my door with less than a 24-hr. notice.*

THE MESSAGE FROM BALA KRISHNAN

Finding lecture rooms for speakers on Saturday night generally involves problems. For that reason I found myself with over fifty people lined up around my rooms and on the stairs. Whenever someone hears of a lecturer who is a bit on the unusual, I am often asked if I can arrange for him to be heard while he is in town. This is how we happened to have a message from Bala Krishnan, who is returning to southern India where he will preach his version of Christianity to the people of India.

At the age of thirteen he came under the influence of Ghandi and served as a non-combatant in the Indian section of the British army during World War II. In order to find an answer to the problems of human misery which he had witnessed, he began studying the teachings and writings of Rama Krishna, Vivekanda, Tolstoi, Ghandi, Abraham Lincoln, Henry David Thoreau, Vinoba Bhave, and Dr. Albert Schweitzer. He covered 12,000 miles visiting holy places and holy men, staying in ninety-six ashrams or monasteries where he sought advice from spiritual teachers of various schools of thought.

During these years he felt that truth was made known to him and since then he has been traveling in many countries of Europe and the Americas where he has been bringing a message of peace, love and brotherhood to man.

Bala's messages go directly to our Christian Bible and are inspired from the words which were taught by Jesus Christ. He was dressed in a typical long white gown with full sleeves which hung to his wrists. He stresses the importance of knowing one's self. According to his philosophy, to do good without knowing the doer only leads to more misery and mischief. He claims our false love and attachment to a particular piece of earth has brought much misery into the world. By identifying ourselves too much with either our Republican or Democratic party we allow ourselves to feel a personal defeat when our party loses. He feels it would be better to accept the verdict gracefully and say, "Thy will be done." Probably one of the strongest points made in this lecture implies the wiseness of "taking no thought." An overdose of thinking not only closes our minds to the help which can be received from the ALL KNOWING MIND but also creates problems which encourage us to live in the past and the future rather than the present.

Bala spent much time stressing that the kingdom of God lies within each of us and to know ourselves we must actually "be still and know that this is so." When this is accomplished it is then we will feel a very real creative joy, a fountain of happiness, which has no opposites, an inexpressible peace, a spontaneous freedom, a true inspiration, and a silent, serene and joyous existence.

The spiritual radiance which came from the man was such that all who heard him felt surely he had found a way to reach the presence of God.

☐ *Bala's message summed up quickly would be, "give love, love, love, and plenty of it without stopping to think about your giving it!" Sounds like our Southern California friend Leo Buscaglia, doesn't it?*

THANKS TO W. RAYMOND DRAKE

While we're on the subject of religion, let's not stop before giving credit to W. Raymond Drake. His numerous books relating to UFOs, mythology, and the Bible are knowledgeable, interesting, and quite convincing. Several are available if you hunt hard. *Gods and Spacemen In The Ancient Past*, *Gods and Spacemen In The Ancient East*, and *Gods and Spacemen In The Ancient West* show the labor of a dedicated man to a subject which will always be of high priority.

Drake attempts to show that spacemen once ruled the earth and over centuries came again and again to keep an eye on our progress. He believes they mated with human beings, have produced offspring, and are responsible for the many legends handed down in different countries which help us to surmise that we are relatives of our brothers from space.

☐ *Later, we'll look at abduction cases in our present time. I find they show that aliens are experimenting with cross-breeding, stealing sperm from men, and swiping an egg or two from a female subject. All this looks like a process we've been through before — maybe forty thousand years ago.*

CHARIOTS OF THE GODS

Erich Von Daniken's *Chariots of The Gods* was such a big seller that it was made into a major motion picture. It has provoked interest about many of the mysteries of the past.

Whether it proves spacemen visited us 40,000 years ago is up to you. Many people believe the giant stone figures on Easter Island relate to space visitors who influenced island life.

☐ *Prehistoric landing strips which can still be seen in the Andes tempt us to think they were made for people who came from far, far away. These authors can't hope to convince everyone. However, if they spark your interest perhaps you'll come up with a better answer.*

TRAVIS WALTON AND THE WOODCUTTERS

On November 5, 1975, seven young men who worked as tree trimmers in Arizona were on their way from work when they spotted an alien craft 25 yards from the side of the road.

Mike Rogers, 28, stopped the truck and they all stared in utter amazement. Twenty-two-year-old Travis Walton of Snowflake, Arizona, jumped out of the car and walked toward the ship. All of his companions shouted for him to come back but he kept going. The ship rocked back and forth in the air — it was smooth and gave off a yellowish-orange light. As he walked nearer the saucer a blue ray shot down from it and he was knocked off his feet. His hands and arms were outstretched and a second later he was gone. Mike stepped on the gas, believing that they were going to be chased. When they realized they weren't followed, he pulled to the roadside. They saw a flash from among the trees and decided the ship had gone. When they found that Travis was gone, they went into the town of Heber, about twelve miles away. The fellows felt no one would believe them and sure enough nobody did. At least not until they took lie detector tests and were questioned by doctors and psychiatrists. Travis Walton could not be found, but five days later he was returned just outside the town of Heber.

He was left on the roadside. He says he saw the UFO take off into the sky. He remembers being hit by something and then waking up in what he thought was a hospital room. Three creatures were standing over him; he panicked and jumped from the table. Again he was knocked out and the next thing he remembered he was on the side of the road and the craft was shooting into space. Travis was interviewed under hypnosis for eight hours and his friends were questioned for another three hours.

☐ *Travis said the creatures looked like well-developed fetuses. They were about five feet tall and wore tight-fitting tannish-brown robes. The beings had mushroom-colored skin and they made no sound. They had domed heads with large eyes and long fingers with no fingernails. Rest assured this won't be the last you'll hear of this contact case.*

THE MISSING PROFESSOR

The event below took place the following week in Campinos, Brazil. On November 13 at 9:30 a.m. Professor Antonio Rjouik, 36, was driving to the University of Campinos where he is head of the mechanical engineering department. Suddenly he developed a violent headache. He stopped the car and put his head down on the steering wheel.

That was the last he remembered for four full days. At 9:30 a.m. on November 17 he was found in an empty lot in the small remote town of Vilhena, 1200 miles away from where he had blacked out. He was in a crouched position, unconscious, and temporarily paralyzed.

Two policemen took him to the Hospital of Mercy, in Vilhena, where he was treated by Dr. Henrique Coulhino. He was suffering from muscular seizures and was in a trance state. The professor was dressed in the same clothes which he had worn on Nov. 13 and they were still meticulously clean and unwrinkled. Because of his outstanding reputation he has been examined by numerous high-caliber doctors. A lie detector shows Antonio Rjouik is telling the truth. Under hypnosis he is not able to give additional information.

The roads on this 1200-mile stretch are so bad that it is estimated to be at least an eight-day trip and even this would be difficult. Mr. Rjouik had never been to this town and had no reason to ever go there. Flights were checked to see if he could have somehow made this trip by air. Even though thousands of pictures were circulated through the area, he had not been seen by anyone.

A check on UFO sightings also produced nothing. The professor said while he was aware of such things it just sounded like science fiction to him.

He is reported to be in excellent health and has never had medical problems. His only reaction to this episode is a somewhat depressed feeling. He is a happily married, well-respected man with a two-year-old daughter.

Police, scientists, and doctors believe there is no logical explanation for this experience and that it must have happened due to a super-normal force. An interesting similarity in many UFO close-contact cases is the stressing of a severe headache.

THOSE TRINIDAD UFO PICTURES

Secrecy in the field of "flying saucers" extends far beyond U.S. boundaries. Perhaps it is carried out to a greater extent here, but researchers in other countries have the same complaint.

An article by Dr. Olave T. Fontes, M.D. has been reprinted in the February 1961 issue of Ray Palmer's magazine *Flying Saucers*.

It carries four photographs which were taken from aboard a research ship at the island of Trinidad, in the South Atlantic. The pictures were taken by a civilian photographer who was a guest on a Brazilian navy ship.

They were shot under the watchful eyes of many military personnel and developed under the strictest observation. It was thought that nearly a hundred persons on shipboard had seen this object and confirmed the photograph to be legitimate.

The photographer spent four hours being interviewed by the military authorities. His pictures were put through every conceivable test and passed 100% in all cases. Because of the large number of civilians on the ship at this time, the authorities were unable to control secrecy regulations and the story front-paged the newspapers for days.

Since the four pictures were taken within fourteen seconds and included tops of mountains, it was possible to estimate speed and other details. A fifth picture, taken at an earlier date by a naval officer, also showed a similar craft.

The photographer described the object as dark gray with a greenish phosphorescent vapor or mist which surrounded it. It appeared to be metallic and solid. Apparently there was no noise from the craft but this could not be certain because of splashing waves and other noises.

The saucer flew with an undulatory movement and changed speed abruptly with no transition, in a jump. Mr. Barauna (the photographer) said he had only been placed under one restriction which he would not be able to tell since he had given his word.

These pictures were taken January 16, 1958, and were only part of a very trying month as more than a half dozen other similar sightings perplexed the scientists who had set up weather observing apparatus on the island.

At one time one of their balloons was sucked into a cloud formation and came out minus its equipment. A few moments later a UFO also emerged from this hideout. Whether it was taken from the balloon or parachuted into some lost place is not known, but it is the purpose of these scientists to have all things under control.

If this 1958 series of pictures weren't enough to convince you — forget it. These pictures were so good, and so well-known and met every requirement that could be desired. No single sighting will do any good unless we capture one in the center of the football field — between Ohio State and Michigan or maybe at the Rose Bowl Game.

THE BUMBLEBEE CAN FLY

No one ever told a bumblebee that it can't fly and because "it thinks it can, it can." Man knows such a design is all wrong and can't figure what gets that big carcass off the ground. What man thinks he can do, he too, can do. It's only his thinking that limits his action.

If man truly wants to reach other planets and far away places, he will, even if he has to redesign his body to do it, that too may not take too long if he keeps fooling around with nuclear weapons....

Scuttlebutt from UFO contacts and other dimensions tell us that space is teeming with life, some similar to ours and much that isn't. Life that occupies the same space as we do, with neither of us being aware of each other, is hard to accept. I guess that's what you call 'what you don't know won't hurt you.'

The May 9, 1989 issue of the *Weekly World News* carries a daylight account of a saucer-shaped UFO which blasted out of the ocean and circled a Japanese freighter for 15 minutes on April 17. This took place 175 miles east of Kanazawa in the Sea of Japan. The 165-foot freighter *Taki Kyoto* suffered some structural damage which occurred from the giant swells caused by the UFO both when it came out of the water and then when it went back in again. Taki Usuda, the 54-year-old Captain, described it as being at least five times as long as their freighter and glowing like a neon. A coastal authority spokesman, Hoshi Ishido, said that the Captain and his crew were calling it an unidentified object, a simple UFO.

In his bestseller *Communion*, Whitley Streiber pictures his abductors as three to four feet tall, large head, no ears, a slit for a mouth, luminous black eyes, and long, thin hands with black, claw-like nails.

A young Pennsylvanian woman who was hypnotized by Professor David Jacobs of Temple University in Philadelphia gave this description: She was lured aboard a UFO by a tiny large-headed creature with large luminous black eyes. Under hypnosis she claimed she had been picked up at ages 6, 10, 11, 17 and 18 and perhaps even more recently. She vowed she had never read about UFOs nor knew anything about them. She believes she was given a medical examination both inside and out. This account is duplicated in many cases where abduction is claimed.

THE ALIEN AT SARANAC LAKE

For many years someone has been describing whomever, or whatever happened to be seen in, or near, a UFO. For instance along in the mid-Sixties a newspaper from Saranac Lake, NY carried a picture of a small alien supported between a local policeman and another person. Both men's names were given and the article assured the reader that more information would follow just as soon as they knew what was to be done with this small bit of robot-looking thing with a helmet and antennas jutting forth from its head. The government was to pick it up and more news was to follow.

Sure enough, the follow-up was soon available. The paper said this was a publicity stunt which had been done to see if they could increase subscribers. I wonder why our newspaper never thought of such a thing?

A science teacher I knew, Dan Haber, took some of his vacation by the way of Saranac Lake to see if he could figure out just what the original story was all about.

No one would talk about the case; the policeman was described in derogatory terms and although they admitted he was still on the payroll, he had been moved from the area and would not be available for comment. Now I doubt if our local police are ready to make that much of a sacrifice for any news sales department. However, there are many stories of little people, bigger people and also the "Bigfoot" tales that just won't go away.

DOCUMENTARIES SUCH AS *Outer Space Connection & Chariots Of The Gods*

Did you see the *Outer Space Connection* or *Chariots of the Gods*? That was back in '75. Such documentaries are very stimulating.

The scenes from the Andes are most impressive and of course there is no natural way in which they can be explained. Huge forms, figures, and roads cover these mountain tops. They are meaningless from the ground and have obviously been made to be seen from above. By whom? That's what we don't really know. Scientists are shown making extensive experiments which show how life might have been brought to earth from other planets. Other experiments show how Kirlian photography is able to picture the life force which emanates from people, plants, and even from the dead hand of a mummy. Mummies have been found which show operations have been made on their skulls which, even today, would be too much of an undertaking. The healing of the bone areas show that patients survived the operations.

A computer has been built by which a chimp can and does "talk" to his trainer by pushing buttons on the keyboard in a proper order. The keys display abstract and otherwise meaningless symbols. It is thought that we too might be able to "talk" to space people through such machinery.

It has been found that the shape of a pyramid seems to draw an unusual energy force that preserves life in the items that are kept within them. Grains of wheat 50 years old sprouted when they were planted. A razor blade regains its sharpness over and over again when kept within a pyramid. The huge stones out of which the pyramids were constructed were moved and maneuvered by means with which we are not familiar.

Numerous pictures of UFOs support the familiar descriptions of unidentified craft. Authors of the book *The Outer Space Connection* make it clear they believe life is somewhere else in the universe and that probably somebody else has been here before, and will be back again.

☐ *By presenting these forerunners to the public, people will be better able to cope with the idea of life beyond our world. This was the process suggested by a panel of scientists known as the Robertson Committee. It is they who pretty much made the rules which govern the way we are informed about unidentified flying objects*

THE JIMMY FLYNN STORY

At the time of Jimmy Flynn's sighting back in 1965, my neighbors Carl and Iola Hansel were spending the winter in Ft. Myers, Fl. and by chance happened to have Dr. John Brown for a doctor. Since he was also one of Jimmy's doctors (eyes), they became well aware of this incident and sent the news clippings to me.

The next time I visited Florida, I managed to locate Jimmy. He wasn't at home but his wife asked me in and showed me a painting that an artist had drawn while Jimmy sat at his side. She was a school teacher and said her students often asked her if she believed her husband. The story had been covered by everyone who ever wrote much more than a dozen pages on the subject. Six years ago, I made up my mind to find out what had happened to Jimmy Flynn in the last fifteen years. It took me about four years to find him, and six months to get him to talk to me. He had had about all the publicity he could handle and didn't much care what anyone thought or believed. Almost everyone whose experience becomes known wishes he had never told anyone anything. The doubters and the professional discreditors do their best to make life miserable. When government and a few eggheads are assuring people that there is no such thing, you are looked upon as somewhat of a "questionable character."

Jimmy is a rancher with a hobby of hunting. He kept hunting dogs and took them down in the Everglades near the Seminole Indian Reservation. It was there that he happened to be camping when three of his dogs spotted a deer. One of his older dogs was inside a wire cage on his swamp buggy but the other one and two younger pups broke loose and disappeared into the swampland. Hunters don't like to lose their dogs and since it was late in the evening he took off in the moonlight to try to find them. He was driving his swamp buggy when he spotted a bright light that zigzagged over the trees and made instant stops at full speed. I don't know what made him think that our engineers had accomplished this feat but he kept watching it for awhile and saw it settle down behind a grove of cypress. The lights from it were so bright that at a distance it looked as if he were approaching a whole town. Jimmy decided the law enforcement officials were watching for poachers; he thought he'd better let them know he was only after his dogs. He kept driving toward it as far as he could and then pulled to a stop and watched it for the next half hour.

It was cone-shaped, approximately 72 feet in diameter, and around 35–38 feet high. The artist's picture showed it to be the shape of a Chinese coolie hat. It had four stacks of windows approximately two feet by two feet that completely circled the ship. The slanted windows gave off a *brilliant* yellow light. Jimmy's hat had a light in the front of it and he carried a flashlight. He decided whatever this was he'd better go offer his help. He left his cooped-up dog and swamp-buggy and took off toward the "thing." When he was within 75 feet, the wind pressure and severe high-pitched whine from the craft kept him from getting nearer. The mechanism of the ship was in the bottom. He could very plainly see through the windows, but nothing or no one was visible. Suddenly a blinding flash shot toward him and that was the last he knew for more than 20 hours. When he came to the following day, he found his dog had gone through a traumatic experience and her pen showed how she had reacted. Jimmy was blind in his right eye and his left eye was badly affected. He managed to maneuver the buggy back to the Seminole Reservation to get help. His older dog found her way back to camp but the two younger ones were never seen again.

He begged his Indian friend to drive him to Lee Memorial Hospital in Ft. Myers, in spite of the fact that the man didn't have a license. Paying the man's fine was the least of Jimmy's worries. A large damaged spot remained for weeks between his eyes just above his eyebrows. Both eyes had to be bandaged for a number of days. X-rays showed no trauma in other parts of his head; he had scratched arms and a badly damaged place on one leg that lasted several months. The eye problem has never completely disappeared, particularly in the right eye.

This was almost a twenty-four-hour experience. He assumed he must have been lying in the sun all day. Everywhere his skin was exposed, it was black. Florida ranchers do not turn black in a day — they may turn beet red and burn. No one ever told him what could have happened to cause this condition.

While he was in Lee Memorial Hospital, under the care of several doctors, temporarily blinded in one eye, damaged in the other — what do you think happened to him? A bunch of sympathetic, well-paid people came in to interview him and collect all his information and medical records. Officials from Homestead Air Base asked him for the location of his sighting, as well as when if, he got out of the hospital, he would go out in the swamp and mark a circle of lime around the outside of the area so they could locate it from the air. When he was finally released in about ten days, he had numerous people who wanted to see the place.

He hauled several hundred pounds of lime into the swamp and marked the area so it could be easily located. The object had carefully chosen where it lowered itself to within five feet of the ground. It came over a knoll which was surrounded by cypress trees. The tops of all these trees were burned and dead, while the bottoms were alive and green. The ground under it was completely burned and bare in a 72-foot circle, which clearly showed its size. He figured its height to be between 35 and 38 feet — measured by the damaged trees. Any Boy Scout could have burned the bottom of the trees and left the tops untouched, but it's a good trick to get up there and burn a circle of tree tops to prove a hoax, including damaging your eyesight for life.

Jimmy took three dozen pictures to show the dead limbs and had someone come in and take a bunch of core samples which were sent to Homestead Air Base. They were so grateful for his help that he never received a thank-you note or any indication they were interested in the case. What he doesn't realize is that long before he was out of the hospital they had all the information they wanted. The people to whom he talked would no longer have the authority to follow the case. When those men left the hospital their work was accomplished.

Meanwhile, Jimmy gets a lot of questionable publicity which make him look like a jerk and he crawls in a hole and waits for our Air Force to come out with this super-human equipment probably hoping he can sue the daylights out of them.... He didn't know anything about UFOs, and still doesn't. He is convinced that this object was a good nuts and bolts construction made by our engineers and thinks they pulled a dirty trick on him when he was just trying to help them. He believed they were in trouble. He was right about one thing — they were in trouble, but not the kind he had in mind. Our government knew this thing was not theirs, but they did not know just where it was from or who owned it. They did know enough to put it under top security classification with a pot full of others with which they did likewise. What else do you expect them to do? How can they answer questions when they don't have the answers?

For more than thirty years they've been filling up their files with this stuff, some of which they have declassified so you can find out a few things for yourself, if you insist. But mostly you don't insist, so you must be slowly spoon-fed for years and years until new generations come along who won't be so horribly shocked when they too may have a sighting. I have no criticism of the way our government has handled this business. I wouldn't have known how to do it better.

A bridge-playing friend told me about her friend who had to go to Buffalo, New York for an unusual cancer treatment. It was somewhat experimental, but she had nothing to lose. It was called Photoradiation Therapy. It used a special dye and light to kill cancer cells. There was one specific demand, the patient MUST remain out of the sun and outdoor light for 30 days or her skin would turn black. I couldn't help but wonder whether the beam of light that knocked Jimmy unconscious could have been related in some way to Photoradiation Therapy?

My sympathy is with Mr. Flynn and many more of these contactees who are brave or foolish enough to admit their experiences. Without hypnosis no one will ever have any idea as to what happened during that long unconscious interlude in the cypress swamp.

After showing Mr. Flynn a video tape of Edward Billy Meier's Pleiadian Beamship (with its accompanying sound tape) Jimmy said he knew that sound. Though the two UFOs were not alike, they both carried the same high-pitched whine. You'll wait a long time before you find more credible experiences than those of the Swiss farmer and Jimmy Flynn.

UFO CONTACT FROM THE PLEIADES

Since 1975, UFO contact from the Pleiades has been one of the most controversial cases on record. An uneducated Swiss farmer, Bill Meier, dared tell the world not only had he taken dozens of pictures of the Pleiades beam ships, he'd been given more than three thousand pages of notes and messages.

If you'd lost an arm and found it necessary to do all that typing with one finger you'd surely be hard-up for publicity to manufacture a hoax. Billy borrowed a camera and bought film by the dozen, was flooded with visitors who swiped some of his pictures, and ended with several assassination attempts. By trying to please the aliens, plus fill requests to satisfy his friends, he lost a caretaker's job and his physical and mental health deteriorated.

The research team of Colonel Wendelle Stevens, Britt and Lee Elders, Bruce Macabee, and others used their own models to try to duplicate the picture which were taken by the Swiss farmer. They were able to show important differences between photographs of models and those taken by Billy Meier.

The *UFO Cover-Up* documentary which aired on October 14, 1988 called his contacts a hoax and claimed he had a UFO model in his barn. The research team and other scientists spent more than 300 days living with this family and watching their every move. Though they made eighteen trips to the place, they were never able to find any indication of a hoax or lack of sincerity. Friends and neighbors confirmed the story and signed sworn affidavits for the investigators.

It seems utter nonsense these men could overlook a UFO model in 300 days with eighteen trips made to Switzerland. This sounds just like a disinformation program of our government.

All of Billy's film was thoroughly checked by photographic specialists. There never was any doubt as to the authenticity of these pictures or movies. No doubt by the time he's dead and gone, Eduard Billy Meier may become a national hero.

UFO FLIES OUT OF THE OCEAN

***Weekly World News*, April 10, 1990**

by Ann Hughey

A saucer-shaped UFO stunned the crew of a tanker when it blasted out of the ocean and circled their ship for fifteen terrifying minutes before vanishing without a trace back into the sea!

According to Sri Lankan newspaper reports, the incident took place in broad daylight in late March, 210 miles south of Matara, Sri Lanka, in the Indian Ocean.

No one was injured but the 175-ft tanker Kim Seng suffered severe structural damage from the towering waves that were kicked up when the UFO rose out of and later returned to the water, the press said.

"It was enormous—at least five times the size of our ship," Rasika Mawatha, the 47-year-old captain of the Kim Seng, told reporters.

"I'd just come up on deck when the huge silver orb flew out of the sea and hovered just off the starboard bow of the ship. We almost sank from the waves it made as it left the water.

"At first, I was so shocked I nearly fainted from fright. My crew was terrified, too. They fell to the deck—covering their eyes and cowering like small children.

"All the ship's instruments went haywire and the needle on the compass kept spinning around and around. I couldn't even use the radio to call for help," he said.

"The spacecraft glowed and pulsated with a silvery light and another eerie beam of light shone from the bottom of the ship. It seemed as if whoever was in the craft was scanning our ship, but for what purpose, I don't know."

After about fifteen minutes, the UFO disappeared as suddenly as it had appeared.

"One minute it was there and the next it had vanished back into the sea in a blinding flash of light," said Mawatha. "It kicked up such huge waves it almost capsized the ship again."

Immediately after the UFO disappeared, the ship's instruments began working again as if nothing had happened.

"I radioed authorities about what had happened and they sent planes and ships to scan the area but they came up with nothing," said Capt. Mawatha.

Officials searched for days but not a trace of the UFO could be found.

"We spent days searching for signs of the alleged spaceship but couldn't find anything," said Adi Chandrakar, a spokesman for the coastal authority.

"Even though we couldn't find any concrete evidence of the UFO, we know that something highly unusual did happen out there because of the damage to the ship.

"Only extremely rough water like you'd experience in a severe storm could cause that kind of damage and there wasn't a cloud in the sky.

"We're calling this incident an official UFO sighting because there's no other explanation for what happened."●

☐ *Note this article in the* News *is dated 1990. It's news comparable to that which Dr. Allen J. Hynek took to Wright-Patterson Air Base when "The Blue Book Project" was in vogue. He suggested this information should be taken very seriously and was told to mind his own business and forget it — after that event, Dr. Hynek started working for "the people" and kept "collecting" from the government! Another 10 article.*

HYNEK AND HIS DEBUNKING SERVICE

By 1965, the Air Force kept Dr. Allen J. Hynek busy denying a barrage of sightings. College girls near Hillsdale, Michigan reported sightings which were stirring up a controversy. An Ohio student in Michigan was a daughter of a friend of mine. She called home in great excitement.

To make it worse, one of those unidentified objects had come down in a swamp area near Dexter, Michigan. It had been seen and reported and needed to be explained. Dr. Hynek was the fall-guy! He scurried up to Michigan and explained to the world "the swamp gas" theory. It all but did him in. From that time on his comments on that subject were low on the totem pole.

When visiting with him later I told him about my military friend who had helped carry a UFO from the jungle. He told me he'd been waiting for years for a case like this. I told him he could keep on waiting. I wasn't about to have a friend lose $10,000, spend ten years in jail, and end up with no pension. These men were under the strictest orders concerning information pertaining to their experience.

By 1977 Dr. Hynek had begun talking about parallel universes, the fourth dimension, or life which exists on an invisible plane. By this theory UFOs wouldn't have to come from far off, but from any place you choose to look. These ships were seen to dive in and out of the water and put on some good sightings for the ship's commander and his crew.

It wasn't until Dr. Hynek had gone to Wright-Patterson with a recommendation for our government sources to get busy investigating one of these cases that he knew why he'd been hired. Both officers and enlisted men were telling him the same story.

Eventually the reply from Wright-Patterson came. He was told to mind his own business and forget about the case. This forced him to take a new approach. He was making a good salary; why not make use of it. From then on he was going to find out all he could concerning UFOs and try to make it up to the people he had conned. Even then he's not above the law — he too would have limits which never would be crossed. I could forgive him for the misinformation but for Dr. Philip Klass, that's another thing. I don't believe the public or our scientists will ever forget how he led them down the garden path.

Dr. Klass shows up at every UFO event he deems worthy of mention and debunks most anything that suits his fancy.

Those who have heard him tell me the audience feels sorry for him and thinks he doesn't know any better. Not me, I think he's a smart cookie. Just like Hynek, he's doing his job and after all it probably pays right pert. If I'm wrong, I'll get down on my sore knees....

After Hynek retired he formed a group called "The Center for UFO Studies." I feel he really did want to do his best to tell the truth. Since his death the organization sounds to me as if a mole or two had edged in to take care of that 25% disinformation for balance purposes. It's OK with me. How would you like making decisions that not only affect all of our country but all of the world?

ALIENS FROM SPACE

After Major Donald Keyhoe's retirement from the Marines he founded "The National Investigating Committee for Aerial Phenomena," known as NICAP. He started writing books one after another; by the time he reached *Aliens From Space* he was a right smart author. When you pick up a book which contains material with which you're familiar it's hard to get excited unless it's very well written.

In 1956, NICAP's intent was to find out the facts about UFOs. By 1957, it was being supervised by a Board of Governors. That's where moles come in — some innocent-looking retired officer wants very much to help. Better be careful — you'll find the wrong decisions being made for you. Vice Admiral R.H. Hillenkotter, former director of the CIA, and Admiral Fahrney made a beautiful membership role. How do you expect to make any decisions when you're being watched about everything you do? Don, do you ever read that "MJ-12" list over and over to see what it looks like? Double agents are the best — they know what's going on all the way. I guess that's all water over the dam. Suppose you had convinced Congress to listen to your files — how would you like it if they start making decisions for you? You'd better keep the admirals; they're a far better bet. The rules under MJ-12 would never have allowed Congress to have a peek at the

National Archives. Just be patient like Ruppelt and wait for one to land on your desk.

Major Keyhoe has devoted half of his life to this subject and no doubt he'll be given plenty of recognition.

☐ *Remember, I wrote most of these articles years ago!*

MAJOR RUPPELT — "BLUE BOOK" AND THE SCOUTMASTER

Late in 1953, Major Edward J. Ruppelt was assigned the job of reviewing old UFO reports. When finished he was given another job analyzing new UFO sightings. This time it was called "Project Blue Book." It was going to solve problems for everybody. The government wouldn't have to answer your questions and "Blue Book" would have all the fun of solving them for you. It wouldn't take long to get an answer unless you happened to have an honest to goodness bona fide UFO experience. In that case the report gets lost — never to be seen again. That's what happened to the angelhair from Marysville, Ohio.

A girl I knew worked in the Blue Book office. She had to go through five locked doors plus one with a guard who demanded to see her picture. In that kind of a place your right hand never knows what your left hand does. You have a job to do, do it.

After a couple of years the government had almost all UFO problems solved. From that time on we were told all interest had been lost in this subject.

One of the highlights of Ruppelt's book is the story of the Florida scoutmaster. I always wanted to interview him, it's one to stay in the records.

The scoutmaster was a young man who had joined the Marines and gotten in trouble. It's bad enough to go AWOL but when you steal a car you've really blown it. Nobody is ever going to believe you no matter how good you try to be. The local Boy Scouts needed a leader and guess who took the job! One night he was taking several scouts home. It just happened that a nice big UFO flew over and disappeared beyond them in a wooded area.

The scoutmaster couldn't resist going through the palmetto palms to see what might be there. He instructed the boys to wait fifteen minutes—if he hadn't returned, they were to go to the nearest house for help. He picked up a machete and a flashlight and took off.

Fifteen minutes passed, the boys saw a round red ball head toward where they believed their leader to be. They too took off.

The scoutmaster had cut his way through the palmetto palms and found himself under a large UFO. It felt like being next to a hot brick building. He drew back from its under-section. Being frightened, he wanted to destroy it or hit it with his knife. That's when he was struck in the head with a ball of red light. His cap, face, hair and arms were burned. He laid unconscious until the boys and police arrived. He staggered back through the palmettos in a dazed and petrified condition.

The boys were questioned and delivered home. The scoutmaster took on a new chapter in his life. There was too much evidence. It was necessary to disqualify the young man. This was easy, you can't sow wild oats and not expect a crop.

Everything looked fine for "Blue Book" until the soil sample under the UFO was checked. The grass was not harmed but the roots had been burned off. The Major figured ways the scoutmaster might have been able to create such an effect.

When he asked a scientist from the Rand Corp. if he didn't believe this was the way the hoax was accomplished — he merely replied, "what do you want, one to come and land on your desk?"

FRANK EDWARDS AND THE NEWS

When I picked up my copy of Frank Edwards book *Flying Saucers, Serious Business*, I thought how much he has done to further the knowledge of UFOs. He carries such a great assortment of sightings which have been covered in various newspapers. My friends Janet and Ed Dicks were among the hundreds of eyewitnesses at Wanaque Reservoir in New Jersey. It was a large white object that hovered over the dam area; they were very impressed.

On February 24, 1961 a man and woman Soviet cosmonaut were launched into orbit and due to a malfunction were never able to return. Suddenly the male's voice burst in saying, "Here, here is something, there is something, if we don't get out, the world will never know about it!" It was clear the couple had seen something nearby that startled them and then terrified them.

In NICAP's files a comparable case, just six weeks later, shows the missile Polaris being launched from Cape Canaveral and tracked down range several thousand miles into the South Atlantic. The official log shows that while Polaris was still rising it acquired a companion which was much bigger than it was. Because of its closeness and size the automatic radar locked onto the wrong object when it veered off into space. According to the log it took the radar fourteen minutes to get off the UFO and back on Polaris.

On the first launching of a Gemini spacecraft April 8, 1984, four controlled objects took positions about the craft. There were two above, one behind, and one below it. They stayed with it for a whole orbit, then took off and headed into space. This required an explanation. (It was that structural pieces broke off from an expendable part of the spacecraft.)

Edwards goes on to show case after case where spacecraft may stop working for weeks or months and suddenly come back into action. It appears they may have been examined by someone else.

Frank Edwards was a good solid news reporter. The material he used came from good old-fashioned newspapers and the NICAP files.

I can't tell you how *Weekly World News* gets its material but I have my own ideas. The following article was printed in the November 15, 1988 *News* by Chuck O'Neil — its headline "UFOs Escort Shuttle to a Safe Orbit." (The alien starships actually showed up on radar during launch and landing!)

> Two UFO "guardian angels" shepherded the Discovery space shuttle and its gutsy crew to a safe orbit — and then four days later, hovered just over the horizon as Discovery landed in a California desert.
>
> This startling revelation comes from a top Soviet astrophysicist who helped monitor the American space shot at the huge Abalakovo radar complex in the Siberian city of Krashnoyarsk.
>
> "Incredibly, the UFOs fluttered around Discovery during its launch phase like a pair of guardian angels determined to protect the five-man crew from any harm," the scientist, who insisted on anonymity, confided to a handful of trusted reporters.
>
> "While the shuttle was in orbit and the astronauts were busily performing their onboard experiments, the extraterrestrials were close by but stayed out of sight," he continued.
>
> "But as soon as Discovery's mission tasks were completed and the crew was preparing for re-entry into the Earth's atmosphere, the UFOs suddenly reappeared and stationed themselves on either side of the shuttle until it was apparent Discovery was headed for a safe landing in the Mojave Desert."
>
> Russian space experts are convinced the two UFOs are "scout ships" from a secret extraterrestrial base on the dark side of the moon, the astrophysicist said.
>
> "And we're sure their presence during the two most dangerous phases of the flight — launch and re-entry — is evidence of their goodwill."
>
> NASA officials refused to comment on the Soviet's mind-boggling claims, but radiotelemetry data collected in Scandinavian countries definitely indicates the presence of two unidentified — and intelligently controlled — objects pacing the first manned U.S. spacecraft to fly since the Challenger tragedy in 1986.
>
> The Russian scientist also disclosed the Soviets had intercepted a mysterious radio message transmitted in Morse code from space after Discovery landed at Edwards Air Force Base. It said "Well done."

☐ *On our 1–10 scale this deserves a 10 if the UFOs were there and a 1 if they weren't. I'll bet they were there.*

SPACE MUSIC DRAWS UFOs
***National Examiner*, August 8, 1989**

A concert of UFO music attracted some surprise guests — an actual fleet of ships from outer space!

The four spaceships dropped by to attend a concert of flying saucer sounds recorded by renowned UFOlogist and former NASA scientist Dr. Fred Bell.

Some astonished concert-goers received the shock of their lives when the fleet suddenly appeared outside the concert hall in Murnau, Germany, and hovered in the early evening sky.

Concert producer Michael Hesemann said: "I could see the saucers, which were about 21 feet across, appear one at a time through the windows of the concert hall. The entire crowd gasped and about 30 people ran outside."

Added concert hostess Frauke Plog: "It was absolutely astounding. The spacecraft were only 50 feet away, and I could feel gentle waves of energy flowing over me, which caused a cut on my hand to heal instantly.

"Several other people and myself were signaling the ETs to land, but after about 10 minutes the four spacecraft suddenly lifted straight up and dashed across the sky. They were gone in seconds.

"Six Air Force jets came screaming out of nowhere, passing over the place where the UFOs had hovered. The jets turned around and zoomed off, chasing the UFOs until they disappeared. And the police cordoned off the entire town and checked everybody, looking for any extraterrestrial visitors."

Bell believes the UFOs were drawn by his new musical release, *Fellowship: The Sound,* which contains real flying saucer sounds that he recorded.

He told the *Examiner*: "This concert was the first time I ever had played *Fellowship: The Sound* through the Fire Star Orb equipment, which has an effect like a negative ion generator. The combination created a frequency which is similar to that of the Pleiadian UFO flying saucers."

Bell, who has successfully passed rigorous lie detector tests regarding his contacts with ETs, said other concerts where he has performed have had the same UFO visitations.●

☐ *This article reminds me of the sound analysis presented by Colonel Stevens in* UFO Contact from the Pleiades, Vol. 2. *A sound engineer's report showed unusual cycles per second which were very hard to explain or duplicate. The sound patterns were recorded on both movie tapes and a recorder which was controlled by Meier's wife. This was accomplished at the same time — quite a good hoax!*

LOOKING BACK

So many things within these pages,
Were written years ago.
And when I re-read them today —
I'm pleased to hear what I did say.

Over all these years I've formed opinions,
It isn't an easy thing to do.
I'm bound to end up with tough decisions —
It's wise to make a few provisions!

I suppose we don't know much for sure —
But that's what life seems about.
You take a look at the facts and choices
And figure which will have more clout!

One thing I've done is ask for help,
I've searched in the highest places —
And if at times I've made mistakes,
I have not missed many bases.

I hope this book won't lead you astray,
I've tried to print truth in the highest way,
And if tomorrow, it should change our day —
It is God who controls — so let us pray!

CHAPTER THREE

More Speakers — Space Probes — UFO Invasion

Getting Down to Brass Tacks . . . 58
More Speakers and More Ideas . . . 59
Maybe You Were There in a Previous Life . . . 59
Reincarnation Shocker — *Weekly World* . . . 59
I Believe . . . 60
Wave of Sightings Sparks Secret Superpower Treaty — *Weekly World* . . . 60
SOS From Dying Planet — *Weekly World* . . . 61
Starship's SOS Stuns Scientists — *Weekly World* . . . 62
Crippled Starship Sends SOS to Earth — *Weekly World* . . . 62
Aliens Plan to Take Over — *National Examiner* . . . 63
Scientists Were Wrong . . . 63
UFO Invasions . . . 64
Bizarre Voices From Outer Space . . . 64
Call For Halt to Radio and TV Signals . . . 64
Swiss Astronomer Claims to Have Received Moon Message . . . 64
Woman Believes She Receives Alien Messages . . . 64
Satellite Orbiting Earth — *Weekly World* . . . 65
Soviets Blast Spaceship — *Weekly World* . . . 65
Scientist Finds Evidence of Visitor From 2081 AD — *Weekly World* . . . 66

UFOs and Crystals

Mystery Crystal Baffles Scientists — *Sun* . . . 67
UFOs Aliens Taught Indian Medicine Woman — *National Examiner* . . . 67
Enormous Crystal Blamed For Devil's Triangle — *National Examiner* . . . 68
The World is a Gigantic Crystal . . . 68
Reporter Believes Saucers Were Nearby — *Public Opinion* . . . 69
Top Scientist Finds Proof of Time Travel — *Weekly World* . . . 69
An Introduction to Time Travel with Sally, Ray, Gidaon and Hodan . . . 70
Charlotte Moberly and Eleanor Jourdain . . . 72
UFOs Are Really Time Travelers — *Sun* . . . 72
Super Jets Travel Back in History — *Weekly World* . . . 73
Screaming Christians — *Weekly World* . . . 73
Two Men Who Sailed Into the Past — *Weekly World* . . . 74
Time Warp Story to Dumfound — *Weekly World* . . . 75
Time Warp Plane Baffles Scientists — *Weekly World* . . . 75
Hypnotized Time Travelers Discover Future Paradise — *Weekly World* . . . 76
Passenger Train Vanishes in Tunnel — *Weekly World News* . . . 76
Time Warps — Poem . . . 77

GETTING DOWN TO BRASS TACKS

It's my purpose in writing this book to show a relationship between UFO printed material of today and that which was received in the 1950's and 60's. It has to be my evaluation of the subject and it does cover a span of forty years of serious research.

I have always found myself leaning towards support for the way our government has handled the UFO problem. That does not mean the way Congress takes care of its responsibilities. Decisions about UFOs are made at a much higher level. It isn't that "MJ-12," is always right; we all have to work on methods of trial and error. I'm willing to give them a B+, or grudgingly an A–. It will be a long sweet day before that becomes a popular decision.

At the time of the forming of the Robertson Committee in 1953, suggestions were made as how to handle this problem. President after President has pretty much followed those rules. If a vote were taken today it would be to release all information and let the chips fall where they may. Not so — people do not know what they want or why they want it. You can't feed people a bunch of lies and half truths and expect them to be able to accept the facts when the cards are on the table.

Each of us has a little protective device that says, "I'm not going to believe this because I don't want to believe this, therefore it isn't true." No doubt we still have someone who will assure us all those pictures of astronauts on the moon were made in Hollywood. It's well known that many people's opinions can't be changed. We have to educate each new generation to consider other concepts which will be more acceptable. This is being done with programs such as *Alf, Starwars, Unsolved Mysteries, Twilight Zone,* and documentaries such as *Chariots of the Gods, What's Going On, UFOs Are Real, Encounters of the Third Kind, The Betty and Barney Hill Abduction,* and many more too numerous to mention. (This was one of the suggestions made by the Robertson Committee.) On October 14, 1988, who do you suppose paid the bill for that two hour documentary on ABC? Somehow it was more important to show *UFO Cover-Up* than all Friday night programs from 8 to 10 p.m., both in the U.S. and Canada. You can bet your boots you helped pay the bill for that one, even if you didn't watch it. Your government took a lot of pains to make sure you know that UFOs are here and that they've brought along their occupants. Did you notice what a clever way they used to take a poll which Uncle Sam didn't dare do by himself? Then you were told, "We're going to give all this to Congress if they want it." You were assured that all evidence would be laid right on the table so they could see for themselves. Did you hear any repercussions? They might as well have shown *Snow White and The Seven Dwarfs* and it would have been much cheaper. Never mind, it will be shown again and we'll decide whether to watch, or go to a ball game.

Three-fourths of all information encourages you to believe — the other fourth or less brings out a doubt in your mind; you can take a deep breath and say to yourself, "I knew it wasn't true." That should be enough to keep you out of the booby hatch. If President Bush were to come on the air and say, "I have great news for you, they're here," that would do it. We'd have broken necks all over the place from some poor souls who would open a window and jump out. I know, I've tried asking people to watch their reactions. My sister said, "I don't want to know or think about it, it scares me." My friend's husband said, "I think they may be there but I've got so many worries I try not to think about it." A retired Lt. Colonel says, "There isn't any such thing, how can you be stupid enough to fall for that stuff, don't you know there's no truth to any news in the grocery store tabloids?" What do you think will happen to him when he finds for the first time in his life he was wrong? And my retired French professor friend said, "I'd always thought you could run for Congress, how could you be foolish enough to believe these false reports?" "Our government has told you there's no evidence for believing in UFOs."

I can remember my husband's reactions. "There are some things we don't bother to examine. We know that all spiritualism is fraudulent." He felt very let-down when he found there were things he had learned that were incorrect. It has made him suspicious of both education and religion. Letters behind a name are sometimes misleading.

As I became more seriously involved I made up my mind to leave no stone unturned. My husband was bombarding me with questions. "Why do you have to look into this, when we know it isn't so?" My answer "Because we've found ourselves wrong in several instances — a judge should look at all the possibilities."

MORE SPEAKERS AND MORE IDEAS

No wonder there was never an end to our speakers. I didn't go much for George King from London; I listened, did my own thinking and have been surprised to find how well it has held up. I've never been one to see a spaceman on every corner but I don't question that they're out there. For years we've been told this is true. It's a BIG subject.

I must accept the possibility that the body of an earth man could be invaded with the mind of an alien. We have charges of possession in case studies by our psychiatrists. Most doctors like to blame it all on split-personality problems. However, when an entity comes through who has died within a few years, one wonders....

A girl named Crystal borrowed the body of a frustrated young man with split personalties. His doctor could chase out the individuals who seemed to be a part of the young man's self but Crystal had been dead such a short time she wasn't ready to leave. She told of the accident which caused her death. Under hypnosis she could tell stories of her life. She and the young man had never known each other. Being very fond of cosmetics, she was able to drag his body to the store counters where she discussed such things. The clerk recognized her voice: it was as if Crystal was there in person! There seemed no way to get rid of her, until she chose to leave.

MAYBE YOU WERE THERE IN A PREVIOUS LIFE

The National Examiner, February 28, 1989. It's attributed to a retired professor of Atmospheric Sciences at Oregon State University. Dr. James Deardorf says, following an abduction, "many people learn they were space aliens in a past life." Instead of yelling "that's not in this country," go talk to the man — why not?

The January 17, 1988 *National Examiner* used this headline "Space beings have been living on earth for millions of years." This one is attributed to Whitley Streiber, who claims to be in contact with aliens. Whitley's books, *Communion*, 1987, and *Transformation*, 1988, recount his experiences with these beings. Go read them—after you've read about twenty others FIRST!

You're never going to get far with UFOs without running into reincarnation. I think I'll print this one "as is." *The Weekly World News* presents many UFO-related subjects. It's my belief that someone sees to it this paper gets a constant flow of material which will keep you up to date. Even if it were 50% made up I'd still consider it good.

REINCARNATION SHOCKER
***Weekly World News*, Dec. 22, 1987**
by Mickey McGuire

Stroke victim Adriano Ramos awoke from a deep two-year coma, speaking an ancient Egyptian language that's been extinct for 5,000 years!

Stunned linguistic experts say they are at a loss to explain how it's possible for a poorly educated Portuguese fisherman to be able to speak the language of 4th dynasty Egypt.

Yet, while under hypnosis in a clinic near Madrid, 54-year-old Adriano revealed that while in his coma he relived an earlier life as Youseff Kabbeh, a Nile River navigator during the 4th dynasty reign of King Snefru.

While language experts may be baffled by Adriano's ability to speak the ancient tongue, his recollection of a past life wipes away the mystery for Gustavo de Cabral, one of Portugal's leading experts in the study of life after death and spiritual transmigration.

"That he once lived in ancient Egypt explains Adriano's extraordinary ability to speak a language that vanished thousands of years before the birth of Christ," Cabral declared.

"When he is under hypnosis, Adriano speaks in his native Portuguese tongue. But once he is revived and seems in full control of his senses, he speaks as Youseff in the language of ancient Egypt. Normally, when people are regressed into earlier lives, they can speak in the language or dialect of that previous existence, but they revert to their normal tongue when revived.

"In Adriano's case, the opposite is true. And that, to me, is solid proof that he is the reincarnation of a man who once lived in the age of the Pharaohs. His case is positively amazing."

Cabral said while Adriano is in a hypnotic state he vividly recalls his life as a navigator on a river boat that hauled cedar logs down the Nile to Dahshur where King Snefru was building the first true pyramid of Egypt.

"He said he, as Youseff, lived in El Iskandariyaa, the city we now know as Alexandria, was married three times and fathered 13 children," Cabral said. "His recollection only goes back to a stormy night when his boat was rammed by another and sank.

"He remembers nothing after that and we presume that was the night that Youseff Kabbeh died."●

☐ *This report tips the scale way over a 9. How would you explain it? Or would you rather believe it didn't happen?*

I BELIEVE

My research leads me to believe we're being fed information of a high and classified nature. I don't have to be right but it makes good sense — government has always been accused of hiding facts from the public. It's a case of being damned if you do and damned if you don't.

I'm convinced President Reagan had a desire to give people every morsel of truth which he dared. He was briefed on all known aspects of UFOs. That doesn't mean he was free to give the report to you. I wonder if he didn't figure a way "to have his cake and eat it"?

At one time most all UFO news was showing up in the *National Enquirer*. Suddenly this changed. Most of such reports were sent to *The Weekly World News*. I can't tell whether there's any connection between the two papers, perhaps it doesn't matter. *The National Examiner* has carried some good accounts as well as the *Sun* tabloid, which manages an article almost every week. *The Weekly World News* puts out some real professional and impressive articles. For all I know, the government may own a slice of any paper they wish to influence.

We've been told that Bill Moore was sent classified film which showed signed affidavits by President Truman and others. It appears this was done so it could be used without official permission. Bill was doing a good job educating the public about UFOs; someone hoped he could keep on doing the same thing. He had help from Jaime Shandera, Stanton Friedman, Bruce Macabee and others. Friedman served 14 years as a nuclear physicist, then spent the next ten years researching UFOs. Do you think he'd be doing this work if government sources objected? Bruce Macabee spent years examining photographs in military service, then went to work for the opposition. Rest assured it isn't without the blessing of all those concerned! These men have put together some good UFO documentaries, just what they were supposed to do — the President didn't dare tell you these facts but he's seen to it that someone else did — even if he can't say a word, which he hasn't. When Ronnie doesn't like something he's pretty apt to let you know.

Of course Bill can't prove these papers are official, but you can bet your bottom dollar the government can't prove they aren't! Nor do they want to — this is a way of bringing the truth to you without the authorities being hounded by a bunch of reporters. This kind of reporting only reaches those who have a desire to know. No one is forced to watch — if you don't like it, pretend it isn't so.

Why do you think our relationship with Russia has improved so much in the last few years? When both countries realized they had equal concerns, they've gotten together.

If you listened to *UFO Cover-Up* on October 14, 1988, you heard an official Russian, inviting an official American, to come on over with them and do some research on their Siberian Project. Do you think that was a surprise and hadn't been planned by the "big wigs" in advance?

Perhaps you should have read the *Weekly World News* on April 14th, 1987. A two-page spread, this article is too well done not to present it as written.

WAVE OF SIGHTINGS SPARKS SECRET SUPERPOWER TREATY
***Weekly World News*, April 14, 1987**
by Mickey McGuire & Vladimir Chienko

In a superpower pact more secret than the A-bomb or the Normandy invasion, President Reagan and Soviet Premier Gorbachev have agreed to combine their military might — to defend planet Earth if it's attacked by space aliens!

The authenticity of the mutual defense alliance was confirmed in a highly classified Soviet military briefing paper leaked to a Western journalist by a top-echelon official in the Kremlin.

The mutual defense agreement calls for both the U.S. and Russia to muster all of their nuclear missiles, supersonic jet aircraft, manned and unmanned spacecraft — including the Shuttle — in an all out operation to repel alien invaders from our skies.

The astonishing pact was signed, sealed and delivered to Reagan and Gorbachev only three days after Alaskan radar trackers confirmed that an immense UFO was plotted as it hovered near a Japan Air Lines 747 jetliner last November. That UFO — described as "bigger than two aircraft carriers" — was just one of literally hundreds of UFO sightings that have been reported from every country since October 1986.

"We have strong reason to believe that there is a definite routine being carried out by what can only be spaceships from outer space," the briefing paper stated.

"There is also intelligence data from our field agents that indicate some of the alien craft have landed on Soviet territory.

"In light of these confirmed reports, the Soviet Union and the United States of America agreed to take prudent steps to insure a united capability to defend Earth in the event of an invasion by alien forces from other worlds."

The paper outlines the "mobilization" of conventional air, sea and ground forces and the immediate dispersal of Soviet and U.S. nuclear-armed submarines.

Of greater importance, however, will be the activation of strategic satellites already in Earth orbit which will fire their laser rays at attacking alien starships while they are still in deep space.

"Everyone has been terrified that President Reagan's so-called Star Wars Initiative posed a threat of world annihilation. But an invasion of Earth by space aliens would bring a global holocaust no one can even begin to imagine," a Pentagon official said. "I cannot help remembering something President Reagan said in 1980," the official continued. "He told the audience, 'We may be the generation that sees Armageddon.' But this pact with the Soviets could be the salvation of Earth."●

☐ *I guess the boys get a 10 for writing this one.*

It isn't just the *Weekly World News* that carried that story. The January 31, 1989 *National Examiner* ran the headline, "Russians Offer to Reveal UFO Mysteries."

The Russians offer to swap stories and ask us to join that excursion to Siberia where a couple of UFOs were seen to explode. Both countries have information which makes them feel we could be invaded by aliens from other worlds. No wonder they want to be sure they aren't on opposite sides!

☐ *In case you're still with me now that we have Ronnie and Gorby on a buddy-buddy basis, let's see if we can find any reasons why this should be?*

Going back to September 10, 1985, *The Weekly World*'s article by Emmet Gruber carried inch-and-a-half-tall letters which say "SOS from a dying planet." "Plea comes from across the Universe!" "Astounded Russian astronomers intercept 80,000-year-old message"....

SOS FROM DYING PLANET
***Weekly World*, Sept. 10, 1985**
by Emmet Gruber

Soviet researchers claim to have intercepted an intergalactic distress call from an alien civilization that had already peaked and was actually dying while sabertoothed tigers still roamed the Earth!

The 80,000-year-old SOS was received and taped late last spring. Only in recent weeks have radio astronomers and language experts found the key to the complex, mathematics-based language and transcribed the frantic plea for help.

Soviet newspapers haven't published a word about the startling signal. But lengthy scientific reports have appeared in two professional research journals, *Radio Astronomy* and *Universe.*

Dr. Victor Kulakov is leading the research team from a state-operated observatory and scientific complex 50 miles northwest of Moscow. He told *Universe* that the signal emanated from some point beyond the galaxy nearest to our own, Andromeda, and was sent by beings that apparently had achieved a civilization no more advanced than our own. "The simple fact that we received and decoded the message proves beyond any doubt that their knowledge and technology were, at the very least, within our reach," commented Kulakov.

"And while they are years of study ahead of us, I can say with some measure of certainty that the death of their civilization was not the result of some cosmic catastrophe.

"It was the result of the civilization turning on itself, possibly with nuclear weaponry."

Kulakov refused to provide either *Universe* or *Radio Astronomy* with a transcript of the message. But he said it began with the question, "Is anybody out there?" and went on to give coordinates pinpointing the location of the planet.

"There was a quite lucid account of apocalyptic devastation, hellish explosions, widespread death and terminal illnesses," said Kulakov.

"A shower of meteors? Possibly. But what strikes me is — and this is just a feeling — is an underlying acceptance of guilt. It's as if the senders of the message are acknowledging blame for what had happened."

"Whatever it was, they apparently had no means to evacuate the remaining population. Space travel was available to them on a limited basis at best.

"The message makes it clear that they were trapped on their world."

A Western expert on Soviet scientific affairs living in Moscow admitted there is a slight possibility that Kulakov's interpretation of the message could be a KGB ploy to scare the U.S. into reducing its stockpile of nuclear arms.

"I emphasize slight," said the expert, who, fearing deportation, spoke on the condition that his name not be used for publication.●

☐ *I believe the article deserves a 10, and that's what it's going to get! In case the article worried you why not forget it and see if it will go away? After all, nobody believes what you read in those papers — if you did, President Reagan wouldn't have dared to allow the continual leakage that seems to flow from other countries. It's so convenient to take no responsibility for what hits the news and eventually be able to take all the credit! I keep hearing the media beefing because they've been tricked into printing "leaked news." More power to them if they can find a way to make use of the "media" — it sounds like a good deal to me!*

STARSHIP'S SOS STUNS SCIENTISTS
***Weekly World*, July 15, 1986**
by Alex Jackson

In one of the most secret projects in history, a joint Soviet-American scientific team is studying a mysterious radio signal from outer space — a distress call sent from a planet or starship 50,000 years ago.

"This is a stunning breakthrough. Our computers have actually translated a major portion of the radio signal," said one U.S. astronomer, who discussed the research with a French freelance news service on the condition he not be identified.

Portions of the amazing message were put together in a reasonably accurate form by the team in April, but have not been published.

"GUIDE US TO FOURTH UNIVERSE. EXPLOSION. WE ARE IN PERIL. WE ARE IN TIME 117.098 IN 12th GALAXY," was the frantic message.

"Very simply, from a mathematical translation, we can assume this was an ancient spacecraft, or even a planet.

"It was looking for some kind of beacon, a signal, to guide them out of danger. This whole thing is mind-boggling," said the astronomer.

"My Soviet counterparts have done the majority of computer translation and we have been working night and day to pinpoint the source of the signal.

"Our initial calculations have shown, and we may be proven very wrong later, that the signal was sent at least 50,000 years ago, maybe longer.

"My colleagues feel we must have more conclusive analysis of the message before we publish a report.

"I disagree.

"Both our governments are briefed on our progress constantly. I feel the whole story should be made public now.

"It is conclusive proof, to me, that mankind is not alone. I only wish that I could go into further detail.

"There is much more to this story and more of the signal to be translated.

"I will say this: when this goes public, it will have one of the greatest effects on the human race in history.

"It could even bring about world peace."

Both U.S. and Soviet government spokesmen refused to confirm or deny that scientific research into an alien message was taking place.

The Soviet spokesman, however, said that "Our government is constantly seeking new information from space, and that includes scanning for radio signals of any kind. It is not inconceivable that our advanced equipment could pick up a message of this sort. I am just not at liberty to discuss it any further at this point."●

☐ *Sure I believe this report — don't sit around and complain that the government didn't tell you these things. It's doing the best it can — and the* News *gets a 10 for it! Did that article do anything to shake you up? If not, let's be a little more specific. On May 26, 1987, Vol. 8, Issue 33, the* News *says, "Crippled Starship sends SOS to Earth." (Real life starwars proves we're not alone!) I thought they proved that last year, maybe it's a good idea to jog a few memories.*

Scientists say, "The desperate call for help originated from the Great Cluster Hercules, or M-31." No use worrying about this one — even if we did hear it, we were still in the cave-man age. This time we've added Germany to our team of experts. 25000 years seems quite a while back; I hope they found a spaceship floating around to help them. Notice this article has no "byline." Sometimes the paper says, "The News *was given or received."*

These are the most impressive. It looks to me as if someone wanted the information to go straight to the top.

CRIPPLED STARSHIP SENDS SOS TO EARTH
***Weekly World*, May 26, 1987**

Startled scientists here on earth have received a desperate SOS from an alien starship blown out of the skies — more than 25,000 years ago!

Experts in the United States, Russia and Germany are convinced the bizarre Mayday message came from a spacecraft attacked by a heavily armed enemy ship around 23,010 B.C., physicist Franz-Herbert Mooser told the Yugoslavian journal *Universe.*

The shocking transmission was intercepted by American scientists at an observatory in the jungles of Puerto Rico and by Soviet scientists at a similar listening post in the taiga region of Siberia, Dr. Mooser said.

"The Russians and the Americans

recorded the message on the same date — Dec. 13, 1986 — and have spent the past six months frantically working to interpret it," the astrophysicist said. Officials in both nations have steadfastly denied the existence of the interstellar SOS, but Dr. Mooser said he was part of an international team of scientists who translated the cry for help.

Dr. Mooser said the transmission apparently originated in or near M-13, a cluster of stars on the outer edges of the Milky Way.

"From what we can determine, the message came from an unarmed passenger ship engaged in interplanetary travel," the scientist said.

"The crippled ship apparently radioed its distress call moments after being struck by some form of missiles or rockets launched by a passing warship from another planet.

"That message has been streaking its way toward earth at the speed of light for the past 25,000 years and it just now reached us."

Dr. Mooser said the Great Cluster of Hercules, where the message originated, is 1.5 billion times farther from earth than the sun.

"But in terms of space, that makes us almost next door neighbors," he said.

The physicist said there is no way of knowing what happened to the ship.

"Even if the message had reached us at the time they sent it, we would have been little help," he said. "Back then, earthlings were still scratching around in caves, still inventing the wheel.

"Woolly mammoths were roaming the earth and some beings 25,000 light-years out in space were pleading for us to save them from disaster.

"They were just wasting their time."•

☐ *The Sept. 18, 1990* Weekly World *repeats this same article with a few abbreviations which do not alter its meaning. Note that U.S., Russia, and Germany were involved in translating such messages. If you've been checking Associated Press articles, you may have noted one carried in the* St. Petersburg Times, *July 20, 1990, on page 5b. It shows names and pictures of five military men along with the name of one woman Sergeant who belonged to the 701st Military Intelligence Brigade at Augsburg, West Germany. All six were being held at Ft. Benning, Ga. They are being charged with desertion. Other articles by AP say they were fined a half month's pay, reduced in rank, and given a general discharge. Is this the normal punishment for six people who are doing "Top Security" work? They are said to have received their training at the Corry Station Naval Technical Training Center in Pensacola, Florida. Scuttlebutt has it they had made up their minds that it was their duty to let the world know what they had found out about UFOs. Anybody with an IQ of over 99 should have known better. I guess they deserve a C- for effort. The* Weekly World *deserves a 9.5.*

SCIENTISTS WERE WRONG

The Weekly World News, January 27, 1987, Vol. 8. Issue 16, states "Scientists were wrong, the expected space war of 1993 is happening now!" Radar scopes have become saturated with an enormous number of targets characterizing an invasion of Brazilian Air Space! The second wave of UFOs to streak though Brazilian skies in less than a year suggests an alien invasion of Earth has already begun. Soviet scientists interpreted a radio transmission from space indicating that the alien society planned to attack our planet on July 6, 1993. All these new sightings made the scientists think maybe it was already here. Since it's already 1989, I guess I'll worry about that later.

ALIENS PLAN TO TAKE OVER?

On August 25, 1987 the *National Examiner* headline was "Space Aliens Plan To Take Over All Earth Governments by 1999." (And the proof is written in the Bible.) In that case it's no wonder Ronnie and Gorby shook hands and decided to cooperate. If you want to read that one, Dr. Irwin Ginsburg has written a book *First Man, Then Adam.* (Dearborn Press). No wonder Ronnie thinks we may be the generation that sees Armageddon! Oh well, my knees hurt and my memory's bad.

UFO INVASIONS

The *Sun* tabloid is right on the bandwagon! An amazing flurry of UFO sightings has convinced some experts that an alien fleet is poised for invasion within the very near future. An article by Francis Shifflett dated March 14, 1989 is adorned by large black letters which read "UFO INVASION!" (Flying saucers ready to attack our world) UFOs first appeared over Asian cities, including Soviet Siberia and Japan. They've been seen in Fresno, California, Cleveland, Ohio, and London, England. It appears that UFOs are showing themselves to larger groups of people instead of isolated rural areas.

BIZARRE VOICES FROM OUTER SPACE

The *Sun*, on December 1, 1987 tells of "Bizarre Voices From Outer Space." These came over Bill Flynn's popular Saturday morning show on High Point, NC, FM station WMAG. A satellite was accidentally knocked out of place. Several messages were picked up by numerous people. Bill doesn't know the answer, he admits the whole thing scares him.

CALL FOR HALT TO RADIO AND TV SIGNALS

The *Weekly World* on August 22, 1988 had an article by Irwin Fisher, "Worried Scientists Call For Halt To All Radio and TV Signals." "Something huge and deadly is out in space — and is stalking us," says Europe's top astronomer.

SWISS ASTRONOMER CLAIMS TO HAVE RECEIVED MOON MESSAGE

Ragan Dunn from the *Weekly World* had an article on December 13, 1988 which said a Swiss radio astronomer claims to have received an SOS from an alien base on the moon! Coded message said, "Help, we've been hit by a meteor." This transmission was received on October 18, 1988 and said the moon base was hit by a fist-sized meteor that cracked a protective shell compromising its artificial atmosphere.

WOMAN BELIEVES SHE RECEIVES ALIEN MESSAGES

On December 13, 1988 *Weekly World* carried this news by Ragan Dunn. He said Mrs. Donna Butts from Kansas is having constant contacts with aliens from a planet in the M-31 galaxy. She believes they have been monitoring our evolution and development since the beginning of human history. They have an important mission that will probably affect our history. They've been contacting her since 1984, and bringing information to give prominent doctors and government officials — there is to be a meeting of aliens and World Governments. The aliens teleport themselves to her and also can teleport her to them. She has "sold" Dr. Scott Corder on her bizarre claim. So, you take it or leave it — personally it doesn't bother me a nickel's worth. If you've read a few boxes full of books over the past few years, none of this information would bother you much.

I feel we've been given this stuff to mull over to see what we can figure out. No matter what the answer is, I've allowed myself to look at all of it. I thank those in charge for allowing everyone a good chance to know what's going on!

If you want something up to date, try this one on for size. The June 13, 1989 *Weekly World*'s headline reads "Satellite Orbiting Earth!" (Scientists fear it was sent by space aliens.) Notice this has been written by a Russian reporter. I wonder if we leak material to them the same as they leak material to us? I haven't seen Dick Kulpa's name before; it looks like more cooperation between two very different countries.

SATELLITE ORBITING EARTH
***The Weekly World*, June 13, 1989**
by Dick Kulpa

Soviet and American scientists say a mysterious spy satellite that began to orbit Earth late last year may have come from another planet!

"It definitely did not originate on Earth," Dr. Maksud Chernova, a Soviet space scientist, told reporters at a news conference in Geneva.

"The satellite was first picked up by our tracking stations in late December and we immediately assumed that it was American.

"Since then we have learned that American scientists began to track the satellite at the same time. And they thought it belonged to us."

The satellite, which is diamond-shaped and appears to be protected by a powerful force field, led the Russians to believe that it belonged to America's Star Wars defense system.

It was only after high-level diplomatic discussions between the Soviets and the Americans that the superpowers satisfied themselves that the satellite was launched by a third party.

A subsequent investigation proved that it did not belong to France, Germany, Japan or any other country with space capability.

According to Dr. Chernova, that left only one other possibility — the satellite came from another planet somewhere in space.

U.S. officials refused to discuss the alien satellite for the record; but highly-respected sources privately acknowledged that it does exist.

They did not deny that it poses "a grave security risk" although they made it clear that NASA does not want the American public to read or hear anything about it.

Dr. Chernova said: "We have yet to get a good, close look at the satellite. But our own satellites and Earth-based tracking stations have found that the probe is unusually large and technologically advanced.

"It appears to have the ability to scan and analyze virtually every aspect of our planet, including life-forms.

"It also contains a transmitter for sending information back to the civilization that sent it into space.

"We have it on good authority," he added, "that America's space shuttle launch next August will attempt to get a closer look at the satellite.

"We in the Soviet Union are planning a launch of our own, possibly in conjunction with the United States."

Dr. Georges Milliard, the French astronomer, is one of more than 200 scientists who have offered to assist America and the Soviet Union in their study of the mysterious satellite.

"The mystery orbiter is like nothing we've ever seen. I believe it may be a spy probe from another world," said Dr. Milliard.

"It obviously traveled a considerable distance to get to Earth and must have been designed and launched a long time ago," he said. "It is only an educated guess, but I'd say it is at least 50,000 years old."•

☐ *No way I'm giving this stuff less than a 10!*

SOVIETS BLAST ORBITING SPACESHIP — OUTRAGED EXPERTS FEAR RETALIATORY ATTACK!
***Weekly World*, September 12, 1989**
by Ragan Dunn (in Geneva)

The Soviet Union incinerated an alien starship with a surface-to-air missile in an attack that has been characterized as mindless aggression — and possibly even an act of war!

Dr. Marcel Cavaleri said the Soviets launched the missile from a silo in Siberia and destroyed the starship while it orbited Earth on June 21.

The Russian government angrily denied the allegation. But Dr. Cavaleri quotes highly-placed NATO sources as having confirmed the launch — and destruction of the saucer-shaped starship in space.

"The Soviet Union must be tried in the court of world opinion for this mindless act of aggression and war," the Swiss physicist declared at a news conference in Geneva.

"There was absolutely no evidence that the starship was anything but friendly. It had been monitored for days at tracking stations all over the planet without incident.

"It is unbelievable that the Soviets would take it upon themselves to attack. The whole world could be held to blame for the aggression.

"Should the extraterrestrials who sent the starship to Earth decide to avenge the attack, every nation and person on this planet will be in peril."

American intelligence sources refused to discuss the incident for the record but privately confirmed Dr. Cavaleri's report.

They said the Soviet missile was launched at 5:05 a.m. Eastern Daylight Time on Wednesday, June 21.

It hit and destroyed the alien starship seven minutes later, at 5:12 a.m., the sources said.

"There was no attempt to establish radio contact with the starship — it was attacked without warning," said Dr. Cavaleri.

"If there were extraterrestrials aboard they never had a chance. The Soviet missile carried a nuclear payload so powerful it actually vaporized the craft."

UFO researchers around the world were outraged by the Soviet action and called on the Russians to acknowledge their mistake.

They also want to broadcast a radio apology into deep space in the hope that the extraterrestrial civilization that sent the starship to Earth will hear it and rule out a retaliatory attack.

"The seriousness of the Soviet action cannot be underestimated," Marcel Koller, president and founder of the Paris-based UFO research group Galaxy, said.•

☐ *Seems to me I've been hearing how we are going to protect the Russians and vice versa with all our goodies we've been stockpiling for years. It looks as if we've forgiven them so we can join forces to fight the bad guys in case they suddenly descend upon us from space. After everyone agrees we have a spy satellite which is able to find out all our innermost secrets — it suddenly disappears out of the sky at 5:12 a.m. on Wednesday, June 21, 1989 and everyone points to the Russians and says, "Look what you did!" Sounds fishy to me — another 10.*

If these papers are telling you some facts, are you going to stand up an scream, "Nobody told us, why weren't we given this information?" I don't believe these articles are there only to sell papers. The paper may well have been paid to print them — Di and Fergie and Marilyn and Elvis are what sell papers.

George Pappas, of *Weekly World News*, wrote the following article, which claims a contact of the future. A coin yet to be made by a man who has yet to be born has caused quite a stir. Before you pitch it — take the time to read why investigators are still in a dither!

SCIENTIST FINDS EVIDENCE OF VISITOR FROM 2081 A.D.

***Weekly World News*, November 5, 1985**

by George Pappas

Eyewitness reports and the amazing discovery of a coin dated 2074 have led researchers to speculate that time travelers visited the ruins of an ancient Incan temple in the jungles of Peru within the past six weeks!

Archaeologist Dr. Jose Sabittini told Peruvian newsmen in Lima there is compelling evidence to suggest humans from the future spent at least several hours at the site.

Some experts — none of whom have had anything to do with the investigation — have publicly branded the incident a hoax.

But Sabittini and a colleague, historian August Benavides, say nothing less than a full-blown study will be necessary to reveal the truth.

The focus so far has been to interview a group of 35 jungle-dwelling Indians who discovered the coin, bootprints and a man's name carved in the trunk of a tree, Sabittini said.

"Skeptics have found it very easy to write this off as a hoax, but they conveniently overlook several crucial facts," he said.

"For a start, the site is 100 miles from the nearest city, Pevas, and is in jungle so forbidding and remote that no outsider could possibly get in without Indian guides.

"For another, they didn't see, as I did, a huge circular area of the jungle that had been flattened to the ground. It looked as if it had been done with a steamroller, but the best explanation I can offer is that a huge object landed there.

"Perhaps it was some sort of craft."

The Indians told Sabittini and Benavides that they were drawn to the site by an unusual smell that grew stronger as they got near.

"These people are quite primitive, but they have been to clinics, and they described the odor as being 'like the inside of a hospital,' " said Benavides.

"We have no idea what that implies."

Sabittini said the coin — which bears the image of a king and appears to be British — could have been minted by a prankster.

But the date, 2074, jibes with the date that was found etched on the tree.

"Someone carved 'Tom Sullivan, July 2081,' and another word that began E-N-G," said Sabittini.

"If all is as it appears to be, that would make the unique coin seven years old." Analysis showed that the coin was made of ordinary copper and zinc. But Sabittini wasn't sure experts would be able to determine if it actually is seven years old. The expert pointed out that several stones had been removed from the temple but could not say with authority that anything else had been taken.

"It's conceivable that someone from the future came here looking for relics," he said. "But at this point, that's just one of several possible explanations for what went on out there.

"Needless to say, we'll be looking into this further," he said. "It's so intriguing to us to think that we might be in the possession of a coin that has yet to be made, delivered to us by a man who has yet to be born.

"It's enough to make you think that everything we have been taught about life, death and human existence — is wrong."●

☐ *This one gets a 5, while we do a little more research!*

Pyramids and crystals go together like bread and honey. UFO contactees describe crystal objects they were given by an alien. They too, saw these pictures. It's as if everyone drinks the same brand of whiskey or else it has to be true.

UFOS AND CRYSTALS

MYSTERY CRYSTAL BAFFLES SCIENTISTS
***Sun*, March 28, 1989**
by Noreen Miller

Excited researchers are trying to determine whether a fantastic beach find is a remnant from a lost civilization, debris from a distant planet or nothing more than an extraordinary hoax!

A pyramid-shaped crystal found on the beach displays distinctly colored moving pictures of human-like creatures dressed in golden hoods.

The backdrop shows an eerie, barren landscape dotted with unusual structures and vehicles similar to saucer-shaped spaceships.

A pair of teenage school boys found the 11-inch crystal half-buried in the sand on a south Florida beach just north of Miami.

The youths turned their incredible find over to authorities. The amazing crystal has reportedly gone to a top-secret government laboratory where scientists are working around the clock trying to determine its origin.

An official cloak of silence has fallen around the object but one insider has leaked some information on Project Jewel.

"This thing could set the world on its ear — if it proves to be an authentic artifact," says the man, who's viewed and probed the colorful crystal.

"The main theory at this point is that the crystal is some sort of transmitter that had been left here by visitors from another planet.

"The color and clarity of the three-dimensional figures are truly fabulous.

"But there are others who view it as proof that Atlantis existed thousands of years ago. They point to the location of the find as an indicator it washed up from the ocean floor.

"If true, that explanation would be a fantastic revelation as well.

"But then we must make sure it's just not an elaborate hoax, one that would make us look like fools."

The source says an answer is expected in the near future.●

☐ *This crystal viewing apparatus is going to show up several times in this book and I'm betting there is one. 9.5.*

UFOs and crystals appear to have some kind of a relationship. The following article suggests this is true.

UFO ALIENS TAUGHT INDIAN MEDICINE WOMAN TO HEAL WITH CRYSTALS
***National Examiner*, June 6, 1989**
by Edward Reynolds

UFO aliens taught an Indian medicine woman how to use crystals to heal.

Now Wanita Windwalker can help cure illnesses ranging from alcoholism to chronic back pain.

Wanita, of Pontiac, Michigan, recalls the evening she drove to a local park with two clients.

Suddenly, two laser-like columns of light touched down on her car, enclosing the vehicle for 10 minutes, she says.

The two clients left for home after the lights disappeared.

But as Wanita began to drive home, she found that even though she was in forward drive, her car was being slowly pulled backward!

Then her car was lifted in the air about 12 feet, where it hovered for some 10 minutes.

She vividly recalls shouting "No, I won't go with you. Release me. I have work to do here."

The car floated to the ground and Wanita drove home. When she reached the front door she encountered a man in a gray suit.

He said, "You are not ready to join us. We will come back another time." Then he vanished into thin air.

Some time later, Wanita says she felt compelled to climb Mount Ida in Arkansas. As she rested at the top, she was drawn to a small clump of scrub trees.

Moments later, she saw a brightly-lit flying saucer. A light beam enveloped her, and the same man in the gray suit appeared and led her to what she describes as a "healer's temple" made of clear crystal.

The man told Wanita she was going to learn how to use crystals. He placed a crystal in each palm and instructed her to cross her hands and look up at the sun.

Wanita remembers finding herself again next to the scrub trees holding the two crystals. She remembers looking at her watch and noticing that two hours had passed.

She then collected 12 crystals, including an 80-lb crystal "generator."

She went down the mountain carrying the crystals as if they were feathers. When she returned home, she says she knew exactly how to arrange her crystals for healings.●

☐ *The Indian medicine woman gets an 8.*

If you don't follow up the clues on these opinions how are you going to evaluate the subject for yourself? The following article has been hashed over about a thousand times more or less — you might as well try this one.

ENORMOUS CRYSTAL BLAMED FOR DEVIL'S TRIANGLE
***National Examiner*, March 8, 1989**
by Jack Pleasant

A giant crystal is responsible for the loss of hundreds of ships and planes in the Bermuda Devil's Triangle, according to a top psychic.

Incredibly, the crystal survived the mysterious destruction of the long-lost continent of Atlantis, said medium Robin Winbow.

The crystal was used by the ingenious Atlanteans to harness the sun's energy, he said. It survived the horrible disaster that destroyed Atlantis about 5,000 years ago and lies deep in the Atlantic Ocean somewhere off the coast of Florida.

"The crystal's power is still a potent force," said Winbow, 49, of Brighton, Sussex, England.

"In certain meteorological conditions, it affects ships and planes. It disorients their controls and causes sinkings and crashes."

Winbow was given the information about Atlantis by his spirit guide when he was helping a man overcome a fear of flying, he said.

Said Winbow: "I learned from a Chinese Mandarin named Ah Wung Chung that the man had led a previous life in Atlantis. He was involved in aircraft design and died in a plane crash.

"His fear of flying remained with him through other lives to the present day."

People today shouldn't be surprised the Atlanteans had airplanes thousands of years ago, he said.

"It was an age of invention," he said. "They not only had long distance craft, but short-range planes. They powered them with the sun's energy.

"This was harnessed by a collection of carefully shaped crystals on the ground, including the huge one that still survives.

"The solar energy in the crystals could be beamed up to aircraft in flight when their power was low."

Some of Atlantis' inhabitants survived the destruction of the continent and reached South America. They took their skills with them.

There could be a connection between them and the animal drawings in the Peruvian desert which can only be seen properly from high in the air.

Winbow believes he has led several previous lives, including one as an American Indian.

Said Winbow: "When I visited the Adirondack Mountains in New York State a few years ago, the area was familiar. I felt a great sense of awe about it.

"It was holy ground to the Indians, a healing place where they would never kill or murder. While there, I also saw several spirits of Indians, although other people were unaware of their presence."

The legendary Atlantis was described by the Greek philosopher Plato in two of his most famous writings.

Atlantis has also been identified with Scandinavia, the Canary Islands, and Palestine, according to *The Encyclopedia Britannica.*

The treacherous 1.5 million-square-mile area of ocean is one of several Devil's Triangles in each hemisphere, according to *The Encyclopedia Britannica.*

The most famous, after the Bermuda Triangle, is the South China Sea Triangle, bounded by Manila in the Philippines, Hong Kong, and Taiwan.

The mysterious area has taken a terrible toll for more than 3,000 years, including two Japanese aircraft carriers and three destroyers that vanished in a calm sea during World War II.

There was no enemy action reported in the area when the vessels disappeared.●

☐ *Maybe about an 8, I don't know much about such things!*

THE WORLD IS A GIGANTIC CRYSTAL

A couple of years ago a Convention of Crystals was held in Texas. Riley Crabb came from New Zealand to present a lecture, "The World is a Gigantic Crystal." Riley is the head of the Border Line Sciences Foundation. This theory dates back to the time of Plato. More recently the Russians brought this up in the youth magazine. Three Russian scientists worked out a grid line theory. About the same time, Christopher Byrd wrote a similar article about crystals in the *New Age Journal.* Ivan Sanderson has also worked out a theory. A scientist in New Zealand agrees with this work.

It's as if our planet is a ball made up of 12 pieces of leather. At each intersection or vortex, a tremendous energy source is formed. This is believed to be responsible for the disappearance of planes, ships and people. For example, those five planes that were sent out from Ft. Lauderdale, Florida, in December 1945 — as well as the ones dispatched to follow them — it was well known this triangle was a danger zone.

The UFOs appear to use these grid lines as a power source. Aime Michel has written a book, *The Straight Line Theory,* which refers to this triangle. The following report which I investigated fits this theory.

REPORTER BELIEVES SAUCERS WERE NEARBY EARLY MONDAY

***Public Opinion*, October 2, 1958**

by Lillian Crowner Desguin

Monday, September 29 set off a flood of "flying saucer" sightings, a number of which were presented in the *Columbus Dispatch*. An interesting picture will be noted if this subject is given close observation. Making a list of the sightings which took place from 4:25 a.m. until 9:15 a.m. we find,

Warren, Ohio-4:25 a.m.; London, Ohio-4:30 & 4:31 a.m.; Hamilton, Ohio-4:35 a.m., Akron-Canton Airport-5:09 a.m.; 2448 Sullivan Ave., Columbus, Ohio-Monday, 7:40 a.m.

Taking your two most distant locations, draw a straight line through Warren and Hamilton, Ohio. You must realize, of course, that a slight difference would be noticed in a geodetic line.

At 9:15 a.m. Monday, farmer Ralph Keys arrived at our door. His farm is one mile east of Flint, on Park Road. He was curious to know if I was familiar with any reason which might cause farm animals to develop a fear complex. Ralph said that he found his herd of cows huddled against the outside of his barn instead of being in their usual pasture. This was odd but not nearly as odd as the results which took place when he tried to get the animals inside to be milked. They wouldn't go. They were frightened. and it was with great difficulty that he managed to have his milking done by the time George Griffith of Galena arrived with the milk truck.

When he explained what happened to George, the problem became more complex. Griffith told him that Earle White, who lives on Alum Creek two houses north of Africa Road, had a worse time than Mr. Keys. At the time he arrived for milk there was nothing to present but the supply from the night before. In fact, White was so provoked he decided to turn the animals loose and forget about it. Keys wondered what could cause such a reaction.

Not having heard any news I could only guess that "flying saucers" had indeed been close. Time and time again similar descriptions are given. I questioned neighbors and tried to find some night owl who might have a story to tell. It was nearly noon before Mr. Keys' cows would go to their pasture, but it was nearer midnight before I was able to show reasoning that these cattle had been scared by UFOs.

One of the most recent UFO books is *Flying Saucers and the Straight Line Mystery* by M. Aime Michel, a Frenchman who has done much investigation in Europe. He finally stumbled onto the fact that flying saucer sightings, over a given time, seem to cover a straight line.

As I looked over the reported sightings, I suddenly realized this was my chance to put the theory to test. The line went approximately through every sighting mentioned (including the two farmer's properties)!

I immediately called Gladys Malone of 2448 Sullivant Ave., in Columbus. The paper identified her as a spotter. She has never read a book on "flying saucers," and she had never seen a "flying saucer" before this weekend. Mrs. Malone was hanging out clothes at 7:40 a.m. when she noticed a silver disk traveling from NE to SW. Please note that these directions were given with absolutely no help from me. At 7:45 two more disks followed, going in the same direction. At 8:10 a cigar-shaped object appeared which was traveling from SW to NE. In the air it appeared about 3 inches long and 1-1/2 inches wide. She felt it must be of tremendous size and very, very, high. The center of this ship appeared blue-green and was surrounded by a red-orange halo. As she watched, it disappeared just as if it had melted. At 8:45 a.m. a second cigar-shaped ship appeared, going from SW to NE. She hardly believed this was the same ship, but admitted it was possible. At 9:15, three silver disks arrived from the SW going NE. Two of Mrs. Malone's sightings were shared by a neighbor. Please note that the straight line of travel may well have lead near the discontented cows.●

Our grocery store tabloids will tell you what happens in many cases. These are what we call Time Warps.

Riley Crabb is a firm believer in UFOs and space people. He thinks they have been here to observe the evolution of our planet. He says they will be here to help us in a time of need.

Here's another one that goes both back in time and ahead to the future.

TOP SCIENTIST FINDS PROOF OF TIME TRAVEL

***Weekly World News*, May 9, 1989**

by Carl Ford

A top scientist claims to have found a 2,000-year-old time capsule that contains a toaster, clock radio and newspaper dated Aug. 22, 2023 A.D.!

And Dr. Charles Frese, the Dutch archaeologist, is convinced that the capsule was planted in the ruins of an East Indian temple by men who traveled back in time from our own future.

"There is no other explanation for it," Dr. Frese told newsmen in Deventer, Holland. "Analysis of the metal capsule indicates that it is at least 2,000 years old. But the contents are items that weren't even invented until the 20th century.

"The newspaper itself is even more puzzling. According to the date, it won't be printed for another 34 years. I still have quite a bit of research to conduct.

"But it certainly looks as if the capsule and its contents were planted by time travelers from the 21st century,"

Dr. Frese claims to have found the brass, football-shaped capsule in the ruins of a 2,000-year-old temple north of Delhi, India, on March 28, 1989.

He initially thought that he had stumbled on some sort of religious icon.

"You can imagine the kind of shock and surprise I felt upon opening the capsule to find a newspaper, a toaster and a clock radio," said Dr. Frese. "At first I thought it was some kind of joke.

"But laboratory tests conclusively proved that both the capsule and its contents are 2,000 years old or older."

The clock radio is similar to ones that are widely available today but its parts are so worn with age that it doesn't work, said the scientist.

The toaster is in similar condition, he added. But the newspaper, which is printed in Japanese, is still legible and speaks of events that are yet to come.

"There is really nothing particularly sensational in the paper, which reports news events that apparently are going to happen in Tokyo in August 2023," said Dr. Frese.

"The implications of this time capsule are staggering," he said.●

☐ *I think time travel is a little beyond me. I'll give it a 5, until I get more knowledgeable.*

AN INTRODUCTION TO TIME TRAVEL WITH SALLY, RAY, GIDAON AND HODAN

In the 1960s I was looking around for UFO stories and related subjects. This experience took place between 1966 and 1976. It was during this time that I met Ray and Sally Seibert. Though I had heard this tale during that time, I was not too aware of the subject "Time Travel." Today, every tabloid seems to find many such tales. I consider them an important part of the information we must face.

I hope you will consider this experience seriously and will also take a good look at the many experiences presented by the tabloids. This individual experience would be better covered in a book — for now I shall try to condense it as much as possible.

Sally and Ray had been introduced to the fad of "table tipping." They asked the table's energy source for a name they might use when addressing it. They were given "Gidaon," pronounced Gi-day-on. The table responded to questions by rising on two legs and hitting the floor — once to indicate yes, and twice for no — and other more complicated methods. After a few months of playing around, they began asking questions about UFOs. Finally they asked for a good demonstration. Having been well satisfied, they gave this energy source the name of "Hodan." He answered Sally's questions mentally and others would record them.

They were anxious to see a good solid nuts-and-bolts UFO instead of something called "Living Light," and pestered their contacts for more information. They were told many of these contacts were unwise and could be dangerous.

At last they were given the description of an area near Parkersburg, W.Va. In due time they found it better to substitute names for towns, roads and their friends. It wasn't wise to lure others into the same experience.

While attending a family funeral in W.Va., Ray found himself alone and within forty miles of the area. The controls had given exact measurements and descriptions of the places mentioned. He calls the town "Elizabeth." He went there and followed directions to a cement bridge on its outskirts. It was to be on Route 54 (fictitious). Starting at this bridge, he was to go 4.3 miles and then follow a road which took off to the left. This was to be followed 2.8 miles to a gravel and dirt road. When he reached the dirt road he drove 1.7 miles to the place he was to park the car. On the left there was a meadow, while on the right was a knoll which he was told was a UFO landing area. All measurements were within one tenth of a mile of being accurate.

A long lane was to lead him to the far side of a hill and it was there he would find a small house and a large barn, with a UFO. It was difficult waiting, but he had been given a definite description of this place. It was to be on a well-kept, kidney-shaped lot with a small house and a large barn. Supposedly the UFO was in the barn; aliens parked it while roaming around the countryside looking for some kind of data.

Sure enough, there it was, looking as if the grass had been freshly mowed. Even though the buildings were of very old vintage, everything about them seemed in perfect shape. Ray remembered he had been told not to show fear or it could be misinterpreted.

He walked to within 45 to 50 feet of the house. He wanted to look in the window. Somehow he couldn't force himself to go closer. He walked all around the house and then went to the barn. Again he found that as much as he wanted to open the door, he felt unable to fulfill his desire. Instead, all he could think about was getting back to the car. He started jogging but found he was in a full run before he had reached his goal. He couldn't leave fast enough! Both he and Sally were glad he was back home.

At this time Ray was working at North American Aviation in Columbus, Ohio. He told a few of his friends what had happened. They answered him they would go back with him and *they* would open that door. They didn't mean sometime — they meant the minute they left work!

And that's why nine of them arrived there at sunset. They had parked their cars by the large meadow that was to lead them around the hill to the much sought after barn. One and a half hours later, all nine were standing beside their cars waiting for the brave one who would go first!

As they started home, one of them said he felt as if someone were watching him. Another said, "If they were watching us, why don't they give us a sign, like shutting off our car engine?" Instantly the car lights, radio, and engine shut off and they were driving in pitch dark. When they came to a complete stop all power immediately came on again. All conversation ceased for the remainder of the trip — they were scared.

The only explanation Sally was given was that all this had been done for their protection. For the next ten years they never went near the site. But on that anniversary, which was July 4th, they decided to see what would happen after ten years. They planned to go alone but told a friend, and soon there were reservations for six at the Holiday Inn just outside Parkersburg.

As soon as they arrived, five out of the six were determined to head for that hill! George and Marilyn had a brand new red Lincoln Continental. He wanted to drive, so all six crowded into one car. They brought a card table along in case they needed to ask more questions.

They found the town "Elizabeth" and the river with the cement bridge, and from then on they only had to follow directions. They measured the mileage but nothing worked. Even though they went back again and again, each time they came up with different answers and no roads! Finally Ray decided there must be another entrance from that location. He carefully figured out where it might be and they made a final attempt. That's how they found themselves seeing a house built on stilts with young ones playing in the yard and pigs living under the front porch. Though they were close to the road, no-one appeared to notice them. George found that he had to cross a large stream of water which covered the road to such an extent Ray had to wade out to make sure they could make it. The car was covered with mud inside and out. As they drove on, they encountered a woman sweeping a dirt path. She was not more than 25 feet away from them. A boy on a bicycle was driving straight toward them down the narrow road within less than 100 feet when he suddenly turned and went across a field. At last they reached the crest of a hill and Ray knew he was there. The meadow had been replaced by woods with large trees. However, he saw the path that led around that hill.

Ken and Ray left George with the girls while they followed Ray's lead.

As they were walking in the lane they were met by a Plymouth car which was probably between a '57 to '59. Even though it was old, it appeared new and was purring like a kitten. Ray said they looked as if they came out of a Grant Wood painting. He pretended he was hunting his old family homestead. The woman told him that this was their home, but their son and family lived there now. He thanked them and said he must have made a mistake.

Meanwhile, Sally also saw the car. She stopped them and asked if they had seen the men. The man said they had, but they weren't from around there. As Sally watched the car go up the nearby hill, it faded into nonexistence.

Ray and Ken continued around the hill. He knew that a large plateau with a house and barn would be there. Suddenly it came into sight. Instead of the well-kept farm he had seen ten years ago, it was old and dilapidated and the siding was falling off. A woman was hanging clothes and a man was working in the garden. Children and dogs were playing in the yard. Rusting farm equipment was nearby. He knew they were the same buildings. No-one paid any attention to them. He felt sure they weren't seen. He believed he had lost his senses. Ray felt depressed and wanted to cry.

Both men were ready to leave. They went back to the car and compared experiences. "Gidaon" told them what they had seen were "thought forms." They only stayed one more day before going back to Columbus.

The story doesn't end there. The next weekend George and Marilyn called to take them out to dinner. George had had this experience. When he arrived home he asked the garage to wash and clean the car thoroughly and remove all the mud, and also to give it a good check-up. When it was returned they told him there was no mud or dirt on the car — but they washed it anyway.

This is what we call a time warp. How can we explain such things? All you can do is read some of these other experiences and see if you know the answer. All I know is that I love the people who had the experience, and trust them very much.

CHARLOTTE MOBERLY AND ELEANOR JOURDAIN

(A 1901 time warp experience)

The *National Examiner*, on April 25, 1989, printed an old-time favorite about people who have traveled back in time, written by Edward Reynolds. He found it recounted in the 1988 *Aquarian Press*. I remember it from many years ago — I will never forget their experience.

Two English school teachers, on vacation, had gone to visit the Palace of Versailles in Paris. No sooner had they arrived than they became lost in 18th Century history. They saw both scenery and buildings which belonged to the past. Even Marie Antoinette was seen sitting on the lawn terrace. Two men who later were identified as her guards told the women where to walk. Another gave directions to the house. Even an old bandstand came into physical reality.

They also were able to identify a repulsive looking man who was seen sitting near a building. He was Compte de Vaudreuil, a pock-marked Creole who was an attendant of the queen.

As I remember, one teacher was the daughter of an English minister, but this didn't help any when she and her companion went home and told their story. Their careers and lives were ruined by those who were unable to accept the impossible. I was interested to note the odd feeling of depression felt by these women. Perhaps we'll be more lenient with them when we find out more about "time warps."

☐ *(I thought it was the thinking or dreaming of those involved in that scenario that made such things appear??) It does seem pretty strong when several different people gave the women directions. Maybe that whole picture continues to exist in another dimension?*

UFOS ARE REALLY TIME TRAVELERS
***Sun*, August 16, 1988**
Special Report by Philip Lane

The most perplexing mystery in mankind's history has been solved: UFO aliens are not extraterrestrials, but human time travelers of our own Earth, and their strange craft are not spaceships but time machines they use to return to the past to study us.

That's the astounding conclusion of a team of six scientists from a top-secret "think tank" in California's Silicon Valley, south of San Francisco, following a seven-year study.

The startling solution to this mystery, which dates back to Biblical times, was revealed confidentially by a prominent member of the high-IQ group who insists he be identified only as "the Professor."

The brainy informant says team members have signed a secrecy pledge with the giant corporation that funded the expensive investigation, promising they will not publicly release all their astonishing findings for fear of worldwide controversy and ridicule.

He says the impact of the astounding discovery would be as powerful as a modern Revelation.

The Professor explains that the conclusions were drawn in part from Albert Einstein's accepted theory of relativity and confirms a principle espoused by mystics for centuries. Einstein said time is the fourth dimension and that a straight line in the universe will ultimately return to its starting point.

Therefore, the think-tank eggheads argue, space travel to distant worlds is impossible.

Time travel, on the other hand, is not only possible but very real.

The Professor says visitors from the future, possessing superior knowledge, cannot reveal to today's world cures for such human miseries as cancer and AIDS because to do so would alter a chain of events that are already in motion.

A visitor from the future could, therefore, prevent his own ancestors from meeting and, by so doing, erase his own existence.

Of course, time travelers look different from us because of natural evolutionary processes.

This explains the strange appearance of creatures associated with UFO aliens sighted around the world.

If the theory is correct, it proves what spiritualists have said all along, the Professor notes: that "the past, present and future are all the same."

This means that what we call space and time are nothing more than illusion.●

☐ *Stick with these articles — I don't know any book which will give you more information. Eggheads ought to get an 8 for effort.*

The *Weekly World News* must pay Ragan Dunn a lot of steak to keep coming up with these articles. If there isn't some truth behind this one, it's up to the doubter to get out there and prove it. Matter of fact, the *News* could offer to take a couple of us along where we might have a chance to judge for ourselves. I think this is a terrific article — if you can prove it isn't true — I'd still send them flowers.

Pictures, and names of high officials are shown and say, "Soviets ex-air defense head, Gen. Alexander Koldunov, lost his job to Gen. Demitri Yozov over the time-travel reports." I'll bet Gen. Koldunov knows whether this is true — providing there is a Gen. Koldunov.

SUPER JETS TRAVEL BACK IN HISTORY
***Weekly World*, November 15, 1988**
by Ragan Dunn

A leading scientist says Soviet and NATO fighter pilots have broken the time barrier and traveled back into our own past!

"This is nothing new — it's been going on for years," Dr. Poks Haglund told reporters in Kalmar, Sweden. "The powers that be would prefer to keep this information secret.

"But I can prove that their pilots have flown over medieval Europe, ancient Egypt, even prehistoric Africa, on flights dating back to the 195Os."

Soviet and NATO spokesmen would neither confirm nor deny Dr. Haglund's report. But Russian sources privately confirmed that former Soviet Air Defense Chief Alexander Koldunov was ousted in 1987 for failing to investigate the time-travel phenomenon.

They also noted that new Defense Minister Dimitri Yazov has demanded immediate updates on any additional developments.

Dr. Haglund himself dismissed official denials as part of a massive coverup. He then produced classified Soviet and NATO documents that describe 274 flights through time since 1959 alone.

Among the most sensational, he said, were::

- Soviet pilot Alexander Ustinov flew a MIG 21 into ancient Egypt on August 23. According to his report, there was a single pyramid on the desert landscape. The foundation of another had been laid.

- NATO pilot Paul Klein reported seeing dinosaurs on a training flight in 1985. He started the flight in northern Europe — but was convinced that he was over Africa when the dinosaurs came into view.

- Soviet pilot Victor Okulov reported seeing a portion of America's Civil War. A student of U.S. history, Okulov felt like he had unwittingly flown a reconnaissance flight over the Battle of Gettysburg in his MIG 25.

- Soviet pilot Yury Yemelyanov was on a routine training mission over central Russia when he suddenly found himself flying at treetop level over medieval Europe. Mounds of human bodies and massive bonfires suggest that he witnessed the devastation caused by the Bubonic Plague.

- An unidentified NATO pilot described a brief but dramatic flight over ancient Rome. He vividly recalled seeing chariots in the street below him — and said the now-crumbling colosseum was new and was filled to capacity.

- A NATO pilot, also unidentified, reported flying into the middle of a WWII air battle over Germany. Both Allied and German pilots saw his jet and scattered, he said.

"None of the trips lasted more than 20 seconds," said Dr. Haglund. "And oddly enough, speed didn't appear to have anything to do with their travels through time. There are reports of pilots breaking the time barrier at both sub- and supersonic speeds.

"It seems much more likely that other forces, such as gravity and resistance, weaken the barrier between what is and what was."

Dr. Hubert Gayan, the French astrophysicist, said Dr. Haglund's report was "most intriguing" and might even explain UFO sightings throughout history.

"The UFOs that our ancestors saw might have been our own planes," he said.●

☐ *How about a 10 for Time Travel?*

SCREAMING CHRISTIANS
***Weekly World*, July 11, 1989**
by Mel van Hoy

Hundreds of people claim to have been awakened in the middle of the night by bloodcurdling screams of men and roar of lions in the Roman Colosseum!

Citizens were so shaken by the incident that they actually petitioned Pope John Paul II to pray at the 2,000-year-old stadium where thousands of Christians were thrown to the lions in the 1st century A.D.

"We don't know what to make of it," Police Captain Marion Caretti told newsmen. The screams and roars lasted almost five minutes beginning at 12:37 a.m. on June 5.

"Hundreds of people were awakened and most of them were terrified." It's possible that the sounds were the work of a prankster with a big tape player and speakers.

"But we have no proof of that. It's purely speculation."

In fact, people who heard the ghostly noises as far as 20 blocks away said cops are out of their minds if they think a prankster was responsible for the screams.

"There isn't a stereo on Earth that could reproduce sound like that," Dino Rizzo, who lives seven blocks from the crumbling stadium, told newsmen.

"The roars of the lions were vibrating in my chest. The screams were blood-curdling. They were definitely made by real men."

Franco R. Tramballi, the Italian acoustics expert, has taken a personal interest in the case. After speaking to more than two dozen witnesses, Tramballi is convinced that the screams were those of Christians who were thrown to the lions by Roman persecutors like the emperor Nero 1,900 years ago.

"Sounds made by people and animals during times of extreme trauma and stress have been known to be heard hundreds and even thousands of years later," said the expert.

"This is a phenomenon that's quite common on battlefields the world over.

"It is quite possible that the screams of Christians and the roars of the lions who ate them are trapped in the Colosseum, possibly for all time."

Pope John Paul has not responded to the request for him to pray at the Colosseum. But one Vatican source said the holy father is taking the ghostly happenings "quite seriously."

Father Gian Soluri of Rome says that is as it should be.

"There isn't a doubt in my mind. Those screams were the sounds of Christians who were martyred in the Coliseum almost 2,000 years ago," he said.●

☐ *You can bet that batch of screaming Christians didn't make it to heaven or they wouldn't be back here yelling their heads off, stuck in a time warp. When you read all these examples of time warps, doesn't it make you wonder? It's worth at least a 9.5.*

TWO MEN WHO SAILED INTO THE PAST
***Weekly World*, April 18, 1989**
by Irwin Fisher

A Dutch yachtsman saw American naval hero John Paul Jones and his British adversary locked in mortal combat on the high seas after he sailed through a time warp — and traveled 200 years into the past!

Peter Brader, owner of the 36-foot sloop *Edo Bettie,* said there was no mistaking Capt. Jones' ship, *Bon Homme Richard*, and the British warship *Serapis*, which fought off the coast of England in 1779.

As horrifying proof that the battle he witnessed was real, Brader told how a stray cannonball sailed over the deck of the *Edo Bettie* — and knocked off a crewman's head.

"I know it sounds like something out of sci-fi movie, but it happened," Braden told reporters in Amsterdam. "The old ships were lashed together and Jones' was burning out of control. The British vessel was still firing her cannon and the balls were whizzing over my sloop.

"We weren't hit but, dear God, one of them took off my mate's head before we left the past and returned to our own time.

Authorities confirmed that the decapitation death of seaman Charles Gortzak, 42, "raised the very real possibility that he was hit by a cannonball," but refused to discuss the explanation given by Brader. The yachtsman himself insisted that his report was accurate. He also provided the authorities with a detailed account of what happened after the *Edo Bettie* left Scarborough, England, on March 12 and sailed through a warp in time in the North Sea.

"We were sailing south for Flamborough Head, about 20 miles down the coast, and anticipated no problem whatsoever," said Brader.

"As we neared Flamborough, Gortzak mentioned that it was the spot where Jones defeated the Serapis against all odds in a battle in 1779.

"The day had been clear up to that point but we suddenly found ourselves engulfed in a sparkling blue mist. Our instruments went haywire and the radio stopped dead. When we sailed back into the light of day there were Jones and the British, battling it out.

"I remember thinking: 'This can't be real.' Then a cannonball shot over my head."

Brader said the *Edo Bettie* was less than 35 yards from the battling ships and had lost both her wind and auxiliary power. He estimated that crewman Gortzak was hit and killed by a cannonball less than a minute after their trip through time began.

The sloop and crew remained in the past approximately eight minutes before the mysterious blue mist reappeared and transported them back to the present.

Belgian physicist Roger Bethune has interviewed Brader and a second crew member who has not been identified in news reports.

Dr. Bethune said, "There is no doubt in my mind that these men are telling the truth."●

☐ *If this is what happens at the vortex of those grid lines, I think I'll stay home. Paul Brader, owner of a 36-foot sloop, and his seaman Charles Gortzok sailed into an eight minute time warp, 200 years in the past.*

Even if it's science fiction, it ought to have a 9.

TIME WARP STORY TO DUMFOUND

***Weekly World News,* June 11, 1989**

by Herb Tennant

WWII fighter vanished in 1942, landed in Russia June 5, 1989 — no gas, and the skeleton of Captain Claus Siegert at the controls.

A German fighter plane that flew over the Eastern Front in 1942 has just landed at a Soviet airport with a skeleton at the controls — 46 years later!

The BF109-G plane appears to be in good condition although it reportedly shows "definite signs of aging."

There was no immediate explanation for the vintage plane's mysterious appearance in Soviet airspace. Russian officials were equally baffled by the skeleton pilot's perfect landing at the Minsk airport the morning of June 5.

"I don't think it's overstating the case to call this one of the greatest riddles in aviation history," Dr. Armel Kleber, the West German WWII military historian, told reporters in Frankfurt.

"The Soviets haven't released everything they know about the plane and pilot. But press dispatches from Moscow indicate that the plane was out of fuel and coasted into the Minsk airport.

"The pilot was identified as Luftwaffe Capt. Claus Siegert, who was listed as missing in action after he failed to return from a mission over the Soviet Union on December 5, 1942. I really don't know what to make of all this. I don't think the Russians do either. All we really know is a warplane that vanished in 1942 has reappeared almost 50 years later."

Soviet authorities were reluctant to divulge more information than was included in sketchy newspaper reports. They did confirm that Capt. Siegert was shot to death while flying the plane.

Judging from the pilot's skeleton and tattered uniform, they estimated that Capt. Siegert was killed at some point during his 1942 mission.

Werner Kalt, a West German physicist, is one of dozens of scientists who have offered to assist the Soviets in the investigation of the phantom plane.

He told newsmen there is "a very real possibility" that Capt. Siegert flew into a time warp after he was shot in 1942 — and just flew out. "It's a compelling notion," said the expert. "If the Russians will allow us to inspect the airplane and what's left of the pilot, we might be able to prove it."●

☐ *How about 9 for the uniform and 10 if I get some bones with it.*

Time warp stories are not new. *The Weekly World* used the following article back on December 24, '85. It's one of the best I've read. Notice that it does not have a by-line.

TIME WARP PLANE BAFFLES EXPERTS

Aircraft found 700 miles and 48 years off course.

A bizarre mystery surrounds a twin-engine passenger plane that was found crash-landed and abandoned in a New Guinea jungle swamp — looking as new as the day it was reported missing almost a half-century ago.

The silver aircraft was identified by its still-vivid markings as one lost on a flight from Manila to Mindanao 46 years ago. Newspapers found inside the downed plane are dated the third week of January, 1937.

An unnamed source in Jakarta, Indonesia, said a team of military aerospace investigators spent several hours inside the "like-new" aircraft and came away pale and shaken over what they found inside.

The chief investigator quickly ordered the area cordoned off with armed soldiers and imposed a total news blackout of the eerie incident.

However, the source in Jakarta had been inside the pristine plane days before the investigators arrived to launch their probe.

"When I first saw the plane. I couldn't believe my eyes," he said.

"I was looking at an airplane that hadn't been in this part of the world since the end of WWII. Yet, incredible as it sounds, it looked like it had just rolled off the assembly line.

"It was virtually new. Its metal fuselage and wings were unscarred and gleaming like a mirror in the sun. It was as if the plane had flown into a time warp that carried it 48 years into the future and 700 miles off course.

"I was certain the door would be difficult to open, but it swung outward easily and without a sound. I stood outside for a second before entering. I was not prepared for what I found — and what I didn't find."

What he didn't find was any sign of life ... or death. Although the plane showed obvious signs of having been recently occupied — empty paper cups, cigarette butts in the ashtrays, a neat-looking, felt fedora, and unyellowed editions of several 1937 newspapers — the interior was deserted.

In one of the ashtrays was an empty pack of unfiltered cigarettes bearing a green label popular in the '30s but discontinued when Americans entered WWII. And the clothing fashions and hairdo styles depicted in a magazine were those of the Depression era.

"But the most astonishing of all was the condition of the plane," the source said. "The batteries were still fully charged. When I threw a few switches, the lights went on.

"There was coffee in a Thermos bottle and it tasted fresh! There were packages of sandwiches that were equally fresh. They could have been made only hours before. It made my skin crawl. It was very spooky. I checked the fuel tanks, expecting to find them bone-dry. But they appeared to be full.

"The plane had come down with its landing gear up. It just skidded along the soft muck until it stopped. It was totally undamaged. With a pilot at the controls, I'm certain it could fly as well as it did almost 50 years ago." The investigation into the plane's past is continuing, according to government sources.●

☐ *Either it's a 10 or a 1. I don't know, do you?*

HYPNOTIZED TIME TRAVELERS DISCOVER A FUTURE PARADISE

***Weekly World News*, April 3, 1990**

by Janice Marks

In mind-boggling research, hundreds of people who were placed under hypnosis have "traveled" into the future and given remarkably similar descriptions of what life on Earth will be like in the years 2100 and 2300.

The amazing similarity of the descriptions convinces psychologist Helen Wambach "that these people are, in fact, experiencing events in the future while under hypnosis."

Miss Wambach, famed for her research on reincarnation, said the subjects describe a world where all disease has been conquered and where the average life span exceeds 200 years.

When death finally does come, they report, it's peaceful and painless.

"But not a single subject of the 1,000 I have worked with so far has painted a totally rosy future world," Miss Wambach added.

The subjects speak of an ecological disaster of some sort that has rendered the air unfit to breathe, killed vegetation and forced people to live in cities covered by transparent domes.

"One fact stands out from all the rest for both time periods (2100 and 2300): There are a lot less people, and over half don't live on Earth but in space colonies.

"Those remaining on Earth are rehabilitating it. One subject said, 'I volunteered to reseed Earth.' "

The reseeding efforts are just barely getting started in the year 2100.

"By 2300, nature is healing the wounds. Vegetation and wildlife are returning," said Miss Wambach. "The air is becoming more breathable.

"One unusual thing in 2300 are feeding stations. You walk into a room in which there are tubes, and you simply 'inhale' food through them.

And there is a very exciting aspect to the Earth's recovery. "A number of my subjects have reported that they are being helped by intelligent beings from somewhere else in the universe, beings who witnessed Earth's difficulties and came in spaceships to assist with their superior technology," she continued.

"Instead, people simply choose to die at some point. But they are not frightened by death at all, describing it as being peaceful and painless.

"The world of the future described by my subjects is at peace, a world recovering from some of its past mistakes and exploring the frontiers of space hand in hand with other intelligent beings."

Psychologist and reincarnation researcher Dr. Leo Sprinkle said: "I'm very familiar with Miss Wambach's work — and it's very exciting. I do think that people are mentally able to travel into the future. Impressive work in the past indicates that this is possible."•

☐ *This article is beyond anything I've experienced! It doesn't look to me as if it should be ignored. I can't judge Miss Wambach — I'm sure she deserves all anyone wishes to give her. Such work is tedious and demands lots of time and patience.*

PASSENGER TRAIN VANISHES IN TUNNEL

***Weekly World News*, June 26, 1990**

by Ann Hughey

A passenger train carrying over 600 passengers entered an 11-1/2-mile-long tunnel — and never came out!

So far, Italian officials have found no explanation for what happened to the 43-car train that disappeared without a trace just south of Bologna.

"It vanished into thin air," said Mario Franchini, the head of the Italian rail authority. "We know it went into the tunnel but it never came out.

"It's just like those ships that disappear in the Bermuda Triangle. There doesn't seem to be an explanation for what happened."

The passenger train was on the last leg of a journey that originated in central Italy and was headed for Bologna.

Authorities know it stopped to pick up and let off passengers a few miles south of the tunnel because the stationmaster radioed ahead to the depot on the other side of the tunnel to say the train was on its way.

One passenger who got off the train at the stop before it vanished recalled that weird things were happening.

"Everything was fine until about an hour before the last stop," said Gerardo Massari. "Then the lights started flickering, the water in the bathrooms wouldn't work and my radio went on the blink.

"I had this really eerie feeling. It was nothing I could put my finger on but something was giving me the creeps so I decided to get off.

"I was supposed to go all the way to Bologna and I'm sure glad I didn't."

The last person to see the train before it vanished was retired farmer Umberto Bosetti, who sits and watches them go by every day.

"I saw the train enter the tunnel," he said. "I really didn't notice anything out of the ordinary except the rumbling ended a lot sooner than it should have. "Trains make a lot of noise when they're in the tunnel. I usually hear them for four or five minutes after the last car goes in but this time I didn't.

"The rumbling stopped after only about two minutes. I didn't think much about it at the time but when I heard a train had disappeared I contacted the railroad authorities. I realized the train must have disappeared at the exact moment when I couldn't hear it anymore. It must have been at the middle of the tunnel."

Officials are still investigating the disappearance but say they're stumped.

"Who knows what happened to it," said Franchini. "We just don't know. Nothing like this has ever happened. How do you lose a train that's over two miles long? It just boggles the mind."•

☐ *I don't believe any country would allow this kind of news to be published without a missing train and at least 599 of those 600 missing passengers. It's about time people get off their "duffs" and look into such things for themselves. The articles that are worth 20s instead of 10s are too numerous to mention.*

TIME WARPS

I wrote a "time-warp" story,
That will give you quite a thrill.
My friends watched a couple vanish,
While they were riding up a hill.

Of course, it's a long story,
That covers ten years or so —
It's perfect for a book or movie,
As you will later see.

If you follow the Weekly World *tabloid,*
And the articles they show —
You'll learn more about this subject,
Than most other people know!

The tabloid tells about a woman,
Found floating on a hunk of ice —
She had her ticket from the Titanic,
And was cold and in a panic!

November's News *you about a soldier,*
Who says he fought in the Civil War —
He was born in South Carolina,
On August twenty-eighth, eighteen thirty-four!

Before you do much laughing —
You'd better examine for yourself.
You've got an awful lot to learn —
That will cause you great concern.

CHAPTER FOUR

Time Travel — Cross-breeding — Astrology and Charts
Noah's Ark — Reincarnation — Bigfoot — And Much, Much More

In Defense of the Grocery Store Tabloid 80
Era of Flying Saucers Started 40 Years Ago — *National Examiner* 81
Crew Survives Fiery UFO Crash — *Weekly World* 81
US Air Force Test-Flying Captured UFO — *National Examiner* 82
Did UFO Give Woman Cancer? — *National Examiner* 82
Homeless Boy is a Space Alien — *Weekly World* 83
UFO Aliens are Living Under Pacific Ocean — *National Examiner* 83
Alien Found Alive in UFO Wreckage — *Sun* 84
Proof ETs Making Test-Tube Half-Breed Babies — *National Examiner* 84
11 Girls Give Birth to UFO Aliens — *Sun* 85
UFO Seen Hovering in Scene From 1928 Movie — *Weekly World* 86
UFO Bases in the Rocky Mountains — *National Examiner* 86
Aliens are Guests of US Government — *National Examiner* 86
Noah's Ark Found? — *Weekly World* 87
Mother Seduced by Alien Toy Boys — *National Examiner* 87
UFO Aliens Rape Our Women — *National Examiner* 88
UFO Led Moses and His People Out of Egypt — *Sun* 88
The Vanishing ETs — *Weekly World* 89
Space Shuttle Attacked By 200 Ft. UFO — *Weekly World* 89
UFO Aliens Saved Burning Barn — *Sun* 90
Drawing of UFO Found in Pyramid — *Weekly World* 90
Space Aliens Fed Farmer — *Weekly World* 91
Huge Angels Seen in Space — *Weekly World* 91
Savage Tribe Ate 6 Space Aliens — *Weekly World* 92
Cop Shoots Space Alien — *Weekly World* 92
UFO Found on Playground — *Weekly World* 93
Ham Radio Operators Hear Secret Calls to Mission Control — *Sun* 93
Space Mummies Found — *Weekly World* 94
Letter From Russia Confirms Discovery — *Weekly World* 94
World's First Space Alien Interview — *Weekly World* 95
Scientists Can Hardly Believe Their Eyes — *Weekly World* 95
Space Aliens Use Spheres of Light to Spy on Us — *Weekly World* 96
Space Rainbows May Be Source Of UFOs — *Sun* 96
UFO Wreck in 1947 — *Weekly World* 97
Tribe Eats Spaceman — *Weekly World* 98
Ancient Video Set Used for Communication — *Weekly World* 98
Libyan Targets Buzzed by UFO — *Weekly World* 98
UFO Dentists Fixed Our Teeth — *Sun* 99
UFO Baby Speaks at 3 Months — *Sun* 99
5,000-year-old UFO Found in Red Sea — *Weekly World* 100
Alien Repairs Crippled Balloon — *Weekly World* 100
I Found Four Bodies After UFO Crash — *Sun* 101
Pigs in Space? — *Weekly World* 101

Small Town Named UFO Capital — *National Examiner* 102
Cops Baffled by a Flying Banana — *Sun* 102
Hot News From TASS: Tourists in Space — *New York Times* 103
Fact, Not Fiction, Says of UFO — *New York Times* 103
Soviets Capture UFO Captain — *Weekly World News* 104
Those Gulf Breeze Sightings — *National Examiner* 105
UFOs Terrorize Russian Town — *Sun* 106
Magic Ray Cures 22 People — *Weekly World* 106
UFO Docs Save Girl's Leg Aboard Spaceship — *Sun* 107
Fishing Trawler Nets UFO — *Weekly World News* 108
Noah's Ark Did Not Land on Mount Ararat — *National Examiner* 108
Minister Ties UFOs to Bible — *Columbus Dispatch* 109
Dr. J.B. Rhine — Mind Over Matter — *Public Opinion* 109
My Interview with Henry — *Public Opinion* 110
2000-year-old Mummy has Artificial Hip — *Sun* 110
First Scientific Proof Astrology is For Real — *National Examiner* 111
Letter From Mabel Trautman 112
Out of Body Traveler Visits 5 Cities Within Seconds — *Weekly World* 113
UFO Landing Bases Discovered Worldwide — *National Examiner* 113
Glowing Space Alien in His Bedroom — *National Examiner* 113
New Arm and Leg — *Weekly World* 114
Astrology Rules Our Lives — *Sun* 114
Shipwrecked with an Alien UFO Pilot — *Sun* 115
Boy Grows New Arm — *Sun* 115
Ghastly Irish Triangle — *National Examiner* 116
ET's Brought Bigfoot to Earth — *National Examiner* 116
Housewife Videotapes Outer-Space Show — *Weekly World* 117
Scientists Examine Bigfoot Baby — *Weekly World* 117
Lost City Powered by Crystals? — *National Examiner* 118
Russian Doctors Deliver Alien Baby — *Weekly World* 118
ET Posse Corrals Bank Robbers — *National Examiner* 119
Man Burned by UFO — *National Examiner* 120
Incredible Powers From Aliens — *National Examiner* 120
Vampires From Space Drank Our Blood — *Weekly World* 121
Human Skeleton on the Moon — *Weekly World* 121
Furry Green Aliens Panic Golfers — *National Examiner* 122
Government Captures UFOs — *National Examiner* 122
UFO Dogfight — *Weekly World* 123
Christmas Message — *Weekly World* 123
10,000-year-old UFO Found in Jungle — *Weekly World* 124
UFOs Stealing Islands? — *Weekly World* 124
UFO Baby Reads Mom's Mind — *National Examiner* 125
U.S. Pilots Flying Captured UFOs — *National Examiner* 125
Nazi Astronauts Return to Earth — *Weekly World* 126
UFO Veggies — *Sun* 126
Underwater UFO Base Found in Pacific — *Weekly World* 127
Crystals — Poem 128

IN DEFENSE OF THE GROCERY STORE TABLOID

In the 1950's and '60's my idea was to find out if flying saucers were real. They were, they are, and they always will be! That's when finding the answers to a million and one questions became a goal.

Bringing in lecturers on all related subjects helped to suggest many possibilities; each possibility raised more individual questions. *Chariots of The Gods*, by Erick von Daniken and W. Raymond Drake's books *Gods and Spacemen of the Ancient Past, Gods and Spacemen in the Ancient East* and *Gods and Spacemen in the Ancient West* all reminded us this topic was nothing new but one we thought belonged to another era of time. These books made us realize that references to such craft are also in the Bible. In all fairness we had to consider *UFOs and the Bible,* by Michigan astronomer M.K. Jessup.

While it was the contactee who convinced us he had seen these things, it was up to us to delve into the why, where, and when.... We thought we had to know, but we alone had to find the answers. It soon became apparent that if our government knew anything, they weren't going to tell us about it.

UFOs seemed to be related to science, math, religion, history and mythology, to say nothing of Atlantis, the Devil's Triangle, Big Foot, etc. Even reincarnation, evolution and the fourth dimension became part of our conversation. Bryant Reeve, in spite of all his letters, wrote *The Cosmic Viewpoint!* People soon forgot George Adamski's *Flying Saucers Have Landed.* Everyone wanted a good solid craft that could be parked in the garage or in the front yard.

When Dr. Allen Hynek and Major Donald Keyhoe decided these objects were for real, they became very verbal and didn't much care who heard what they said. The last time I heard them speak at a MUFON Convention in Dayton, Ohio, Dr. Hynek spoke about the fourth dimension and Major Keyhoe was upholding abduction cases which formerly he had tried to avoid.

In the 1970's I brought the UFO subject up to date in a column I wrote for the *Public Opinion* in Westerville, Ohio. It seemed foolish to keep repeating too many of my ideas or beliefs. By then UFOs were presented in many books and other publications.

It was some time before I began clipping papers and watching to see where I could find the most up-to-date material. We all had copies of Keyhoe's "National Investigating Committee of Aerial Phenomena" and the Lorenzen's bulletin, "Aerial Phenomena Research Organization."

There were other publications both here and in England, besides a good out-pouring of books. Eventually I began to compare the items from the tabloids to other sightings and cases which were presented. I found many good sightings which were covered in everyone's report.

If the tabloids were inventing their stories at least they did a better job and were getting the same information across to the public. They lost some of their readers with headlines that would curl your hair; if you took the trouble to read them it seemed to me they had a lot to say.

For the last five years I've been comparing their information with that taken from other papers, books, and my own research. I believe the tabloids have won. A half-dozen papers seemed to agree on the same cases. I found any number of reports which I had every reason to think were true. It is my idea to publish some of these articles; in some cases I've had to shorten their fancy headlines.

After watching the sports events who judge individuals on a 1 to 10 basis, I thought this might give you an idea how I feel about each report — this causes many of them to be listed as a 5 or 6 in order to show you some that I consider a 10. It doesn't mean that one is better than the other but that I know more about some cases than others.

There are so many doctors and scientists who are named, pictured, and quoted. I would certainly want to give much more credit provided I could prove these statements. I'm taking for granted many of these comments are true.

ERA OF FLYING SAUCERS STARTED 40 YEARS AGO
***National Examiner*, June 2, 1987**
by Patrick Cotter

It was 40 years ago that the term "flying saucers" was coined, helping usher in a new era in the history of mankind.

Although UFOs have been reported above Earth for centuries, it was veteran pilot Kenneth Arnold's sighting on June 24, 1947, that sparked the descriptive phrase that popularized UFOs — and led to scientific investigation of the fascinating phenomena.

Arnold was flying a search and rescue mission in Washington's Cascade Mountains when a flash of light caught his eye. "I observed a formation of nine very bright objects," he reported, "flying very close to the mountain tops and traveling with tremendous speed. I could see no tails on them, and they flew...like a saucer would if you skipped it across the water." The next morning, a newspaper coined the expression "flying saucer," and Kenneth Arnold had his place in history.

Although many who claimed to have had close encounters back in the 1950's and 1960's were ridiculed, it is now perfectly acceptable to discuss UFOs, says Timothy Green Beckley, who has been a dedicated UFOlogist for more than 20 years.

"You can believe in them without people saying you're crazy," he told the *Examiner*. "People want to hear more about UFOs. Celebrities are interested in the whole phenomenon — just look at Shirley MacLaine."

Early UFO contactees were laughed at when they spoke of what the extraterrestrials revealed during channeling, in which a spirit or higher intelligence speaks through a human, the use of crystals for healing, and reincarnation.

"But now all these things are very popular," says Beckley, of New York City. "Awareness of these phenomena came through the space people. The message has gotten through.

"People don't fear UFOs any more, like they did in the 1930's, when Orson Welles' *War Of The Worlds* radio broadcast terrified thousands. Now people think of aliens as friends after seeing movies such as *Close Encounters of the Third Kind* and *ET*."

Beckley believes the aliens are technologically advanced long-lost relatives who are keeping an eye on us.

"We should take seriously their current warnings about how we might blow our planet up and wipe ourselves out," he goes on to say.

"What they predicted before has already come true."●

☐ *In all fairness, I don't see how I could rate this lower than a 9.8 and I feel guilty by not making it a 10. I find nothing wrong about it. There is nothing to criticize.*

CREW SURVIVES FIERY UFO CRASH
***Weekly World News*, June 16, 1987**

Five space aliens have been hospitalized for the treatment of burns covering up to 90 percent of their bodies following a fiery UFO crash in central China, a UFO research group reports.

Jacques Pretet, president of the Paris-based Citizens for Truth in UFO Reporting, said documents obtained from military sources behind the Bamboo Curtain called the survival of the aliens a priority, but offered no prognosis.

Chillingly, the medical effort has reportedly been condemned by high-level Soviet and American officials, who believe the creatures are dangerous and should be killed or allowed to die.

"The survival or deaths of these five aliens has truly become a global concern," said Pretet. "Mikhail Gorbachev, Ronald Reagan, and the militaries in both of their countries have taken an intense personal interest.

"I have it on authority that envoys of the Soviet Union, U.S. and at least five other countries will meet with the Chinese in Geneva to discuss the situation. The meeting will take place within the next four weeks."

In a preliminary agreement hammered out in Peking, Chinese doctors have agreed to keep the superpowers briefed on the aliens' medical progress on a weekly basis, said Pretet.

According to the documents, the information is considered so sensitive that it will be conveyed via military couriers to prevent telephone wiretaps and satellite-signal intercepts, the UFO expert said. If the description of the aliens in the Chinese documents is accurate, the creatures are identical to nine others who were pulled from the wreckage of a starship the Soviet Union in 1985, said Pretet.

A classified report smuggled into Yugoslavia at the time said the aliens looked like human children with three shocking exceptions — they appeared to be sexless, were covered with microscopic, flesh-colored scales and had no mouths.

The fate of those injured aliens remains a mystery, although Pretet believes the Soviets kept them alive long enough to conduct studies, then exterminated them and preserved them on ice.

The Soviets refused then, and now, to discuss the incident. And the Chinese, Soviets and Americans are apparently working together to suppress information about the Chinese crash, Pretet told reporters.●

☐ *Do I believe this? Put it this way — I have no reason not to believe. Not depending upon the grocery store, there are dozens of different sources which make me feel that we have dead aliens, live aliens, and just plain aliens! Why do you think a nuclear physicist like Stanton Friedman, would spend the last 25 years doing research on UFOs and then show up on a UFO documentary supporting such things?*

I'll give it a 8.9 rating.

US AIR FORCE TEST-FLYING CAPTURED UFO
National Examiner, **May 30, 1989**
by Edward Reynolds

A top-secret US government report reveals that the Air Force is test-flying a captured UFO!

And space alien visits to US air bases overseas are becoming more and more frequent, according to a top UFO investigator.

Because the National Security Agency flatly refuses to discuss the document, it adds to the belief that the revealed details are genuine.

Top UFO investigator Clifford Stone of New Mexico has received a copy of the partly-censored report.

It reveals that:

In 1959 "the United States established primitive communications with aliens."

In 1964 a US Air Force intelligence officer arranged a meeting point with two aliens in the New Mexico desert and spent three hours with them exchanging information.

In 1972 the US government initiated Project Snowbird in Nevada to test-fly a recovered alien aircraft.

Says Del Newman, a leading British UFO expert: "The US Air Force bases at Mildenhall and Woodbridge, England, and the nuclear power station at Sizewell, England, are areas of interest to visitors from space."

Others near the Air Force bases have had their own disturbing share of UFO encounters.

Janet Richards, a former schoolteacher, was driving near Blyburgh, England, with her 23-year-old daughter Cathy one evening.

She says: "We were talking about this and that when I noticed a sort of ball of white light in the sky. We got out of the car. There was a humming sound and the light came toward us and passed overhead."

Nurse Melanie Hartley, of Bury St. Edmunds, England, had a similar experience.

Says Hartley: "It was about 11 p.m. and I noticed a very bright light reflecting on the hood of our car. Both my daughters were in the back and they saw an object to the left and above the car."

Hartley says the object was saucer-shaped and about the length of three buses.●

☐ *This top secret report probably has been leaked! It has long been suspected that the UFO experience of Betty Cash, Vicki Lindrum and grandchild might have been caused by a faulty captured UFO with mechanical problems. Betty has serious radiation problems with cancer; some feel the craft she saw may have been one captured by our government. I believe it deserves an 8.5.*

DID UFO GIVE WOMAN CANCER?
National Examiner, **February 14, 1989**
by Edward Reynolds

Did UFO aliens give Betty Cash cancer?

Outspoken Betty believes they did — and she blames the US government as well.

Betty claims she was driving down a lonely country road in west Texas with her friend, Vicki, and Vicki's young grandson, Tobey, when the youngster noticed mysterious lights above the pine trees.

A huge, diamond-shaped spacecraft hovered near them, flames shooting from its bottom like a blowtorch. Betty says she got out of the car and stood paralyzed in the UFO's beam for 20 minutes.

Recalled Betty in a recent TV interview: "When it moved, it made a swishing sound. There was also a deafening beep that I still hear in my mind at night, and my skin was burning."

Suddenly, Betty says, a squadron of helicopters appeared on the scene. The women identified them as belonging to the US military.

Said Vicki: "They were trying to escort the spacecraft. It looked like they were going to collide."

Then the spacecraft whisked over the trees and vanished, the helicopters right behind.

"I was too sick to go to work the next day," Betty recalls. "My eyes were swollen shut, and there were welts on my head and face. I thought I was going to die."

At the hospital, Betty was treated for burns. Weeks later, she had lost patches of skin on her face, and half of her hair fell out.

Then, in 1983, Betty was diagnosed as having cancer. She underwent surgery, but doctors were uncertain if they'd removed it all. Now, each passing day is another victory for the tormented woman.

Said Betty: "I'm mad as hell and disappointed with the government of the United States."

Top UFOlogists speculate the spacecraft was a secret weapon developed by the military, or the craft was given to the US government by the ETs.●

☐ *There is little question about this sighting. It was carried in many places. I can't rate it less than a 9. I don't know of any serious investigator who doubts this story. I hope that a 9 rating won't imply I am critical in any way.*

HOMELESS BOY IS A SPACE ALIEN

***Weekly World*, November 22, 1988**

by Ragan Dunn

Govt. expert says waif was abandoned by UFO crew!

A youngster who wandered into an East Indian village with a badly injured leg may be a space alien — who was abandoned by a UFO crew!

That's the word from government spokesman Kalipada Banswal, who claims to have created a human identity for the child so he could be adopted by a scientist in Myjore.

"The boy cannot be identified because of the sensitive nature of his background," Banswal said. "But I can assure you that he is not human.

"Medical tests indicate that he has two hearts and an unknown type of blood. By his own admission he was abandoned by his own extraterrestrial friends and relatives.

"They apparently felt like his injury would slow down their exploration and study of our world."

Banswal said the government officials became aware of the boy after he turned up alone and disoriented in a farming settlement north of New Delhi on October 15.

The child had a badly injured leg and was taken to a regional clinic, where doctors determined that he had an extra heart and a blood type never before seen in a human being.

"The boy stands out here because his skin is pinkish-white, but other than that he looks like any other human being," said Banswal.

"Doctors at the clinic wisely alerted federal officials, who immediately took the boy into custody for his own protection."

Banswal said the extraterrestrial youngster was eventually taken to a government hospital where doctors treated his leg and interviewed him extensively about his background.

The official said he wasn't privy to everything doctors learned from the boy.

He was told that the youngster hails from a planet in our own galaxy, possesses no special powers other than a keen intelligence and is not considered to be a security risk.

"His progress and behavior as an adopted child will be closely monitored by our government," said Banswal, "but it appears that he's going to do just fine.

"It's hard to imagine why extraterrestrials with the technology to visit and explore Earth would abandon a child simply because he had a bad leg," he continued.

"It apparently has something to do with their belief in the survival of the fittest. Maybe that's why they are so advanced. Maybe they get rid of anybody who doesn't meet a very high standard of extraterrestrial excellence." U.S. officials refused to comment on reports that a scientific team from the States has jetted to India to interview the boy.

But one highly placed source within the Indian government confirmed that it has.

"We have also had inquiries from the governments of the Soviet Union and France," said the official. "Needless to say we are proceeding very carefully. The boy may not be human, but his well-being is at stake."●

☐ *I will give this article a 4.9, only because there is no way to know the truth. Maybe, for all I know it may deserve a 10+, or a 1-!*

UFO ALIENS LIVING UNDER PACIFIC OCEAN

***National Examiner*, May 2, 1989**

by Linda Decker

Space aliens from the Pleiades star system are living under the Pacific Ocean!

That's the mind-haggling discovery of a top-notch UFOlogist, once a prominent NASA scientist.

Dr. Fred Bell reports that he was astounded one evening to witness an enormous flying saucer emerge from the ocean as he sat with friends in his living room overlooking the water at Laguna Beach, California.

"It was a huge, flat, silver disk that came out of the water next to Elisso Pier," Bell tells the Examiner. "The water depth must have been about 25 feet where the craft emerged."

He adds: "It was traveling slow enough for me to observe that the front of the extraterrestrial ship was raised in the manner of the kinds of flying saucers that come from the Pleiades."

The Pleiades are the star system around which our solar system revolves every 27,827.5 years, says Bell, who worked with German rocket genius Wernher Von Braun, developer of the Saturn V that put American astronauts on the moon.

Bell says he's been in contact with ETs from the Pleiades for over 20 years. And they have revealed only to him highly sophisticated technological inventions used in their civilization.

Just as incredible, a US government insider reports that more than 40 alien races have been using Earth as a way-station for water and natural resources.

Says the insider: "Extraterrestrials are frequent visitors to Earth because there are very few planets that contain the extraordinary variety of chemicals."

Adds the source: "It has been documented that a number of aliens utilize the hydrogen contained in water as fuel for their long journeys to other galaxies.

"Corroborating evidence demonstrates that a reptilian species of extraterrestrials has built underwater bases located in Blue Lake, New Mexico, where they refuel their spacecrafts for intergalactic journeys.

"An unusual number of UFO sightings have been recorded near Blue Lake. Witnesses report that the spacecrafts have long tubes that appear to draw up large quantities of water.

"However, this reptilian species also utilizes human beings for food and other energy resources. The increase in disappearing children is due to this alien species preying upon humans, just as we kill cattle for our food."●

☐ *I hate to tell you but I believe you're going to find more evidence to give reason for worry about this report. How about an 6.5 for the time being?*

ALIEN FOUND ALIVE IN UFO WRECKAGE
***Sun*, April 4, 1989**
by Ben Snark

Stunned scientists investigating a mysterious explosion found a crashed UFO spaceship — and in the most amazing discovery of modern times, rescued an alien survivor from the wreckage!

Amazingly, the shocked authorities say he's human!

"The creature was definitely humanoid in form," says Dr. Jian San, "but evidently he belonged to a species more highly evolved than our own."

This mind-boggling closest of close encounters began with a strange and violent firestorm reported by villagers in a remote desert region.

A team of scientists sent into the area to investigate soon located the source of the disturbance: a large crater in a valley strewn with wreckage.

"The material was metallic, of a strange alloy not found on Earth," says Dr. Jian, "and the structure of the ship, as close as we could tell, was an immense disk."

Several hundred yards away were the bodies of two of the crew members, and a third was still alive!

"We were overjoyed," recalls Dr. Jian. "We never expected to find anything this important.

"Their bodies were thin and short, around five feet tall, and the skin was gray and scaly.

"Their faces were strangely pear-shaped, with broad foreheads and narrow chins.

"Their noses were more pointed than ours, their ears were perfectly round, and their mouths were very small, almost non-existent. They also had an extra thumb next to the little finger.

"The survivor sat staring at us with huge yellow eyes and beeping submissively."

The alien and its dead comrades were rushed by helicopter from the remote region in China to a research facility in Chung-king, where doctors attempted to treat its injuries.

As the amazed doctors probed the alien's body, he began to speak, repeating their own words.

"He was listening to us speak among ourselves and he was learning our language instantly," says Dr. Jian, a note of awe in his voice.

"He had a very limited vocabulary, but we had no trouble understanding him.

"He must have had an extraordinary intelligence to be able to analyze and learn our language so quickly."

The creature spoke in a high-pitched voice, telling the scientists his spaceship had been sent to investigate Earth.

He said he was an inhabitant of a planet similar to ours, located in a distant solar system revolving around the star Sirius, 8.7 light years away.

"He told us fascinating stories about his planet," says Dr. Jian.

"Life had emerged there a hundred million Earth years before life began on our own planet.

"His ancestors had been nearly identical to humans, but the planet's current population is far advanced," explains the scientist. Unfortunately, the alien was immediately stricken with measles apparently contracted from one of the scientists.

With no immunity from Earth's diseases, his body was quickly ravaged and despite the doctors' best efforts he died in several days.

"It was tragic," says Dr. Jian.

"But his body has been preserved and will be exhaustively studied."

The staggering encounter was kept secret from the West until Dr. Jian released some of the details at a recent medical conference in the U.S.

"The alien had one important message for us before he died," adds the scientist.

"He said his society had advanced to the point where war and disease were wiped out.

"This too will happen on Earth," he adds.●

☐ *I find little reason to doubt this article. However, without a body you can show everyone in town, I will have to give it a 7.5. It deserves much more because of the information that reaches every person who bothers to read the report. I believe this kind of leakage may be a deliberate form of education.*

PROOF ETs MAKING TEST-TUBE HALF-BREED BABIES
***National Examiner,* June 2, 1987**

UFO aliens are making mixed-breed babies from humans they kidnap, experiment on, and return to Earth, says a top researcher.

The ETs, from an astonishingly advanced, but genetically endangered civilization, may be taking sperm, eggs, and even fetuses from pregnant women to help revitalize their dying race, says author Budd Hopkins in a mind-boggling new book, *Intruders* (Random House, 1987).

Using hypnotic regression, he has helped UFO abductees unlock the secrets of their harrowing ordeals, in which ETs seem to treat humans in much the same way people use lab animals.

"A central goal of UFO abductions, I now believe, is the apparent interbreeding of an alien species with our own," writes Hopkins, an artist who has investigated more than 125 cases over the past 12 years.

He believes that the accounts of abductees indicate that the extraterrestrials, for all their technological superiority, are in a desperate bind.

"It is possible that the very survival of these extraterrestrials depends upon their success in absorbing chemical and psychological properties received from their human abductees," Hopkins adds.

He describes the general pattern of the abductee experience as has been revealed in hundreds of hypnosis sessions:

"An individual, male or female, is first abducted as a child. During that experience, a small incision is often made in the child's body, apparently for sample-taking purposes, and then the child is given some sort of physical examination."

A series of contacts follow over the next few years. Sperm samples may be taken from young males, and eggs taken from young females. Some cases even suggest artificial insemination has taken place for some women.

"In the cases in which artificial insemination is attempted, the women are apparently re-abducted after two or three months of pregnancy and the fetus is removed from the uterus," Hopkins explains.

Sometimes, however, women are abducted at the time of ovulation, and their eggs are apparently fertilized and grow into fetuses outside the womb.

Men have also been abducted, and their sperm has been taken. One of the most complete abduction stories comes from a 28-year-old Kathy Davis, who lives with her two sons outside Indianapolis, Indiana.

Her description, under hypnosis, of how the aliens probed her body, eerily matches that of a modern day medical procedure used to take eggs from women, says Dr. John Burger, director of gynecology and obstetrics at Perth Amboy Hospital in New Jersey.

Kathy also recalled being allowed to see a hybrid human-alien child that the extraterrestrials said was her own daughter, apparently grown from an artificially-inseminated fetus taken from her during a 1977 abduction — about the same time a confirmed pregnancy suddenly, and inexplicably, terminated.

"She looked like an angel," said Kathie. "She had really big blue eyes and a little teeny-weeny nose and she was pale except her lips were pink. And her hair was white and wispy and fine.

"I'm pretty sure somebody told me I should be proud. I know everybody was happy with me. It was like a little piece of her they left with me 'cause they had to take her away. I know I'm going to see her again. They told me so. But I wish it was going to be sooner than I think it will be."●

☐ *This is a 10 article. It may come from a grocery store tabloid but there is much evidence to support everything that is given. If you want to know the truth about this subject read it very carefully.*

11 GIRLS GIVE BIRTH TO UFO ALIENS — SOVIET AGENTS SNATCH THEM AWAY!

***Sun*, June 13, 1989**

After describing astonishing close encounters with UFO space travelers, 11 teenage girls have given birth to monstrous alien babies!

The hideous infants are being held in a top-secret research facility after they were snatched away by Soviet agents.

Their mothers, all between the ages of 14 to 18, were scattered throughout the nations of Eastern Europe.

A 15-year-old, identified only as Tanya, gave an account that is typical of the extraordinary experiences the girls reported.

"I woke up to find my bedroom flooded with shifting patterns of colored light," she remembers. "I looked out the window and saw a tremendous rainbow-colored glowing ball, almost the size of our farmhouse, sitting in the field."

Seduced by the strange, other-worldly beauty of the spacecraft, Tanya left her house and walked towards it. A door opened up in the side of the ball and three pudgy creatures emerged.

"They were no more than four feet tall, but very fat," Tanya recalls. "They had a copper-like color. But their mouths and the huge lids of their eyes were bright green.

"When they spoke, it sounded like baby talk. They made me laugh."

The roly-poly aliens motioned to Tanya to enter their ship. Inside, the amazed teen found herself surrounded by a giant black dome, with pinprick points of light, like stars, shining on the ceiling.

At this point, her recollection of the experience grows dim. "All I can remember was getting into a metal box, like a coffin," she says. "The stars swirled around the domed ceiling.

"Next thing I knew, I was lying in the cool grass, watching the glowing ball disappear into the night sky."

In the next several months, Tanya, like the other 10 girls, began to feel her body undergo a strange set of changes. Her waistline grew, and she felt something moving inside of her. But the Plovdiv, Bulgaria teen knew little about sex, and it was her parents who realized she was pregnant.

"They never listened to a word of what happened," Tanya says. "Instead, they accused me of terrible things."

But Tanya's parents began paying attention to their daughter's strange story 10 months later when she gave birth to a horrible copper and green creature!

Shocked Dr. Vaskar Flibjin delivered the grotesque infant. "The baby was fat and round, with a large flat head, hard metallic skin and piercing orange eyes," he notes. "It just lay there, blubbering.

"We hardly had a chance to examine it before a group of Russian scientists, along with local police, arrived to take it away for research somewhere in the Soviet Union."

According to sources in Russia, 11 babies in all are now being held at a secret military hospital.

Soviet officials are extremely concerned, the sources add, because there have recently been additional sightings of the rainbow-colored UFO.●

☐ *For the present this gets an 8.5 but not because it isn't true.*

UFO SEEN HOVERING IN SCENE FROM 1928 MOVIE!

***Weekly World*, April 11, 1989**

A silent movie filmed in 1928 and never released clearly shows a UFO hovering over the cast!

"It's not a prop — it's real," Gerard Tesson, director of Bartlett's Film Museum, told reporters in Paris. The saucer-shaped craft shows up on a 22-second segment of film and the actors on the set don't even seem to know that it's there.

"The craft is at treetop level and motionless for the first few seconds. Then it begins to move slowly out of the field of view."

According to reports, Tesson discovered the UFO while he reviewed the obscure, untitled movie after finding it in the basement of the museum.

The black and white romance melodrama was conceived and directed by Robert Gaits, who died shortly after the completion of the film and was not able to edit it for release.

Catherine Martin, the Paris-based UFO researcher, has seen the film but stopped short of saying whether the UFO is authentic.

"It appears to be real," she said.

"But I want to study the film further before I stick my neck out."•

☐ *How about a 5 for this one?*

UFO BASES IN THE ROCKY MOUNTAINS!

***National Examiner*, March 21, 1989**

UFO aliens have established refueling bases throughout the Rocky Mountains, according to some of the dozens of folks who have sighted strange spaceships in the area.

Evelyn Moe and her son Eugene are just two of the sane and sober citizens from Montana who have spotted UFOs in recent years. They saw three shiny spacecraft moving in formation near their home in Helena.

"They looked like two soup bowls inverted on one another," Eugene declared.

"They hovered there for some minutes and then disappeared with incredible speed."

It is believed that more UFO sightings have occurred in Montana than in any other state, though many of them go unreported.

"I don't want people around town to think I'm crazy," said an excavation contractor from eastern Montana, who admitted seeing a UFO only on the condition that his name not be revealed.

"Don't tell anyone, they'll think I'm senile," said another man — an elderly gent who spied a UFO hovering above the hotel where he lives in Paulson.

And elk hunters Tim Newgard and Jim Vert say a UFO followed Jim's pickup for 21 miles along a road between Elmo and Nirada.

Said Jim: "What was so absolutely amazing is the way it moved from point A to point B with lightning-fast speed. It also did this vertically."

A mountain man known to locals as Spike thinks he knows the reason for the abundance of UFO sightings in the surrounding area. "I've watched them for years," he said. "I believe they are using part of the Rocky Mountains for refueling bases. Lots of people have seen UFOs in these parts. But Montana people don't like to be scared. We don't really like to talk about it too much."•

☐ *These UFO bases are described all over the place. The report does well to get a 7.4. It may be so, but what about California, Mexico, Nevada and New Mexico, Utah, etc.?*

ALIENS GUESTS OF GOV'T.

***National Examiner*, Feb. 21, 1989**

by Edward Reynolds

A UFO alien has been living on a secret base as a guest of the US government since 1982.

And two other ETs of the same species have resided at the base at different times since 1948, exercising "complete control," according to government "agents" Condor and Falcon.

In the late 1940's a space alien was captured in the desert of New Mexico after his flying saucer crashed, according to Condor.

A secret panel of US government officials, MJ-12, struck a deal with the ET, whom they named EBE, or extraterrestrial biological entity. EBE was said to come from the Zeta Reticuli star group.

The agreement held that the US government would not disclose the alien's existence as long as the alien did not interfere with our society. Also, the alien was given a base in the Nevada desert.

Later, two more aliens came to the US as part of an "exchange program," according to Falcon. One of the aliens has been living at the base since 1982.

Falcon says he obtained most of his top-secret information from an MJ-12 text referred to as "The Bible."

The Bible is said to contain autopsy reports of dead aliens recovered in the 1940s UFO crash, ET briefings, and other vital technological data.

And, according to Falcon and Condor, whose credentials were reportedly verified by UFO researcher Bill Moore, documentary film producer Jaime Shandera, and a Los Angeles TV newsman, the ETs have written the so-called "Yellow Book," which offers details of their planet, solar system, and culture.

According to the book, ETs have a universal religion with the universe itself as supreme being. They enjoy many forms of music, but especially like ancient Tibetan-style songs. Their IQ has been measured at the genius level of 200 and they have a lifespan of 300 to 450 years.

The space aliens eat Earth food, preferring a steady diet of vegetables. Their favorite snack, however, is a dish of strawberry ice cream.

Falcon, who claims to have personally met one of the ETs, was fascinated by an octagon-shaped crystal, which, when held in the alien's hand, produced pictures within it of his planet and even Earth as it appeared millions of years ago.

Condor and Falcon have agreed to

hand their mind-boggling findings over to Senate investigators. The agents are calling for a complete Congressional investigation so the truth can at last be told to the American people.●

□ *The above material given was presented on ABC TV October 14, 1988. I believe it to be 100% true. I know a scientist on that panel well enough to be sure — he never would have been there if he hadn't known it to be true. It's worth a 10 in my book.*

NOAH'S ARK FOUND?
***Weekly World*, April 18, 1989**
by Ragan Dunn

A Soviet scientist claims to have found Noah's Ark along with the remains of intelligent, two-legged lizards in Asia's Gobi Desert.

"Make no mistake about it, this is the scientific coup of the century," Dr. Alexei Makeyev said in Moscow.

"We have found what is left of the great ark and the remains of lizards that walked upright and appear to have been intelligent but did not survive the ship's voyage. We have yet to determine what killed them.

"We do know that they died before they were able to mate and produce offspring because the species is extinct today."

The alleged mid-March discovery of the ark in the western section of the Gobi touched off a controversy among scientists around the world.

Some, like French ark expert Louis Metz, insisted that the one true ark is located on or near Turkey's Mount Ararat and could not possibly have been found in the Gobi Desert.

Others, like Belgian archaeologist Ernst Haller, said the ark was just as apt to be in the Gobi as anywhere else. And he personally believes that the Russians have found it.

"All but a small section of the ark is buried under tons of sand but geographical scans indicate that at least 35 percent of the vessel is intact," said Dr. Makeyev. "We feel sure that we can get it out," he continued. "But for the moment I am more interested in the fossil remains of the two lizards that we found on the deck of the ark than the ark itself.

"Judging from various bones and skull fragments, we can see that the male stood about 8 feet tall and the female was only slightly shorter.

"Both creatures had unusually large heads, which means that they had larger brains and much greater intelligence than you would expect to find in a lizard. I'm tempted to call them lizard people."

Dr. Makeyev had no timetable for excavating the ark but Western experts agreed that it could take up to 10 years to complete the operation, due to the fragility of the aged vessel.

The Russian also declined to discuss the religious implications of his recent discovery.

He did say "You don't have to be a Christian to recognize the importance of finding Noah's Ark. There is no need to bring God into it.

"This is science, not religion," he added. "So let's not lose our perspective over this."●

□ *I've read about so many arks that I'm ready to wait awhile before I go for this one. Maybe it's worth a 30, but for now its only a 5.*

MOTHER SEDUCED BY ALIEN TOY BOYS
***National Examiner*, Sept. 13, 1988**
by Fred Down

A 40-year-old woman claims she was seduced by two alien toy boys.

The unfortunate mom of four was abducted from her bedroom by two silver-suited youths and dragged into a field, she said. There was a ship about the size of a bus on the grass and everything was lit up like an amusement park.

Said the nearly hysterical woman: "I went through a door into a white room. There was a bed with a sheet over it and they made me lie down.

"They shackled my legs and I smelled something sweet. I felt a needle go into the upper part of my left arm. Then I blacked out."

There is medical evidence that the woman was physically abused, according to UFO expert Philip Mantle.

"We'll put this woman under hypnosis," he said. "We believe she had some sort of sexual intercourse with them.

"It is very difficult for her because she has a common-law husband and the kids," he added.

The woman was petrified when the aliens said after the terrifying experience that she could have a baby.

The woman still has terrible scars from the ordeal, said neighbors in Blackpool, England. Sex with her hubby has become repugnant.

She has nightmares, recoils when someone merely touches her on the shoulder, and suddenly cries hysterically for no apparent reason, they added.

The woman's husband knows she went through a terrible ordeal and is trying to help her as best he can, said a close friend.

But many men don't understand the depth of a woman's mental and physical reactions after she has been sexually violated. Their relationship is being threatened by the tremendous strain and it could be on the rocks, she added.

"If you were to joke about it, you could say she is the first in Britain to find an alien toy boy," said Mantle. "And what if she had an alien baby?"●

□ *I'm only going to give her a 4, but I'll bet she thinks it's worth a 10! Don't think for one minute that I don't believe this "could be" one of those crossbreed experiments! That doesn't mean she necessarily had sex with one of those critters!*

UFO ALIENS RAPE OUR WOMEN
***National Examiner*, Sept. 13, 1988**
by Edward Reynolds

Space aliens are attracted more to human women because they have a higher "love vibration," than men, according to research gathered by a top UFO investigator.

And an increasing number of women all over the United States report that ETs are materializing in their bedrooms and raping them, reveals author Brad Steiger, 52, of Scottsdale, Arizona.

Writes Steiger in his intriguing new book *The UFO Abductors* (Berkley, 1988): "I first began receiving letters revealing the UFOnauts' extraordinary interest in our planet's females in 1966.

"The letters all had a monotonous sameness about them, yet they contained a strong note of urgency, and they came from all sections of the country."

One bright female college student wrote that a flying saucer hovered over her car while she was driving to her parents' farm.

Just hours after the sighting, the young woman said she was aware of something in her bedroom as she was preparing to retire for the night.

She claimed she had not fallen asleep before she felt something fondle her.

"I wanted to scream, to get out of bed, but I was unable to move," she recalled. "I remember nothing more until I awakened the next morning, but I have reason to believe that something made love to me while I slept.

"I believe this incident was associated in some way with my sighting the UFO."

A young California woman claimed she was raped and impregnated by an ET. Writes Steiger: "There is also a deposition by her doctor who testifies to having treated the young woman for the premature delivery of a stillborn baby that seems to be the product of highly dubious mixed breeding."

Barbara, a research assistant to New Zealand UFOlogist John Stuart, claimed she was raped by an unseen entity for more than two hours shortly after she and Stuart had seen a grotesque misshapen entity while investigating a UFO report.

The assistant said she smelled a strange odor the moment she stepped into her room.

And while taking a bath, she felt unseen eyes following her every move. Then, as she put on her pajamas, an "invisible something" touched her on the shoulder.

She found herself paralyzed.

UFOlogist John Keel believes cases of UFO sexual liaisons are a variation on the incubus phenomenon. An incubus is explained as a spirit or demon thought to cause nightmares by raping women in their sleep.

Keel told Steiger: "Induced hallucinations seem to play a major role in these cases.

"There maybe considerable validity to the theory you expounded in one of your books that semen is extracted from human males in some succubi events and that this same semen is then introduced to human females in incubi incidents.

"The true nature and purpose of this operation is completely concealed behind a screen of deliberately deceptive induced hallucinations.

"Early fairy lore is filled with identical cases, as you know. And such sexual manipulations are an integral part of witchcraft lore."●

☐ *I know these things happen, but I think I'll give it a 6.5. I believe the cross-breeding is done more by instrument than by hanky-panky!*

UFO LED MOSES & HIS PEOPLE OUT OF EGYPT
***Sun*, November 22, 1988**
by Robert Webb

Bible student reveals Moses and the Israelites managed to escape Egyptian soldiers through the desert with the help of a guiding light — from outer space!

A UFO hovering above the fleeing hordes of former slaves showed them the way out of Egypt and aided them while they were being pursued by an angry army on horses and chariots, according to a Biblical researcher.

"The Bible makes references to a pillar of cloud and a pillar of fire that helped the Israelites travel by day and night," explains Anton Corbon, an ancient-astronaut expert and Bible student.

Moses and his people were met by the mysterious object after being released by the pharaoh whose country was undergoing a series of plagues.

"The cloud was probably a sparkling UFO leading the way during the daytime, while the pillar of fire was the same object with burning lights to guide them at night as they wandered through the desert to the Red Sea," says Anton.

The out-of-this world object came to their aid once again when the Egyptians changed their minds and pursued Moses and his people.

"The Bible says the pillar of cloud made it dark for the Egyptians but gave light to the Israelites so they could flee," Anton notes.

The historian also says the incredible powers of the ancient astronauts may have played a role in the parting of the Red Sea. He claims space aliens helped the Israelites to set the human race on a new path, but Biblical scholars call Anton's theories "a lot of nonsense" and say the Bible specifically states the Lord made these things possible.●

☐ *This surely is worth an 8.5.*

THE VANISHING ETs

***Weekly World*, November 8, 1988**

by Laurel Bowie

Five pip-squeak space aliens shot it out with ray guns in a Wild West—style showdown on a remote Peruvian plateau — and when the smoke cleared, the peewee ETs had all vanished into thin air!

"They had ray guns, or laser guns, like something from an old science fiction movie," said mining engineer Eleodoro Solari. "But there was nothing fictional about this.

"They were shooting at each other from behind boulders, and every time one of them was hit he'd just disappear like he'd never been there."

Unsuspecting Eleodoro and his partner Pedro Berrospi stumbled onto the bizarre spectacle while conducting a mining survey in an isolated region of Peru's Altiplano Plateau.

"We had seen a rather strange object in the sky a few minutes earlier and Eleodoro said it must be a UFO — and then we both laughed," Pedro recalled.

"But we drove our four-wheel drive in that direction just to look. We came over a little rise and there they were — the strangest creatures I've ever seen, shooting at each other with some kind of high-tech ray guns."

The gawky little gunslingers stood no more than 4 feet tall and their skin was sliver colored, the bewildered witnesses later told reporters.

"Their eyes were blank like poker chips and there wasn't a single hair anywhere on them," Pedro said. "Their voices were very shrill, and they moved around like clumsy children."

The weirdo warriors were shooting it out from a distance of three yards, three of them on one side and two on the other.

"There may have been many more of them earlier, because every time one was zapped he would vanish right before our eyes," said dumb-founded Eleodoro, 44.

"After two minutes or so, there was only one of them left. And then he vanished, too — for no reason at all.

"We were so stunned, we just sat there in our truck, wondering what to do."

Eventually, the wide-eyed engineers drove to the village of Uncaypa, 23 miles away, and told cops about the alien gunplay. "We went to the area and searched for guns, but we found nothing," said police chief Carlos Souza. "But there were very high levels of radiation around, so I'm convinced something unexplained occurred out there.

"I have known Eleodoro Solari for 20 years and he is no nut. If he says there were strange creatures out there shooting at each other with space-age ray guns, I believe that is exactly what happened."●

☐ *I guess Eleodoro Solari ought to get at least a 3 for being such a good guy.*

SPACE SHUTTLE ATTACKED BY 200-FT. UFO!

***Weekly World*, May 2, 1989**

by Jack Tremont

A 200-foot UFO buzzed last month's space shuttle flight and there are even more serious allegations that a pair of bug-eyed extraterrestrials took control of the craft while they inspected its cargo!

London's respected *Daily Star* newspaper, which has a circulation of 1.3 million, broke the story that included sensational testimony from an impressive stable of scientists and UFO researchers who claim to have tapes of conversations between the shuttle and mission control.

In a mind-blowing interview, former NASA mission specialist Bob Oechsler of Baltimore, Md., stunned *Daily Star* readers when he revealed that he was in possession of a tape that described the shuttle's UFO encounter.

The veteran space flight specialist, who worked at the famed Goddard Space Flight Center located near Washington, D.C., refused to say where he got the explosive tape.

But he told *The News* in a telephone interview that he has commissioned a sophisticated voice-print analysis to determine if it really is the shuttle telling mission control: "Houston, this is Discovery. We still have the alien spacecraft under observation."

NASA officials and the astronauts themselves vehemently deny the UFO reports and all allegations of a coverup. But according to the *Daily Star*, Oechsler says NASA bosses are "lying through their teeth."

Of the astronauts themselves, Oechsler commented: "These men are so well trained I suspect they could pass a lie detector test."

The *Daily Star* rocked Europe by additionally reporting that a ham radio operator claims to have heard a shuttle astronaut say: "Houston, we have a fire," which is widely believed to be a NASA code word for a UFO.

Those reports, while sensational, paled before yet another allegation from Dr. Marcel Ponte. In Paris, the president and founder of the watchdog group UFO Truth, said he can prove that space aliens boarded the shuttle and inspected its cargo — a $60 million satellite.

He also claimed to have heard an alleged conversation between the shuttle and mission control that says:

"Houston, this is Discovery. We have alien spacecraft 200 feet. Blue. Cargo hold. Controls useless. A pair. Bug-eyed. We are invaded...."

The brief transmission was allegedly made when Discovery was in the 20th hour of its five-day mission. Nothing more was said about the extraterrestrials or alien spacecraft.

And that led Dr. Ponte to speculate that NASA chiefs ordered the astronauts to resume communications on a classified channel.

He also called for an immediate investigation and full disclosure of the facts.

"The world deserves an explanation — not another coverup," said Dr. Ponte. "The UFO threat affects every man, woman and child on Earth.

"No agency or government has the right to keep vital information like this secret."

Incredibly, NASA information chief Carr insisted that no explanation is forthcoming.

"Why should NASA or the astronauts explain anything?" he told *The News.* "This is absurd — an elaborate hoax at best."

A spokesman for the British Unidentified Flying Object Research Association, in Burgess Hill, England, said he will reserve judgment until all the facts are in. "NASA would never admit the encounter even if there was irrefutable evidence," the source said.

BUFORA chairman Anthony West told *The News:* "I think it is quite possible that the astronauts saw something that they didn't expect."●

☐ *If the government wanted this to be a secret it would have been a secret. It is in print so you can read it. How about an 8.4.*

UFO ALIEN SAVED BURNING BARN

***Sun*, November 1, 1988**

by Robert Webb

Space creatures came to the rescue of a desperate farm couple who feared their entire livelihood would be destroyed by flames but then watched in fascination as their barn was repaired.

"I stood helplessly thinking our barn would be burned to the ground, but then a miracle happened," declares Wilbert Guerton. "A spacecraft put out the fire!

"The occupants hopped out and for the next six hours, my wife and I stood in amazement as they rebuilt the entire barn."

Wilbert, 43, and Helene, 37, were awakened in the middle of the night by the horrifying blaze and ran to the barn to save the animals.

"There was nothing we could do, but seconds later the whole sky lit up and hovering above the barn was a brilliant blue spacecraft," Helene remembers.

The two were so frightened they raced back to the house. "But one by one we saw these creatures walking out of the ship which was parked in mid-air just above the barn," Wilbert recalls.

"All of a sudden, a bright yellow light covered the barn and smothered the fire. The animals were saved, but the place was a complete wreck.

"Then the creatures went to work."

Wilbert describes the half-dozen aliens as being tall, with slender arms and legs, and helmet-like heads.

"We never got close because we were still scared," he says, "We couldn't call anyone because our electricity had been mysteriously turned off.

"But in a matter of six hours, they had completely rebuilt the barn. The ship then shot away and disappeared in seconds."

Wilbert wonders if the aliens saved their farm near Essen, West Germany, because they accidentally burned it.

"We don't know what caused the fire," he notes. "Maybe they were performing experiments and started it.

"But we can never thank them enough for making the barn look as good as new."●

☐ *The names and pictures of the people involved are shown — the important part of this article is they believed this happened — hypnosis and complete investigation should follow. Just in case that barn is still there, it ought to have a 4.*

DRAWING OF UFO FOUND IN PYRAMID

***Weekly World*, June 21, 1988**

by Ragan Dunn

A scientist claims to have found a drawing of a "flying saucer" on the wall of an Egyptian tomb!

"This is it — this is the evidence we've been looking for," Dr. Isadora Demazure told reporters in Paris. "Space aliens really did contact the ancient Egyptians.

"This drawing proves it, once and for all."

The expert refused to say exactly where the drawing is located other than to say she found it in a 3000-year-old tomb on the banks of the Nile.

She acknowledged that some of her colleagues would like to inspect the tomb before declaring the drawing authentic.

But she insists that it is genuine — and claims her still photographs and video-tapes prove it.

"The spaceship appears to be of classic UFO design," Dr. Demazure said. "It rather looks like an upside-down dinner plate with a lip or a rib running around its lower edge.

"There is a cockpit or observation deck on top covered with a clear dome. There is also a lighted dome underneath, but there are no visible life-forms.

"I have no doubt that this is a spaceship," she added. "There is nothing else it could be."

Fragments of an unusually strong and lightweight metal found in the tomb have so far defied analysis, said the expert.

"But there is a very real possibility that they are extraterrestrial in origin," she continued. "They certainly aren't familiar to us.

"They are nothing like we have ever seen before."

The expert is currently negotiating with a major European publisher who wants rights to the photos and video-tape she shot inside the tomb.

Dr. Demazure refused to say how much she has been offered. But publishing sources say she'll get at least $75,000 for the photo package, maybe more.

Queried by newsmen, Egyptologist Andre Lafont called Dr. Demazure's discovery "interesting but anticlimactic."

"UFO researchers and Egyptologists already know that extraterrestrials were in contact with the ancient Egyptians," he said.

"Space aliens gave them many aspects of their culture. They helped them build the pyramids."●

☐ *A good cave picture ought to be worth a 6 just in case it's there.*

SPACE ALIENS FED FARMER
***Weekly World*, February 7, 1989**
by Sharon Fader

A farmer says space aliens treated him to a feast of foods from all over the universe, including pig-like intestines, syrupy white wine and fat green eels!

"I don't care if you believe me or not — I had dinner with aliens from outer space," Gerald B. Voisart, 52, told reporters in Bastia, France.

"I caught four of them snooping around in a pasture and they asked me to join them in a meal on their spaceship. The food was pretty good and they said it came from all over the universe.

"When we finished up dessert they escorted me out of their UFO and flew away."

The farmer's story was viewed with some skepticism in Bastia but he stuck by it — and even provided newspapers with a list of what they got to eat.

The menu allegedly included:

A foul-smelling soup made from a plump green eel that the aliens called "bronk." "It tasted," said Voisart, "like mushrooms in chicken broth."

Deep-fried intestines, from an animal the farmer was told resembled a pig.

A whole broiled animal that was the size and shape of a hamster. Only the heart was eaten. The rest was discarded. "The aliens said the little animal was very rare and expensive," said Voisart. "I thought it tasted like soap."

Giant green lizard roast. "They said they brought it from their home planet," said the farmer. "It was very good, like pork sausage."

Wine, both red and white, came from a vine-covered world at the edge of the universe. "It was thick and syrupy," said Voisart. "And much too sweet."

A dessert of a mouse-sized animal that had to be crunched whole, like a hard candy. "It tasted like a mixture of sugar and hot sauce," said Voisart. "You wouldn't want to eat a whole bunch of them. But one or two were all right." Oddly enough, the farmer said the extraterrestrials offered him some after-dinner mints that were made by a chocolate company in Britain.

He also got to keep a souvenir from his dinner — one of the small metallic tubes that the aliens used in place of forks.

"The aliens had real big foreheads and big mouths and their eyes didn't have pupils," said Voisart. "Their skin was lily-white and they wore loose--fitting red suits.

"Their shirts didn't have sleeves. They looked like tank tops." Voisart said the aliens' spaceship was saucer-shaped and silver. The interior was dimly lit, he added, and the only thing on the main deck was a big round table.

Aviation authority spokesman Catherine Lemoine would neither confirm nor deny reports that a UFO showed up on radar the day Voisart claimed to have had dinner with the aliens.

"We did receive 20 reports of a UFO sighting," she said. "But I am not at liberty to say whether they were related to this farmer or not."●

☐ *He's right — nobody is going to believe him; a good imagination is worth a 2 to me!*

HUGE ANGELS SEEN IN SPACE
(Soviet Cosmonauts stunned)
***Weekly World News*, Oct. 22, 1985**

Six Soviet cosmonauts say that they've witnessed the most awe-inspiring spectacle ever encountered in space — a band of glowing angels with wings as big as jumbo jets!

Accounts of two bizarre sightings by Russia's leading space travelers are contained in a top secret report smuggled out of the country by a Soviet scientist who defected to the West earlier this year.

The defector, who asked not to be identified, said the report was classified because Soviets fear its release would damage the credibility of their space program.

"They would prefer to write off the sightings as hallucination or some form of unexplained natural phenomenon," said the former Soviet space scientist.

"But the evidence seems to indicate that what they saw was more supernatural than natural."

Startled cosmonauts Vladimir Solevev, Oleg Atkov and Leonid Kizim said they first saw the seven celestial beings last July, during their 155th day aboard the orbiting Salyut 7 space station.

They said they were performing medical experiments in their cramped quarters when a brilliant orange glow engulfed the craft, leaving them temporarily blinded

When their eyes adjusted to the light, the space travelers peered toward its source — and got the shock of their lives. "What we saw were seven giant figures in the form of humans, but with wings and mist—like halos as in the classic depiction of angels," said the cosmonauts in an account signed by all three.

"They appeared to be hundreds of feet tall with a wing span as great as any jetliner.

"Their faces were round with cherubic smiles and they were all identical. We were totally mesmerized."

The cosmonauts said the band of angels followed their capsule for about 10 minutes and then vanished as suddenly as they had come.

But 12 days later the glowing figures returned and this time they were seen by six Soviet scientists.

Cosmonauts Svetlana Savitsaya, Vladimir Dzhanibevok, and Igor Volk had joined the others on Salyut 7.

"We were truly overwhelmed," the lady astronaut was quoted as saying. "There was a great orange light and through it we could see the figures of seven angels. They were smiling as though they shared a glorious secret. But within a few minutes they were gone and we never saw them again."●

☐ *Those seven angels ought to be worth at least a point a piece, but until I see one of those Cosmonauts on TV they're only going to get a 3.5 for all of them! Pardon me guys — can't give all these articles such high marks — I had to pick on something.*

SAVAGE TRIBE ATE 6 SPACE ALIENS
Weekly World, **March 21, 1989**
by Ragan Dunn

South American cannibals murdered and ate six space aliens who came to Earth on a mission of peace in 1936!

That's the word from Swiss anthropologist Fritz Greder, who actually spoke with an elderly savage who dined on one of the extraterrestrials 53 years ago this spring.

"It's a fantastic story but one that I am convinced is true," Dr. Greder told reporters in Zurich, Switzerland. "The cannibal chief I spoke with is almost 100 years old but his mind and memory are sharp.

"He clearly recalled the arrival of the aliens in a silver starship in 1936. He also remembered that the creatures were killed and eaten because they behaved strangely and lost the tribe's trust.

"He said the extraterrestrials tasted like frog's legs or fish. But humans, he told me, taste like pork." Dr. Greder claims to have met the cannibal chief while studying tribal life in the jungles of Brazil late last year.

The incredible story came to light after the old man warmed up to the scientist during their long conversations on the tribe's history. The chief told Dr. Greder he had a secret to share — and proceeded to describe the bizarre alien encounter that had unfolded 53 years ago.

"He told me that the alien arrived during a time of terrible tribal warfare," said Dr. Gredler. "He said that they were no bigger than children but their flesh was a deep, rich green.

"They spoke to the tribesmen in their own jungle language and insisted that they had come to Earth on a mission of peace.

"They got along well with the savages for a day or two but the cannibals became suspicious and ate them after they were caught examining a child."

Dr. Greder said he inquired about the extraterrestrials starship and got "a strange reply." The old chief told him that it glowed bright white and vanished a few hours after the extraterrestrials were killed.

The expert plans to publish a full scientific report on the ill-fated close encounter later this year.

"I'm sure that the cannibal chief's story is accurate," he said, "and it really is a shame. These savages felt guilty about what they had done — and that's why they kept it a secret all these years."•

☐ *Anybody who is 100 years old deserves a 5 whether he ate an alien or not!*

COP SHOOTS SPACE ALIEN
Weekly World, **December 8, 1987**
by David Barr Scribner

An 80-year-old cop mistook a space alien for a burglar — and shot the creature dead!

Luiz Sabioni defended his actions on the grounds that the alien he found in a warehouse in Bara Mansa, Brazil, threatened him with a laser weapon, said newspapers.

But military officials who investigated the incident say the alien was unarmed — and no bigger than a 5-year-old child.

"This is a catastrophe," Sgt. Mario Hargreaves told reporters before the government clamped a lid of secrecy on the incident.

"There is every indication that the alien came here on a mission of peace.

"It's not being an alarmist to say that his death might spark an inter-galactic incident.

"That fool cop ought be taken out and shot himself."

Sabioni has been stripped of his duties pending the outcome of a massive investigation by his superiors in Barra Mansa and the military officials, newspapers said.

He is under orders not to discuss the incident.

But reports obtained by Brazilians for Truth in UFO Reporting say the cop blew the extraterrestrial away on the loading dock of a wholesale food distributor on November 2.

"The alien was shot square in the forehead," said Orlando Zenobio, founder and president of the respected group.

"Some of its features were destroyed by the bullet but it clearly came from deep outer space. His skin had a bluish tint and was marked by thousands of small bumps, like a pebble grain.

"The eyes were quite small and were set close together in the head.

"The nose and mouth were also extremely small. It had two small slits for its ears.

"There's no telling where the body is now," he added. "I imagine the military has it and if that's the case, it will never be seen by civilians again."

Reports that a UFO appeared over Barra Mansa on the night the alien was shot have not been confirmed by military authorities even though dozens of people claim to have seen one.

"There may or may not be a connection," said Zenobio. "All I can say that our group will be pressuring the government to make all the facts known."•

☐ *I ought not to give that fool cop more than two points for shooting an alien, but it seemed to me David deserves 6 points for writing the article.*

UFO FOUND ON PLAYGROUND

***Weekly World*, May 24, 1988**

by Henry Weber

A researcher claims to have found a UFO so small that an adult could hold an entire fleet in the palm of his hand!

"When I first saw the thing I thought it was a golden beetle but there's no mistaking it now," Dr, Alfredo Chavez told reporters in Lima, Peru.

"The technology to build something like this is almost inconceivable," he added. "Our microchips are like garbage can lids compared to the components that were used to build this machine."

Dr. Chavez said he found the tiny spaceship while investigating an unusual UFO encounter just west of Lima.

According to reports, an insect-sized UFO and at least three others like it buzzed a playground, causing six children to be treated for minor radiation burns.

While searching for clues in the playground, Dr. Chavez stumbled on the golden, saucer-shaped spaceship. Radiation levels were dangerously high within a foot of the tiny UFO.

He actually had to put it in a special lead-lined container for safe transport to his lab back in Lima.

"It's a remarkable piece of work," said the expert. "X-rays show it to contain a single, circular room lined with miniature computers and all kinds of unusual instruments.

"There is no evidence of life aboard the little craft," he continued.

"That leads me to believe that it is an unmanned probe or the crew escaped before I found it. If there were crewmen they could be running around that playground right now. We've been searching for them and will continue to do so."

Dr. Chavez said the casing of the UFO is made of an unusually strong and lightweight plastic. Although the ship is obviously disabled, it somehow maintained a surface temperature of 145 degrees Fahrenheit, he said. His own study complete, the expert plans to turn the UFO over to the military for more sophisticated analysis. The tiny craft will be studied by air force experts.

"There's no telling how much information we can get from this single little spaceship," said Dr. Chavez. "It may be the key to a revolutionary technology.

"We may not be able to duplicate the technology, of course, but we might be able to determine where the ship came from, how it got here and even more important, what it was doing around those children. Time will supply the answers."●

☐ *That UFO is awfully small, I think I'll give it about a 3. Remember, it may be a 10.*

HAM RADIO OPERATORS HEAR SECRET CALLS TO MISSION CONTROL

***Sun*, May 16, 1989**

by Ken O'Hara

Shocking evidence proves that the space shuttle Discovery was contacted by UFO aliens as it flew during its latest mission!

Experts say a UFO followed the ship during its five-day flight and that the alien craft "locked" onto the shuttle's controls at one point, causing a sudden loss of power.

Discovery's five-man crew reported to NASA ground control that they were being trailed by an "alien spacecraft" — and astonished ham radio operators throughout America say they picked up the conversation!

One radio ham in Baltimore claims that he taped the top-secret chats between NASA ground control and Discovery pilot Colonel John Blaha.

The ham claims Col. Blaha can be heard saying: "Houston, this is Discovery. We still have the alien spacecraft under observation." The radio exchange allegedly occurred exactly 20 hours and 45 minutes after Discovery blasted off from Cape Canaveral in Florida.

The space shuttle also reported losing its power at the time of the sighting — which is proof that the alien craft cut into the shuttle's power supply, say experts.

Another radio ham in Ohio says that he picked up Col. Blaha telling mission control: "Houston did have a fire" — believed to be a secret NASA code word for UFO.

And a third ham radio buff says that he heard NASA order Col. Blaha to change radio frequencies before saying any more information about the UFO.

Col. Blaha and NASA officials have angrily denied making any contact with UFOs during the Discovery mission, but experts are convinced that the Baltimore ham's tape is genuine and the eerie encounter actually occurred.

Sources say NASA has a policy of denying UFO sightings, no matter what the evidence might show.

Former NASA mission controller Bob Oechsler says that space agency officials are "lying through their teeth" about the UFOs.

"Only one man got a tape, but it is backed up by other radio hams who also heard the conversation," he says.

"The facts are simple — either NASA is lying or the tape is a hoax.

"We are having a tape print analysis done and when we get the results of that, NASA will have to make the facts public."●

☐ *I believe this to be about an 8.*

SPACE MUMMIES FOUND

Weekly World, **October 1, 1988**

by Ragan Dunn

Soviet scientists claim to have found the mummified remains of 600 space aliens in a peat bog in northern Siberia!

"This is the scientific discovery of the decade, if not the century," Dr. Gennady Kharlamov told reporters in Moscow.

"The proximity of the remains to those sabre-toothed tigers and wooly mammoths suggests that the aliens arrived on earth at least 30,000 years ago.

"We have yet to find evidence of a space vehicle. But that merely indicates that the extraterrestrials were teleported to earth or dropped off with no immediate means of leaving.

"The challenge before us now is to find out what happened to them after they arrived.

"They were wiped out, possibly by disease, before they had a chance to establish a base of operations.

The expert's theories played to mixed reviews among Western scientists, several of whom doubted that the remains were extraterrestrial.

Dr. Didier de Seydel, the French anthropologist, speculated that the bodies were those of prehistoric nomads who never ranged beyond the wastelands of Russia's Siberian Yamal Peninsula.

Dr. Kharlamov countered that theory with x-rays that showed the bodies to have oversize skulls and eyesockets and nine fingers on each webbed hand.

"These are not the skeletal systems of human beings," he said. "Even if the extra digits and enormous eyes are disregarded, we still have to consider the fact that their skulls and brain capacities were greater than those of modern man."

Dr. Kharlamov refused to pinpoint the location of the peat bog where the bodies were discovered "as a matter of state policy."

He did say that the remains have been taken to a research facility within the Soviet Union for further analysis and study.

"We fully intend to keep all parties and nations apprised of our finds," said the expert.

"At present we feel sure that extraterrestrial beings tried to establish a colony here on earth.

"The questions before us now are why — and will they try again."●

☐ *Those mummies are pretty far up in Siberia to be worth very much — how about a 5?*

LETTER FROM RUSSIA CONFIRMS DISCOVERY

Weekly World, **January 31, 1989**

by Alex Jackson

The Soviets have discovered the corpses of seven monkey-size aliens in Afghanistan and taken them to Moscow for scientific study, says a letter received by a Russian soldier's family.

He said the Russians also have the charred wreckage of the aliens' spaceship, which crashed in a ball of fire on a hillside 46 miles south of Kabul.

The incredible letter was mailed from Afghanistan with the help of a Swiss businessman who forwarded copies to newspapers throughout Europe. It was dated November 3 and was first published in France and Germany on December 21.

The letter described the aliens as being the size of monkeys with long pointy ears and tiny eyes. It went on to say that their horribly burned bodies were shipped to Moscow where they are almost sure to undergo scientific investigation, the European newspapers said.

Dr. Albert Estager, the French UFO expert, called the discovery of the spaceship and bodies "the most important UFO development of the decade."

He also called on the Soviets to share what information they have about the extraterrestrials with researchers in the West, many of whom have already asked Moscow if they can see the bodies firsthand.

So far the Soviets have remained tight-lipped about the alleged starship crash and recovery of its crew. Repeated phone calls to European embassy officials went unanswered.

And here in the States, officials at the Soviet Embassy in Washington didn't return call from *The News* to either confirm or deny the discovery.

But the Kabul *Times* reported that a heavily guarded caravan of Russian Army vehicles, including a refrigerator truck, passed through Kabul in early November, destination unknown.

There also were unconfirmed reports a few days earlier that some type of space vehicle had crashed in the hills 50 miles south of Kabul.

Adding even more credibility to what could be the scientific discovery of the century is a newspaper report out of Paris, France.

The newspaper *La Croix* reported in early November that Dr. Vladimir Tolsky, one of Russia's top pathological scientists, was abruptly called back to Moscow.

Tolsky had been on vacation at a resort on the Black Sea.

Text of letter from Russian Soldier:

"Dear Mother: I hope you are as well as I am. Last night I and 30 of my comrades were taken at night by truck 75 kilometers south of Kabul.

On a hillside was the burned wreckage of a spaceship and the bodies of seven little men no taller than 3 feet, about the size of a monkey.

They were horribly burned and had huge pointed ears and tiny eyes. They were bald with no eyebrow or eyelashes.

Their naked bodies were being placed in plastic bags and loaded into a refrigerator truck. Tags attached to their toes said they were bound for Moscow.

When my sergeant saw me looking he chased me away. "These are men from Mars," he said. "Don't look!"

I and my comrades worked through the night loading the spaceship wreckage on the trucks. When we finished we were told not to tell anyone.

With love, your son."●

☐ *I think Alex deserves at least an 8.5 for this one. If he made this one up he's on the ball!*

WORLD'S FIRST SPACE ALIEN INTERVIEW
***Weekly World*, January 24, 1989**
by Ragan Dunn

An internationally known French journalist claims to have gotten the world's first interview with a space alien!

Vincent Blanc says he conducted the 25-minute question-and-answer session in the courtyard of his home south of Marseilles.

The extraterrestrial reportedly told the newsman that UFO aliens from at least 14 planets are actively involved in the study and exploration of Earth.

Even more incredible, he said that these creatures are planning to take full or partial control of our planet and its resources within two years.

"I don't want to sound immodest but I have to consider this one of the most important interviews ever conducted," Blanc, who has written for virtually every major newspaper in Europe, told newsmen in Paris.

"Parts of the interview are so shocking," he added "that they should be read in the company of others, preferably family members or people you love.

Blanc says the interview was conducted in French when the alien mysteriously showed up on his doorstep on the morning of December 4.

The creature had blonde hair and blue eyes, he continued, and looked like a three-year-old child. He allegedly spoke in a high-pitched monotone and answered the following questions before he glowed bright blue and disappeared.

Q. Who are you? Who do you represent? Why are you here?

A. I am Bertan speaking for the inhabitants of Det. You do not know us but we have known you since the beginning. You used to be insignificant. Now you have something we want.

Q. What do you want?

A. Cooperation. Resources. Land and wealth.

Q. You have come to steal from us, to plunder planet Earth?

A. We have come to share with you, to cure your illnesses, to banish your strife, to bring you heaven on Earth. We can also bring you the wrath of hell. The choice is yours to make.

Q. How can you help us? And what must we do to get that help?

A. Fourteen extraterrestrial civilizations are actively interested in your planet. Each will have demands but we can come to terms together. This is a large and fruitful planet. In one year or in two years we will meet to discuss our futures together.

Q. What if the people of Earth reject your efforts?

A. The people of Earth are not foolish. If they do not cooperate they will be banished. The universe has many planets. You may be sent to any one of them. We can accomplish our mission here without you.

Q. What if you are resisted militarily?

A. Your weapons are useless against us. If you use them, you will only hurt yourselves. You saw our power in your Soviet Union when a nuclear power plant exploded in Chernobyl. You have seen our power in the AIDS virus you fear so much. We also have weapons to terrify, to shred each nerve — to bring horrors out of your worst nightmares.

Q. Why haven't you contacted us before?

A. Your leaders are aware of our presence and we have engaged them in negotiations. I emphasize that we come in peace. We ask you to prepare for us.

Journalist Blanc conceded that it is impossible to prove that his interview with the alien actually took place, and several skeptics have accused him of fabricating the whole thing.

"I was a skeptic myself," he said "until now."

One man who believes the reporter is UFO researcher Pol Seydel. The Paris-based expert said: "UFO activity has been at an all-time high over the past year and I suspect that these extraterrestrials intend to contact us on a formal basis any day now."●

☐ *That certainly seems to jibe with what Mr. Blanc is telling us. I don't doubt that he got that interview at all. I'm not sure about this French journalist, but the information sounds pretty accurate so he gets an 8. My own research with Mr. X convinces me that I must not underestimate this newsman. I would have had to give Mr. X a 10 plus and giving less than an 8 just ain't cricket!*

SCIENTISTS CAN HARDLY BELIEVE THEIR EYES
***Weekly World*, November 8, 1988**
by Ragan Dunn

A Swiss scientist claims to have photographed a gigantic extraterrestrial monster drifting through space — and he now fears that it might be headed for Earth!

The incredible pictures were filmed through a high-powered telescope aimed at Mars. Some experts are already calling them the most important scientific photographs ever made.

"This is the biggest breakthrough in space since man landed on the moon," astronomer Erben Basel told reporters in Geneva. "It had to be a billion-to-one chance that we would see anything — so this is a little short of a miracle. Judging from the shape, depth, and proportion, I would say the monster is at least 200 feet long and 50 feet wide.

"At times it appears to have the saucer-shape of a classic UFO. But the picture series we also have indicates that it can change form.

"In some photos it actually looks like a giant one-eyed sea snail propelling itself through space."

Dr. Basel refused to say how fast the alien object is moving and would not speculate about its estimated time of arrival on Earth.

But he did say: "Scientist around the world are studying the Swiss photographs and tracking the creature as it approaches Earth to determine if it is indeed a threat." Experts are also said to be considering what impact it might have if it crashes or lands on our planet. Dr. Richter C. Pretet, the French biologist, said that a living creature the size of the object Dr. Basel photographed could alter life as we know it if it was able to survive in Earth's atmosphere.

"It's too early to say what we are dealing with but not too soon to think about it," he said. "We should be prepared for any possibility. We cannot face this crisis from a position of ignorance."

Soviet and American space officials were very tight-lipped about the Swiss photographs and would neither confirm nor deny reports that they are secretly sharing vital information about them.

Dr. Basel did say that the Swiss government discussed the photos with both countries and subsequently warned him not to talk with the press but he ignored the warning.

"I'm jeopardizing my career but something of this magnitude must be a part of the public record," said the scientist.

"I can only hope that the superpowers can and will attempt to deal with it. It's out of my hands now."●

☐ *How about a 5.5 until that monster gets a little closer?*

SPACE ALIENS USE SPHERES OF LIGHT TO SPY ON US!
***Weekly World*, December 27, 1988**
by Ragan Dunn

Space aliens are spying on individuals politicians, military installations and anything else that interests them with bugging devices that fly!

That's the mind-blowing claim of top UFO expert Paul Rhein, who says the extraterrestrial bugs look like spheres of light and have been spotted in places as diverse as the Kremlin, Cape Canaveral and Washington, D.C.

"The implications of this phenomenon are staggering," the West German researcher told reporter in Stuttgart. "There is evidence to show that these unmanned spy ships can read our thoughts as well as monitor our speech and activities of all kinds.

"They were photographed while observing the launches of both the Soviet and American space shuttles. They have also been seen at sports events and over seats of government such as the Kremlin, Paris, London, Peking, and Washington D.C."

Rhein said the space bugs are generally described as being disc-shaped and ranging from the size of a silver dollar to four feet across.

They were first encountered back in the 1960s, he added, and have been seen with increasing frequency since.

In one dramatic encounter, a tiny disc hovered over a Soviet submarine on maneuvers in the Pacific, totally disrupting its electronics, said Rhein.

The discs also caused alarm when they appeared at this year's launches of the Russian and American space shuttles.

But they don't limit their spying to space and military operations. They watch regular people as well.

"There are literally thousands of reports of individuals having encountered the discs," continued the expert. "Thankfully no one has been injured."

Rhein has his share of skeptics, some of whom have suggested that the discs are merely reflections of lights or crafts that are manufactured by men.

But Rhein insists that the discs are sent here from mother ships that record and process information the spy ships beam back from Earth.●

☐ *I was hunting for an excuse for upping the value of this article when I received a letter from Jack Grant. He sent me some UFO material from the* Columbus Dispatch *plus news of his summer's vacation. In between was a comment which is so apropos that I can't resist quoting it. August 17, 1989 — "George Adamski and I never had our pictures taken together but I think Helen Reeves had a picture of Desmond Leslie and me taken at Vet's Memorial when he gave a lecture there. Also in that picture was a strange white ball that was over our heads in the background. Helen said at the time the picture was taken there was nothing visible."*

I didn't know Jack at that time, but I was there when the picture was taken. Later that evening Jack brought Desmond to our midnight dinner party. Helen and Bryant Reeve were very interested. As I remember, they went back to the Veterans Building to see if they could find any reason for the strange phenomena. These balls of light were spying on anything and everything long ago.... Thanks to Jack for reminding me —I'll give this a 9.9.

SPACE RAINBOWS MAY BE SOURCE OF UFOs
***Sun*, January 17, 1989**
by Robert Webb

Huge bright arcs stretching across millions of miles through space may be launching pads and refueling areas for thousands of fleets of UFOs traveling about the universe.

The glowing blue arches have baffled astronomers — some speculate the cosmic rainbows could be created by a massive galaxy bending light from a galaxy directly behind it.

However, other experts believe the newly-discovered space arcs billions of light years from Earth are either produced or used by advanced civilizations traveling through space.

"The colorful arcs seen the through a cluster of galaxies may serve as an energy source by space aliens, explaining how these advanced beings are able to travel light years in such a short time," says Dr. Ethan Almu, a scientist who studies UFOs in Kolding, Denmark.

Such enormous quantities of light would be invaluable to space travelers.

"Advanced civilizations would most probably be able to harness energy from light and use it to perform tasks that baffle us.

"It is possible the advanced beings created the light themselves, since the arches have only recently been discovered by our astronomers.

"But wherever the source, it is a phenomenon that could not be ignored by outer space visitors," adds the scientist.

Swiss UFOlogist Conrad Reimas calls the discovery of the space rainbows the greatest breakthrough in the history of UFO study. "We have mounds and mounds of evidence showing UFOs have visited our planet," he notes. "But we also know these visitors must come from light years away, since no other life forms appear to exist in our own solar system.

"Where do they come from and how do they get here?

"The bizarre appearance of these space arcs offers us some answers," he points out.

"Light is certainly an extraordinary energy source we ourselves hope someday to use to the fullest potential.

"Advanced creatures able to fly through the universe as easily as we drive on the highways have more than likely conquered this source," the UFO expert concludes.●

☐ *A for effort — give it a 5.*

UFO WRECK IN 1947
***Weekly World News*, January 14, 1988**
by Ragan Dunn

Expert says Harry Truman inspected bodies of dead aliens.

A British politician says the US government recovered the bodies of four extraterrestrials and the wreckage of their starship in 1947 — and he has the secret report to prove it!

"The United States has been involved in a massive cover-up of alien contact for better than 40 years," said the politician, who asked to remain anonymous when he gave copies of the document to reporters in the House of Lords.

"This is bigger than any mere Watergate," he added. "This is a cosmic Watergate — and it's time the truth was told."

The papers, signed by President Harry Truman — who saw the dead aliens — were addressed to the most powerful figures in Britain.

Then Prime Minister Clement Atlee got a copy, as did Winston Churchill, King George VI, the Queen Mother, and select members of the House of Lords.

The leaders' reactions reportedly ranged from shock and amazement to outright fear. The document itself stressed the need to keep the recovery operation secret to avoid "a massive religious backlash and worldwide panic."

It went on to describe the extraterrestrials in chilling detail. "Four small human-like beings apparently ejected from the craft before it exploded and crashed in America's southwest," said the report.

"All four were dead and decomposed due to predators and exposure to the elements before their discovery.

"The beings were between four and five feet tall.

"They wore tight-fitting silver jumpsuits. Their heads were disproportionately large with oversized brown eyes slanted in the head.

"Their noses and mouths were mere slits. They had small holes for ears."

The document went on to say that pieces of the starship were strewn for miles. Analysis show fragments to be a strong and lightweight metal but were otherwise inconclusive.

The report did not pinpoint the location of the crash nor did it say where the bodies and fragments were taken.

But the likeliest destination was Wright-Patterson Air Force Base in Dayton, Ohio — where the bodies of four more humanoids were taken after a second starship crash 10 years later.

Though the U.S. Government has never confirmed either crash, UFO experts are convinced that both wreckage and bodies have been recovered and are still preserved.

In fact, a super-secret government agency code-named PI-40 keeps tabs on alien visitors and briefs U.S. Presidents on UFO developments past and present, the British source said.

Gerber Pasche, founder and president of the Swiss UFO watchdog group Alien Encounter, was appalled to learn of the cover-up.

He told reporters that the governments of the United States and Britain should be held accountable and tried in the court of world opinion.

"The irony of all this is that everybody knows what's going on — we've known for years," he said. "Space aliens exist and have a deep and abiding interest in our planet.

"This is a concern of all mankind — not just superpower leaders."●

☐ *No argument about this one — it gets a full 10.*

TRIBE EATS SPACEMAN

***Weekly World*, August 11, 1987**

A gentle green-eyed space alien was sent to Earth as a goodwill ambassador, but his message of peace and love was lost forever — when a band of harebrained cannibals ate him for lunch! Swedish scientists Sten Karlsson and Ulf Ahlberg learned of the scaly-skinned spaceman's bizarre fate while investigating an outbreak of food poisoning among slap-happy savages deep in the Amazon jungle.

"We went to the village to determine why seven people had died of a violent intestinal ailment," Ahlberg told *Universe*, a scientific journal.

"We came away convinced beyond a shadow of a doubt that there had been an occurrence out there to stagger the imagination — that these people actually cooked and ate an extraterrestrial."

Members of Brazil's head-hunting Hurucua tribe told the anthropologists that seven warriors died after dining on a man-like creature who arrived in a dazzling copper-colored craft that landed in a clearing outside their village. The savages were so awed by the little ET, who told them in their native language (a form of Guarani) that he came from a distant planet to make friends with the people on Earth, that many of them fell to their knees in reverence, sending the tribe's witch doctor into a rage.

"The witch doctor was so incensed that he ordered warriors to kill the spaceman and eat him, and that's just what they did," Karlsson said. "They stabbed him with their spears and roasted him over a bonfire.

"Seven of them feasted on his body — and they paid for their lunch with their lives."

The natives gave the astonished scientists what was left of the alien's remains.●

☐ *Let that be a lesson — don't eat spacemen! How about a 5.5?*

ANCIENT VIDEO SET USED FOR COMMUNICATION

***Weekly World*, May 17, 1988**

by Ragan Dunn

An archaeologist says the color TV set he found in an Egyptian tomb is at least 4,000 years old and may have been brought to Earth by space aliens!

Dr. Harold Lueger said the ancient set differs from those manufactured today in several ways. For starters, it is designed to monitor only one channel.

It also has four triangular screens, one for each side of its gold-trimmed titanium cabinet.

"This is the most important archaeological find since King Tut's tomb," the expert told reporters in Geneva, Switzerland.

"Obviously those ancient Egyptians didn't have the materials technology or need to build a television set. It must have been given to them.

"And when we think about who might have given the device to them, we have to look to a civilization from outer space."

Dr. Lueger refused to disclose where he found the set, other than to say it was nestled in the corner of a previously undiscovered tomb on the banks of the Nile.

The television and other artifacts were judged to be almost 4200 years old after testing, he said

And while the set no longer works, the solar cells that once powered it do.

Electrical engineer Richard Monet inspected the TV and concluded that it is at least as sophisticated as the sets of today, said Dr. Lueger.

In fact, he is now trying build a duplicate of the device on the chance that a working model night pick up TV signals from another planet, just as he believes the ancient receiver did.

In the meantime, Dr. Lueger plans a return trip to Egypt to search for more evidence of extraterrestrial contact with the ancient Egyptians. "There's no telling what they left behind," he said. "We might even find a television camera, a VCR or blueprints for the pyramids."●

☐ *This one is really far out — it may be so, but I don't know — so we'll give it a 5.*

LIBYAN TARGETS BUZZED BY UFO

***Weekly World News*, May 20, 1986**

by Elizabeth Russell

After the stunningly successful American air strike on Tripoli, Libyan gunners fired at a new target — a wedge-shaped UFO that cruised around the burning city for several hours, a top correspondent reports.

Franz Scheyder, an East-German journalist based in Tripoli, quoted Libyan military sources as saying that the unexplained machine gun fire that followed the strike was directed at the greenish-blue UFO.

Libyan Radio originally claimed that the target of the fire was American fighters. But the Pentagon angrily denied the charge.

Privately, both Libyan and American authorities hustled to gather intelligence on the UFO.

According to Scheyder, the alien craft appeared briefly on Italian radar screens at the same time American F-111 fighters were flying over the Mediterranean on the last leg of their mission to Libya.

"The clear implication is that an extraterrestrial intelligence observed the American strike force and later assessed the damage," said Scheyder. "The question is why? What was their interest?

"And why did the UFO appeared in broad daylight?"

The Libyan sources told Scheyder that they took "clear and numerous photographs" of the UFO but refused to let him see them.

The journalist said he was told that the craft was greenish blue, shaped like a wedge and performed impossible mid-air maneuvers — such as 90 degree turns — with incredible speed and precision.

"Needless to say, shooting at the thing was like throwing darts at a freight train," said Scheyder. "If the Libyans did hit it, it wasn't apparent.

"I'm told that it cruised over Tripoli for several hours, sometimes at treetop level, before it disappeared." The sighting in Libya came on the heels of what European UFO experts have described as "unprecedented UFO activity" in and around Afghanistan, Nicaragua, South Africa, Iraq, and Iran, said Scheyder.

Curiously, all those countries are political or military hot spots that directly or indirectly involve the superpowers: America and the USSR.

"It is as if the world is at the brink of Armageddon and somebody or something has taken an interest," Dr. Axel Hertlein a German UFO expert told Scheyder.

"There is nothing in the history of UFO research to compare with the number of sightings that are being reported from these troubled places.

"At this point the only questions in my mind are when are they going to make contact or in some other way interfere?"●

☐ *This will have to be another 5 — which means I don't know too much about what happened. Personally, I believe it to be a 10.*

UFO DENTISTS FIXED OUR TEETH
***Sun*, September 13, 1988**
by Garry Messick

Along with the abduction, two men also got extractions when they underwent a thorough dental exam performed by UFO aliens!

"Take us to your molars!" could have been the demand of the space creatures when they picked up Marc Jahns and Timothy Ruckers, who were hiking through the Wrangell Mountains on their way to hunt Dall sheep and mountain goats.

"We were headed back home when I heard Tim gasp and I turned around to see this thing floating slowly to the ground," recalls Marc, a 36-year-old father of three.

"It was a glowing saucer-shaped object. We were never so scared in our lives.

"It was even more terrifying when three little gray-skinned men with huge heads came out of that thing and grabbed us.

"We couldn't do anything because we were somehow frozen, couldn't move a muscle."

Next, the two hunters were pulled into the alien craft by a powerful energy force and soon found themselves on long cushioned tables.

The aliens then proceeded to probe the mouths of the helpless men with dental-type instruments.

"The creatures seemed to talk to us without opening their mouths, and they scolded us for not taking better care of our teeth," Timothy claims.

"Then they said one of my back teeth would have to come out, and suddenly they yanked it out like nothing.

"There was no pain at all. They took two teeth out of Marc." Following the examination, they escorted their patients back outside.

The saucer then lifted off and disappeared within seconds. Authorities say they have no reports of other UFO sightings in the remote mountainous area, which is east of Fairbanks, Ak.

But the men insist they're willing to take lie-detector tests, and Marc's wife Adrienne swears her husband is missing two wisdom teeth he once had.●

☐ *I've got about 4 or 5 fillings I'd like to have replaced. If I thought It would do any good I'd go down by the river and sit on the bank for a few hours. I'll give this about a 4.5.*

UFO BABY SPEAKS AT 3 MONTHS
***Sun*, February 25, 1986**
by Diane Amery

A UFO baby born to an Earth woman is being worshipped as a god because he talks in complete sentences at only three-months of age.

Five months before the baby was born, its mother, Rosa Martinez, claimed she was raped by a UFO alien who had landed in the dirt behind the wooden shanty she and her husband had built.

The man and woman were sleeping in their beds when they suddenly heard a strange buzzing noise outside.

Mysterious lights were flashing, and they went out into the yard to see what was going on.

"A giant being which resembled a human except it was about nine feet tall, came toward us," says Armand, the husband. "I heard my wife scream, and then I fell unconscious."

The woman reported the experience to police in their small village located just outside of Hidalgo, Mexico.

"The authorities laughed at me," says Rosa. "They thought I had been cheating on my husband, and I was making up this story so he wouldn't kill me.

"Even when my husband spoke to them, they still wouldn't believe us," says Rosa sadly.

"They thought we were crazy," she cries.

Within a week of the incident, Rosa knew she was pregnant. "I was certain the infant had been fathered by that horrible space alien," said the lady.

"My husband and I went to the police again, but they still refused to believe us," Rosa says.

Rosa had given birth to three children before, and she and Armando are no strangers to the effects of pregnancy.

However, they claim this pregnancy was more difficult and more riddled with side-effects than any previous ones.

"I could never get enough to eat," says Rosa. "It seemed the more I ate, the hungrier I became."

She would hallucinate a lot while she was carrying the child, and often became confused and disoriented.

"Then I went into labor after just five months," she said. "At first I thought I was going to lose the child, but it came out a normal-looking, healthy boy."

The baby, named Carlos, started saying its first words almost immediately, and by the time he was three months old, he was speaking entire sentences also.

"The child says when he reaches his first birthday, his UFO father will come to claim him," says Rosa.

Meantime, residents of this small village are making pilgrimages to Rosa's home to see the amazing talking infant.

Some of the more superstitious people even say he is a god, and they plan to erect a shrine to him.●

☐ *I never have heard whether the dad came back to get that kid — therefore he'll have to settle for a 2.2, but when the UFO comes back for him he gets the remainder of the 10.*

5,000-YEAR-OLD UFO FOUND IN THE RED SEA
***Weekly World News*, July 5, 1988**
by Irwin Fisher

A top German scientist claims to have found a 5,000-year-old starship on the bottom of the Red Sea. The expert says the hull is cracked.

But the interior appears to be intact — and its nuclear engines are still hot enough to turn sea water to steam.

"The discovery of the UFO is an amazing achievement," Dr. Verlag Kiemel told reporters in Cairo, Egypt.

"We now have concrete proof that extraterrestrials visited Earth in antiquity. If we can get the ship up we might be able to duplicate the technology and build one of our own." Dr. Kiemel said divers discovered the UFO after a storm kicked up sand on the floor of the Red Sea.

The expert refused to pinpoint its location. But he did say that it is in 60 feet of water off the coast of Sudan.

The portion of the UFO that has been exposed suggests that it is shaped like a flattened cigar, he added. Algae and silt have stained the hull.

"Sand samples taken from the area indicate that the ship is at least 5,000 years old," said Dr. Kiemel. "but the nuclear engines contain unspent fuel and are still hot enough to boil the water around them.

"We won't know for sure until we get it out of the water, but it doesn't appear that there are any bodies aboard."

The governments of Sudan and Egypt have refused to comment on the expert's reported discovery. But he has applied for permission from both countries to begin a recovery operation, newspapers confirmed.

The discovery of the ship comes in the wake of dozens of archaeological discoveries relating to extraterrestrial contact with ancient humans.

UFO researcher Erich Hassold, of Wiesbaden, West Germany, commented: "The evidence that space aliens visited Earth and early man is irrefutable.

"Anybody who thinks otherwise has his head in the sand or he's crazy."●

☐ *You'd do well to get a 5.0 out of this one. I have a feeling we're never going to hear any more about it.*

ALIEN REPAIRS CRIPPLED BALLOON
***Weekly World*, December 6, 1988**
by Irwin Fisher

A cross-country balloonist says a space alien saved him from a certain and grisly death by repairing his hot-air blower at an altitude of 7,000 feet!

"I know it sounds crazy but a space alien really did save my life," Lennart Horling, 46, told reporter in Motala, Sweden.

"He came alongside my disabled balloon in a small silver spaceship and then materialized along side me in my basket.

"He was no bigger than a three-year-old child and he had only two fingers on each hand. But he immediately sensed that my blower was broken.

"And he repaired it like he had been doing it all his life." Horling said the mid-air drama unfolded on a solo flight from Motala to Sala, Sweden, on October 25.

Halfway through the flight the blower that forces hot air up into the balloon to keep it aloft sputtered and stopped. "I was terrified," said Horling. "I started losing altitude immediately and all I could think about was crashing to the ground.

"I was actually saying my prayers when I saw a bright silver speck on the horizon. It got bigger and bigger until it came to a stop and began to hover less than 50 yards away.

"Just then the alien appeared in my basket. At that point I didn't know if what was happening to us was a dream or real."

All doubt vanished when the tiny alien went to work and began repairing the blower, Horling said.

"After about five minutes, he got it working again, and my balloon leveled off.

"I tried to thank the alien and offered him my hand."

The creature hesitated for a moment, he continued, and then both he and the spaceship flew off and disappeared.

The balloonist described the alien as looking exactly like a human child with the exception of his two-fingered hands. UFO researcher Sven Carlsson said the description of the alien confirmed that Horling had had a close encounter — because 14 other people independently claim to have seen the same alien over the past year.

"This is the first time the alien has

saved anyone's life but I think it's obvious that he is most interested in humans," said the expert.

Added Horling: "I get down on my knees every night and thank God for that alien.

"If he hadn't come along when he did, I would be dead."•

☐ *This one is cute and deserves a 6 on general principle. I'm sorry Lennart, I believe you, but no one else is going to....*

I FOUND FOUR BODIES AFTER UFO CRASHED

***Sun*, June 20, 1989**

A rabbit hunter was shocked out of his boots when he bagged a quarry of a very different nature — four space aliens whose dead bodies he ran across the morning after thousands of people reported seeing a UFO crash out of the nighttime sky.

At least 2,000 folks in southern Indiana, western Kentucky and northern Tennessee are said to have witnessed a spectacular light show that literally shook the earth.

One man from Owensboro, Kentucky says he and his wife saw a "huge ball of light hovering in the sky" before it suddenly "broke into fragments that plunged to the earth."

This witness, who asked to remain anonymous, claims the fiery display was accompanied by a loud noise "like a sonic boom.

"It looked like whatever was up there exploded, and the different parts crashed to the ground."

Officials from the National Weather Service and Federal Aviation Administration have written the amazing event off as a meteor shower, despite the claim of 23-year-old Mason Hutchinson that he discovered the bodies of four non-human creatures in the vicinity of the crash the next morning.

Mason was hunting for rabbits near Mammoth Cave in southwest Kentucky — the center of the area where the witnesses reported the mysterious sightings and a longtime hub of UFO activity — when he stumbled across the bizarre corpses.

"The bodies were badly charred," says Mason, a construction contractor who lives near Bowling Green. "But they appeared to be two-legged, two-armed beings with elongated, oval-shaped heads that had antennae sticking out of them.

"They were each about four feet tall, with round bodies and three eyes—one on the forehead just above and in between the other two eyes.

"My truck was too far away to carry the bodies, so I hustled back there and drove to find help."

But when Mason and friend Sherm Lundeen returned to the site about two hours later, the bodies were gone.

"They just plain disappeared," astonished Mason insists. "I know the buzzards didn't get them, and animal predators would have left some kind of remains behind."

Declares Mason's buddy, Sherm: "I've known Mason for 20 years and he's a straight guy. If he says he found four dead UFO aliens, then that's just what happened."•

☐ *There have been other cases where the bodies were gone when the "finder" came back to recover the bodies. My guess — an alien craft may have taken care of the situation. How about 6?*

PIGS IN SPACE?

***Weekly World*, June 27, 1989**

by John Thompson

A leading scientist says pigs should replace men in the exploration of space because they are expendable — and their internal organs are very much like those of men. And if Dr. Claude Pochon gets his way, the first Earthling to step onto a faraway planet like Venus, Jupiter or Pluto could be a pig!

"It makes a lot of sense," Dr. Pochon, the Swiss astrophysicist, told newsmen in Geneva. "Pigs can test the effects of extended space travel without risking the lives of men.

"Pigs are expendable. If they survived a trip to Venus, Pluto or beyond, we could follow up with astronauts.

"Even if they died, such a launch would add volumes to our understanding of extended space travel.

"For that reason alone, I'm sure that one day pigs will fly." Dr. Pochon's ideas were surprisingly well received in Europe, where scientists in such diverse fields as biology, physics, medicine and space geography have agreed to establish an international task force to study the feasibility of sending pigs into space.

Even NASA, America's usually tight-lipped space agency, has expressed some interest in the plan.

"The safety limitations that are built into our space program are definitely a hindrance," said one NASA insider. "If we replaced human astronauts with pigs, we could accelerate our exploration of space 10 times over.

"Pigs are very much like humans physically," he added. "If they fared well on extended space flights and planetary expeditions, we could safely follow up with men.

Animal rights activists, like the Frenchman Phillip Voisart, have already vowed to fight Dr. Pochon's space-pig proposal tooth and nail.

Jean Ortner, the Austrian UFO researcher, is planning to resist the idea as well.

"My great worry is that we might actually land a pig on an inhabited planet," said Ortner.

"The aliens who live there would think that pigs are the most intelligent beings on Earth.

"I don't think we can risk giving them that impression," he said.•

☐ *Now that NASA is going to get little cash — we're going to buy some pigs to take a trip. I'll bet they don't ask the pigs first — 5 is my going rate for pigs.*

SMALL TOWN NAMED UFO CAPITAL OF WORLD
National Examiner, **June 27, 1989**
by Wayne Ruple

Even the police chief swears he has seen a flying saucer in a small southern town that has become the UFO capital of the world.

Worldwide attention focused on Fyffe, Alabama, population 1,400, recently after police chief Junior Garmany and assistant chief Fred Works spotted a crescent-shaped UFO a few miles west of town.

The officers followed the object for 12 miles, keeping in contact with other departments in surrounding towns where reports of the UFO were flooding in.

"It seemed to always stay the same distance ahead of us," Garmany told reporters.

On their return to Fyffe the two officers pulled to the side of the road and got out of their car.

Works said: "We saw an object low on the horizon which looked like an airplane to begin with. It came right straight towards us and went straight overhead at about 1,500 feet."

He added: "It appeared to have had three big floodlights or something on the bottom of the object. The UFO never made a sound. It appeared oblong, roundish."

A nearby Lickskillet resident was so frightened, he fired a shotgun at the object as it passed overhead at treetop level.

Days later, two Grove Oaks residents, six miles north of Fyffe, watched a UFO as "big as house" hover over treetops near their home.

And Bonnie Bishop and her son reportedly saw a UFO in woods behind their Silverhill, Alabama home that did the strangest thing.

They claim a door underneath the object slid open and a large beam of light lit up the ground as if it were searching for something.

Said Bonnie: "It never made a sound."●

☐ *Look, you guys. This one has been carried in local papers, TV and other places. Pretend you saw it in the Associated Press. We'll give it a 9.*

Here's a quote from the March 4, 1989 Associated Press — "This is unreal," Police Chief Junior Garmany said Friday night while he watched bumper-to-bumper traffic in the town of 1,000 people in northeastern Alabama. "We've never had traffic like this." Fyffe got on the UFO circuit February 10, when a woman reported seeing a strange light in the sky and police later reported seeing a large lighted object passing silently over them. Numerous other sightings have been reported since then.

☐ *Don't tell me the* Examiner *made up their story, but the one from AP is O.K.*

COPS BAFFLED BY FLYING BANANA
***Sun*, April 18, 1989**

A banana-shaped spacecraft quickly split as authorities approached, leaving stunned onlookers baffled by the silent ship that gave them the slip.

Eyewitnesses say the UFO was bigger than a jumbo jet and was covered with green, white and red lights.

"There was a red light on each end and a white light in a line between them," says one resident of Fyffe, Alabama, where the craft appeared one evening. "The top of the curve was outlined in green light."

Police Chief Junior Garmany personally responded to the reports and got a first-hand look at the hovering banana.

"We got out of the car and we turned off the engine," recalls the chief. "When we started towards it, it began moving away."

The officer estimated the craft's speed at between 300 and 400 mph. The peaceful town of Fyffe is located in northeastern Alabama.●

☐ *This is a true article and you read it in the* Sun. *A 10 please.*

HOT NEWS FROM TASS: TOURISTS FROM SPACE

***New York Times*, October 10, 1989**

by Esther B. Fein

"Scientists have confirmed that an unidentified flying object recently landed in a park in the Russian city of Voronezh," *Tass* said in a straight-faced news report. "They have also identified the landing site and found traces of aliens who made a short promenade around the park."

The authorities in Voronezh, some 300 miles southeast of Moscow. could not be reached tonight for comment. A spokesman for *Tass,* reached by telephone tonight, said the report was neither a hoax nor a joke. "It is a serious dispatch," the night duty officer at the agency said.

The press agency has seemed to undergo a bizarre metamorphosis in the last year or so. In addition to its traditional role of dutifully reporting the comings and goings of Soviet leaders, and often condemning those of American officials, *Tass* has taken to writing supermarket-tabloid sensationalism with all the seriousness due a superpower summit meeting.

People in the Soviet Union have long been attracted by the mysterious and the occult, and lately the authorities seem to be feeding this interest. Two of the hottest programs on state-run television these days are psychic healers who promise to cure everything from obesity to leukemia, in person or via the airwaves.

There seems to be a particular fascination here with outer space — quite apart from the Soviet obsession with the American "Star Wars" program — and in February 1984 the authorities here set up a Commission into Abnormal Phenomena after a "flying cigar" was spotted near the city of Gorky, east of Moscow.

A much talked about report: last summer in the newspaper *Sotsialisticheskaya Industriya* told of a milkmaid's encounter with a stubby-legged alien in the Perm region of Central Russia.

Indeed, tonight's report was presented with a straight face and with technical descriptions worthy of a major scientific discovery. Genrikh Silanov, head of the Voronezh Geophysical Laboratory, said in an interview with *Tass* that the landing site was identified "by means of bilocation."

According to Soviet reference books, bilocation is an extrasensory method of tracking objects or people invisible to the human eye.

Tass said Voronezh residents reported that the aliens visited the place after dark at least three times. They arrived in a large shining ball, or disk, and emerged through a hatch, accompanied by "a small robot," and went for a "short promenade about the park."

Tass also reported that witnesses claimed to have seen "a banana-shaped object in the sky and a characteristic illuminated sign." It said such descriptions had been reported in the American magazine *Saga*, a regular in barbershops and bowling alleys.

And to dispel any notion that the Voronezh witnesses had been influenced by reports in *Saga*, *Tass* said "it is unlikely residents of Voronezh could have read the magazine.●

☐ *Perhaps only the prestigious* New York Times *can publish this account of a UFO landing and retain the respect of every opinionated reader who scans its pages. It isn't that the news is so different — but it certainly is presented with a sincerity that lets the world know aliens have landed. These excerpts from the* Times *should shake the shoulders of those who are still blindly hiding from the reality of what life may expect in the twenty-first century.*

FACT, NOT FICTION, SAYS OF UFO

***New York Times*, October 11, 1989**

by Esther B. Fein

MOSCOW. It is not a joke, nor a hoax, nor a sign of mental instability, nor an attempt to drum up local tourism by drawing the curious, the Soviet press agency insisted today in discussions of what it called an extraterrestrial visit to southern Russia.

Residents of the city of Voronezh insisted today that lanky, three-eyed extraterrestrial creatures had indeed landed in a local park and gone for a stroll and that a seemingly fantastic report about the event carried Monday by the official press agency *Tass* was absolutely true.

"It was not an optical illusion," said Lieut. Sergei A. Matveyev of the Voronezh district police station, who said in a telephone interview that he saw the landing of the UFO on Sept. 27.

Lieutenant Matveyev confessed that he had not actually seen the aliens, but said he saw the spaceship and "it was certainly a body flying in the sky," moving noiselessly at a very high speed and very low altitude.

To be honest, Lieutenant Matveyev said, he was a little skeptical himself when he first saw the object. "I thought I must be really tired," he said. "but I rubbed my eyes and it didn't go away. Then I figured, in this day and age, anything is possible."

Using the sensationalist tone that has lately infected the once-staid *Tass,* the press agency today provided more details of the UFO landing in Voronezh, a city some 300 miles southeast of Moscow.

According to *Tass*, and a report today in the newspaper *Sovetskaya Kultura*, two boys and a girl from a local school — Vasya Surin, Zhenya Blinov and Yuliya Skolokhova — were playing in a park on the warm evening of Sept. 27 when suddenly, at half past six, they saw a pink shining in the sky and then spotted a ball of deep red color about 10 yards in diameter. A crowd gathered, "and they could clearly see a hatch opening in the lower part of the ball and a humanoid in the opening."

The three-eyed creature, about nine feet tall and fashionably dressed in silvery overalls and bronze boots and with a disk on its chest, disappeared, then landed and came out for a promenade with a companion and a robot.

The aliens seemed to communicate with each other, producing the mysterious appearance of a shining triangle, and activated the robot with a touch.

Terrified, a boy began to scream, but with a stare of the alien's shining eyes, *Tass* said, the boy was silenced and paralyzed.

After a brief disappearance, the three returned, but this time one of the "humanoids" had "what looked like a gun" by his side — a tube about two feet long that it directed at a 16-year-old boy. The boy, whose name was not given in the report, promptly vanished, but reappeared after the alien embarked in the ball.

Vladimir A. Moiseyev, director of the regional health department, said in a telephone interview that despite reports of widespread fear in the city, none of the witnesses had applied for medical help. But he said that "certainly we are planning to examine the children." There was no explanation why, with the passing of two weeks, such an examination had not yet taken place.

Mr. Moiseyev, like other authorities in Voronezh, the editors of *Tass*, and indeed many of its readers, treated the report as a serious scientific phenomenon. No extra men are assigned to patrol the area because the department is short-handed, said the duty officer at the local Interior Ministry department, who identified himself only by his last name, Larin, but he said troops would be dispatched "if they appear again."

The *Tass* correspondent covering the case of the mysterious visitors to Voronezh, Vladimir V. Lebedev, seemed insulted that anyone would treat the story with anything but the full seriousness that it was given by the agency.

In a telephone interview, Mr. Lebedev described conversations with dozens of witnesses and with experts who had examined the evidence and spoken to the children. He said there were about three landings of the UFO between Sept. 23 and Sept. 29.

In the latest development, not yet reported by *Tass*, Mr. Lebedev said that Genrikh M. Silanov, head of the Voronezh Geophysical Laboratory, today asked the children to draw what they had seen.

Though isolated from one another, he said, the children all drew a banana-shaped object that left behind in the sky the sign of the letter X. Such descriptions, Mr. Silanov said, were reported as typical of UFOs in a 1976 article in the now defunct American magazine *Saga*. Mr. Silanov said today that a rock that was reportedly found at the site and described as being not something found on earth was actually a form of hematite, which is found in various parts of the Soviet Union.

While not a witness himself, Mr. Lebedev said he had visited the site. "The traces were still seen," he said. "I could see holes of a clear shape that resembled the footprints of an elephant."

He said his reports from Voronezh would continue.●

☐ *Note the article from the* Sun, *April 18, 1989, which is above the* New York Times *report. It says the chief of police from Fyffe, Alabama was called about a UFO sighting. He observed a craft that looked like a large flying banana. This story was reported in many papers. The Russian sighting is not the only one that describes aliens with three eyes. The* Weekly World News *dated April 20, 1987 tells of a factory worker, his wife, and child who reported being sucked up into a gigantic cone-shaped Chinese hat by a light beam. Refer to article "Family Abducted by UFO." This family was from the Szechwan province of China. The aliens were described as having featureless faces with three huge white eyes in their foreheads and were not more than three feet tall.*

SOVIETS CAPTURE UFO CAPTAIN
***Weekly World News*, Nov. 7, 1989**
by Derek Clontz

The captain of the shimmering silver starship that landed in a Soviet park earlier this month was captured and is now being held prisoner by the KGB.

That's the word from a Russian ham radio operator who saw the ball-shaped craft land in Voronezh on Wednesday, September 27, and watched as Soviet agents strong-armed the extraterrestrial captain and spirited him away.

Heavily-censored reports of the incident were first published by the official Soviet news agency *Tass* and later picked up by Associated Press and published in newspapers across the U.S.

But they only confirmed that the starship landed — and totally disregarded the violent criminal tactics of the KGB.

"The captain of the UFO is in a Soviet jail and God only knows what the Russians are going to do with him," said Jacques Powers, a ham radio operator who spoke with the Soviet ham from his base in Paris.

"My contact said the extraterrestrial was dressed in shiny red overalls — the others were in silver — and obviously in charge. He was taken by the KGB while he and his crew were surveying the landing site.

"He offered no resistance. He was actually very gentle. But the agents hit him with a club, stuffed him in the back of a black van and sped away," he said.

Powers refused to identify the Soviet ham for fear the KGB would arrest him, too. But hams in France, Sweden, Italy, and Japan also heard the man's report and backed up what Powers said in published reports around the world.

Not surprisingly, Soviet officials denied the allegations and went on to say that the *Tass* and Associated Press reports about the landing of the spaceship were "fabrications."

But media analysts know better. Though censored and controlled by the Soviet government, the *Tass* news agency is considered to be exceedingly accurate.

And eyewitnesses who discussed the incredible encounter with Western journalists backed up both *Tass* and

A.P. reports that the starship landed while hundreds of people watched.

The aliens that emerged from the ship were said to be 9 to 12 feet tall with extremely small heads.

They were reportedly accompanied by a fireplug-shaped robot that took air and sea samples.

And they remained in the park for approximately 4 minutes before KGB agents arrived and arrested the captain of the ship.

According to the Soviet ham, the remaining aliens and robot ran back to their ball-shaped ship, which seemed to take on the form of a disc as it moved away and disappeared.

Genrikh Silanov, head of the Voronezh Geophysical Laboratory, gave even more weight to the reports when he conducted tests at the landing site that proved extraterrestrials had been there.

A 60-foot depression and four deep dents left where the starship landed clearly showed that the craft had touched down in the park.

Two small rocks that fell out of the ship were tested and found to be unlike anything on Earth, he said.

Western intelligence experts would not comment on any of the reports for the record — even after a team of experts from the Soviet Union's prestigious Academy of Sciences were dispatched to the landing site.

But privately they agreed that a spaceship landed in the Soviet Union. And they expressed grave concerns over the fact that the starship captain had been arrested.

"This is a very delicate and dangerous situation," said one Washington-based intelligence expert. "The Russians don't know who or what they are dealing with — nobody does.

"There could be reprisals. And if there are, the entire world could be held to blame for this intergalactic act of espionage."

Fears that the Soviets could get information of military significance from the alien are not unfounded, he added.

"There's no telling what kind of technology these extraterrestrials are privy to," he said.

"The Russians could get information that would render the Star Wars defense system obsolete before we get a chance to finish it." Stu Henderston, founder of the Belgian UFO research group Galaxy, agreed "that this time the Russians have gone too far."

He also called on Soviet chief Mikhail Gorbachev to release the alien captain "before it is too late."

Ironically, the landing of the craft may have been prompted by U.S. psychic Andy Reiss.

As reported in the *News*, the California seer and millions of Americans telepathically asked space aliens to land in Chicago on Oct. 2. The starship touched down in the Russian park a few days earlier on September 27.●

☐ *Note that the* News *tells us that the Russians are printing their own tabloids. They need to educate their people just as is being done in our country. It is thought both the U.S. and Russia have made trade-off agreements with visiting aliens. Perhaps someone forgot to notify the KGB before they whacked the captain and stuffed him in a van.*

The following article says Soviet sightings are a hoax, but those at "Gulf Breeze, Florida" are real. Andrus, International Director of Mutual UFO Network says, "Gulf Breeze is definitely one of the cases that defy any explanation."

THOSE GULF BREEZE SIGHTINGS

***National Examiner*, November 7, 1989**

by Diana Hardcastle

Recent reports of UFO sightings in the Soviet Union are being denounced worldwide as a hoax — but UFO investigators here have conclusive proof that flying saucers are hovering over a small US town.

That's the opinion of top UFO investigators who have viewed incredible photographs of flying saucers taken by residents of Gulf Breeze, Florida.

"Where are the pictures?" asked American UFOlogists when *Tass*, the official Soviet news agency, reported last month that three-eyed creatures had emerged from a spacecraft and taken a walk in a Russian park.

No photos were taken of the alleged Soviet UFO landing, and the only eyewitnesses were children.

The Gulf Breeze sightings, on the other hand, were reported consistently — and caught by cameras between Nov. '87, and May '88, and expert Walter Andrus believes the case is one of the biggest breakthroughs in the UFO world. "I am convinced the photos are genuine," Andrus says. "They would be extremely difficult to hoax.

"My belief is that the aliens chose this place to show themselves. They made no attempt to hide — they wanted to be seen and I'm sure they'll be back."

Nearly 140 residents of the coastal community reported a UFO sighting during the six-month period.

Local builder Ed Walters took several photographs of the alien craft.

One spectacular shot shows a cylindrical spacecraft with flashing lights projecting a blue laser beam down to the ground.

Another captures a craft hovering only a few feet above a highway. And Walter's wife also snapped him with just a towel around his waist, yelling at a spacecraft to leave him alone.

"I have researched hundreds of cases over the years and 70 to 80 of them are either hoaxes, delusions, hallucinations, or identifiable objects," says Andrus, international director of the Mutual UFO Network.

"But around 20% defy any explanation, and the Gulf Breeze case is definitely one."●

☐ *No argument — I believe it's a 10.*

UFOs TERRORIZE RUSSIAN TOWN

***Sun*, December 5, 1989**

by Francis Shifflett

The alien spacecraft, which caused a world-wide panic when hundreds of witnesses watched it land in a Russian town, was tracked on radar back to a secret UFO base — in the United States!

That's only one of the shocking details covered up by the Kremlin in what may be the most amazing alien encounter of recent times.

Other facts verified by the Russian army and police are that space aliens have kidnapped 26 people from the town of Voronezh, and 25 of them have never been seen or heard from again!

The one who returned, a crippled girl, was found hours later thousands of miles away, dazed, but with her leg deformity mended!

Despite the spirit of openness, known as *glasnost*, that is reportedly sweeping the Soviet Union, officials are taking great pains to keep the truth from the public.

A filing clerk at the Soviet news agency *Tass* was arrested by secret police and charged with selling a classified report on the amazing incident to Western sources.

The world's eyes focused on Voronezh after it was reported that a dark red ball measuring about 10 yards in diameter descended from the sky and landed in a park.

Stunned onlookers watched in amazement as a hatch opened and two aliens and a robot emerged.

The aliens were over nine feet tall and had small heads with three eyes.

They were dressed in silver overalls and bronze boots and wore strange metallic disks on their chests.

After a quick walk around the park, one of the pinhead spacemen aimed what appeared to be a gun at a boy in the crowd.

The boy disappeared, but reappeared after the spaceship took off.

That boy was one of the lucky ones, according to an army official at a nearby military base.

"An identical spaceship touched down on at least three occasions following the first landing," he notes. "The same aliens used their guns on onlookers, causing them to materialize aboard the UFO.

"We have evidence that the abducted citizens were then transported to secret medical bases, where they were used as guinea pigs in bizarre medical experiments."

Although hundreds have seen the ball-shaped UFOs, only one kidnapping victim was released by the aliens.

A crippled 27-year-old woman, identified only as Yuliya, was taken aboard the spaceship in Voronezh.

Hours later, she was found in the remote Siberian village of Yakutsk, thousands of miles away from her hometown.

And the aliens had fitted her with an amazingly-advanced artificial leg!

But the most frightening part of the story is that a radar station tracked the UFO that abducted Yuliya to a location in the Aleutian Islands of Alaska, in U.S. territory!

In addition to the Aleutian Islands base, Soviet Air Force radar stations have revealed that UFOs are also arriving and departing from several locations in the frozen Siberian wilderness.

"We have noted a great deal of alien activity in three sectors of Siberia," claims the military intelligence source.

"Air Force reconnaissance flights and spy satellites have photographed giant silver domes at these sites that are emitting high amounts of infrared radiation."

Although at this time the U.S. government has not publicly acknowledged the existence of the Alaskan base, a high-ranking Pentagon official confirms that a top-secret investigation is underway.

"Like the Russians, our satellites transmitted photos of a large dome-like structure on one of the uninhabited Aleutian Islands," he states.

"We've also intercepted strange radio communications consisting of grunts, beeps and moans.

"The U.S. Military is in constant contact with the Russians regarding these UFO bases," the official adds.●

☐ *If you feel all these Russian articles are manufactured for lack of something better to do, well it's OK by me, but I'm going for a 10!*

MAGIC RAY FROM UFO CURES 22 PEOPLE!

***Weekly World*, December 5, 1989**

by Mickey McGuire

At least 22 sick and crippled people were miraculously cured when they were bathed in an eerie greenish light that pulsated from a gigantic UFO hovering over their city!

Official reports from western Turkey said the incredible cures began moments after the silvery, saucer-shaped spaceship streaked silently down from the heavens to hover for more than an hour just over the rooftops.

And what is being hailed as the most sensational photograph ever made of a "flying saucer" was taken by a Turkish soldier home on leave.

"There is no doubt the photograph is real," declared a Turkish official in the city of Manisa. "Hundreds of people here saw the UFO. They saw it arrive and they watched it depart.

"But even more amazing than the photograph is the overwhelming evidence that something from the ship healed at last 22 sick and crippled people."

A physician, Dr. Mehmet Nadi, said he talked to a woman named Inisa Tokap, whose 46-year-old husband Alaattin was miraculously cured of crippling arthritis that had kept him bedridden for years.

"With tears streaming from her eyes she told me how his twisted limbs slowly straightened as the UFO's greenish light washed over his frail body," Dr. Nadi recalled.

"She said when the light from the UFO touched him the pain vanished from his body and his gnarled twisted fingers slowly began to become relaxed and began to straighten.

"His feet and toes became straight and he was able to stand and walk for the first time in years."

Dr. Nadi said he has examined several other patients and found them completely cured of their ailments, including Kamal Yilmaz, a middle-aged man who had been in a stroke-induced coma for months.

"I couldn't believe my eyes when Kamal came walking into my office as healthy as an ox," he said. "I've known him for years, but I made him show me some identification. I just couldn't believe it was true. But it was."

Medical officials from Ankara are now in the area to examine dozens of other people who also have reported being cured by the strange light.

"So far, we know of several people who were dying of cancer who now appear to be completely cured," one doctor confirmed. "But only time will tell us if the cures are permanent or merely some kind of coincidental mass remission."

Another doctor confirmed that a 9-year-old boy identified as Hasan Koru, comatose and near death with total kidney failure, awoke and got out of bed after the mysterious light filtered through a window swept over his still body. Other doctors verified that a woman blinded by cataracts regained her sight, a man deaf since birth had his hearing restored and a day-old infant girl dying of some undiagnosed malady now appears to be normal and healthy because of the miracle light.

The UFO, which hovered over the village for about 70 minutes before it suddenly streaked off into space, is believed to be the same spaceship that landed in a Soviet city about 1,300 miles to the north on September 27.

The *News* revealed in its November 7 issue that the captain of the spaceship was captured by KGB agents when the aliens left their craft after landing in a park in the city of Voronezh.

"It would be too much of a coincidence for two UFOs to be making such dramatic visits within weeks of each other," one Turkish official declared.●

☐ *Another 10 for the* Weekly World News. *Even Kathrun Kulman couldn't pull off the miracles these three-eyed aliens produce!*

UFO DOCS SAVE GIRL'S LEG ABOARD SPACESHIP

***Sun*, December 5, 1989**

by Dr. Bruno Grosse

According to the woman who knows them best, the space aliens who've terrorized the Soviet Union can't be all bad — they gave her a brand new leg that allowed her to walk again!

Yuliya, a 27-year-old Voronezh resident, was the only person to return after being kidnapped by a UFO. Authorities have withheld her last name.

Crippled from birth due to a deformed leg, Yuliya used her crutches to hobble to a field near her home when neighbors spotted a bright red ball floating down from the sky.

"Two of the spacemen came out and pointed guns into the crowd," she recalls. "Yellow rays shot out and people hit by them disappeared. All I remember is screaming, and then a yellow flash."

Semi-conscious, Yuliya found herself aboard the UFO, which according to Soviet military sources, flew to a secret alien base in the Aleutian Islands of Alaska. The woman recalls only bits and pieces of her ordeal, which occurred while she was in a dreamlike state.

"I was lying on a glowing glass platform and I heard humming and felt pressure on my leg," she says. "When I looked up I saw people from my neighborhood with tubes in their bodies that were attached to giant blinking computers."

Despite her horrifying description of the alien hospital, Yuliya says that she was never afraid, and that no one around her seemed to be in pain.

Only four hours after her disappearance, villagers of Yakutsk, a small town in Siberia, discovered the woman lying in a nearby field. The townspeople, who on the previous night had seen strange lights in the sky, rushed her to authorities.

Though stunned and confused, Yuliya was found to be in perfect health. But the real surprise came when doctors examined her leg and found the bones had been replaced with a strange metal!

She was flown to a military hospital near Moscow where the Soviet Union's top physicians studied the astounding artificial leg.

"It was advanced beyond anything modern medicine could ever conceive," says a member of the scientific panel. There was an exact metal substitute for every single bone, even the tiny ones in the knee and ankle joints.

"Even more incredible was the way the girl's existing muscles, tendons and nerves had been attached to the metal leg.

"The skin had been opened up and stretched around the metal skeleton. Although her leg is larger now, and has two large holes drilled into either side of the knee, it functions perfectly."

After telling officials in Moscow everything she knew about her alien abductors, Yuliya returned to her home in Voronezh. For the first time in her life, she is able to walk unaided.

She feels nothing but gratitude toward the aliens.

"They've done for me something doctors could never do: they've allowed me to live a full life," she says. "I know they'll eventually release everyone else unharmed. I've told the army officers that we have nothing to fear from these creatures, but no one believes me."●

☐ *I wish I were able to show you the picture of this girl and her new leg — and the scars and the incisions. If you pick up a copy of the* Sun *you can see for yourself. I think our governments want us to aware of the numerous miracles and medical achievements which are taking place in UFO contacts. A 10 for Dr. Bruno Grosse.*

FISHING TRAWLER NETS UFO

***Weekly World*, July 4, 1989**

by Robert Buckner

A team of renowned scientists and medical specialists from around the world is examining a human-like creature that survived a spectacular UFO crash just 62 miles southwest of Kodiak, Alaska.

Sketchy military dispatches intercepted by radio operators on a trawler fishing further out to sea than usual because of the recent oil spill near Valdez indicate the spacecraft crashed into the sea on May 31 or June 1.

The crew of another fishing vessel accidentally netted a 25-foot shiny black capsule that broke away from the starship after the crash.

Stunned crewmen notified military authorities after they found an injured alien inside.

"What they're saying is, this thing is a little over 5 feet tall and looks a lot like a human being," said Jerzy Faron, who monitored both military and civilian reports.

"He has eyes and a nose and mouth, but no ears and no hair and no teeth. And he only has three fingers on each hand. They said he's moving around, but he's obviously suffered some injuries and the doctors aren't sure how to treat him."

A Coast Guard official in Alaska denied any knowledge of a UFO crash or the recovery of an alien astronaut.

"I've heard rumors, but as far as I know there are no little green men around here," said the official, who asked not to be named.

But Jerzy Faron and other members of the trawler crew say radio dispatches indicate the alien was whisked to an undisclosed hospital for treatment and is being kept under heavy 24-hour guard.

"They've brought in doctors and scientists from all over Germany, France and even Russia, I think," Faron said.

"They were speaking to one doctor in Polish — I'm Polish myself — and I heard them say that keeping this thing alive might be the most important mission of their lives."

Meanwhile, military officials are desperately trying to determine what happened to the main body of the ill-fated spaceship.

"They want the technology, and they want to find out if there are anymore aliens down there, either dead or alive. They don't figure that one little fellow came all this way alone," Faron said.●

☐ *This one gets a 9 because I have no reason to doubt its validity.*

NOAH'S ARK DID NOT LAND ON MOUNT ARARAT

***National Examiner*, June 20, 1989**

by Phil Brennan

Noah's Ark did not land on Mount Ararat.

Instead, the huge ship came to rest on Doomsday Mountain, 17 miles away from Ararat, where a team of archaeologists and scientists discovered its remains.

Moreover, the ark was not made of wood, but of reeds covered with cement, is far bigger than biblical experts thought, and far from being hidden, is still clearly visible thousands of years after it came to rest on dry land when the waters of the great flood receded. Explorer David Fasold tells the incredible story of the discovery of the ark's remains in his gripping book, *The Ark of Noah* (Wynwood Press, 1988).

Using sophisticated electronic and other equipment, Fasold uncovered the skeleton of the gigantic prehistoric craft, showing for the first time the ark's twin-prowed shape and its true size and composition of cement-covered reeds.

Scientists and biblical experts have ignored the ark, uncovered by an earthquake in 1948, because its location and size seemed to contradict biblical accounts.

Fasold, however, shows that the remains are consistent with biblical and other historic sources.

The remains are those of a craft 516 feet in interior length. The Bible describes the ark as being 300 cubits long, and uses the Hebrew version of the cubit in translating the length to 450 feet.

Fasold, however, writes that Moses, who wrote the Bible's story of the flood, was educated in Egypt and would have used the Egyptian version of the cubit, which would make the ark the exact size of the remains—516 feet.

The remains are not on Mount Ararat, but on Mount Mahser Dagi — Doomsday Mountain — 17 miles from the traditional resting place of Noah's ark.

The Bible, however, does not say the ark landed on Mount Ararat, Fasold points out. It says only that the ark landed on the "mountains of Ararat."

The author quotes a Turkish farmer as saying he knows a ship when he sees one, and the remains are obviously those of a ship. Fasold also knows a ship when he sees one — he's a former Merchant Marine ship's captain.●

☐ *It's the newest "Noah's Ark" article I've seen — for that it's a 7 and for the possible 516 ft., another 1 — an 8-point for the ark.*

MINISTER TIES UFOs TO BIBLE
***Columbus Dispatch*, April 22, 1989**
by George W. Cornell, A. P.

(Book says visits from space may explain miracles)

NEW YORK AP — Smile indulgently about it if so inclined. That's OK with the Rev. Barry K. Downing, but he firmly maintains that UFOs are real and that they have key religious significance.

He says recognizing the existence and operations of unidentified flying objects could do much to strengthen faith and renew confidence in biblical accounts.

"It would establish scientific plausibility for the whole biblical field," he said.

Downing, a Presbyterian pastor with a scientific bent, said government equivocation has caused skepticism about UFOs.

He theorizes that activities of UFO-borne "higher beings," likely from another dimension rather than other planets, are indicated in biblical events ranging from guiding the Israelites from Egypt to Christ's ascension.

Downing, 50, an Endwell, N.Y. pastor, has a bachelor's degree in physics. After completing Princeton Theological Seminary, he got a doctorate at the University of Edinburgh in Scotland on relations of science and religion.

He explains his ideas about UFOs and eternity in a new paperback edition of his book *The Bible and Flying Saucers*, issued by Berkely Books.

"What is clear through the biblical material is that God's will for the Jews, and eventually for all mankind, was 'revealed' by beings from another world," he writes.

"Usually these beings looked very much like ordinary human beings (they almost never have wings)... Once the 'package' of biblical religion had been delivered, man became responsible for the distribution of the contents."

Downing said a hovering, UFO-like "cloud" by day, and glowing "pillar of fire" by night guided the Israelites out of Egypt. It projected some propulsive force that parted the Red Sea and led them for years across the desert, he said.

Other events he sees as carried out by UFOs include: The fire-like phenomenon on Mount Sinai in which Moses received the Ten Commandments, the Prophet Elijah taken to heaven in a fiery chariot, the Star of Bethlehem, the engulfing light of Jesus' transfiguration, his being "lifted up" at his ascension and the blinding visitation of Paul en route to Damascus.

"All these were UFO types of reports," Downing said. ●

☐ *Everybody has a right to get in here with a theory. This one ought to bring an 8.5. It has lots of thinking and research behind it.*

The following is an article I wrote January 4, 1962. Recent published articles imply that we are doing this kind of research with other countries such as England and Russia. It is taken more seriously nowadays.

DR. J.B. RHINE — MIND AND MATTER
The Public Opinion

Dr. J.B. Rhine and his laboratory of assistants have been piling up stacks of evidence to prove that mind does control matter. All this has been proven mathematically. However, the weak spot is that no one has been able to offer enough proof to show a practical way of accomplishing positive results.

Norman Vincent Peale has been preaching this theory for years. He too knows that matter can be influenced, but here again a good sure way to accomplish this goal is quite a problem.

A Los Angeles development engineer, Roy A. Crain, claims to have developed a principle by which the mind can learn to (1) influence the behavior of electrical instruments, (2) control favorable throws of dice or the turn of the wheel in roulette, and (3) influence objects in motion.

Crain calls his discovery Subjective Physics. (That area where the observed results show, mathematically, the influence of a purposefully created psychological climate.)

For many years Crain was a free-lance development engineer in industry. Experiences finally convinced him that "something" (Crain calls them happy accidents) influenced the work being done by individuals who were working at jobs which required some new technique to fulfill their needs.

In 1958 he began a series of experiments trying to prove that matter could be controlled. His success was slow but steadily increased. Finally he has reached a stage where he has offered $5000 to the person or organization who can prove he cannot support his claims — with the stipulation that if they fail they will donate substantial effort and funds for the development of a program to explore the science of subjective physics.

The more complex the experiments have been have led to far higher percentages of success. It has been found that anxiety and complacency have led to lowering positive results while emotional stress tends to increase success.

The all-important rule that Crain found necessary was that, having once established in mind that which he wished to control, it was then wise to withdraw the attention to another area, simply imagining another dream picture to replace the objective experiment.

His results have been so fantastic that letters from the Duke University Parapsychology Department indicate that he is one of the very few persons whom they have found able to obtain results over a long period of time. It is also unique because of his theory of how he is able to obtain his outstanding results. ●

HENRY'S STORY

The following article was published on February 21, 1963. It concerns an interview I had with Dr. Henry Smith, a retired skin specialist. Formerly he was President of the Theosophical Society. I heard him give a series of lectures and was so impressed I asked him to have lunch with me. He was reluctant to tell me this experience. I had given him all the right answers; I have never been more impressed and have no doubt as to the truth of this article. He assured me he NEVER told this to an audience! If he is still with us, I hope he forgives me for giving his name. This is only a small part of his story. It began back in Chicago when money was about as hard to find as hen's teeth!

Hunting UFOs have led me down many pathways. This is one that I shall never forget!

I was tempted to write a full coverage of several of my columns — this one in particular.

MY INTERVIEW WITH HENRY

Public Opinion

Years ago, while lunching with a retired doctor, an M.D., we were discussing phenomena. He told me it had been a great struggle for him to go into medicine because of financial problems.

As he was about to give up, he thought, "If I am to go into this field I must have some sign to convince me this is wise."

A freshly cut rose fell into his lap. Since he was alone there was no one to confirm his story, but for 30 years he kept the rose as a reminder of that day. Years later while he was in his office talking to a woman who claimed to be an atheist, he had another such experience.

This woman gave lectures on her "unbelief." She told the doctor it would take some demonstration to convince her otherwise. As she finished her sentence she received her demonstration. An armload of dew-wet cut daffodils fell out of the air and onto his desk. The woman did not remain an atheist!

The doctor had mentally asked where these flowers came from and in return was shown a puff of smoke which filled the room with an incense of sandalwood. During the years he had other experiences which were also impressive.

I haven't the nerve to try to explain what happens in these instances but it does seem to me there must be life in other dimensions which we do not perceive.●

2,000-YR-OLD MUMMY HAS ARTIFICIAL HIP

***Sun*, July 4, 1989**

by Ken O'Hara

Staggering proof that the ancient Egyptians had medical technology rivaling 20th century medicine has been found in a 2,000-year-old mummy that has a perfectly-fitted artificial hip!

British scientists studying a mummy on loan to them from the Egyptian government were startled to discover that the advanced medical procedures carried out on the corpse included a hip-joint implant!

Archaeologists have long suspected that the ancient Egyptians had the most advanced techniques known to mankind at that time. They were absolutely astounded when they came across the highly-advanced metal work on the perfectly-preserved mummy after taking extensive x-rays.

"The new evidence of the artificial hips is just further proof that the ancient Egyptian civilization of 2,000 years ago was comparable in many ways to the 20th century," says anthropologist E.T. Baird.

"The surgery and precision needed for fitting artificial body parts requires great medical and engineering skill.

"We'd like very much to discover what kind of anesthesia, if any, they used when implanting the artificial hips.

"We know that the Egyptians had scientific skills beyond our wildest imagination, but each new discovery only adds to our amazement and awe of their achievements."

Baird dismisses speculations the metal implant was put in there as a hoax in recent years.

"Our studies show the tissue surrounding the hip replacement was totally untouched since mummification," he explains. "This amazing operation is probably the first attempt at high-tech medicine."●

☐ *I'll bet they used hypnosis to do it — and the aliens probably showed them how while they were lifting stones for those pyramids. It's worth a 9, without the hip joint.*

ASTROLOGY AND NUMEROLOGY

FIRST SCIENTIFIC PROOF ASTROLOGY IS FOR REAL

National Examiner, **April 25, 1989**

by John Turner

A top astronomer has rocked the world of science with amazing new evidence that astrology is for real, proving that the stars really do control our destiny.

It's all because of magnetism, says eminent scientist Dr. Percy Seymour.

"Astrology isn't bunk," he declared. "I'm staking my reputation on that."

Dr. Seymour carried out years of research to prove beyond a doubt that ancient wise men got it right when they devised the horoscope to predict and interpret our lives.

The clincher was significant research into birth signs and personality traits by French psychologist and statistician, Dr. Michel Gauquelin.

"He proved conclusively that successful people in certain fields were born when their birth signs were under the influence of certain planets," says Dr. Seymour, who is principal lecturer in astronomy at Plymouth Polytechnic, England, and a fellow of the prestigious Royal Astronomy Society.

Seymour has written astronomy textbooks for universities, but it's his latest book, *Astrology, The Evidence of Science*, just published in Britain, that's exploded like a bombshell.

"The movements of the stars, the planets, and the sun and moon have a profound effect on the lives of every man, woman, and child on this planet," says Dr. Seymour. "And it's all because of the way they change the Earth's magnetic field, molding our personalities through biological effects."

The Earth is like an enormous magnet, explains Dr. Seymour, but what few people realized, until now, is the enormous impact on our lives that magnetic field has.

"That field — the magnetosphere — is influenced by the gravitational pull of nearby planets the same way the moon's pull affects the tides in our oceans which can be predicted in a tide table.

"We know that magnetic forces induce electrical impulses. and we know that the human brain, even when it's like a blank magnetic tape forming in the womb, is an electrical apparatus that functions on minute electrical impulses.

"That's why the position of the stars at birth do 'label' our personalities.

"Think of the zodiac as a traditional telephone dial. Sure, the planets are constantly changing their position against the background of the zodiac, but they're still dialing the same sign.

"And I'm speaking as a hard-headed scientist for whom facts, not superstition, must be the basis of belief."

WHAT YOUR BEST CAREER SHOULD BE, BASED ON DR. SEYMOUR'S STUDIES

Dr. Seymour compiled a scientifically accurate horoscope based on his detailed study. He points out that it only gives a broad picture because research into astrology has only just started.

This list can help give people pointers as to what type of career would suit them best. Jobs listed under each sign are ones that statistical analysis of millions of subjects has shown to be the ones that attract and satisfy the highest proportion of people born under that sign.

ARIES (Mar. 21-Apr. 19): Personality — active, dynamic, confident, inventive. Occupation — sportsman or athlete, dentist, mechanic, fireman.

TAURUS (Apr. 20-May 20): Personality — constructive, determined, problem-solving. Occupation — accountant, architect, farmer, baker.

GEMINI (May 21-June 21): Personality — ambitious, humorous, independent, lively. Occupation — author, journalist, commercial traveler, teacher.

CANCER (June 22-July 22): Personality — supportive, understanding, protective of others, inspirational. Occupation — cook, social worker.

LEO (July 23-Aug. 22): Personality — not afraid of making tough decisions, leader, forthright, and loyal. Occupation — actor, musician, manager.

VIRGO (Aug. 23-Sept. 22): Personality — obliging, helpful, analytical; tends to be a perfectionist. Occupation — clerk, cashier, optician, typist.

LIBRA (Sept. 23-Oct. 23): Personality — diplomatic, sees both sides of an argument. Occupation — hairdresser, beautician, tailor, dressmaker.

SCORPIO (Oct. 24-Nov. 21): Personality — energetic, tough-minded, able to learn from mistakes. Occupation — doctor, miner, policeman.

SAGITTARIUS (Nov. 22-Dec. 21): Personality — restless, curious, wide-ranging interests. Occupation — sportsman, lawyer, minister.

CAPRICORN (Dec. 22-Jan. 19): Personality — Systematic and a good organizer. Occupation — civil servant, engineer (civil), politician, miner.

AQUARIUS (Jan. 20-Feb. 18): Personality — sociable, understanding, open-minded. Occupation — electrician, radiographer.

PISCES (Feb. 19-Mar. 20): Personality — generous nature, warm and loving, independent, artistic. Occupation — actor, musician, artist, bartender, fisherman.●

☐ *We brought in everybody and that included an astrologer. My birthday is June 6, 1911. You can check the chart and see how it works for you. I think Dr. Seymour has a 9 coming for all his labor.*

In looking through my pictures and papers I came across the following letter from Mabel Trautman. Since Mabel came to visit our group and gave numerous readings to our members, I thought you might be interested in this chart which she sent to me. Besides, I don't want anyone to think that the Reagans and Shirley are the only ones who can have an astrologer! Mabel did charts on both astrology and numerology. I assume this must be a combination as it refers to a lot of numbers. She told us she had made charts for many of the stars. One is so well known that everybody knows him.

May 31, 1971

Dear Lillian:

When I had finished with the fine work on your chart I had even more 6's than when you and I worked it out and talked about it one afternoon.

You surely are a mixture of Metaphysics and the Arts. You have Pisces on the Asc. which is Psychic — Moon in Libra which is art — Sun in Gemini, hand ability — Mercury and Saturn in Taurus, more art. You should give it as much time as you can spare. I can now see why it was too bad you did not get the artistic training as a youngster....

With 6 of your planets out of 9 below the line of the chart indicates your later years will be your very best. Gemini never grows old. They are the Peter Pans of the Zodiac, so you have plenty of time yet.

Venus in Cancer — In this sign Venus wants the comforts of life, wants the little things taken care of. This is a fine position for Venus. In art and music the feelings are deep and quiet and often melancholy. Here in Cancer she is often humorous and good natured — popular and loved by many.

You are fortunate that you do not have any difficult aspects from Mars this year when he transits through Aquarius. This is a headache in almost every chart. You have very little of this influence.

Saturn, the planet of obstruction, will move across your Sun through the second half of 1972 and all of 1973 and this will be a good period to take care of Lillian. Your Sun is very well aspected so it can't do you much harm.

The period between June 6 and September 11 this year is very good for you.

You are the born artist — 1972 is going to be a good year for you in your art work.

You are now living in the name of Desguin and it is a very good name to guarantee a good ending to the life — which is a bad thing to see in any chart to have a negative closing to the life.

Mars in you first house gives you a lot of energy. You are a serious individual and would like to feed the world and take care of a lot of people who need attention but you must also take care of Lillian for she has some good periods in her life ahead and they can bring her much satisfaction.

Gemini does not always work well for a lot of people but it is an asset in your chart, since it is the hand ability to you that you need in your work. Many Gemini people have unfortunate charts for it needs good aspects to get the good out of the sign, but you sure have just what it takes to put it to work.

I only found one period in your life that was negative and that was between age 52 and 57. Could have been one earlier but I did not work too far backward.

Be glad to answer any questions.

Love and blessings,
Mabel T.

OUT-OF-BODY TRAVELER VISITS 5 CITIES WITHIN SECONDS
***Weekly World*, September 6, 1988**
by Ragan Dunn

Some Soviet scientists say an out-of-body traveler visited five European cities in two seconds flat!

The psychic appeared in each city for only a split second. But he was seen by over 60 witnesses who were waiting for him at preassigned spots.

"This is the most sensational display of out-of-body travel on record," Dr. Vladimir Borisov, who supervised the experiment, told reporters in Moscow.

"The implications are staggering," he added.

"What we learn from this man might even be able to help us conquer space.

The man, Ivan Tolstik, has been the prime figure in Soviet psychic research since 1978. Considered by many to be the world's leading clairvoyant, he has spent the past decade perfecting his control of the out-of-body experience.

The latest experiment was conducted on July 12. After going into a self-induced trance in a Moscow facility Tolstik allegedly left his body and visited Trier, West Germany; West Berlin; Bourges, France; Rome; and London — virtually at the speed of light.

The visits were witnessed by 67 people who claimed to have seen Tolstik's shimmering, translucent form appear briefly at predetermined rendezvous points, Dr. Borisov said.

"The most intriguing aspect of the experiment took place in Moscow," continued the expert. "When Tolstik lapsed into unconsciousness and began his travels, his body temperature plunged to a mind-boggling 71 degrees.

"His pulse rate fell to one-third its normal rate and his brain activity almost stopped dead. It was like he had willed himself into a state of suspended animation.

"Had he been a patient in a hospital, most doctors would have written him off as dead. But he was fully aware of everything that happened. He correctly described the weather in each of the five cities he visited and repeated things that I had said while he was unconscious in the lab."

American officials refused to comment on the experiment "until full data an reports are in." But privately they were only too willing to talk — and unaimously praise the Soviet experiment.

"America treats psychic research as a joke and always has," said one expert.

"I hope this report scares us Americans because it proves that the Soviet scientists are light years ahead of the U.S.

"And sooner or later, what they have discovered is going to pay some very big dividends."•

☐ *I've got a couple of friends that were able to do that — If they said they did, they did, so these people get a 9. I read in the papers that any countries are getting around to checking out such possibilities.*

UFO LANDING BASES ARE DISCOVERED WORLDWIDE
***National Examiner*, November 8, 1988**
by Edward Reynolds

UFO landing bases are being discovered in dozens of nations around the globe.

The bases, precise rings of flattened crops and grass, are about 30 feet in diameter and have been found primarily in industrialized countries, including the United States, Great Britain, Australia, Japan, and Italy.

Scientists have ruled out hoaxes as a cause because of the sheer number and size of the circles and their different locations.

A team of scientists has discovered more than 70 in Great Britain alone.

Some of the circles have small satellites of flattened vegetation, north, south, east, and west of the main ring.

Researchers, armed with infrared cameras, videos, and other recording apparatus, are monitoring the landing bases to capture man's first official glimpse of the space beings.

Vegetation flattened by flying saucers is slow to grow back, reports America's top UFO investigator, Budd Hopkins, of New York City.

Soil at a UFO landing zone in Indiana had a lighter color and was less dense, according to laboratory analysis. To duplicate the effects, soil had to be heat-treated at 800° Fahrenheit writes Hopkins in his intriguing book *Intruders* (Random House, 1987):

"I photographed the area in late May 1985, nearly two years after the original event, and the mass of the circle was still almost devoid of vegetation."•

☐ *I feel it's important for you to realize these UFO bases are world-wide. Sometimes it seems repetitious to print so many of these accounts. When you see different papers and different people saying the same thing, I hope you will take it seriously! 9 for Reynolds and the* National Examiner.

GLOWING SPACE ALIEN IN HIS BEDROOM
***National Examiner*, June 7, 1988**
by George Glidden

Malcolm Bourne had a close encounter of a very weird kind in his bedroom.

Bourne, 41, was awakened in the early morning by heavy footsteps and strange mumblings.

Lurking near his closet was a six-foot-tall space alien dressed in dazzling white robes.

There was no face in the huge oblong head, just a glowing yellow light.

The ET's chest beamed powerful laser beam lights, much like in a modern-day discotheque.

Said Bourne, of Shropshire, England: "I was terrified. It was talking to itself in a strange beeping tone and walking around the room as if confused."

Added Bourne: "I thought my days were numbered. I had no idea what it was, but I knew it was after me."

In a desperate effort, Bourne summoned up his courage, leaped out of bed, and made a dash for safety.

Recalled Bourne: "At that moment the whole vision seemed to vanish in a circular swirl of white smoke. I knew nothing about UFOs beforehand and was really something of a cynic.

"That's before I saw an alien."

Bourne has the comfort of knowing that his description is similar to that of other sightings of aliens taken by the British Unidentified Flying Objects Association.

But the respected churchgoer fears that the space alien is going to return soon.

And he knows he is defenseless to stop it.

Said Bourne: "Thirty years ago, if some brave soul came forward with a story like mine, he would have been carted off to the loony bin. But at least today there is serious study being put into the UFO contactee experience."•

□ *Many readers won't take this article seriously. I am including it because I'm aware of too many others that more or less duplicate the experience. Sometimes I wonder if these writers themselves believe the stories they are required to print — if not, they had better start believing. I think they are doing a great service for the world knowledge of mankind. A 9 please!*

NEW ARM AND LEG!
***Weekly World*, June 14, 1988**
by Ragan Dunn

A man who lost an arm and a leg in a car crash stunned doctors when he sprouted a new pair of limbs!

"Everybody wants me to say something about it — but what on earth can I say?" Dr. Charlotte Timar told reporters in Bourges, France.

"Worms regenerate body parts. So do starfish. But I've never heard of a human being doing it. At least not until now."

The mind-boggling medical drama began to unfold after Robert Sauvage's left arm and right leg were severed in a horrifying collision with a logging truck last November, said newspapers.

Attempts to reattach the limbs were unsuccessful. And when Sauvage regained consciousness, Dr. Timar had to tell the young man that the best doctors could do was fit him with a pair of artificial limbs.

"I've never seen such a violent reaction in a patient," said Dr. Timar.

"Mr. Sauvage absolutely refused to believe that he would have to go through life as an invalid.

"He looked me straight in the eye and said with steely determination: 'I've had two good arms and two good legs all my life — and that's not going to change now.'

"What happened next, I still have a hard time believing," she continued. "Within days a pair of small appendages were growing out of the stumps where his arm and leg had been. These new growths looked just like mushrooms," said Dr. Timar.

"Within a week the appendages were much bigger and had the form of the limbs they ultimately would grow to replace."

Now, six months later, the young man's arm and leg are close to full size.

He had about 65 percent use of them at the moment. But Dr. Timar expects that percentage to improve with time. "We are looking for a physiological explanation for the regeneration of these limbs," she said.

"But to tell you the truth, I don't think we're going to find a thing.

"I spoke to a psychiatrist who thinks we'd be better off seeking a psychological explanation.

"He thinks the answer, if there is one, lies in the power of this young man's will and mind."•

□ *This article was written in 1988. Recently I have read that doctors are studying ways in which they could cause such growth to occur. When will they ever begin to recognize the power of mind and suggestion? UFO occupants have already learned a lot of these things. Refer to the section on rescue and healing. A 9.5.*

ASTROLOGY RULES OUR LIVES
***Sun*, June 28, 1988**
by Robert Webb

Top space expert confirms: Star Wars have erupted within the scientific world because of a top astronomer who believes our lives are in fact ruled by the stars.

Scientists have long been skeptical of astrology, but Dr. Percy Seymour, a confessed skeptic himself only five years ago, announces:

"Scientific research shows people born when the planets are rising in the sky, or are just past their peak, will be leaders in their fields.

"I am positive the stars rule our lives."

Dr. Seymour notes people born under the planetary influence of Mars will be military leaders, top executives, physicians and sports champions, while those born under Jupiter are more likely to succeed as journalists, playwrights, actors and politicians. Saturn breeds physicians and scientists.

"I changed my mind because of facts," says Dr. Seymour, lecturer in astronomy at Plymouth Polytechnic in England.

"Now I want to prove to other people stars do have an influence on us. And, if anything, my scientific background has given me an even greater understanding of how it works."

He has even established Jesus Christ was born under a triple conjunction of Jupiter and Saturn in the constellation of Pisces, an event which only occurs every 900 years, and signals the birth of a great leader. The star the three wise men followed was Jupiter.

Each of us has a special relationship with the star we were born under.

"Each planet is playing a tune, which creates a harmony within the whole universe," Dr. Seymour points out.

"That note can be tuned into by humans and animals through a very sensitive aerial located in the nervous system.

"After all, it's the wiring of the nervous system which determines person's character, and it is the pulsing of the electrical circuits which act as receivers to the stars.

"It's almost as if we have our own personal telephone number directly linked to our individual star," he concludes.●

☐ *Another 9 for the doctor.*

SHIP WRECKED WITH AN ALIEN UFO PILOT
***Sun*, July 18, 1989**
by Joe Frick

What started out as a solo voyage in the South Pacific became a long, wondrous adventure for a shipwrecked sailor who was stranded on an island with a crash victim from a UFO!

"We worked, lived and survived together for six months until a ship from has planet arrived, taking me to civilization and bringing him home," claims Arthur Mailan.

Arthur's sailing vessel crashed into rocks off the island east of Fiji during storm and he managed to reach shore.

"I was there for a few days wandering through the woods and wondering if I'd ever be rescued, when I spotted him standing by a tree," recall Arthur, 38.

"Huge green eyes the size of doughnuts stared at me. I almost passed out from shock, but we both stood face to face for several minutes.

"He was four feet tall, had a bald head and yellowish skin, three long fingers on each hand and was wearing a suit made of strange materials."

Filled first with fear, then excitement, Arthur began trying to communicate with the creature.

"He guided me to the site of his crashed UFO. It was huge, but completely destroyed. He showed me where he had buried his fallen comrades. We couldn't speak to each other, but I felt a great deal of sorrow for him.

"Because the accident had destroyed everything in his ship, this highly-advanced creature was completely helpless on the island. In honor of Robinson Crusoe, I named him Friday."

From the wreckage of the spacecraft the two men built a strong shelter.

"It was made of material that protected us against the strongest winds and rain," says Arthur. "It also contained some kind of substance that kept us warm in cold weather and cool during the heat of the day."

Arthur, an experienced adventurer, introduced his new friend to the tropical fruits on the island and taught him the possible dangers of certain plants.

"During the whole time, he was working on his radio equipment, and finally made contact. Help arrived one morning in a giant circular craft."

Arthur says Friday led him into the ship, where he met other aliens, and in a matter of moments he was taken to northern New Zealand before the craft lifted off again.

Back home in Bundaberg, Australia, people believe shipwrecked Arthur is the victim of delirium, but not Malcolm Crale, a friend who watched Arthur sail away in Fiji.

"He was obviously stranded somewhere for six months and then managed to get back," Malcolm notes. "Who rescued him?"●

☐ *This shipwreck is worth a 10 even if it's science fiction and more than 10 if it isn't. The description is too good for a compulsive liar. The eyes, the color, the fingers, the bald head, the size, and the clothing are believable. The equipment which showed unusual qualities is interesting and the emotion shown toward his companion is convincing.*

BOY GROWS NEW ARM
***Sun*, July 25, 1989**
by Ken O'Hara

In an astounding occurrence that defies medical knowledge, a remarkable youth who lost his arm in a gruesome automobile accident has stunned doctors around the world by growing a brand new limb!

Wonder boy Timmy Carlson, 12, had his left arm amputated after the car he was riding in was demolished by a tractor trailer.

Timmy's father Andrew suffered two broken legs in the grisly mishap.

"The two of them were a horrible mess when they were brought into the emergency room," recalls Dr. David Harris.

"We had to amputate the boy's arm almost immediately. His arm was literally hanging off when he got to the hospital."

Timmy spent the next three months in a hospital near Wellington, New Zealand, where he underwent extensive rehabilitation therapy every day.

"Tim never complained," says his dad.

"Whenever the therapists would ask him how his arm felt, he said he felt like it was still there.

Medical experts say that an amputee often feels sensations where his amputated limb used to be, so they discounted Timmy's declarations that he still had feelings in his arm.

After extensive testing, however, they concluded that he was indeed growing new skin and bone matter to replace his lost arm!

Suddenly, during his eighth week in the hospital, Timmy's new arm started growing by leaps and bounds!

"The small stump by his arm was

two inches long at one point, and a few weeks later it was nearly the size of a normal arm," says growth specialist D. Trevor Hansen.

"Lower forms of animal life regenerate lost body parts, and perhaps his genes contain some remarkable ability to do the same thing.

"We think the new arm formed from a little piece of living tissue left near his shoulder blade, and we've done a biopsy to examine the contents.

"His extraordinary growth hormones must have sent growth signals to his arm," he adds.●

☐ *I couldn't resist another article about a boy growing a new arm — I've got a half dozen places where I want to grow some new parts — I think I'll give him a 9.5.*

GHASTLY IRISH TRIANGLE
***National Examiner*, July 18, 1989**
by Glen Troelstrup

A ghastly Irish Devil's Triangle is swallowing ships. That's what officials say is happening in the Irish Sea. Robin Boyder, a British maritime official and expert on sea disasters, says "It's the Bermuda Triangle all over again. These are mystery sinkings. We don't know the cause or causes."

Eighteen fishing trawlers have disappeared there since 1983 in relatively calm conditions.

The few survivors claim their unfortunate vessels suddenly were pulled under the waters between Britain and Ireland without any warning.

Thirty-seven sailors have died in the sinkings.

The latest ship was the 145-ton Belgian trawler Tijl Uilenspiegel. She went down abruptly some 50 miles off the northwest British coast with all five hands aboard.

The Coast Guard in Liverpool reported the trawler's experienced crew was using modern radar and navigation equipment, visibility was good, and only a light breeze was affecting the area.

The ill-fated vessel reported no problems. No distress signal was sent. All the that was recovered later were the bodies and some fishing gear.

The British Coast Guard reported only that a wreck was marked on charts near where the Tijl Uilenspiegel disappeared.

George Falces, a member of the British Parliament, called the Irish Sea "a Bermuda Triangle for fishermen." He demanded an official inquiry into the mystery situation.

He protested: "Boats have been lost without a trace and it is getting suspicious."

Foulke noted that half of the victim vessels were loft in an area where NATO submarines hold exercises. But British Coast Guard and Defense Ministry officials responded sharply that there was absolutely no submarine activity in the area at the times of the 18 sinkings.

Boyder added: "Something's happening out there. Men are dying and we don't know how. It's tragic. We need answers. And we need them soon."●

☐ *This is something that seems to occur in a number of places around the world. Beside this Triangle near Ireland and the one near the east coast of Florida, there's one near Japan. Is it crystals or pyramids or submarines... I don't know. Glen gets an 8.5.*

ET's BROUGHT BIGFOOT TO EARTH
***National Examiner*, July 18 1989**
by Edward Reynolds

Bigfoot creatures could be experimental animals UFO aliens brought to earth in order to test the environment before colonizing.

That's the incredible explanation given by Walt H. Andrus Jr., international director of the Mutual UF Network based in Sequin, Texas.

And it is one shared by top UFOlogist Timothy Green Beckley, editor of New York-based UFO Universe magazine. He says there is a definite link between Bigfoot and UFO sightings especially throughout Pennsylvania Ohio, and New Jersey.

More than 600 people in Pennsylvania reported seeing UFOs or strange creatures like Bigfoot in 1988, according to a report in *The Pittsburgh Press.*

A 67-year-old disabled Army veteran from Wilpen, Pennsylvania, tells of a chilling encounter he had with a Bigfoot while on a fishing trip at Loyalhanna Creek, the site of numerous UFO sightings.

Sam Sherry says he stood within 20 feet of the beast, which he estimates weighed 700 pounds and stood six and a half feet tall with arms nearly down to its ankles.

Sherry claims the creature put one arm on his shoulder and another on is back as he turned to get in his car. Fortunately, he was able to drive away.

Beckley says one of the most sensational Bigfoot sightings of recent times places the creature inside UFO, and is verified by an area investigator for the National Investigations Committee on Aerial Phenomena.

According to Beckley, University of Wisconsin professor J.M. Bostrack says after a number of interviews with farmer Frederick Bosak he is convinced of the elderly man's sincerity.

Bosak claims he saw a transparent UFO on the side of the road while driving toward his farm. He pulled alongside the craft and peered inside.

The Wisconsin farmer was quoted as saying: "All I know for sure is that he had thick reddish-brown hair covering his face and arms. This heavy layer of hair appeared to extend downward to the region of his chest...."

He added: "The eyes—I doubt if I'll ever be able to erase them from my memory. They were big and round, really protruding."●

☐ *There are too many UFO sighting which in someway relate to Bigfoot. For that reason this suggestion will have to be given consideration. If we are in someway related to space-aliens — it shouldn't be surprising to find Bigfoot too, may have played a part. I think I'll go for a 9 on this one.*

HOUSEWIFE VIDEO TAPES OUTER-SPACE SHOW

***Weekly World*, August 1, 1989**

by Willie Grice

A 36-year-old housewife claims to have videotaped a television show from outer space.

And shockingly enough, a team of six scientists who studied the seven-minute tape agree that the program did not originate on Earth.

"We don't know what to make of it," Dr. Peter Wolfrath, the radio astronomer who led the team, told reporters in Lugano, Switzerland.

"We do know that the program was taped during a period of unusually heavy sunspot activity which could have steered a stray television signal to the woman's set.

"Beyond that we are as baffled as she is. The characters vaguely resemble human beings but with baseball-sized eyes and large fleshy ears.

"There isn't much action. The characters just stand there. And the dialogue — if you can call it that — is nothing more than clicking and squealing noises like dolphins make.

"Needless to say we are continuing to study the tape. All we can say now is that it didn't originate on earth."

Marta Gerber told newsmen that she taped the strange television program by accident.

"I set the VCR to record while I was out shopping but that's not what showed up on the tape," she said. "When I got home and tried to play back my show there were two minutes of static and snow. Then the picture got clear and these monsters came on. They didn't do much. They just stood around and made clicking noises.

"At first I thought someone was playing a joke. But when I called the television station and told them about the tape they acted like I was some kind of a nut.

"Then I called the newspapers and they wrote about it. After that Dr. Wolfrath got in touch with me and asked if he could study the tape.

"I was glad to give it to him. It gives me the creeps. I'm still mad that I missed my soap!"

The tape has generated interest among scientists around the world. One expert French astrophysicist Philip Lemoine, says the tape — if genuine — is "the strongest proof yet that life exists in outer space.

"If we picked up one of their signals there's a good chance that they could be picking up ours," he added.

"If that is the case we'll do everything within our means to open lines of communications with these beings while we have this chance."●

☐ *Here's another original report. If Willie made this out of thin air, he needs to go to Hollywood where he's really needed. Not only is it interesting — it's convincing. I'm going to turn our satellite dish towards "The Pleiades" and see what happens. It's worth at least a 9.5*

SCIENTISTS EXAMINE BIGFOOT BABY

***Weekly World News*, October 10, 1989**

by Ragan Dunn

Dutch anthropologists claim to have captured a Bigfoot baby in southwest China. The boy is only a few weeks old. But he can already sit up.

He also has gigantic six-inch feet and is covered with a thick mat of brown hair!

"Bigfoot exists — and we have him," Dr. Jan Brader told newsmen in Amsterdam

"It is still too early to assess his intelligence but the creature is definitely smarter than an Ape. The only question in our minds is how long he can survive in captivity. He seems to be healthy and happy today but that could change overnight."

Dr. Brader and his team reportedly captured the baby Bigfoot while studying native cultures near Cangyuan, on China's border with Burma, on September 15.

The boy's Bigfoot mother actually turned, ran and abandoned the baby when the Dutch anthropologists stumbled on the lair in a forest clearing.

"The other was at least 8 feet tall and could have crushed any one of us with her bare hands," said Dr. Brader. "At first she stood fast and tried to frighten us away with horrible screams.

"When we refused to leave, she seemed to have a change of heart. She left the baby in the clearing and ran into the woods. Her maternal instincts were overcome by fear."

Dr. Brader said the baby showed no fear of humans and willingly returned to civilization with the team.

The Chinese government has a strict policy on the protection of its native cultures and would never have allowed the visiting anthropologist to leave the country with the Bigfoot boy.

So Dr. Brader risked his freedom, and possibly even his life, to smuggle the boy back to Holland.

The child is now the focus of an intensive scientific investigation in Amsterdam — where experts from four countries, including France and the United States, are trying to determine where the Bigfoot baby belongs on the evolutionary ladder.

"The boy isn't human. He isn't ape. He appears to be in between," said Dr. Brader. "He's only a few weeks old but he already weighs 32 pounds. He's as strong as a 5-year-old and he climbs like a monkey. He also appears to be a quick learner and can already drink from a cup. Sometimes I think we've found the missing link between humans and their ape ancestors."

Geneticist Charles Dekker is

assisting Dr. Brader in the study of the Bigfoot baby. And while he admits the experts are "navigating uncharted waters." He believes the boy will stand 9 feet tall as an adult — an weigh almost 600 pounds.

"This is one of the greatest scientific discoveries ever," said Dr. Dekker. "And as scientists we must exercise extreme caution in the study of the boy.

"We have no right to make him over in the image of a human or into something that we want him to be.

"We must let the Bigfoot boy develop as normally as possible. That is the challenge we face."●

☐ *At last we have a team of scientists who have managed to bring a baby Bigfoot back from the wilds of China to Amsterdam, Holland. How can one doubt the kind of information given in this article? For years we've been told to ignore this subject — it was for the birds! This baby is going to get a 10 until Dr. Jan Brader comes out and claims it was all a mistake.*

LOST CITY POWERED BY CRYSTALS?

***National Examiner*, August 22, 1989**

by Julie Golden

Incredible evidence that computers were used more than four million years ago by the lost civilization of Atlantis has stunned scientists around the world.

The archaeological discovery of an ancient computer made entirely of crystal is boggling scientists, who say it is far superior to space-age technology.

Records found in the excavated computer have convinced some researchers that it was built by ancient engineers from Atlantis, the legendary advanced civilization thought to have been destroyed by a flood million of years ago.

The staggering find was unearthed last year during an archaeological expedition headed by Linda Waldron, an expert in ancient civilizations. Investigations conducted over 25 years led Waldron to believe that the island of Bikini, off the coast of Florida, had been the hub of the Atlantian civilization during its golden age. The island is actually the tip of one of the world's largest undersea mountains.

"I had been excavating an underwater region off Bimini where several artifacts previously had been found at the opening of a sealed-off cavern," Waldron told the Examiner.

"On this trip, we finally gained access into the cave. It turned out to be a 30-foot-high, dome-like hall.

"A flat table-like structure made of solid quartz crystal was near the center of the room," the 43-year-old archaeologist explained. "It appeared to have fallen over, and an unusual shaped object, hidden by seaweed and sand, was resting against it."

At first, the expedition team couldn't identify the seven-inch hexagon-shaped object. Then, several months later while Waldron was examining it under sunlight, the instrument began to vibrate in her hands.

"I had rubbed my fingers across an unusual set of pink and green markings that are remarkably similar to the laser bar price coding used at supermarket check-out counters," said the New York City-based researcher. "The object began to give of a high-pitched frequency that eventually became inaudible to my hearing.

"That's when it began to transmit information. It turned out to be consistent with geographical data on volcano eruptions occurring in the area more than five million years ago."

Said the physicist who accompanied the expedition "We've never seen anything like it before. The computer memory is formed by the pattern of the crystal and is virtually indestructible. The records have been preserved."

The computer is apparently activated by a touch — sensitive mechanism charged with solar power and contains a kind of artificial intelligence that interacts with human brain waves.

"It literally reads your thoughts and transmits the information requested directly into your brain," Waldron said.

Scientists have compared the find with the discovery of the Rosetta Stone, which unlocked the secrets of ancient Egypt.

"Now we can finally learn the secrets of the lost civilization of Atlantis," Waldron said.●

☐ *Of all the articles on crystals — this is the one that makes me wonder if maybe it's really on the level. Somehow I feel as if I've read this tale a long time go — I think I'll give it a 9.5 just in case.*

RUSSIAN DOCTORS DELIVER ALIEN BABY

***Weekly World*, September 5 1989**

by Ragan Dunn in Geneva

Soviet doctors incredibly claim to have delivered the alien baby of one of nine extraterrestrials rescued from the wreckage or a starship in July!

The stunning development came to light in a classified report that was smuggled into Yugoslavia after the sensational story of the aliens rescue appeared in the *News*.

Yugoslav sources said the birth of the infant in a top-secret facility near Moscow took the Soviets by complete surprise. The newborn creature was so grotesque, they added, that doctors initially refused to believe that it could possibly be alive.

In an official memo addressed to Soviet research scientists, Dr. Sapar Kurylev said the newborn looked nothing like the adult aliens and that even they appeared to be shocked by its appearance.

"I supervised the delivery from beginning to end," he wrote. "But when the thing began to squirm and rear its head, all I could think was, 'Oh my God, it's alive.'

"It was so ugly and misshapen. It looked like a reptile, a reptile that sprang to life in the screaming agony of a nightmare." A log of the alien baby's progress and behavior contains four hourly entries followed by a handwritten autopsy order. It is not clear, however, whether the infant died of natural causes or was killed by scientists.

"The suggestion that the baby was killed may be between the lines, but it appears throughout the report," biophysicist Milorad Gusavac said.

"There is no doubt that the Soviets were shocked and maybe even a little frightened by whatever it was the alien mother brought into the world."

Gusavac said the infant's birth weight was 3 pounds, 7 ounces. It was slightly longer than 13 inches, and the shape of a football.

"It apparently had three appendages, legs or arms, that were covered with a thick coating of scales," he said.

"The head was similar to that of a lizard, with tiny black eyes, no nose and a single nostril. Skin color was described as being bluish."

As reported in *The News* earlier, the adult aliens look like human children with the exception that they don't have mouths and are covered with microscopic, flesh-colored scales.

The latest documents to surface in Yugoslavia made scant mention of the adult.

They did contain a brief reference to the mother, who reportedly recovered from the delivery of her baby within minutes and showed no remorse over the death of her child.

"It would seem that the aliens have recovered from the injuries they suffer in the crash and perhaps have been moved to another facility," said Gusavac.

"We knew their priority was to get them healthy so that they could concentrate on finding some means to communicate.

"If that's what they're working on now, let's hope they succeed soon. Maybe then the Kremlin will go public with all this — and give the world the whole story."●

☐ *The possibility of this being true is too great for me to discredit it. The quote beside it, from another paper, repeats the visual description. Those microscopic scales sound familiar and aliens often appear to do their talking by telepathy, but how the alien mother had her baby without any sex involved is about six chapters ahead of me. We seem to run into cases where a mouth cavity doesn't go anywhere. Whether they can take food through their body, or maybe their skin, I don't know. Their "innards" seem quite different from ours ... Ragan isn't going all the way to Geneva for less than a 9.5.*

ET POSSE CORRALS BANK ROBBERS

***National Examiner*, Sept. 5, 1989**

by Gus Vandermeer

A quartet of desperate bank robbers are safely behind bars thanks to a law and order posse of extraterrestrials.

The robbers staged a bold daytime holdup and made a clean getaway. But they hadn't reckoned on the long arm of the law being able to reach them all the way from outer space.

In fact, the police were as surprised as the bandits when the getaway car, with the robbers and loot inside, materialized on the steps of the local jail, says Detective Ramon Puentes.

"You should have seen the looks on their faces," says Puentes, who happened to be there when the car suddenly appeared.

"Of course, I guess I must have looked pretty amazed myself," he adds. "I had absolutely no idea what was going on."

But Fernando Alvarez, a UFO researcher investigating sightings in the mountain near where the robbery took place in northern Peru, knew instantly what had happened when he learned the details.

"As soon as I found out, I knew I had to interview the robbers," he told a Mexican freelance reporter.

"I immediately suspected they had gotten too close to a UFO base and the aliens simply moved them to a place where they wouldn't be any more bother—jail."

The robbers, Zavier Leal, Francisco Sanchez, Edwardo Tolendano, and Juan Jose Garza, confirmed Alvarez's suspicions.

"We had the perfect hideout in the mountains. No one could ever find us there," Sanchez told Alvarez. "We saw UFOs going in and out every day.

"It's like an airport up there. Of course, the authorities deny there is an such thing. But how are they going to deny it now?"

The robbery went perfectly until the robbers decided to take a different route to their hideaway just to make sure the police would not be able to trace them there.

"That seems like it was our big mistake because we almost ran into three UFOs parked right on the road," said Sanchez. "Actually, they seemed to just pop up off the ground when we got close, so we wouldn't have hit them.

"Suddenly there was a glowing light all around us. The next thing I knew we were sitting in the car in what seemed like a huge hall with lights blinking and flashing. And then all of the sudden we were on the steps of the jail. I was almost glad to be there. At least I knew where I was."

Alvarez believes that the extraterrestrials teleported the car aboard the spacecraft, but when they realized that, the men inside the car were robbers, the ETs made them all rematerialize where the police couldn't possibly fail to capture them — the police station!

"We have been after these men for quite some time," says Puentes. "I'm not saying that Alvarez is right, but I have no other explanation that can account for how they appeared out of thin air.

"What I would really like to know is if there is any way we can get the extraterrestrials to make this a regular practice.

"It would certainly make our job a lot easier."●

☐ *There ain't no way I'm not going to give this 10! It's possible, plausible, and practical. There is much evidence of many UFO bases. A few more hijacked bank robbers deposited at police headquarters could make UFOs mighty popular in Peru.*

MAN BURNED BY UFO
***National Examiner*, Sept. 19, 1989**
by Wayne Diaz

A stunned vacationer was horribly burned by a UFO when he tried to talk with its inhabitants.

Stephen Michalak originally believed the flying saucer was an experimental aircraft experiencing mechanical problems. But when he approached the object a jet of hot air scorched his shirt and chest, reveals UFO expert Timothy Good.

Michalak watched the UFO land in a secluded area near Falcon Lake, on the Manitoba-Ontario border while vacationing in the area in 1967, says Good, author of *Above Top Secret: The World-wide UFO Cover-Up* (Grafton Books, England, 1987).

Michalak watched the 12-by-5-foot object for nearly half an hour, then a door opened on the craft and he heard two human-sounding voices inside.

Believing the object to be an Earth craft, Michalak called out and asked the unseen visitors if they needed help.

Receiving no answer, Michalak approached and began examining the outside of the craft. The lower rim of the vehicle suddenly shifted and Michalak saw what appeared to be an exhaust vent.

Without warning, Michalak was struck with a blast of hot air, which set his shirt on fire. He stumbled backward, tearing off at the seared clothing and watched the mysterious craft silently fly away.

As he started the long walk back to his hotel, Michalak's head began to throb and he was overcome with nausea. He took the next bus home and promptly entered the hospital.

The physical symptoms of Michalak's close encounter were severe, Good notes. He was unable to keep food down for weeks, and he lost 22 pounds. His blood lymphocyte count dropped briefly, and he was stricken with what appeared to be hives.

Most peculiar, however, was the strange gridlike burn pattern on his chest-shaped exactly like the mysterious exhaust vent from which the blast had come.

Dr. Horace Dudley, former chief of the Radioisotope Laboratory at the US Naval Hospital in New York, speculates that Michalak received a short, intense blast of radiation with X-rays or gamma rays.

If this is the case, Dudley adds, Michalak was lucky to survive this encounter. Longer exposure would almost certainly have killed him.●

☐ *I want to include this article because I have one like it. In 1965 Jimmy Flynn tried to help a UFO he thought was in trouble. Fortunately he was unable to get close enough to be burned.*

When he tried to signal, he received a ray of light in the forehead which both blinded him and left him unconscious for nearly 20 hours. He too, spent a week in the hospital. Stephen gets a 10 from Jimmy!

INCREDIBLE POWERS FROM ALIENS
***National Examiner*, Sept. 19, 1989**
by Glen Troelstrup

An amazing clairvoyant got her incredible powers from aliens.

A frightening encounter with a UFO changed her from being an average kid into a remarkable psychic.

"The beings I met in an English meadow still contact me regularly, in my dreams," says Jean Reynolds Franklin.

After her strange UFO experience in 1937. Eight-year-old Jean alarmed her parents by accurately predicting the deaths of friends and relatives.

"I even had a dream in which I foresaw WWII, including the evacuation of Dunkirk, and the German V-bombs," Jean recalls.

She adds "With the aliens' help, I've been able to publicly predict, years ahead, such phenomena as the great droughts in Ethiopia and the hole in the ozone layer."

She recalls: "I learned not to talk about these things at school because the other children would call me mad and pelt me with stones. But sometimes I felt it was my duty to speak out!"

During the 1940 London Blitz, she had a terrifying sense of coming disaster only seconds after joining neighbors in an air raid shelter.

She begged them to leave it.

"But they laughed at me, so I left alone," she says. "Next morning, I learned that a bomb hit the shelter, killing the entire family."

Jean's first UFO contact came after looking up to find what she then called a large, silver house on stilts looming over her. A platform descended and three tall men dressed in red, stepped down. One carried her inside the UFO.

"I was frightened and wanted to escape," she recalls. "But I couldn't. My limbs seemed frozen.

Jean says the UFO's exterior was the size of a small house but its interior appeared much larger.

She recalls being placed in a molded chair, facing a dazzlingly bright light and experiencing unique thoughts and visions. Then she was taken to an enormous pyramid and wandered its dark corridors for hours until she found a door which opened to the meadow where she had been.

Jean, now of Hobart, Tasmania, foresees a bright, largely peaceful, and prosperous future for mankind.

She says there'll be many UFO sightings soon, leading to thousands of space aliens walking among us; aircraft will be wingless there'll be world government and two-hour work weeks, and industrial ugliness will give way to majestic buildings, parks and forests.●

☐ *The psychic Uri Geller says his psychic abilities began when he was a child after having contact with such craft. Based completely on my own judgment, I must give this a full 10. Many times I have given a lower number than I thought it deserved.*

VAMPIRES FROM SPACE DRANK OUR BLOOD!
***Weekly World*, March 14, 1983**
by Laurel Bowie

Two terrified miners were captured by a band of thirsty space aliens who drained more than half a gallon of their blood and greedily drank it down!

Mystified miners Sergio Razuri and Fernando del Pozo said the bug-eyed vampire aliens also took samples of their skin, hair and fingernails before setting them free.

"We don't know if they were doing some sort of scientific research or what," a shocked Sergio, 41, told reporters in Lima, Peru.

"But they sure seemed eager to drink our blood, and when they did, they really seemed to enjoy it. In fact, they almost fought over it as they passed it around."

The victims' spine-chilling adventure began as they crossed a remote region of Peru's Altiplano Plateau while conducting a mining survey.

"We came over a rise and there was their spaceship sitting there on metallic tilts like something out of a science fiction movie," recalled Fernando, 48.

"Our jeep sputtered, then stalled, and suddenly we were surrounded by seven or eight little aliens, all of them about 4 feet tall with big eyes and silver skin.

"They pulled us out of the Jeep and hustled us up a ladder and onto the spaceship. They were very firm, very businesslike."

The peewee ETs strapped the horrified miners to separate tables and drew more than a quart of blood from each of them.

"They nearly drained us dry," said Fernando. "They had two huge beakers of our blood, and they started passing them around for everyone to drink, like some big party.

"They'd been so somber, but when they started drinking they got smiles on their pinched little faces. It was a very frightening experience."

Once they'd guzzled down the blood the pint-size vampire aliens took skin scrapings, nail clippings and hair samples from the miners, then ushered them back to their Jeep.

Still trembling from their erie encounter, the men drove to the nearby village of Uncaypa to report the incident to authorities.

"I've examined both these men and they appear to have been through quite an ordeal," said village doctor Miguel Vela Sanchez. "As strange as it seems, I'm certain they really were the victims of vampires from another planet."•

☐ *I hate to tell you — but I believe this article deserves a 10.*

HUMAN SKELETON ON THE MOON
***Weekly World News*, Nov. 28, 1989**
by Ragan Dunn

America's Apollo 11 lunar module photographed a human skeleton on the moon when it landed there in 1969.

That's the blockbuster claim of Chinese astrophysicist Dr. Kang Maopang, who first stunned the world when he released pictures of bare human footprints on the moon at a news conference in Beijing last winter.

The scientist claimed to have received those photos which were so secret the Apollo 11 astronauts didn't even know they existed from "an unimpeachable U.S. source."

The photograph of the human skeleton was included in a second batch of photos and documents he received from the same source this fall.

"The Americans have conspired in a cover-up of monumental and possibly even criminal proportions," Dr. Kang told newsmen in Beijing.

"They hid photos of bare human footprints on the moon for 20 years and managed to keep the human skeleton secret even longer.

"The implications of what they found up there are staggering," he continued. "But the Americans apparently felt that nobody else in the world is privileged enough to share the information."

Dr. Kang's allegations stunned U.S. space and intelligence experts, one of whom went into hiding after reporters tried to question him in a Washington. D.C. restaurant.

Other sources also refused to comment — even when told that the Chinese expert has copies of over 1,000 NASA photographs that clearly show bare human footprints and a human skeleton on the lunar face.

Intriguingly, the skeleton appears to have been wearing jeans. Judging from the position of bones, it seems likely that the person it belonged to was at least partially dismembered and met with a violent death.

It is also probable that the skeleton was transported into space long after the person was killed. The decomposition of bone and flesh would not have been possible in the airless atmosphere of the moon.

The Chinese expert further noted that the age of the skeleton cannot be estimated without analyzing the bone firsthand.

"Like the footprints on the moon, these photos were taken by a remote camera aboard the lunar lander and were given to me by an American source who is beyond reproach," said Dr. Hang.

"I am also in the possession of classified documents and letters that describe the footprints as being fresh and the skeleton unquestionably human.

"The question that must be answered is how the footprints and skeleton got to the moon. The obvious implication is that extraterrestrial lifeforms were involved but we'll never know unless the Americans release all the information they have."

The documents Dr. Hang quoted from are stamped "top secret" and dated Aug. 3, 1969, which means they were written just two weeks after astronauts Neil Armstrong and Buzz Aldrin landed and walked on the moon — in boots — on July 20, 1969.

Large portions of the text have been blocked out. But it's clear that U.S. experts agreed extraterrestrials had something to do with the bare footprints and skeleton on the moon.

Repeated attempts to get officials at any level of government to address Dr. Kang's report were unsuccessful.

Explained a Washington source: "Nobody's going to say anything until President Bush gives the go-ahead. This isn't any ordinary cover-up. It makes Watergate look like a Sunday School picnic. It's that damn big."●

☐ *I think this is another example of the way our government feeds us information. First they give it to a well-respected foreign scientist so he can send it back to us. A percentage of people will be aware of the news, others will be sure it's "pure bunk" and will carefully avoid it. It's probably a clever idea. "Information" by a somewhat similar method is the way material was given to Bill Moore. It barely makes a ripple on the thought waves around us. Another 8 until we see the blue jeans!*

FURRY GREEN ALIENS PANIC GOLFERS

***National Examiner*, November 7, 1983**

by Glenn Troelstrup

Furry green ETs have terrorized golfers on three separate occasions.

Astonished U.S. and other players have encountered the strange six-and-half foot-tall, monkey-like creatures at a famous international course.

"It was unreal — from out of the mist came these three bright green creatures!" says John Harris, of Taupo, New Zealand.

The breathtaking sighting happened as he and two friends were about to tee off at the famous Wairakei course, 140 miles southeast of Auckland.

"The things actually stood still for awhile. But when we got about 55 yards away, they took off.

Their recent amazing experience came several months after we U.S. golfers spotted the bizarre ETs, but were too afraid of ridicule to report them. Only later were they aware of a first sighting in 1984.

"We saw some movement in the bush up to the left," says expert golfer who asked to be identified only as Chuck. "As we got closer, we spotted what looked to be a couple of big hounds — only they were green.

"We carefully moved closer, but then they spotted us, made a weird, high pitched, squeaking sound, and darted into the trees."●

☐ *Kinda cute — particularly if you can see the picture that goes with it. A 5 for the little green aliens.*

GOVERNMENT CAPTURES UFOs

***National Examiner*, Dec. 19, 1989**

by Stanley Donaldson

One of America's top aviators is convinced that the government has captured at least 30 UFOs.

And, he says many have been test-flown by American pilots. John Lear, the son of Lear jet inventor William Lear, is a renowned airline captain who has flown more than 150 different types of aircraft over the years.

The one craft he has not flown however, is a flying saucer.

But other pilots have, Lear states — as a result of a top secret government program called Protect Redlight.

According to Lear, who says he has contacts within the government intelligence community, more than 30 UFOs have been acquired by federal agents since 1947.

And not all of the craft were captured following a crash. "The U.S. government has been in business with little gray extraterrestrials for about 20 years," Lear states.

"In exchange for technology we promised to ignore their abduction of humans and mutilation of cattle.

The space aliens snatch people, Lear explains, because their digestive systems have started to die, and they need human hormones and enzymes in order for their race to survive.

The ET's process human and animal parts in giant chemical-filled vats located in underground alien bases around the world.

Three of these bases, states Lear, are believed to be located in New Mexico.

"We are in deep, serious trouble and the public need to know about it now," he warns.●

☐ *Laugh all you like, if this makes you feel good. But — this is more or less the story I've been getting for some time. In order to reach more people, articles such as this one need to be fed to them. It is only the repetition, and the assurance that this material is coming from high sources, that will eventually convince readers that it is time to wake up. Worth about a 10.*

UFO DOGFIGHT
Weekly World, **December 26, 1989**
by Marc Jubert

Spectacular starship dogfight lasts 57 minutes, say stunned eyewitnesses.

Three alien starships engaged in a spectacular dogfight and disintegrate in midair in the first known battle between UFOs ever!

The stunning aerial assault was witnessed by more than two hundred African villagers who watched for nearly an hour as the eerie scene unfold lighting up the night sky over Kenya.

French aviation expert Louis Bujon arrived in Kenya with a team of researchers one day after the incident occurred.

"Never before has there been a UFO encounter that was so well documented," Bujon told newsmen.

"We also have confirmation from Cairo that the three craft appeared on military and civilian radar screens and vanished simultaneously." Bujon said his researchers have interviewed dozen of witnesses — including tribal chief Karanja Njoroqe and will remain in the field until all those who saw the dramatic incident have been contacted.

According to Bujon, villagers in the Rift Valley north of Mount Kenya noticed an unusual light in the sky at about 9:20 p.m.

Bujon said that a second light suddenly appeared beside the first and then both began to take shape as UFOs as they slowly descended toward Earth.

"By this time there were between 200 and 300 people watching from the ground," he said. "They described the approaching craft as round brightly-lit objects. At this point a third craft, much larger than the others, approached rapidly from the south."

According to eyewitness accounts, the larger UFO fired what appeared to be beams of light at the other two craft, destroying one.

"The remaining saucer circled around and returned fire with what we can only assume to be some type of laser weaponry from the descriptions that we have received," Bujon commented.

"At precisely 10:17 p.m. both craft disappeared in a tremendous flash of light."

Bujon said he does not believe the explanation offered by some scientists that what the villagers actually witnessed was a meteor shower.

"Evidence does not support that conclusion he said. "This as a skirmish in an interplanetary war. •

☐ *Wouldn't you like to think that aliens have learned not to fight like dogs and men? Not likely. The Bible reminds us that there are forces of light and forces of darkness. No matter what it was, this is one more article that tells us of aliens who like to point things at each other and watch what happens. With two to three hundred people watching for an hour this ought to be worth a 9.5.*

CHRISTMAS MESSAGE
Weekly World, **Jan. 2, 1990**
by Irwin Fisher

American scientists have reportedly received a Christmas message from a dying planet. Portions of the 45-second transmission were garbled.

But it clearly stated that the extraterrestrials who sent it had visited Earth. It went on to warn that men must learn to live in peace before we destroy ourselves and our planet just as they have destroyed their own.

"It's almost as if we received a Christmas message from God Himself," said a Washington-based intelligence source familiar with the message.

"We picked it up at listening post in Puerto Rico and California on December 15. And while we have yet to determine exactly where it came from, there are strong indications that it originated from a planet in our own Milky Way.

"There is absolutely no possibility that the message is a hoax. The radio telescopes that picked it up are aimed into space and are designed to ignore signals that originate on Earth."

U.S. officials refused to discuss the message for the record in spite of the fact that it came to light in a report published by Dr. Werner Kanbach, the radio astronomer from Wiesbaden, West Germany, and was confirmed by the intelligence source.

Dr. Kanbach refused to say where he got his information. But it is commonly known that he has served as a consultant to Americas' space program since the late 1960's.

According to Dr. Kanbach the alien Christmas message was received at 12:03 a.m. Eastern time on December 15.

Parts of the transmission were unintelligible. But Dr. Kanbach provided this transcript.

"Greetings... wishes to the planet Earth... season of peace... harmony, destruction of our planet and species... warning... learn from our mistakes... war and hatred here and on Earth... your fate will be ours... act before it is too late."

"Portions of the message are missing, but the thrust is clear," said Dr. Kanbach. "A dying extraterrestrial civilization is most interested in the future of our planet.

"They are warning us to mend our violent and aggressive ways before we destroy ourselves like they have destroyed themselves.

"We have no way of knowing exactly what happened on their planet But it certainly seems that they waged global war and fear we will one day do the same.

"The implications of such a message are almost beyond belief," continued the expert. "These aliens have literally given us a glimpse of our own future.

"They have also given us a chance to change our way before it is too late."

Repeated attempts to get copies of the tape or a more detailed analysis from U.S. officials were denied.

And after his initial report and interview, Dr. Kanbach refused to discuss the message further apparently under pressure from American intelligence operatives in West Germany.

Meanwhile, UFO organizations around the world are calling for "full and immediate disclosure of all the facts."

"The message is for all men," UFO expert Karl Scholz said. •

☐ *Don't tell me you don't know people who would flip their lids if they were sure this message really took place! This looks like a clever way of letting you know the truth. It's worth at least a 9.5, probably more.*

10,000-YEAR-OLD UFO FOUND IN JUNGLE
***Weekly World News*, April 3, 1990**
by Boyd Ray

Soviet scientists claim to have found a 10,000-year-old starship in the African jungle — but there's more.

Strange metal documents recovered from the site indicate that the space aliens who brought it here went on to establish a colony.

And that means their descendants might still be living on Earth today!

"This is a scientific discovery of the first magnitude," Dr Alexei Ivanov told scientists and newsmen at a conference in Moscow.

"The spacecraft alone proves that extraterrestrial life-form had the technology and desire to reach our planet thousands of years before the pyramids were built in ancient Egypt.

"And the documents indicate that they had every intention of establishing a colony that might still be here today.

"The value of what we have learned cannot be overestimated," he continued. "It could change forever the way we think about ourselves and the universe."

For security reasons Dr. Ivanov refused to pinpoint the location of the ship, but he did say that it was found in the jungles of Uganda on February 19.

He described the craft as being U-shaped with downfolded wings ending in huge cargo-carrying pontoons. He said the starship was 250 ft. long and in remarkably good condition considering that sophisticated dating tests show it to be at least 10,000 years old.

"It was completely dismantled on the site so that we could bring it to the Soviet Union for study," continued the expert.

"The unusual metal documents are also under scrutiny. We haven't been able to translate any of the text.

"A series of pictures inscribed in the metal shows a band of tall, slender humanoids starting on a journey north.

"The pictures also show these humanoids at work and play in a village of pyramid-like huts. That seems to indicate that the extraterrestrials did in fact colonize Earth.

"Because these documents show the aliens living in pyramid-like structures, we are also considering the possibility that their descendants eventually migrated to Egypt and helped design and construct the pyramids there more than five thousand years later in 2700 B.C."

Whether the alien colonists interbred with humans, died out or went into hiding are key questions that the Soviets will try to answer as they study the starship and documents in the months and years to come.

"It is also conceivable that we can duplicate the technology that we find in the starship and build a similar craft of our own," Dr Ivanov told reporters.●

☐ *This UFO has been mentioned by the* News *in another article. It's about time you start taking it seriously. I do. Another 10.*

UFO STEALING ISLANDS?
***Weekly World News*, January 9, 1990**
by Damon Ray

Aliens are stealing tiny South Pacific islands at the rate of 15–20 a year.

That's the claim of geologist Halston Schultz, who says extraterrestrials suck the islands into the holds of massive starships and "take them to God knows where."

"It's theft, plain and simple," Dr. Schultz told newsmen in West Berlin. "None of the stolen islands were inhabited. But it's only a matter of time before these aliens take an island with people on it."

The expert's report touched off a storm of controversy among scientists, some of whom said there is little or no basis for his claims.

Dr. Shinltz countered the skepticism with a mountain of evidence including a confidential CIA report that says 45 to 60 South Seas islands — some no bigger than pinheads on a map — have mysteriously vanished in the past three years.

The documents say "that there is almost certainly an alien connection.

"It makes sense," said Dr. Schultz. "If aliens came from another planet to study Earth, they would definitely want samples of our soils.

"By taking entire islands they would also get thousands of animals, insects and microscopic life-forms to study.

The islands that have vanished have been small and in many cases unnamed.

"Sailors first noticed that they were vanishing in 1987. At the same time airline and air force pilots from several countries began to report seeing numerous large UFOs near Fiji and American Samoa, the area where the islands disappeared.

"The implication is that these spaceships have the ability to pull entire lands into their holds with some kind of antigravity device or tractor beam," said Dr. Schultz.

"There is no other explanation."

U.S. officials would neither confirm nor deny that the secret documents obtained by Dr. Schultz are genuine.

Privately, one source conceded that the CIA is investigating the disappearances of small islands southwest of American Samoa. "Something's going on out there."●

☐ *Remember that UFOs can pick up most anything — you haven't forgotten those 26 elephants that were plucked out of the zoo, have you? It's a good bet some of those big stones in the pyramids had a little help of this kind.*

Don't throw this out unless you're darn sure you're right — it deserves about a 9.

UFO BABY READS MOM'S MIND
***National Examiner*, January 20, 1990**
by Chet Antonini

A baby born with amazing powers is the offspring of an alien, says his proud mom.

The little boy, named Klaus, is shocking doctors by his ability to read his mother's thoughts, levitate high into the air, and move toys with his mind.

"I had a feeling something could be different about this baby," said mom Doris Lehn. "I was pregnant for 11 months."

When Klaus was born doctors were intrigued by his fine features and uncanny strength.

"He looked more like a miniature adult than a baby," said Jason Marer, who delivered him.

"And within a few days he was playing with toys hardly designed for a newborn."

When he was only two weeks old he successfully put together a complicated jigsaw puzzle. Then, as his mom stood in open-mouthed astonishment, Klaus made each little puzzle piece march back into the box.

But at six months, the little guy made his mom shriek in terror when he levitated in mid-air after falling off a jungle gym.

"I couldn't believe my eyes — he was just hanging there," he recalled. "After a few moments he gently touched down."

Since then, there have been three other occasions when baby Klaus has hovered in mid-air, just above his crib.

The most recent incident was witnessed by the family priests. "I almost fell out of my chair when I saw it!" said Father Patrick Dalgleish.

"It's obvious Klaus has supernatural powers. I still can't believe what I saw!"

Doris says Klaus is the result of a mating that took place aboard an alien spacecraft.

"I was walking home one night when I saw a bright light in the sky above my head. The next thing I remember was lying in a dark room surrounded by a strange TV monitor and flashing lights. The memory is vague but I'm sure that's when I became pregnant."●

☐ *The story is beside a picture of a beautiful baby named Klaus. This is one more article that claims an infant is able to levitate and move objects. If this is so, it's time someone else got busy with an investigation. Somewhere, somehow, someone knows whether there's any truth to this report. It's up to that person to come forth with the information that isn't printed here. This is only worth a 5 without more facts.*

U.S. PILOTS FLYING CAPTURED UFOs
***National Examiner*, April 10, 1990**

Alien starships are being tested at a maximum security government base in Nevada, says a top scientist.

"What they've got at that base is actual physical contact with another planet and an alien intelligence," says engineer Bob Lazar who worked at the hush-hush desert fortress codenamed S-4 in the 1980s. "It's real, it's here and it's now.

"What's going on there is one of the most important events in world history."

Lazar says that every day he and other scientists were piled into a windowless bus and driven to the remote compound nestled in the mountains near Groom Lake.

Heavily armed guards then led them to their laboratories housed in enormous camouflaged hangars with sloping doors that held captured alien flying saucers.

"When I first saw one of the crafts I was spellbound," the scientist says. "But I was gruffly told to keep my eyes to the front and to walk quickly past it.

"Later I got to see it in operation. The bottom of the globe glowed and hissed like high voltage does on a round metal sphere. Then it slowly lifted off the ground.

"There was no noise, no exhaust, no propeller. Even the hissing stopped at about 20 or 30 feet.

"I saw a total of nine saucers, each one different, so I gave them all simple names. There was the top hat, the jello mold, and the sport model. There was even one that looked like a guided missile.

But Lazar says he will never forget the shock he felt when he was first allowed to look inside one of the craft.

"It had really small seats," he says. They were tiny, like they were made for children — or very small alien creatures, he noted.

Before making his sensational claims public, Lazar and five others sneaked past the grim-faced security guards to videotape the craft in flight.

The amazing footage shows one of the craft soaring above the mountaintops before disappearing.

Lazar claims are backed up by other scientists who say that salvaged alien discs are routinely stored at the test site. A form of radar operator at the base claims he once clocked a UFO doing 7000 mph. Then he was ordered to turn off his radar sensors.

Lazar says he was later subjected to intense psychological pressure to keep him from talking about his work.

"The government is terrified that the secrets of base S-4 will leak to the American public," he declared.●

☐ *You'll find this same material given on the "We The People" program on WCCF radio, Punta Gorda, Florida and a couple of hundred other stations it reaches. If you go back and look at former news presented by the* National Examiner *and other tabloids, you'll realize you should have known this long ago. A 10 for the* Examiner.

NAZI ASTRONAUTS RETURN TO EARTH
***Weekly World News*, April 17, 1990**
by Nelson Mann
(Special Correspondent)

Nazi astronauts launched into space on a suicide mission ordered by Adolf Hitler in 1943 have returned to Earth 47 years later!

That's the word from NASA sources who say that the three space pioneers were in surprisingly good health after their splashdown in the Atlantic on April 2 and are now being interrogated at an undisclosed military facility in the United States.

The sources added that NASA is studying the Nazis' bulb-shaped space capsule in an attempt to figure out how the astronauts — now in their 60s — survived the impossible mission.

"It's incredible, but the astronauts haven't aged a day since they left," said a NASA insider.

"We've got thousands of questions and very few answers," he said.

"The simple fact that Hitler and the Nazis launched men into space in the 1940s is mindblowing enough," he continued. "But the fact that the astronauts survived a 47-year flight is almost beyond human comprehension.

"There's no telling what we can learn from these men. I do know that they are going to put us light-years ahead of the Soviets, just like the Germans were light-years ahead of us."

NASA, military and government officials angrily refused to discuss the report, promising to "ruin" a reporter who accused them of a cover-up.

The insiders themselves admitted that details are sketchy. But they confirmed that the Nazi astronauts were launched into deep space on a suicide mission ordered by Hitler himself.

The rocket that propelled the men to space had three stages and was a modified version of the powerful V2 rockets Germany used for bombing missions during World War II.

Both versions were designed by German rocket specialists who were instrumental in developing Soviet and American space programs after the war, including Werhner von Braun.

"Von Braun knew the Nazi astronauts were up there but to my knowledge he never said a word about it," said the second NASA source, who knew von Braun personally.

"Of course, he never expected them to return to Earth because they were on a suicide mission. Their space capsule was equipped with heat shields and parachutes for re-entry and splashdown but that was apparently for show.

"Before they were launched from the German rocket base at Peenemunde, Hitler sent them a telegram that they still have today. He thanks the men, who were then in their early 20s, for making "the ultimate sacrifice' for Germany. Hitler obviously expected them to die in space."

How the astronauts managed to survive the marathon space mission and get their capsule back to Earth are mysteries that may not be solved for years to come, said the sources.

When U.S. naval vessels picked the men up in the Atlantic their space capsule contained neither food nor water, the sources explained.

"We don't know what the hell went on up there. In a way, it's like something out of the "Twilight Zone," said the first source. "We don't know where the capsule went — it certainly wasn't orbiting Earth or we would have spotted it decades ago.

"We don't know what the astronauts ate and drank. either. We've been throwing around a lot of terms like 'black hole, time warp. suspended animation, even extraterrestrial intervention.'

"The fact is, we don't have any explanations."●

☐ *That "Special Correspondent" impresses me. There is nothing to gain by printing such an article and everything to lose. I have found that much material which the* News *has printed is true. Therefore to print this stuff without reason would be ridiculous. Einstein has told us what would happen to someone who spends years in space — this isn't the first time evidence of "not aging" has been shown in this book. Our government is getting desperate — they must start telling the truth, and you must start accepting scientific facts. A 10 for the* Weekly World.

UFO VEGGIES
***Sun*, April 10, 1990**
by Maurice Bender

A farmer whose gigantic 20-lb. tomatoes are as big as pumpkins says he learned the secret of growing monster vegetables from green-thumbed space aliens!

Grateful Mario Cordato claims the aliens' amazing growing method saved his failing farm from certain bankruptcy.

"And the amazing thing is growing huge vegetables is so simple," says the 47-year-old farmer and father of six.

"I don't know why I never discovered it myself. I owe everything to those men from the heavens."

A team of government agricultural experts has visited Mario's farm and confirmed that his vegetables are out of this world in size, color and taste.

Mario's crop yielded tomatoes weighing from 12 to 23 pounds and zucchini ranging from two to three and a half feet long. One head of lettuce was larger that a basketball and weighed more than five pounds.

"Not only are the vegetables unusually large in size, their nutritional content and flavor quality is excellent," says state official Hector Redonda.

"However, Mr. Cordato is being difficult about revealing his secret.

"He keeps insisting that he was taught how to farm superior vegetables by space aliens. This, of course is outrageous."

Investigators are now testing the soil of Mario's 40-acre farm which lies northwest of Melo, Uruguay hope to identify unusual chemicals or fertilizers that could be responsible for the miraculous harvest.

But Mario claims they're searching in vain.

"I learned the secret last May," he recalls. "My harvest had been pitiful and my wife and children had gone to a special evening Mass to pray for a better crop.

"I was sitting in the field when I spotted a shooting star. It kept getting bigger and suddenly I realized it was coming towards me. It settled in a nearby grove of trees.

"I was frightened but curious, so I ran over. When I got there, I found a large metal sphere about 25 feet high. A door opened and three man-like creatures came out.

"They were no more than five feet tall and wore silver suits. Their skin was very white and they had no hair or ears."

"I don't recall them making any sounds, but it seemed like the were talking in my head."

Mario claims the space aliens told him the correct time to plant, the pattern of plowing and the exact amount of fertilizer to use.

"They said timing and positioning is everything when it comes to growing crops," he says.

"And the exact time and position varies each year. Before the left, they promised to return this year to instruct me for my next crop, Mario adds.●

☐ *How do I know there's a state official named "Hector Redonda" in Uruguay?*

I don't and neither do I know whether those 12- to 23-pound tomatoes are "for real." I do have a feeling that "space beings" are going to teach us a lot of things — this may be one of them. You'd better believe ETs have been here before and helped make us what we are today and probably will continue to be a part of our history — forever. And that's a long time — a 10 for the Sun.

UNDERWATER UFO BASE FOUND IN PACIFIC

***Weekly World News*, May 8, 1990**

by Nicolai Dubinin

The captain of a Russian destroyer stared in amazement as a 30-foot-long metallic-looking cylinder rose slowly out of the sea and hovered silently in midair 50 feet away from his ship.

Then the eerie object shot upward effortlessly and veered off toward the open sea as if driven by incredibly powerful rockets that made no sound.

The incident is one of 200 sighting of UFOs that emerge from under water, all fully documented by a special scientific commission that was appointed by the Soviet government to investigate UFOs.

The sighting was reported by Captain Nikolai Petrov, the commander of the 9,000-ton destroyer Vladimir Vorobyev. It occurred about 2 a.m. Jan. 16, 1990, in the Sea of Japan off the port of Vladivostok.

"Capt. Petrov reported to naval authorities that he had found evidence of an underwater base manned by aliens from outer space," said Dr. Boris Azhazha, head of the special UFO commission.

Petrov told officials the UFO was metallic gray, with no visible potholes.

He said he watched it for more than three minutes as it bathed his ship in a glow like moonlight. After six more encounters with UFOs, all within the same 20-square-mile area in the Sea of Japan, Capt. Petrov submitted a 160-page report of what he'd seen.

In his report, he described a 600-foot "mother ship," also cylindrical, which he said is the home in space for the underwater UFOs.

"Twice he had observed the mother-ship and watched it deliver its cargo of flying submersibles," Dr. Azhazha said. "The smaller craft were squeezed out of the mouth of the cylinder as if it were a toothpaste tube. The returning craft were sucked in the opposite end."

In another startling case, a UFO popped out of the water and actually scraped the hull of a Soviet exploration vessel near the Kamchatka Peninsula.

"The ship got quite a jolt as the spacecraft emerged," Dr. Azhazha said. "There was no damage to the ship or to its expensive electronic equipment, although everybody on board was shaken up.

"The record of the incident was signed by the captain, every member of his crew and all 20 members of the scientific expedition aboard.

"The aliens would like to have bases on Earth goes without saying," he said. "But hiding from us is not easy unless they're under water."

He speculated that the UFOs may be carrying out explorations to find new sources of minerals.●

☐ *I can't begin to tell you the importance of this article. The* Weekly World *carries a picture of the Russian destroyer Vladimir Vorobyev. Everything in this account could be checked and probably has been.*

It was a comparable sighting, back in the days of Bluebook that convinced Dr. Allen J. Hynek that UFOs were truly with us and that our government was using him to assist in their cover-up. The biggest difference in these two reports is that Hynek's tale was given by a shipload of American military, while this 1990 report is from the crew of the Japanese Navy and their scientists. Numerous books and articles lead us to conclude that there are UFOs which are able to go in and out of the water and others that indicate actual underwater bases. Some suggest a tie-in with former civilizations such as Atlantis and Lemeuria. A wonderful way to give this information to the public without having to admit it's true! A 10 for the Weekly World *and "probably" another 10 for our government!*

CRYSTALS

What do you know about crystals?
They are used in various ways.
Many places use them for healing,
It usually improves how they're feeling.

They're beautiful around your neck,
Are made into dangling earrings.
I would hate to be without my light,
And it's crystals that dazzle, with color, at night!

I hear that crystals have lots of power,
But I don't know what they do —
I'm not very knowledgeable about such stuff,
I haven't studied them long enough.

I do know they've been found in the ocean,
And appear to influence certain things.
It is said they send out lots of power,
It's good we don't buy it by the hour!

The Aliens carry a crystal gadget,
That works like a TV set.
When it's held within your hands —
It triggers pictures at your command.

You can see way back in history,
When our earth was very young.
It shows just what has happened to us —
No wonder folks make such a fuss.

It also shows where the Aliens live,
And what their development has done.
I'd like to rent one for a whole weekend —
It certainly sounds like fun!

CHAPTER FIVE

Reincarnation — Dreams — Possession

Reincarnation or the Recycling of Souls 130
A Dream Come True 130
Ohio Woman Reborn After 76-Year Interval — *Weekly World* 132
Pacochea 132
Two-month-old Baby Speaks 8 Languages — *Weekly World* 133
Civil Rights Leaders Reincarnated as Holocaust Victims? — *National Examiner* 133
Girl is Reincarnation of Movie Star — *Weekly World News* 134
Reincarnation of Chieftain's Son — *Weekly World* 134
Baby Boy Born With Wooden Leg — *Weekly World* 135
Coma Man Wakes Speaking Ancient Greek — *Weekly World* 135
Baby Born Wearing Dead Dad's Ring — *Sun* 136
Baby Born Talking — *Sun* 136
Born With Ring — *Weekly World* 136
Is Boy Reincarnation of Robert E. Lee? — *Weekly World* 137
I was Billy the Kid — *Sun* 137
Born Wearing 3,000-year-old Anklet — *Weekly World News* 138
Born Again — *Weekly World* 139
200-year-old Bullet Found in Baby's Chest — *Weekly World* 139
Boy Thug Returns as Dog — *Weekly World News* 140
Living Two Lives — *Weekly World* 140
Death of a Soldier — *Weekly World* 141
Dead Dad Reborn as own Son — *Sun* 141
Baby Born Speaking in Dead Dad's Voice — *Sun* 142
Murdered Child Reborn — *National Examiner* 143
Sally — Reborn as Ruth 143
Reincarnation Nightmare — *Weekly World News* 144
Baby Girl Locates Fortune — *National Examiner* 144
Dead Girl Reborn as Younger Sister — *National Examiner* 145
Memories of Zachary Stoddard — *Sun* 145
Machine to Recall Past Lives — *Weekly World* 146
The Reincarnation of Natalie Wood — *Sun* 146
Baby Born with Artificial Heart — *Weekly World News* 147
John and the Oxen — Poem 148

REINCARNATION OR THE RECYCLING OF SOULS

Why am I going to show you a series of reincarnation experiences? From 1949–52, your government had an alien—not Alf, but another one—hidden away as a guest, one who was able to give much knowledge in many directions. One of his disclosures was on the recycling of souls, or reincarnation. The alien has been described as child-like with the mind of a thousand men.

Linda Howe's new book, *An Alien Harvest,* will tell you all you need to know and more than you want to hear. She is just one more person who has been used like putty in the hands of her government. Someone has to do this job; she's done it well.

For some years I've been convinced President Reagan would do all in his power to release UFO news—he did—now President Bush is doing his part. You are given news on this subject every day.

Linda Howe published only 1,000 copies of her new book. It is not a beginner's book. It is by far the most knowledgeable material on the market. When you're given the facts but no confirmation for those facts, you can't prove what you know. It's very clever: those who want to know will know, and those who can't take it will grasp for floating straws.

A DREAM COME TRUE

When I was in the third grade 70 years ago, I sat across the room from a blond curly-haired boy. Nearly fifty years later we met again. He was a math professor at Ohio State University; I was writing UFO articles. Dr. Merriss Cornell had dreamed of a childhood so unlike his own that he wanted to find out what caused it. He could see a town, the houses and the people. He could feel dirt squish between his toes; no matter where he looked he found nothing that resembled those in his dream.

One day he thought, "The next time I dream that dream I'm going to try to find out the name of that town." That's the way to do it! He hypnotized himself. Sure enough, the next time he had the dream his mind told him, "I wish I knew the name of this town." Instantly, he knew it was Gates Mills. He forced himself to wake up and write it down. That ended his dream—but it didn't solve anything. He had no idea where "Gates Mills" might be. One day while looking at a map he noticed a Gates Mills east of Cleveland, Ohio. He wondered if that could be the place.

When he told me about his problem I suggested we ask a friend if he would try a little hypnosis on Merriss. John Reich, a CPA, had a hobby of using hypnosis. We rounded up a dozen friends and circled around to watch what would happen.

Merriss was an excellent subject, he went under so quickly John felt he was pulling his leg. He remedied that by getting a needle and giving him a few sharp jabs. Having been told he wouldn't feel anything, Merriss didn't flinch. Then he was told to relax and think about his former dream. He was asked if he would like to know more about it—the answer was "yes." He was given the suggestion to go deeper and deeper asleep. John said, "I want you to put yourself back into the dream as you have experienced it. Can you tell me your name?"

Merriss: *Rellie.*
John: What's the rest of your name?
Merriss: *I can't remember. It's Sh... it's a hard name.*
John: How does your mother say your name?
Merriss: *Loud!* (John had to give up.)
John: How old are you?
Merriss: *Eleven.*
John: Do you have brothers or sisters?
Merriss: *I think I am alone.* (He did describe a boy friend named Rick.)
John: What does your father do for a living?
Merriss: *Bends wires, bends wires, rakes.* (Later we found there was a hay rake factory that had burned in 1904.)
John: Tell us about your mother.
Merriss: *She's pretty.* (Wore her hair up in a bun on her head.)
John: Where do you go to church?

Merriss: (A traveling minister came to town but not every week.)
John: Can you describe your house?
Merriss: (Describes a "widow's walk" on top of the house. There was lots of carving on his house.)
John: Can you tell me about your bed?
Merriss: *It rattles!* (Probably corn husks.)
John: Do you go to the store for your mother?
Merriss: *Yes.*
John: Do you buy bread? (Trying to trick him.)
Merriss: *No.*
John: Do you buy your food in cans or boxes?
Merriss: *Boxes.*
John: Tell us what you see in the store.
Merriss: *A big block of cheese on a wooden table and a coffee grinder.*
John: Describe your grocer.
Merriss: *He has a beard.* (His name was McIntosh.)
John: What year were you born?
Merriss: *1880.*
John: How old were you when you died?
Merriss: *About 16.* (In this life Merriss was born in 1911. Children who die early in life often are born again within a few years. This happened in another case.)
John: What caused your death?
Merriss: *Pains—pains in stomach and side—everything got black.* (Probably appendicitis.)
John: Where were you buried?
Merriss: *Cemetery outside of town.*
John: Describe your tombstone.
Merriss: (motioning in a curve) *Round on the top.*
John: Will you read the name on your tombstone? (Trying everything to get last name!)
Merriss: *Rellie.* (Couldn't get more.)

When I found his tombstone it was round on the top and said "Rellie 1880–189?," I couldn't tell whether it was a 5 or 6, it was sandstone and so worn. There was no last name. Later I found that children often were buried with the parents names on a stone beside them. It was quite common at that time. Apparently his parents left "Gates Mills" and there was no one to take responsibility for that lot. I went back twice to try to check records. The second time I was told the grave had been destroyed and sold to a new owner. No name showed up on the lot number. The store had burned down; even there I could find no records. All I could find were the ornate houses with their bric-a-brac and decorations.

Merriss told about going into the city with his father in a spring wagon. When asked about the name of the place—he spelled (without being asked) "Cleaveland." This is the first time we knew it was in Ohio. A friend who was with me was a retired school teacher. The following day she dug out some books and found that Rellie could spell—Cleveland had been named after Moses Cleaveland. The spelling was later changed to Cleveland for mapping purposes.

I believe "Gates Mills" dates back to 1820. It was a true experience; I felt I was going back in history. As we drove into the graveyard on a sloping hillside, I saw some small rounded tombstones and walked to the first row at the lower side of the slope. I didn't look at more than three markers before I found one that said "Rellie 1880–189?". I couldn't tell for sure about that last 5 or 6!

As you read the following articles perhaps you'll understand why I gave so many 9's and 10's.

OHIO WOMAN REBORN AFTER 76-YEAR INTERVAL
***Weekly World,* March 6, 1990**
by Susan Jimison

Nothing has been the same for 41-year-old Georgia Rudolph since she went on a trip two years ago—and visited the town where she died in 1914!

The Atlanta divorcee knew she had lived there before when she recognized every turn in the streets of Marietta, Ohio, and could find her way unguided from one end of town to another.

She could describe buildings that had stood there in the early 1900s when she lived in Marietta as Sandra Jenkins.

"It's not spooky to me anymore, but at first it scared me to death," said Mrs. Rudolph, a nurse. "I didn't believe in reincarnation—it went against my teachings.

"But after my trip to Marietta I couldn't let this thing go. It was a fixation with me. I don't know what reincarnation is, but I know this has taught me a lot."

The plump brunette says the first indications that she had lived before came when she began having flashbacks to her other life at the age of 5. In a recurring dream, she saw herself standing in front of a church in a long white dress. She was about 15 years old. From the church she walked several blocks to a cemetery, following a path to her grandmother's grave.

"I've had the dream about 800 times," Mrs. Rudolph said. "Sometimes I dream it once a month and then I dream it over and over again. It's very clear."

When she began to draw, she often drew the same picture, the mother-of-one recalled. It was a young woman wearing a light green dress of the Victorian era, with high neck and long sleeves. All through her life, she would remember names of people and places she'd never seen.

The name "Marietta" was among these. Only when it occurred to her in 1979 that "Marietta" was a place and not a person did Mrs. Rudolph make up her mind to visit the town. That visit changed her life.

"I thought something was seriously wrong with me," she said. "I went to a psychiatrist who hypnotized me back to my early childhood and that's when Sandra came out. I told the doctor I was Sandra Jean Jenkins and that I was 12 years old. I was born in 1895."

In later hypnosis sessions, Mrs. Rudolph found out Sandra had drowned herself at the age of 19 after her boyfriend died, leaving her alone and pregnant. A search of Ohio records turned up little information on Sandra, but did confirm that a Jenkins family had lived in Marietta.

"I found a 1908 family photograph with an unidentified girl in it," she said. "The girl looks about 13, just the age Sandra would have been at that time. I'm convinced it's her.

"And when I went back to Marietta, I found the cemetery and the church from my dream. I found a house and garden belonging to the relatives of the Jenkins—just like the one I used to draw as a child."

Mrs. Rudolph believes many people have lived other lives but are afraid to admit it. She's speaking out in the hope that she can convince others to talk about their past lives, too.●

☐ *Note the similarity of this research and that of Dr. Merriss Cornell of Westerville, Ohio—a 10 article. Perhaps you saw this shown on* Unsolved Mysteries?

This next article was one I had published on November 24, 1960. I had several cases which were remembered in a dream or by conscious thoughts. This is one where the woman actually hypnotizes herself in order to find out the truth concerning her experience. If she had used a hypnotist no doubt she would have remembered much more.

PACOCHEA

How far does your memory reach into the past? Sometimes events in our lives jar the sub-conscious until we conjure up mental pictures which do not belong in this life. Many of such experiences stem from recollecting dreams which keep hammering away at our minds.

Others seem to be brought into reality by circumstances which remind us of experiences which may have happened to us in a previous time, or existence.

Recently a friend of mine mentioned how at the age of nine or ten, she had been hit in the head with a portion of a cow-stall which had come loose from the fastenings. The animal, being of a nervous disposition, struck the wooden stanchion so that the child was knocked unconscious and suffered a serious concussion.

After a few days of hovering between life and death she pulled through the ordeal and slowly came back to normal. One of the first things she said to her mother was this wasn't the first time this had happened to her.

Her mother assured her that she had never been injured before but the girl insisted. She could remember an accident when she was very young. In her mind was a picture of herself at the age of not more than three.

She said horses were running toward her and that they trampled her beneath their feet. She saw blood running from her head and face; all this seemed so real that she was positive this event had actually happened.

Her mother questioned as to other memories of her life; all were quite accurate except for this description. Even though she has nothing to confirm her story, she will never relinquish the idea that such an event happened to her.

My comment was this: "Why don't you concentrate and tell me just what happened one moment before this experience and also afterwards?" If memory tells us such a thing, there is no reason not to know more than one scene of this event. Her answer was that she had never thought about it.

She sat and concentrated and before long said, "I see wigwams and a big kettle boiling on a tripod. There are horses running and it looks like a stampede. I have a long dress on and I am very little. The horses knocked me down, injuring me seriously."

The next thing she remembers is a woman whom she knows to be her mother running toward her. She is taller than the mother she has known in this life, yet she is sure that this woman is also her mother. The woman wore a long black dress and cried frantically "Pacochea, Pacochea."

When she reached her, the child saw fear and horror written all over her face. She knew that her mother stooped to pick her up but from then on her mind drew a blank.●

☐ *If you feel that a certain experience happened to you, try to remember other details which may also lurk in the shadows of your mind.*

TWO-MONTH-OLD BABY SPEAKS EIGHT LANGUAGES
***Weekly World News*, Dec. 15, 1987**
by Kathryn Hruska

A baby girl who speaks eight languages has child development specialists baffled, but experts on reincarnation have an explanation for her bizarre talent—they say she has lived before!

Two-month old Sofia Petkov of Pleven, Bulgaria, has aroused interest and controversy among scientists in Eastern Europe. She became famous when her doctors reported in the Journal of Child Psychology that the little child can speak fluent Latin, English, Spanish, French, Bulgarian, Lithuanian, Russian and an obscure Arabian dialect of ancient Egypt.

Videotapes of the child's abilities have been sent to major universities in communist bloc countries and experts have been invited to comment.

"At an age when most children can barely form basic syllables, Sofia has mastered complex languages," said Dr. Boris Androchov, a child psychologist specializing in language skill formation.

"Never has there been a case of such extraordinary dimensions.

"We have studied the child carefully and can offer no explanation for her advanced development. We have never seen anything like this before."

The head of Moscow's Reincarnation Society is convinced 11-pound Sofia was born with her extraordinary abilities. Nicolai Tovashpin says the child has lived many times before and has brought her knowledge of languages from previous lives along with her at birth.

"Her parents, Ivan and Aleksandra, say that the child appeared to be listening intently to them from the first moment they spoke to her," Tovashpin said.

"Her first sounds were recognizable words and they came early, when she was just a week old.

"The parents report their daughter was speaking in full sentences in one month and that she was using several languages by that time. She described memories of living in other places and other times. She appears very intelligent and can carry on a conversation in all eight languages."●

☐ *If this one bothers you pretend the* News *made it up. If not, try the next column on for size—I've watched my subjects under hypnosis as they were regressed into other lives! It's interesting, to say the least. That baby deserves a 10 if the* News *isn't kidding us.*

RIGHTS LEADERS REINCARNATED HOLOCAUST VICTIMS?
National Examiner
by Christopher Luke

Tens of thousands of baby boomers—many of whom are active in civil rights and the peace movement—are reincarnated Jews who died in the Holocaust.

That's the amazing revelation of religious leader and paranormal researcher Rabbi Yonassan Gershom.

Gershom heads the Shevet Shalom (Tribe of Peace) ministry in Sandstone, Minn., a group that combines traditional Jewish rituals with New Age teachings.

He says he has met over a hundred people who believe they died in the Holocaust, with more coming forward every day.

"The majority, born between 1946 and 1953, are now in their mid-30s and 40s," he notes. "It is possible these souls came back as quickly as they could to work for peace on earth so that the horrors they had been through could never happen again.

"It is no accident that World War II was followed by the civil rights movement, the peace movement, women's liberation, and other struggles for equal rights."

Gershom says most of the people he's met with past-life memories of the Holocaust are not Jewish this time around.

They have come to believe they died in the Holocaust through every possible means, including dreams, visions, deja vu, past-life readings, intuition, spirit guides, automatic writing, and psychotherapy.

"Some cases are more probable than others," he explains. "Some interviews seem to click and send shivers through my soul, while others do not."

Gershom emphasizes that these reincarnations could have major implications on the future of mankind.

If these people's stories are true, the world could be moving toward an era of unprecedented peace and love.

Says the rabbi: "World War II could have been Armageddon, which would mean we are now moving toward the Messianic Age."●

☐ *I'll give it an 8.*

GIRL IS REINCARNATION OF MOVIE STAR
***Weekly World News,* April 25, 1989**
by Laurel Bowie

Stunned psychic researchers are convinced a glamorous movie star killed in a tragic car crash is alive again—in the body of a shy 3-year-old girl!

Remarkable little Nandi Weeakodny is so familiar with the life of former film queen Rukmani Devi that she can recite thousands of the dead actress' lines word for word.

"The evidence is so overwhelming there can be no doubt that this girl is the reincarnation of Rukmani Devi," investigator Dudley Sabaratnam told reporters in Amparai, Sri Lanka.

"She has told us so many things about Rukmani's life that are true but were never made public—so many things she could have known only if she had been Rukmani in another life.

"And you have to remember that she's a 3-year-old baby and could never be coached to pull off a hoax of this magnitude."

Radiant Rukmani was the Liz Taylor of Sri Lanka before a horrifying head-on car crash snuffed out her life near the village of Amparai where, a year later, little Nandi was born to businessman Bandula Weeakodny and his wife Sirimavo.

"Nandi seemed perfectly normal to us until one afternoon when we turned on television to watch one of Rukmani Devi's movies and suddenly our little girl was reciting the lines right along with Rukmani," her mystified mom recalled.

"She was only 2 at the time and she'd never seen the movie before, but she knew every line by heart.

"After that, every time she saw a picture of Rukmani or saw her on television, she'd say, 'That's me, Mommy, that's me.' And she told us the most detailed stories about Rukmani's life and things the actress had done."

Eventually, Nandi's parents asked Buddhist reincarnation experts to look into the dark-eyed child's puzzling past. And researchers were staggered by what they found.

"What we have seen here is truly amazing," said investigator Sabaratnam. "This girl even told us what Rukmani was wearing the day of her accident—details that never appeared in any newspaper.

"She's told us about Rukmani's childhood and about her romances and about her squabbles with directors and fellow stars. She is wise and knowledgeable far beyond her tender years," he said.

"When we add it all up, there is only one conclusion: This child has provided the most incredible proof of reincarnation the world has ever seen."●

☐ *I'd be lying if I didn't think the kid deserves a 10. There are many cases that have been recorded by well-known doctors in our country.*

REINCARNATION OF CHIEFTAIN'S SON
***Weekly World,* May 28, 1989**
by Valerie Rae

In an amazing case of reincarnation, a 6-year-old girl startled her parents by recalling her previous life as the son of a village chieftain.

Not only did little Gayani Gunawardene convince her parents of her past life as a young man named Bandara Pannamp, but she led them to the village of her previous life.

And she solved the mystery of how, as a young man, she had died in 1969—14 years before she was born in her present body in 1983.

Even more startling, she revealed where she had been during the 14-year gap between her death and her rebirth.

"I was in the sky like a bird," said little Gayani, who lives with her parents in Columbo, Sri Lanka.

"But I was not a bird. I was just floating like a bird."

Gayani's mother Manel and father Lionel had no inkling of their toddler's previous existence.

And when Gayani began talking about her grandmother, the parents thought it was just wishful thinking—because Gayani's grandparents were dead.

Then Gayani began babbling strangely about her other father, her grandmother, the place she had lived, her life as Bandara and how he had drowned.

Finally, an uncle convinced her parents to take the 75-mile trip to the village Gayani talked about.

When the family arrived at the village, an excited Gayani yelled "Stop," leaped out of the car and ran to a house. She banged on the door and when an elderly man answered, she jumped into his arms yelling, "Father, I am your son Bandara."

Her parents explained what was happening to the stunned older man, who was the village chief. He let little Gayani guide him through his house pointing out things that she couldn't possibly have known.

When the little girl grabbed a small wooden elephant from a shelf and identified it as her old toy, the old man burst into tears and hugged the girl. "My darling son Bandara, you have indeed returned," he said.

Later, Gayani told her first father and current parents how 25-year-old Bandara had died. Police had found his body in a drainage ditch and assumed he had accidentally fallen in and drowned.

But Gayani said Bandara was jumped by robbers who beat him and tossed him into the ditch where he drowned.●

☐ *Libraries have cases comparable to these by well-known doctors and specialists in this field. Take a good look at them. If this is a hoax the paper still deserves a 10.*

BABY BOY BORN WITH A WOODEN LEG

***Weekly World*, April 4, 1909**

by Ragan Dunn

Incredible new proof of reincarnation, say experts

Scientists say the birth of a baby with a wooden leg is the most dazzling proof of reincarnation ever!

"This is it—this is the proof we've been waiting for," Dr. Karl Magnusson, the paranormal researcher, told newsmen in Halden, Norway.

"The baby was born on March 2 with one normal leg and another made of heavily-weathered oak. Analysis has proved beyond doubt that the wooden leg is at least 250 years old.

"That means it was made and initially worn in the 1700s when pirates sailed the high seas."

The report Dr. Magnusson gave touched off an immediate controversy among scientists, several of whom suggested the 7-1/2" wooden leg might have been fitted on the child, 8-1/2 lb. Tore Frederickson, after he was born.

But Dr. Magnusson produced strong evidence to support his claim, including an eyewitness report from Dr. Carl Jorgen Haland, the obstetrician who delivered the baby.

"I brought the infant into the world with my own hands and I still have a hard time believing what I saw," said Dr. Haland. "The mother's pregnancy proceeded without a hitch.

"The delivery of the baby—head first, legs and feet last— was flawless. But when he emerged from the womb there was the peg leg attached by a leather strap firmly above the knee.

"The stump itself actually had a nasty scar. It looked as if the infant had lost the leg and had it stitched up by someone other than a doctor."

Martha Frederickson, the baby's 18-year-old mother, was not available for comment, but Drs. Magnusson and Haland confirmed that she had been treated for shock.

Meanwhile, Dr. Magnusson was consulting with several reincarnation experts to determine how to go about studying the baby without interfering with his development.

"The infant will almost certainly have memories of a past life when he is old enough to speak but we must proceed carefully with our study," said the expert.

"The potential for psychological scarring is really quite pronounced when you're probing the past life of a child, especially when the physical evidence—the stump of a leg—is there for him to see.

"In that regard we will do everything possible to help the child lead a normal life. He will be fitted with a modern artificial limb as soon as he is old enough to walk.

"And he has already gone home with his parents, although their address cannot be made public because they don't want to be hounded by reporters.

"Above all, they do not want their baby's leg photographed. He is, after all, a human being—not a freak."•

☐ *This one gets a 10 as soon as I see the wooden leg.*

COMA MAN WAKES SPEAKING ANCIENT GREEK

***Weekly World*, May 24, 1988**

by Ragan Dunn

A truck driver who snapped out of a four-month coma speaks ancient Greek—and thinks the year is 500 B.C.!

Now, Harland Baker, 53, is the focus of an intensive scientific investigation. Experts say he may be living proof of reincarnation.

"The Harland Baker who slipped into a coma in January is not the Harland Baker who woke up four months later," psychologist Birger Gayan told reporters in Agen, France.

"The man we are dealing with today has no recollection of his own life.

"He truly believes that he is a merchant who lived and died 500 years before Christ was born."

The truck driver's incredible transformation began when he sustained head injuries in a car crash and went into a coma on January 4, said Dr. Gayan. The man didn't suffer any permanent damage.

But when he awoke on April 14 he insisted that he was a Greek merchant named Pasalaris.

He spoke an ancient Greek dialect rather than his native French, requiring a university expert to translate. He didn't even know his own wife or son.

"The transformation was complete," said Dr. Gayan. "Mr. Baker—Pasalaris—almost went into shock before he got used to his surroundings.

"He pined for ancient Athens and constantly inquired about his Greek colleagues, family and friends. When his own wife tried to hug him, he recoiled and accused her of being a harlot."

Historian Isidore Gregoire interviewed Baker and called his knowledge of ancient Greece "phenomenal."

"He is a living, breathing textbook," said the expert. "We're going to learn a great deal from him. And yet I'm told he has only a high school education."

Dr. Gayan is now examining historical texts in hope of finding references to a merchant named Pasalaris so he can check Baker's story.

"What he tells us holds up under hypnosis," he said. "But finding independent confirmation would go a long way toward proving that he really is the merchant incarnate.

"I really do have mixed emotions about all of this," he added. "If Mr. Baker has become a merchant from ancient Greece, we have a golden opportunity to study reincarnation, not to mention our notions of how people lived and thought 25 centuries ago.

"On the other hand we would have lost Mr. Baker. His family would be devastated."•

☐ *If it happened, it's a 10. There's about eight chances out of ten that it did. However, this may also be another case of body snatching, rather than a life he has lived...after accidents the owner of the body sometimes deserts its vehicle and a waiting soul see his chance to get back into the physical.*

BABY BORN WEARING DEAD DAD'S RING
Sun, **November 15, 1988**
by Robert Webb

A newborn wearing a wedding band around his fingers astounded doctors who don't know how it could've gotten there when it was buried with the baby's father!

Brandon Hoeffe came into the world with the gold wedding band that once belonged to his father Martin, who died a few months before in an auto accident.

The ring, which included Martin's initials and the wedding date on the inside, is believed to be a symbol of Martin's reincarnation as his son.

"Martin has returned to me as my child, it's a reincarnation miracle!" the baby's mother Agatha, 26, cries with joy.

Reincarnation expert Phyllis Eilsen agrees.

"Reborn souls often provide a sign as they leave Heaven," she explains.

"It can be in the form of a birthmark or unexplained knowledge.

"But this is extraordinary! A material transformation from a past life!"

Dr. Nels Rudgran delivered the infant at Agatha's home near Bremen, West Germany, with the help of Agatha's sister Diedre.

"I pulled the infant out, then handed it to Diedre," the doctor recalls. "When I next looked at the baby, the ring was on tightly around its fingers."

The band wouldn't come off and they were concerned about cutting off the circulation in the fingers, so they rushed the baby to the hospital where doctors were finally able to remove it without causing injury.

The doctors say the baby is lucky to still have his fingers, and charge someone deliberately put the ring on after birth.

"It's possible the ring was taken from the coffin before Martin was buried," Dr. Rudgran admits. "Maybe Diedre wanted to make her sister feel better and believe her husband was still with her.

"She could've put it on while I was looking at Agatha but that would've been only for a few seconds, and I remember seeing the ring on Martin's finger during the funeral."●

☐ *There are too many cases of this kind to throw out the rings, bracelets, and wooden legs. Another 10 as far as I'm concerned.*

BABY BORN TALKING
Sun, **January 24, 1989**
by Arthur Dale

A baby's first words proved the last word in his parents' stormy relationship. Before a delivery room full of shocked witnesses, the newborn disputed his dad's claim to fatherhood

"Instead of crying, the little guy looked directly into his papa's proud face and said 'You're not my father!' " swears Dr. Bernard Kondash.

"The poor guy was devastated and, needless to say, we were all stunned."

The 8-lb. 4-oz. boy hasn't blurted a word since his birth. But his opening line was more than a mouthful as far as Joe Mucheck is concerned.

The 20-year-old mechanic's rigorous work schedule kept him away from home for long periods, and he suspects his wife of cheating.

In fact, when wife Tonelle broke the news of her pregnancy, he did a bit of quick math and says the numbers didn't quite jibe with his travel schedule.

But thoughts of fatherhood nevertheless made him a happy man. "I believed a baby could make things all right." Joe recalls. "What a fool I was. She's been a cheater all along—I know it!"

Tonelle, 25, denies any wrongdoing, but isn't heartbroken over the split.

"Any man who believes the mumblings of a newborn baby can't be playing with a full deck," she says from her home near Debrecen, Hungary.

She believes people in the delivery room were hearing things. "I don't have to defend myself," says the angry mom.

Joe wants no part of either mother or child. "It's time to start a fresh life," he says bitterly.

"Would you want to play father to a boy who doesn't even recognize you as his dad? It pains me that she had the nerve to name him after me."●

☐ *There are other cases like this—a baby girl gave another name and date from long ago. This too, did not last. The family hoped to use hypnosis when the child was older. How about a 9?*

BORN WITH RING
Weekly World, **August 16, 1980**
by Ragan Dunn

An obstetrician says he delivered a baby girl with an engagement ring on her finger!

"As God is my witness that child was wearing a diamond," Dr. Rolf Wendel told reporters in Hasselholm, Sweden.

"We delivered her by Caesarean section and she had it on when we pulled her out. She held up her little hand as if to display it. Then it fell off.

"A lot of people say this is proof that the child was reincarnated. Maybe she was, maybe she wasn't. All I know is that she was born healthy and happy with a ring on her finger.

At least six nurses and assistants claim to have seen the exquisite Victorian diamond after it hit the floor in a Hasselholm hospital and rolled under a heart monitoring device.

One other witness, Nurse Birgitta Stern, said she saw it on the child's finger before it slipped off.

Neither the child nor her parents were identified in reports.

In a statement issued through the hospital they confirmed that Dr. Wendel and his staff had presented them with the ring — a size six — which has been appraised at over $25,000.

Jeweler Sven Jansson told reporters that he would buy it on the spot. He says the ring was crafted in Spain around 1875. The central diamond is surrounded by six smaller diamonds and the diamonds total weight exceeds 2 carats.

Paranormal expert Marianne Lindgren has spoken with the parents about the possibility that their child has lived before and somehow brought the ring into her new life.

"We are watching the child's behavior closely for any sign that she has lived before," said the expert.

"So far she hasn't done anything out of the ordinary. But I suspect that she'll provide us with a wealth of knowledge when she is old enough to speak and think on her own."

Medical historian Peter Schultz noted that there are at least a dozen other instances of reincarnated souls bringing material possessions into their new lives.●

☐ *Would you pay $25,000 to create a hoax of this kind? The baby or parents will certainly keep the ring—you'll have to admit it's a good trick. Your only chance is to say the whole event never happened. In that case it's a 1, or a 10, take your choice.*

BOY, 2, IS REINCARNATION OF GENERAL ROBERT E. LEE

***Weekly World News*, February 7, 1989**

by Laurel Bowie

A baby born in rural India speaks English with a Southern drawl and is so familiar with the U.S. Civil War that experts are convinced he's the reincarnation of Confederate General Robert E. Lee!

"There is no question that this child is the great General Lee reborn," said top psychic researcher Sieghard Ehlen, 60, who's studied the astonishing tot for the past nine months.

"In my many years of work, this is the most convincing case of reincarnation I've ever seen."

The tot

— speaks little of his native tongue, but chatters on and on in English, a language he's never heard in India;

— has the accent of a Civil War southerner, spicing his speech with words like "y'all" and "y'heah";

— salutes where shown pictures of Confederate soldiers;

— constantly asks researchers to bring him "Traveler," General Lee's horse;

— refuses to answer to the name Chander—but responds eagerly when anyone calls him "Lee" or "General";

— snaps to attention when he hears the song "Dixie";

— gazes intently at pictures of famous Civil War battles—and identifies the battles with unerring accuracy.

"When he started rattling off the names of those battles, like Gettysburg and Antietam, that's when we knew for certain that we had a genuine case of reincarnation," Ehlen told reporters. "There is simply no other explanation for that, or for so many of the other things we've seen in this child."

The chubby-cheeked little Chander came to the attention of experts after a village doctor took him to specialists in New Delhi to find out why he was babbling in English.

"My colleagues in New Delhi recognized that there was something unique going on with this child and they summoned me," said Ehlen, a West German psychiatrist and reincarnation researcher.

"I quickly realized this was the most exciting case I've ever encountered."

Ehlen said he's been granted permission to take the amazing babe to his clinic in West Berlin for further study over the next year.●

☐ *Maybe it's a hoax, then again maybe it isn't! It's a 1 or a 10. If you ask your favorite alien he'll tell you it's a 10.*

I WAS BILLY THE KID

***Sun*, March 22, 1988**

Billy the Kid secretly buried a treasure in gold and jewels just before his death, and now a woman who claims she was the famous outlaw in a previous life is a millionaire after finding the incredible stash.

Marsha Thompson, 34, is a housewife who became a fan of hypnotic regressions after taking a class near her Vancouver, British Columbia, home.

Most of the past lives she experienced with the help of hypnotist Arthur Kelvell were all quite boring, she explains.

However, one recent regression put her smack in the middle of the bloody Lincoln County War of 1878, where Billy the Kid sealed his reputation as the West's most murderous punk.

Historians are at a loss to explain Marsha's find, but she certainly can.

Hypnotically regressed to her past life as Billy, Marsha says the treasure was a payoff he planned to use as getaway money.

He had it with him at the old Alexander McSween home in Lincoln, NM—site of a three-day siege before the house was burned to the ground.

Everyone but Billy was killed, and despite the raging fire he managed to unearth the stash of gold bars and jewels he had buried in one corner of the kitchen.

The Kid had secretly amassed the fortune, which Marsha found without a minute's hesitation.

Billy had buried the leather bag containing the treasure near a rocky outcrop like an Indian's face, about 40 inches below the ground, in the desert about five miles from the battle scene.

"Dr. Kelvell had regressed me a dozen or so times over the last few months, and I was having a ball with the experience because I'm a history buff anyway, and this regression business is just a real insight into what things were really like back then," says Marsha, the mother of two.

"But all of the lives were ordinary. I'd be washing clothes, or trapping furs, or wandering along some road in France trying to steal an apple. Nothing very exciting.

"Except, a couple weeks ago, I found myself in the middle of this gun battle, flames all around, and other men dropping like flies around me."

Without realizing it, Marsha lapses into the persona of "Billy the Kid."

"I ran into the kitchen to dig up the treasure, and ran for safety," says Marsha, a bank auditor.

"I was the only one who got away and the place burned to the ground. I hid it so I could go back for it in case I was caught.

"But after that, Pat Garrett stayed on my tail and I could never get back. I figured I'd go back after the treasure some day, and take the money to Mexico.

"Then, of course, Garrett ambushed me in a hotel room, and shot me to death before I even saw him. And the gold and jewels waited all these years for me to come and get them."

Marsha shakes her head, realizes the lapse, and grins at her luck.

The leather bag contained more than 100 gold coins, gold chains weighing about three pounds, and 43 diamonds, emeralds and rubies set in rings and necklaces.

"Billy the Kid" never robbed banks or trains, and historians are at a loss to explain how he got the treasure.

Owners of the property are claiming ownership of the stash, says Marsha.

However, on her lawyer's advice she had obtained a signed agreement allowing her to keep 90 percent of her find.

What will she do now?

"Pay for my kids' college, buy a car, and spend time finding out who else I was," she says, laughing.●

☐ *Maybe Marsha planted all that loot in the desert so she could prove she had been Billy the Kid? Not likely—she ought to get at least a 9.*

BABY BORN WEARING 3,000-YEAR-OLD ANKLET

***Weekly World News*, March 29, 1989**

by Laurel Bowie

Amazing baby Aisha Sabry was born with a tarnished, 3,000-year-old Egyptian anklet on her tiny leg—and experts say the mind-boggling birth provides the most astonishing evidence of reincarnation the world has ever seen!

"This is sensational. It's the proof we've been waiting for," psychic scientist Herman Gallad told reporters in Alexandria, Egypt.

"This child has lived before. There is no other logical explanation for all the circumstances present here.

"She has given us all a reason to rejoice."

Dark-eyed Aisha came into the world January 3 in an Alexandria hospital, the third daughter of Egyptian janitor Mohsen Sabry and his wife Kamala. Dumbfounded doctors say the birth was perfectly normal except for the ancient anklet found dangling from the baby's leg.

"The anklet was obviously very old and much too large for a baby's ankle," said Dr. Osman Rashad, who delivered the bouncing babe. "It could have slipped right off her leg during birth but for some unexplained reason, it didn't.

"We were all flabbergasted, to say the least. Since there seemed to be no medical explanation, we asked the people at the Institute of Alexandria for help."

Stunned scholars examined the strange silver anklet and found it bore the cartouche—or emblem—of King Ramses II who ruled Egypt from 1292 to 1225 B.C.

And archaeologists, using a sophisticated dating process, have determined that the mind-boggling relic is indeed more than 3,000 years old.

"There is no doubt that it is authentic," said noted scientist Mahmoud Badawy.

"It is a very ornate piece of jewelry from a very opulent period in Egyptian history.

"It's precisely the type of ankle ornament worn by Ramses' favored ladies. The only questions now are, is this one of the King's ladies reincarnated? And if not, how did the anklet wind up on the body of this newborn, 30 centuries later?"

But to reincarnationist Herman Gallad and other experts in the supernatural, the answer is obvious.

"We have never had such clear and convincing evidence of reincarnation or transmigration of the soul as we have here," Gallad said.

"Try as they might, the doubters will be able to find no other possible explanation.

"This discovery should be a time of rejoicing for all of us. We believe if this child has lived before and will live again, so will you and I."●

☐ *The aliens who have been asked, tell us this is true. I'm not sure how many 3,000-year-old anklets it will take to convince about 50% of our population. The anklet gets a 10.*

BORN AGAIN

***Weekly World*, February 14, 1989**
by Sharon Fader

In a startling case of reincarnation, an 11-year-old girl who died in a motorcycle accident has been reborn! Incredibly, experts and family members say little Inoka Shamalee is the reincarnation of Milani Chandrika, who died eight years before Inoka was born.

"I was Milani's fourth grade teacher and knew her well," said Gana Jayakody of Minuwangoda, Sri Lanka.

"This little girl knows things only Milani could know. And she talks in the same manner as Milani. I am stunned. Milani died many years before, yet after talking to this little girl it is as if Milani has come back to life."

Indeed, Milani's parents are convinced that their daughter has been reborn in little 4-year-old Inoka.

Inoka identified Milani and Milani's relatives from old photographs. And she wandered about Milani's village pointing out areas Milani frequented when she was alive.

More shockingly, Inoka pointed out the exact spot where Milani was killed on a motorcycle.

Yet Inoka was born in the village of Pethiyagoda eight years after Milani's death and had never been to the dead girl's home in Minuwangoda.

And she's only 4, and unable to read any newspaper or article that could have referred to the dead girl.

Born to a poor family, Inoka first shocked her parents, M.S, and Rota, when she began talking about her previous life as Milani, whose family was in a higher economic class.

"It was much better," Inoka told her parents. "We had electricity, painted walls and a large radio."

She talked of having brothers and sisters named Shamlie, Bandu, Sudu and Loku.

Finally, her parents took Inoka on the long trip to Milani's village.

Inoka insisted on visiting the temple and chief priest Loku Hamuduruwo. It turned out that the priest had been the dead Milani's religion teacher.

He was stunned when Inoka began talking to him of things that only Milani could have known. Then Inoka went to Milani's house.

"Where is my doll?" she asked Milani's mother Mahima.

Then she asked for "her" marbles and glass bangles, toys that were dear to the dead Milani. Then after a long talk and many questions Milani's mother embraced Inoka as her long lost daughter Milani.●

☐ *All of these reports have had pictures and names of people who are discussed in the articles. It's much more impressive—another 10.*

200-YEAR-OLD BULLET FOUND IN BABY'S CHEST!

***Weekly World*, September 29, 1987**
by Susan Jimison

Doctors treating an infant born with a heart defect were shocked when they operated on the 8-month-old boy and found a 200-year-old musketball buried in his chest.

The child, an unidentified American boy, underwent treatment in France, improved dramatically after removal of the old bullet, which has been described as a British musketball fired during the American Revolutionary War era.

"The mother could offer no explanation for this bizarre occurrence and had never suffered any injury during her pregnancy," said Dr. Andre Maynaud, a general surgeon specializing in pediatric care who reported on the bizarre case at an international symposium.

"Experts have told us the musketball is genuine."

"We can think of no logical explanation for how a piece of iron manufactured over two centuries ago could end up inside the body of a baby at birth. We have only the wildest theories, only the most bizarre conjectures."

Maynaud said his young patient has caused a sensation among reincarnationists who believe the boy may be a soldier killed fighting in the American Revolution and was reborn again this January.

The doctor has been contacted by two psychics who have identified the baby as a reincarnated soldier who died in 1775, he said.

However, medical experts are withholding judgment on the strange case, pointing out that calcium deposits in the body have been mistakenly identified as shrapnel or metal in the past.

"The baby was born underweight and in difficulty," Maynaud told a conference in Brussels, Belgium. "We believed he suffered from heart abnormalities that caused him to suffer breathing and pulse irregularities."

"We stabilized him and waited as long as possible to do surgery so that the child could build up weight for the operation. At eight months we went in to correct the deformities and found no abnormalities. The problem was caused by a half-inch ball of metal lodged near the aorta."

Maynaud said the baby has done very well since surgery and had developed completely normally. At the parents' request, no more information has been released about the child or his background.

Word of his condition spread locally, however, and aroused the interest of paranormals and reincarnation experts. "These people are convinced that the baby is beginning a second life after having died in the American Revolution," Maynaud said. "Psychics who claim to have communicated with the spirit of the dead soldier say the man was 19 years old and engaged to be married when he was shot in the chest in 1775.

"They say he wanted very much to live again, and that he chose to come back as this child. Who knows? It may be true. There's no other rational explanation for this case."●

☐ *This is another example comparable to the slave bracelet on a baby girl, or the engagement ring on a baby girl, or the father's wedding ring on the man's son—to say nothing about the pirates wooden leg which he drug back from another lifetime!*

The only way you can fight these articles is to yell, lies, lies, lies, it's your only defense—5, for the baby and another 5 for the bullet.

BOY THUG RETURNS AS DOG
Weekly World News
by Maurice Bender

In one of the most mind-boggling cases of reincarnation ever reported, a mother and father say their dead teenage son has been born again in the body of a cocker spaniel.

J.W. and Sara Aratki say the dog showed up on their doorstep out of the clear blue and proved it was the reincarnation of Soma Aratki, who was killed by a boar in 1986, by:

— licking and barking at a picture of the boy that the couple keep on a table;

— going directly to where Soma Aratki's bed had been and falling asleep;

— bringing home a bronze neckband that the boy wore before his death;

— whining and whimpering in the presence of a young woman that Soma Aratki was accused of raping;

— returning several bracelets and a necklace that the boy had stolen from a neighbor years earlier.

"The dog is our son, there is no question about it." J.W. Aratki told newsmen in Kirdalla, Sri Lanka.

Buddhist monk C.B. Dehigabba, an expert on reincarnation, agrees that the spirit of the dead youth now lives in the body of the brown-eyed spaniel.

"In our religion, reincarnation is accepted as fact," explained the monk. "Just as it is possible that a spirit may pass from one human body into another after death, so too may a spirit pass from a human to a beast. But for a human's spirit to pass into a beast, the man must have been very evil during his life.

"Soma was evil through and through."

And the villagers of Kirdalla agree that Soma was a bad boy, a local juvenile thug and thief. During the last three years of his life he was suspected of raping the 12-year-old daughter of a woodcutter, stealing the jewelry of the village headman's wife, burning the hut of a local holy man and various thefts.

Few of the villagers mourned the boy's death three years ago. It was just four months ago that Soma's parents were stunned when, after hearing a scratching on their door, they opened it to find a cocker spaniel sitting there.

The parents were shocked to find the bronze neckband of their dead son around the neck of the dog. The neckband had been missing when the boy's body was found. The dog leapt on Mrs. Aratki, licking her as if she were its long lost master. Then it walked over to where her son's sleeping mat had been and went fast asleep.

Over the next weeks, the parents and villagers were stunned by the dog's behavior. Every morning, the cocker spaniel ran to the door of a hut and lay there whining and whimpering until the teenage girl who lived there came out to pet it. It seemed as if the dog was begging forgiveness from her.

In his investigation, the monk Dehigabba learned that the girl was the one Soma was suspected of raping.

One day, the village headman was shocked speechless when the dog walked up to him carrying a little rag bundle. Inside were the bracelets and necklace stolen by Soma years before.

"When an evil person's spirit goes into the body of a beast, it is not just punishment," the monk explained.

"It is a chance to repent. The dog's friendly acts show that Soma is trying to make up for his old evil life in his current dog's life.

"If he does enough good in his dog's life, he will be reborn as a human."•

☐ *A case like this sounds as if the spirit of the boy took possession of the dog's body. I am reminded of the story of a horse that was able to answer questions by various maneuvers. Then again, I've read of a bird that was trying hard to get a message across. I suppose if one wanted badly enough, one might use any vehicle available that could be made to work. "A" for effort in presenting the case. It looks like an example of possession of the dog's body to me.*

LIVING TWO LIVES
Weekly World, **January 7, 1986**
by Helga Schmidt

Psychiatrists are baffled by the bizarre case of a 32-year-old West German nurse who complains that every night while she sleeps she lives another existence—as an American schoolmarm in 1842!

The woman, who doctors refused to identify to protect her privacy, is undergoing treatment at a private clinic in West Berlin after she attempted suicide because of her "reincarnation syndrome," according to a report in a professional journal.

"She is terribly upset by this phenomenon and has suffered severe depression and loss of self-confidence in the eight months since her ordeal began," said the woman's psychiatrist, who asked to remain unidentified.

"She has become frightened by the fact that no matter what—she always becomes another person in her sleep. She feels she is possessed."

The divorced mother of two first began experiencing her bizarre symptoms last March. She became aware that her dreams were repetitive and invariably involved a middle-aged woman named Joyce Reading Scott who lived near St. Louis, Mo.

"The woman I dream about lives in a rural area in a cold and drafty cabin," she told her psychiatrist. "She is sick with a nagging cough and her life is dreary and lonely.

"She teaches a group of eight children who walk long distances to her cabin over country roads. She is paid a small salary, but exists mostly on gifts from her students' families."

The woman told her doctors that she tried sleeping pills and a switch to the day shift at work to try to shake her "other life" but could not avoid dreaming of Miss Scott each night. She consulted a psychiatrist and when weeks of therapy resulted in no improvement she had a breakdown and attempted suicide.

"We admitted her as an in-patient and in the course of our work with her we observed her as she slept," her psychiatrist reported. "What we found was astonishing. She really seems to become someone else—someone who lived in another hemisphere about 100 years ago!"

Psychiatrists found that soon after falling asleep, the woman enters a trance-like state in which her eyes are open and she is able to speak. In this condition she speaks perfect English, using American slang.

She has a nagging cough and appears tired and ill.

When questioned about her circumstances, the woman—who in the trance state insists she is Miss Scott—describes life as it was lived in frontier America more than a century ago.

"She says that John Tyler is President of the United States and that she's teaching her pupils about a new invention called the steam engine," the psychiatrist said. "She was most impressed by the coronation and marriage of young Queen Victoria of England. which received great coverage in American periodicals in 1837 and 1841.

"We have invited American linguists to listen to tape recordings and they agreed that the woman's accents are exactly those of a mid-westerner in the 1800s. Yet we know that this woman can speak no English at all.

"It's the most incredible thing I've seen in 25 years of practicing psychiatry. If you had told me three months ago that I could ever believe in reincarnation, I'd have laughed. I am not laughing now."

Psychiatrists say they are baffled by the woman's condition but hope to help her accept her dual existence through counseling.●

☐ *Give the nurse a 9 for baffling her psychiatrists. Who knows whether this is possession or reincarnation?*

DEATH OF A SOLDIER
***Weekly World*, April 7, 1987**
by Susan Jimison

Archaeologists have discovered what may be the most conclusive proof of life after death ever—the corpse of an Indian soldier who died 130 years ago and is living again today, reincarnated as a 7-year-old boy.

The scientists, a team of four from Palacky University in Czechoslovakia, reportedly followed the instructions of little Charan Varma of Lucknow, India, to find the corpse in a shallow grave. The child insisted that the body was his in a previous life and studies of the corpse appear to confirm his claims, says the New Delhi *Press Syndicate*.

"The child says he was killed by British soldiers while fighting in the Sepoy Rebellion in 1857," a *Syndicate* reporter wrote.

"He told scientists he was shot twice in the chest, bayoneted repeatedly and slashed with sabres by British troops.

"Examination of the mummified corpse confirms that the body received extensive and fatal wounds that would support the boy's claims. The body is of a man in his 20s who died in the 1850s. The skeleton showed scars on the ribs, consistent with deep stab wounds, markings on the legs and arms consistent with sabre wounds and the fragments of two bullets in the chest cavity.

"Scraps of cloth and a tarnished brass belt plate in the grave match descriptions of the uniform of sepoy soldiers of the 1850s."

The Palacky University archaeological team was involved in a dig of prehistoric Indian home sites near Lucknow when news of the child's remarkable claims reached them. Little Charan said he had lived as Mahdu Pylee in his previous life. Pylee, the child claimed, was a native soldier—or sepoy—who died during the Indian Mutiny at the age of 27. He had been buried in an unmarked grave near the village of Sitapur, India.

"We interviewed the child and we were deeply impressed," said Dr. Karol Tyl, a member of the scientific team.

"The boy offered to lead us to the site where Pylee was buried, a place more than 60 miles from his home.

"He took us to an abandoned farm near Sitapur and pointed out a spot near a ruined house where a small mound was visible. When we dug into the mound, we found the remains of a man who had been buried there for a century and a half."

Indian newspaper coverage of the Charan Varma's reincarnation story has been extensive, but details of the archaeologists finds are expected to be published some weeks from now, Tyl told reporters.

"This is the first conclusive evidence ever found that reincarnation is real, not imaginary," Tyl said. "We want to be sure that our work remains above reproach.

"We will publish the results of our finds at the Pylee grave site in professional journals soon. But we have no doubt that what we've uncovered is the most important proof ever found that people can die and live again."●

☐ *We are told soldiers who've died accidental deaths and children often come back sooner—it seems to represent unfinished business. Maybe he found the wrong grave—give him a 9.*

DEAD DAD REBORN AS OWN SON
***Sun*, April 21, 1987**
by Sondra Delaney

Tragically facing premature death from cancer, a loving husband beat death by arranging to be reborn to his wife as his own son.

The boy's mother says she's convinced her son and her late husband are one and the same, and claims she has the evidence to prove it.

"My husband Eric and I always believed in reincarnation," Anna Kirstham reveals, "and now my 4-year-old son—our son—has proved to me it does exist.

"He is the spirit of my husband come back to life."

After studying with a psychic at a spiritualist center in their hometown of Bonn, West Germany, Anna explains, she and her husband learned that souls actually decide where they will be born in their next life.

"We had wanted children anyway and even his terrible diagnosis of liver cancer didn't deter us.

"Then we had the idea of having Eric reborn in our child." Eric died six months later at the age of 35, and within 24 hours Anna was impregnated with a sample of his sperm that had been previously frozen.

"Our spiritualist told us souls must make a choice within a couple of days as to where they would be reborn.

"Luckily, the timing was right and I became pregnant right away."

Nine months after the death of his father, Eric Jr, was born and Anna, 33, was overjoyed.

Now that the boy is 4 years old, Anna has decided to go public with her amazing story, because she finally has proof he is the reincarnation of her late husband.

"I believed it all along," she insists, "but since he can talk now, it's become obvious to others who knew Eric Sr. as well, that father and son are the same.

"We visited the architectural firm where my husband used to work, and little Eric broke away from me and ran right into his dad's former office.

"Later, as we were walking down the hall, he spied a row of award plaques on the wall and started jumping up and down and pointing to one in particular. It was the one his daddy had won."

Another time, Anna recalls, she was visiting her old college roommate who she hadn't seen in seven years, when her son called her friend 'Bunky,' out of the blue.

"I had introduced her to him as Gloria, but when he called her by the nickname my husband used to use, she turned white as a ghost. I had never used that name in my son's presence.

Then at a family reunion at her house, Anna says her son and his cousins were playing with blocks in another room when suddenly her mother-in-law let out a scream.

"We all raced in, and saw that Eric Jr. had built a remarkably sophisticated skyscraper with his blocks—it looked just like a building my husband had designed before he died."

Spiritualist medium Gretel Rietzl says she, too, is convinced. "At Mrs. Kirstham's request, I attempted to contact the spirit of her late husband, only to be told by my spirit guide that he walks again on this Earth—in the body of his only son.

"It's not unusual for souls who die to be reborn and meet loved ones again. But this is the first time a couple actually planned it in advance."●

☐ *Give dad a 9 for convincing his wife he's here again.*

BABY BORN SPEAKING IN DEAD DAD'S VOICE

***Sun,* July 15, 1986**

by Richard Dominick

A young widow began screaming in horror after giving birth to a baby girl who called to her with the voice of her dead husband.

Madeline McKay, 24, who lost her husband five months earlier in an automobile accident, had to be sedated by doctors.

She is now under medication, suffering from intense shock. "The whole thing is unbelievable," states nurse Gertrude Johnson, who was in the delivery room at the time.

"That baby just looked over at her mother and began speaking in a man's voice.

"The mother started screaming, I started screaming, and another nurse ran from the room.

"It was like the Devil was coming to life in that baby," adds Nurse Johnson.

Doctors in the delivery room of the London hospital confirm the baby began speaking in a man's voice just moments after she was born.

"I was holding the infant," says Dr. Harrison Perrette. "It was amazing because I could feel it trying to twist itself around, to have a look at her mother."

Dr. Perrette admits to being shocked into silence when he realized the baby was speaking in an adult male's voice.

"She looked over at her mother and in a clear voice said. 'Hello, Madeline. It's Roger; I had to see you again.' "

"That's when the woman began screaming that her baby was speaking in the voice of her dead husband.

"I was so frightened, I believe my heart stopped for a moment," he adds.

At that point, several of the nurses began to scream as the baby continued speaking.

"I don't believe Madeline ever heard what the baby was trying to say," says Dr. Perrette. "She went immediately into shock.

"I was so stunned, I just kept standing there holding the baby, too shocked to do anything," he admits.

Several other doctors, hearing the commotion, ran into the delivery room and sedated Madeline.

"She was shaking incredibly, crying and screaming that her dead husband was alive inside her baby," says Dr. Kevin Boswell.

"It was terribly eerie."

Since the child's birth Madeline is being kept isolated, suffering from shock, while hospital doctors are examining the infant girl.

"Every once in awhile the girl lifts her head and asks out loud in a man's voice where his wife Madeline is," says Dr. Perrette.

"Other than that, the infant has not said anything else." Hospital officials, claiming the incident was nothing but an elaborate hoax, ordered a search of the delivery room in hopes of uncovering a hidden recording device.

They discovered nothing out of the ordinary.

"I don't normally believe in reincarnation," states Dr. Perrette "but in this case, the evidence is hard to contradict."

He intends to have Madeline meet with her baby after the shock wears off.●

☐ *This sounds like another case of possession. He may leave the body later on—give Richard the 8.*

MURDERED CHILD REBORN
***National Examiner*, June 27, 1989**

A murdered child was reborn with a scar where his throat had been cut.

The incredible case is one of many documented by famed psychic researcher Dr. Ian Stevenson, a world-famous psychiatrist who has taught at the University of Virginia for the last 32 years. It is included in the fascinating book *The After-Death Experience,* (William Morrow, 1987) by Ian Wilson.

Ravi Shankar lived in one of the crowded suburbs of Kanauj, India. Ravi's father was Ram Gupta, but, shortly after his second birthday the boy began saying he was really the son of a barber called Jageshwar.

Ravi told his stunned family that in his previous life as Jageshwar's son he had had his throat cut by a washerman called Chaturi and a barber called Jawahar.

As proof, Ravi pointed to a birthmark on his throat, which looked exactly like a knife wound. He also kept asking for the toys that he had owned in his previous existence.

Convinced that their son was telling the truth, Ravi's parents began to investigate his bizarre story.

They discovered a barber living nearby named Jageshwar whose son, Munna, had been murdered at age six, just as Ravi had described. Munna was murdered six months before Ravi was born.

A washerman named Chaturi and a barber named Jawahar—the names Ravi had supplied—had been accused of murdering Munna, but charges were dismissed for lack of evidence.

In exploring near-death and after-death experiences, Wilson reaches the conclusion that the strongest evidence for life after death is made by cases of spontaneous communication with the dead, such as dream contact and post-mortem phantoms.●

☐ *The* Examiner *gets a 10.*

The following article is one I had published in the *Public Opinion* on December 31, 1959. It was the experience of Mrs. Ruth Myers who lived on the outskirts of Westerville, Ohio.

SALLY—REBORN AS RUTH

If it hadn't been necessary to chase down the details concerning unidentified flying objects, no doubt I would never have run into the side issue of hypnosis. But, it was, and I did, and that's how I happened to witness a subject under hypnosis who was just as interesting as the much-discussed Bridey Murphy.

To see a grandmother suddenly become a three-year-old required quite a change in personality. Our subject became frustrated when asked too many questions too fast and this caused her to suck her thumb and pull at her skirts in a typical child-like manner. The name she gave changed entirely and bore no resemblance to the one she now possesses.

In order to get many details of interest it was necessary to suggest an advance in age so that she might give this information better. Sally told us that she lived near Piketown or Piketon, Ky., and that she was born in 1850 and died in 1865 from a lung condition. When advanced to the age of fourteen she found it very difficult to breathe, which made me so uncomfortable I could hardly bear to watch.

Instead of coming from a large family like her own, she told that she was daddy's little angel, that her sole purpose in life was to be a lady. She had only one brother and he had been sent north to study to be a doctor.

Later she told that he was in the South with lots of men and that she didn't understand what it was all about. Her father just sat and shook his head and said that it would never do, never do—this was near the time of her death.

Sally's mother died with heart trouble a year before her daughter and apparently the father was close to a nervous breakdown. The girl said her mother was a music teacher—this made us hope that we might have a star pupil at the piano. However, the grandmother disappointed us, she had been unable to study the piano because of an injured hand.

The description of her home, family, colored mammy, mode of travel, etc. left us in a complete daze, for no Hollywood artist could put on an act to equal the reality which we were shown.

When I tried to find a town by this name, I found that such a place did exist, but that the name was changed to Pikeville in 1879. So many names and details were given that we decided to drive there. It was like going into another world, it was one of the earliest settlements and has a setting which is unique.

The subconscious mind contains many surprises which no doubt will be given to us in the future. The person under hypnosis is not aware of what is told and is often dumbfounded when given this information.

A number of our friends were grateful to Ruth for having shared this experience with us. As Ruth became a frustrated three-year-old, my husband sat by holding his head in his hands saying, "It beats the hell out of me—it beats the hell out of me!"

This is only a bird's eye view of the actual case and deserves many pages to do it justice.●

BABY GIRL LOCATES FORTUNE!
***National Examiner*, April 3, 1990**

A 10-month-old baby led her parents to a fortune in gold and silver jewelry and ornaments buried centuries ago on their family farm.

The astounding discovery catapulted the family from borderline poverty to unimaginable wealth.

And now they are having the last laugh on neighbors who ridiculed a family legend that wealthy ancestors had buried precious jewels on the property.

From almost the minute she began to crawl, little Isabella Lagorda always headed straight for a pond on their farm near Cuzco, Peru, revealed her mother, Anna Maria.

Last month, Isabella grabbed her mom's bracelet and threw it into the pond.

The next day, when the family raked the pond in search of the bracelet, they hit something hard that turned out to be an antique chest.

"It was incredibly well-packed, sealed with wax and amazingly airtight," Felipe told a reporter.

"I had a devil of a time opening it and then you can't imagine how stunned we were.

"Incredible gold and silver jewels, all in perfect condition, nestled inside.

"I nearly fainted dead away."

Police estimate the jewelry is worth almost $1 million.●

☐ *In due time the child may recall many memories. She probably is a former family member. Hypnosis is a science that is badly neglected and under-estimated. A million dollars is worth a 10.*

REINCARNATION NIGHTMARE
***Weekly World News*, October 10, 1989**
by Arthur Wade

At the very moment of her birth, an infant girl stunned her delivery room doctors and nurses when she revealed a past life—by speaking Old English in the anguished voice of a young woman being burned at the stake as a witch!

Seconds after the infant gasped her first breath of life, a loud, bloodcurdling scream shattered the quiet of the delivery room. The newborn child continued to howl, then began to writhe in agony. Suddenly, in the voice of a young woman suffering the torments of hell, the infant began to babble:

"Hath not the devil from my own mouth flown and cleansed my body? Why dost thee shame me before the Almighty God? My body is clean, yet thee wishes that mine bones be charred unto ashes that thou wouldst scatter them upon the winds.

"Satan has abandoned me, yet, unto the fires of Lucifer thou condemn my soul. I am not a witch...no longer am I the mistress of Incubus. Still, now do the flames scorch mine naked feet. In Salem there is no mercy.

"Soon, thy fires of hate will surround me and consume my mortal body. Yet though I die, mine God in Heaven shall taketh me unto His bosom and I shall liveth with His angels."

The infant suddenly vented another horrible scream that slowly faded to silence. As the doctors and nurses stood in shocked disbelief, the infant began its normal wails of life.

That incredible drama of reincarnation unfolded in less than a minute in a delivery room of a hospital in Anklam, East Germany. But for Doctor Eloise Pilot, the seconds seemed an eternity.

"That poor infant's first scream of agony left us all frozen with such terror that is beyond imagination," Dr. Pilot told reporters. "It stabbed into our hearts and brains like a searing hot dagger.

"And when the infant began to speak, the voice filled the delivery room. I have tried to shut it out. But it will live with me until the day I die."

Experts in witchcraft, who have studied the words of the infant as related to them by Dr. Pilot and her delivery room staff, are convinced that the voice belonged to a woman who had lived—and died—before and had been reborn in the infant.

"It is not the classical case of reincarnation," explained Michael Trebose, a self-proclaimed warlock (male witch) and a lifelong student of the Black Arts. "Usually, a previous life is recalled when the person of the present recalls events of one or more previous lives.

"This can happen when the person recalls places and events where there should be no recollection at all.

"They know the names of people who have been dead for centuries.

"They describe in the fullest detail the rooms of houses and shops that no longer exist, though records prove they once did exist.

"From the baby's speech and the mention of the place 'Salem,' this is the reincarnation of a young woman who was burned at the stake—in Salem, Massachusetts of colonial America."

Trebose said the woman had probably been one of the teenage girls accused, tried and convicted of witchcraft during the inquisition that raged through New England in the late 1600s.

Dr. Pilot said the identity of the infant girl as well as that of her parents is being kept secret and said the hellish episode in the delivery room probably will never be revealed to the child.

"She should live a normal life," he explained.

"But someday, I fear, the terrible memory of that agonizing past life will come back to torment her."●

☐ *If you don't believe Dr. Eloise Pilot is on the level in the* News *picture showing the doctor holding the new baby girl—why don't you trace the story and go straight to the source?*

Even though the family's name is being protected, the doctor and staff should be adequate proof that this event took place under their crew in a hospital delivery room, in Anklam, East Germany. This one sure gets a 10 in my book.

DEAD GIRL REBORN AS YOUNGER SISTER
***National Examiner*, July 4, 1989**

A dead girl was reborn as her younger sister!

The reincarnated girl's imminent arrival was even announced to her father by a disembodied voice.

According to *Fate* magazine, the case attracted the attention of the nation's leading reincarnation researcher, who analyzed every aspect of the case.

Dr. Ian Stevenson, a nationally renowned psychiatrist at the University of Virginia, thought the case of Susan Eastland, of Idaho, merited a full-scale investigation. He told her story in his book *Children Who Remember Previous Lives* (University Press of Virginia, 1987).

Three years after six-year-old Winnie Eastland was struck by a car and killed, Susan was born.

But even before her birth, the family knew that there was something unexplainable about Susan.

Winnie's sister, Sharon, dreamed that her dead sister was returning to them. Later, her father sensed that Winnie was soon to be reborn. A disembodied voice told him that Winnie would return.

Susan first spoke of her past life when she was two years old. Asked to give her age, she consistently responded that she was six—Winnie's age when she was killed.

Susan often behaved like the sister she never knew, and she took a strange interest in two of her mother's photographs of Winnie.

Mrs. Eastland said Susan seemed to have paranormal information linking her to her dead sister.

One example was a ritual that Winnie used to take part in. Mrs. Eastland kept cookies in a jar with a cat lid. When the children wanted some cookies, they played a game in which they asked the cat for cookies and their mother would tell them in a high-pitched voice the number of cookies they were permitted to take.

When Winnie was killed, Mrs. Eastland packed up the cookie jar. But when she took it out several years later, she discovered that Susan was familiar with the game.

Susan's recollection continued into her early teens, much longer than other cases of children recalling past lives which Stevenson has studied. The famed researcher said that children usually stop talking about past lives when they are about five years old.●

☐ *This one isn't from India or China or Timbuktu and Dr. Ian Stevenson has long been known for his work in this field. How about a 9 for the cookie jar?*

MEMORIES OF ZACHARY STODDARD
***Sun*, March 20, 1990**
by Francis Shifflett

A man who was stuck on the head has more to worry about than an ugly lump. The blow sent him back to a past life in the early 19th century!

Stunned scientists say 46-year-old Neal Mitchell's journey in time is the best evidence yet for reincarnation.

The incident began innocently enough when Neal, an electrician from Cornwall, England, made the mistake of slamming the door behind him when he entered his favorite pub. The impact caused a heavy wooden carving to tumble down from a shelf above the door and smash him in the head.

"He sort of blacked out and we helped him up," says Keith Brown, a friend of Neal's. "When he came to, he looked at us and asked us who we were.

"We figured he just had a little amnesia, but when we walked him home he began acting very strangely.

"He was scared to death of cars and screamed and tried to run away whenever one came near."

Back home, it soon became apparent that Neal's injury was very severe. He didn't recognize his wife, Patricia, or their two children, and was terrified by electric lights and appliances.

After Neal refused to leave his bedroom for several days, his worried wife consulted Dr. Carter Boren, a famed specialist on amnesia.

"At first I suspected that he suffered from amnesia," says Dr. Boren. "But then I realized he had taken on a whole other personality.

"He identified himself as Zachary Stoddard, a 33-year-old shoemaker in Boston, and told me the year was 1812.

"His recollections of life in the early 1800s were so vivid, I began to consider the possibility that he might be for real."

Dr. Boren conducted a detailed series of interviews, and then had researchers in Boston check the city archives for a Zachary Stoddard.

They found records of a shoemaker by that name who had lived in the city at that time and died in 1812 of pneumonia when he was 33.

"I was so amazed that I immediately made arrangements to take him to Boston," says Dr. Boren. "It wasn't easy, since he was terrified of the world outside of his room. "He had to be tranquilized for the flight."

But Neal's fear and deep depression vanished as he entered an old part of Boston. He walked briskly through the streets, excitedly pointing out monuments and telling of his experiences at a time when America was young.

Unfortunately, Neal was suddenly brought back to earth when Dr. Boren took him to see Zachary's grave in an old Boston churchyard.

"I didn't realize he hadn't yet accepted his death," says Dr. Boren. "When he saw the gravestone, tears filled his eyes.

"He became aware that he was a prisoner, trapped in time."

Neal has since been taken back to England, where he seldom ventures from his room. He is still a stranger to his family and friends.

"All he wants is to go back to his own time," says Dr. Boren, "even though he knows it's impossible.

"At this point, the only thing we can do is try to teach him how to live in a world 178 years ahead of his own," Dr. Boren adds.●

☐ *Now and then we find an experience which indicates a person loses recognition of the present and reverts to a former life-time. If the above case were the only one, it would be easier. Such experiences should be thoroughly researched. Zachary deserves a 10.*

MACHINE TO RECALL PAST LIVES

***Weekly World,* May 22, 1990**

by Nelson Mann

German scientists have developed a reincarnation machine that enables users to recall past lives in startling detail!

Drs. Helmut Bogel and Max Dietz say the device, code-named L-261, electronically probes through layers of consciousness until it reaches the area of the brain where memories of previous lives are stored.

They also predicted that home versions of the machine will be available to the public within five years.

"The machine will make it possible for everyone to examine their past lives and has already provided us with the most startling proof of reincarnation ever," Dr. Bogel told newsmen at a press conference in Oelde, West Germany.

"In preliminary studies it has enabled test subjects to recall as many as 100 past lives with amazing clarity," he added. "One subject actually spoke to us in 35 languages and dialects she had learned in 38 past lives."

Drs. Bogel and Dietz refused to say how L-261 works or discuss the principles used to develop it. They did reveal that the device is the culmination of 25 years of research.

They went on to say that they intend to sell smaller versions of the machine, which looks like an upside-down bowl of spaghetti, to the public beginning no later than 1995.

"We think L-261 is the most important technological breakthrough since the computer," said Dr. Dietz. "It's startling proof of reincarnation and is obviously going to change the way we view human history, lives and consciousness forever."

Darlene Kohl is one of 75 people who volunteered to test the device in studies conducted over the past six months.

Frightened at first, she quickly came to grips with memories of her past lives and now calls the experience "the most rewarding of my life.

"When they put the helmet and probes on my head I had second thoughts and almost bolted from the chair," said the woman. "But as soon as they turned it on a pleasant tingling sensation ran through my body.

"I was wide awake but I couldn't keep my eyes open and I began to see all these images like I was dreaming.

"The next thing I knew I saw myself huddled around a fire with cavemen. It was thrilling because I remembered being there thousands of years ago."

As the probe continued Miss Kohl recalled 22 past lives that she led in Greece, Rome, China, Mexico, America and Europe.

As each life unfolded she was able to speak in the language peculiar to the country and period in which she had lived. She also provided researchers with historical details that she couldn't possibly have known unless she had experienced them in past lives.

"Miss Kohl has only a ninth-grade education but provided us with historical data worthy of a university professor," said Dr. Bogel.

"We got similar results with all our test subjects and I concluded that L-261 is an unqualified success.

"This technology will change the lives of everyone who uses it," he added. "All of history is going to unfold before us."●

☐ *This exclusive article from the* News *may be a "breakthrough" which will allow locked up information in our minds to come to the surface of our consciousness. To understand the development of a soul would surely be a gift of the greatest value. Who would wish to continue a life of crime and cruelty if he felt this would lead to a repetition of these sad experiences. I will look forward to making this a 10.*

THE REINCARNATION OF NATALIE WOOD

***Sun,* May 29, 1990**

by Martha Beasley

A beautiful dark-eyed baby girl is revealing amazing details of the glamorous life and tragic death of Natalie Wood—and stunned scientists are convinced she's the reincarnation of the deceased movie star!

Little Ingrid Elvsgunder began speaking at the unbelievable age of four months, and announced that she was Natalie Wood.

"I've always scoffed at these so-called cases of reincarnation," states Dr. Henryk Neilson, Ingrid's pediatrician. "But this child is so remarkable she's made a believer out of me."

Ingrid's mother Annika was shocked when she first saw her newborn infant.

"The baby was born with her eyes wide open," says Annika. "And what a pair of eyes they were! They were so large, so deep and such a beautiful dark color. Her hair was dark too."

Four months after Ingrid was born, Annika heard a strange sound from the baby's bedroom.

"I thought she was crying at first, but when I came closer, I realized she was singing a song in English," Annika says. "I couldn't believe it—it was 'I Feel Pretty' from the movie *West Side Story.*

"Ingrid sang for several hours. When my husband Hermann came home, she was talking about Hollywood and the movies."

Astounded, Hermann called Dr. Neilson and insisted he examine Ingrid at once.

"I never saw anything like it," says Dr. Neilson. "The baby was speaking English in an adult woman's voice.

"I took her hand, looked into her eyes and asked, 'Who are you?' She said, 'I am the reincarnation of Natalie Wood.' "

In the days that followed, Dr. Neilson assembled a team of top psychologists and psychic researchers to interview the baby at a Stockholm hospital.

The child correctly answered every question they asked her about the life and career of Natalie Wood.

"She talked about her favorite films, and the stars she enjoyed working with," says Dr. Neilson. "She asked us to send for her husband, Robert Wagner, because she was very eager to be reunited with him.

Eventually, the subject of her death came up.

The baby recalled the fateful night of November 28, 1981, when she mysteriously disappeared from her yacht and drowned off Catalina Island.

She claimed she was standing on the deck when someone creeped up behind her, hit her on the head and pushed her overboard. For several hours she clung to a dinghy which broke away from the yacht, carrying her farther and farther out to sea.

Exhausted, she eventually lost her grip. Then all went black.

"She never saw who hit her," says Dr. Neilson. "And her parents refuse to let us ask her any further questions about her death.

"Perhaps when she's a little older she'll be able to give the police in California some valuable clues." ●

☐ *My main concern is whether the personality of Natalie Wood entered that body before birth or afterward. These memories of other lifetimes often fall by the wayside in a few years. This case looks to me as if the baby girl is going to hang on to that personality. I think it's possible. As a rating from 1–10, I'd say this is a 25.*

BABY BORN WITH ARTIFICIAL HEART

***Weekly World News*, June 26, 1990**

by Laurel Bowie

Adorable Angie Emiliano is a bouncing, bright-eyed baby girl who seems perfectly normal in every way but one—the amazing babe was born with a mechanical heart!

Dumbfounded doctors discovered the artificial heart beating away in Angie's tiny chest just minutes after she came into the world last March.

And specialists summoned to study the little girl say there is simply no scientific explanation for the bizarre turn of events.

"We're stumped—absolutely, totally stumped," baffled Dr. Benito DeMita told reporters in Rome, Italy.

"To have a baby born with such a sophisticated mechanical heart in place of a flesh-and-blood heart defies all reason. This procedure runs counter to all the laws of medical science. We're so bewildered we're even prepared to consider the possibility of supernatural influences here."

Angie's parents go even further.

They are convinced their first-born is proof positive of life after death. "She has to be the reincarnation of someone who received an artificial heart in a past life," insists doting dad Antonio.

"What other explanation is there? This is not something that happens as a simple freak of nature.

"I think now we can say for certain that people live and die and are reborn."

But Dr. DeMita says the answer is more complicated than that. "This heart is much more sophisticated and advanced than anything I've ever seen," said the mystified specialist.

"I just can't imagine where it could have come from. It seems to be functioning every bit as well as any natural heart and that in itself is baffling."

The child's heart is working so well, in fact, that the docs have given her a clean bill of health. "She's eating, she's growing and the little bundle is cute as a button," says her proud mom Maria.

"Of course, we wish she was perfectly normal like other babies, because we worry about whether her heart will eventually wear out.

"But we know our little Angie is something special and we plan to treat her like she's special." ●

☐ *There is no way I'm going to believe the* News *is so hard up for customers it has to make up an article like this one! My bet is that the* News *has a story and it's about time someone listened! One more 10 for the article and another 10 for the paper.*

JOHN AND THE OXEN

Once we did an experiment,
With lights directed on us.
It showed us many shadows and traces
Which helped to form, and change our faces.

One of mine was a small child,
Somewhere from four to six —
He'd been hit by a wagon wheel,
And was in an awful fix!

His face was smashed and bloody,
Those viewing — knew he was dead.
It wasn't horses beside that wagon —
But a pair of oxen, instead.

DeDe said, "I see a man named John,
I don't know who or why —
He certainly knows the reason,
That this child had to die."

No one paid much attention,
After all, this was done for fun —
We didn't understand what had been seen,
It might as well have been a dream.

But after forty years have passed,
A relative had a break at last —
He found our name in a telephone book,
And was thankful he'd done the work it took.

His family lives in Rome, New York,
He wanted to know about mine —
Where had we been all these years,
Could I fill in this time?

I rounded up some papers,
And a lot of pictures too —
I gave him lots of dates and things,
And hoped that this would do.

I sent him a picture of our family home,
That had built about eighteen-seventy.
I didn't know what good that would do —
But it's still there, and I am too.

He wrote right back, and sent one to me,
Of their family home in Jefferson County —
We took one look, and there we saw,
Our house, as plain, as it could be!

Relatives had cut our house —
It was made, to fit together.
Both houses stand, but aren't so grand,
Because of time and weather.

There was John, in front of the house,
Standing with his team of oxen.
And in the wagon his family sat —
I wondered if I could be a part of that?

I called my relative in New York
And said, "Could this possibly be?"
Can you find out, did John lose a child?
I wonder if it could have been me?

He called me back, and this he said,
"A boy of five was lost!"
His father John, took out his gun —
And shot those oxen dead.

CHAPTER SIX

UFO Kidnappings — World Abductions

Government Blasted for Failure to Probe UFO Kidnappings — *National Examiner* 150
Close Encounter That Changed a Man's Life — *Sun* 150
Children Abducted by UFO — *Weekly World* 151
A UFO Sucked Us into the Sky — *Weekly World* 151
Woman Kidnapped by Alien — *National Examiner* 152
UFO Aliens Kidnap 1,400 Farmers — *National Examiner* 152
Aliens Seek Human Blood and Body Parts — *Weekly World* 153
Couple Encounter UFO Alien Beings — *Sun* 153
Bizarre Tales of 200 UFO Kidnap Victims — *National Examiner* 154
UFO Kidnap — *Weekly World* 154
600 Missing Kidnap Victims — *Weekly World* 155
Spacemen Kidnapped My Science Teacher — *Weekly World News* 155
Skydivers Disappear into Thin Air — *Sun* 156
Tossed Back for Being Too Fat — *Sun* 156
Slave Traders From Outer Space — *Weekly World* 157
UFO Aliens Kidnap Farmer's Sheepdog — *National Examiner* 157
UFOs Have Abducted at Least 2,300 People — *Sun* 158
Two Fishermen From Mississippi 158
Green Aliens in Spaceship Sucked Me Up — *National Examiner* 158
Baby Glows in the Dark — *Weekly World* 159
Family Abducted by UFO — *Weekly World News* 159
Elephants Snatched by UFO — *Weekly World* 160
Man Snatched From Cabin by Space Aliens — *National Examiner* 161
UFO Aliens Kidnap Bride — *Sun* 161
Abducted by Blue-Goggled Space Aliens — *National Examiner* 162
Bride and Groom Spend Honeymoon in UFO — *Sun* 162
UFO Aliens Steal 4-1/2 Hours of Teens' Lives — *National Examiner* 163
Woman Recalls UFO Abduction — *National Examiner* 163
Cop Vanishes After Taking Alien's Picture — *National Examiner* 164
Family Plucked Off Earth by UFO — *Weekly World News* 164
Two "Lost" Hours Found Four Years Later — *National Examiner* 165
Baby's Father From Outer Space Says Scientist — *Weekly World* News 166
UFO Buzzes Jet — *Weekly World* 166
UFO Aliens Kidnap Couple — *National Examiner* 167
Space Aliens Examine Kids — *Weekly World* 168
I Took a Ride on a Starship — *Weekly World* 168
6-Year-Old Boy has 2 Hearts — *Sun* 168
UFO Ride at Carnival — *Weekly World* 169
UFO Snatches Plane, Then Disappears — *Sun* 170
UFOs Kidnap Earth Women to Breed Half-alien Children — *National Examiner* 170
UFOs are Raping Earth Girls — *Sun* 171
UFOs and the Ostrich People — *Sun* 172
Hubby Fined $110 For Killing Wife — *Weekly World* 172
Excerpts From Cynthia's Letter 173
Grandmother Made Blind by Aliens — *Weekly World* News 173
Alien Captured in Russia — *Sun* 174
Loses Face — *Weekly World News* 175
Beamed up by Giant UFO — *Weekly World* 175
Girls Give Birth to UFO Babies — *Sun* 176
Kidnapping — Poem 177

GOVERNMENT BLASTED FOR FAILURE TO PROBE UFO KIDNAPPING

***National Examiner*, June 21, 1988**

by Edward Manzi

A top criminal lawyer claims law enforcement officials fail to take seriously citizens' complaints of abductions by space aliens.

Peter Gersten, 45, has sued the federal government a number of times since 1977 to obtain UFO documents under the Freedom of Information Act.

The New York City attorney told the Examiner, "If a dozen people said they were taken hostage by a motorcycle gang, their claim would stir an investigation, but the same cannot be said for people who claim to be abducted by extraterrestrials."

Added Gersten: "If you go to the police and say you were kidnapped by space aliens who communicated by mental telepathy, do you think the cops will take you seriously?"

Gersten said he sues the government because he believes the public has a right to know about UFOs.

"I could prove in a court of law that UFOs exist," he said. "There is sufficient evidence.

"What they are and where they come from is a matter of speculation."

Gersten, whose personal library contains more than 5,000 government documents on UFOs, would like to get his hands on about 60 documents held by the Central Intelligence Agency and another 140 by the National Security Agency.

"Obviously they think if they release the documents they will compromise the way they gather information, or it could be they are hiding something," said Gersten.

The UFO investigator believes abductions by space aliens are linked more to a supernatural intelligence than to extraterrestrial beings who ride around the galaxy in spaceships.

And as for UFOs, Gersten speculates they may be terrestrial, secretly manufactured by the US and Soviet governments, using the latest technology.

Said Gersten: "I like mysteries. That's why I'm a criminal trial lawyer and investigate UFOs."●

☐ *Sometimes I think Peter Gersten is just fooling around having fun. He knows the government is going to release whatever suits its best interest. Perhaps this kind of publicity is what officials want. High up officials do not want to keep UFOs a secret. They are forced to do it. It is you who make this tactic necessary. How about a 7.5 for Peter?*

CLOSE ENCOUNTER THAT CHANGED A MAN'S LIFE

***Sun*, January 5, 1988**

by Phil Brennan

A remarkable UFO sighting changed a veteran policeman's life forever.

Early on November 28, 1980, while on routine patrol in Todmorden, England, Alan Godfrey, then 33, saw a strange object in the road ahead. He stopped about 90 feet away from it and got out of his police car.

Up ahead he saw a metallic, diamond-shaped craft silently hovering several feet above the road.

The lower part of the UFO was rotating slowly. There was a row of windows around the upper part, and the whole craft glowed with an eerie silver light.

Startled, Godfrey tried to reach the police station on his walkie-talkie, but got nothing but static. He tried his car radio, but, mysteriously, that wouldn't work either.

Unable to communicate with his superiors, he sat and sketched the object, which he said was about 20 feet wide and 14 feet high.

He finished the sketch, looked up, and was stunned to find himself at least 300 feet farther down the road, far beyond where the object had been, and the UFO was nowhere in sight.

Back at the station, he discovered it was later than he'd thought—minutes had simply vanished from his life—one of his new boots was slit open, and he had a small burn mark on the sole of his foot.

The next day he heard that three police officers from a near-by town had also reported seeing the object.

Four years later, because Godfrey was still shaken by his experience and unable to get it out of his mind, his superiors retired him on a pension for disability suffered in an earlier and unrelated incident.

"When you've had an encounter such as I had, it changes your whole outlook on life," Godfrey told reporter Ralph Barker of England's *Sunday Express* newspaper.

"All I can say is that I know I saw what I saw."●

☐ *I have no idea how many police abductions are on record; I'll bet it's a bunch. They are so available at the right time. I hope to cover a number of them. Some of my friends are going to remind me there is no "Alan Godfrey" — all such stuff is made up by those tabloids! In case they may be wrong — we'll give this an 8.*

CHILDREN ABDUCTED BY UFO

***Weekly World*, October 6, 1987**

by Julio Enriquez

Four lucky children were taken aboard a UFO and shown the wonders of the universe on a three-day journey into outer space, civilian and military authorities report.

"Adults lie. Teenagers lie. But children this age are incapable of lying, at least like this," said Roderigo Ortiz, special investigator with the police department in Concordia, Argentina.

"From all appearances they did spend time on a genuine starship. They actually traveled into space and saw the sights like ordinary tourists.

"At one point they thought God was taking them to heaven as He—whatever 'He' was—stood behind the controls of the craft."

Newspaper reports of the amazing drama identified the children as 8-year-old Maria Molero, her sister Emma, 6, and brothers Jorge, 5, and Carlos, 3. According to the children and a half dozen eyewitnesses, a 75-foot, saucer-shaped craft swooped over the field they were playing in on August 9 and sucked them into the craft after hitting them with a burst of bright blue light.

"A great golden ship took us up in the sky and it was driven by God—I know it was God.

"He wore golden robes and had long silver hair and was shiny all over," said Maria Molero, the oldest.

"He was a nice man and told us to call him Lalar. He showed us the moon and other places in the sky and said they were the stars."

The other children confirmed her account and said they were scared "for just a little while. He scraped our faces with a little stick and stuck us with a needle but he didn't hurt us at all," said Jorge Molero.

"I liked the bedrooms because the beds were soft and way up high," added Emma Molero.

Little Carlos Molero, the youngest, said: "There were a million buttons and lights. The man looked funny because he had a real big head and two big yellow eyes. He is our friend."

Because of the difficulties of interviewing children, authorities have yet to determine everything that happened during their three days aboard the spaceship. It does appear that they underwent some sort of medical testing, however, because needle marks and scrapes were still visible on their cheeks after they got home, officials said.

A military spokesman would neither confirm nor deny reports that a UFO was picked up on radar the day the children were abducted and the night they were brought home.

"We are investigating and the facts will be made public when they are known," he said. "The children are being interviewed now.

"We hope to have some solid information soon," the spokesman said.

The children's parents, Emilio and Carmen Molero, declined to comment.

UFO researcher Armando Azparen has not spoken to the children personally because the military has refused his requests for an interview.

"But from what I have read in the newspapers," he said, "I believe that these children are telling the truth."●

☐ *This UFO abduction story covered the front page of* Weekly World *on October 6, 1987. I decided to watch the newspaper racks in a large Wal-mart store, south of Punta Gorda, Florida. Though these papers were placed near the cash registers in the front of the store they did not sell out by the end of the week. Critics of these papers tell you these headlines sell papers. Is it people are not concerned over abductions? Perhaps they don't believe there are abductions. Do you suppose our government investigated this case? You bet they did! Once a government source reaches a story it's right hard to get much information. People involved are sworn to secrecy. Those who know make sure someone knows the truth. They often leave signed sworn statements. It's the best they can do! I believe this to be a 10—since I can't prove any of these statements, I'll still give it a 9.5.*

A UFO SUCKED US INTO THE SKY

***Weekly World News*, Dec. 15, 1987**

A fiery red UFO abducted a carload of shrieking tourists and dumped them in the countryside 60 miles away ....

Louis and Jane Verdeyen and pal Fernand Matrige told Italian authorities they were confronted by the saucer-shaped craft while traveling along a mountain road northeast of Venice.

The vacationers said the craft disabled their rented car with a blast of reddish light as it swooped overhead.

Then it hit them with a beam of thin green light that pulled them into the belly of the starship like metal shavings to a magnet.

"Thank God they didn't harm us," Verdeyen, 41, said. "The whole thing lasted only about 10 minutes. But I'll tell you this—those were the most terrifying minutes of my life.

"My wife Jane was so scared that she went into shock."

Matrige, 36, added: "We were driving along a winding mountain road about 11 p.m. when the countryside was lit by a bright led light.

"Just then our engine sputtered and stopped. We all got out to see what was going on and looked up at the sky. There was a 25-foot flying saucer hovering about 60 feet above us.

"We jumped back in the car and were trying to start it when the UFO sprayed us with a green light that lifted us straight up off the road.

"Louis said something obscene and Jane screamed until she passed out. Me, I prayed like the dickens. I told God I'd be a good Christian until my dying day if he'd get us out alive."

A few seconds later Matrige got his wish. The UFO stopped over a country road and gently dropped the vacationers off. Incredibly, their car started right up. They drove two miles to a service station and learned they were 60 miles away from the spot where they were abducted a few minutes before.

A UFO expert speculated that the tourists unwittingly approached an extraterrestrial operation of some sort and were whisked away to keep them from witnessing it.●

☐ *If you believe the* News *is lying, or these tourists are all make-believe, pretend you're reading fairy tales—in time you may change your mind. That many people deserves a 9. This is not an unusual report.*

WOMAN KIDNAPPED BY UFO ALIENS TALKS TO ANIMALS!
***National Examiner,* August 30, 1988**
by Edward Reynolds

A housewife kidnapped by UFO aliens can now communicate with dolphins and whales.

And Marianne Cascio Shenefield can tell if someone has had an encounter with a space being and if UFOs are nearby. She can also tell if someone is sick, physically or mentally, according to a top psychotherapist.

Marianne, 46, told the *Examiner:* "I never wanted to be this way. I was very happy. I feel like the aliens have used me as a sort of guinea pig in a cruel experiment."

The experiment began in 1952 when Marianne was 11. She was playing in a field and suddenly heard someone behind her. Later, she told her parents she met a strange little "Chinese" boy dressed in a "scuba diving suit" who came from a "car from Heaven" and led her into a "compartment" for an examination.

Her parents thought she had been molested. Marianne was disoriented and refused to go to school. Six months later, she fell victim to an eye disease that slowly blinded her.

Marianne said she was again abducted in 1972.

Said the Agawam, Mass. housewife: "They told me I was the perfect candidate for the experiment they needed."

Two years later, while riding in a friend's car, Marianne said a dark blue spiral of light struck her in the eyes, restoring her vision.

But that night, Marianne's vision faded and was replaced by a barrage of colors and symbols that prevented her from sleeping. Household objects levitated and electricity shot out of a refrigerator, according to eyewitnesses.

Marianne, who now sees colors and symbols 24 hours a day, was tested by prestigious paranormal researcher Dr. Andrija Puharich, the scientist who has worked with world-famous psychic Uri Geller. Incredibly, she was able to write in Hebrew and ancient Egyptian hieroglyphics despite having no formal education.

Psychotherapist Patricia Sable of Hartford, Connecticut, who has written a book about the housewife, calls Marianne's gift "brain sight." Sable said Marianne can pinpoint illnesses with startling accuracy.

Said Sable: "Marianne also has an amazing ability to communicate with animals, but she especially likes to work with dolphins and whales."

The sea mammals are on a "frequency" that produces color sequences which Marianne translates.

"I don't receive the information in sentences," said Marianne. "It's more like knowing, a feeling. The whales tell me they are very much concerned with their own survival."

Marianne said a person's aura also triggers her colors, and she can tell if the person has been abducted by ETs or is sick in some way.●

☐ *I find no reason not to believe this article and many reasons to believe.... The majority of cases examined show that we are being used as guinea pigs by the aliens who come here—just as we would do if we were able to go to them. How about a 7.9?*

UFO ALIENS KIDNAP 1,400 FARMERS
***National Examiner,* August 9, 1988**
by Gregory Bangs

Are space aliens responsible for the mysterious disappearance of 1,400 people?

That's the question facing police and a UFOlogist in Sha Tin, China, where 1,432 residents have vanished from farms and villages in the past three years, half of them between the ages of 7 and 16.

UFOlogist Wong Watin, 52, sees a connection between the disappearances and a rash of UFO sightings.

Wong saw a brightly-lit UFO in December, 1987, about 80 feet by 60 feet, and shaped like a watermelon. It apparently had no windows or any means for the ETs to view the outside.

The UFO stood in a field about 50 feet from the bushes where Wong, an herbalist by profession, routinely picked berries. He crouched low in a ditch and watched in amazement as the UFO rose silently from the ground and zoomed into the sky.

At first Wong suspected the UFO was a Soviet spy plane, but when hundreds of peasants began disappearing, his suspicions turned to ETs.

Wong is now convinced space aliens are kidnapping human beings and performing strange genetic experiments.

Four dazed teens, who had apparently blacked out for several hours, were discovered wandering the countryside with circular burn marks on their arms and legs.

One of the teens, a 16-year-old girl, claimed gray-skinned ETs with big heads and large black eyes stole her unborn baby, according to police.

And a schoolteacher reported that she saw a UFO moving slowly a few feet above the ground toward a pupil on his way home. She grabbed the child and they hid in some bushes.

But people in Sha Tin are panic-stricken, Wong says. They no longer leave home at night and they walk in groups of 10 to 20 during the day.

One farmer said he saw a UFO in his pasture. After it zoomed into the sky, he claimed a horse and cow were missing.

Another farmer, Cheng-Wu, 55, said he found four of his best cows mutilated. One of the cows had an incision in its head and its brains were missing.

Said Cheng: "There were no signs of poachers. The fields were very muddy and they would have left tracks. This is all a mystery to me."

UFOlogist Watin believes spacebeings experimented on the cows, lifting them into their spacecraft with a strange beam of light and placing them back in the field when they were finished.•

☐ *After forty years of research and having read dozens and dozens of books on UFOs and related subjects, I find no reason to question any remark made in the above column. If this is a created article it comes about as near the truth as you are apt to get. I hate to admit it but I'm afraid this is worth a 10. This material is not made up by the tabloids. It's your best researchers that come up with this kind of stuff!*

ALIEN KIDNAPPERS SEEK HUMAN BLOOD AND BODY PARTS, WARNS EXPERT
***Weekly World*, April 28, 1987**
by Alex Jackson

An expert on UFOs says reports of astonished earthlings being kidnapped and used as "medical lab rats" by highly intelligent, space aliens from another solar system are not uncommon.

"I've heard of at least 300 documented experiences from Europe, America and Asia in recent years," said Dr. David M. Jacobs, a history professor at Temple University in Philadelphia. "The extraordinary encounters I'm familiar with seem to involve aliens from another solar system because of the type of medical testing that was involved."

Space aliens have been visiting the planet Earth for 20 or more years and they already know many of the things that earthlings were captured and examined for, the professor said.

"It appears we are dealing with a civilization from another system that is advanced—very advanced. That would mean also that the problem of distance in space isn't meaningful anymore," said Dr. Jacobs.

"The aliens have no qualms about abducting earthlings and taking blood and body part samplings," he said.

"They seem to be especially interested in our reproduction process."

Dr. Jacobs said the super smart aliens who kidnap people around the world are probably quite capable of conquering Earth if they wanted to.

"Encounters with space aliens are becoming a global phenomenon," he said. "The scope and numbers of the reports are very frightening to me."

People from all walks of life, all races, ages and from all educational levels are reporting close encounters with aliens, said Dr. Jacobs. "These people are just plain folks. They're not crazies."•

☐ *I get a little fed up with those who tell me there are no people back of these sightings and articles. This is one I'd like to tell someone to put up or shut up. O.K. Alex, this one is worth a 10, and no one can blame you for it.*

COUPLE ENCOUNTERS UFO ALIEN BEINGS
***Sun*, May 2, 1989**
by Ken O'Hara

A suburban couple contacted by giant golden-haired space aliens who want to save mankind from destroying earth say the U.S. government is engaged in a "cosmic Watergate."

Michael and Aurora El Legion say the friendly UFO visitors only want to warn about the dangers of nuclear war and pollution that threaten us.

But political leaders are covering up the evidence and government agencies are instructed to downplay UFO sightings.

The Scottsdale, AZ couple speak to audiences all over the world about their hair-raising experiences.

Michael recalls his first: "I had fallen off a pier in Oceanside, Calif., and suddenly I heard a high-pitched noise.

"There were bright lights surrounding me, and I was quickly rescued by a spacecraft hovering in the fourth dimension above Earth."

Michael says his second contact with the aliens came in Los Angeles, when the beings told him that 300 to 400 million "star people" actually live on this planet!

Aurora had her first encounter with the space visitors when she was eight and living in Michigan.

"Somebody entered my home, searched around and leaped out of my bedroom window," she recalls.

"I looked outside and there were two spacecraft on the ground. I believe a burglar was in my house and the aliens scared him away," she points out.

Aurora had her next encounter years later when she was speeding down the road in her car but couldn't stop when she came to a red light.

The terrified woman recalls a moment of "absolute silence" after she zoomed past the light.

Certain she was about to crash, she suddenly found herself parked in a deserted gas station—and neither she nor her car were scratched at all!

She says the unexplained moment of silence was really the aliens protecting her from harm!

"There is no question about it—beings from other worlds do exist," Aurora maintains. Michael says the aliens are closely watching over us hoping that man doesn't destroy his own planet.

"They will intervene only if necessary" Michael says, adding: "They will remove those who want to leave this planet."•

☐ *There are so many cases like this one. It's unfair not to cover all types of contacts and abductions. I can't give this more than a 5 but be assured there are dozens more like it.*

BIZARRE TALES OF 200 UFO KIDNAP VICTIMS
National Examiner, **July 12, 1988**
by Georgina Gold

A policeman is medically examined aboard a huge alien spaceship.... A woman is paralyzed by the touch of a strange three-fingered alien and held hostage aboard a UFO.... A supermarket manager is drawn into a strange encounter with a mind-reading spaceman....

These are just a few of the amazing UFO kidnappings reported by 200 people and documented in the new book *Abduction* (Robert Hale Publ., 1988), by top UFO expert Jenny Randles, who says she believes the incredible stories.

"All the witnesses I've spoken to have been very sincere," says Randles.

To former British policeman Alan Godfrey, there is no doubt about UFO kidnappings because he was taken aboard a UFO and medically examined.

Early one morning, he was called out to locate a herd of straying cattle in the countryside near London, England.

Suddenly, right in front of his car was an oval-shaped object hovering above the road.

The next moment, the policeman found himself half a mile farther down the road with no idea how he got there. Glancing at his watch, he also noticed that, unaccountably, 14 minutes had passed. He decided to contact a local UFO investigation team.

Under hypnosis, he recalled floating in a room and being medically examined by small beings with lamp-shaped heads. They were supervised by a tall human-like being in a white cloak who said his name was Yoseph. The aliens spoke to Godfrey telepathically and told him that one day they would return. Then he was returned to his car.

A 20-year-old supermarket manager also had a close encounter of the mysterious kind. He was walking home one night near London when he spotted a light that flashed and turned into a greenish, bullet-shaped object.

As the beam hit the ground, a tall being in a silvery one-piece suit materialized. It glided toward him and moved its hands down his face, giving him the sensation he was being drawn out of his mind.

Eventually the figure returned to the beam and was pulled up into the bullet. Years later, the man still gets the urge to visit the spot and stare at the night sky.

From Boston, Massachusetts, comes another chilling account of UFO abductions.

Joann Berte was kidnapped by strange three-fingered aliens who paralyzed her with their touch and then took her aboard an alien craft to observe a mysterious operation being performed on her friend.

"I was immobilized," she told a source. "I couldn't move or speak."

Aboard the alien craft, Joann saw a small, three-fingered alien in an incubator. She was then brought to a glass-enclosed platform where she observed her friend lying on an operating table with tubes extending from her body.

Joann reported "They didn't ask permission. They just took us away."●

☐ *These papers don't have to make up such stories there are too many available—anything less than a 9 is an insult. All serious researchers know that such abductions are not uncommon.*

UFO KIDNAP!
Weekly World, **May 31, 1988**
by Henry Weber

A 39-year-old secretary vanished from the face of the earth less than 24 hours after she told friends that space aliens were trying to abduct her!

Now authorities are trying to figure out if Jackie Smith is in hiding or in the clutches of the extraterrestrials who allegedly had been tailing her.

"Either way it's an alarming situation," UFO investigator Jenny Randles told reporters in Warrington, England. "The young woman who disappeared is not some kind of UFO nut.

"Her friends and co-workers say she is rock solid. When she told them space aliens were after her they believed her."

The woman's boss, Andy Egan, recalled how terrified the woman was the day before she vanished.

"She turned up at the office in a panic," he said. "She said she was driving along in her Toyota when it was whisked into the air and mysteriously transported 'to a different place.'

"The next thing she remembered was waking up in the car about six hours later with blue dots on her ankles and neck."

According to a co-worker Sally Warren, Miss Smith also said that several "strange beings suddenly appeared in her car" a few seconds before the vehicle was transported through the air.

Miss Smith described the aliens as being 'tall, manlike and extremely muscular, with small round heads and four eyes,' her friend said.

"The blue dots on Miss Smith's ankles and neck are classic signs of testing by aliens," said Mrs. Randles. "She may be in hiding, terrified they'll come back to get her.

"It's also possible that they already have come back and Miss Smith is now with them."

The young woman's mother, Rose Smith, is frantic. She said her daughter used to telephone her everyday come hell or high water—but hasn't called since she disappeared.

"Something bad has happened to her, I just know it," said Mrs. Smith, 66, of London. "Jackie isn't the kind to play a joke of any kind, much less something so upsetting as this.

"What if those spacemen did get her?" she sobbed. "I pray to God that they bring her back unharmed."

Government officials refused to discuss Miss Smith's disappearance and referred questions to police.

Police spokesman Michael Fletcher said detectives are baffled by the disappearance. There is no evidence of foul play. And a search of her house revealed that all of her clothes are still there. "She left in a hurry," Fletcher said. "Her car is in the driveway. Her checkbook is on a dresser.

"I've never been a big believer in UFOs," he said. "But this case makes me wonder.

"Maybe they do exist and maybe they are coming down to Earth. It's not a pretty thought."●

☐ *If this article makes you laugh don't laugh very hard. Better yet—don't laugh where people can see you and remind you of it later. I'll drop this to an 8 in case Miss Smith is hiding some place. I think it's more likely she just ain't here no more.*

600 MISSING KIDNAP VICTIMS
***Weekly World News*, August 4, 1988**
by Henry Weber

Dr. Carlos de Melo says the victims come from almost every country in the world and range in age from 6 to 85.

They appear to be in good health, he added, although several bear scars of surgical experiments—most of which were conducted on the brain.

"This is the scientific discovery of the century," Dr. de Melo told reporters. "These poor people have experienced a close encounter of the worst kind.

"They were abducted by extraterrestrials. One has been missing since 1926—he has not seen his wife and children in 62 years."

Brazilian military officials refused to comment on the researcher's claims, although press reports indicate that the victims are currently being debriefed at a military installation in Bel Horizon.

American intelligence agencies are rumored to be involved in the operation, but sources will only confirm that "a small contingent of specially-trained officers have been sent" to Brazil.

Dr. de Melo says he found the kidnap victims massed in a jungle clearing 75 miles north of Rosario Oeste, near Brazil's border with Bolivia, on June 9.

He initially thought that he had stumbled on a religious cult. "There were men, women and children, some old, some young, huddled together in the jungle," said the expert.

"A few were totally disoriented, having no idea where they had been or why they were in the jungle. Others were fully aware of their circumstances. They were cautious at first, but eventually asked for government assistance to get back to their respective homes."

Dr. de Melo alerted government officials, who directed the army to helicopter the victims back to civilization. It is not yet known why they were released by the aliens.

According to Dr. de Melo, the victims were taken to a distant planet where they were used in medical experiments, as slave labor and in zoos.

Several allegedly told the expert they worked as interpreters at listening posts monitoring radio signals from Earth.

Dr. de Melo said he repeatedly questioned the victims about the extraterrestrials themselves but was told that any discussion of them "would result in death."

Swiss UFO researcher Gerald Bischof said the 600 kidnap victims are the first to be returned to Earth. "This is definitely a milestone," he told reporters, "but we still have a crisis.

"Tens of thousand of people are abducted by aliens each year. If we begin serious study of these kidnap victims there's no telling what we can learn about the aliens and their civilization.

"By those standards, these 600 are a drop in the bucket. Many, many more are missing still."●

☐ *I think there is little reason not to believe this to be true. Just in case it isn't, it's still worth a 9.5. There is reason to believe our government has approved some temporary abductions by the aliens.*

SPACEMEN KIDNAPPED MY SCIENCE TEACHER
Weekly World News

Sound Off Column printed this letter on Nov. 17, 1987. It refers to an article which was carried on Nov. 3, 1987.

Editors: I was both delighted and stunned to pick up a Nov. 3 issue of *Weekly World News* and see the story about Masao Sekoya, the science teacher who was abducted by a UFO.

I was fascinated because Masao was a teacher of mine while I was an exchange student in Japan four years ago, and even though I haven't been in touch with him for more than a year, I still consider him a dear friend.

I know a lot of people scoff at the notion of spaceships and believe that anyone who says he's been aboard one is a nut case.

I guess I was pretty skeptical myself until now.

But one thing I know for certain—if Masao Sekoya says he was abducted by aliens, he was abducted by aliens. Masao is one of the most sober, brilliant and (if you'll pardon the expression) down-to-earth men I've ever known.

He is a hardworking man with a lovely wife and three children, and he would never risk bringing dishonor upon his family by concocting such a story.

You mention that authorities are investigating the incident and I hope you'll give us a follow-up report when the investigation is done.

R.O. Toledo, Ohio.

Japanese authorities have been questioning Sekoya in secret for more than a month now, and our sources tell us they believe his encounter may prove to be one of the authentic and revealing of all time. – Editors.●

☐ *A Japanese science teacher is abducted while walking in a park. This by itself is just one more unconfirmed abduction. Even with his picture we can't be sure Masao Sekoya is really who it says he is. But when the* News *gives you a letter from a schoolboy in Toledo acknowledging this man was his science teacher while he was an exchange student—now that's real impressive! What do you think? This is a 10.*

SKYDIVERS DISAPPEAR INTO THIN AIR

Sun, **July 5, 1988**

by Michelle Tupper

A pilot and two witnesses claim they watched in bewildered shock as three skydivers parachuted from a plane and disappeared into thin air—without ever touching the ground.

The vanishing trio—Jean-Luc Denier, 29, Claude Belmonde, 33, and Paul Souree, 28—were friends and business partners who were making their first solo jumps from an airplane.

The pilot is Francois Lenueve, 44, principal owner of the skydiving school where the three beginning divers had taken lessons.

He says he took the plane to an altitude of about 1,000 feet over the French countryside near the town of Albi, where they dived while school co-workers Jacques Granday, 30, and Catherine Lyniere, 24, waited on the ground.

"All three parachutes opened properly," the pilot recalls "and it appeared they had made successful dives.

"I lost sight of them when they went into a cloud bank, but after I landed the plane, I discovered the skydivers were nowhere to be found."

"Catherine and I watched as they went into the cloud," Jack Granday adds, "but they never came out. We all scratched our heads and stared at each other in amazement."

Catherine is convinced the divers were snatched from the sky by a UFO. "I've read that UFOs often hide in clouds," she notes. "I've also read that they can make themselves invisible.

"It had to be a UFO that got them. That's the only possible explanation for what happened."

Not according to French authorities.

"We think foul play was involved," says police detective Charles Mordan.

"The victims were partners in a mail-order business that handles large quantities of cash, and the only witnesses to their so called disappearance are three people who also work together.

"We haven't established an exact motive yet, but the opportunity for murder was certainly there.

"We will investigate this matter further before we close the books on it."•

☐ *Michelle deserves at least a 9 for 3 missing people. If they show, they'd better have a good story.*

Cloud abductions are not uncommon. Often people are returned miles from where they were taken. One case I remember is of a man who jumped from a plane and his parachute didn't open. He was found sitting on the ground with an unopened chute not knowing what happened. There are many UFO rescues.

Another case is of a doctor and his wife who were attending a wedding. It was a long trip. They were followed home by another car. Upon arriving without them, their friends retraced the route. The next day the missing couple found themselves miles from their destination. They only knew they were sitting in the car in an unfamiliar location. Their car was confiscated for examination. They had been seen driving into a cloud and then disappeared. I think the UFOs got them. Anyway they get an 8.9 from me.

TOSSED BACK FOR BEING TOO FAT

Sun, **June 14, 1988**

by Fred Sleeves

The startling adventures of a woman abducted by a UFO ended abruptly when the disgruntled aliens tossed her out of their spaceship because she wasn't an ideal specimen for their wild experiments.

In truth Helen Moranthul, a 445-pound chubby, says the space visitors disposed of her because she was too fat.

"I was never so thankful for my weight," says the terrified woman, still shaken by the incredible journey.

"They had me on a table and were trying to squeeze me through a large tube.

"I was obviously a guinea pig for their hideous lab experiments! Inside the tube were pointed instruments that were moving up and down which were probably meant to stick into my body.

"They had given me some kind of drug and I was too paralyzed to scream."

The ghastly nightmare began when Helen, a 43-year-old housewife, was allegedly kidnapped in her own backyard near Wakefield, England.

Her husband, George, was working late in a chemical plant that night when Helen noticed a bright yellow light outside.

Helen remembers only being sucked up by the light into a spaceship after she walked out back.

"I was helpless as these tall, dark figures were grabbing and probing my body with instruments," she says.

"They stuck something in my mouth and I became completely paralyzed."

After the aliens tried unsuccessfully to push their fleshy subject into the tube, they became annoyed and roughly removed her from the table.

"The next thing I remember was lying in the grass in my yard," Helen insists.

Although George says his wife was probably hallucinating from diet pills she has been taking, Helen insists her rotund figure saved her life.

"I'm glad I'm fat," she declares. "If I wasn't, I'd probably be in a tube somewhere in space like the other missing people snatched by UFOs."•

☐ *Every once in awhile a man gets booted out of a UFO because he's too old to be useful. This is the first person I've seen who got away by being too fat! It's not fair to give her less than a 6.*

SLAVE TRADERS FROM OUTER SPACE

Weekly World, **July 5, 1988**

by Henry Weber

Space aliens kidnap as many as 10,000 people a year and the situation is going to get worse as their need for slave labor increases!

That's the word from Dr. Atle Spoor, who says the extraterrestrials used to nab misfits and transients but are now beginning to target white collar workers and the middle class.

"I don't want to be a prophet of doom, but I can envision a day when the entire human race is in danger," the expert from Amsterdam told reporters.

"As it stands, 10,000 men and women vanish every year to prop up the economy of an alien civilization."

According to reports, Dr. Spoor based his claims on the study of thousands of missing person reports in the files of European police departments.

Strangely enough, almost 18 percent of the missing people claimed to have seen a space alien or UFO shortly before they disappeared.

"The obvious implication is that these people were tailed and then kidnapped by the extraterrestrials," he continued. "In the past year we have seen that an increasing number of these people belong to the middle and upper classes, which suggest that the aliens are now using slaves in white collar occupations."

Swiss UFO expert Hugo Jenzer applauded Dr. Spoor's report "as a story that must be told."

"The Soviet Union is fully aware of the extraterrestrial slave trade and even published a brief paper on the situation in 1984," he said.●

☐ *This won't be the last one of these articles you read. There are many missing people. Another 9 for Henry. (Don't be mad. I know it's worth more.)*

UFO ALIENS KIDNAP FARMER'S SHEEPDOG

National Examiner, **July 5, 1988**

by Mark Stevens

UFO aliens kidnapped his sheepdog, a stunned farmer told police after receiving a surprise visit from spacemen.

Coy Luna, 60, said he was planting potatoes when another dog and his faithful German shepherd began barking at a shiny, globe-shaped UFO that had landed in a hayfield near his house.

Luna told the *Examiner*: "It was sparkling all over and was so bright you could hardly look at it. The UFO was about seven feet tall and 15 feet in diameter.

"It looked like it was covered with tinfoil."

The farmer said the German shepherd took off after the UFO and when the dog got within 30 feet of it, the spaceship shot straight up. A minute later it had vanished.

Luna, of West Point, Tennessee, said he had list taken out a big bowl of food and water for his 14-year-old sheepdog before the UFO landed. Luna believes the UFO snatched up the pooch because the dog has been missing since the sighting of the alien spaceship.

"The sheepdog was close to the spot where that thing landed and he never leaves home," Luna said.

"He always stays by the German shepherd. The shepherd is about to go crazy, and so am I. I've never seen anything like it before and never want to again."

Added Luna: "I'm not seeing or imagining things and I haven't had a drink or nothing."

Sheriff's Deputy Tim Jackson confirmed that Luna was completely sober.

Said Jackson: "I made him go over the story seven or eight times and he had the same story each time. He never varied and he wasn't and hadn't been drinking."

Luna said he got a good look at the UFO.

"It had a door on the side of it, about half the size an ordinary house door," he recalled. "There was a window in the middle of the door. No space beings left the spaceship and none appeared to move inside."

UFO experts are conducting tests at the landing site, Luna said. One UFO expert from Nashville told Luna there was an 80% chance the spaceship would return.●

☐ *So they took a dog. Wait till you read about what has happened to other animals. A dog is only worth about a 5. Just think of all the ducks and elephants and cows and horses etc.!*

UFOS HAVE ABDUCTED AT LEAST 2,300 PEOPLE
***Sun*, August 2, 1988**
Special by Joe Frick

People taken aboard UFOs give such terrifyingly similar accounts of their abductions, more scientists than ever are convinced the outer space ordeals are true.

Most abductees report they're carried up by beams of light that float them into spaceships. They're given physical exams by eerie, gray creatures with large heads and black eyes.

David F. Webb, a solar physicist, has compiled descriptions of some 2,300 abduction experiences.

Webb, who works under contact with the U.S. Air Force in Bedford, MA and investigates UFOs in his spare time, points out the accounts "are very consistent," which leads him to believe the stories, whether they're real visits by ETs or psychological phenomenon.

Decades of reported UFO abductions reveal the astounding similarities.

Ernest and Martha Throne of Sonora, CA remember being in their car one night when the engine shut off and they rose slowly and floated in the air! Martha recalls ending up on an examination table where the creatures looked her over.

They were later returned to their car. They kept their secret for 10 years and still have the wrist watches they were wearing that night. Both are frozen at 7:30—the exact time they spotted the aliens!

Marguerite Carnes also reports "being lifted through the air and into a small hatch" under a saucer from her back yard in Michigan in 1929.

She was examined by creatures with "yellowish-gray bodies," large heads and "big, black eyes" before she was returned to her back yard as the ship sped away.

Budd Hopkins, a UFO author, conducts counseling sessions to help people overcome the trauma of being kidnapped by UFOs. He says the "phenomenon is real" and investigations must continue.●

☐ *Abductions follow the same pattern all over the world. Since this was marked a special, I'd better give it a 10. I can't understand how anyone can criticize it.*

THE TWO FISHERMEN FROM MISSISSIPPI

The two fisherman from Pascagoula, Mississippi, deserve their experience to go down in the records. In 1973 they were fishing when their abduction took place. Two alien-like beings came out of a craft and escorted them in for an examination. The beings floated above ground and therefore they thought of them as being robots. These floating aliens are too numerous to call them all robots. It's one of their best abilities.

Charles Hickson and Calvin Parker were given all kinds of tests. Their case is typical except their conscious memory is greater than many others.

Remember the Mexican Chauffeur that the Reeves encountered in Mexico? Those aliens floated across the muddy ground while Salvador was getting wet and muddy. It's no wonder he chickened out when asked to go in and see their ship.

GREEN ALIENS IN SPACESHIP SUCKED ME UP
***National Examiner*, Feb. 9, 1988**
by Edward Reynolds

Carlos Diaz was sucked into a spaceship examined by slender green men, and abandoned near a roadway hundreds of miles from his home.

That's the amazing revelation of Pedro Romaniuk, 53, director of the Argentine Cosmobiophysic Institute, which conducted an exhaustive investigation into the astonishing case.

The mind-boggling event began after the 28-year-old waiter left his night job in the early morning hours.

As Diaz was crossing a railway yard, he was blinded by a bright light and his body became paralyzed. After being sucked 10 feet in the air, he passed out.

When he regained consciousness he found himself kneeling in a brightly-lit round room with transparent plastic-like walls and no furniture.

Oxygen streamed out of holes in the floor. Diaz discovered that when he moved away from the air flow, he became nauseous.

Under hypnosis Diaz told UFO investigator Romaniuk: "Suddenly three creatures with a human appearance entered, moving softly. The first thing I noticed was the green coloring of their faces and heads."

Added Diaz: "The heads had no trace of hair, eyes, mouth, ears, or nose! They were about six feet tall, slender, and their bodies were covered by a sort of rubber.

"They had two arms like ours, but they were very grotesque because they had no hands or fingers, just stumps with little suckers on the end."

Incredibly, Diaz says the green men used the suckers to painlessly pull clumps of hair from his head, chest, and arms!

And, hours later, he woke up on the side of a highway, 420 miles from home.

Diaz was taken to a local hospital where he submitted to a series of examinations and tests. No physiological or psychological damage was found, although signs of physical experimentation were apparent.●

BABY GLOWS IN THE DARK
***Weekly World,* June 20, 1989**
by Laurel Bowie

Bouncing baby Maury Joffre seems to be a perfectly normal little boy in every way—except that he glows bright green in the dark!

Dumfounded doctors say they don't have the foggiest notion why the 3-month-old infant gives off an eerie glow when the lights go out.

But the mystery is heightened by the bewildering disappearance of Maury's dad, who vanished into thin air shortly after the bizarre babe was conceived.

"We have done every test available and we still don't know what causes the unusual luminescence emanating from this little boy," Dr. Marc DuMont told reporters in Bern, Switzerland.

"The baby is not radioactive. He seems healthy in every way, with only one intriguing characteristic to distinguish him from other babies his age—his body shines like a green Christmas tree light in a dark room.

"His mother seems to be normal, so we would truly love to locate his father in hopes he could fill in some of the missing pieces of this puzzle."

Maury's mystified mom said she met the boy's dad a little over a year-and-a-half ago at the ski resort where she works outside Bern.

"He was a captivating man and we eventually had an affair," bartender Berniece Joffre recalled.

"I loved him and he told me he loved me but he always talked in riddles when I asked him anything about his past. That always made me a little nervous." The day Berniece, 16, learned she was pregnant, she showed up at her boyfriend's lavish apartment and found him gone. And she hasn't seen him since.

"It's like he just vanished off the face of the earth," said the shaken lady. "He took nothing with him but the clothes he was wearing.

"His furniture, his luggage and most of his clothing are still in the apartment, but he's never returned.

"I reported his disappearance to the police and even hired a detective to look for him but there's been no trace.

"He seems to have appeared out of nowhere just days before I met him and then just dissolved into thin air.

"He told me his name was Andre Lemoine and that he worked in real estate, but I don't know if any of that is true." For while baffled Berniece searches for her lost lover, doctors continue efforts to learn why her bouncing baby boy glows green in the dark.

"Thus far, we're in the dark ourselves," admitted Dr. DuMont. "We still hope his missing dad will show up and provide us with an answer."•

☐ *I wonder if this account of a baby which glows in the dark could belong to one of those critters? The green baby gets a 7.5.*

FAMILY ABDUCTED BY UFO
***Weekly World News,* April 28, 1987**
by Doug Gardner, China Corresp.

Peking — A family of three was kidnapped by child-size space aliens and examined like laboratory guinea pigs aboard a cone-shaped starship, according to a top-secret report.

The incident occurred on March 7 during a UFO sighting in the Szechwan province of China that was reported in newspapers around the world.

"The family is undergoing psychiatric and medical testing at the moment. The mother and father are in their early 30's and the child is 9 years old. Their story is incredible," said a psychologist who worked with the family for nearly a week after they were found dazed and wandering by a roadside near their hometown of Ping Wu in central China.

The psychologist, who asked not to be identified because of the tight security surrounding the incident, described tape-recorded interviews with the family from March 9 to 15 at a Peoples' Republic hospital in Chengtu.

"The man, a factory worker and part-time farmer, said he was awakened around midnight by a high-pitched hum that seemed to be just outside his small two-room house.

"He went outside to investigate, followed by his wife and child who were also awakened. They were nearly blinded by a beam of yellowish light coming from a huge reddish-orange object that hovered above them, slowly spinning. The woman said it was shaped life a gigantic straw hat.

"The hum grew so loud that it became painful and they covered their ears, according to the man.

"They then described a floating feeling as if they were being sucked into the craft by the light beam. All three blacked out.

"The woman said she was first to regain consciousness and found herself naked and strapped to a steel table by metallic bands.

"Her husband and son were on duplicate examining tables about 18 inches high. She said the room was circular with 5-foot ceilings.

"The woman said she began to scream hysterically, but her husband and child remained unconscious. She said she was shaking all over and felt alternately hot and cold. She said the light in the room was purple in hue.

"A tiny hatchway in the wall opened and five creatures she described as child-like and barely three feet tall entered the room.

"They looked human in shape with proportionate arms and legs but their faces were featureless except for three huge whitish eyes in their foreheads. She described their skin as transparent blue color that seemed to deepen from time to time.

"The creatures said nothing but immediately took blood from each of their arms.

"They then inserted long needles into their knee and ankle joints but she said there was no pain.

"Her husband and child awakened but seemed to be in a trance, like a half-sleep.

"She tried to speak to them but she could make no sound, only mouth the words.

"Electrodes were taped to their skulls and the woman said they were almost deafened by the same high-pitched hum they heard outside their house. She said the vibration was extremely painful and she kept trying to scream to the creatures. One of the creatures then took what looked like a scalpel and made a long incision in the child's thigh.

"The boy winced and blacked out.

"She said that the cut was healed seconds later when one of the aliens passed a pencil-like instrument over it.

"The woman said the creatures then took clippings of their hair and fingernails.

"The room went pitch-black and she felt as though she were spinning on a very slowly turning merry-go-round. She said her sense of time was distorted. The spinning might have been minutes but she recollects that it might possibly have been days!

"The next thing that any of them remembered they were walking along the roadside about seven miles from their home. They felt nauseated and the child vomited several times. They also reported blurred vision, numbness and ringing in their ears.

"They were picked up by a passing bus and taken to a medical clinic by the concerned driver. They were then sent here to the hospital in Chengtu.

"These people have experienced something amazing. I only hope someday their whole story will be known. I imagine they will be hospitalized for several more months.

"They still suffer terrifying nightmares sweats and racing thoughts."

Editors at *China Daily*, the official government newspaper, reported the UFO sighting at length. But the paper refuses to comment on the abduction until all medical findings are in.●

☐ *The experience of Jimmy Flynn—which I've included—happened in 1965. His description in both shape and sound is comparable to this one. He has never been under hypnosis. Therefore we don't know what happened to him in the 20-hour gap following his sighting. This location was south of route 80, in the Florida Everglades near Homestead Air Base. The China story gets a 9.5.*

ELEPHANTS SNATCHED BY UFO
***Weekly World*, July 26, 1988**
by Henry Weber

A UFO kidnapped a herd of elephants from a safari park while horrified witnesses watched.

"We don't know what to make of it," Police Maj. Oscar Merino told reporters in Lugo, Spain. "It sounds like something out of a science fiction novel.

"But 40 people say they witnessed the abduction. And the fact remains, 26 full grown elephants are missing."

The bizarre drama reportedly unfolded in broad daylight at the African safari park just east of Lugo. According to witnesses, a 250-foot UFO with purple lights on its edges seemed to appear out of nowhere over the park.

Then it sprayed the grazing elephants with a beam of orange light and pulled all 26 into its belly at once.

"I thought the whole thing was being staged when the UFO first appeared," said Imelda Gil-Casares, who was driving through the park with her children.

"But when the elephants started rising up in the air I knew it wasn't a joke. The kids were screaming and laughing but I was speechless.

"I wanted to put the car in reverse and escape but I was too frightened."

The entire incident lasted less than two minutes, Mrs. Gil-Casares and other witnesses said. After that the starship, which was said to be silver and shaped like an upside-down bowl, disappeared.

Park officials refused to comment on the alleged abduction. However, Madrid-based UFO researcher Jose Diaz Salazar has spoken at length on the case. He says space aliens have abducted over 200 exotic animals from zoos and safari parks around the world in the past six months alone.

"It's a trend that government officials worldwide are aware of," he said.

"Hardly a week passes when we don't have at least one new report of an animal abduction. The extraterrestrial collectors obviously have a growing interest in Earth and its animal life."●

☐ *There's no way to leave animal snatching stories out of the picture. It isn't just elephants it's animals. Sometimes they siphon off their blood, mutilate their carcasses or do beautiful jobs of surgical work on their body parts. They manage to do this without leaving clues as to how they accomplish such feats. Often sightings of UFOs are seen near places where such events have happened. Twenty-six elephants are a lot of elephants — it deserves at least a 9. If you don't feel this is worth a 9, pick up a June 26, 1990 copy of the* Sun. *This was written by Maurice Bender, and describes a large circus elephant being kidnapped by a UFO in a big beam of bluish light. This abduction was watched by dozens of observers. The elephant's name was Gina and she belonged to the "Zarafis Circus" which was being presented in Somber, Yugoslavia.*

MAN SNATCHED FROM CABIN BY SPACE ALIENS

National Examiner, **Nov. 15, 1988**

by Edward Reynolds

Christopher Young will never forget the morning he was snatched by UFO aliens and subjected to a terrifying medical examination.

The good-natured college student was living in a small cabin in the foothills of California's Sierra Nevada mountains between semesters.

He had gone to bed early one evening, sleeping on a thin foam rubber pad laid out over a rickety wooden floor.

Young got up early in the morning, when it was still dark. As he lay back down to sleep, he sensed something across the room.

In a split second, a space being's thought penetrated his mind. He was told he was being taken captive.

The space being pinned Young to the floor and roared into his ear, paralyzing him instantly. Then he felt as if he'd left his body; he passed out. What followed he would not remember until 10 years later, after being hypnotically regressed.

Young recalled that he had been surrounded by four-foot-tall aliens with oversized hairless heads and big, black, shiny eyes. The aliens beamed him aboard their spaceship and placed him on an examining table.

An alien stood over him and slid a foot-long needle up his nose. The needle penetrated his upper sinus and made a sudden pop. Young saw a sudden flash of light and lost consciousness. When he woke up, he found himself lying on his stomach with two aliens examining him.

"You are now complete," the leader told him.

Moments later, Young was transported back to the ground, feeling very happy. He believes the aliens may have made him feel that way to lessen the trauma.●

☐ *Sometimes I think there's a million and one comparable cases to this one. Lots of these people don't want to use hypnosis to know what happened—more likely they want to forget. It probably is true—it's worth an 8 because it is so typical of the many UFO abductions.*

UFO ALIENS KIDNAP BRIDE

***Sun,* January 31, 1989**

A wedding day was rocked by terrorists from outer space who snatched a screaming bride from the arms of a startled groom and whisked her away from the church.

The entire wedding party looked on in stunned silence as Eva Danneberg, 23, was abducted by a pair of strange-looking creatures in tight-fitting one-piece uniforms.

Hubby Adolph saw the weird characters approach his new wife and thought it was some sort of prank being pulled by his buddies.

But his smiling expression turned to absolute fear when they grabbed Eva's arms and she began yelling for help just before the trio disappeared suddenly in a bright flash of light.

Some of the horrified onlookers say the beam of light appeared to come from and return to a triangular-shaped craft with red, white and blue flashing lights hovering just above the church.

"Until that day, I never believed in UFOs," remarked the astonished groom after the experience outside the West German City of Munich.

"But there is no other explanation for what happened to my poor Eva."

Authorities are treating the disappearance as a regular kidnapping—despite the large number of eyewitnesses.

"I admit we have no leads at this time," said police Sgt. Gunter Lubke. "It's a very strange case, but we can't consider it an alien abduction.

"We are professionals and that just doesn't happen outside the movies."

The mother of the bride doesn't care what police think, she just wants her daughter returned.

"We pray nightly for our Eva," said teary-eyed Marlene Hannecker. "I'll never forget what those...those things looked like."

The still-shaken women says the abductors had odd-shaped hairless heads, large eyes and slits for a nose and mouth.

"It all happened so fast," moans Marlene. "Why did they have to single out my daughter?"

Lubke vows police will harshly punish the culprits behind what he calls an elaborate hoax.●

☐ *I wonder if they'll give the aliens a couple of years in jail—that'll fix 'em. The heck with the police—they don't know everything. Let's give it a 9 and hope they bring her back someday.*

TRAUMA OF TWO MEN ABDUCTED BY TWO BLUE-GOGGLED SPACE ALIENS

***National Examiner*, October 18, 1988**

by Edward Reynolds

Two men were kidnapped by squat, blue-goggled space aliens and subjected to six agonizing hours of psychological experimentation, reveals a top UFO researcher.

And now everything the terrified victims drink bubbles up like champagne.

The men, Don, a truck driver, and roommate Jack, a retired piano teacher, have told their amazing story on a two-hour tape to Colin Norris, director of the Australian International UFO Research Organization, reports Aussie columnist John Pinkney.

"We became aware something odd was going on," said Jack. "We'd wake up to find our roof TV antenna had spun around to face the opposite direction. I climbed up several times and tightened the clamps, but then the antenna would swing around again."

Next, the men said, eerie-looking people began popping up behind their house near Murray Bridge, South Australia, peeking through windows and fiddling with a huge hot water tank.

"Then one night they burst in," recalled Don. "The venetian blinds shot up and two short men with hairy sweaters and blue-tinted goggles stared in at us.

"The next thing we knew, we were inside their spaceship." Added Don, "It was bitterly cold. When I complained, one of the aliens explained that was the normal temperature where they came from.

He talked in clicking sounds, but I could understand him inside my head."

The men were led to a rectangular room where they were tested. "They sat me at a table and asked me to press a plastic switch repeatedly," Don explained. "This released two kinds of small plastic cups which rolled toward me.

"The aliens told me to place certain cups which were made of a glassy material, to the left of me and to crush the other cups with my right hand. When I did this, the latter cups dissolved into powder which quickly vanished.

"According to my watch, they kept me doing this from 1 a.m. to 7 a.m. The next day I could hardly bend my aching arms."

The men were made to drink a sugary concoction and they blacked out. When they awakened they were sitting at their kitchen table.

Incredibly, a doctor who examined the men after their ordeal reported that their skins had yellowed and that they had strange swellings under their eyes.

And tests confirm the duo had indeed suffered an unusual form of trauma.

Neighbors reported seeing glowing red over the area weeks before the abduction.●

☐ *This is a cute tale and deserves a 6.5 whether it's true or not. After forty years nothing about UFOs surprises me.*

BRIDE AND GROOM SPEND HONEYMOON IN UFO

***Sun*, November 15, 1988**

by Fred Sleeves

A newlywed couple went on a whirlwind romance like no other when they were snatched from the Earth and forced to spend their wedding night in front of an audience of extraterrestrial scientists.

Hector and Regina Loperro say they began their honeymoon as prisoners in a UFO spaceship.

"Hector always promised to take me around the world, but not out of it," declares Regina, 23, who manages to keep her sense of humor despite the harrowing experience.

"We were trapped like laboratory rats in a huge room while these awful things stared at us," she recalls.

"They actually wanted us to mate while they watched because they were studying human behavior, they told us."

Hector, 25, and Regina vanished minutes alter the evening ceremony as they were walking to their car south of Jalapa, Mexico.

Stunned guests who were still celebrating report seeing a huge white light overhead before the couple disappeared.

"Regina and I were hit by the light as we were leaving and suddenly felt ourselves being pulled into the sky," Hector says.

"We ended up inside a spaceship which had sucked us up. There, surrounding us, were these small thin green creatures with huge circular eyes, long arms and hands with what looked like suction cups at the ends of them."

The aliens communicated with them through mental telepathy and wanted them to perform sex so they could see how Earthlings reproduced.

"We refused," Regina states emphatically.

"Hector stood by me the whole time protecting me from those fiends," she adds proudly.

After being examined during the whole night with a variety of strange laser-like instruments, Hector and Regina say they were suddenly returned near their car the next morning.

Although they reported the abduction to police, one officer believes that the two "did too much celebrating" after the wedding.●

☐ *This case would be very simple to check out. Nobody in their right mind is going to make up such a tale after a wedding. I doubt very much that this story is a hoax. The bride and groom deserve a 9.5.*

UFO ALIENS STEAL 2-1/2 HOURS OF TEENS' LIVES

***National Examiner*, Nov. 22, 1988**

by Edward Arnold

David Oldham will never forget the night he and two buddies "lost" two and a half hours, and he found love.

It was the same night a UFO hovered above their car. Oldham was 16. His friends weren't much older. They were riding around trying to kill time and pulled into an isolated road.

That's when the teenagers saw a huge light that appeared to sit on a grove of trees.

Recalled Oldham: "It was as though you could just climb up on the trees and reach and touch it with your hand. It felt that close."

The boys froze and stared in wonder. Finally, one or two of them suggested they should leave.

They drove to a nightclub near Greensboro, N.C. At the door they asked what time it was.

And like an episode straight from the *Twilight Zone,* they realized they could not account for more than two hours of their evening. Oldham cried himself to sleep that night but didn't know why.

It wasn't until nine years later, in 1975, when Oldham was hospitalized after a car crash and had nightmares that he sought answers to the UFO mystery.

Under hypnosis the teenagers' harrowing ordeal came to light. Oldham recalled: "All of a sudden out of the distance I saw a shadow of a person, and, naturally I freaked. The being came at me and I was unable to move. He looked me in the eye and didn't know what to do.

"Through telepathy he told me to close my eyes and relax, that I was frightened, and that there were other people who wanted to see me."

Oldham was taken aboard a flying saucer and placed in a dimly lit room. A group of space beings (SBs) stood over him and passed a strange instrument over his body.

The SBs levitated Oldham and moved him to another room, where they questioned him telepathically. They showed him images on a screen, much like a slide show.

Finally, he was led from the spacecraft and set free, but not before he began crying.

The alien asked why he was showing such emotion and William replied: "Because I've never felt love like this before."

Now 37, Oldham believes that one day mankind and the UFO will walk together in harmony and share love.●

☐ *Do I think these boys are real people? Probably. Do I think they know everything that happened to them? Probably not. I think it's worth a good fat 8.*

WOMAN RECALLS UFO ABDUCTION

***National Examiner*, Sept. 8, 1987**

by Eddie Bea

A housewife reveals that UFO aliens performed unspeakable experiments on her when they abducted her four different times between the ages of 9 and 20.

Shirley Coyne, 47, stunned listeners with her tale during a recent UFO international symposium in Washington, D.C.

The first abduction Coyne knows of took place when she was 9. Later encounters occurred at ages 16, 17, and 20.

"They did some things I'd rather not talk about," she says.

"I was taken from my bed by two beings who were 2-1/2 to 3 feet tall," she explains. "They came into my bedroom. It was like they were floating not walking. I had no control.

"They took me aboard their craft and gave me a very painful examination. They did all kinds of little experiments on me. I have a scar on my thigh where they took a sample of tissue."

Coyne, a mother of two, and her husband, George, first got interested in UFOlogy when there was a rash of UFO sightings in their neighborhood in 1983.

The Coynes saw a UFO themselves as they drove home one night at about 1 a.m.

"I slowed the car," says George. "It started going parallel to us, just over the houses.

"We were not afraid. I wanted to get a message to them. I threw my mind into a blank so I'd be receptive to anything they wanted to send."

But the glowing metallic spaceship merely cruised along beside their car for a short distance and then disappeared.

That sparked the Coynes' interest, and they began to investigate.

George says: "The first thing we tried to do is disprove it." As part of their research, Shirley underwent hypnotic regression.

It was during these sessions that she was able to remember the experiments performed by beings with gray-white skin and "very, very big eyes" aboard the walnut-shaped spacecraft.●

☐ *There is no point in using these articles if I don't tell you what I think—I think this deserves a 9.5 and I don't think it has anything to do with the* National Examiner *making it up. It was a well-known case long before they used it.*

COP VANISHES AFTER TAKING UFO ALIEN'S PICTURE
***National Examiner*, Sept. 22, 1987**
by Enrique Ramon

A terrified cop was reported missing just weeks after encountering an extraterrestrial and taking its picture.

Jeff Greenhaw, 26, was answering a call from a woman who said a UFO had landed near her home when he was startled by a spaceman on an isolated dirt road.

Said the Falkville, Alabama, police chief: "It was just standing there in the middle of the road. I got out of my patrol car and said 'Howdy, stranger,' but he didn't say a word."

Added Greenhaw: "I reached back and got my camera and started taking pictures of him. I was scared stiff, but he didn't move, so I had a chance to take five pictures.

"Then I flipped on the switch for the blue lights and when they started flashing, he took off running down the road. I jumped in my car and took off after him, but I couldn't even catch up with him in the patrol car. He was running faster than any human I ever saw."

Greenhaw said that the metallic-suited alien didn't have any features on its face and had a point on top of its head. It ran like a robot, but made no noise.

"I want to think it was somebody's idea of a joke, but then again some things about it I just can't understand," he told reporters before his disappearance.

"You'd naturally think it was a joke but the way the thing moved and the way the suit fit so well is hard to believe. I just wish I could forgot about it though; I'd be able to get a lot more sleep."

Unfortunately the encounter did not end there.

A few days later, his wife got a call from someone who claimed to be the "spaceman."

"He told her he was going to get me for taking his picture," Greenhaw said. "I just laughed."

But in the space of only a few weeks, his car engine blew up for no apparent reason.

He got threatening phone calls from individuals claiming to be the notorious men in black, many who wanted him to publicly declare that the photos were fake.

When he ignored the threats, his mobile home burned to the ground.

He left the Falkville police department in 1973 and that's when he vanished.

Recently there have been reports that Greenhaw might still be living in Alabama.

And the MIB are preying on others like Greenhaw who have had close encounters, according to top UFOlogists.

Although their origin is unknown, the warning is always the same: discontinue UFO research, surrender all photographs and maintain silence—or else. ●

☐ *This is a much publicized case and should be taken very seriously. Those who criticize these papers should do some research on their own. Anyone should be entitled to a few mistakes and exaggerations. This has happened to many people.... Jeff is just one of the many who have been heckled by the MIB (the Men In Black). I don't think this is a popular thing to do anymore. It's probably worth a 9 or more. The CIA is our most likely culprit.*

FAMILY PLUCKED OFF EARTH BY UFO
***Weekly World News*, March 15, 1988**

Their blood-curdling ordeal, already labeled the Nullarbor Incident, is unquestionably the best documented close encounter of the fourth kind ever reported.

One expert on sightings of alien craft said an of official report claiming the UFO was nothing more than a meteorite shower is preposterous and a scandalous attempt at a coverup.

The expert cited evidence that clearly proves the encounters were genuine. They are:

– the car they were riding in when it was snatched up by the glowing UFO is heavily dented where its roof came in contact with the alien craft;

– scientists are at a loss to identify the talc-like dust that covered the car when police found it;

– descriptions of the odd-shaped UFO given by the trawler captain and crew who also encountered it hundreds of miles away are identical in every respect with those given by Mrs. Knowles and her three grown sons;

– and all efforts by investigators to prove the two separate sightings coincidental hoaxes or a bizarre case of multiple hysteria have been miserable failures.

"We were a bit skeptical at first," said police Sgt. Jim Furnell.

"I've always had reservations about UFOs. But after investigating, we're treating the reports very seriously."

For the Knowles family, the minutes that would change their lives began ticking off in the predawn hours as they traveled a barren highway across Australia's vast Nullarbor Plain on a trip from Perth to Melbourne.

Suddenly a shimmering craft streaked out of the sky and followed the Knowles' car as it raced down the road at 120 m.p.h. before clamping itself to the car's roof.

"I reached out and touched the thing," the 48-year-old mom told reporters. "It felt warm and spongy and it smelled like dead bodies."

Her 24-year-old son Patrick said he heard a humming and then saw a dark mist begin filling the car.

"We started yelling and screaming, but our voices had changed," he said. "They were deep voices and very slow like in a dream.

"Then the craft picked our car up and started to shake it!

"We had our dogs with us and they went crazy. Then the thing released us and the car slammed to the ground so hard it burst a tire."

The glowing UFO hovered near the car for several minutes before it suddenly shot into the heavens with a fantastic burst of speed.

The terrified family drove 400 miles

to the town of Ceduna where they reported their harrowing encounter to Sgt. Furnell., Unknown to the Knowles family or to Furnell, at about the same time but far to the south, the skipper of a fishing trawler was reporting that a shimmering, dome shaped starship had hovered for several minutes over boat in the Indian Ocean.

The skipper and the crew to a man said that when they tried to speak, their voices were very deep and their words seemed to be spoken in slow motion! ●

☐ *This case remains under critical investigation. It's worth at least a 9.5. The Knowles family experience has been well-published in many papers, not just by* Weekly World.

TWO 'LOST' HOURS FINALLY FOUND FOUR YEARS LATER

National Examiner, **1988**

by Edward Manzi

Puzzled by stains and rips on her dress, scuffs on his shoes, and strange marks on their car, Betty and Barney Hill had somehow "lost" two hours while driving through the mountains on a crisp autumn evening.

That blank period would not be filled until four years later when the two submitted to hypnosis and their story made headlines. Later it became the theme for a movie and a popular book, *Interrupted Journey,* which detailed the couple's horrifying abduction by space aliens on September 19, 1961.

The Hills, of Portsmouth, New Hampshire, told of being captured by creatures resembling short, bald humans with big eyes, no ears, and high foreheads. They said they were taken into a spacecraft, examined with strange instruments, and released.

"They put a needle-like instrument in my navel," recalled Mrs. Hill. "The procedure was unheard of then, but now doctors do it every day."

The space beings (SBs) removed her dress and apparently spilled something on it, leaving pink stains that have defied analysis.

Two particular aspects of the Hills' account have given it a high degree of credibility, even among skeptics.

The first is a star map that Betty Hill drew following her hypnotic sessions. Mrs. Hill said it was based on one shown her by the alien leader. Astronomers say the map corresponds closely to a view of the sun and neighboring stars from a few light years beyond the Zeta Reticuli star system.

Incredibly, a number of the stars Mrs. Hill drew were unknown to astronomers until 1969, eight years after the Hills' experience.

The second significant feature is that the Hills' abduction account is strikingly familiar to ones given by dozens of other people and follows a familiar pattern.

Abductions usually begin with the appearance of a dazzling white light. Victims black out at the hands of their alien captors but remember the experience while under hypnosis. The abductees find themselves inside a spaceship and are given chilling medical examinations.

Descriptions of the aliens are fairly standard. They stand about four to five feet tall, have grayish, white skin, and round, shiny black eyes set in oversize, bulbous skulls.

UFOlogist Budd Hopkins, a renowned New York artist, stands out as the chief chronicler of abduction cases. In 12 years Hopkins has recorded thousands of hours of interviews with more than 135 subjects.

One of those subjects, Kathie Davis, is the centerpiece of his latest book *Intruders* (Random House, 1987). In 1983, Davis, 24, a mother of two, lived in an Indianapolis suburb called Copley Woods.

One morning she found a large, circular scorched area in the backyard. In the months that followed, nothing would grow there. Davis later discovered that a spaceship had landed in that spot.

Under hypnosis she said the aliens thrust a needle into her ear. Hopkins speculates the SBs were implanting a tiny device by which they could track her.

Even more disturbing, Davis revealed that during her teens the SBs had visited her and performed an unforgettable gynecological procedure, after which she became pregnant.

Hopkins has photographs of small, scooplike scars on the backs, arms, and legs of more than a dozen subjects who believe they have been abducted. He speculates the SBs may be taking cell samples.

And he concludes the SBs are possibly breeding with humans to strengthen their bloodlines, which may be weakened.

Said David Jacobs, a history professor at Temple University in Philadelphia: "The possibility that these people are saying things that actually occurred to them must be taken seriously. You cannot say these are just crazy people and it just couldn't have happened."

Dr. Leo Sprinkle, psychologist and professor of counseling services at the University of Wyoming, has provided hypnotic sessions for alleged UFO abductees and contactees for more than 20 years.

Sprinkle told the Examiner: "If we don't want to believe these stories, we can reject them. If we do want to believe we can accept them. If we don't know, we have to keep investigating." ●

☐ *If you criticize this article forget it. This includes the best research done in the UFO field. I wouldn't dare to give this less than a 10.*

BABY'S FATHER FROM OUTER SPACE SAY SCIENTISTS

***Weekly World News*, March 21, 1989**

by Gordon Caine

Scientists investigating a series of UFO sightings around Mt. Everest have found an incredible starbaby they are convinced was fathered by a creature from outer space.

"The boy is about the same size as a human baby of about 8 months," said Dr. Wah Singh, "but any resemblance to a human ends right there.

"The baby walks and runs as easily as any adult. He can also lift small objects by pointing his finger at them. And he sets fires with a laser-like beam that shoots out of his eyes."

Dr. Singh said the child has an oversized head, eyes with cat-like pupils, large, tapered ears and a wide mouth.

Even more astounding, Dr. Singh said x-ray studies show the child does not have human internal organs—other than a stomach-like tube terminating in another tube similar to human intestines.

"The youngster has no heart, kidneys, appendix, pancreas, lungs — nothing," Dr. Singh said.

"Instead, there is a single mysterious organ about the size of a walnut in his chest.

"Medical experts conclude it is a combination of all the necessary organs and glands."

Dr. Singh, a noted lecturer at European universities including the Berlin Institute of Research, said the starbaby and his teenage mother were found living alone in a hut outside a mountain village at the base of Mt. Everest, on the border of China and Nepal.

"The young woman had been expelled from her village because she had become pregnant out of wedlock," the scientist said. "She delivered the baby herself and supported herself and the child by begging."

The girl told Dr. Singh and his assistant of a nighttime visit by a beautiful, strange man from the stars.

She said she became unconscious and has no memory of the sexual encounter. Dr. Singh said the region in which the starbaby was found is one of the busiest UFO areas in the world.

"We were simply gathering information on these objects in the sky when we heard of the baby, " he said.

"Villagers spoke of the strange baby, about 8 months old, who never cried and walked as easily as an adult," Dr. Singh said.

Dr. Singh said the mother and child were being readied for a trip to East Berlin where a careful study of the starbaby will be made by top German scientists.

"The scientific community is particularly interested in the multi-purpose organ in the child's chest," he said. "It appears to do the job of many human organs. In many cases it seems to do that job far better.

"We also want to know how he is able to levitate objects and set fires with his eyes. Of course, he may have even greater powers as he gets older. There's no telling what he will be able to do when he grows up.●

☐ *No comment. 8.5.*

UFO BUZZES JET

***Weekly World News*, May 9, 1989**

by Dick Donovan

Passengers aboard a high-flying jet were hurled from their seats just like rag dolls when their plane briefly plunged several hundred feet—after a terrifying encounter with a UFO!

The swift British TriStar jet fell like a rock before its pilot Bob Taylor was able to regain control of it.

The blood-curdling plunge came a split second after the jet, carrying 140 passengers, was buzzed by a blazing UFO that streaked out of the night sky like a comet.

The alien encounter took place as the TriStar flew 30,000 feet above the Mediterranean isle of Sardinia on a flight from Malta to London. Passenger Susie Walton witnessed the UFO fly-by.

"I glanced out the window and saw what appeared to look like a glistening, multicolored cloud that left a vapor trail behind it," 25-year-old Susie recalled. "Then all of a sudden it vanished and our plane plunged earthward.

"I thought it was the end. It was terrifying. Some passengers started praying, and I grabbed the man sitting next to me. I was sure we were going to crash."

But seconds later, its veteran pilot had the huge jetliner under control and climbing back to its assigned altitude.

At least a dozen other passengers saw the UFO as it swooped silently past the jet less than 100 yards away.

"It was glowing red and green and yellow...like a huge oblong cloud," passenger Rita Bathgate said. "It looked like what I imagine the American Space Shuttle to look like when it plunges into the atmosphere from outer space.

The pilot also discounted the possibility that the mystery invader was another earth-based aircraft.

"It was traveling too fast to have been another plane as we know them," he declared.

"We probably will never know what it was. But it most certainly wasn't a plane. I've never seen anything like it."●

☐ *How long do you think papers can make up sightings like this and get by with it? You'll notice your government never bothers to come out and tell you these are all a bunch of lies. The tabloids are doing just what the government needs done. I'll bet President Bush gives Quayle the job of getting down on his knees every night and thanking God for the job they've done. The pilot deserves at least a 8.9 for keeping the plane under control.*

UFO ALIENS KIDNAP COUPLE

National Examiner, Nov. 25, 1986

by Catherine Magrini

A couple underwent hypnosis to relive a mind-boggling abduction by seven-foot-tall extraterrestrials—and convinced a top UFO investigator their experience was terrifyingly real.

Angelo Ricci, 42, and his 37-year-old wife, Grazia, were vacationing at the resort town of Cadore in the Italian Alps when an alien spacecraft touched down nearby.

But the couple from Verona, Italy, remembered nothing of the bizarre two-hour encounter that followed until deep hypnosis unlocked their memories, explains Professor Antonio Chiumiento, president of the Italian Center for UFO Studies.

"I am totally convinced that the Riccis are telling the truth," he told the Examiner. "I haven't the slightest doubt they really did experience a close encounter of the third kind."

The complete loss of memory concerning events in the two-hour period was the result of a temporary amnesia the aliens induced in Ricci, an economist, and his wife, a teacher, to protect them, says Chiumiento.

"The Riccis were questioned twice separately and twice together," adds Chiumiento. "None of the details were contradictory or at odds with each other's version."

This is what they recalled, as described by Mr. Ricci:

"We were sitting at the edge of the woods when we noticed an extraordinary light descending rapidly toward us. I looked at my watch. It was 12:50 a.m.

"We saw it was a luminous white disc, about 30 feet in diameter. It landed almost in front of us, only a few yards away, without making the slightest sound. We were dumbfounded.

"I looked at my watch again and I was stunned. About 10 minutes bad passed, yet my watch now said 3:00 a.m. Grazia and I had no recollection of anything during those two hours. Yet we both felt exhausted and were thoroughly confused."

The Riccis inspected the spot where the craft had landed and saw the grass pressed down and blackened. They returned to their lodging where, unable to sleep, they discussed the incredible experience.

Mrs. Ricci remembered having read newspaper reports of recent UFO sightings in the area and recalled that Professor Chiumiento had been mentioned in them.

They called him the next morning and arranged an interview. The professor persuaded them to undergo hypnosis to reveal what had transpired in the blank two hours.

Mrs. Ricci's account, which was fully matched by her husband's, follows:

"Two human-like shapes approached us. They were at least seven feet tall and clad in some kind of gray fabric jumpsuits that covered all but their heads.

"Their heads were elongated and their faces were oval and very pale. They had no hair. Their eyes glowed like phosphorus, making it almost impossible to look at them.

"Their ears were close to their heads and pointed. They appeared to have normal noses. The creatures had a slit where the mouth would be.

"They walked toward us and picked us up, each carrying one of us in his arms. We were completely limp, with no control over our muscles or movements. Yet my mind was functioning and alert, and I felt aware of everything.

"A feeling of terror swept over me—and, as though the being sensed it or even knew it from inside my brain, I could feel the being talk to me to calm me down.

"Yet there were no words spoken. It was as though this creature could communicate without saying anything. The being didn't seem menacing after that, and I was filled with wonder and awe at what was happening.

"They carried us inside into what seemed a large laboratory, pure white and full of strange instruments and gadgets. Batteries of little colored lights glowed and blinked in panels around the wall.

"We were placed on reclining chairs, like those dentists use but more advanced in design, with buttons and lights built into the sides and they began to perform some kind of testing on us.

"They swung down various devices from overhead and positioned them above our faces and bodies. I was filled with dread, but then I realized nothing they were doing hurt at all.

"I have no idea if they scanned our minds or took any fluids or injected anything. There were no marks or bruises. They simply pointed things at us and studied whatever it was their instruments told them about us.

"This lasted perhaps an hour, maybe longer. I lost all sense of time. They seemed to know exactly what we were feeling and thinking.

"The two beings never spoke to each other, but I got the idea they were communicating and comparing notes in some way we could not understand—as though they were on a separate channel.

"Then they switched their instruments off and carried us back outside into the night, to the very place we had been sitting. I have no recollection of a take-off. They seem to have blanked that out, so we wouldn't remember too much or see which way they headed."

Although the Riccis suffered nightmares, sudden nighttime awakenings and feelings of dread in the weeks following their abduction, they experienced no physical problems, ailments, rashes or marks on their bodies, says Chiumiento.

He obtained samples of the dead grass where the spacecraft landed for analysis and learned from aviation and military authorities that no aircraft had been in the area the night of the Riccis' close encounter.

Chiumiento also discovered there had been at least four other sightings reported of a strange, glowing aircraft in the area that night.

"In my 10 years of UFO research, I have never been involved in so explicit a case of alien contact as that of the Riccis," adds the researcher.

"The Riccis told me they used to ridicule UFO reports. They never believed a word of them. Their encounter has left them badly shaken and no longer in doubt.

"The incident has convinced them that superintelligent life forms are out there—and that they know who we humans are."●

☐ *Typical—all investigators have heard this same story repeatedly. Ho hum, another 9.*

SPACE ALIENS EXAMINE KIDS

Weekly World, **November 1, 1988**

by John Blackburn

Shocking new evidence discloses that heartless space aliens have been snatching terrified tots from their beds for monstrous medical experiments, warns a top UFO investigator.

"We've long been aware that adults are being abducted for these abominable tests, but now we're getting more and more reports of cases involving children," said Budd Hopkins, author of two books on alien kidnappings.

In one horrifying incident, a New Haven, Conn., woman's 2-year-old daughter constantly blubbered about a monster hiding in her bedroom, according to the UFOlogist.

"Just as most any parent would do, the woman told the child she was having bad dreams. One day, though, the girl cried out in terror as she ran from the bedroom and into her mother's arms—pursued by a small humanoid figure with large black eyes.

"The alien was right behind the youngster, the mother told me, almost as if it was on the verge of merging its body with the daughter's. However, the mother screamed and the alien disintegrated before her eyes. Later, the little girl complained the 'monster' had 'burned' her arm and 'hurt' her finger.

"Sure enough, when the woman examined the girl, she found wound marks on her arm and finger."

The fact that there are a growing number of reports of child snatchings may not mean more kids are being abducted now than in the past, according to Hopkins, just that adults are finally paying attention to the terrifying tales told by children.

"Perhaps it's been going on for a long time and has been dismissed because we figure the kids are just having nightmares," said Hopkins.●

☐ *So they've been checking kids for years. This shows up in many UFO books that have been written. Believe me, the tabloids don't have to do much work to give you this report. I'll give John about 8.5 for that subject.*

I TOOK A RIDE ON A STARSHIP

Weekly World, **October 4, 1988**

by Chuck O'Neil

A world famous UFOlogist who's investigated hundreds of close encounters has startled scientific colleagues by revealing for the first time his own amazing childhood voyage beyond the stars.

"It happened when I was a fifth-grader and growing up in a small town in Colorado," recalled University of Wyoming psychologist Dr. Leo Sprinkle, 57.

"I was aboard a space vehicle of some kind, looking out a large window at the stars rushing by. A tall man—at least I think he was a man—was standing beside me, his hand resting on my shoulder.

"He said to me: 'Leo, learn to read and write well. Then, when you grow up, you can help people learn about their purpose in life.'"

Incredibly Dr. Sprinkle, who has hypnotized nearly 200 persons to help them recollect their eerie—and sometimes horrifying—subconscious memories of encounters with space aliens, wasn't aware of his own bizarre UFO experience until he himself went through a hypnosis session in 1980.

"Even today when I visualize that fantastic sight of those stars rushing toward me, it gives me a thrill," the psychologist said. "I think: 'Wow! I'd like to see that again.'"

Some of the individuals Dr. Sprinkle has hypnotized have recounted tales of well-meaning space visitors on a peaceful mission.

These sessions have produced descriptions of aliens who are here merely to monitor our progress.

But others describe chilling experiences of being used as unwilling guinea pigs in frightening medical probes. Dr. Sprinkle said he is sure it is a "benevolent invasion" whose purpose may not be revealed for generations.

"Not only are they measuring us physiologically, but they're also assessing us psychologically, trying to determine what they can do to help us catch up to their advanced level of knowledge," he explained.

"It's still a mystery, though. We don't have the answers. Quite often, we don't even know the questions."●

☐ *I have a rough time with my friends who can't believe there is such a thing as a "Flying Saucer." I am always told all names of doctors and scientists are made-up and I should know better. This is one I'd like to talk them into putting their money where their mouths are. Naturally I'll give it a 10.*

6-YEAR OLD BOY HAS 2 HEARTS

Sun, **August 2, 1988**

by Crandall McIntosh

Astonished doctors admit a miracle youngster with two hearts may have been fathered by a UFO alien, confirming what the boy's mother has claimed for six years.

Pretty and petite Lu sing Suan, 23, says she has endured the cruel taunts and vicious ridicule of her family and former friends ever since the birth of her only child — a boy named Hu Linn — six years ago.

Lu Sing maintains she was made pregnant by a visitor from outer space who abducted her near her home in Loho, in the Chinese province of Honan, and took her aboard a UFO for several days before releasing her.

Acquaintances of Lu Sing admit she vanished for nearly a week at the age of 17, but always said she was staying with a mystery boyfriend.

When she gave birth to a baby boy just four months after her disappearance, even her mother and father scoffed at her outlandish abduction story. They branded her a liar, pointing to the boy's normal appearance.

Doctors noticed right away the lad was anything but normal, however, when they discovered he was born with twin hearts — one in the standard position on the left side of his chest, and one toward his back on the right-hand side.

"No one had an explanation," Lu Sing recalls. "They all said the other heart would dissolve into Hu Linn's body in time. But it never did."

Now there is additional evidence that Hu Linn is not entirely of this world.

"After extensive tests on the boy, I have concluded he is not 100 percent human," explains Dr. Mei Ling Lang. "Not only is there the presence of the dual hearts, his skin tissue is also composed of a substance foreign to anything recognizable by modern medical science.

"It is a condition that defies medical explanation other than to say that since his mother is clearly of the human species, his father must have been some sort of alien life form," she states.

British UFO expert Lane Stevens, who examined Hu Linn at his mother's request four years ago and has monitored the child's condition ever since, says it's about time folks started believing her.

"Perhaps now people will stop harassing Lu Sing and her son," he observes.

"The child is certainly no freak of nature. He is the apparent offspring of a human mother and an alien being.

"And, with two hearts, this endearing youngster has more love in him than any human I've ever met. He should be allowed to grow up in peace."●

☐ *I believe we are given articles like this to see how much we will believe without actual proof. This way we may have some knowledge but no way to prove what we think. I believe we are given enough information to prove them either true or false. I think we can give him a 9 just in case he's really there.*

UFO RIDE AT A CARNIVAL
***Weekly World*, June 13, 1989**
by Joe Gibson

Dozens of carnival patrons got the shock of their lives when they climbed aboard a saucer-shaped "thrill ride" that turned out to be a UFO!

Officials said the 67 men, women and kids could have been kidnapped or killed if the alien crew harbored evil intentions.

Fortunately, the shaken passengers were all released unharmed after a brief but breathtaking ride aboard the brightly lit orange and blue starship.

"It's a miracle we got them back alive," Police Capt. Arne Pedersen told reporters in Askim, Norway.

"We were powerless to help them after they boarded the craft.

"It was up to the extraterrestrials to take care of them at that point. Thank God, they did."

The mind-blowing drama allegedly unfolded just after dusk at the Wulffossen Carnival, one of Norway's largest. According to reports, the carnival featured 32 major rides—not including the UFO.

"I don't know how in the hell it got there," Elling Mykland, carnival chief, told reporters. "The first time I saw the thing it was taking off.

"Everybody on the midway started pointing and screaming: 'How much does it cost to ride that?' "

The Norwegian authorities warned the UFO passengers not to discuss the incident with reporters.

But Jan Bach, one of the first people to board the starship, defied the order under threat of arrest.

He said he climbed a metal ramp and was met by "a blond, blue-eyed child in a silver jumpsuit who accepted my ticket and pointed inside the vehicle. I went into a circular room and stood against the wall," said Bach. "Other people were coming in behind me and they did the same.

"We figured that it was going to spin us around. But when the room was full, the ramp closed. The next thing I knew a second kid in a silver jumpsuit walked into the middle of the room. He gazed up at a small blue light on the ceiling. Then we took off."

Bach said the passengers quickly realized that they weren't on any old ordinary amusement park ride. "Everybody stopped talking and laughing and it got real quiet," he said. "Then one woman looked around and said: 'We're on a UFO!' "

The entire ride lasted less than a minute but Bach is convinced that the starship took the passengers into space and around the world. The alien spacecraft landed in a hay field about two miles away from the carnival. The ramp was lowered.

And when all the passengers had gotten off, the starship rose straight up and disappeared.

Government officials refused to discuss the incident pending the outcome of an investigation. They did confirm that there were hundreds of reports of a UFO sighting on the night the starship allegedly appeared at the carnival.●

☐ *There is no reason on God's green earth this report can't be checked for truthfulness. Until someone comes out with evidence that this sighting is a hoax it's going to get a 9. I'll bet a nickel it deserves a 10.*

UFO SNATCHES PLANE, THEN DISAPPEARS

***Sun*, August 30, 1988**

by Charles Van Nues

Several befuddled witnesses swear they watched in stunned amazement as a pyramid-shaped UFO plucked a small private plane from the air in broad daylight as it approached an airport runway.

Airport officials confirm a twin-engine aircraft owned and operated by veteran pilot Mitchell Lanning suddenly disappeared in mid-air, and puzzled searchers admit they haven't been able to find any trace of the plane or its four passengers.

"This is a most perplexing situation," observes air traffic controller Trent Rogerson, who was on duty at the private airfield near Perth, Australia when the mysterious incident occurred.

"One moment the plane was clearly visible to the naked eye at an altitude of approximately 800 feet, and the next moment it had vanished.

"According to my equipment, there were no other craft in the area, but something snatched that plane right out of the air.

"I'd think I was cracking up except five other people witnessed it too."

The five are two mechanics working in a hangar at the airport, a pilot and his passenger who were preparing to take off in their own plane and Mitchell's wife, Susan.

She was waiting on the ground for her husband's plane to land.

They all say a huge, shiny UFO suddenly materialized from a cloud bank over the airport and whisked the descending airplane away in the blink of an eyelash.

A search party was immediately dispatched to comb the surrounding area, but found nothing. Another search party sent out the next day had the same results — no sign of wreckage, no trace of Mitchell or the three businessmen he had picked up in Melbourne.

"I pray every night that whoever has my husband will bring him back to me," heartbroken Susan says.●

☐ *I keep looking for cases that are so good they can't possibly be ignored. Among my mile-high stack of clippings, I found this one I had overlooked. There's no reason this hasn't been headlined in every newspaper in existence — it could be proved either true or false and should have been. It's worth a 10+.*

UFOs KIDNAP WOMEN TO BREED HALF-ALIEN CHILDREN

***National Examiner*, August 29, 1989**

A top doctor has been serving as gynecologist to female UFO abductees.

And he warns that alien scientists are grabbing women and using them as human incubators in bizarre genetic experiments.

"We feel there are probably hundreds of women throughout the United States who may have been used in this way," says Dr. Richard Neal, of the Southern California UFO Research and Support Group.

For the last 10 years, Dr. Neal, a noted obstetrician and gynecologist, and his associates have examined dozens of women who were abducted by UFOs, forced to submit to painful examinations, and injected with alien sperm.

"There is a substantial amount of evidence that these events have resulted in pregnancies," warns Neal, of Los Angeles.

Neal says once aliens take a woman on board they paralyze her with a powerful drug and then, using a telescopic tube, impregnate her with alien sperm. The aliens then return a few months later to retrieve the half-formed, half-breed fetus.

Afterwards, the aliens track their subjects for years, following signals from transmitters inserted in victims' noses.

"I recommend that known abductees watch for any evidence of recurrent nosebleeds that can't be explained," says Neal. "These beings are coming into people's homes at night and doing this—it's not limited to a lonely isolated spot out in the desert—it's happening in the homes of people."

And no one is safe from the aliens, says Neal.

"It's across the board," he says. "They seem to hit everyone people in the entertainment business, politicians, farmers, blue collar workers, truck drivers—they don't seem to focus in on one specific type."

Neal says women aren't the only ones at risk from the UFOs. Aliens are also collecting bone marrow, blood samples, and even sperm from men they catch.

"I guess they can use that for in-vitro fertilization in their own labs. They're getting eggs from females and possibly do similar research work," he says.

Neal says he does not know why this is happening.

"I would say they're not evil, but they're not good," he explains. "They're indifferent. It's just like they have a job to do and they're doing it.

"They could be the people that brought about the missing link from a Neanderthal man to Cro-Magnon man. For 500,000 years, man stayed the same and then all of a sudden he changed to Cro-Magnon and then to our present Homo sapiens, and I think it was done through some type of intervention."●

☐ *You read it in the* National Examiner! *If there is anything incorrect in it, I couldn't find it. Don't ever come to me with complaints you weren't told these things—you were. The* Examiner *gets what it deserves—a full 10.*

UFOs ARE RAPING EARTH GIRLS
***Sun*, September 5, 1989**
by Ted Holiday

Aliens from outer space have raped thousands of innocent young girls, flying back to other planets with most of their offspring while leaving at least 50 "star babies" to roam among us!

That's the claim of UFO experts who say that hypnosis has helped some women recall the out-of-this-world lovemaking that impregnated them with half-human, half-alien babies.

"It is true. There have been cases of women having intercourse with aliens and becoming pregnant as a result," says Sheridan Lane of the East Anglican UFO/Paranormal Research Association in England.

"I don't know how many cases there are, but it has happened world-wide."

Noted UFO researcher Dr. Gerald Polsky says that there have been 52 reported sightings of "star babies" in the U.S., Mexico, Finland, and Australia.

The half-human, half-space alien beings look almost like normal human beings, he says, except for the fact that they have abnormally long faces.

"I'm sure that most people never even suspect that they know one of these special beings," says Dr. Polsky. "But if you know an extremely intelligent person with a very elongated face, chances are that its father is not human."

According to Polsky and Lane, the "star children" were conceived after their Earth mothers where abducted and taken to spaceships, where they were rubbed with a strange sexual stimulant and forced to have sex with UFO aliens.

"The teens recall being on a spacecraft and having their bodies rubbed with a kind of jelly," explains Lane.

"It is believed that this is some kind of aphrodisiac, because no matter how repelled she may be feeling, she somehow feels stimulated at the same time.

"Intercourse then takes place and the girls become pregnant."

Lane says that some of the Earth moms were flown to another world to give birth—and then brought back to Earth, leaving their babies behind.

"Or, they become pregnant," she says, "and early on in the pregnancy, dream they are giving birth to a child with the skin of a reptile.

"When they wake up they aren't pregnant anymore. It's as if they had suffered a miscarriage."

The UFO expert and her research team believe that this group of mothers were taken back to the space ship in a dream-like state, where they delivered their babies. The newborns were then snatched away by the aliens—and the mothers never even knew what happened.

The babies who were abducted by the alien rapists were hideously deformed, according to the UFO trackers, who say that the nearly human star children were scattered throughout the Earth for a special purpose.

"They will someday become leaders of the first Earth colonies in outer space," predicts Dr. Polsky.

"They were left on Earth so that they can understand human beings and help them adjust to living in space with aliens when the first space colonies are established."●

☐ *The* Sun *and the* Examiner *are obviously kissing cousins. They seem to share their news and do an excellent job. This is another 10 article and shows that both papers are in agreement on the material they present. It also shows that I'm in agreement with them!*

Perhaps these cross-breeding experiments sound far out to you, but remember this kind of information also came from a former music teacher, Elizabeth Klarer, who hails from South Africa. Even in the days of Adamski in the 1950s, Elizabeth made comments which are equally appropriate with today's UFO news. Her claim to have borne an alien son on another planet, at that time was far out—but today it seems like nothing she has said can afford to be dismissed. Cynthia Hind, from Harare, Zimbabwe, Africa, made the following comments concerning Elizabeth Klarer. The following quote is from a recent letter:

> Elizabeth Klarer is a very nice lady. I have known her for a long time and have always respected her for her gentle ways, her many talents and her genuineness. I think she is a very determined person too and I cannot for one moment believe that she would make up all these lies about her trip to Meton and the son she bore Akon; she is not the sort of person who would ever admit to having an illegitimate child. She just does not come from that generation.
>
> On the other hand, I do find inconsistencies in her story. Some things do not tie up with others; some statements are not the same as they were before. But then no-one—not even those who are much younger—could be expected to remember everything they originally said and confirm this about 25 years later.
>
> The major problem here is whether Elizabeth Klarer's experience was a real one or one of imagery. Unfortunately for Klarer, there is no physical proof. She has produced a ring which she claims Akon gave to her. I have seen the ring and it is charming and has a sort of Victorian-era acceptability to it. On the other hand, I think all the stones are obtainable on Earth so it could have come from anywhere. But for those of you involved with spiritualism, there are apports — could this be something like that?

UFO ALIENS—NEW EVIDENCE SHOWS OSTRICH PEOPLE CAME FROM OUTER SPACE
***Sun*, September 26, 1989**
by Francis Shifflett

Descendants of space aliens have been living on Earth for centuries—in an African tribe known as the Ostrich people!

The natives' bizarre two-toed feet are evidence of their amazing alien past, claims famed anthropologist Dr. Etienne Charbonal.

"After we gained their trust, the tribe revealed to us what is unquestionably Africa's last and greatest mystery," says Dr. Charbonal. "In the jungle outside of their village, there is a demolished UFO.

"The tribe goes there to worship, conducting a strange ceremony in which they pray to their ancestors."

Located in an isolated jungle region of Zimbabwe, the Ostrich people number about 100. Each member—man, woman, and child — exhibits the shocking foot deformity.

Despite their awkward appearance, the two-toed feet are surprisingly nimble. The toes can be used like fingers to pick up objects. And the large size of their feet aids the Ostrich people in keeping their balance when trudging through jungle mud.

Since the natives are shy and elusive, little was known about them before Dr. Charbonal's landmark expedition.

"We arrived in their village with the goal of observing the people in their day-to-day lives," says Dr. Charbonal. "This proved to be difficult at first, since they were very suspicious and didn't come out of their huts for days.

"But gradually they began to lose their fear and approached us. They became wonderful hosts, feeding us and giving us shelter at night."

The explorers even witnessed the birth of a two-toed baby.

"In the past, the few researchers who had observed the Ostrich people believed that their strange feet were the result of a genetic mutation," says Dr. Charbonal. "Since we had not discovered anything to the contrary, we had to accept this explanation. But then something amazing happened."

It was during the night of a full moon that Dr. Charbonal's team was wakened by the natives, who were naked and had painted their entire bodies glowing silver. The awestruck explorers followed the tribe into the dark jungle. After several hours, they came upon a large, shining silver dome.

"It was badly smashed and covered with vegetation," says Dr. Charbonal. "The tribe began dancing wildly around it and singing songs to their 'ancestors from the sky.'

"The dome was like nothing of this earth."

The incredible ceremony continued until the first light of dawn. Then the weary Ostrich people led the explorers back to their village.

On the way, an elder told Dr. Charbonal that about 200 years ago, the large "spinning sun" had fallen from the sky, bringing the tribe's ancestors to the remote jungle area. That was all anyone remembered.

More will be known when the French team returns to the jungle to study the crashed UFO.●

☐ *I keep watching for articles with a location that can be found and verified. Author Cynthia Hind has written a book on UFOs; she has traveled many miles in Africa to check out these sightings. Several reports from our tabloids have been within her reach. She was surprised to find these Ostrich people do exist. Their two-toed feet bear no resemblance to our feet. I wish I were able to show you a picture of them— get a copy of the* Sun, *the article and pictures are well worth it.*

Cynthia lives in Harare, Zimbabwe. I sent her the following article, which she was able to verify. I will print a part of her letter so that you will realize the work that is done by the tabloids. And by the way—Cynthia also was able to verify the existence of the Ostrich people.

HUBBY FINED $110 FOR KILLING WIFE!
***Weekly World News*, Oct. 24, 1989**

"Your young wife got what she deserved," said a hardhearted judge who fined her burly husband $110—for beating her to death.

"Every woman should mind her man and do what he says," said Magistrate John Russell. "Total obedience to your husband is a virtue."

Fragile Francine Chapusa, 28, was brutally punched by her 205-pound husband, Laimon, because she refused to go home and fix supper.

"He had been drinking beer all afternoon at a bar on a farm," said Harare, Zimbabwe, Police Inspector Kip Kabala. "She was with him, but he wouldn't allow her to drink." Witnesses told cops the drunken hubby ordered her to go home and prepare supper for them and their three children, who had been left alone.

When she refused to leave without him, Chapusa, 56, sent her reeling across the room with a fist to her face.

He yanked her to her feet, punched her in the stomach and threw her out the front door of the bar. Then he kicked her and dragged her home.

The drunken hubby pushed her inside, pinned her to a wall and beat her with a stick. She died a short time later.

Chapusa was charged with second-degree murder but released without bail so he could care for their children.

"The victim was asking for trouble by the way she behaved," said Magistrate Russell. "Chapusa's behavior was extreme, but he definitely was provoked into uncontrollable action."

Sending Chapusa to prison would make the children virtual orphans and send a wrong signal from this court to other wives who would ignore their husbands' wishes, said the judge.

"Since you have no previous record, Mr. Chapusa, I fine you $110 and place you on probation for one year," said Magistrate Russell.●

EXCERPTS FROM CYNTHIA'S LETTER:

With regard to the cutting, which I return herewith, this is absolutely true. They might have printed it in a more sensational way than it was presented by the press here, but it is quite true that some Judge—no, it wasn't a Judge, but a Magistrate, said what he did say. It was absolutely disgusting, I thought so at the time, and a travesty of justice and I believe there was such an outcry in the press, letters to the editor and dozens of comments from women all over. But the African male is very chauvinistic and he believes the woman's place is in the home and subjected to the man. What a cheek. Of course, if he had beaten her, then perhaps one could understand a totally chauvinistic magistrate's remarks, but he KILLED her. I must try and find out what happened, but I believe something did come of it all, and the man was given a much heavier sentence. I will try and find out from some journalistic friends of mine what happened eventually, but it goes to show, the *Weekly World* is printing the truth. I wonder who is sending them these items from our newspapers — perhaps they pick it up themselves?

Incidentally, it was not a Judge who gave that ruling. It was a Magistrate. They have these small courts where a Magistrate presides and then the person can appeal to a higher court. But I must tell you that there are many travesties of justice, Lillian, but what can one do? They have to learn, the same as anyone else. I often pick up the paper to find that someone has been fined or gaoled for witchcraft, cutting up the body of a dead child and sometimes KILLING a child to use its genitals or other parts of the body, i.e. the tongue, the brain, the nipples. Horrible, but Africa is still very primitive and one cannot change these people overnight!

☐ *My* Oxford American Dictionary *defines a Magistrate as a minor judge, which is near enough not to criticize the* Weekly World News. *I hope many people will understand why I am doing so much to uphold "The defense of the grocery store tabloids!"*

Even though this article has nothing to do with UFOs, it shows the sincerity of the material presented. These papers must have many different contacts to feed their hungry editors and their flocks...how about a 10 for Cynthia and Lillian?

GRANDMOTHER MADE BLIND BY SPACE ALIENS

***Weekly World News*, Nov. 28, 1989**

by Jack Alexander

I was skeptical of Marianne Shenefield's psychic powers while interviewing her on the phone, but not anymore.

"If you can zap TV sets and pop lightbulbs by looking at them, perhaps you could give me a sample of your powers over the phone," I asked.

Believe it or not, the phone system went dead within five seconds. I called back, wanting still more proof.

Five minutes later, the phone went dead again. And the power in the *News* building went off for three or four minutes.

I called Marianne back. "I'm sorry, but you asked me to do it," she said. "I do have the power to blow circuits." She made a believer out of me.

An encounter with aliens 37 years ago left Marianne totally blind—but with amazing psychic powers!

In an exclusive interview, the 48-year-old Mississippi grandmother relived that frightening experience and made these startling revelations:

The United States and most of the world is inhabited by visitors from other planets "who come and go as they please."

These extraterrestrials have a grayish color to their skin, but otherwise look, act and talk like us. Most, but not all of them, mean us no harm.

They are superintelligent beings with enormous powers to cause tornadoes, hurricanes, and even earthquakes.

"I've been deathly afraid lately because of Hurricane Hugo and the California earthquake," she told the *News*. "It could be Mother Nature...or it could be them."

Marianne was 11 when she was abducted while playing in the backyard of her parents' home in Agawam, Mass.

"A small Oriental-looking boy in a greenish-black skindiving outfit with a large metal helmet put his hand on my head," she said. "I felt like I was floating as he led me to a silver spaceship.

"Another alien sat me in front of a large TV screen that showed my internal organs and brain waves.

"I screamed for my parents, but no help came. I was so terrified I threw up all over one of the aliens. Then they tried to attach a hose with something like an oxygen mask to my mouth."

The six aliens had grayish skin and spoke English in mechanical-sounding voices. After testing her emotional responses by pressing buttons on a silver box, the aliens left her on a hill near her home, dazed and disoriented.

"They warned me to look away when they took off," she said. "I remember seeing a bright flash of light."

Five months later Marianne's sight deteriorated. The diagnosis: bilateral degeneration of the macula, a genetic disease usually afflicting the aged.

"Since I have no history of this eye disease, doctors speculate rays from the TV screen on the spaceship either created my blindness or speeded up the deterioration process." Marianne has been blind for 37 years, but has the incredible ability to see the energy mechanisms in people, animals and plants.

A renowned expert on psychic phenomenon, Dr. Andrija Puharich, says Marianne has developed an extraordinary psychic power because of the alien encounter and resulting blindness.

"Marianne is psychic. She can read what you're thinking by observing the aura of your body," said Dr. Puharich. "Psychics believe the aura is an atmosphere that surrounds a person like a halo and is invisible to most people."

Dr. Puharich and two other psychiatrists say Marianne is "for real." They have taped her alien encounter experience while she was under the influence of sodium ambethal, a truth serum.

"My powers allow me to spot aliens because they have a different aura. Their body mechanisms are different."

Marianne has seen space aliens walking the streets of Boston as recently as five years ago. She saw several in New York City and one alien knocked on the front door of her home in Mexico in 1974.

"I know some of your readers will think I'm a kook, but for whatever reasons, the space aliens made me blind and psychic. I can explode a TV or pop a light bulb by just looking at it.

"And I can literally see right through people," said Marianne.●

☐ *All grandmothers deserve 10s.*

ALIEN CAPTURED IN RUSSIA
***Sun*, May 15, 1990**
by Francis Shifflett

Several months after an extraterrestrial spaceship kidnapped residents of a Russian town, Soviet troops have raided a UFO base in Siberia—and captured one of the aliens alive!

Russian authorities are keeping a tight lid of secrecy on the developments to avoid worldwide panic. But they have privately informed top U.S. officials, in the new spirit of cooperation that exists between our two countries.

"The truth of the matter is that this is only the tip of the iceberg," says a top Pentagon official, on the condition that his name not be disclosed.

"We have reason to believe that this facility was only one of several alien bases operating in the U.S. and Russia.

"The important thing is that we have finally come face to face with one of the creatures that have been living alongside of us.

"The Kremlin has provided us with an image of the alien and detailed information about its body structure."

The astounding chain of events that led to the space alien's capture began with a flurry of UFO activity in the Russian town of Voronezh.

In an incident that was reported around the world, a glowing red ball landed in a city park and two tall, three-eyed creatures and a robot emerged. One of the aliens fired a ray gun at a boy standing nearby, causing him to disappear. The boy eventually reappeared when the spaceship took off.

Later it was reported that 26 residents of the town had disappeared in similar encounters. Soviet radar traced the UFO abduction ships to bases in both Siberia and Alaska.

When satellite photos revealed a large silver dome in the desolate Siberian wilderness, an elite squad of Soviet soldiers and scientists was sent to search for the base.

"As soon as our helicopters landed on the frozen wasteland, we saw the giant silver dome in the distance," reports a high-ranking Soviet officer who agreed to speak about the mission.

"Unfortunately, the aliens quickly sensed that they had visitors and decided to flee."

The stunned squad watched in amazement as the dome opened up and a huge glowing ball blasted off and disappeared into the sky.

"After we recovered from the roar of the takeoff, we entered a tunnel that led to the dome, which we expected to be uninhabited," says the source.

"Inside we found a giant open area the size of a football stadium, filled with blinking lights. Then we heard a strange moan and noticed a large figure lying motionless on the ground."

The troops cautiously approached the creature, which was apparently left behind and wounded by the blast of the spaceship taking off.

It was over seven feet tall, with long thin arms and legs. Its most remarkable feature was its gigantic silver head and large jet-black eyes. It was dressed in a tight green jumpsuit with a strange insignia on its chest.

The squad airlifted the alien to a Russian military base for medical treatment and study.

Scientists have constructed residences in the area of the base and are now conducting a detailed investigation of the abandoned structure.

Meanwhile, sources report that the creature's health has improved. It prefers to eat iron-rich soil and speaks in a high-pitched language that sounds like human baby talk.

"So far, efforts to communicate with the alien have been unsuccessful and it has not provided any clues to the whereabouts of the abducted Russian citizens," says the Pentagon official.

"The Soviets have asked for American assistance in studying it, but our government has decided not to become involved for the time being. Quite frankly, we fear that a captive space alien could spark an intergalactic war if its buddies try to rescue it."●

☐ *The purpose of this article is to convince you that we do have aliens both alive and dead. And that there are bases of them in many places on this planet. The constant repetition of these facts is the only way it can be hammered into the heads of Earthlings!*

Why would a number of papers print the same story if all this is make-believe? How else can our government inform us on such a controversial subject? You have a chance to think for yourself. Do it—probably a 10. Be grateful to these tabloids, they deserve it.

LOSES FACE

***Weekly World News*, June 5, 1990**

by Pete Sanders

A 40-year-old woman says space aliens sliced off her face with a laser scalpel and left her in a field to die!

And while medical authorities can't vouch for her story, they admit that somebody or something seared Gloria Garcia's face right off her head, leaving nothing but ugly scar tissue behind

"The woman suffered unimaginable trauma but we are at a loss to explain what happened or why," said Dr. Jayme Santiago Ramos, the woman's physician.

"She says the damage was done by extraterrestrials who took her aboard a starship.

"Maybe that happened. Maybe it didn't. I'm more concerned with the patient's health and figuring out how to give her a new face. She almost died from the shock."

Mrs. Garcia is the first to admit that her story sounds farfetched. But as she puts it: "I wouldn't lie about something like this."

In her statement to police, the woman said she was standing in front of her home in Belo Horizonte, Brazil, when a saucer-shaped UFO appeared overhead.

She said she started to run but blacked out only to awaken on an examining table aboard the ship.

"Hideous men with long noses were standing all around me, talking in a language I didn't understand," said Mrs. Garcia. "I begged them to let me go but they wouldn't listen. I tried to get away but I couldn't move.

"I was screaming when a machine came down from the ceiling and stopped in front of my head.

"One of the men waved a strange flashlight and a red light shot out and cut into my face.

"The pain was so bad I begged God to let me die. But He wouldn't let me die. I just fainted.

"And when I woke up I was in a field near my house. I didn't know it then, but my face was gone. They cut it off and kept it like it was a mask."

Military officials have questioned Mrs. Garcia several times but refuse to comment on their investigation.

Reports that a UFO was spotted over Brasilia at the time of her alleged abduction remain unconfirmed, so there may or may not be a connection.

"Nobody knows what to make of it," said Francisco Barros, a UFO researcher based in Rio de Janeiro.

"Extraterrestrials rarely harm humans. Why they would want this woman's face is beyond comprehension."●

☐ *So you think you want to know about these things? This is not a typical UFO experience, thank goodness. However, there is almost no reason to doubt this woman's story.*

Laser surgery is a specialty of aliens. It's usually animals—they lose many parts and are left dead in fields. The Weekly World News *deserves a 10 for publishing it—hunt up a copy and look at that woman's face!*

BEAMED UP BY A GIANT UFO!

***Weekly World*, October 31, 1989**

by Laurel Bowie

Terrified Dr. Tino Ciuni and his family were captured by aliens and held prisoner for seven electrifying hours—after a fiery red spaceship sucked their car into the sky!

The stunned surgeon, his wife Sophia and his brother Roberto were driving down a lonely mountain road northeast of Venice, Italy, when the saucer-shaped starship suddenly loomed in front of them.

"The thing was bathed in bright red lights, so brilliant we had to cover our eyes to avoid being blinded," recalled trembling Tino, 39.

"As soon as the object appeared, our car conked out on us. And the next thing we knew, we were being lifted into the air and drawn toward the ship like we were in the grip of a powerful magnet.

"Poor Sophia screamed and we all grabbed onto each other for comfort. We didn't know what was happening, but we knew we were totally helpless."

Bewildered police say the incident marks the second time in two years that travelers have reported being sucked into the underbelly of a bizarre spacecraft in the remote mountain pass.

In 1987, a carload of Belgian tourists told cops they were beamed into the sky by a scorching-red starship that air-lifted them to a spot 60 miles away before dropping them off unharmed.

"There is definitely something going on out there," said mystified investigator Indro Bonifazi. "Right now, we just don't know what to make of it."

The still-shaken Ciunis said their car was drawn gently against the underside of the 40-foot UFO and held there through the night.

"As we were raised up, the red lights that had been so bright softened into an orange glow," astonished Tino told reporters.

There were porthole-type windows in the bottom of the craft and we could see faces moving around in them—little blob-like faces.

At first we were all hysterical, but soon a strange sensation of calm came over us. We all had the same feeling, like people in the craft were trying to communicate with us, to tell us that everything would be all right.

"We continued to pray, but we all began to feel less terrified for our own safety."

The frantic family's adventure into the unknown ended at dawn when their car was gently lowered back onto the roadway.

"The car started immediately and we drove away—almost like nothing had ever happened," said the dumbfounded doctor.●

☐ *Surely, surely the good doctor has better things to do than make up stories like this one. I don't doubt this experience any more than I question whether we'll have to pay income taxes next year. How about a 9.9.*

GIRLS GIVE BIRTH TO UFO BABIES
***Sun*, April 24, 1990**
by Bruno Grosse

UFO panic has gripped a city where five young girls have given birth to grotesque, green-skinned alien babies!

The girls, from 7 to 10 years old, previously described horrifying close encounters with alien visitors whose spaceships have been spotted by hundreds of residents over a wide area!

Now four months old, the alien babies are kept in a private wing of a Caracas, Venezuela hospital. Doctors report that the five are highly intelligent and have already begun communicating with each other in a strange high-pitched language.

The sensational saga began over two years ago when a group of purple, triangular-shaped UFOs were seen flying low over Caracas in formation.

Police received dozens of eyewitness reports, but none were as strange as those given by five girls who claimed to have been taken aboard the UFOs.

"Normally, we would dismiss such tales as the products of overactive imaginations," says Police Captain Donaldo Ramirez. "But all five girls, who had no knowledge of each other, told remarkably similar stories.

The account of a 10-year-old, identified only as "Anita," was typical.

"I woke up late at night when I heard a kitty cat meowing outside," she says. "I got out of bed to go look for it.

"When I opened the front door, I saw a bright purple light coming from the park across the street. It was so pretty I walked over to it, even though I was afraid."

Spellbound, Anita approached a triangular spaceship the size of a house. It emitted a deep humming sound and bathed the surrounding trees in an eerie purple glow.

"Three little men with green skin and big yellow eyes came out of the purple house," Anita recalls. "They danced around on the grass, meowing like cats and jumping up and down. It made me laugh so hard I fell down."

Vaguely, as if in a dream, Anita remembers being carried into the spaceship.

Inside, dozens of tiny aliens surrounded her, hissing and touching her with four-fingered, clammy hands. Then a sweet-smelling mist filled the ship and Anita lost consciousness.

A neighbor found her in the park the next morning, asleep under a tree. Her parents took her to the police after she described her strange ordeal.

"We gave Anita and the four other girls complete medical examinations, but failed to find anything unusual," says Ramirez. "Five months later, we were stunned to learn that they were showing signs of pregnancy.

Dr. Rafael Tamayo, an obstetrician, was called in to examine the girls.

"Since none of the girls was old enough to conceive, it appeared that all of them had been implanted with embryos, much like surrogate mothers," he states.

"The strangest thing was that these embryos had taken control of their body functions. Any attempt to abort them would have killed the girls.

"As much as we hated to, we were forced to let nature take its course."

All five girls gave birth on the same day, one Dr. Tamayo will never forget.

"I delivered one after another green-skinned, eight-fingered slimy creature," he recalls.

Each strange infant was more hideous than the one before it.

At the end of the day, all five infants looked at us with their wide-open yellow eyes and cackled like crows. Now they're speaking in a strange language."

Meanwhile, the purple UFOs continue to appear.●

☐ *I'm trying to present what I think is probably true...I believe one is probably true and could be checked. It's worth a full 10 to me!*

KIDNAPPING

Do I believe Aliens pick up kids?
Oh yes — I think they do.
It isn't only kids they get,
Perhaps they may get you!

Sometimes they just examine you,
To see how you are made.
Now and then — you may disappear,
And never be seen again.

But mostly they just poke and probe,
To see what they can find.
It seems their parts need some repair —
One thing for sure — they need more hair!

But that is neither here nor there,
There's not much we can do —
Let's hope the ones who do get you,
Give back more than they take from you!

Of course, a man may lose some sperm,
And a girl and egg or two —
They may implant some seeds of theirs,
That may help brains — but not our hair!

So if you acquire something awful,
Just yell "Rape, it was a UFO,"
You may win out in a court —
It's probably useless to report!

CHAPTER SEVEN

Space Probes From Heaven

Phone Line to Heaven — *Sun* 180
Space Probe Records God's Voice — *Weekly World* 180
Space Probes Take Photos of Heaven — *Sun* 181
Pilot Enters Heaven During Devil's Triangle Flight — *Weekly World* 182
I Was Taken to Heaven in a UFO — *Weekly World* 182
John's Dream — Rescuing Souls — *Public Opinion* 183
UFOs Come From Heaven — *Sun* 183
Woman 'Dies' and Goes to Heaven — *National Examiner* 184
Loving Old Couple Experience Paradise — *Weekly World* 184
Baby Born Talking, Describes Heaven — *Sun* 185
Life After Death Proof — *Weekly World* 185
Angels — *Poem* 186

PHONE LINE TO HEAVEN

***Sun*, August 2, 1988**

by Michelle Tupper

A noted scientist claims he has invented a mind-boggling new machine that makes it possible to talk directly with spirits from the great beyond.

Dr. Wilhelm Von Schmid, on sabbatical leave from Hamburg University in West Germany, says he will unveil a prototype of the amazing machine for fellow physicists at a conference to be held this fall in Zurich, Switzerland.

The 46-year-old scientist, who is best known for his work in magnetism and force fields, says he became interested in beyond-the-grave communication after the death of his mother last year.

"My aunt convinced me to attend a seance to contact the spirit of my mother," he recalls.

"I had always been skeptical of such things but agreed to keep an open mind.

"To my astonishment, the medium was able to conjure my mother's presence and talk to her.

"But when I tried to do the same thing later on my own, I failed.

"So I set out to build a machine capable of tapping into the same universal energy source used by the medium to contact the spirit of my mother.

"At the risk of sounding immodest, I believe I have accomplished that aim.

"You see, science in recent years has been able to actually detect and measure this energy, which was once thought to exist only in the psychic realm.

"My invention utilizes this energy in much the same way as a message is transmitted from one place to another over telephone wires.

"It was simply a matter of hooking into the force field inherent in the atmosphere and all matter."

Von Schmid claims anybody—when armed with the knowledge of how to operate his machine—can "call up" the spirits of departed loved ones and carry on a conversation with them.

He plans to demonstrate this capability at the upcoming symposium.

"This isn't advice you'll find in people's homes," he observes.

"It's much too expensive and complex.

"But it could go a long way in bringing traditional and psychic sciences together as one, which is essential if we are to fully understand the universe in which we live and die."●

☐ *What man can think of, man can do. It's only a matter of time until somebody is going to figure a way to do this — when he does he's going to get a 15 instead of a paltry 10.*

SPACE PROBE RECORDS GOD'S VOICE

***Weekly World*, November 29, 1988**

by Ragan Dunn

(Incredible 12-second message was beamed to Earth from far beyond the solar system)

A space probe that shot dramatic photos of heaven earlier this year has now recorded the voice of God Himself, a top scientist claims.

Dr. Kurt Bauer, the German astrophysicist, says that the 12-second message beamed from the probe back to Earth is both direct and clear.

According to the Soviet tape, it says: "You have worlds to explore. The universe and everything in it is yours. But heaven is Mine. You must stay away."

"This could easily be the most important message in the history of mankind," Dr. Bauer told reporters in Magdeburg, West Germany.

"It not only proves the existence of a God in heaven, it shows that He is interested in and has some great plan for men.

"There isn't a doubt in my mind that the Soviet tape is genuine," he continued. "The voice itself is almost indescribable. It's like hearing a hundred baritones and a symphony orchestra rolled into one."

Tight-lipped Soviet officials would neither confirm nor deny Dr. Bauer's report. They did say the German expert has worked closely with Soviet space scientists since 1979. They also acknowledged "he would have access to the tape-recorded voice of God if it did, in fact, exist."

Kurt Bauer made international headlines last May when he revealed that the Soviet probe had photographed heaven after it passed Pluto on a voyage into deep space.

At the time he said the probe flew through a rainbow-colored tunnel and emerged over a great walled city that literally glittered under an intense golden light.

The probe's photos also showed people filing through the gates of the city as if they were entering heaven for the first time.

Dr. Bauer concluded that the images were identical to those described by people who have died and gone to heaven before doctors were able to bring them back to life.

"The probe beamed hundreds of photos to Earth before it malfunctioned or was disabled by some outside force," said the expert. "Oddly enough, it began to function properly again in October and that's when it recorded the voice.

"The craft is headed out into the far reaches of space. It's almost as if it was guided out of heaven by the hand of God and put back in its place."

Dr. Batter said the Soviets have no plans to release photographs of heaven or the tape for the foreseeable future. They say the voice could be a radio transmission originating on Earth and the photos merely space debris catching the light of the sun.

One man who hopes to persuade them otherwise is French clergyman Hubert Domon. "We must pressure the Russians into giving them to us."●

☐ *I'm sure not going to give God less than a 10!*

"DEAD PEOPLE SEEN ALIVE IN LOVELY CITIES AND PARKS"

"SPACE PROBES TAKE PHOTOS OF HEAVEN"

Headlines like these cause people to turn away from the grocery store tabloids. Without reading further, one is convinced this is just another silly made-up article. Had it said "Space Probe Scientists are Dumbfounded" some might have read a few more paragraphs. You are told this information is being kept secret for now in hope of avoiding a world-wide panic. Many believe this is nonsense, but those people don't know what they'd be told. If you announce yes, we are having space visitors — you'll have one million and one more questions to which you won't know the answers.

These papers are serving a very useful purpose. Suppose there was a probe that passed through the asteroid belt and was sending pictures back to earth?

PROBE TAKES PHOTOS OF HEAVEN
***Sun*, April 25, 1989**
by Francis Shifflett

A probe deep into the outer reaches of our solar system has sent back amazing pictures of a mystical realm that, some scientists are convinced is heaven!

Although an official report hasn't been released, stunned administrators confirm that the pictures show a shining city of the dead!

"This information is being kept secret for now in hopes of avoiding a world-wide panic," says a top official on condition he remains anonymous. "The discovery is so earth-shattering it will soon be viewed as the most important event in history.

"Not only have we discovered what's out there in space, we've also answered the eternal question of what happens to us after we die."

Launched in the mid-Seventies, the space probe had passed the asteroid belt and was sending back pictures and readings of outer space.

"The probe was functioning normally," notes the source, "but suddenly we began receiving data that indicated the probe had entered a cosmic 'dust storm', a vast haze of debris apparently resulting from the disintegration of a planet.

"Luckily, it proceeded undamaged and we became very excited at the prospect of viewing the first images ever taken within a cosmic storm."

But nothing could have prepared the excited scientists for the jolt they were to receive when the pictures from the probe began coming in.

"We stood there in disbelief," says the high-ranking official. "It was too fantastic, too impossible to be true.

"Yet right in front of us were pictures of a beautiful city of crystal buildings and lush gardens — teeming with human beings!

"All of this in the midst of a dismal storm in outer space, near no sun or planets, near nothing.

"And yet, there was a mystical other worldly quality about these pictures, and we knew we were not looking at any place on Earth."

When asked to describe the pictures, the usually talkative scientist finds himself at a loss for words.

"To begin with," he says, "the landscape was filled with giant angular buildings. The buildings appeared translucent and luminous.

"Large tropical-looking vegetation was arranged in orderly gardens between the buildings and wide crystal streets.

"Closer shots revealed that the streets and gardens were teeming with people. They were dressed in fine clothing, but some of the fashions were from a bygone era.

"They all seemed to be enjoying the prime years of their lives, although they were of different ages and different races. Their faces literally glowed with peace and tranquility."

Suddenly, readings from the probe indicated it had slipped back into outer space.

Efforts by mission control to turn it back towards the strange city were unsuccessful.

Months of intensive study led the scientists to conclude the probe had somehow passed into another dimension upon entering the dust storm.

"We believe this dimension is what is commonly referred to as heaven," says the official.

"Many people who've had near-death experiences have given exact descriptions of this place.

"Since the probe sensed a complete absence of physical dimensions, such as land mass and atmospheric composition, we have concluded that this wonderful place exists purely within a spiritual realm.

"With no star or sun nearby, some of our scientists believe the brilliant light that suffuses everything in the pictures is the presence of God."●

☐ *True or false — it's good enough to deserve a 10.*

PILOT ENTERS HEAVEN DURING DEVIL'S TRIANGLE FLIGHT

Weekly World, July 21, 1987

by Pete Wheeler

A German fighter pilot says be flew into heaven while crossing the Devil's Triangle in 1938!

Edward Braucker, now 69 and dying of cancer, spoke for the first time about the incident to his doctors in Gunzberg, West Germany.

They contacted a psychiatrist who interviewed the old man under hypnosis and declared: "There is every indication that Mr. Braucker had a true paranormal experience on the flight he described in 1938.

"His account of heaven closely parallels the experience of people who have died on the operating table and have been brought back to life."

Braucker himself told a German magazine: "I remember everything like it was yesterday. I was test-piloting a disguised Messerschmitt 109 on a flight from Cuba to the Bahamas when I entered what looked like a white, glowing tunnel of a cloud.

"I remember thinking how unusual that was, because the weather was ideal and everywhere else the sky was blue and clear.

"Then I heard a calm voice say, 'Don't be afraid ... go back ... only the dead can enter.' At first I thought I was losing my mind. But then I saw figures taking shape in the clouds — figures I couldn't believe I was seeing. First, my dead mother appeared, smiling at me like she did when I was a baby.

"My grandfather was there too, holding hands with my grandmother and cousins.

"My family knew I would be joining them. They seemed assured. An incredible sensation of calm and peacefulness came over me as I flew out of the cloud and saw it vanish behind me.

"I knew then that death was nothing to fear.

"In fact, I often think that the cancer I have cannot kill me because I am already dead.

"The cancer is merely the vehicle that will deliver me to heaven."

Braucker, an ace who is credited with downing 42 enemy aircraft during World War II and made a fortune in the business world later, said he never before spoke of his experience for fear it would hurt his career.

"Now that the end of my life is near I felt like I owed it to the world to talk about it," he said.

"I want people to know that heaven is real and every man, woman and child who dies is going there. It's God's gift to humanity. It is an astonishing place."

Dr. Rudolf Neumann, the cancer specialist who has been caring for the pilot, said: "Mr. Braucker may or may not have gone to heaven but of one thing I am sure — the cancer he has is very advanced and painful. Most people in his condition cry out for morphine — but he refuses to take any medication whatsoever. He says he feels no pain."●

☐ *Surely that pilot deserves at least a 9.*

I WAS TAKEN TO HEAVEN IN A UFO

Weekly World, May 16, 1989

by Cindy O'Neil

A respected young doctor says a UFO picked up his soul and flew it to heaven when he went into a coma after a skiing accident in the Austrian Alps!

Even more incredible, Dr. Marc Lamot says every starship that visits Earth is piloted by glowing white angels who do nothing but ferry the souls of the dead from here to the hereafter.

"UFOs are tools of the Lord. I know, because one of them took me to heaven," Dr. Lamot, a general practitioner, told reporters in Vienna.

"When I went into a coma my soul drifted up into the sky and an amazing sense of peace came over me.

"Just then a saucer-shaped starship flew into view. A door opened, I was drawn inside. Then I was met by a beautiful, glowing woman who told me she 'came of God.' She told me not to be afraid. She said: 'We have come to take you to heaven.' "

The mind-blowing drama allegedly unfolded after Dr. Lamot slammed into a tree while skiing in the Austrian Alps. Doctors confirmed that he was admitted to a nearby hospital in a coma.

They also said that he remained unconscious for six weeks before they were able to snap him out of it.

"Six weeks isn't a long time but it seemed like an eternity because I was in heaven," said Dr. Lamot. "The UFO trip itself seemed to be over in an instant, but it was obvious that we had traveled deep into space.

"Heaven looked like a bright, white cloud that just seemed to be floating in a sea of black.

"When we arrived, the angel pilot said: 'We must leave you here. There are other souls to be brought.' "

Dr. Lamot said another angel led him through a tunnel of light into heaven itself, which looked like "a city in ancient Greece."

He said that he met his dead mother and father and several other friends and relatives. Then his angel escort "told him: 'Now you will become part of the light.'

"It is very difficult to describe what happened next," said Dr. Lamot. "I lost all consciousness. There wasn't a thought in my mind. All there was was a sense of utter well-being. It was perfect bliss.

"I wanted to stay forever. But my body was still on Earth. When I began to snap out of the coma I could feel myself drifting out of the 'light.'

"The next thing I recall is the UFO pulling me out of the light and up into its belly. I was met by an angel who told me that I must go back to the state of the living.

Psychiatrist Phillip Pretet examined Dr. Lamot after he came out of his coma and is "95 percent sure that his soul was spirited to heaven in a UFO."

"There is a very slight chance that he was dreaming," said the expert. "But if you listen to him describe his experience you can't help but believe that it happened.

"His story is very similar to those that are told by people who die temporarily but are brought back to life.

"The only difference is that most of these people feel like they are drawn into heaven by a mysterious, unseen force.●

☐ *I have never heard of anyone else having claimed that he was taken into the after life in a UFO.*

Doesn't this remind you of my following article? A 9, please.

This article is taken from one I wrote for the *Public Opinion* in Westerville, Ohio, December 25, 1958.

JOHN'S DREAM — RESCUING SOULS

In 1958, I found myself in a conversation with a well known, brilliant young man. He said, "I haven't read much about saucers, but I'm sure they exist."

Since the age of five or six, he had dreamed of piloting a dish-like ship through space. Always in color, always approximately the same, the dream would recur several times a week. Twenty-five years of the same dream puts a lot of reality into the unreasonable. At the time this began, such stories had not become fashionable.

Feeling sure that it was he himself he was seeing, it was hard to figure why the man in his dream was so different in appearance. He had Mongolian features, hair to his shoulders, wore a uniform like a ski-suit with straps across his chest and boot-like shoes. Sailing into a sea of darkness, he would find groups of people whose confused faces filled him with a feeling of compassion. A section of his "upside down dish" would open and people would file in much like filling an elevator. Then the door would close, he would adjust the controls, and in a short time his carload would be landed on an orange planet. Everything but the buildings seemed to be this color.

When the ship arrived, his passengers filed out, never to be seen again. Each load had different faces. During all these trips not one word was spoken by anyone. His only feeling was that of compassion; theirs, of confusion.

Occasionally he would enter a very modern building, the doors of which opened as he walked toward them. Often he went down a long corridor only to awaken, never knowing just where this led. One point seemed very certain to him. He had seen cities in space. It doesn't sound like firm footing, but perhaps in another dimension that too, wasn't necessary. I couldn't help smiling at the similarity to other tales which are told.

Maybe John was one of those reincarnated spacemen I keep reading about. It was 31 years ago I heard this dream.●

UFOs COME FROM HEAVEN
***Sun*, April 4,1989**
by Joe Frick

(A Flying Saucer Expert claims they're bringing angels to earth)

Faithful UFO spotters swarm to a countryside shrine where they pray night after night for the arrival of the alien visitors they believe are sent from heaven!

Members of the religious cult believe the sightings should be revered instead of feared — because they are actually angels dispatched on an earthly mission from God!

The solemn seekers intermingle with a number of other regular visitors to the Hudson Valley area where nightly sightings have been commonplace space the early '80s.

Among the others who gather along the New York suburbs and farmlands are UFOlogists, people wanting a glimpse of a spacecraft, or volunteers willing to be taken aboard.

But it's the God-fearing UFO worshippers who've constructed the riverbank shrine, adorned with religious articles and circled with candles.

These true believers meet nightly, join hands and dance around their monument, hoping the angels will swoop down from the heavens to join their ceremony.

Some worshippers bring religious trinkets to trade with the visitors, while others carry crosses and Bibles.

"We are living in the last days, and the unexplained lights in the sky are angels watching over us before the end," claims a man who calls himself Morven, leader of the group which congregates nightly near the Hudson River.

"When the time comes, the angels will descend and lift those of us who believe into the heavens.

"Whenever there's a calamity in the world, you'll notice these sightings become frequent. It will happen more often until there'll be nothing but chaos. The angels will be our only salvation and we'll be here to be saved."

Other experts and amateur UFO buffs who come to the Hudson Valley are more optimistic. Whether the objects are friendly alien ships or secret government aircraft, they keep watching the skies to find a reason for the incredible number of UFO sightings.●

☐ *Sounds better than the ones that are killing our animals and swiping our people. It ought to get at least an 8.*

WOMAN 'DIES' & GOES TO HEAVEN

National Examiner, **June 27, 1989**

by Edward Manzi

A tragic car accident left Mary Agnes Patton teetering on the brink of death, while her spirit floated away from her body and went to Heaven.

She says God sent her back home with a mission to evangelize, but He kept her 10-month-old baby and the 78-year-old man who hit her car.

The accident happened on Mary's 40th birthday. Husband Don had phoned, asking her to meet him in town. So she bundled baby Sarah into the car and headed into Lancaster, Ohio.

Two miles from home a dark sedan ran a stop sign and smashed into the car, leaving it in a twisted heap against the limestone embankment.

A burly truck driver, who had stopped to help, cradled tiny Sarah in his muscular arms.

Tears in his eyes told the gathering crowd the infant was beyond help.

Then a nurse from a nearby town attended to Mary, who lay limp on the road, face-down and bloody.

Later, doctors credited the nurse's fast action with saving Mary's life.

For three days in February, 1966, Mary lay unconscious and responded to no one. She couldn't. Her spirit was up on another plateau, a beautiful park.

Recalls Mary, now a garden columnist with the Los Angeles *Herald Examiner*: "I was blissfully going toward some beings who were coming toward me with arms outstretched.

"There were fruit trees in an orchard off to my right and wonderful fragrances of trees that were both in bloom and in fruit. There was orchestral music, and a choir was singing."

She adds: "Then a big golden presence appeared at my right side, and I was enveloped in indescribable love. I looked up but could not see the face of God. But I knew His love.

"A beautiful, deep, compassionate voice said, 'It is not her time.' Then I woke up in the hospital in such pain that I knew Sarah could not have survived. At least I didn't want her to suffer the way I was."

Mary, now 63, tells the *Examiner* she has no fear of death because she has been there and knows its beauty. She says she has recently come to realize how God wants to use her.

She says: "He wants me to let people know that God is there for them."●

☐ *Another description of Heaven — this one is worth more than a 9 to many who read it.*

LOVING OLD COUPLE EXPERIENCE PARADISE

Weekly World, **June 27, 1989**

by Phil Billings

An elderly husband and wife died and went to heaven hand in hand and saw exactly the same things — before doctors revived them in one of the most dramatic life-after-death experiences on record!

Medical records and physicians confirm that Sergio and Antonia Lanza, both 70, were dead for at least 35 minutes after deadly natural gas from a leaking pipe filled their two-bedroom apartment in Napoli, Italy.

The couple were revived at the Napoli Metropolitan Clinic after a neighbor found them slumped over in chairs and called for an ambulance.

When the Lanzas awoke, they excitedly told staffers that they had gone to heaven. They also said that they had grown younger along the way.

"I used to be afraid of death but now I know there is nothing to fear," said Mrs. Lanza. "Sergio and I will always be together.

"And we won't be old and feeble. We'll be young — like we were in heaven."

Psychiatrist Salvatore Oliva has talked with the couple extensively since Drs. Dario Spinoza and Alfredo Ambrosino revived them at the Napoli Clinic.

He believes there is "a very good chance" that they really did go to heaven. "There is always an element of doubt in cases such as this," said the psychiatrist. "But in this instance we have statements from two doctors and medical records to prove that Mr. and Mrs. Lanza did, in fact, die.

"We also know that they shared a strikingly similar near-death experience. They both tell us that they went to heaven together.

"They go on to say that they grew younger after they died and actually entered heaven as teenagers.

"I don't think they would have shared such an unusual vision if their experience had been purely psychological."

The couple's description of their shared experience is similar to those given by other people who have died and been brought back to life.

In interviews, the Lanzas said they were watching TV in their apartment when they lost consciousness and then died from exposure to the leaking gas.

"It was like falling asleep," said Lanza. "At first there was nothing but darkness. But then we both floated upwards until we emerged into a room of bright light.

"We suddenly realized that we were holding hands. I looked at Antonia and she looked at me and we couldn't believe our eyes. We felt so light and airy. We were perfectly at peace. But more than that, we were young again."

The Lanzas said they walked up a stairway to the gates of an enormous white city and saw "so many faces, all of them happy and young."

But just as they began to walk through the gate they were stopped by an unseen hand. "Nobody said anything," said Mrs. Lanza. "But Sergio and I instinctively looked at one another.

"And without speaking, we realized that it wasn't our time to enter heaven. We immediately began to float downward. Everything got black. Then we were on Earth, coughing and gagging.

"The doctors were there and giving us oxygen. We were alive again."

The Lanzas' 54-year-old son, Indro Lanza, is convinced that his parents' story is true.

"I've never seen such a change in anyone," he said. "They used to be afraid to live and afraid to die. Now they seem to be totally at peace. They are happy and contented for the first time in their lives."●

☐ *What makes this article so special is that two people had an identical experience while both were unconscious. Worth an 8.*

BABY BORN TALKING — DESCRIBES HEAVEN

***Sun*, October 31, 1989**

by Kathy Hart

Heaven is a warm, serene place where fortunate souls live a beautiful existence surrounded by peace and harmony. That information comes from the mouth of a baby born talking!

The sensational incident, witnessed by startled doctors and nurses, is proof of reincarnation, according to investigators.

Baby Myra Delorio came into the world not wailing but talking up a storm — about the place she had just come from.

In a quick succession of sentences, the baby described what it was like in Heaven, recalls shaken Nurse Carla Brunatti.

"At first I thought someone was playing a trick, but then I looked at the baby's mouth and saw it was speaking.

"The remarkable baby was saying something about the warm light she had come from, how it was such a great feeling and how everyone was living in peace.

"After a few moments the baby fell silent, then started crying. It was as if she suddenly realized she was now in the real world, instead of heaven."

Myra's ecstatic mom Teresa remembers being shocked when she heard her child speak moments after delivery.

"I was frozen, as was everyone else, when I heard her say those beautiful things," says Teresa, 23. "But after she started crying, and I held her in my arms, I realized a miracle had taken place.

"I think because she was a few weeks early and I had to be rushed to the hospital, she still felt like she was in the other world when she came out."

Psychic investigator Paul Ralone agrees after interviewing witnesses at the hospital in Taranto, Italy.

"Two doctors who were there swear they heard the baby speaking, although they're scared to speak publicly about it," says Ralone.

"The nurses are more open, and everyone has the same story. The baby spoke about the serenity, warmth and beauty of heaven, and how the souls lived in harmony.

"The infant was still mentally in heaven when she arrived and wanted to speak about it.

"Then she stopped when the reality of this world hit her. But it proves the case for reincarnation."●

☐ *Talking baby deserves a 9. She gets a 10 if she talks 2 days instead of two minutes! Another case that we must make a choice of reincarnation or possession?*

LIFE AFTER DEATH PROOF

***Weekly World*, January 2, 1990**

by Martha Atkins

Terry Smith is living proof there's life after death — she died last May and then came back to tell about it!

Terry says she was only dead for a few minutes but that it was a wonderful experience and changed her life for the better.

"All I could see was this bright light at the end of a tunnel and then I heard this male voice say, 'Are you ready?' And I said, 'Heavens, NO!' "

Terry, 35, had just returned from a wedding with her boyfriend, Jim Baidokas, when she had an allergic reaction to something she ate. They were watching TV in her Lima, Pa., home when she leapt off the couch and clutched her throat.

"I can't breathe," Terry gasped. "Please — call the ambulance."

She said Jim realized they didn't have time to wait for an ambulance and rushed her to the hospital.

"I was blue from the belly button up," said Terry.

Jim took Terry's pulse as they neared the hospital but there wasn't any. Paramedics rushed to revive her but by this time, Terry wasn't feeling any pain.

"I was very panicky when my throat closed up," said Terry. "I struggled and fought against it at first. Then I just let go and I was very serene.

"I was kind of floating over the Earth. I had no weight and I was transparent. There was a bright light and it was very peaceful. I wasn't afraid at all.

"That's when I had my conversation with the superior being. He asked me if I was ready to go and I said no," said Terry.

"I was wondering if he was going to let me go back," said Terry. "And he did."

Terry woke up in the hospital a few hours later with an extremely sore throat. She was hooked up to life-support machines and spent two days in intensive care. She says it took her almost three months to physically recover from the experience.

But she says she's glad she had the experience because it made her put her life in order and took away her fear of dying.

"It's given me a lot more confidence because I feel so good to be here. I've gotten more laid back," said Terry.

"I've made a will. Everything in my house is clean and ready if I were to die tomorrow. Now that I've experienced it, when my time comes I'll be ready. I'll just let go and go. I'm no longer afraid to die."●

☐ *Just one more person to tell you how life has changed for them after a death experience. After reading so many reports and the effects felt by those who claim them, it's easy to see why many people believe they too will have such an experience. A 9 for Terry Smith.*

ANGELS

Everyone believes in angels,
Most have different opinions.
The "Hubble Scope" claims there are places,
Where angles were seen with beaming faces.

They were brilliant orange, with great big wings,
It must have been an awesome thing.
They were spotted near an old star cluster —
It probably gave NASA quite a fluster!

Imagine seven, eighty-foot angels,
With wings as large as airplanes!
They were pleased to know they'd been observed,
It's a way that earthlings can be served.

Russia spotted a band of angels,
When on a mission in space.
It helps bring our countries together —
When astronauts see such a face!

I want to see an angel just like me,
With beautiful wings and a halo —
Then I could see what I might be,
If all works out in eternity!

In the '60s, Roy Eugene Davis, author of "This is Reality" and other books, came to lecture at our UFO group. In this photo, Lillian Desguin greets Mr. Davis front of the Intergalactic Looking Society headquarters in Flint, Ohio. Mr. Davis is now with the Center for Spiritual Awareness, in Lakemont, GA.

Dr. Everett R. Walter, Director of VPRI, UFO educator, researcher, engineer, and applied mathematician.

Headquarters of the Intergalactic Looking Society, in 1958, in Flint, Ohio.

Paul E. Desguin and Lillian C. Desguin, building our observatory for the International Galactic Looking Society. Those 500 bull-nosed blocks! (See Part One; "Astronomy and the Intergalactic Looking Society.")

Notice the big "tube" we procured from the Highway Department. (See Chapter One; "Astronomy and the Intergalactic Looking Society.")

Lillian Crowner Desguin and Paul Eugene Desguin, 50th Anniversary. Lillian has spent over four decades researching the UFO phenomenon.

Cynthia Hind, author of "UFO–African Encounters." Mrs. Hind has been interviewed in numerous countries as well as been a featured speaker for "MUFON" in the United States. Mrs. Hind resides in Harare, Zimbabwe, Africa. (See Chapter Six; "Excerpts from Cynthia's Letter.")

Professor Merriss Cornell, retired from Ohio State University, Columbus, Ohio, where he taught mathematics for many years. (See Chapter Five; "A Dream Come True.")

Bryant and Helen Reeves, authors of "Flying Saucer Pilgrimage" and "The Cosmic Viewpoint." Upon his retirement from American Motors, Bryant, a graduate of Yale University and M.I.T., decided to track down the truth about flying saucers.

Jimmy Flynn and his Swamp Buggy, in 1990. (See Chapter Two; "The Jimmy Flynn Story")

The Bruce Stevenson sighting at Circleville, Ohio in February 1948 and the March 1965 Jimmy Flynn experience were sufficient to forever put to rest the question as to the existence of UFOs. The sincerity of these men, to me, is beyond question!

Lillian C. Desguin visiting with Major Donald E. Keyhoe while he was in Westerville, Ohio to present a lecture on UFOs. Major Keyhoe was the founder of NICAP and gave many lectures, in addition to having a very long list of books to his credit. (See Chapter One; "NICAP.")

Jack W. Grant, from Columbus, Ohio, recently retired from the Columbus Galvanizing Plant. After 44 years of research on Unidentified Flying Objects, Jack has become an authority on early contact cases. He intends to publish his collection of personal letters received from George Adamski concerning his experiences. (See Chapter One; "Jack and George," "Jack W. Grant and the Saucers," "Kentucky's Little Green Men.")

WEEKLY WORLD
NEWS

600 South East Coast Avenue • Lantana, Florida • 33462 • (407) 586-0201

May 9, 1989

Mrs. P. E. Desguin
565 Tarpon Terrace
Harbour Heights, FL 33983

Dear Mrs. Desguin,

Thank you for your interest in Weekly World News and your recent request for permission to use articles from The NEWS in your research.

You hereby have my permission to use these articles in any way you see fit and I understand that The NEWS will be given proper credit.

Thank you again for your interest.

Sincerely,

J. K. Chappelle for

Joe West
Editor

JW/skc

The Public Opinion, Inc.

130 GRAPHIC WAY WESTERVILLE, OHIO 43081
(614) 882-2244

TO WHOM IT MAY CONCERN:

In July 1958 THE PUBLIC OPINION became the first newspaper to carry a weekly column on the controversial subject of (Unidentified Flying Objects). Eventually the paper received special recognition for being the only one in America which regularly published a column on this topic.

Lillian Crowner Desguin attended the old elementary Vine Street School in Westerville, Ohio during 1920 and 1921. The Crowner family home is one of the few houses left on Park Road, four miles west of State and Main. For more than forty years Mrs. Desguin has covered many miles in search of legitamate experiences and contact with U.F.O.'s. She is 100 percent convinced of the reality of these objects and the occupants who travel within them. This was a popular column and was carried from 1958 to 1963 and brought up to date again in 1975 and 1976.

A. Jean Courtright

A. Jean Courtright
Publisher

CHAPTER EIGHT

The Faces Found In Space
The Three Faces of Mars, Venus and the Moon

Probe Finds Face on Mars — *Weekly World News* 188
Probe Finds Face on Venus — *Weekly World News* 188
Third Face in Space Found on the Moon — *Weekly World News* 189
Space Probe Sends Photos of Messages Carved on Martian Surface — *Weekly World News* 189
Jungle Tribe Worships Face on Mars — *Weekly World News* 190
Voyager 2 Photographs "Identical" Face on Neptune — *Weekly World News* 190
Stone Face Found in Antarctica — *Weekly World News* 191
Claims African Tribe Came From Mars — *Weekly World News* 192
Canals on Mars are Full of Fish — *Weekly World News* 192
Mysterious City Found Near Face on Mars — *National Examiner* 193
Town Found on Venus — *Weekly World News* 193

Bigfoot

Chinese Team Closing in on Bigfoot — *Weekly World News* 194
Bigfoot Lives — *Sun* 194
Bigfoot Spooks Loggers — *National Examiner* 194
Two-Headed Bigfoot Terrifies Town — *Sun* 194
Furry Space Aliens Mated With Earth Women — *Weekly World News* 194
Bizarre Beings Lurk in New England Triangle — *Sun* 195
Mysteries on Bigfoot — *Weekly World News* 195
Bigfoot Family Found — *Sun* 196
Soldiers Discover Living Breathing Baby Bigfoot — *Weekly World News* 196
I Killed a Bigfoot — *Weekly World News* 197
Baby Bigfoot — *Sun* 197
Courageous Bigfoot Rescues Family — *National Examiner* 198
Hairy Spacemen Kidnap Cop — *Weekly World News* 198
Giant Bigfoot Captured Alive — *Sun* 199
Starving Hunters Rescued by Gentle Giants — *Weekly World News* 199
Bigfoot Saved My Life — *Weekly World News* 200
Giant Bigfoot Sightings Alarm Indian Village — *National Examiner* 200
Crash Survivors Rescued by Bigfoot — *Weekly World News* 201
Bigfoot From Outer Space — *Weekly World News* 201
I Talked, Ate and Slept With Bigfoot — *Sun* 202
Bigfoot Is My Buddy, Swears Hermit Trapper — *Sun* 202
Bigfoot Tribe Kidnaps Five Kids — *Sun* 203
I Came Face to Face With Bigfoot — *Weekly World News* 203
Bigfoot City — *Weekly World News* 204
Bigfoot to the Rescue — *Weekly World News* 204
Bigfoot Saved Me From Being Buried Alive — *Sun* 205
Bigfoot Lives in China — *Weekly World News* 206
Claims to Have Seen Bigfoot Skiing — *Sun* 206
Bigfoot Rescues Boy From Alligator's Mouth — *Sun* 207
Bigfoot Cured My Arthritis — *Sun* 207
UFOs Killed All the Dinosaurs — *National Examiner* 208
Ranchers Kill Monster From Prehistoric Past — *National Examiner* 208
Those Carved Faces — *Poem* 209

THE THREE FACES OF MARS, VENUS AND THE MOON

I'm convinced the *Weekly World News, The Sun,* and *The National Examiner* are not going to feed us all lies in order to sell papers. I believe they have a good basis for most of the news they print. If the results are variable that's understandable.

Since 1920, we've had reports of radio signals from Mars (according to the *New York Times*). In 1924 these signals were transferred to photographic film which revealed a crude image of a face. It is similar to one photographed by the Viking probe in 1976.

This article was written for *Weekly World* by Ragan Dunn — and was published on September 27, 1988. "The Face On Mars — A New Shocker." This same picture has been carried in many places. I feel I would be stupid to try to discredit it. If it's true we certainly need to pay more attention to the *News*; it surely is worth a 9.

PROBE FINDS FACE ON MARS
***Weekly World*, Sept. 27, 1988**
by Ragan Dunn

Martians were communicating with American scientists in the 1920s and the proof is in any large library for everyone to see!

Back issues of *Scientific American* magazine and the *New York. Times* clearly state that researchers were receiving radio signals from Mars between 1920 and 1924.

Transmissions received at listening posts around the world showed the messages to be composed of a mysterious code-like series of dots and dashes.

And even more astonishing, when the dots and dashes were transferred to photographic film they took the form of a crude face just like the crude stone face America's Viking probe photographed on the surface of Mars in 1976.

"I'm not the least bit surprised that scientists were receiving such messages in the 1920s," said Dr. Ludin Psche, the Swiss astronomer.

"I am firmly convinced that the stone face, the so-called Martian sphinx, is used to house radio and television transmitters.

"It is my contention that a Martian civilization has been transmitting messages to Earth and beyond for half a million years, which is the estimated age of the Martian face."•

☐ *I have a feeling someday this will be worth a 10.*

PROBE FINDS FACE ON VENUS
***Weekly World*, February 7, 1989**
by Ragan Dunn

A Soviet scientist claims to have found a stone face on Venus that is identical to the stone face on Mars!

"This is the most important extraterrestrial discovery ever," Dr. Alexei Pushkarev, the Soviet astrophysicist, told reporters in Moscow.

"There is no doubt that these faces were designed by the same architects and they were probably built by the same workers.

"The question we've got to answer is why they put these monuments on barren planets. It's almost as if they left them there as markers to guide other space explorers such as ourselves."

Dr. Pushkarev's report got mixed reviews from Western scientists, some of whom doubted that a stone monument on Venus could be a mirror image of one on Mars.

The Soviet expert countered that criticism with dramatic photos of the Venusian face that were taken by Russia's Venera 9 and 10 space probes in 1975 but weren't properly interpreted until now.

The pictures are every bit as sharp as those America's Viking probe took of the Face on Mars in 1976. And they clearly show a massive stone structure that looks like a man wearing a giant helmet — which is identical to the structure on Mars.

"Nobody has doubted the Viking photos," said Dr. Pushkarev. "So why do they question those that were taken by Venera?"

Dr. Claude Ludin, the Swiss astrophysicist, doesn't doubt anything. In fact, he called the implications of twin faces on Venus and Mars "staggering."

"The faces prove beyond any doubt that an extraterrestrial civilization exists and is active in our own solar system," said the expert.

"They also suggest that Mars and Venus were once inhabited by intelligent beings. Why else would somebody or something build monuments if there were nobody around to see them?"

The surface temperature of Venus is over 900 degrees, which prohibits manned exploration in the foreseeable future. But Dr. Pushkarev made it clear that the Soviets will spare no expense to get more information. "We are monitoring the planet with sophisticated radio receivers," he said. "Many scientists believe that the face on Mars houses a gigantic transmitter. We want to know if the Venusian face is sending out signals, too."•

☐ *This is a 9.*

I hope you read these articles carefully — I do. The June 6, 1989 issue of *Weekly World* has a scoop with these headlines. "Soviet Astronomer's Shocker — Stuns the Scientific World." Big letters tell you...

THIRD FACE IN SPACE FOUND ON THE MOON!
***Weekly World*, June 6, 1989**
by Terry Anderson

Soviet scientists claim to have found a stone face on the moon that is identical to the stone face on Mars!

The discovery of the mysterious monument stunned researchers, who are still reeling from the discovery of a great stone face on Venus earlier this year.

"These faces are like stepping stones through our solar system," Dr. Alexei Blinov, the astronomer, told newsmen in Moscow.

"They obviously were built by the same creatures.

"The questions we must answer are 'Why?' and 'What do the faces mean?...' "

Dr. Blinov and a colleague, Dr. Vladimir Shepel, photographed the lunar face while conducting a routine telescopic survey of the moon on April 18.

The face on Mars was photographed by America's Viking probe in 1976. And while the Venusian face was spotted by Russia's Venera 9 and 10 space probes in 1975, the photos weren't properly interpreted until January 1989.

The Soviets did not release photos of the face on the moon. They did pinpoint its location — Mare Nectaris — leading to stepped up scrutiny of the region by astronomers around the world.

"The face on the moon appears to be smaller than its mile-long counterparts on Venus and Mars," said Dr. Shepel. "But the features, including two large, oval eyes, chiseled nose and stylized helmet, are exactly the same.

"All the faces are ancient, at least 500,000 years old," he continued. "Whoever or whatever built them had an incredibly advanced civilization before mankind even existed.

"They had mastered the technology necessary for interplanetary flight and massive construction projects. And there is no doubt that they visited Venus, Mars and the moon.

"The fact that they left behind monuments is not something that we can easily explain. But it would appear that they wanted other interplanetary travelers to know where they had been.

"And perhaps, where they were going."

U.S. officials refused to comment on the Soviet report. But there has been widespread speculation that the Magellan probe, launched from the space shuttle Atlantis in May, was specially designed to study the face on Venus.

The Russians themselves indicated that they will send a manned flight or a probe to the moon to study the face more closely. But they did not say when such an expedition might be launched.

Gerits Brader, the Dutch astronomer, has called on America and the Soviet Union to create an international task force to study the stone faces more closely.

He told reporters in Amsterdam: "These monuments might have been constructed by a lost civilization — or one that is still thriving today. It is imperative that we find out everything we can."●

☐ *This is either a 1 or a 10 — I don't know.*

Now that you have all the needed information about the carved faces from Mars, Venus, and the Moon, note the warning given to Earth from Mars.

SPACE PROBE SENDS PHOTOS OF MESSAGES CARVED ON MARTIAN SURFACE
***Weekly World*, May 9, 1989**
by Ragan Dunn

A Soviet scientist says the Phobos II space probe photographed a warning that was written on the barren surface of Mars shortly before it mysteriously stopped working on March 27.

The forbidding message appears to be carved out of solid rock. The warning says — "Stay Away" — and seems to be aimed directly at mankind!

"There is intelligent life on Mars and this proves it," Dr. Viktor Borisov, the Soviet space scientist, told newsmen in Moscow at a large press conference.

"We do not yet know if the inhabitants of Mars intentionally tampered with or destroyed the Phobos craft. We do know that the challenge before us now is to open a line of communication with these beings and arrange to meet with them.

"The message on the planet's surface clearly warns us to stay away — but I'm sure we can reason with these Martians and possibly even establish diplomatic relations if we make radio contact before we mount an expedition to the planet."

Dr. Borisov's report stunned scientists in the West, many of whom agree that the Phobos probe made one of the most important discoveries in the history of space exploration before it suddenly stopped working.

Photographs transmitted back to Earth before the probe went on the blink clearly reveal words on the surface of Mars.

The message, which is written in English, says "Stay Away" in letters that are half a mile long and 75 yards wide.

They appear to be chiseled out of solid rock and are so monumental that they almost certainly were cut with laser tools, Dr. Borisov said.

"Unlike the stone Face on Mars, which was photographed by America's

Viking probe in 1976 and is very old and weatherbeaten, the message on Mars was made recently," continued the expert.

"I would imagine that it was created in response to the growing number of probes we are sending to Mars. The planet's inhabitants obviously want us to stay out of their affairs.

"I don't want to accuse anybody of anything at this point. But it is conceivable that the Martians destroyed the Phobos probe themselves."

Dr. Borisov refused to say how the Soviets plan to go about contacting the Martians but he acknowledged that they are already at work on the task.

Dr. Jean Leydel, the French radio astronomer, is one of a dozen scientists worldwide who have offered to assist the Soviets in the effort.●

☐ *Why do you think the Russians are interested in less war and more research? Perhaps the* News *publishes this stuff to scare the daylights out of you! Another 9 for the message!*

JUNGLE TRIBE WORSHIPS THE FACE ON MARS

***Weekly World*, January 24, 1989**

by Ragan Dunn

Members of a South American tribe know all about the Face on Mars even though they've never seen it!

That's the claim of West German anthropologist Wilhelm Scharke, who says the savages and their ancestors actually worshiped the monument for 400 years before America's Viking probe "discovered" it for the world in 1976.

"These people are among the most primitive on Earth but they know more about the Face than most scientists," the expert told reporters in Alzey.

"From what I understand they have worshipped the Face for at least 400 years. And they insist that their knowledge of it 'came from the stars.' "

Dr. Scharke said he discovered the tribe 200 miles north of Barra do Garcas, Brazil, in late September.

He instantly noticed that the masks they wore resembled the Martian monument. But he chalked it off as a coincidence until a tribal elder asked him to kneel at the altar of their "Sky God King" which had the identical chiseled features and helmet as the Face.

"I inquired about their God and was stunned by the old man's reply," said Dr. Scharke. "He repeatedly referred to the Red Planet, which we know as Mars.

"He also talked about messengers from heaven who gave his people the 'Light of Truth' and brought them images of the Sky God King.

"There's no doubt in my mind that their God is the Face on Mars.

"The challenge before us is to find out how they heard about it.

"These people or their ancestors might have been in contact with extraterrestrials from Mars or some other planet in our solar system."

Dr. Scharke's report got mixed reviews from his colleagues. One went so far as to call the similarities between the Face on Mars and the tribe's masks and myths "an interesting but meaningless coincidence."

Undaunted, Dr. Scharke vowed to return to the Amazon to see if he can prove that the tribe and the Face are linked. "These primitive people might be able to help us make contact with an extraterrestrial civilization," said the expert.

"Wouldn't that be something? To think that people who've never ridden in cars or flown in planes might be our ticket to the stars is really amazing."

The Brazilian government refused to comment on the expert's report. But one official, who requested anonymity, was particularly intrigued by it.

"Many jungle people have UFO myths," he said. "Personally, I don't doubt that this tribe has made contact with space aliens."●

☐ *At the present the South American tribe gets an 8 — when Dr. Scharke returns to the Amazon next time, he'll get a 10.*

VOYAGER 2 PHOTOGRAPHS 'IDENTICAL' FACE ON NEPTUNE

***Weekly World News*, Sept. 19, 1989**

by Mickey McGuire

'Stone image is IDENTICAL to others found on Mars, Venus & the moon,' says scientist.

A computer-enhanced image beamed back to Earth by the Voyager 2 space probe clearly shows a stone-like face that pulsates in the gaseous, wind-whipped atmosphere of Neptune — and it's identical to those found on the moon, Venus and Mars!

That's the mind-boggling claim of Alexei Blinov, the Soviet astronomer who stunned the scientific world when he discovered the moon face and matched it to the faces found earlier on Venus and Mars.

The *News* reported the Soviet scientist's astonishing discovery in our June 6 issue.

The face on Mars was televised to Earth on September 3, 1976, minutes before America's Viking landed on the planet's surface, and was published in newspapers across America. The Venusian face was discovered by the Soviet space probes Venera 9 and 10 in 1975.

"These images transmitted by Voyager 2 are incredibly sharp and richly detailed," Dr. Blinov declared. "there is absolutely no doubt that it is identical to the faces on the moon, Venus and Mars.

"The faces are indisputable proof that early space travelers or extraterrestrials had visited the planets and left those immense monuments as stepping stones for others to follow through the galaxy."

U.S. officials have flatly refused to comment on the Soviet claim and no photos have been released in the U.S. However, there is growing speculation that a future manned flight to Mars from a NASA space station on the moon will investigate the face on Mars.

During Voyager's Aug. 25, 3,000-mile approach to Neptune's surface, highly sophisticated television cameras scanned its vast surface and beamed picture signals back to Earth.

"Those signals were received by super sensitive antennas to several sites on Earth and relayed to NASA's Jet Propulsion Laboratory in California," Dr. Blinov explained. "I was able to intercept those signals at my observatory. When the signals were processed by the imaging computer, the pictures they produced were beyond my wildest expectations.

"More than 11 photos show the stone-like face that has been photographed on the Moon, Venus and Mars. And all four faces are identical. Each has the same large oval eyes, the chiseled nose and the strange-looking helmet.

"Whoever carved those magnificent faces belonged to a superior extraterrestrial civilization that existed long before man walked on the Earth.

"We may never know who left the faces or where in deep space they came from. But it appears they wanted future planetary travelers to know someone had been there before them."●

☐ *It's hard for me to believe a Soviet astronomer would continue this kind of a hoax. I wonder if he dares to give that report to the Russian papers? If the original report of the face on Mars is true, I'll bet he's on the level about the face on Neptune. I'm inclined to think this may be worth a 9.5.*

STONE FACE FOUND IN ANTARCTICA

***Weekly World News*, May 29, 1990**

by Robert Oates

German and American scientists have found a stone face under polar ice that's identical to the stone face on Mars.

The mile-long monument also matches stone faces found on the moon, Venus, and Neptune. And that suggests that the people or creatures who built them were capable of interplanetary travel over 500,000 years ago, when the images were believed to have been made.

"The faces were clearly made by the same hands. The challenge before us now is to find out who made them, and why."

Drs. Phillip Lentz and Dieter Horne discovered the stone face under 3,500 feet of polar ice while conducting a seismological survey of Antarctica in April. The monument's features were recorded by an instrument that uses sound waves to map geological formations under the Earth's surface.

And those features clearly mirror the helmeted, human face that America's Viking probe photographed in 1976.

"Other probes photographed stone faces on the moon, Venus and Neptune between 1975 and 1989 and they are all the same," said Dr. Lentz, who holds advanced degrees in geology, astronomy and physics. "The key question is whether the Antarctic face was the first monument or the last," he continued. "If it was the first, we can assume that a technologically advanced society existed on Earth 500,000 years ago and left to colonize space.

"If it is the last monument, it seems likely that extraterrestrials visited Earth and might still be here today.

"It's pure speculation," he added. "But we humans may be descendants of those extra-terrestrials.

"Either that, or they may still be here on Earth, in hiding, today."

Drs. Lentz and Horne plan a second expedition to Antarctica next spring and hope to learn more about the massive monument at that time.

It is also believed that NASA is planning an expedition of its own, possibly before the end of June.

"It will be years before we can get a man to the moon or Mars to study the faces there," said Dr. Flentz. "But this isn't like the faces in space. This is in our own backyard.

"It is an opportunity that can't be ignored."●

☐ *By repetition I hope to convince you that such articles have to have a foundation of truth.*

There is no point in the tabloids repeating this information year after year unless there is a good reason to believe there is an element of truth in them. There is literally no doubt as to the existence of this face on Mars.

Because of this I am inclined to think those same faces may also have been carved on Venus, Neptune and the Moon as well as this buried one under our polar ice cap. We owe these tabloids more than words can tell for sharing information that is so meaningful to all of us. And we can thank our government for allowing this to be. The combination of all 5 faces surely deserves a 10.

CLAIMS AFRICAN TRIBE CAME FROM MARS
Weekly World, **July 12, 1988**
by Ragan Dunn

Scientists claim to have found a jungle tribe that came from Mars 176 years ago — in 1812!

At least three of those original extraterrestrial colonists are said to be alive.

And according to reports, their spaceship is still hidden in undergrowth on the outskirts of their settlement east of Kisangani, Zaire.

"This is the scientific find of the century," Dr. Signe Winslof told reporters in Boras, Sweden.

"The extraterrestrials have totally acclimated themselves to a primitive jungle existence in Africa. And yet they still possess the knowledge and technology to travel through space and colonize other planets."

The expert said he and half a dozen colleagues discovered the 50 Martian tribesmen on a routine study of Zairian cultures in late April.

The extraterrestrials were secretive and standoffish at first.

But they eventually began to trust the scientists and showed them the rusted remains of a silver, crescent-shaped starship, he said. The tribe's historian reportedly said that 25 colonists fled Mars in 1812 to escape a virus that threatened to wipe out the entire Martian race.

"The Martian tribesmen are black and look just like humans with the exception of their eyes, which are completely white," said Dr. Winslof.

"They show a fondness for hoops and circles. They use the shape as an adornment for their bodies and as designs for their houses.

"They speak a typical African dialect among themselves, but communicated with us in both Swedish and English.

"The aliens told us we were welcome in their settlement as long as we did not interfere in their internal affairs or primitive way of life."

Just why the extraterrestrials choose to live as savages in the jungle isn't clear. But Dr. Winslof believes it might be "a kind of revolt against the highly technical, impersonal lives they and their ancestors led on Mars.

"They still have detailed maps of Mars and our solar system," he continued. "But they made it clear to us that too much discussion of their past was off limits.

"Their background is something they can't or won't bring themselves to talk about in detail."

Dr. Winslof said he and his associates plan to return to the village by August and publish a full scientific report with photographs by December.●

☐ *Here's one that could be a 1 or a 10 —I'm going to try to do some research on this one.*

I am trying to show you that Mr. U.S. Citizen is being shown the truth about UFOs and related subjects. He is being protected by allowing him to make a choice. This allows a person who has a need to know the potential of knowing, and the one who needs not to know can rely upon his Uncle Sam to tell him if it's true. The trouble is, it's much like playing Russian Roulette — the gun may go off at anytime. We were lied to before, why would we believe now?

NASA is also getting a shot in the arm. I doubt if they'll want to break any UFO news to you! Read for yourself the following article about a U.S. space probe's shocking discovery!

CANALS ON MARS ARE FULL OF FISH
Weekly World, **January 17, 1987**
by Ragan Dunn

Government bigwigs clamp lid of secrecy on incredible findings, says top scientist.

The surface of Mars is etched with canals that are full of water and teeming with fish!

That's the word from Swiss physicist Marcel Bischof, who says he can prove that the superpowers have known about the waterways and marine life since America's Viking probe landed on Mars in 1976.

"This is the biggest scientific coverup since the United States went to work on the atom bomb," Dr. Bischof told newsmen in Geneva.

"There is life on Mars and both the Soviets and Americans know it. They conspired to keep the information secret to avoid world panic." Soviet and American officials denied the charges but Dr. Bischof produced a mountain of evidence to support his claims.

In addition to photos that show water-filled canals on the planet's surface, Dr. Bischof said he had top secret documents that describe Martian marine life, including "millions of fish."

Those documents also implied that the canals are not natural formations and might have been constructed by "intelligent beings not unlike men themselves."

"The accomplishments of America's Viking probe were much more significant than the public was made aware of," said Dr. Bischof.

"These documents prove that the craft located and analyzed samples of water. It also used an underwater camera to photograph enormous schools of slender, golden fish.

"The implications of such a discovery are staggering," he continued. "The existence of life on another planet means that we are not alone in the universe.

"It means that mankind is much less important in the universal scheme than we had ever imagined." UFO researcher Roland Cavelti of Fribourg, Switzerland, called Dr. Bischof's report "most enlightening."

"When are the superpowers going to learn that they can't keep us in the dark?" he asked. "It's high time they came clean and admitted this coverup.

"The public has a right to know — even if it does cause world panic."●

☐ *I don't know Swiss physicist "Marcel Bischof," but if you do, he and Ragan Dunn ought to have a 10.*

MYSTERIOUS CITY FOUND NEAR FACE ON MARS

***National Examiner,* November 1, 1988**

A mysterious city and pyramid have been found on Mars!

Top scientists say the dwellings are near an amazing Sphinx-like face carved into a mile-long rock.

Photos taken by NASA's Viking spacecraft of the unusual formations indicate they may have been built by an intelligent civilization that has since disappeared, says Brian T. O'Leary, a former astronaut and an expert on the Red Planet.

Mark Carlotto, an optical engineering expert, said a computer enhancement of the Viking photos shows that the city, pyramid, and face appear to have been carved by ETs and not by violent Martian windstorms.

Said Carlotto of critics' charges the formations are just a photographic illusion: "It's extremely unlikely that it's a trick of light and shadow."

Incredibly, the pyramid could be a fortress, says Richard Hoagland, founder of The Mars Project, an organization of top scientists. Hoagland believes a nearby cliff could have been part of an astrological marker.

A line drawn from the center of the city, across the face to the cliff, would line up exactly with the sun at the start of Mars' summer solstice, as it would have occurred 500,000 years ago, Hoagland said.

And Hoagland insists such an alignment is unlikely to have been natural.

Said the prestigious researcher: "Geologically, the odds are one in 300,000 that this would be here by chance."

Former astronaut O'Leary says NASA should send another spacecraft to Mars as soon as possible.

"We must go back to Mars and photograph it at a higher resolution," he said.

O'Leary said he asked Soviet scientists to take a look at the formations, but their spacecraft were not technically designed to study the Cydonia region of Mars, where the sites are located.

Researcher Hoagland said NASA spotted the face in the Viking films more than 10 years ago, but never took it seriously enough to investigate.

Said Hoagland: "There is such a bias against something like this that there was no official attention given to this data."●

☐ *Well, well, how about a 7?*

TOWN FOUND ON VENUS

***Weekly World News,* April 11, 1989**

by Ragan Dunn

A Soviet space probe photographed a Wild West town complete with horses, wagons and people on the surface of Venus, stunned scientists report.

"There is life on Venus — human life — and we have absolutely no explanation for it," Dr. Yury Srednev, the Soviet space scientist, told reporters in Moscow.

"Photographs beamed back to Earth show that the town is situated in the middle of a Venusian desert and is typical of those that were built in the American West in the 1880s.

"Surface temperatures on Venus are in the 900 degree range and the atmosphere is laden with sulfuric acid. But the town appears to be constructed of ordinary wood.

"And the people and horses there are definitely thriving even though the planet is airless."

The Soviet report stunned scientists, especially those in the West. Ralph Laurent, the French physicist, called the discovery of a town and life on Venus "the scientific scoop of modern times."

American experts agreed but were tight-lipped, even after seeing copies of Soviet photographs that clearly show a Wild West town resembling Dodge City from the 1880s, with cowboys, horses and wagons on the planet's surface.

"The possibility that the pictures were faked does exist," said one U.S. space official. "But the Soviets have nothing to gain by perpetrating a hoax.

"Even if they did, it seems highly unlikely that they would use an American-style town rather than a Soviet city or village.

"This is like something out of the *Twilight Zone,*" he added. Dr. Srednev refused to discuss the mission of the probe in detail but he did confirm that it was the latest in a series of Soviet probes that have photographed Venus since the 1960s.

He also declined to comment on speculation that the town was built by extraterrestrials who visited the American West in the 19th century or intercepted a television signal that showed what Wild West towns looked like.

It is not clear when — or if — the Soviets will send their next probe to Venus. But Simon Drost, the Dutch UFO expert, called on the Americans and Soviets to pool their knowledge, equipment and resources and get one there fast.

"We've got to find out what that town is doing on Venus," said Drost. "It isn't the kind of knowledge we can live without."●

☐ *The Town Found on Venus article sounds like the one those two English school teachers found when they went to visit the Palace of Versailles and ended up in the 18th century. If that could happen here — maybe it could happen on Venus? How else can you account for life in a 900 degree temperature? I guess Venus could have "time warps" if we can have them here on earth. It reminds me of that "Heaven" probe we have on file.*

This is one of those 5s I told you about.

BIGFOOT

When someone offers enough money for one of these critters — surely someone will figure a way to haul one into Grand Central Station. There are so many of these sightings they're almost a dime a dozen. The popular thing to do is laugh and pretend all of them are made up to fill empty gaps in the news. The articles are convincing, so sincere, so numerous, I can't believe all of them are false. If one is true then there's no reason that many of them aren't true. If you had clippings with all the following headlines, which would you choose as illustrations?

CHINESE TEAM CLOSING IN ON BIGFOOT
***Weekly World News,* Nov. 18, 1987**

Hair samples collected over a four-year period prove beyond doubt that Bigfoot exists, say Chinese scientists — they plan to capture one within weeks!

☐ *Maybe so — I still haven't seen one on TV. It doesn't have a by-line but it's a mighty fine article. I wouldn't wish to discredit a word of it.*

BIGFOOT LIVES
May 23, 1989, by John McGraw

Amazing photos prove it. Expert animal tracker catches beast taking a cool shower in a mountain pool.

☐ *This one will sell remarkable film footage. For fifty bucks it looks like a better investment than trying the stock market. I'm tempted.*

BIGFOOT SPOOKS LOGGERS
***National Examiner,* July 14, 1987**

Terrified loggers claim they were attacked by a huge bigfoot creature ... crossed the road in two single steps.

TWO-HEADED BIGFOOT TERRIFIES TOWN
***Sun,* March 7, 1989**

A double dose of horror plagues a terrified town ravaged by a two-headed Bigfoot! A team of scientists has been sent to the village outside Bombay, India to investigate the sightings.●

FURRY SPACE ALIENS MATED WITH EARTH WOMEN
***Weekly World,* April 25, 1989**
by Henry Weber

"Amazing wolf people are their offspring," says scientist.

Wolf people living in Mexico and China were fathered by space aliens like Chewbacca, the hairy extraterrestrial in *Star Wars!*

That's the claim of Dutch geneticist Peter de Vries, who spent two years studying the furry people and now says they are only half human — at best.

"Humans and space aliens have mated and these wolf peoples are the result," the expert told newsmen in Amsterdam. "They are stronger than men. They are smarter than men.

"But the feature that truly sets them apart is the thick brown hair that covers their bodies and faces. It makes them look like wild animals.

"But it is proof of their extraterrestrial heritage. There is no other explanation for it!"

The geneticist's report raised eyebrows in scientific circles but he produced strong evidence to support his claims.

Tests clearly show that the wolf people have 52 chromosomes — six more than human beings — and genes that are at least twice the size of those found in men.

Even stranger, the mothers of the wolf people all claim to have had close encounters with UFOs or hairy aliens like Chewbacca, the Wookiee in the sci-fi movie *Star Wars,* before they had their babies.

"There are currently 28 wolf people,

ages 4 to 27, in Hotien, China, and Nuevo Laredo, Mexico," said the expert.

"You would think they would be treated like freaks or outcasts. But their superior strength and intelligence has helped them avoid such a fate.

"They have IQs of 225 plus. Four and 5-year-olds can lift as much as 200 pounds. I saw a teenager pull a tree out of the ground with his bare hands."

Dr. de Vries heard about the wolf people from a fellow scientist in 1987 and immediately began his study.

He has yet to determine, however, why they would appear in Hotien and Nuevo Laredo — thousands of miles apart.

"There are other troubling questions," he continued.

"Were their space alien fathers rapists or did they seek to have offspring with human women as part of a master plan?

"What possible reason could these creatures have for interbreeding with humans?"

While Dr. de Vries continues his research, the wolf people are bending over backwards to live normal lives.

They allowed Dr. de Vries to interview them but refused to accompany the scientist back to Amsterdam to undergo further testing.

As 27-year-old wolf man Zbang Xin put it: "We deserve the same rights and respect as human beings.

"We are not guinea pigs."●

☐ *The accompanying pictures of these people were convincing. It has long been suspected there is some kind of a relationship between UFOS, Bigfoot, and us. The showing of Chewbacca in* Star Wars *helps people to adjust to such possibilities. Sounds like a 9 to me.*

The May 17, 1988 *Sun* has an article by Joe Frick which credits a Bigfoot in helping to save a man's life. A contractor whose single engine plane crashed in British Columbia, made his way to a road with the help and verbal prayers of a Bigfoot. Many UFO conversations appear to be telepathic; I wonder if this might have been the case. Hypnosis would help.

BIZARRE BEINGS LURK IN NEW ENGLAND DEVIL'S TRIANGLE

***Sun*, July 5, 1988**

by Christopher Luke

(Scared residents say they have seen tall, furry, man-like creature).

This area is known as the Bridgewater Triangle and includes Brockton, Taunton, Rehoboth, E. Freetown, Middleboro, and Abington.●

MYSTERIES ON BIGFOOT

***Weekly World*, December 22, 1987**

by Allan Trexler

Soviet scientists claim to have solved the world's greatest mysteries and have delivered their findings to world leaders for possible global action in the future.

The 1,500 page report explores UFOs, Bigfoot, the Devil's Triangle and Atlantis and is signed by a dozen of the Soviet Union's leading researchers, including famed physicist Anotoly Shalnev and Vladimir Ptashnikov.

Incredibly, the study links UFOs, the Devil's Triangle and Atlantis with extraterrestrial activity on our planet both past and present.

Bigfoot does exist, said the Soviets, as the missing link between modern man and our primitive ancestors, the apes.

"This revolutionary study is only the beginning," Dr. Shalnev said in his preface to the shocking report.

"It is the beginning of a new era of research that should include the greatest minds on Earth. Extraterrestrials are operating here in great numbers and have been for centuries.

"It is imperative that we find the means with which to communicate with them if we expect to have control over our own destinies.

"Establishing relations with Bigfoot is vitally important. These creatures are our link with the past, just as aliens will be our link to the future."

Swiss journalist Claude Ludin obtained two copies of the hush-hush Soviet report from a source behind the Iron Curtain.

He is currently negotiating with a major European publisher who is seeking rights to the document. But he agreed to provide excerpts of the Soviet's study and findings "as a gift and service to mankind."

Here, in alphabetical order, is the crux of the report.

As world leaders in the search for the lost city, the Soviets scanned the Atlantic from Great Britain to Africa's Gold Coast before determining that Atlantis lies some 400 miles west of Portugal.

A research team led by oceanographer Boris Sturua found the remains of a city on the ocean floor. And contrary to popular belief, the architecture did not mirror that of the ancient Greeks.

"It is suggestive of an incredibly advanced technology," said Dr. Sturua. "Building materials range from concrete to unusually durable plastics.

"The remains of streets and avenues suggest the use of monorails for transportation. We managed to recover a statue that depicts a human being in conversation with an alien life-form.

"The alien is humanoid, extremely slender and has an enormous, bulb-shaped head. There is little doubt that Atlantis was a colony of extraterrestrials. It would appear that most if not all perished in some natural disaster."

Anthropologist Melor Ivanov led the team that sought contact with Bigfoot in China, India, South America and Canada. Attempts to capture one of the creatures alive failed.

But two were shot dead. And the study of the body and brains of the hairy, 7-foot creatures clearly showed them to be man-like, even more so than the apes.

"These beasts are clearly out of step with the evolution of all other life-forms on the planet," said Dr. Ivanov.

"They have a dim intelligence below that of men but higher than that of forest-dwelling apes.

"It is my belief that they are mankind's closest relatives. It is as if they are the cave men who survived the ages without evolving. The most surprising aspects of the Bigfoot phenomenon are the creature's sophisticated cultural and social systems."•

☐ *Too hard to judge, 7 is the best I can do.*

BIGFOOT FAMILY FOUND
***Sun*, December 8, 1987**

Research team claims to have lived with caveman Yeti in a secluded cave in the mountains. These Soviet Yeti are smaller than the ones generally described. A book has been written by Marie Jeanne Koffman — *The Sasquatch, and Other Unknown Humanoids.*•

☐ *Looks like we have a cousin from way back.*

SOLDIERS DISCOVER LIVING BREATHING BABY BIGFOOT
***Weekly World News*, March 4, 1986**

A Chinese Army expedition to the Himalaya Mountains has stumbled across one of the greatest finds in scientific history — a living, squalling, Bigfoot baby.

Although given only a brief mention by China's official news agency, an interview with one of the doctors now involved with the incredible creature was smuggled out of the country by a Swiss free-lance medical writer.

In the interview, Dr. Liu Tien-chi, a researcher at the Peking Institute of Science, said the beast-baby is "still alive and flourishing" in a secret clinic in Shansi province, where it was taken after it was found last December.

"We have not yet been able to determine its age," Dr. Liu told the Swiss writer. "That is mainly because the creature is unique and we have nothing to base an estimate on.

"However, when it was found, we believe it was between 5 and 18 months old. It measured three feet six inches tall and weighed 72-1/4 pounds. It has since grown another 13 inches and more than doubled its weight."

Dr. Liu said the creature is a female and has been named Yang-sin.

He estimates that if she grows to maturity, she will be at least seven feet tall and weigh about 900 pounds.

"She is the most amazing specimen of life anyone has ever seen on this earth," he said. "She is a throwback to the early evolution of man — more animal than human.

"She can stand upright and she can walk. Her feet are as human as my own. They have very human toes. Her body is covered with a very thick coat of fur that is only now beginning to molt. It will be replaced, I am sure, with the long, scraggly, gorilla-like hair reported by those who have sighted full grown specimens.

"Only her face is bare of hair. And she has the most remarkable eyes I have ever seen on man or beast. They are like deep, black pools with tiny glints of red. It is almost as though some primeval fire is burning inside her head."

Dr. Liu Said the amazing beast was found by an expedition of engineers surveying the site for a new satellite tracking station in the lower reaches of Mount Gosainthan, a towering Himalayan peak on the China-Nepal border.

"They found her in a cave, lying on a bed of thick, matted hair we believe came from her mother.

"She was flown by helicopter to the Shansi clinic and immediately put on one of the life-support machines we use for experimental chimpanzees," said Dr. Liu.

"Now she seems to be doing very well. She is eating and she is growing. In another six months, if all goes well, photographs and data will be released to scientists throughout the world.

"Then everyone will see our incredible Yang-sin, the most astonishing creature that has ever lived — and still lives today on the face of earth," he said.•

☐ *We've been waiting three years to see that baby Bigfoot. Where is she? Why can't we have a follow-up on such an interesting case?*

These are the ones we fuss about — it may be a 1 or a 10, who knows? Until more is released it's anyone's guess.

I KILLED A BIGFOOT
***Weekly World*, April 4, 1989**
by Max Mabry

In an incredible life and death battle on the slopes of Mt. Everest, a Sherpa guide fought and killed one of the legendary man-ape monsters of the wild — a Himalayan Bigfoot!

Armed only with his courage, wits and a determination to survive, the 27-year-old Tibetan Sherpa spent three desperate hours trying to escape the crazed beast that was tracking him like an animal. Finally, he had to stand and fight.

"I had kept moving up the mountain," the guide, Torban Lodang, told newsmen. "When I got to about the 9,000-foot level, my way was blocked by a slope of solid ice.

"I knew that before long the Bigfoot would catch up with me. I decided to wait — to save my strength for the fight I knew I had to win."

Lodang's nightmarish ordeal began after he had set out to recover the body of a climber that had been spotted three weeks earlier by a Japanese expedition.

"I was working along the face of the mountain," Lodang said. "Suddenly I came upon some footprints in the fresh snow. They were huge and had been made by bare feet. I knew at once that it was the track of the Bigfoot.

"But I was troubled about one other thing — there were fresh bloodstains on the footprints."

Lodang said he followed the tracks for about two hours before he realized that the trail had made a large circle.

"Suddenly I realized that the Bigfoot was behind me. I was no longer tracking the beast — the beast was tracking me. My best chance was to reach a base camp at the 10,000-foot level. I began to climb."

But Lodang's escape route was cut off by the icy slope — 1,000 feet from the base camp.

"Now there was nothing I could do but wait for the Bigfoot to find me. Suddenly it was there — looming up like some fantastic monster.

"It was at least 8 feet tall and covered from head to foot by long, shaggy hair that was splattered with its own blood. I could see its fangs, as long as a leopard's, and eyes that glowed like red-hot coals.

"As soon as it saw me, it raised its massive arms above its head. The creature screamed and charged me. I had to fight.

"But at the last minute, I leaped aside and tumbled in the snow. The beast stumbled a bit and then turned, screamed out its rage and charged again. I realized it was weak from loss of blood. So I had a glimmer of hope.

"As the monster charged me, I hurled my body at its knees, hoping it would fall in the snow and give me time to flee.

"The beast stumbled over my body and landed on the icy slope. Its massive body plummeted down the ice and hurtled over the edge. The drop-off there is 3,000 feet. I knew the Bigfoot must be dead."

The next morning, Lodang returned to his village of Tungpu to tell his incredible story. He now believes that the Bigfoot had been shot and wounded by someone and had gone mad with pain. ●

☐ *Very few Bigfoot stories are like this one. Perhaps it was the condition that caused such a reaction. If that creature was in a dead heap some place he should have gone hunting for him. No body — maybe a 5.*

The Sun *has some photos of a Bigfoot baby. It is widely believed the father of the one-year-old is an extraterrestrial. Mothers report being captured by metallic creatures that they believe to have been robots. If you are following UFO cases it becomes obvious experimental cross-breeding is taking place.*

BABY BIGFOOT
***Sun*, February 28, 1989**
by Francis Shifflett

Despite a horrifying appearance at the time of birth, an amazing baby Bigfoot has become the darling of the town as he reaches his first birthday.

Incredibly, the furry youngster is already the second bigfoot baby born in a farming community.

Experts believe that they're both the result of UFO experiments!

But the understandable fear and concern of the townspeople has given way, at least temporarily, to a sudden sense of fondness.

They are taken by the cuddly little creature which they say is as cute as a button.

"He's a real-life teddy-bear," declares the child's mom Lan Xiu.

In more ways than one, baby Bigfoot resembles any other one-year-old child.

He's normal in size and weight. Like human children he is bright-eyed, inquisitive and playful.

A mass of black fur covers the entire boy's body. Present since birth, the furry coat has grown substantially in his first year.

His mom is forced to trim it every week to prevent the child from disappearing into a giant ball of fur.

Baby Bigfoot never cries, says Mom Lan, but emits a strange high-pitched yapping. She admits her strange son can be extremely mischievous at times.

"He's able to climb and crawl into all sorts of strange places," the mother says. "Sometimes be runs into a room and seems to literally disappear.

"I know he's hiding, but God knows where."

The most frightening thing about the odd child is the mysterious set of circumstances that resulted during the time of conception.

Classified top-secret by the Chinese government, Lan is totally forbidden to discuss them.

But a UFO expert, Yon Jean, reveals that the Bigfoot baby's father was probably an extraterrestrial.

"There have been widespread UFO sightings in remote parts of Sichuan province where the two Bigfoot babies were born," he states.

"Both mothers reported similar experiences of being captured by metallic creatures which they believed to be robots".

"They were taken aboard the spaceship and strapped to a large machine that made them both pregnant."

Mom Lan would only release one detail of her strange ordeal: "All I can say is that I was never really frightened. I felt a strange sense of contentment."

UFO reports in the area have increased since the births of the two Bigfoot babies.

Officials are warning women to stay indoors at night to avoid future Bigfoot babies.

Dr. Jean strongly advises caution. "These babies may be cute right now," the expert notes. "But there's just no telling what they might grow into."●

☐ *Names of family with pictures plus a baby can't be ignored — this is worth a fat 9.*

COURAGEOUS BIGFOOT RESCUES FAMILY
***National Examiner,* December 6, 1988**
by Gus Vandermeer

A heroic Bigfoot saved a vacationing family from a ferocious grizzly bear that chased them up a tree.

Takeo Nishimura, 35, says he and his wife, Oyako, 32, and their son, Tadashi, eight, and daughter, Kiko, five, owe their lives to the bravery of the giant, fur-covered, ape-like Good Samaritan.

"I had heard of Bigfoot but never expected to actually see or be rescued by one," Takeo notes.

The Nishimuras, of Tokyo, Japan, were camping in the wilds of northwest British Columbia when they encountered an enormous bear.

"We had just finished breakfast when my son saw the bear coming through the woods toward our campsite," Tokeo explains. "We scrambled up the nearest pine tree as fast as we could.

"After gobbling up the lunch Oyako had packed, the bear came right over to the tree, reared back on its hind legs and snorted at us. It stood at least nine feet tall. We were terrified.

"Then the grizzly cocked its head, sniffed the air, and wheeled around to see a Bigfoot monster standing there, holding a long, heavy club.

"The Bigfoot was almost as tall as the bear. He seemed to appear out of nowhere, but I instantly felt he would protect us. I could see intelligence in his eyes.

"He bashed the bear on the shoulder with the club, knocking it away from the tree. Then, before the grizzly could attack, he landed a severe blow to its foreleg.

"The bear limped away, snorting and growling. The Bigfoot creature looked at us in the tree, apparently figured we would be all right, and vanished into the woods as quickly and mysteriously as he had appeared."

Still trembling with fear and astonishment, the Nishimuras climbed down from the tree and left the forest, stopping at a nearby ranger station to report the amazing encounter they had witnessed.

"The forest ranger told us we were incredibly lucky. Bigfoot monsters are very shy and do not often approach humans. We are just thankful this one was there when we needed him. I wish I could shake his paw and thank him in person for chasing that bear away."●

☐ *This sounds like a real honest-to-goodness experience. In case it is, it deserves a 9.*

HAIRY SPACEMEN KIDNAP COP
***Weekly World,* December 20, 1988**
by Dick Donovan

Rookie cop Martin Cohen says he was kidnapped by "furry" space aliens during an evening stroll — and dozens of witnesses say his story is true!

The 21-year-old British bobby said he was bathed in a glowing purple light that beamed him skyward as he walked in a park in Roundhay, an English village north of Leeds.

"It was about 10:30 p.m., and I was walking to the Mansion House Hotel to have a drink with a friend when suddenly I saw a purple glow," Cohen said.

"The next thing I knew I was being carried off the ground. My body went numb and my head started spinning.

"Then I saw forms that appeared to be women. They looked like they could be human. Then I just blacked out."

From Cohen's description the furry creatures looked like *Chewbacca,* the Wookiee in *Star Wars.*

Cohen says he has no recollection of where he was taken or what happened to him from the time he blacked out until he came to, sprawled on the ground, eight hours later.

Cohen's unconscious body was found early the following morning by park jogger Mike Cotran, 23, who said he saw a glowing purple light less than 100 feet in front of him.

"At first I thought I was just seeing things," Cotran said. "Then I noticed the body of a man on the ground. There had been no body on the ground before the light appeared.

"My first impression was that it was a dead body. I was very frightened and in a state of shock. When the man I now know to be Martin Cohen came to, he was very weak and in a cold sweat.

"He just kept rambling on and on about being 'somewhere else'...about having a weird experience."

Even before Cohen's shocking abduction story was made public, several people reported seeing the ominous purple glow shimmering in the park near the Mansion House Hotel.

"We had many calls from people who wouldn't identify themselves," said Angela Friend, an investigative reporter for the Yorkshire *Evening News.*

"We made a careful investigation into the story, but weren't able to come up with much, " she told *The News.*

"It's just one of those things that can't be proved or disproved. It's a real mystery."●

☐ *Much effort and expense is involved in bringing these reports to you — read them! That cop deserves an 8.5.*

GIANT BIGFOOT CAPTURED ALIVE; HUNDREDS SEE IT

***Sun*, January 24, 1989**

by Joe Frick

Bigfoot experts remain mystified by the young beast put on public display before hundreds of witnesses after it was captured by a railroad crew in the Canadian wilds.

An entire nation was enthralled by the banner headlines splashed across the front page of the Victoria *Daily Colonist* in 1884 asking what was this "strange creature."

It all began on a hot summer day when a freight train traveling through the Fraser Canyon in British Columbia, Canada, came upon what appeared to be a man lying beside the track.

An alert engineer put on the brakes and the train stopped within yards of the body.

But the figure suddenly leaped to its feet, giving a loud, sharp bark before climbing up a steep slope.

The crew chased it up the embankment and cornered the injured beast, which had run out onto a projecting shelf of rock and became trapped.

Terrified at what they were seeing — a half-man, half-beast — the men decided to try and capture it.

After several efforts they managed to rope the howling creature.

Arriving back in Yale, B.C., the crew turned the beast, which they nicknamed "Jacko," over to stunned stationmaster George Tilbury.

Word of the capture spread rapidly and a reporter from the Victoria *Daily Colonist* rushed to Yale. He could scarcely believe what he saw.

"The creature is something of the gorilla type," he reported. "He may truly be called half man and half beast."

At 8-foot-2 and weighing about 600 pounds, the hairy, black beast possessed extraordinary strength, he said.

"Apparently he is still young and the only sound he makes is half growl and half bark."

Hundreds of people came to see Jacko, but the creature's identity remained a complete puzzle to everyone.

Before researchers could study the animal, Jacko suddenly vanished. George, a silent eccentric, refused to discuss the beast's disappearance.

Observers speculated Jacko either escaped or died.

Whatever the case, Bigfoot experts realize that science missed a perfect opportunity to examine one of the greatest mysteries of the world.●

☐ *I'll bet a nickel the government got there first. It's hard to get your story — when the big boys beat you to it! Without the creature, it only gets an 8.*

STARVING HUNTERS RESCUED BY GENTLE GIANTS

***Weekly World News*, November 5, 1985**

A party of hunters, lost for weeks in the unexplored jungles of Borneo, stumbled out of the bush with an incredible tale of their rescue — by a hairy, ape-like tribe of Stone Age cave men!

In a news dispatch from Surabaya, Java, the six hunters said they were hopelessly lost and near death from starvation when they were found by a band of cavemen.

"They saved our lives, that's for certain," the news story quoted one hunter. "If we hadn't been damned near gone when they found us, we probably would have shot them dead on the spot — if we still had our guns."

"They were a fierce-looking lot and they grunted like wild boars. But they were gentle as lambs."

The hunters, not identified by name, are members of an exclusive club of wealthy Argentine sportsmen known for their searches for adventure.

The hunter said his group lost all their supplies when their canoe hit a submerged log and overturned on a branch of the Barito River that winds through the jungle skirting the eastern slopes of the Muller Mountains.

The hunters struggled on through the bush for 14 days before their agonizing hunger brought their trek to a halt. Too weak to walk any longer, they settled in a clearing to await the fate they knew would soon come.

"We were lying in the grass and all of us were just about out of it when, suddenly, I felt myself being swept up in powerful arms. I opened my eyes and looked into the most frightening face I had ever seen.

"It was definitely human, yet it had strong, ape-like features. It was huge and its head was massive, with a protruding brow ridge and a high, sloping forehead. The face was almost completely covered with hair. It reminded me of a picture I had once seen of Neanderthal man.

"I must have passed out because the next thing I remember is waking up in a large cave.

"Later, they gave us raw meat and water, and bearskins to warm us. There were at least 100 of the cave people living together."

"They could only grunt like animals, but somehow they seemed to know what we needed.

"We stayed in that cave for 16 days while we regained our strength.

"Then one day, they loaded us up with dried meat wrapped in deerskins, took us to the river and pointed the way back to civilization.

"A two-week trek brought us to a village."

The six hunters have vowed never to reveal the location of the Stone Age cave dwelling to protect the cave people from the outside world.

"They are the survivors of earth's earliest days," the hunter explained. "They survive only on animal instinct, yet it was that instinct that saved our lives."●

☐ *Most convincing and enjoyable — deserves a 9.5.*

BIGFOOT SAVED MY LIFE

***Weekly World*, December 31, 1985**

by Stan Kaplow

Terrified explorer Emil Stainer clung to an icy ledge high in the storm-swept Himalayas and stared death in the face for three agonizing hours before being rescued — by a giant, lumbering Bigfoot!

"There is no doubt the creature saved my life," the shaken Stainer told a scientific journal in Belgrade, Yugoslavia.

"I had watched my companions plunge a thousand feet down the mountain and could feel the ledge slowly crumbling beneath my feet. I knew I couldn't last much longer.

"I had given up all hope of life when the beast appeared from out of nowhere to save me."

Stainer's hair-raising adventure unfolded while he and seven other Yugoslav meteorologists were conducting weather studies near Mount Everest in Nepal.

Stainer and two colleagues, Dusan Imre and Ivan Meden, were setting up their equipment on a shelf six miles from base camp when horror struck.

"We thought we were on safe footing, but suddenly the ice and snow gave way under us," the 31-year-old scientist recalled.

"It happened so fast. Dusan and Ivan screamed and fell into the precipice. I knew automatically that they were dead and I thought I was going to die with them.

"But I started to slide and fought desperately to hang on.

Somehow I wound up unhurt on a ledge about three feet wide and 30 feet down."

The frightened father of four huddled on his precarious perch for hours, staring a thousand feet straight down the mountain and thinking about the loved ones he'd left at home.

"To me, all hope was lost," Stainer said. "I knew no one would find me there.

"Then I heard a commotion from the shelf above and when I looked up there was the yeti peering down at me. He was massive, at least 8 feet tall and completely covered with hair.

"It was like something out of science fiction. Suddenly he began lowering one of the safety ropes we'd left on the ledge. I grabbed the rope and tied it under my arms and around my waist. He waited patiently, never making a sound, and then slowly and carefully pulled me to safety.

"He was so strong my weight was like nothing to him. He pulled me onto solid ground and then lumbered away."

Stainer made his way back to camp and a search party was organized for the missing scientists, but their bodies were never found.

"The only thing we found on the ledge was what was left of the gear and the largest footprints I have ever seen," said another weather expert, Stipe Skrbek. "They measured 23 inches from heel to toe.

"We were tempted to follow the prints but our first concern was the search for our friends.

"By the time we gave up the search, the snow had wiped out the prints. But none of us who saw them doubts that what Emil has told us is true — his life was saved by the creature the natives call yeti."●

☐ *I don't have the advantage of having a picture of the man whose life was saved. However, somewhere in the* Weekly World *files you'll find one. Yeti gets a 9.9.*

GIANT BIGFOOT SIGHTINGS ALARM INDIAN VILLAGE

***National Examiner*, October 10, 1989**

Eight-foot-tall Bigfoot are terrorizing remote Indian villages.

And the growing number of sasquatch sightings is alarming native residents who have known for years that the giant creatures inhabit the forests around Canada's Lake Winisk.

A huge creature stirring in the bushes recently scared Caroline Yesno while she swam in the lake. When she reported the sighting to the police they discovered the 14-inch-long footprints of a sasquatch.

"A number of tracks were clearly visible," said Police Constable Jeff Simpkins, of the Ontario Provincial Police's Northwest Patrol.

That night, as Bobby Wabasse paddled a canoe on his way to battle a forest fire, he came face to face with the monster crashing through the brush.

"He saw a shadow about 20 feet from the shoreline and he saw an object moving that was eight feet tall and erect," said Simpkins.

Just two weeks earlier, Harvey McKay spotted a bigfoot at least seven feet tall and covered with long brown hair.

"I saw this thing that looked like it was trying to cross the road," he said. "When it ran away, it moved kind of slow-motion fashion ... it was big and didn't move too fast, but ambled along with long strides."●

☐ *Doesn't it seem reasonable that someone should tell us the truth concerning "Bigfoot"? When we are told there is no such thing — and then all these people claim to have such experiences — isn't it time we deserve a reasonable explanation?*

October 3, 1989, by Ben Snark, carries an article with additional information concerning this article. How much must these tabloids feed you before you investigate for yourself? Of course this information is worth a 9.5.

CRASH SURVIVORS RESCUED BY BIGFOOT

***Weekly World*, October 1, 1985**

Arequipa, Peru — Two prominent geologists injured in a plane crash high in the Andes Mountains told authorities they were watched over by a hairy, lumbering Bigfoot which approached their crash site seven times to toss them food.

Dr. Alberto Gomes and his wife Teresa were rescued after spending three bone-chilling days and nights in a remote region of El Misti, a 19,150-foot dormant volcano in southern Peru.

"We had a close encounter with a creature we thought lived only in legends," Gomes told investigators from his hospital bed.

"He was 8 feet tall and very shy, but there is no doubt in my mind that he was doing everything he could to keep us alive."

The two Brazilian scientists were on a routine survey flight when their plane developed engine trouble and plummeted to the ground, killing pilot Vicente de Souza, 38.

Gomes, 51, suffered a broken ankle and two broken ribs. Mrs. Gomes, 39, suffered internal injuries and severe facial lacerations.

"We could barely crawl, but we managed to drag the blankets and warm clothes out of the wreckage," Mrs. Gomes said later.

"Then we bundled up in the snow to spend the night. I never prayed so hard as I did then. I was certain we were going to die out there."

Shortly after daybreak the next morning, the scientists said, they were awakened by rustling in the brush — and spotted a Bigfoot standing at the edge of the clearing 30 yards away.

"It was a cross between a man and an ape," Gomes told police. "He was covered with matted brown hair from head to foot. Our hearts were pounding because we could barely move and we knew he could kill us if he wanted to."

But instead of charging, the monstrous creature flung several handsful of berries and slender roots toward the injured couple and then fled into the brush, they told investigators.

"We ate the berries, then used melted snow and a pot from the plane to boil the roots," Teresa Gomes recalled. "They were very edible, even tasty."

That night, she said, the Bigfoot reappeared and tossed them two small fish, which they cooked and ate.

"Before the rescuers got there, he came back five more times and brought us roots and berries," Gomes said. "We never heard him make a sound except for the noise he made running through the brush. He was our silent savior.

"He just brought us food and ran away."

A rescue party spotted the geologists' emergency beacon three days after their plane went down and rushed them to a hospital in Arequipa, where they are recovering from their injuries and the effects of exposure.

Police said natives have reported more than a score of Bigfoot sightings in the El Misti region over the past five years, but some lawmen remained skeptical of the Gomes' account.●

☐ *This one makes me feel good — pretend only one of these articles is true — any one of them contains earth shaking news. What do you want—one to walk into your living room? This rescue deserves a 10.*

BIGFOOT FROM OUTER SPACE

***Weekly World*, 1988**

by John Blackburn

Bigfoot is a space alien, startling new evidence reveals.

Stunned residents of a remote wilderness community on Lake Winnipeg in northern Canada have actually seen the hairy, 9-foot-tall creatures stepping out of UFOs at secret landing sites in the area.

And incredibly, the Royal Canadian Mounted Police have made plaster casts of monstrous, telltale footprints left behind by one of the extraterrestrial beasts.

"We've had to put up with the mysterious visits of these terrifying half-man, half-ape creatures for at least 20 years," said Gerald Valiquette, a 31-year-old back-woodsman who lives along the northern reaches of the meandering Poplar River, 200 miles northeast of Manitoba's capital, Winnipeg.

Amazingly, several of Valiquette's neighbors have reported watching in horror as giant UFOs landed at the river's edge and unloaded their unearthly cargoes of huge beasts that walk on their hind legs and are covered with smelly, thick mats of long, stringy, dark hair.

"I myself have been chased by one of these creatures — and narrowly escaped with my life," the backwoodsman disclosed.

"I was hunting one day several years back when, suddenly, this huge, man-like thing reared up about 60 feet in front of me. It was definitely a Bigfoot. I've lived in the wilderness all my life and I'd never seen anything like it before.

"I turned on my heel and ran through the woods. I could hear the huge beast, crashing through the underbrush behind me in pursuit. I ran faster, thought my lungs would burst, when, suddenly, it gave up the chase. I'm not a coward, but I've never hunted in that particular spot since. In fact, I avoid it."

Earlier this year, after a rash of UFO sightings in the Poplar River area, a Mountie patrolling the region made two plaster casts of 15-inch-long footprints.

A Canadian anthropologist who has examined the casts said he knows of no earthly creature that could have made the prints.●

☐ *There are reports that connect some Bigfoot with UFOs. I can't ignore it and will have to give it an 8.5.*

I TALKED, ATE AND SLEPT WITH BIGFOOT

***Sun*, October 13, 1987**

by Richard Dominick

Explorer Claude Lenault came face to face with a Bigfoot monster while trapping fur in western Canada near the Washington State border. He befriended the half-man half-beast, and the two ate, slept and even spoke to each other before going their separate ways. This is his astonishing story:

Claude says he was checking traps in a heavily wooded area when he suddenly spotted the enormous creature standing on its hind legs. It was partially hidden by the trees, but for the veteran hunter and trapper there was no mistaking it.

"All my life I dreamed of meeting this great creature," recalls Claude. "My father would tell me stories about him when we went out hunting together when I was a child, but never in a million years did I ever think I would actually see Bigfoot!"

Claude, of French-Canadian descent, walked slowly toward the beast.

"I didn't want to frighten him off."

When the trapper got within a few feet, the animal held up a trap in his right forepaw and handed it to Claude.

"I started to laugh," says the trapper. "The creature startēd laughing, too. That's when I knew I had nothing to fear." Claude describes Bigfoot as at least 8 feet tall.

"He probably weighed about 400 pounds. He was built like a man in every way except his body was covered by a coat of thick, dark fur."

Because the sun was beginning to go down, Claude decided to set up camp right there where he found Bigfoot.

"I put my knapsack down and began building a fire.

"Bigfoot watched my every move, and I showed him how I started the blaze by first igniting some dry leaves. When the fire began to crackle, he sat down on a log and made a groaning sound which reminded me of the sort of noise a dog makes when you're gently stroking its stomach."

The trapper says he pulled a package of freeze-dried food out of his backpack and began to cook it.

"I wasn't sure if that was the proper thing to feed Bigfoot, but it was all I had."

Seconds later, Bigfoot held out a dead rabbit with his left hand.

"I couldn't believe my eyes, Claude says, shaking his head. I immediately skinned the animal and skewered it.

"Then Bigfoot used his hands to explain to me he had found the rabbit in the trap earlier."

Man and beast dined together, and when the fire started to die down, Bigfoot simply grabbed a sapling tree, uprooted it and dropped it down on the flames.

Eventually the trapper fell asleep. When he awakened the next morning, there was nothing left of Bigfoot but his tracks leading into the forest.

"I'm sure Bigfoot realized I wanted to bring him to civilization, but he just wanted to be free," says Claude.●

☐ *I'm a real sucker for this story. I can't believe there isn't an element of truth in it — no wonder I believe in UFOs. By the way, along about this time I'm hoping you're beginning to believe too. A 9.5 for Claude and Richard.*

BIGFOOT IS MY BUDDY, SWEARS HERMIT TRAPPER

***Sun*, September 20, 1988**

by Fred Sleeves

The isolated life of a mountain man has been made richer by an old pal who visits him to share meals and conversation near a warm fireplace. The guest is quite different from others who stumble upon the cabin, however. He's a huge, hairy Bigfoot!

"He comes to my cabin three or four times a year," says Caylan Brown, a 44-year-old Canadian trapper in northern British Columbia.

"Each time he brings a freshly-killed animal. I skin it and cook it, and we have a nice meal together.

"Then we sit down and talk. He grunts and uses sign language. I speak to him and he seems to understand what I'm saying.

"Some years I see more of him than I do other humans," he notes.

Sasquatch hunters who've discovered footprints near the isolated cabin have been grilling Caylan for information, but he tries to keep them away because he respects his friend's privacy.

"I think that he's brought here by a flying saucer," explains Caylan. "I always see a few in the sky shortly before Bigfoot comes.

"Once I saw a flying saucer on the ground. It took off and disappeared when I came near, but I ran into my old buddy Bigfoot a few minutes later.

"I pointed up to the sky and asked, 'What was that?' He grunted and hugged himself. I don't know what that means, but I'm sure Bigfoot and the flying saucers are connected."

Several UFO sightings have been reported near the area, and experts have long suspected a link because Bigfoot and UFO reports often come together.

Caylan first met his 8-foot-tall buddy several years ago while hunting. He was terrified at first, but got up enough courage to offer the hairy creature some food, and the two became friends.

"I see him and have supper with him so many times, I gave him a name. I call him Charlie. He likes that very much and smiles whenever I call him by name.

"Charlie doesn't talk much, no more than a few grunts, really," says Caylan.

"But I know he's real intelligent. He knows what I say and he's able to make his thoughts known to me. He's as much a person as you or I.

"He comes more often in the winter and likes to sleep over in the warm cabin after supper.

"But what the hell, it's cold outside. If you came, you'd probably want to sleep over, too," the trapper adds.●

☐ *I think this is a pretty nice article. The trapper and Fred deserve at least a 9.5, don't you agree?*

BIGFOOT TRIBE KIDNAPS FIVE KIDS

***Sun*, April 21, 1987**

by Crandall McIntosh

An angry tribe of Abominable Snowmen swept down from the Himalayan Mountains, invaded a small village, kidnapped five children from a schoolhouse, then hightailed it back to their isolated domain, says a New Delhi, India, newspaper.

It was the latest in a series of attacks by the normally peaceful Yeti, shaggy half-men, half-beasts who are Asian cousins of North America's Bigfoot monsters.

Schoolteacher Zana Rampunr, 25, says she could only watch in stunned horror as the herd of hairy creatures burst into her classroom, tied her to a chair and hauled away five of her screaming, flabbergasted students.

"It was a nightmare," Zana says.

"Eight Yeti barged right into our little one-room schoolhouse and kidnapped the children.

"Two of them bound me with ropes to my chair, and another guarded the door while the rest of them picked up the children in their furry arms and took them away.

"The Yeti acted frantic and crazed, quite unlike the way they have been depicted in books and legends."

Indeed, experts are at a loss to explain the Yeti's recent bizarre behavior.

"The Yeti, more commonly known as the Abominable Snowman, is usually a shy, solitary creature," notes Dr. Walter Henshaw, a professor of anthropology at New Delhi University. He has devoted his career to the study of the bewildering beasts.

"They have inhabited the Himalayan region for centuries, yet there was never a report of them banding together in tribes until the past few months.

"They are incredibly intelligent, and have the ability to speak, according to people who claim to have heard the Yeti calling their names in the night.

"That's another thing. Previously, the Yeti had never been sighted in broad daylight. They appeared only during darkness hours, usually just before dawn," says Henshaw.

"Lately, several tribes of Yeti have been seen in or near various villages. There have been reports of unprovoked attacks upon livestock and pets, as well as random vandalism," according to Henshaw.

"The invasion of Miss Rampunr's schoolhouse is the latest and most drastic example of their suddenly mysterious and violent behavior."

What has caused the formerly mellow Yeti to go on the warpath is anybody's guess, Dr. Henshaw explains.

"I can't explain this new and frightening phenomenon," he says.

"But I have a gut feeling that the terror has just begun," Henshaw adds.

Meanwhile, the grief-stricken parents of the abducted children, who range in age from 6 to 11, say they will organize search parties and journey into the rugged, snowy mountains in an effort to rescue their youngsters.

"We will hunt the Yeti down and kill them for what they have done to our children," declares one villager.

"These invasions must be halted immediately," the villager adds.

Citizens in neighboring villages are also bracing themselves for possible future attacks.●

☐ *With pictures and names and information, I can't discount such a tale. I may be wrong but this report looks good for a 9.5.*

I CAME FACE TO FACE WITH BIGFOOT!

***Weekly World News*, Dec. 16, 1986**

World-renowned adventurer brings back proof of massive creature who rules mountains of Tibet. A double-page spread with a picture of Reinhold Messner shows the importance attached to this article.

Record-setting mountaineer Reinhold Messner has returned from his latest Himalayan conquest with an astonishing account of his encounter with the most elusive creature on earth — the man-ape known as Bigfoot!

And he has vivid photographs that prove beyond any doubt that his incredible story is true!

But even without photos, those who know Messner — the only man to climb all 14 of the highest peaks in the world — know him as a man of integrity and courage, not given over to fantasy.

His brief but frightening encounter with "Yeti," as the beast is known in Tibet, came during his assault on Mt. Lhotse. He had just reached the 12,000-foot-level when be saw something moving across the snow only a few yards away.

"It was huge, much bigger than me and covered with thick, dark hair," the dashing, 42-year-old climber said. "We came to within 40 feet of each other and, I admit, I was scared.

"It was making grunting noises that I didn't understand. It moved with very long strides, sometimes walking upright like a human, and at other times down on all fours like an animal. But it didn't have a tail, and if it was an animal, it was like no other known to man."

However, some anthropologists believe the Bigfoot encountered by Messner is a survivor from the Stone Age known as Gigantopithecus, a veritable King Kong of an ape that towered over the primitive humans that all but hunted them into extinction.

The scientists believe that some of the giant creatures may have fled into the Himalayas, adapted to the harsh environment and managed to reproduce in small numbers for millions of years.

Bones of that beast were recently uncovered in China, Tibet and Vietnam, indicating that Gigantopithecus could very well have survived into the 20th century.

"I had always thought it was a legend fabricated by the natives," Messner said. "The more I traveled these mountains, the less I believed in the monster. But I have seen it. I have photographs of its footprints. It was Bigfoot.

"It must weigh about 450 pounds. Its footprints measured 17 inches long and 5-1/2 inches wide. It has long arms and reddish-brown hair all over its body and it smells of blood. What the Tibetans say about Bigfoot is true. I know. I've seen it."●

☐ *Another 9 for Bigfoot.*

BIGFOOT CITY
***Weekly World News*, February 17, 1987**
by Alice Dominguez

South American scientists are mounting an expedition after reports of an astounding new find — a complete city inhabited by Bigfoot creatures!

Scientists, anthropologists and primate specialists from major universities in Peru and Bolivia, have gathered in the city of Santa Ana, Peru, in the Andes, where the Bigfoot settlement was discovered.

"Following the disclosure of extraordinary evidence of a 'Bigfoot city' inhabited by over 200 individuals, the scientific community has moved to conduct a thorough investigation," said a press spokesman for the team in announcing the expedition. "The study team is expected to leave for the mountain of Nevado Salcantay within the next two months."

According to the press release, the "Bigfoot city" was discovered by a team of mountain climbers exploring a remote Andes area. The climbers reported their find to the Peruvian government upon their return, and authorities alerted scientists.

The climbers — eight men and women from an international climbing club — are still in Peru in anticipation of an attempt on 20,574-foot Nevado Salcantay. Their descriptions of the Bigfoot settlement appeared in the Peruvian press and sent shockwaves throughout the scientific community worldwide.

"We became lost in a blizzard on the eastern slopes of the mountain and mistakenly headed east and north toward an unexplored region," one of the climbers, Kitsunobe Abe, is quoted as saying.

"When the blizzard ended about 48 hours later we discovered we were way off in a region of Peru where our guides had never been.

"We descended to a warmer, snowless valley and in one corner of this we spotted a canyon wall riddled with clefts and caves. We decided to take shelter for the night and approached the caves.

"To our amazement we found they were inhabited — by at least two or three hundred beasts."

The climbers said the Bigfoot city they saw contained scores of cave dwellings. Some clefts in the rocks were packed with supplies of roots and nuts and obviously served the inhabitants as storage bins.

Bigfoot young, accompanied male and female adults along well-trodden pathways or streets and the entire settlement bustled with activity.

"The reports of the climbers indicate that the Bigfoot city dwellers have a well-developed sense of social communication and give evidence that the beasts are capable of at least a rudimentary society and civilization," said the press release.

"This is the first time proof of such sophisticated development among the creatures has been found. We intend to do a long-term study of the city and its inhabitants and we expect such research will reveal a number of important facts about Bigfoots and will help us understand primitive man."

The climbers described the creatures as being from six to seven feet tall and covered with smelly thick mats of long, stringy, brown hair.

The beasts seemed peaceful and completely nonviolent. There were no signs of weapons for hunting or war, the release said.●

☐ *If one of these reports deserves a 9, it appears they all should share the wealth.*

BIGFOOT TO THE RESCUE
***Weekly World News*, Nov., 1985**

Gravedigger Efrain Arachi was only moments away from being eaten alive by a savage flock of giant condors. But he was saved by another awesome creature of the wild — a mountain Bigfoot!

Bellowing his rage with the fury of a rogue elephant, the hairy Goliath shielded the terrified gravedigger with his massive body and killed the crazed vultures with crushing blows from his bare fists.

A news dispatch filed in La Paz, Bolivia, reported that Arachi was digging a grave below the snow line of Illimani, one of the highest peaks of the Bolivian Andes Mountains, when he was attacked by more than a dozen of the enormous vultures.

Carcasses found at the grave site revealed the average size of the birds to be about 6 feet from tip of beak to tip of tail with wingspans measuring between 13 and 16 feet.

Equally amazing, the loose dirt Arachi had excavated from the grave bore the clear impressions of immense footprints made by a creature who must have stood at least 10 feet tall and weighed close to 1,000 pounds.

The La Paz news story carried this firsthand account of Arachi's encounter with death and his rescue by a creature that he described as "half man, half animal."

"I had finished digging the grave and I was moving the coffin onto the lowering ropes when something blocked out the sunlight," the 49-year-old Aymara Indian said. "I had heard nothing, but when I looked up I saw a great condor coming at me with its talons reaching out to claw my face.

"I flung my arms up over my eyes, but I was knocked to the ground.

"At once, other devil birds swooped out of the sky to attack me.

"I looked around for some place to hide, but there was none ... except the coffin. I crawled inside and flung myself down on the corpse.

"But the coffin was made of woven twigs and I knew the condors could easily rip it to pieces. In seconds, the beasts were tearing the twigs away with their beaks and claws.

"Then I heard a thundering roar of rage that shook the ground like an earthquake.

"Then I saw the hairy beastman charge into the clearing with his arms flailing the air. The condors flew at him in a furious attack.

"But he had the strength of a hundred men and he easily beat them off.

"The fight went on like that for only a few minutes before the remaining condors flew off. As I lay in the coffin, I looked up and saw the creature staring down at me. I was certain it was now my turn to be torn limb from limb.

"But it had not come to harm me, it had come to save my life. It made a grunt, then just walked away."●

☐ *Both UFOs and Bigfoot do their share in being a friend to man. I'll give the birds an 8.*

The preceding article reminds me of an experience of a friend of mine. Jack Pickering went on a hunting trip down in the West Virginia hills. His family owned some unused property which was quite isolated. A long lane led back to an old cabin. When he was walking down this lane he heard a slight noise. Glancing up, he saw a large blue-black bird diving straight for his head. Its wingspread covered the entire width of the road. He knew it intended to attack him — there was no time to lose. He dove between its feet and lay flat on the ground. The bird had lost its chance; there was time to seek shelter.

Jack thought it looked more like a condor than anything else but didn't know what it was. While he was there he saw a round UFO that flew low over the treetops. It reminded me of John Keel's Mothman story.

My friend is no longer with us; but he told his cousin what had happened and warned him not to hunt there. He never had the nerve to tell others such a weird and frightening tale.

BIGFOOT SAVED ME FROM BEING BURIED ALIVE
***Sun*, August 16, 1988**
by Robert Webb

Slowly sinking into what he thought would be a ghastly death, a hunter was quickly rescued by the hunted when a giant ape-man yanked him from the deep mass of mud sucking him in.

Roger Bodersal had been stalking the hairy Bigfoot creature four days and nights till be finally spotted the beast running through the swamp.

"I thought at last my journey had come to an end, but soon it was my life that was ending," remembers Roger, a 53-year-old Canadian who suddenly found himself hopelessly caught in wet quicksand.

Roger, a Bigfoot researcher, had traveled from his home in Vancouver, B.C. to the jungle forests of Venezuela to search for a legendary Bigfoot-like creature reportedly terrorizing the Indian villages.

Known as the Kanaima, the creature haunts the remote area near the Brazilian border on the Coroni river.

Roger followed the tracks of the creature through forests and swampland before finally spotting a 7-foot-tall ape-like monster about 50 yards in front of him.

The creatures have been known to chase humans when they're in groups, the expert notes, but this one fled. Roger ran after it until his legs got caught in the mud.

"At first I thought I'd pull myself out and give up my search, but in a matter of seconds I was plunging into the mud," he recalls. "When it got up to my chest, horror swept over me. I knew I was going to die.

"The quicksand was up to my chin when suddenly I felt two strong hands on my head pulling me up.

"It really hurt, but the thing yanked me out completely. As I lay dazed on the dry ground, I looked up to see the hairy creature a few feet away.

"It stared at me with yellow eyes, then ran off." Roger says he no longer intends to look for the Kanaima. "These creatures only want to be left alone, and yet this one saved my life, a man who was hunting him down," he adds. ●

☐ *Robert, if you made that up — congratulations! It's easy to see why people who have been befriended by Bigfoot are reluctant to do anything which might harm them. Another 9 please.*

BIGFOOT LIVES IN CHINA
Weekly World News, **October 4, 1988**
by Dick Donovan

A team of 100 top Chinese scientists say they've found a half-human, half-ape creature known in America as Bigfoot.

News reports in Shanghai's respected *Wen Hui Bao* newspaper said the team's research proved that hair samples found in the forests of Hubei province could only have come from the shadowy beast the Chinese call Wildman.

Peasants who have seen him speak of a lumbering brute standing at least seven feet tall, with long, dangling arms and a massive, powerful-looking body covered in a matted, shaggy blanket of reddish hair.

Despite numerous sightings dating back 3,000 years — sightings that include not only the wildman of China and America's Bigfoot, but the Yeti of the Himalayas and the Sasquatch of Canada as well — no one has ever before come up with proof that such creatures actually exist.

Then in June, a research team composed of 100 of China's top scientists scoured the mountain forests of central Hubei province in a massive effort to solve the mystery.

When they returned to Shanghai, they brought with them hair samples unlike any they had seen before.

These samples underwent weeks of chemical analyses and atomic testing at Huadong University and at the Shanghai branch of the Chinese Academy of Science. The tests were supervised by the head of the China Wildman Research Center, Professor Liu Minzhuang, whose documentation of China's Bigfoot sightings is extensive.

Then the team finally released the results of those tests — and stunned the scientific world.

"The distribution of trace elements in the Wildman hairs is different from that of modern man, black bear, orangutans and other animals," the newspaper report said.

"This objectively proves the existence of the Wildman (who is) a rare and advanced primate similar to man."

The report explained that the tests showed the levels of calcium, iron and copper to be higher in the creature's hair samples than they are in the hair of nine other mammals, including man.

"The evidence is in and it is irrefutable. Wildman, Bigfoot or Yeti... whatever you prefer to call it...is a creature that roams the Earth today," declared anthropologist Chen Sun Chang, a member of the research team since 1984.

"It's only a matter of time now before an expedition goes back to the Hubei forests to bring back a living specimen.

"But proving that the creature really does live must go down as the greatest discovery in the history of Man."●

☐ *Another 9, but so help me when they get him under lock and key, he gets a 10!*

CLAIMS TO HAVE SEEN BIGFOOT SKIING
Sun, **May 16, 1989**
by David Durend

Awesome sightings of a mighty Bigfoot skiing down the slopes and even escaping a search party with the skill of an Olympic champion are convincing experts the legendary creature is far more intelligent — and athletic — than they ever imagined!

Dozens of eyewitness accounts of the hulking, hairy giant on skis have brought researchers from around the world to the slopes of the Canadian Rockies in northern British Columbia.

"Although witnesses are terrified when they see this eight-foot creature whiz by them, it appears he's only out for enjoyment," says Bigfoot investigator Warren Brunar.

"He doesn't bother anybody. He just slides down the hill with poles and skis he apparently made himself!

"People say be looks too large for the skis, even clumsy at first. But he manages to weave around the trail and lean from side to side like a real pro."

Lone skier David Durend was taking a break on the slopes of a resort northwest of Prince George when he caught the most shocking sight of his life.

"I saw this huge, hairy object coming toward me," he remembers. "At first, I thought it was some guy clowning around on his way to a ski party.

"But when he got right on top of me, I realized I was looking at a real-live Bigfoot! He was the biggest creature I'd ever seen, covered with hair from head to toe.

"He was using large branches for poles and had two big pieces of wood for skis. He was moving along with the strength of 10 men. I sure wish I could ski like him."

Just as Bigfoot disappeared around a bend, several excited skiers followed behind, giving chase.

"I went after them and found them minutes later, exhausted," David recalls. "They'd been chasing Bigfoot for some time before I saw him.

"They were hoping to capture him, but they said he was just too fast."

Another witness, teenage skier Cathy Marneau, claims she was getting up after falling when she saw the gargantuan creature coming at her at full speed.

"I crouched down and he just leaped over me, then sped down the hill," she says, adding: "I think there'll be a lot more sightings of Bigfoot now that he's skiing, because he enjoys it and knows nobody can catch him."●

☐ *Dozens of accounts have brought researchers to the Canadian Rockies in northern British Columbia in hopes of seeing him — he sounds real to me — another 9.*

BIGFOOT RESCUES BOY FROM ALLIGATOR'S MOUTH

***Sun,* June 6, 1989**

Lost in the Florida swamps, a child was facing a hideous death in the jaws of a monster alligator when he was rescued — by a giant Bigfoot creature!

The entire mind-boggling incident was witnessed by 10-year-old Kevin Hoagland's parents, who watched helplessly in horror and amazement.

"Don't tell me that Bigfoot doesn't exist," declares Kevin's grateful mom Marcia, 36. "He saved my baby's life."

The Hoaglands had been camping deep inside the Florida Everglades when Kevin wandered out of the campground and into the 'gator-infested swampland.

"We panicked when we couldn't find him," says dad Norman. "We quickly set out to look for him ourselves."

Out in the swamp, the frenzied parents shouted for their lost child and scoured through the marsh for any sign of his disappearance.

Then came the boy's cry from the distance. Racing over, they saw a scene out of a parent's worst nightmare.

Kevin had fallen into part of a lake disguised by reeds. As he splashed and struggled to free himself from the thick vegetation, a dark shadow glided towards him through the murky water.

"I could see it was a giant alligator," recalls Norman. "But I was so paralyzed with fear I couldn't move."

"At that moment there was a tremendous sound of crashing reeds and a flash of black burst from the forest."

"It was an animal covered in shaggy fur, about eight feet tall. I thought it was a bear at first, but it walked upright and had a face like a chimpanzee."

The swamp creature splashed past the screaming child and confronted the 12-foot 'gator, which reared out of the water and opened wide its gaping jaws.

Water flew everywhere as monster battled monster. In a matter of seconds, the reptile was beating a hasty retreat.

"The Bigfoot picked up Kevin, who was in a state of near-shock, and slogged out of the water. He put Kevin down softly at our feet," says Marcia, who was both terrified and relieved when she arrived on the scene. "His eyes met mine and they seemed sad, and almost human."

His mission accomplished, the monster hero trod off into the swamp, leaving his powerful musky scent hanging heavy in the air.

Investigators say the amazing rescue gives them new clues in the search for the Everglades Bigfoot.●

☐ *A Bigfoot who can rescue a kid out of an alligator's mouth gets a 10 all day.*

BIGFOOT CURED MY ARTHRITIS

***Sun,* July 19, 1988**

by Stanley Donaldson

A British tourist says a friendly Bigfoot cured her arthritis when she became lost in the wilds of Oregon.

Amanda Fielding, 66, was visiting the U.S. on a backpacking tour of our national forests when she decided to leave her tour group for a few minutes and do a little hiking on her own.

However, she quickly became lost and wandered around for nearly two hours, unable to find her way back.

"I was horrified," recalls Amanda. "I had enough food for only a day or two, and the sunlight was starting to fade.

"I yelled and yelled, but I guess no one heard."

Amanda's bad dream turned into a nightmare when the rheumatoid arthritis in her right leg suddenly flared up in the dampness, making it impossible for her to walk.

"The pain was incredible," Amanda says. "I couldn't put any pressure on it at all. It felt like someone was stabbing me in the leg with a red-hot poker."

Amanda huddled between two big logs as the chilly night approached, unable to move or even build herself a decent shelter.

Then she saw what at first she thought was a man emerge from the dense underbrush.

"I was about to call out to him when I saw that it wasn't a man at all, but a Bigfoot," Amanda states. "He was about 8 feet tall, covered with really dirty, matted hair, and he smelled terrible.

"I just sat there, scared to death. I couldn't run or even move because my leg hurt so badly."

After several minutes of silent scrutiny, Amanda's unexpected guest ambled over and gently prodded her with one big finger.

"I winced when he touched my knee, and it was as if he somehow knew what was wrong," says the matronly vacationer with a smile.

"He disappeared into the forest for several minutes, then came back with a fistful of different kinds of plants all mashed together.

"I knew then he wasn't going to hurt me, so I pulled up my pant leg and he applied the poultice with the gentleness of a country doctor."

Amanda says the strange herbal concoction began to work almost immediately.

"I could feel the pain literally draining from my arthritic knee," she states.

"It was absolutely incredible. I've suffered from rheumatoid arthritis on and off for nearly 20 years and no painkiller has ever worked as well."

Amazingly, Amanda's hairy friend stayed with her until morning, protecting her from the varied wild animals that patrol the forest at night.

"I felt completely safe in his presence," Amanda notes.

"I tried to talk to him, but he just sat there, staring and listening. He was the most gentle creature."

Amanda's guardian disappeared into the woods as the first rays of daylight filtered through the forest canopy.

Her leg much improved, Amanda slowly hiked through the underbrush until she found a trail, then followed it to a forest ranger's camp and safety.

"No one believes me," says the grateful granny, "but I know what happened. That gentle giant cured my arthritis.

"I haven't had a flare-up since, and I go hiking nearly every weekend.

"It's a miracle even my doctor can't explain."●

☐ *Boy oh boy, do I wish a gentle giant would come along and put some crushed leaves on both of my knees! Amanda's Bigfoot gets a 10.*

UFOs KILLED ALL THE DINOSAURS
National Examiner, **August 1, 1989**
by Christopher Luke

The mighty dinosaurs were wiped off the face of the Earth by an invasion of UFOS, according to startling new scientific evidence.

For decades, debate has raged about what caused the dinosaurs to suddenly disappear an estimated 66 million years ago.

Some scientists believe a rash of volcanic eruptions was responsible for the incredibly rapid extinction of the once-great species of gigantic creatures.

Other researchers argued that an enormous object from outer space — possibly a huge comet or asteroid — slammed into the Earth, killing the entire population of dinosaurs and at least two-thirds of other existing species.

Now, an amazing new discovery has convinced many scholars that UFO aliens invaded our planet during that prehistoric era, snuffing out virtually every life form in existence, including the dinosaurs.

"Evidence has been uncovered indicating Earth was attacked by extraterrestrial forces during the end of the Cretaceous period," declared Mexican archaeologist Felipe Montez recently at a scientific conference in Lima, Peru.

"It is my opinion that this invasion was responsible for the previously unexplained overnight extinction of the dinosaur species."

Montez said he bases his astounding conclusion on artifacts that were discovered at a dig in the central Mexican desert.

The artifacts, which Montez said are of extraterrestrial origin, were found through the process of carbon dating to be some 66 million years old.

"I will have more to say on this exciting subject after the completion of more tests," Montez promised.

"But all preliminary indications point to the very real possibility that space aliens brought about the abrupt end of the dinosaur era with a violent attack upon Earth."●

☐ *It's a little hard for me to go along with this one. I lean towards the theory that our earth got out of balance by an over accumulation of ice or something. It seems to me a good hard flip would be enough to spread dinosaur bones from here to South America or wherever. How can you tell an alien artifact anyway? Just because its carbon dating is 66 million years old doesn't prove where it came from — or does it? I believe I'd rather cope with a space alien than a polar flip — what about you?*

I suppose I'd better give it a 5.

RANCHERS KILL MONSTER FROM PREHISTORIC PAST
National Examiner, **August 1, 1989**
by Christopher Luke

A pair of shocked ranchers killed a colossal winged monster believed to be a gigantic survivor of the prehistoric past.

The ranchers described the amazing creature as resembling a huge alligator with a long tail and immense wings.

They encountered the exhausted beast in the desert near Tombstone, Arizona, and killed it with gunfire, although it supposedly attacked the men with its huge, razor-sharp teeth before it died.

A local newspaper said the monster measured an astounding 92 feet long, with a wingspan of some 160 feet.

Although this astonishing encounter allegedly took place nearly 100 years ago, reports of other prehistoric creatures have continued to the present day.

In the early 1960s, a couple driving at night through Trinity Forest in California saw what they thought at first was a plane in trouble, but then decided was a bird.

They said the soaring monster looked like a pterodactyl — the giant flying reptile that lived during the dinosaur era.

Pterodactyls appeared about 150 million years ago. They lived in flocks in coastal areas, and their jaws were equipped with sharp, powerful teeth.

They flourished for 85 million years and then supposedly died out. Or did they?

In 1976, dozens of sane and sober witnesses reported seeing prehistoric flying reptiles in Texas.

At least five people identified what they saw as pteranodons, a type of pterodactyl that were the largest flying creatures known to science.

Fossils of these prehistoric monsters have been found in Texas, but they're supposed to have been extinct for 65 million years.

Is it possible some of them could have somehow survived to terrorize modern man?●

☐ *Or could these animals have been caught in a "time warp" suddenly to materialize before stunned witnesses?*

Remember that big bird my friend Jack was attacked by down in West Virginia? He didn't know what it was. If you can have "Nessie" somewhere over in a lake in Scotland — we ought to be able to have our own "time warp" and have an occasional by-gone critter show up long enough to cause a stir. Besides, that's nothing compared to a whole western town getting photographed on Venus! A few prehistoric monsters and aliens aren't going to cause me to lose much sleep. How about another 5?

THOSE CARVED FACES

If you want to know about "The Face on Mars,"
Please read the following pages.
If this isn't enough, watch what NASA will do,
To let you know that they know too —

In a couple of years NASA's going back,
To photograph what they already know —
They can't tell you they've had this stuff
Hidden in files, fifteen years or so!

Next time when we fly past Mars,
You'll be told lots of things.
It's been decided — you should know —
That others reached Mars, long ago!

And if you live through that surprise,
Perhaps then, you should know —
That Venus, too, has had that face —
Brought there by another race!

After that, if you can take some more,
Perhaps you'd like to know,
That Neptune, too, has had her share,
That same carved face — has been left there.

Gossip has it that on our moon,
Someone has found a smaller face.
It has been carved with identical lines —
Were all these made by an Alien race?

Do you think those early settlers
Forgot that we were here?
Down under the ice at the South Pole,
There's another face awaits its role!

CHAPTER NINE

Healings and Rescues — The Devil's Triangle
Time Travel — Atlantis

Seeing Through Metal Etc. — *Public Opinion* 212
UFO Ship Saves Climbers — *Sun* 213
Leading Scientists Raised 25 People From the Dead — *Weekly World* 213
UFO Beams Corpse into Sky — *Weekly World* 214
Beam From UFO Revives Dead Man — *National Examiner* 214
Space Aliens Cure Teen's Muscular Dystrophy — *Weekly World* 215
Aliens Cured AIDS Case — *Weekly World* 215
UFO Rescues Girl — *National Examiner* 216
Rescued by Supermen — *Weekly World* 216
UFOs Helped Rescue 3 Trapped Whales — *Sun* 217
Schoolboy Claims UFO Aliens Cured Acne — *National Examiner* 217
Space Alien Cures Dying Child — *Weekly World* 218
Devil's Triangle Shocker — *Weekly World* 218
Dead Passengers and Crew Land in Brazil — *Weekly World* 219
Buried at Sea in 1926 — *Weekly World* 219
Phantom Squadron Prowls Sky Over Devil's Triangle — *Weekly World* 220
Space Alien Docs Healed My Cancer — *Weekly World* 220
Shipwrecked Fisherman Gets Younger Since Rescue in Devil's Triangle — *Weekly World* . . 220
Russian Cosmonauts Return to Earth Years Younger — *Weekly World* 221
Atlantis Found 80 Miles From U.S. — *Sun* 221
The Devil's Triangle — *Weekly World* 222
Atlantis Found — *Weekly World* 222
Ray from UFO Cures 22 — *Weekly World* 223
Examiner World Exclusive — *National Examiner* 223
The Custodian at Tokyo Computek — *Poem* 225

HEALINGS AND RESCUES BY ALIENS AND BIGFOOT

I've picked out a bunch of miscellaneous articles on healings and rescues. Supernatural experiences seem to abound around the Devil's Triangle and Atlantis. Whether it's a gateway to eternity seems questionable — but there's no doubt unusual experiences take place in that area. Long before some of these tabloids were born there was plenty published on these subjects. For instance, the following article is one I wrote for my column back in March 29, 1962. As you can see the event took place back in 1954.

SEEING THROUGH METAL ETC.

***Public Opinion,* March 29, 1962**

After reading Dr. Hermann Oberth's "Discussion on UFO's," in which he singles out the contact story of Carl Anderson and states that he would be willing to bet 100–1 that this man was not only normal but actually experienced "something," I felt you might be interested in a resume of the Anderson book. It is titled *Two Nights To Remember.*

On April 3, 1954, Carl Anderson, his wife Stella, his children, Betty Ann and Bobby, his brother-in-law Jim and Jim's wife Terry, another brother-in-law Harold and his wife Eleanor, all took off for a weekend camping trip near Desert Hot Springs, Calif.

Carl led the parade and was responsible for the final camping ground location. He felt he had been both guided by an inner voice as well as physical pressure on his steering wheel.

Their camp equipment was set up on what seemed to be the bottom of an ancient dry lake bed. It was about the size of a small landing field and was hemmed in on all sides by mountains.

Carl and his family set up a tent and cots but the other couples slept in their cars. Harold and Eleanor were 30 feet away while Jim and Terry were about 20 feet farther in distance.

At 3 a.m., Carl, Stella, and Betty Ann found themselves sitting straight up in their beds. As they sat wondering what had awakened them, the tent slowly began to disappear until it became absolutely invisible.

Hovering a few inches above the ground was a large shining disc. Carl estimated it to be 60 feet across and 30 feet in height. It had five windows or port holes which were visible from their location.

For 15 minutes the family found themselves completely paralyzed. Harold and Eleanor had the same experience and found that their car also became invisible. Jim and Terry were farther away and remained asleep.

Bobby Anderson did not awaken. Carl felt he could hear mumbled voices but did not see anyone. Eventually they heard a slight humming sound and the dull fluorescent light which surrounded the craft changed to an orange cast, then a bright red color.

The ship rose straight up in the air and went faster and faster, finally changing to a brilliant bluish white. The tent began to reappear and once again they were all able to move. Carl felt they had been prevented from going too near a craft which might have been dangerous.

Eighteen months later, Carl, Stella and Jim went to another desert location hoping to make contact with the ship again. Again Carl felt he was led to a camp ground. It was a small lake bed clearing, 500 yards across and surrounded by huge boulders. They had decided to keep warm in sleeping bags and soon found it necessary to crawl in.

As they watched the sky a bluish white light came streaking toward them, turning a dull green, then white, and then gave off a faint glow like a halo. It came nearer and nearer until it was about 100 feet off of the ground.

Stella became panic-stricken and ran to the car screaming, "Oh my God!" Immediately the craft shot high above them. After calming Stella, Jim lit a red flare and held it high over his head signaling the ship to come back.

Once more the ship came back when suddenly Jim threw the torch to the ground. The red hot chemicals had dripped on his thumb causing a severe burn. Jim cried, "Oh God; why did this have to happen?" The craft suddenly brightened and completely disappeared. It was time to treat the thumb. In amazement they found the burn had been completely healed. Not even rubbing it with coarse sand caused any discomfort.

Each of these people have published sworn statements to show sincerity to those who doubt.●

□ *There are many reports of healings that have been reported over the last thirty-five years. It doesn't seem reasonable that people make up such a variety of tales. This story is full of clue after clue that makes it appear to be a real experience. Seeing through metal or objects continues to be mentioned in a number of UFO contacts dating from the Fifties to the present day.*

UFO SHIP SAVES CLIMBERS

***Sun*, April 11, 1989**

by Ben Snark

Stranded on Mount Everest and battered by high-altitude winds, three frostbitten mountain climbers were facing an agonizing death when they were rescued — by an alien spacecraft!

Now safe on lower ground, the thankful mountaineers can only marvel at the astounding episode they experienced on the top of the world.

"It's beyond comprehension," declares Yoshio Nakamura, 34. "Perhaps our still being alive is the best testimony to the fact that it really happened."

The ill-fated Japanese expedition up the world's highest peak proceeded without a hitch until the three seasoned veterans left base camp for their final assault on the summit.

"In the blink of an eye, black clouds had filled the sky," explains Keno Keiji, 32. "The temperature dropped from 17 degrees to minus 31, accompanied by blinding snow and vicious gusts of wind.

"If that wasn't enough, Yoshio misjudged a step and tumbled down an embankment, breaking his leg."

Keno and fellow climber Hiro Watabe, 30, carried injured Yoshio to a flat area, where they set up their small tent. Inside they huddled together in a vain attempt to fight off the frigid temperature.

"I couldn't say how long we stayed in there," notes Hiro. "We had lost all feeling in our hands and feet and were weakened by the thin air. We knew we were doomed."

Hours later, Keno crawled out of the tent to check the weather when he was met by an extraordinary vision.

"There was a huge silver circular object several hundred feet above us," he says. "It hovered completely still, despite the powerful wind.

"Then a compartment opened in its underside and a round disk about 20 feet in diameter slowly descended to the ground next to me."

Hiro came out of the tent and watched in amazement as a metal door opened on the smaller craft to reveal six alien creatures.

"They were no more than four feet tall and covered with a metallic gray fur," Hiro recalls.

"They had large heads and prominent pointed ears, but the most striking thing about them was their giant green eyes, which pierced right through you.

"Without a thought, we went on board. Then three of them climbed out, got Yoshio and carried him in."

The door closed and the awe struck mountain climbers felt the capsule rise. Around them, thousands of lights blinked in a fascinating array of colors.

"The creatures crowded around us and stared at us, chirping in a high-pitched tone," says Hiro.

"In a short time the capsule's door opened. We were on a green field near a village in the shadow of Mount Everest.

"They let us out and then silently took off."

Native villagers soon came to the weary climbers' aid and took them to a hospital in Kathmandu, Nepal, where they are now recovering.

"The strange thing was that the villagers saw the craft descending, but weren't surprised," states Yoshio. "Evidently, these aliens are a common sight in that region."●

☐ *This is no big deal, if you really want to check it out you could — whether true or false, it's still a big story. Somebody deserves a 9. I can't tell whether it's the mountain climbers or Ben — it all sounds good to me.*

LEADING SCIENTISTS RAISED 25 PEOPLE FROM THE DEAD

***Weekly World News*, August 8, 1989**

by Karl Stack

Leading scientists have raised 25 people from the dead by exposing their bodies to radiation and powerful magnetic fields.

That's the word from the European science journal *Pathology* which flatly stated that the scientific team working anonymously in Greece has "pushed medicine to its final frontier."

"This is the greatest medical achievement of all time," said Dr. Nikos Karvela, the Greek physician who wrote the article for *Pathology.*

"The experiments prove that mankind really does have the power and know-how to raise the dead. And while these men cannot promise immortality, they have certainly shown that we have a second chance at life."

Dr. Karvela's shocking report and comments touched off a rumbling storm of controversy among the scientists around the world.

In one particularly scathing attack, French physician Andre Levell called the Greek doctor a "huckster" and the experiments a "hoax."

"I knew I would be criticized when I agreed to speak for the researchers, who are remaining anonymous to avoid the ethical constraints and reprisals they would face if they were working out in the open," said Dr. Karvela.

According to the expert, seven scientists from France, West Germany, Belgium and Japan set up a research laboratory a few blocks away from a major hospital in Athens in 1987.

By a mutual agreement with the hospital, they received the bodies of over 100 people to test their theory that the dead can be revived when exposed to short, controlled bursts of radiation and powerful magnetic fields.

Since the experts began their work, 25 people have been revived.

The patients ranged in age from 5 to 65 and were pronounced dead up to five hours before they were raised from the dead.

All but two of those patients are alive today, Dr. Karvela said.

"The success rate of 25 percent is impressive but work remains to be done," he continued.

If the success rate holds or improves, they will then go public.●

☐ *I wonder if our scientists have been reading UFO articles? What these scientists claim to be doing is just what these UFO cases claim to have done. Do you suppose they're doing the same thing? How about a 9?*

UFO BEAMS CORPSE INTO SKY
Weekly World News, **April 22, 1989**
by Henry Weber

Space aliens took dead Hector Morillo aboard a starship and brought him back to life while his family watched in disbelief!

"It's a miracle from heaven," Marta Morillo, the man's wife, told reporters in Juarez, Argentina. "Doctors said my Hector was dead and there was nothing they could do for him.

"But those space creatures have powers greater than that of any man. They gave my husband the most precious gift of all. They gave him back his life."

The drama allegedly unfolded three days after Morillo, 46, suffered a fatal heart attack, said newspapers.

Father Celiar Rodriguez was actually conducting the dead man's funeral when the silver-gray starship swooped down from the sky and sucked his wife, son and daughter aboard with a greenish white tractor beam.

"The coffin went up, too," said the priest, "and I could hardly believe my eyes.

"The family cried out for help but we were alone in the cemetery and there was nothing I could do.

"I prayed for God to protect them on their journey."

When the family vanished in the belly of the ship the UFO took off over the horizon, said the priest. He reported the incident to local authorities, who the priest said, acted like "I was a lunatic."

Their laughter stopped abruptly six days later, said newspapers, when Morillo walked back into town with his family in tow.

Curiously, their only recollection of the experience was the initial meeting with the aliens, "who were shaped like human beings and floated in air like smoke."

"When we found ourselves on the outskirts of town it was as if we had awakened from a long, dreamless sleep," said Mrs. Morillo.

"We went directly to Father Rodriguez and told him what happened but he was as confused as we were.

"He told us that some things are not for men to understand. He said the Lord works in mysterious ways."

Morillo himself pointed out that he feels better and healthier now than ever before in his life.

"I am rejuvenated," he continued. "But if you're asking me to explain what has happened, I can't. For some reason my life has been given back to me. I am so grateful to those space creatures.

"Now it is up to me to make the most of the time I have left."

Manuel Bernaus, president of the Argentine Institute for UFO Research, said the family's experience is "a compelling new chapter in the study of UFOs."

Dr. Hernando Hualde, who originally pronounced Morillo dead, refused to discuss the incident, said newspapers.●

☐ *This has happened in other places — even in the graveyard! There are many cases of rescue. If this really is true there's no number big enough for it — if not, score 8 for Henry!*

BEAM FROM UFO REVIVES DEAD MAN
National Examiner, **August 23, 1988**

Minutes after he was declared dead, an elderly man returned to life when he was sprayed by a beam from a passing UFO.

"There is no doubt in my mind that my husband was dead," said Maria da Souza, 72. "He had a heart attack and was not breathing for over 15 minutes. It's a miracle he's alive. He was given a second chance by the aliens."

According to da Souza, her husband, Delfim, 80, suffered a fatal heart attack as they were taking a Sunday stroll through a park outside of Rio de Janeiro, Brazil.

"Suddenly, Delfim grabbed his chest and was gasping, da Souza told an Italian freelance journalist.. "He collapsed on the ground and passed away."

A passing motorist stopped her car and ran to the elderly couple's aid.

"I used to be a nurse and I know what signs to look for to see if somebody is dead or alive," said Maria de Santos, 53. "This man had no pulse, no heart beat and he was turning cold."

De Santos draped Mr. da Souza's body with a blanket from her car, then drove toward the city to notify medical authorities.

"I was devastated," said da Souza. "I was kneeling next to my dead husband's body crying. That's when I heard a strange noise over my head."

Less than 100 feet above, da Souza said she saw a UFO hovering in the sky. Terrified, she still refused to run for cover.

The spacecraft hovered about 75 feet above da Souza and her husband's corpse. da Souza started screaming at the UFO to go away.

Suddenly, the bottom of the UFO opened up and a yellowish beam shot out of the hatch.

"It felt warm and it started to relax me," Mrs. da Souza recalled. "The next thing I knew, Delfim was stirring. I ripped off his blanket and his eyes opened. He was alive."

The UFO disappeared just before police arrived. ●

☐ *Sometimes I think people really don't want to know ... Score another 8, whatever.*

If you feel like laughing at the articles which follow this report from *Weekly World* — at least read them carefully.

SPACE ALIENS CURE TEEN'S MUSCULAR DYSTROPHY
***Weekly World,* August 23, 1987**
by Margret Pfander

A 16-year-old girl was taken aboard a UFO and cured of the muscular dystrophy that was killing her, say newspapers.

At least 12 people claim to have seen the gigantic orange starship spirit away wheelchair-bound Patil Deka, as she watched her younger brothers play soccer in a field near Udipi, India.

For the next eight days the young woman's family and friends grieved as if she was gone forever.

But their sorrow turned to joy when the young girl burst through the door of her mother's home in Udipi and cried: "I'm cured, Mama, I'm cured!"

Dr. Victor Bele, who diagnosed Miss Deka as having muscular dystrophy in 1982, confirmed "that something truly miraculous has happened to her."

"The disease is progressive and hers was in a very advanced stage," he continued. "The wasting away of her muscles was almost complete.

"She hadn't walked in over two years and her neck was so weak her head dropped over to her shoulders and chest. But now she's walking and talking like any other girl her age. I have no explanation for it.

"But she really is cured of this horrifying disease."

The young woman's recollection of her encounter with the aliens is remarkably clear.

"One minute I was watching my brothers play and the next minute I was in the spaceship," she said.

"I was in a round room that had a silvery ceiling and walls of bright blue light. Nobody spoke to me but I know people were there because I could see the silhouettes of bodies in front of the light.

"They were very tall and had large oval heads. The last thing I remember was one of them moving toward me with his arms raised straight up.

"Suddenly I felt very hot and then I passed out. When I woke up I was standing in front of our house."

Chitra Deka, the girl's mother and a devout Catholic, has since denied that the girl was abducted by space aliens, and insists that the UFO was a manifestation of "the Holy Virgin."●

☐ *You can't please everybody. I guess that's what I'd call score 10 for the Holy Virgin!*

ALIENS CURED AIDS CASE
***Weekly World,* May 10, 1988**
by Henry Weber

An overjoyed mother-to-be says space aliens took her aboard a spaceship — and cured her of AIDS!

"They saved my life and the life of my baby," Sylvia Manisco, 29, told reporters in Florence, Italy. "My own doctor's said we were doomed and there was nothing they could do for us.

"But those strange men knew exactly what to do. They used all sorts of strange lights and instruments to cure me of AIDS."

Dr. Eugenio Lauro, the woman's obstetrician, confirmed that she contracted AIDS from a blood transfusion but miraculously she no longer shows any sign of having the virus.

The doctor refused to discuss her alleged encounter with extraterrestrials but conceded "that something miraculous must have happened to have given her this cure."

Mrs. Manisco herself insists that she was abducted by a group of space aliens who subjected her to terrifying but painless medical procedures before releasing her. She was unharmed.

"I found out that I was pregnant and had AIDS on the same day in March," said Mrs. Manisco.

"In fact, I had just about made up my mind to take my own life when two men with long pointed noses and ears knocked at the door of my house. When I answered they looked at me with piercing black eyes and motioned for me to follow. I wanted to resist but couldn't. They seemed to have a power over me that I couldn't shake off."

According to newspaper accounts, the woman said she followed the strangers into a forest near her home and was taken aboard a saucer-shaped UFO that was "a pulsating bluish color, about the size of a school bus."

Once inside, the aliens ushered her into a dark circular room, where she was placed on a padded table and strapped down.

"For the first time I was afraid and started to scream," said Mrs. Manisco.

"When I did, two other men came into the room and pointed a strange looking flashlight at me.

"One of them pulled a large instrument and light down from the ceiling and pointed it in my face.

"I didn't feel any pain but the men were so frightening I must have passed out."

An astonished Mrs. Manisco woke up — sitting in her own front yard!

Three hours had passed. And the only evidence that anything had happened to her was a single needle mark in her right temple, newspapers reported.

"Whoever or whatever those men were, I want to thank them from the bottom of my heart," said Mrs. Manisco.

"I remember them in my prayers every night. I owe them everything."

Eugene Kahler, the noted French UFO researcher, called the woman's story "remarkable, especially in light of similar incidents that have been reported world wide over the past five months.

"At least 18 people say extraterrestrials have cured them of deadly afflictions since Christmas," he told reporters.

"It's a bit premature to declare this a trend. But we're going to have to take a closer look at these amazing occurrences."●

☐ *How do you expect the government to tell you a case of AIDS is curable? The riverbanks would be lined for miles with willing customers.*
This is either a 10 for Sylvia or another 10 for Henry.

UFO RESCUES GIRL

National Examiner, March 12, 1985

by Gus Vandermeer

Kindhearted aliens swooped down and rescued a young girl from being buried alive just as her coffin was being lowered into the ground.

As the priest gave the final blessing over the body of Teresa Saravia, 17, an enormous UFO appeared over the gravesite in a cemetery near Barboza in the Philippines, scattering the terrified funeral procession.

Eyewitnesses say the craft hovered over the coffin, which was suspended in mid-air, and lowered a gangplank to the ground.

Eusebio Malanipa, Teresa's uncle and one of the pallbearers, says three aliens descended and examined the casket. One of the three four-foot-tall extraterrestrials then guided the coffin from the grave with a device that "looked like a remote control panel for a television.

"I was so frightened I couldn't move," he says. "I thought they were on some kind of gruesome kidnap mission and that we were next.

"The alien being then held the gadget over the casket and the lid came up. I couldn't bear the thought of them disturbing the remains of my poor little niece.

"The alien waved that little gizmo again and suddenly my niece sat up. I thought I was going to have a heart attack.

"She was as alive as you or me.

"Poor Teresa was bewildered. Here she was, sitting in a coffin over her grave with three strange looking creatures smiling at her like she was some prize catch.

"When she realized that she was neither dead or sleeping, she let out a wail that made those little extraterrestrials nearly jump out of their skins.

"They didn't know what to make of it. Here they had saved her from certain death and she was crying like she had lost her mother.

"Mama, mama," she sobbed.

"Her mother heard the cries even though she had run away.

"She rushed back to the grave and lifted her daughter out of the coffin without so much as a glance at the aliens.

"Then suddenly she realized that these funny little men had saved her child and proceeded to hug them.

"This was too much for the extraterrestrials.

"They beat a hasty retreat to their ladder, quickly scurried up the gangplank and disappeared into their UFO.

"The craft was gone in seconds and everyone who had run away came back to help celebrate Teresa's return from the dead."

Government officials are investigating the astonishing mission of mercy, but there is no need for any inquiry as far as Mrs. Saravia and Teresa are concerned.

"Those little men are perfect angels," says Mrs. Saravia. "We would have buried my little Teresa alive if it had not been for them. I think they should investigate the boneheaded doctors who said my lovely daughter was dead.

"I think they are the ones who should be buried alive.

"Just let them see how it feels."

Plucky Teresa — a real-life sleeping beauty — has been quick to shake off the terrifying experience.

"I was scared when I woke up in that box," she says.

"But I know my mama will never let that happen again.

"I wish those strange men would come back so I could thank them. I was afraid of them at first, but I'm not anymore."•

☐ *You all can't live with this one — pretend you didn't read it. As you see there are numerous cases of this kind. Who knows — maybe it really is a 10??*

RESCUED BY SUPERMEN

Weekly World, October 13, 1987

A German U-boat commander in World War II kept a diary that tells how he and two other men were rescued and taken to the lost city of Atlantis after their vessel sank in the North Atlantic in 1944, say newspapers.

Armin Schmitt, 73, died of a heart attack in Magdeburg, East Germany, on September 6 and under the terms of his will the secret journal was opened at that time.

The amazing journal reportedly details what Schmitt claimed was a three-day stay in the undersea city. It further says that Atlantis is inhabited by superbeings who live under domes and possess a technology that is far superior to that of men.

"The diary is a mind-boggling document, one that could unlock the mysteries of Atlantis once and for all," said historian Otto Hopf of Oberhausen, West Germany.

"If this information is accurate, there is every reason to suspect that Atlantis not only exists but is still thriving on the ocean floor."

Hopf is one of four historians who was chosen to study the diary by Schmitt's relatives, who live in West Germany and have requested anonymity.

He confirmed that it was probably written on or around the dates mentioned in it. But he says it will take "a concerted international effort to determine if it is a true report or fabrication."

The diary, in part, goes like this:

December 24, 1944. Christmas Eve. Somewhere in the North Atlantic. Forced to abandon ship after bombing run by American plane.

Found myself in sea with crewmen Bernard Mayer and Willie Boll.

Other crewmen presumed lost. Our life jackets saved us until rescue ship rose from sea like a giant ray.

Taken aboard by strange men with sickly white skin, large hairless heads and deep blue eyes. They wore tight flesh-colored suits and spoke in English, French and Greek before trying German.

We were relieved and terrified. Boll passed out.

December 25, 1944. Awoke in brightly lit circular room surrounded by strange men like the ones who rescued us. Ate tasteless greens and drank water from ceramic glass. Toured city with guide. Like ancient Greece come to life.

Columns, broad avenues, no cars, no Christmas.

December 26, 1944. Hosts very kind and exhibit strange psychic powers. Our answers to questions are known to them even before we speak. Guide opens doors by looking at them.

They are afraid to let us stay longer.

According to Hopf, the diary goes on to say that the German crew was taken to the ocean surface and set adrift in an unmarked raft.

They were captured by an American ship and later were released at war's end.

"The diary states that the three men swore themselves to secrecy. But why they did that isn't clear," said Hopf. "We have found that Boll died in a car wreck in Starnberg (West Germany) in 1958.

"All we know about Mayer is that he is somewhere in Poland. We are trying to find him now, of course, but the real quest is to relocate Atlantis.

"I have called on my colleagues around the world to pressure their governments to help.

"I hope they respond."•

☐ *A number of UFO books describe beings taken under water to places which are inhabited. No one knows if these are 'pipe dreams'. There are plenty of them. As a book it's worth a 10 — as a report, it better go down to a 7.5. Someone knew all the right answers when writing this article.*

UFOs HELPED RESCUE THREE TRAPPED WHALES

***Sun,* December 20, 1988**

The sensational rescue of three California gray whales was performed with some unexpected and mysterious assistance — from UFO aliens!

Long-range observation and eyewitness accounts back up reports of alien involvement with the rescue of the whales that were trapped by ice near Point Barrow, Alaska, notes astronomer and UFO expert Keiji Nakamura.

"Normally, aliens take a strictly hands-off approach to a situation where their presence might be discovered," says Dr. Nakamura.

"Perhaps they were touched by the plight of the whales and impressed by the cooperation between American and Soviet authorities."

The three whales were discovered trapped in a steadily shrinking circle of open water and locked in the freezing Beaufort Sea.

Local Eskimos worked with state and federal authorities to try to free them, but hopes dwindled as one attempt after another failed.

"When it became clear that one of the whales, nicknamed 'Bone' by the Eskimos, was not going to make it, the aliens must have decided to act," Nakamura points out.

Bone disappeared one night and was presumed drowned.

But that was the same night that local inhabitants reported strange lights both in the sky and under the ice.

"The aliens went in there and hauled Bone out to open water and safety," Nakamura explains.

"Their spacecraft work very well underwater.

"They could've saved all three, but they didn't want to raise suspicions of their presence and they saw an opportunity to foster cooperation between the U.S. and the Soviets in saving the other whales."

The visitors further helped by creating an unseasonably warm shift in the weather, which helped the Eskimos keep open the ice-holes that the whales were using to breathe.

"The power of their UFO engines is vast," says Nakamura.

"They could have melted the ice if they wanted to, but once again, they hate to arouse suspicion.

"However, water radiation levels were up slightly, and that tipped us off that submersible UFOs were lurking beneath the surface."

The extraterrestrials were able to keep the whales alive until Soviet icebreakers were able to arrive and free them.•

☐ *Well maybe — it does seem as if the aliens ought to have done their share in that rescue ... An 8 for cooperation.*

SCHOOLBOY CLAIMS UFO ALIENS CURED HIS ACNE

***National Examiner,* April 4, 1989**

UFO aliens cured his acne, claims a 15-year-old schoolboy.

And Martin Kelswasky said his face is free from spots and the dreaded aftermath — deep scarring.

Kelswasky said that while walking through some woods near his New Zealand home, a creature from outer space zapped his face.

Said the teen: "A furry alien that looked like Bigfoot shined a flashlight on me. My pimples vanished instantly. So did the space critter. Before I could thank him, he was gone, poof!"

Kelswasky's parents are less sure about the space alien encounter, but they're mighty happy their son's acne is gone.

"He was always being teased at school," said his mom. "I suppose now they'll laugh at his UFO story. I'm just glad he's happy. That's all that matters.•

☐ *If Martin's pimples are gone he won't care whether this is a 5 or 8.*

SPACE ALIEN CURES DYING CHILD

***Weekly World,* May 13, 1986**

A Mexican couple claim they were visited by a space alien who miraculously cured the cancer that was eating their 6-year-old daughter alive.

Accounts of the sensational incident that appeared in Mexican newspapers were careful to point out that the couple's claims were undocumented.

But a mountain of circumstantial evidence — including a doctor's assurances that the child no longer has a trace of the deadly cancer that was killing her — seem to support the incredible story, the newspapers said.

Yolanda and Edgardo Castaneda told reporters that the extraterrestrial appeared on their doorstep on March 22, two weeks after cancer-specialist Escar Perdomo told them little Gloria Castaneda's cancer was inoperable.

"It is a miracle from God and the heavens," Mrs. Castaneda was quoted as saying. "He saved our daughter's life and made her well forever."

The Castanedas said the alien — who was humanlike, stood about 7 feet tall and wore a glistening black suit — walked into their tiny house near Teocaltiche shortly after dusk.

They said he hesitated momentarily, then hit them with a paralyzing beam of greenish-blue light that shot from the palm of his hand.

The couple said they could not move but were fully conscious as the alien left the room and returned with their daughter.

"He moved like a figure in a dream," said Mrs. Castaneda. "He carried Gloria in his arms and placed her on the kitchen table."

For two hours the creature spoke gently to the girl in a strange language, said the couple. Then he placed two glowing metal tubes next to her temples.

Five minutes later he removed them, they said, "and Gloria jumped up and hugged him."

"He looked at us and blinked his eyes, and when he did, we could move again," said Mrs. Castaneda. "He told me in our language: 'She is well.' "

The couple said the creature departed in a black bullet-shaped craft about the size of a school bus.

Dr. Perdomo confirmed that Gloria shows no sign of ever having had the cancer that "was so bad she would have died within weeks. I have no explanation for her cure and I'm not going to speculate," he said. "Stranger things have happened."●

☐ *If you think these papers printed all these articles to fool you and to sell their papers — you'd better think again. What is being printed ties in with documentaries which are being presented on this subject. They wouldn't be shown if your government didn't hope and pray you'd be watching. An 8 for the tall alien.*

DEVIL'S TRIANGLE SHOCKER

***Weekly World,* September 29, 1987**

by Stuart Kern

Three fishermen who vanished in the Devil's Triangle reappeared a year later — one of them miraculously cured of the hideous physical deformities that plagued him since he was a child!

Even more incredible, the men insisted that the date was December 6, 1986, when they turned up in the Bahamas on August 27. Two actually had to be treated for shock when they learned that, in fact, the year was 1987.

"This is one of the most intriguing cases ever to come out of the Devil's Triangle," a top French psychologist told reporters in the Bahamas.

"In my opinion these three men spent the past 11 months in limbo.

"Time had no meaning as we know it. And they brought back verifiable proof of the experience.

"In addition to the antiques they claim to have gotten off a phantom ship that saved them from drowning when their own boat sank, there is evidence that one of them was the beneficiary of a remarkable operation to rebuild his face and chest, which were severely burned when he was a child."

He identified the fishermen as Panamanians Carlos Giraldo, 27, Jose Torres, 42, and Ciceron Moya, 46 — all of whom are now being questioned by experts sent by the U.S. government.

The psychologist said: "The men told me their ordeal began when their boat started taking on water during a storm on Sept. 26, 1986. They were only 65 miles north of the Bahamas.

"Their radio wasn't working and they fired flares to attract help. What happened next sounds incredible — but they say an 1850s clipper ship appeared from a mist and took them aboard.

"At first they thought the ship was a replica of one the Americans sailed over a century ago. But the crew wore the authentic, old-fashioned uniforms of American sailors.

"And they used archaic words that the Panamanians, who know modern English, could barely understand."

Eerily, only one member of the ghost ship's crew dealt directly with the fishermen. Without a word he led them to cabins, past crew members who seemed to stare right through them.

Then he took the deformed sailor to a doctor, who knocked him out with a strange orange liquid — and somehow made him whole again.

"What happened next isn't clear," said the psychologist. "The fishermen said they spent what they thought were the next 10 days in a dream.

"Actually, 11 months passed before they found themselves on a dock in the Bahamas. They had no idea how they got there, no idea where they had been.

"All they had to show for their time aboard the clipper were two brass buttons from a uniform, an old metal fork and a pewter mug. A historian examined them and says they are quite authentic, the kind American sailors would have used around 1850."●

☐ *When you hear someone say, "I know something is happening, but there's a good reason for it and it can be explained," put that person right to work and let him find out the reason. Give him a job running down some of these cases. The article is worth a 9.*

DEAD PASSENGERS AND CREW LAND IN BRAZIL

***Weekly World News,* Nov. 14, 1989**
by Irwin Fisher

Aviation authorities say a commercial airliner that flew out of Germany in 1954 has landed in Brazil with 92 skeletons aboard!

And while officials refuse to speculate on the where-abouts of the plane for the past 35 years, several respected scientists, including paranormal researcher Dr. Celso Atello, say Santiago Airlines Flight 513 almost certainly entered a time warp and just flew out.

"There is no other explanation," Dr. Atello told newsmen in Brazil.

"Flight records show that the aircraft left Aachen, West Germany, on the morning of Sept. 4, 1954, and then vanished over the Atlantic on its way to Porto Alegre later that day.

"At the time aviation authorities assumed that it had crashed. But the plane landed in Porto Alegre a few weeks ago on October 12.

"It was piloted by the skeleton of its captain and all the crew and passengers were dead. Officials don't want to discuss explanations. But they cannot deny that this airplane had defied the laws of space and time. And God only knows how a skeleton managed to land it."

Santiago Airlines went out of business in 1956 and executives who are still alive didn't know enough about the flight to comment.

Brazilian aviation officials themselves confirmed that the vintage Lockheed Super Constellation aircraft "appeared out of nowhere" and landed at an airstrip west of Porto Alegre.

They said that its powerful turboprop engines were still idling when personnel found the skeletal remains of 88 passengers and a four-man crew, including Captain Miguel Victor Cury who was still clutching the controls.

Government agents are known to be investigating the mysterious flight. But they refuse to discuss anything about the airplane or the course their investigation is taking.

The official shroud of secrecy has outraged Dr. Atello and other experts, who are now calling on the Brazilian government to let civilians assist in the investigative effort.

Roderigo de Manha, a retired physics professor in Porto Alegre, said: "The public has a right to know everything about this plane and the government has a duty to tell them.

"If this plane did enter a time warp and there is evidence to prove it, the entire world should be told. Something like this could change the way we view our world and alter science as we know it.

"It is a crime to keep information like this secret — especially from the relatives of the people who perished on Santiago Airlines Flight 513."●

☐ *If you're going to dig into this subject you know that "Time Warps" are going to be with us for a long time. There are too many of them — do you suppose some dentist still has records of those passengers? It surely is worth more than a 9.*

BURIED AT SEA IN 1926

***Weekly World,* March 28, 1989**
by Edwin Fisher

A 54-year-old yachtsman who died and was buried at sea in 1926 was found alive and well in the Devil's Triangle last month — on February 26!

Michel-Yves Gayan was frightened and disoriented when the crew of a Panamanian fishing vessel found him bobbing in a white canvas body bag 75 miles south of Bermuda.

He knew his name and seemed to have vivid recollections of his life, which ended when he died of cancer in a Bermuda hospital 63 years ago and began all over again last month.

"There is no doubt that the man is who be says he is because we have a death certificate, complete with fingerprints, to prove it," Dr. Harold Jensen, who examined the man in a Bermuda clinic, told reporters.

"Don't ask me to explain why or how this man came back to life. I have absolutely no explanation for it. Greater minds than mine are working to solve that mystery right now."

Documents on file in Bermuda confirm that Gayan, a Frenchman, moved to the island in 1918. He developed cancer in 1923 and asked to be buried at sea when he died.

His wish was carried out on March 24, 1926. The record clearly shows that Michel-Yves Gayan was wrapped in white canvas and tossed into the sea south of Bermuda, in the Devil's Triangle, on that date.

What happened to Gayan in the years that followed has yet to be determined. Judging from pictures taken before his death, it doesn't appear he has aged. But in interviews with Dr. Jensen, the man was not always lucid and spoke in fits and starts.

He reportedly recalled a lengthy encounter with "glowing white angels." But it wasn't clear whether he was describing space aliens or people in heaven, Dr. Jensen said.

Panamanian fishing boat Capt. Gabriel Diaz added to the mystery by saying Gayan was disheveled and panicky when he was plucked from the sea.

"Gayan's first words were 'Where am I?' And he was very nervous," Capt. Diaz told reporters.

"When we asked him what he was doing in a body bag, he told us he was dead. He kept referring to the year 1926. And he told us about his life in France and Bermuda up to that date."

The fishing vessel took Gayan to Bermuda and turned him over to the authorities, who escorted him to Dr. Jensen's clinic.

He has since been jetted to the Zurich Psychiatric Institute, where Dr. Charles Greder is trying to find out what happened to Gayan after his death in 1926.

"The man has been through something that the human mind can hardly comprehend," said the expert. "He is having great difficulty coping with what happened to him and is not yet able to tell us everything he knows.

Dr. Greder says it could take months to learn all there is to know about Gayan. He expects to publish a full scientific report on the patient and incident in the Devil's Triangle by late summer or fall.●

☐ *How do you expect the government to come out and tell you this kind of stuff? It was bad enough to have Jesus calling Lazarus to come out of his tomb. Well, maybe a 4?*

PHANTOM SQUADRON PROWLS SKY OVER DEVIL'S TRIANGLE
***Weekly World*, December 15, 1987**
by Mickey McGuire

A ghost squadron of World War II Navy Avengers that vanished without a trace in the Devil's Triangle 42 years ago has been seen by crewmen aboard a South American freighter!

"The planes flew back and forth in perfect formation just a few feet above the waves, as though searching for a place to land," one deckhand said of the eerie encounter.

"I know everyone will think I'm mad, but I saw those phantom planes with my own eyes.

"Their engines didn't make a sound, but they were there, flying back and forth like in slow-motion and as silent as a whisper."

The five torpedo bombers of Flight 19 flew off into oblivion on December 5, 1945. They roared down the runway at Fort Lauderdale Naval Air Station at precisely 2:10 p.m., on a routine two-hour patrol that would take them 160 miles east, 40 miles north, then 120 miles straight back to their base.

Except for a few garbled, frantic radio calls, the squadron was not seen or heard from again — not until a few weeks ago when crewmen aboard the *Caribe Tiger* had their eerie encounter 35 miles off the South Florida coast.

"The pilots and two crewmen were clearly visible in each of the planes except one," another deckhand said. "In that plane I could only see two figures.

"They flew right over the ship, but they never looked at us."

The crewman, who had been on the bridge at the time, said when the squadron flew overhead the freighter's radio, compass and other electronic navigation equipment suddenly went haywire.

"Everything on board went wild," he said. "The compass started spinning like a top."

Ironically, in one of his last garbled messages, the squadron flight leader, alarm clearly evident in his voice, said, "We don't know which way is west. We can't be sure of any direction."

And one point that clearly identifies the five planes as those of the lost squadron is the fact that the freighter's crew could see three men in every plane ... except one.

Avengers normally carry a pilot and two crewmen. But on that fateful day that Flight 19 made its flight into the unknown, one plane lifted off with only two men aboard.

"We saw the planes for at least 15 minutes," the *Caribe Tiger* crewman said. "One minute the sky was clear from horizon to horizon. Then they were there, flying very slowly, almost drifting like a cloud.

"Then the airplanes turned and vanished from sight."

The freighter's encounter with the squadron came to light when the *Caribe Tiger* docked recently in Algiers.●

☐ *Everybody knows there aren't any such things as ghosts — or are there? Here's a 5 for the ghosts.*

SPACE ALIEN DOCS HEALED MY CANCER
Weekly World, March 28, 1984

Editors: Your story a couple of weeks ago about space aliens invading our hospitals to conduct research on humans came as no surprise to me.

You say they're doing all sorts of horrifying things to human patients, but my experience with them was just the opposite.

I went into a hospital in Chicago with stomach cancer and the doctors said there was nothing they could do to help me. I was dying.

But one night a team of alien doctors came to my room and worked on me — and two days later I was miraculously healed.

My earthly doctors couldn't believe it. But thanks to these alien invaders who were the gentlest doctors I've ever had, I've never been better. —

T.T., Springfield, Ill.●

☐ *If it works don't knock it — it sure was worth more than 8 to the patient.*

SHIPWRECKED FISHERMAN GETS YOUNGER SINCE HIS RESCUE IN DEVIL'S TRIANGLE
***Weekly World*, March 10, 1987**

The wife of a fisherman rescued from the Devil's Triangle seven months ago says that since her husband's ordeal he has undergone a startling physical change — and is growing younger by the week!

In the most bizarre phenomenon yet associated with the weird, mystery-shrouded Triangle, the unidentified Florida resident, 45, has lost his wrinkles, regained his hair and regrown teeth lost years ago. The man — now undergoing tests in a prestigious clinic — has yet to find a doctor who can explain the mysterious rejuvenation, his wife says.

"Jim has always worked outdoors as a construction engineer and the constant years in the sun aged him prematurely," the woman told medical writer Robert Penn in a recent interview. "He was 45 but looked 10 years older, though he was in excellent health, an outdoorsman and fisherman. Now he looks 30, if that. It's scary. The doctors can't figure it out, but Jim and I believe it's somehow associated with the Devil's Triangle." The woman — who agreed to tell her story on condition that neither she nor her husband be identified — said her husband was lost at sea last September after his fishing boat went down in the Devil's Triangle near Bermuda in the Atlantic Ocean.

The man was able to inflate a small raft and drifted for nearly two weeks before he was found by the boaters.

"At first he was weak and exhausted from his ordeal, so if anything he looked older," said his wife, a mother of two. "But after a week or so, he felt great. Then he began to feel a surge of energy. Before too long we could see he was looking different, too.

"All his lines and wrinkles disappeared. A small scar on his ankle he got as a child faded away and the sagging areas under his eyes and chin vanished.

"His receding hairline has grown back and his body seems to become more youthful every day. It's like something out of that movie *Cocoon* where the old folks grew younger."●

☐ *I've got a good notion to send my 80-year-old husband down to that Triangle and see what happens. If it works, I may go down myself. Sounds too good to be true — it's still worth a 7.5.*

RUSSIAN COSMONAUTS RETURN TO EARTH YEARS YOUNGER

***Weekly World News,* June 20, 1989**

by Beatrice Dexter

Soviet cosmonauts who returned to Earth last December after a year in space are physically and mentally years younger than they were on blast-off.

That's the shocking claim of Japanese biologist Akihito Ozawa, who says American astronauts in their 40s would undergo the same physical changes-returning to Earth after a few years in space with the bodies of 30-year-olds.

"Russian scientists are stunned by the results of physical tests on cosmonauts Musa Manarov and Vladimir Titov," Dr. Ozawa told the Kyoto *News Press*. "We've heard the Russians found remarkable changes in the men's conditions after they had spent 366 days in the Soviet space station.

"At present no one has a clue as to what causes the men to actually undergo a reverse in normal aging patterns.

"Whatever it is, it is clearly associated with space travel and may offer valuable information to help us prevent old age here on Earth."

Soviet scientists made a routine announcement in January indicating that the cosmonauts were in excellent health, but behind the scenes their findings were anything but routine, Dr. Ozawa said.

"Titov and Manarov showed evidence of stronger heart muscle action, better eyesight, a more vigorous metabolic rate and overall improved cardiovascular function," the scientist said.

"Manarov had developed thicker hair growth on his scalp and Titov — who was missing a molar — found that the tooth regrew.

"Their mental reflexes are quicker. Far from the decline the scientists expected, the cosmonauts had undergone an improvement in their conditions. They were younger in every way than they were when they blasted off a year ago."

Dr. Ozawa believes the cosmonauts' miracle rejuvenation was the subject of a hush-hush conference held recently in Moscow, and he expects the Russians to announce their discovery soon.

"This is an incredible finding," Dr. Ozawa said. "They know it will have enormous impact and they will want to reveal their discovery — and impress the world with it. They won't be able to keep it an official quiet for long."●

☐ *I hope the Russians won't keep it a secret very long! These articles all may be 10s as far as I know. This 7.5 is just a way of saying I have to wait and see. Why not go out in space for awhile — we won't have to get wet splashing around in a boat!*

ATLANTIS FOUND 80 MILES FROM U.S.

***Sun,* June 6, 1989**

by Francis Shifflett

An extensive oceanographic survey has revealed shocking details of an ancient underwater city located only 80 miles off the coast of Florida!

A remote-controlled probe even photographed strange humanoid beings that scientists believe are inhabitants of the mythical lost continent of Atlantis!

"We've detected unmistakable signs of an ancient civilization at the lowest depths of the sea," notes Dr. Anton Adir, leader of the research project.

"Amazingly, there are indications that the city is still inhabited by intelligent life."

Using the latest satellite technology, scientists were able to pinpoint the underwater city alongside the chain of islands that make up the Bahamas.

"When I looked at the first sonar-generated map, I felt as if I was looking at a map of Paris," says Dr. Adir. "It was easy to make out details of towering cathedrals, stately monuments and broad thoroughfares."

Since the city was located at a depth inaccessible to divers, a photographic probe was sent down.

Scientists watched breathlessly as it relayed images of a lost world never before viewed by human eyes.

"The blackness was so dense that the light of the probe could only illuminate a small area" explains Dr. Adir. "Still we were able to view elaborate buildings with huge pillars. Mystical hieroglyphics were etched into the stone."

But the real surprise was yet to come.

"As the probe rounded a corner, it suddenly showed two scaly grey creatures swimming by," the French scientist recalls. "They were almost human in form, yet they had flat, webbed arms and legs that looked like fins.

"Their heads were the size of human heads, although their eyes were tiny and appeared not to function. They had gill slits on the sides of their necks.

"They soon sensed the probe and darted away."

Dr. Adir believes a thriving community of the creatures has existed for thousands of years in the eerie city.

"The islands now known as the Bahamas were once part of a continent which sank around 50,000 years ago, taking its whole civilization with it.

"Evidently, the inhabitants survived by evolving features that allowed them to live underwater, and they continue their civilization up to the present day!"●

☐ *One of these days we may find where Atlantis really is — 7.*

THE DEVIL'S TRIANGLE

Weekly World, **November 8, 1988**

by Ragan Dunn

The Devil's Triangle is a gateway to eternity — that opens 16 times a year!

That's the mind-blowing claim of Dutch physicist Ludwig Hamming, who interviewed 75 people claiming to have had supernatural experiences in the Triangle, and determined that half of them came within a hair of entering the hereafter alive.

"This is the most incredible proof of life after death on record," Dr. Hamming told reporters in Amsterdam.

"Thirty-seven of the people I spoke with had amazingly similar glimpses of an afterlife while they were flying or sailing through the Devil's Triangle.

"In almost every case they encountered severe wind or electrical storms and blacked out — only to find themselves walking into a black tunnel that ultimately led to an open space bathed in a brilliant white light.

"Many of these witnesses went on to meet dead friends and relatives. Others said they were escorted out of the tunnel by either God or Jesus Christ.

"In one case a man's dead uncle told him he had indeed found eternity. But he insisted that his nephew go back through the tunnel to the world of the living."

Dr. Hamming's amazing report touched off a storm of controversy among scientists around the world. According to newspapers, German physicist Dr. Heinrich Englehard was especially critical, describing the Dutch researcher's study "an intriguing flight of fantasy."

"I expected criticism and it certainly does seem like I'm getting it," said Dr. Hamming. "But I can assure you that my work is serious. And I do have quite a body of evidence to support my belief that the Devil's Triangle is a portal to a world beyond our own.

"From my interviews and on-site studies I have found that this portal opens with astonishing regularity. I am also convinced that thousands of pilots, sailors and vacationers who have vanished in the area actually made it into paradise alive.

Dr. Hamming went on to say that many of the people he interviewed had seen unmanned boats and airplanes at the end of the tunnel. "It is my belief that these are the ships and planes of men and women who vanished in the Devil's Triangle, never to be seen again." Dr. Hamming's study also led him to believe that the mysterious gateway opens at least 16 times a year.

He has theorized that the openings coincide with magnetic and gravitational fluctuations that have long been known to occur in the Triangle. But he has not yet been able to calculate when or if the gateway will open again.

Dr. Phillip A. Voisard, a Swiss paranormal researcher, spoke highly of Dr. Hamming's research. He told reporters, "The results of his study should compel us to rethink everything we have ever believed."●

☐ *Even if it is a gateway to heaven it still gets a 7.*

ATLANTIS FOUND

Weekly World News, **Dec. 6, 1989**

by Geoffrey Shane

Salvage ship discovers 'lost continent' near the Azores in Atlantic.

A skipper of a salvage vessel searching the Atlantic Ocean for sunken freighters has made the most incredible discovery in modern history — he has found the lost continent of Atlantis!

Fifty-three-year-old Reyes Miaga said a deep-sea television sled being towed by his salvage ship *Talia* revealed what appears to be ruins of one of the lost cities of the fabled Atlantean continent that vanished more than 11,000 years ago.

"There can be no doubt whatsoever that the lost continent was there beneath my ship, just east of the Azores," Miaga told the *News* after his vessel had arrived in Lisbon, Portugal.

"The camera clearly showed great stone buildings and huge pillared temples ringed by statues. We cruised over the area for a distance of 10 miles above what could only have been a wide, curving boulevard with smaller avenues branching out like the spokes of a wheel. There is one particular area of concentric circles of huge rectangular stones which proves beyond a shadow of a doubt that I had found the lost world of Atlantis.

"The shape and the pattern of those stones could not have been made by nature. Anyone familiar with underwater geology knows they had to have been made by man."

The existence of Atlantis was first revealed 2,400 years ago by the Greek philosopher Plato.

He described Atlantis as a "great civilization" founded on advanced technology, engineering and architecture. His description of islands far out in the ocean may have been what prompted Columbus to go in search of new lands.

"Plato said Atlantis was a great continent larger than Asia Minor before it was destroyed by a great flood," Miaga said.

"In recent years, the ruins of temples, pyramids and circular roadways have been found in the Bahama Islands," said the captain.

"There can be no doubt that the ruins found off the east coast of America and the ruins that I have found belong to one vast land mass that now lies below the surface of the Atlantic Ocean.

"And that great land mass can only be the lost continent of Atlantis."

Miaga, who took part in the underwater search for a hydrogen bomb carried aboard an American plane that crashed off Portugal several years ago, said he plans to return to the site of his discovery with a deep-diving research submarine.●

☐ *If such facts are true, wouldn't you think every headline would be spreading the news? One wonders whether anyone wants us to believe ... Or are we supposed to think these tales just may be true?*

The skipper only gets a 5 until he can convince a bunch of well-known scientists.

RAY FROM UFO CURES 22
Weekly World, **December 5, 1989**
by Mickey McGuire.

At least 22 sick and crippled people were miraculously cured when they were bathed in an eerie greenish light that pulsated from a gigantic UFO hovering over their city!

Official reports from Turkey said the incredible cures began moments after the silvery, saucer-shaped spaceship streaked silently down from the heavens to hover for more than an hour just over the rooftops.

And what is being hailed as the most sensational photograph ever made of a flying saucer was taken by a soldier.

"There is no doubt the photograph is real," declared a Turkish official in the city of Manisa. "Hundreds of people here saw the UFO. They saw it arrive and they watched it depart.

"But even more amazing than the photograph is the evidence that something from the ship healed at least 22 sick and crippled people."

A physician, Dr. Mehmet Nadi, said they talked to a woman named Inisa Tokap, whose 46-year-old husband was miraculously cured of crippling arthritis that had kept him bedridden for years.

"With tears streaming from her eyes she told me how his twisted limbs slowly straightened as the UFO's greenish light washed over his body," Dr. Nadi said.

"She said when the light from the UFO touched him the pain vanished from his body and his gnarled, twisted fingers slowly began to become relaxed and began to straighten.

"His feet and toes became straight and he was able to stand and walk for the first time in years."

Dr. Nadi said he has examined several other patients and found them completely cured of their ailments, including Kamal Yilmaz, a middle-aged man who had been in a stroke-induced coma for months.

"I couldn't believe my eyes when Kamal came walking into my office," he said. "I've known him for years, but I made him show me some identification. I just couldn't believe it was true. But it was."

Medical officials from Ankara are now in the area to examine dozens of other people who also have reported being cured by the strange light.

"So far, we know of several people who were dying of cancer who now appear to be completely cured," one doctor confirmed. "But only time will tell if the cures are permanent or merely a kind of coincidental mass remission."

Another doctor confirmed that a 9-year-old boy, identified as Hasan Koru, comatose and near death with total kidney failure, awoke and got out of bed after the mysterious light filtered through a window and swept over his body. Other doctors verified that a woman blinded by cataracts regained her sight, a man deaf since birth had his hearing restored and a day-old infant girl dying of some undiagnosed malady now appears to be normal and healthy because of the miracle light.

The UFO, which hovered over the village for about 70 minutes before it suddenly streaked off into space, is believed to be the same spaceship that landed in a Soviet city about 1,300 miles to the north on September 27.

The *News* revealed in its November 7 issue that the captain of the spaceship was captured by KGB agents when the aliens left their craft after landing in a park in the city of Veronezh.

"It would be too much of a coincidence for two UFOs to be making such dramatic visits within weeks of each other," one Turkish official declared.●

☐ *By printing these UFO articles, you are given about 20 times as much evidence as if they were printed separately. There are so many, it's hard to pick and choose, and to show you what you'll find when you look into the subject. How about a 9.9?*

EXAMINER WORLD EXCLUSIVE
National Examiner, **April 17, 1990**
by Jim Hogshire

Two Iranian jet fighters went down in flames after being destroyed by a giant UFO.

The fighter planes were threatening an unarmed Iraqi 747 jumbo jet carrying 290 passengers when the UFO swooped to the rescue.

Suddenly it opened fire with what were apparently laser weapons, hitting one of the fighters on its portside wing and the other in its engines.

Secret tapes of radio transmissions obtained by an *Examiner* correspondent tell the story of the dramatic life-and-death battle over Iraq's swampy Shatt-al-Arab region last May. And they reveal the stunning intervention of the alien craft to save the stricken super jet.

"It happened so quickly none of the passengers realized what had happened," said a member of the jumbo jet's crew.

"When we landed, myself and the rest of the crew were taken aside by a high government official and told not to breathe a word to anyone about this."

The hush-hush tapes reveal that Captain Ghawar Al-Tosheh radioed Iraqi military forces at nearby Basra airbase: "Mayday! Mayday! We have two Iranian F-5s on our tail. Request assistance."

Although the Iraqi air force quickly scrambled its own planes, it was clear the 747 was doomed.

"Those fighter jets are heavily armed and capable of climbing 50,000 feet per minute," said one military observer on the scene. "The Iraqis were dead ducks."

The Iranians said they intended to destroy the plane in retaliation for the Iraqi bombing of a major city two years ago.

As the pilot of the lumbering jetliner tried valiantly to escape his attackers, he pleaded with the Iranians not to shoot them down.

"We beg you for mercy," said the pilot. "These are innocent lives on board. We are not a warplane."

But the Iranian pilots were unmoved.

"You are flying under the flag of the evil Iraqi government," they declared.

"We beg of you," said the Iraqi captain.

"You have one more minute," replied the Iranian pilot.

There was radio silence for 10 seconds before the Iraqi pilot called the airbase.

"Basra, Basra, we have an unidentified craft in our radar. Is this you?" he asked.

Seconds later the UFO's powerful beams obliterated the Iranian fighters.

UFO experts theorize the aliens moved to prevent the attack after picking up Iranian threats to destroy the plane. The captain of the 747 agrees.

"That UFO saved the lives of all 290 passengers," said Captain Al-Tosheh, who landed the jet safely at the airbase.

"We are at a complete loss to explain it but they seem to have acted out of compassion. They obviously meant to rescue us."

An Iraqi military spokesman said: "Two Iranian jets recently crashed and burned, apparently while on a training exercise. We do not know what caused the incident."●

☐ *How much do you have to be told so you'll understand these articles are published for you to read? This account indicates that more lives were saved than all others I've read given in the tabloids. Most extraterrestrials are more apt to help someone than harm them. I want this one to have a big fat 10.*

THE CUSTODIAN AT TOKYO COMPUTEK

The September 25th issue of the Sun,
Has a picture of a janitor who's become
The most famous man in a Japanese firm,
After he was abducted on his way home!

Sam says he was so stupid —
He couldn't count his money,
But after his abduction —
He became a manager of production!

Now Sam has a little lump,
Right in the middle of his forehead.
The Aliens have inserted a box,
That's considered to be unorthodox.

After a leave of absence to visit the doctor,
He thinks he'd best be careful —
The scientists want to take it out,
To solve how this thing came about.

Sam isn't taking chances,
He's been promoted to president.
As long as he keeps that thing there —
He won't worry about his lack of hair!

CHAPTER TEN

Personal Opinions After 40 Years
Epilogue — Special Sightings

UFOs Watched Japs Bomb Pearl Harbor — *Sun* 233
UFO Expert Says Mass Sightings Were Genuine — *National Examiner* 233
Amazing UFO Photo — *Weekly World* 234
Hubble Telescope Shows UFO Fleet — *Sun* 235
Killer Cloud Melts City — *Weekly World* 235
President to Meet with UFO Abduction Victim — *Sun* 236
Doc Says Teen is Child of Space Aliens — *Sun* 237
UFO Returns Coeds Kidnapped in 1966 — *Sun* 237
UFOs Are Not From Other Planets — *Sun* 238
Nazi U-Boat Captured by U.S. Navy Ship — *Weekly World News* 238
Alien Cousins? — *Poem* 240

PERSONAL OPINIONS AFTER 40 YEARS

Our planet appears to be one of many the Creator has chosen as a school where he can experience and understand His own creation.

Mary Baker Eddy, in *Science and Health,* sums it up this way:

> There is no life, truth, intelligence, nor substance in matter,
> all is Infinite Mind and Infinite Manifestation, for God is All in All.

This is a convincing statement. It indicates everlasting life. I believe most of us accept it is that spark of life within that enters this bit of dust we are, that enables us to come and go as the Creator wills it.

It seems likely that the God-self of an individual records its life experiences and is the best to judge how it may improve itself so sooner or later it may return to the Father who has created the universe and all within it.

The arrival of Jesus — the Christ on earth, has helped guide Christians, who believe him to be the "way-shower" back to the Father-Creator. Those whose faith and devotion are sufficient, may find themselves at the portal of a shining city of gold and crystal where the love of God will care for their every need. Others may find themselves searching for material bodies to inhabit while they go merrily on from one life to another trying to understand themselves and their Creator. Eventually all will return where they belong....

Do you remember the account of Mr. X and the captain of a spaceship? During their elongated and interrupted conversation the captain said they used our planet as a penal colony. I asked Mr. X if this meant the transference of bodies — or souls. His answer was he didn't know, because it was just a statement. The greater part of their visit concerned the mechanical make-up of the spacecraft.

I was reminded of the dream of the young man who for years saw himself piloting a dish-shaped ship to an orange planet. His description of zombie-like people whom he picked-up in space made me feel they were "lost souls." No words were ever spoken — he opened a door — they filed in, the door closed and eventually he released them and never saw them again. All he felt was compassion, all he saw in their faces was confusion.

This made me wonder if the alien captain had been hauling souls instead of physical bodies —and if spacecraft are interested in rescuing bodies, or souls? Perhaps it's both. I suppose a body, or a soul, might have similar vibrations.

I find little reason to doubt the cross-breeding which is being done by aliens with our people. Their IQs are said to run 200 or so. That ought to improve the 75s some of us are blessed with. I'm not sure about the change in physical bodies. Mr. X and I both wonder whether the captain he saw was seen or heard by anyone but himself? The same thing could be said about the contacts of George Adamski, Truman Bethurum, Reinhold Schmidt and others.

I believe some aliens are able to appear with any body form they wish to present! They are masters with hypnosis. Our doctors have a rough time breaking through the suggestions which have been given contactees.

Travis Walton was petrified when he saw the bug-eyed mushroom colored aliens; they were forced to change their appearance. The next thing he knew he was seeing men who looked like himself. So how do we know what's real and what isn't?

We've been told that marking and cross-breeding is done so that better equipped physical bodies can be used to reteach and start a new civilization (in case of a catastrophe). I wonder how many times this has happened before? I'm not sure it sounds like much of a favor to live under those new conditions. Perhaps the ones that are left are in need of reliving their former experiences, after not having quite made the grade.

The experience of the Mexican chauffeur which is given in Bryant and Helen Reeves book, *Flying Saucer Pilgrimage,* happened in 1953. The description by Salvador of the living conditions of these aliens is interesting. Some contactees have written books, much of which was received under hypnosis, and others were consciously remembered. Salvador spent several hours with the aliens. The following comments are ones I found convincing:

1. They had white faces and were about 4 feet tall.
2. Wore loose-fitting outfits much like corduroy which were tight at the neck, wrists and ankles; material also covered the feet.
3. Wore a thick bluish belt about 3 inches wide with holes in it; sometimes lights flashed on and off. He was told it was used to contact them and warn of danger.
4. They carried a helmet which had small wires running from the earpieces. (The belt and helmet match a description given me by a woman minister who said she and a friend were near an alien who ran within 3 to 4 ft. of them. The alien ran above the ground and floated up across the top of a fence. This sighting included a spacecraft which was seen by a stable-boy and a policeman. It was in New York State.)
5. Salvador accompanied the aliens toward their spacecraft. They walked above ground while he was getting wet and muddy. If he was lying, he knew a lot of the right answers.
6. The alien's hair was fine, thin, gray and shoulder length. This goes along with Adamski's description — also the four South American children who were kidnapped ... I'm convinced the aliens allow themselves to be seen to suit the desire and need of the observer.
7. The aliens claimed to come from a "place of much space" (literal translations from Spanish).
8. Claimed their place was much more inhabited than here. There were no uninhabited areas in their towns and all buildings were continuous.
9. Claimed each house had a patio area where they were able to have a well and garden.
10. Power was generated from productive centers which took advantage of inexhaustible solar rays — it was used to run their vehicles.
11. Streets never crossed at the same level — sidewalks were made of endless belts running in opposite directions.
12. Did not have big trees or tall buildings.
13. Aliens told Salvador there are men who look, eat, and dress like we do, who live among us ... it is their job to report all data about wars, progress, life and government back to their planet.
14. The aliens said they had gone through our stage of living thousands of years ago — they went on to describe their own government ... it will be interesting to read the "Yellow Book" that "Falcon" told us about in the documentary *UFO Cover-Up*. (If that ever happens!)
15. All conversation was in Spanish. It is obvious most contacts are made by telepathy. Most people believe the conversation took place in their own language. Usually one alien appears to do all the talking.

The suggestion that aliens live among us is not unusual, but remember, this contact dates back to 1953! Recently contactees have been shown a crystal object which acts much like a television and is able to show our past history as well as that of the aliens on their home planets.

Supposing we do have other life forms of some sort appearing in our earthly experience of existence? And supposing all of them differ to some extent in their own life experiences. In case we are quite a way down on the totem pole in scientific knowledge, how do you think that will affect the ego of those who believe they are sitting on the top of all truth and knowledge? Probably most churches believe that God is truth, but they certainly don't agree on what God is — what are we going to do with the beliefs of the aliens? Heaven forbid we have to send some missionaries to Neptune to tell them they should do away with that duplicate Sphinx-like face — probes have found carved on Mars, Venus, and the Moon, as well as Neptune. Of course we can pretend the faces aren't there — but for goodness sake, don't investigate — that's the apple you aren't supposed to eat. Over and over I hear someone say, "I'm aware of this information but it simply doesn't interest me." The same people will tell you our Government should tell us all they know about such subjects. Why should you be told something which you have no desire to know?

When I paint a picture I have to decide what colors go together to create a work of art. How do I make a choice? If I wish to use a lot of brown shades, I know it will be appropriate to use some reds, blues, and yellows because they are all related to the make-up of my brown paint.

With the discussion of UFOs, I need to know what topics to use to assure I have not strayed from my subject-matter. Just as shades of red, yellow, and blue produce my browns, I know that the subject-matter in the discussion of UFOs is unlimited. As far as I know there are no holds barred!

To leave religion out of this book would be like taking the red out of the brown paint. It wouldn't work. To ignore economics, politics, ecology, and all sciences — as well as our lifestyles and behavior patterns, would be like removing the yellow from the shade of brown I desire.

Everything we do, or think, or believe, has an appropriate place in *Flying Saucer Opinions.* Therefore, bear with me so I may express my personal feelings concerning some of the many aspects that come into my life experience.

I've read many reincarnation cases during the last forty years. I'm so thankful there were no abortions for me to have to mull over. I wonder what it would be like to think the vehicle I was carrying could have been occupied by someone I might have known and loved at some stage of my development, wherever that might have been. There are so many people who have gone out of my life — I think how much I would like to bring them back again. I wonder if this is the way the author of Brigadoon felt?

Much of my life has been planned out in detail. When I met my husband I carefully scrutinized him and decided "this one will do." Then I set out to fall in love — when I felt perhaps we could afford a baby — that's when No. 1 son arrived. It may have taken six months, but both he and we knew he came by invitation! Surely the love vibrations put forth in such a case must be felt. Five years later No. 2 son was planned and wanted just as much ... every lick I did for him was a pleasure — how could these children owe me anything? The pleasure was all mine.

It's difficult to reach out and up-date sources on UFO-related subjects. However, some of my friends are more able to do this than I am. Baird and Marjorie Wallace have just returned from a lecture trip to the island of Barbados where interested researchers gathered at the seaside for many informative talks. Baird is an engineer with an automotive company in Detroit, Michigan. Marge is a former librarian. I was sent a tape made from one of their many speakers, Dr. J.J. Hurtak, a scientist and author.

Having already finished most of my comments in this book I was interested to listen to a man who has done extensive research into all aspects of this field. He has been involved with many of our top scientists. I couldn't help but feel pleased to find his words and thoughts to be so compatible with my own. Dr. Hurtak spent time living with monks in different Ashrams in the East. He shared himself in observing religions of the world. All people appear to have experienced contacts with aliens who have left their imprints on civilizations. While recognizing the various kinds of contacts which reach our news, he feels there is danger of over-estimating some of the scientific aliens whose high IQs may have furthered scientific accomplishments, but who may not have the necessary spiritual background to balance life experiences.

It is well known that negative results may come from "visiting aliens" as well as positive results in other cases. It's much like answering the door bell not knowing who is on the other side. The trick is to be aware of these beings and still remember there is a fifth dimension that goes beyond the life forms that fill all space, whether you are aware of them or not.

Dr. Hurtak refers to the God-Energy as the "Living Light" and feels everyone should see himself as belonging to this source in order that the "Holy Spirit" may infiltrate our very being, that we too will be able to pour forth "Unconditional Love."

Our ecologists tell us in order to live and thrive on this planet, it's necessary to protect all forms of life to assure they too may continue their material existence. The Creator has so carefully balanced His Creation that to destroy any species of the many lifeforms throws off the necessary balance to protect all life. For as surely as we fail — we destroy ourselves. Thus we must continue with the positive and negative make-up from which all life manifestations are formed. It is of little wonder that the well-known Dr. Albert Schweitzer believed so strongly in "A Reverence for Life." We must learn to live and share with all!

By the time one reads Dr. Charles Hapsgood's theories in *The Earth's Shifting Crust,* and those of Immanuel Velikovsky in *Worlds in Collision* — to say nothing of all the scientific hoop-la written about the black holes in space that may gobble us up someday — why should I worry about a few thousand aliens who apparently have their own problems?

EPILOGUE

When I think about the best way to summarize what I've been trying to say, I think of the *UFO Coverup* documentary, which was presented on ABC on October 14, 1988 from 8 to 10 p.m.

The time choice alone told its importance. The fact it was carried in Canada at the same time should have given another clue. How important must it be to have preferential treatment over all prime time shows? What do you suppose the bill would be to monopolize all those stations?

In spite of the advertizing, in spite of the immense coverage, I was amazed to find the low percentage of those who listened. It becomes obvious that UFOs are not a high priority with those around us. This has a great deal to do with the low-key technique which the government is forced to use. No matter how much effort has been made to acquaint the public, as long as UFO topics are officially ignored, people will continue to act much like busy ants scurrying through their daily routine.

If, without further warning, a situation arrives which causes the world to know "these things are here," I shudder to think how ill-prepared people will be to cope with the situation! Perhaps there's little we can do about it — but the recognition that life is all around us and we are such a small part in the whole design is bound to jar the daylights out of all of us! It's time to "wake up" and think — don't wait for Uncle Sam to blow a siren!

UFO Cover-Up was carefully developed and presented. It shows the White House was buzzed by UFOs on July 26, 1952. There was nothing officials could do, they didn't know who it was, or what it was. Not knowing how to answer questions which were asked, Project Blue Book was born.

Colonel Robert Friend was in charge of Blue Book for a five-year period. He and Colonel Wm. Coleman were interviewed on this documentary. Rest assured they weren't there because they thought UFOs were non-existent. Col. Coleman told of his 1955 sighting in Alabama where he and his crew saw a UFO which was approximately 70 ft. in diameter and 15 ft. in height. Though they were debriefed and the case was filed, years later when he checked Blue Book files he found his case was missing. This was the way Blue Book operated — they solved all sightings which were possible as long as they could get away with it. When a sighting was too hot to handle they had "moles" (unregistered personnel) whose job was to ferret through the files and remove these unexplainable cases. By doing this, Project Blue Book was able to close its doors on UFO investigations. From that time on, UFOs became handled as a covert operation.

Dr. Richard Hanes (20 years with NASA) tells *UFO Cover-Up* of his more than 3000 cases of reports, some of which formerly were from unbelieving officers. Their close sightings caused them to bury their egos and confess their sightings.

With Dr. Hanes was Capt. Neil Daniels, a 35-year pilot for United Air Lines. He told of his March 12, 1977 sighting of a UFO which was several hundred feet in diameter. Both he and his passengers saw this craft. They were within an eighth of a mile when he attempted to show it to his flight engineer. The response was, "I don't want to see it and I don't want to know about it!" How many times have I heard this reaction?

Cover-Up invited a Russian journalist and investigator to join them from Moscow. Be assured he had the blessing of both our government and his. Later, when he invited our scientists to come over and work with them, it was no surprise. During the last year we have had reports that show such projects are proceeding. Sergei Bulantsev went on to describe several close sightings and abductions. Even to a couple of rosy colored aliens who emerged from a UFO and told his two-man audience not to be afraid, they would not be harmed. (Not an uncommon message, usually given by telepathic means.)

Sergei described a beam of light from a UFO which when shown directly on a group of houses, appeared to make them vanish from sight. Also we have case after case where a beam of light made viewing possible even through metal.

A Russian scientist, Leonard Nikishin, said in 1984 Russia asked for those having had UFO experiences to please notify the government. Over 20,000 replies were somewhat of a surprise. The scientist also believes we will soon meet extraterrestrials, perhaps sooner than we think! (This is what I call "playing with a loaded deck.")

The well-known case of Betty Cash, her friend Vickey, and grandson Tobey, were on deck to tell about being badly burned by a UFO. They believed it to have been operated by our own men. We are said to have a craft which had belonged to the aliens. It was thought to be in difficulty and was about to crash. Twenty-three helicopters arrived to surround it — fortunately it recovered and was rescued. This is not so with Betty Cash: she is very ill with serious cancer problems. This isn't all — she says she is "madder than hell" at our government! It's hard for me to believe that our government would have taken this kind of a chance — on my scoring chart, I wouldn't have given it more than a 5!

UFO researcher Bob Barry presented Canadian films which show the unorthodox movements of a UFO. (This program was designed to show most everything you need to know, and DON'T.)

It was after the 1947 UFO crash referred to as the Roswell Incident that the real "cover-up" began. Dead aliens and parts were carted away and hidden indefinitely. President Truman created MJ-12. Those on this list were responsible only to him. As they died or committed suicide, they were replaced by others. The strain of this secret knowledge is hard on the best of them.

Paul Shartle, formerly with an audio visual program, and Robert Emenegger, author of *UFOs Past and Present,* were invited to talk about our government's exchange program and Emenegger's tale of a craft which landed at Holloman Air Base. Paul Shartle claims he saw film of three alien beings landing at Holloman Air Base. They were met by Base officials. A few weeks later we began an exchange program with the aliens. (Whether this date was April 25, 1964 or May 1971 doesn't matter much — the important thing is whether it happened at all!)

The pseudo names "Falcon" and "Condor" are said to be government men whose job is to inform the public the truth about UFOs and the government. (I believe this to be true.) It had to be done this way; if the government admits the truth you will flip — if you are told the truth and the government remains silent, you may assume this is another hoax, if it were true Uncle Sam would have told us so! Don't kid yourself — you're being given plenty of evidence.

Who do you think would want to show you those complicated charts of alien bodies and all their "innards"? Remember you didn't hear one dissenting word from your government which told you to ignore the whole thing or, "Oh that was just a bunch of 'hog wash'!" "Falcon" says we have three visiting aliens in a Nevada base. He also tells us that a book called the *Yellow Book* has been written by our visiting aliens and tells all about their society, surrounding planets, and details of many kinds. The thing which most impressed him was a crystal which when held in the hand of the alien showed dimensional pictures of their life on another planet and a history of mankind as it has gone through its development. (Does this remind you of the messages about crystals in this book?) Contact cases have mentioned this ability of crystal use. The grocery story tabloids have given you information on this topic. Did you ignore it?

When we are told the life span of some of these aliens is as much as 350 to 400 years and their IQs run over 200 — who is it wants you to know this? Why are you told we've had dead aliens and live aliens for years? Who is it wants you to know? Wake up! Make it a little easier for the guy at the top!

President Bush, having been vice president as well as head of the CIA, has been on the privileged list "to know" for years. He must be a strong character not to have ended up in the "booby hatch" long ago.

UFOs WATCHED JAPS BOMB PEARL HARBOR
Sun, **February 6, 1990**
by Ben Snark

Japanese fighter planes weren't all that filled the Pacific sky on the morning of December 7, 1941. An entire fleet of UFOs watched the attack on Pearl Harbor!

That's the astonishing revelation of Bob Baumgartner, who alleges that the UFO presence at the Battle of Oahu is the U.S. military's biggest coverup in history!

Bob, 71, was a 23-year-old Military Policeman on guard duty at Pearl Harbor during the Japanese sneak attack, and he's still haunted by that morning.

"Even though hundreds of both Americans and Japanese viewed five spaceships at the height of the battle, the U.S. military has kept silent," says Bob, who since became a leading investigative journalist.

Six years ago, he decided to conduct in-depth research to uncover once and for all the complete story of Pearl Harbor. After interviewing dozens of survivors and sifting through thousands of official documents, he has assembled definite proof that hovering alien spaceships watched the surprise attack.

"It was before dawn when I began hearing explosions in the distance," Bob recalls.

"Within minutes, Japanese planes were everywhere."

Bob managed to find cover in a bunker. Then all hell broke loose.

"Plane after plane swooped down and strafed us with machine gun fire," says Bob. "I thought I was a goner for sure.

"As I looked up into the fiery sky to ask God for forgiveness, I noticed two giant silver disks hovering almost directly above me. They both had to be at least 100 yards in diameter."

Bob later found out that he wasn't the only one who had seen the flying saucers.

"Servicemen on both the U.S. and Japanese side reported the spacecraft," he says. "The Americans thought they were secret Japanese weapons.

"In fact, Japanese war files reveal that one of the planners of the attack, General Takashi Kozamura, ordered a retreat when he saw the mammoth flying saucers, but was over-ruled by General Tomoyuku Yamashita."

Still, the Pentagon has refused to confirm the UFO incident.

But through the Freedom of Information Act, Bob found reference to it in recently declassified files.

"An Army Air Force report reveals that five disk-like structures were sighted above Pearl Harbor," Bob says. "The explanation was that they were on a surveillance mission for 'an unknown and possibly extraterrestrial power.'

"The report goes on to state that 'the unidentified flying objects continued to hover after the enemy planes departed, appearing to survey the damage.

'They then disappeared into the upper-atmosphere at a high rate of speed,' " Bob quotes.●

☐ *Any investigator that can get his carcass off a chair ought to check this article for himself. By allowing such evidence to be in print certainly credits government sources for not having covered up this report. If you have read this, and still feel it's no big deal and doesn't matter — well, perhaps it doesn't, it's a little late to worry about it now ... on a scale of 1–10 it looks like a 35 to me.*

The Gulf Breeze sightings in Florida carry such strong evidence surely it will go down in ever-lasting history. It is so impressive, it will require "moles" to undermine and discredit, in order to smooth the feathers of the unbeliever.

With the identity of "Falcon" and "Condor" made known, these men, too, must be discredited to protect the government's role. This is done by "moles" who infiltrate organizations and see we are given "disinformation." It's the only way! You will have to learn to think for yourself — no one else will do it for you.

When I found the following clipping I felt it expressed my own feelings so well that I'm including it in hopes you too will be impressed.

UFO EXPERT SAYS MASS SIGHTINGS WERE GENUINE
***National Examiner*, August 22, 1989**

Mass sightings of UFOs are not a hoax, says a top Navy scientist.

The sightings of dozens of UFOs occurred over a six-month period in the small town of Gulf Breeze, Florida.

A number of residents took pictures of the mysterious objects, which are now being studied by experts.

Dr. Bruce Maccabee, a Navy scientist considered to be the world's top UFO expert, said: "They would be extremely difficult to hoax, I and others looked for irregularities which would prove that hoax techniques were used. I could find no convincing proof, I say they are real."

Researcher Philip Manile said. "The pictures are the biggest ever breakthrough in the UFO world.

"UFOlogists are putting their reputation on the line by stating that they are genuine."●

☐ *It is believed spaceships visited the small town of Gulf Breeze between November 11, 1987, and May 1, 1988 and were witnessed by 140 residents.*

Following the presentation of *UFO Cover-Up* in October 1988, I've been interested to see what would be given for an encore in 1989. The *Cover-Up* program hardly shook any leaves off the bushes. In fact, one wonders bow much of an audience it did have?

Along about December, 1989, somehow the *For the People* program, which is carried on WCCF-AM radio in Punta Gorda, Florida, began receiving questions concerning the validity of the cover-up information. After the arrival of a few crates of mail in response to those calls, the producer, Chuck Harder, shelled out a few thousand in the right places and presented the results in his 1990 winter issue of *For the People* magazine. Thanks to that, he probably won't be taking any vacation soon. He has managed to condense this material into a package which can be read at one sitting. Whether that's advisable is another thing. It is so well-done, it's a good bit like trying to eat a week's food supply in one meal.

The $15.00 fee for joining the group entitles you to receive all sorts of Consumer News, whether it's real estate, lawsuits, job hunting or other problems. The UFO material has been an extra tid-bit thrown in for good measure.

For the People is carried on nearly a couple hundred stations including Alaska as well as shortwave radio worldwide. I took one look at this magazine, called a dozen people and said, send him $15.00 immediately; it doesn't matter whether you can receive the station — he deserves it. His magazine is the best bargain I've seen all year. I wonder if someone else did that too? No vacation Charlie, just stay home and tend the mail. Besides, the next issue is carrying an article by nuclear physicist Stanton Freeman. I'm not at all sure that Chuck Harder isn't one more pawn that government sources are using to bring the UFO subject to the attention of their fledglings. That's fine, as long as they're both happy — what does it matter? A 10 for Charley and a 10 for the government.

AMAZING UFO PHOTO
***Weekly World News*, Feb. 13, 1990**
by Tim Stern

A UFO hovered over Egypt's Great Pyramid for three mind-blowing minutes, apparently searching for a relic or beacon that was planted when the structure was built 5,000 years ago — in 2680 B.C.

That's the claim of French and Danish archaeologists who photographed the starship as it scanned the pyramid with a laser at dusk on January 12.

The researchers also watched the spacecraft retrieve a small black box from the base of the pyramid before it disappeared.

"The UFO came for that black box," Dr. Jacques Claire, the French archaeologist, told newsmen in Cairo.

"Even stranger, the alien pilot and crew didn't seem to care who saw the starship. It hovered over us for three minutes, scanning the pyramid and ground around it with a blue laser.

"The UFO zeroed in on the north face of the structure and pulled a small black box from the sand at the base up into the hold of the ship.

"Before it disappeared we got a photograph. I don't think it's overstating the case to say it's the most dramatic picture of a UFO ever."

UFO experts around the world tended to agree. After computer studies indicated that the photo was not a composite or hoax, researchers flatly called it proof that space aliens do exist — and are interested in planet Earth. Jorgen Bering, Dr. Claire's Danish colleague, went even further than that.

He believes the UFO may have been manned by the descendants of space aliens who helped design and build the pyramid in 2680 B.C.

"There is no other explanation," said the expert. "That black box wasn't a suitcase. It had to be a beacon that led them to the pyramid or a relic left by their ancestors in ancient times."

Scientists have long believed that space aliens had something to do with the design and construction of the pyramids.

"In my mind that proves it."

Egyptian officials conceded that a UFO was picked up on radar on the evening of January 12 but refused to discuss the incident pending the completion of an investigation.

Intelligence sources in the Soviet Union and United States also confirmed that Mikhail Gorbachev and President George Bush had been informed of the close encounter.

"We may have seen the last of the starship or it might turn up here again tomorrow," said Dr. Claire.

"I only wish that the aliens aboard had approached us.

"I want to know what was in that black box. I want to hear them tell us why they were here."●

☐ *If by now you are still in doubt of the reality of these extraterrestrial craft, well, perhaps it doesn't matter. Que sera, sera. The Creator's creation goes on through eternity.*

HUBBLE TELESCOPE SHOWS UFO FLEET

***Sun*, July 10, 1990**

by Francis Shifflett

Moments after being released into orbit by the space shuttle, NASA's Hubble telescope beamed back horrifying pictures of a fleet of UFO warships headed for Earth!

Several top NASA officials have now confirmed the shocking sightings, despite orders from the highest levels of government to keep quiet.

"The Hubble telescope has revealed 43 unidentified objects flying towards Earth in formation," says a mission control specialist who declined to be identified. "Our tracking station has been sealed off to the public and is now functioning under direct orders from the Pentagon.

"In addition, governments around the world have been notified of this frightening new threat."

The $1.55 billion Hubble telescope is the United States' most expensive telescope and is 50 times more powerful than any telescope on Earth. After the Space shuttle deployed it into orbit 380 miles above Earth, scientists prepared to peer into distant realms of the universe.

"We began scanning various sectors of the galaxy, testing the equipment," states the NASA specialist. "We had barely started when we noticed an alarming pattern of 43 lights arranged in a triangle.

"Complete silence fell over the room. Then I heard someone gasp as the images were magnified.

"I looked at it and couldn't believe my eyes. It was easy to make out 43 spike-shaped spacecraft. Judging from the formation they were flying in, they appeared to be warships heading into battle.

"According to our calculations, they were traveling toward Earth at a high rate of speed!"

NASA chiefs called an emergency meeting and then issued a statement claiming that a malfunction on the Hubble telescope had prevented it from sending any images back from space. The agency claimed it would take several weeks before the telescope could be put into working order.

"That was simply a ploy to gain time," says the source. "We contacted the Defense Department and began tracking the UFOs.

"We know that if they maintain their present rate of speed, they'll arrive on Earth in less than a year."

Sources report that a possible defense strategy against the potential threat was discussed during the recent summit between President Bush and Russian leader Gorbachev.

"We can't be absolutely sure that these beings are hostile." says the NASA source. "But if they intend to take over the Earth, we must put up a fight."●

☐ *I've been reading about that bunch of ships that are headed our way for a long time. I thought maybe they were the ones that were supposed to pick us up when all Hell breaks loose on our planet? Besides NASA has known about them for a month of Sundays — it wasn't as if it were any big surprise. If they expect to educate people, it might be wise to begin printing such stuff in the* N.Y. Times *where it would be read. Until NASA starts displaying their photographs in the news, this has to rate a 5.*

KILLER CLOUD MELTS CITY

***Weekly World*, July 17, 1990**

by Max Tanner

A mysterious black cloud turned an entire city and everyone in it into a shimmering pool of water, stunned scientists report.

"Explanations? How do you explain something like this?" chemist Yen Chi-fu told newsmen who visited what's left of once-bustling Telingua, China.

"The handful of people who witnessed the disaster from a safe distance can only tell us that a black cloud appeared at a very low altitude and settled down on the city.

"When the massive cloud moved on a few minutes later Telingua and its 35,000 residents had been reduced to water. We don't know what was in that cloud, but whatever it was makes acid rain look like bathwater."

The mind-blowing incident reportedly took place on June 9 and a team of over 200 scientists, researchers and support personnel have been trying to figure out what happened since.

The startled experts initially believed that the mysterious cloud was composed of chemicals or gases that escaped from an upwind factory but they were unable to find a shred of evidence to support the theory.

Analysis of water that was left behind after the cloud passed through Telingua was inconclusive. Even more baffling, the killer cloud vanished after it rolled out of the city and it hasn't been sighted since.

"We are at a complete loss," said chemist Yen. "What happened to this city and its inhabitants is beyond comprehension.

"The cloud could have come from anywhere. It could have contained anything. We just have no idea."

The Chinese government has declared Telingua a disaster area and is currently limiting access to authorized personnel only.

It is not yet clear how long the investigation will last, but state department spokesman Hu Xian Xin says it could last a year or longer.

"We intend to get to the bottom of this," said the official. "There is an explanation and we will find it."●

☐ *Now why would anyone write a silly article like that? Is it for publicity? Come to think of it, haven't I heard someplace that we're about 98% water? In that case, maybe it wouldn't be much harder to make water out of us than to make wine out of water?? Is this a fictitious name of a town or perhaps misspelled purposefully? Did 100 people disappear instead of 35,000 such as shown in the News?*

Clouds are sometimes accused of kidnapping people — but never turning them into water! Any black cloud that abducted 35,000 people would surely fall down with all that weight! Wouldn't it?

I couldn't find "Telingua" on the map of China but I did find "Telingha." When I try to pronounce either word in English, both sound about alike. It was interesting to note "Telingha" is in a mining area. It is located about 100 miles north of the 36th parallel and about 400 miles N.W. of the city of Lanchou which is on the 36th parallel. Max only missed this place by one letter and surely deserves an A for effort.

The above special articles which I have chosen are there to keep this book up-to-date, as well as to say that perhaps they have been given to inform us; if not, thank goodness! If so, Que Sera Sera.

PRESIDENT TO MEET WITH UFO ABDUCTION VICTIM
Sun, Oct. 8, 1991
by William Rock

The American government is anxious to meet face-to-face with a Colombian farmer who says he was abducted by aliens and given an important message for President George Bush.

More than 3,000 people recently gathered at a village outside Bogota to hear 37-year-old Luis Rodriguez recount his frightening close encounter with a gigantic UFO. Among the curious were said to be several American scientists and intelligence agents.

"The CIA and Mr. Bush himself are taking Rodriguez very seriously," says one government insider. "His story sounds fantastic but I understand he's already passed a lie detector test.

"I've been told he'll soon be jetted to Washington for a debriefing. If his story holds, he'll then get his chance to relay the alien message to the President.

"The message contains some reference to the dangerous unrest in the Soviet Union and the shakiness of that nation's leadership."

Rodriguez allegedly told a friend that the aliens fear the Soviet Union's vast nuclear arsenal will fall into the wrong hands, leading to a global conflict.

The extraterrestrials want to step in and preserve world peace, the farmer says.

"A nuclear holocaust would render earth a useless desert," says one top UFOlogist.

"Apparently these aliens have been monitoring world events and realize a potential for disaster exists in the Soviet Union.

"No one knows who has their finger on the button. Things could heat up as the struggle for freedom and control rolls on." Rodriguez says he was tending his fields when the saucer-shaped craft zoomed into view and bathed him in a super bright beam of light.

The trembling farmer next remembers being surrounded by six strange-looking creatures.

"They only stood about five feet tall and they spoke in a strange language, but for some reason I could understand what they were saying," he says.

"They told me I was to be a messenger for them. That I must go back to my homeland and meet with Cardinal Mario Revollo. My next mission was to speak with George Bush. I don't know how long they kept me on the ship before they let me go."

Other villagers reported seeing a bright light shoot across the afternoon sky.

About six hours after Rodriguez was reported missing by his wife, he was found unconscious in a ditch five miles away from his farm.

"American scientists are itching to get their hands on Mr. Rodriguez," says a top secret *Sun* source.

"If the aliens are going to play an active role in world events, we certainly want to know how and when they'll intervene.

"We're all for world order, but we also don't want to find ourselves manipulated by some advanced race of ETs."

Rodriguez says that before his trip to Washington he must see Colombia's Cardinal Revollo. That meeting is expected to take place in Bogota within the next few weeks.●

☐ *The* Sun *shows a portion of this article being published in Bogota, Columbia, by REUTERS. It's so easy to discount a tabloid — don't discount REUTERS. The* Chicago Tribune *broke the story in the U.S. All government needs do is ignore or deny any knowledge, while you have the advantage of having been told. Of course, I believe it's a 10 — it's the same story I've been given for years! There are others who have felt they too should give out these messages.*

DOCS SAY TEEN IS CHILD OF SPACE ALIENS

***Sun*, Oct. 29, 1991**

by Mike Jones

A 13-year-old girl has such bizarre physical features that doctor think she's the off-spring of space aliens.

"She is one of the most remarkable curiosities in medical history," Dr. Bruno Hegal says about amazing Diana Krueger.

"Among other things, Diana has two hearts, blood with a copper rather than an iron base, and two sets of eyelids. The copper-based blood is similar to that of certain sea animals, such as lobsters. Her inner eyelids are retractable and transparent, like those of fish, reptiles and lizards."

What's more, her lungs are enormous and are equipped with mysterious organs the researchers believe can draw oxygen from water.

"In other words, she seems to have many characteristics of an amphibian — such as a frog," explains Dr. Hegal, head of a German research team examining the Bavarian schoolgirl. "We believe she can breathe in water as well as out."

Biologist Werner Haupmann, a member of the research team says:

"If she is an alien at least one of her parents came from a planet that is primarily water and where intelligent life is amphibious, possible reptilian."

The girl's parents are not known, according to police. "She was only a few weeks old when she was found abandoned in a barn by Anna Krueger, her foster mother," says police spokesman Hans Duegel.

Rather than allow her to be sent to a state orphanage, the Krueger family adopted and raised her.

"What the doctors are saying about Diana comes as a shock," says bewildered Anna Krueger. "She was always a normal child, except for the fact that she was never sick."

Diana's remarkable physical characteristics were discovered after she fell recently from a moving powerboat, struck her head — and was under water for more than a half hour before divers found her body at the bottom of a freezing mountain lake.

"The paramedics were stunned to find her blood was still flowing and its oxygen level was close to normal — despite the fact her heart was not beating," says Hegal.

Shortly after being taken from the water, the girl's heart started again and she acted quite normal. The astonished medics called Hegal's research team.

"We learned later that her second heart, which is located below her liver, had continued to beat and that her mysterious lungs had taken oxygen from the water," Hegal explains.

"Although she appears to be humanoid, she is not 100 percent human. She is quite likely a hybrid, with one of her parents coming from another world.●

☐ *To choose a few of the many good articles which are given is difficult. I picked this one because much cross-breeding is being done. It may be necessary in order to continue physical life. The aliens appear to have reasons for their actions.*

There are many visitors, perhaps from different dimensions. Their deeds may not be the same. The picture of the child and doctor are very convincing! They both deserve a 10.

UFO RETURNS COEDS KIDNAPPED IN 1966

***Sun*, Oct. 29, 1991**

by John Coffin

Three missing women who suddenly turned up after 25 years have stunned authorities with their claim that they were kidnapped by a UFO and taken to heaven.

The three, college students at the time, disappeared while walking along a farm road in 1966. They were given up for dead by relatives and police.

But they mysteriously reappeared on the same road — looking exactly as they did 25 years ago!

They say a UFO had taken them — not to another planet, but to another dimension where they met dead friends and relatives.

"I don't know what to make of it," says Margot Tercee, the mother of one woman.

"She looks exactly like my daughter, Denise, behaves the same, and remembers things only she and I know."

Police say the trio's dental records and fingerprints also match those of the missing students.

"They took us so that we can tell everyone that there is life after death," says Denise.

"UFOs are not space ships but the 'angels of death' who gather the souls of the dead and transport them to heaven."

Veronique Farneau notes: "After the time we spent on the other side, I'm not afraid of death anymore. I just can't wait to see my grandfather and grandmother again."

Denise, Veronique and Pauline Villiers — who were between 19 and 21 when they disappeared — told police in Limoges, France, they were "sucked up" by some type of alien craft while walking on the road near their school at night.

"I looked up just in time to see this spinning disk-like object with flashing lights hovering about us," Denise recalls.

"We were suddenly in a bright, white room. We were communicating with creatures, but they weren't wholly physical. It was as if we were in between the material and spiritual world. We were finally taken to heaven."

The girls say everyone they had known who had died was waiting when they stepped off the UFO.

"Everyone looked so happy," says Pauline. "My younger brother, who died from leukemia when he was 8, was the picture of health."

At the end of their stay, the girls were engulfed in a bright light and were told they were being returned to Earth to reassure people there is a purpose to life and a reward in the hereafter.

But when they returned — at the same spot where they had been abducted — they couldn't believe 25 years had gone by.

Political and religious leaders admit

they are confounded.

"They have been identified by their parents and that identification is supported by official records, including fingerprints and DNA tests," says Roman Catholic Cardinal Josef Bruneau.

"If this is a hoax, it is elaborate beyond belief. Based on the evidence we have and what they have told us, we have no other choice but to believe their stories."●

☐ *If you've read this article you may understand why our government handles the UFO situation as it does. I know only a few people who would bother to read through it twice. Even so, it's the same information I've been hearing for years. This case could easily be checked out as there is plenty of information given. Never do I read reports that ALL these cases are a bunch of "malarky"! I fully believe the government wants you to read them! The Sun carries pictures of the three girls who were abducted. Since I have no valid reason for doubting — it's worth a 10 to me!*

UFOs ARE NOT FROM OTHER PLANETS

***Sun,* Nov. 5, 1991**

by Mike Jones

Visitors in UFOs are not from outer space but from a thousand years in the future, a top physicist reveals.

"They're here to study us, just as our archaeologists study ancient cultures like the Egyptians, Greeks and Sumarians," says Alexander Siboranky. "UFOs are time machines, not spacecraft."

Soviet officials became very upset with Professor Siboranky's discovery five years ago, and the KGB threw him in prison.

Now freed with other political prisoners following the collapse of Communism, Siboranky says our future descendants "are very interested in this period" in mankind's history.

The professor claims he made his remarkable discovery by "eavesdropping" on communications between the UFOs with a "light-wave collector."

The collector was originally intended to study distant galaxies too far for ordinary telescopes.

The device allowed him to "freeze" UFOs and light-wave communications signals so he could take photos of the time machines and record their communications.

"It slows things moving too fast to be seen with the naked eye down to a perceptible speed," Siboranky explains.

"They discuss us as though we are cave-dwelling savages," the scientist says.

"They don't want us to know they are from the future. They want us to believe they are from outer space."

In deciphering the conversations between the time machines, Siboranky says he learned that "some great catastrophe will be taking place within the next 100 years which will result in most of our history being lost to future generations."

The professor says he doesn't think the men from the future have any intention of preventing the catastrophe.

"They're afraid that if they do they will change their own history," he points out.

The Russian physicist has agreed to discuss his findings and his light wave collector with American scientists soon.●

☐ *This article is a couple chapters ahead of my knowledge, but — nothing surprises me anymore. I'm inclined to believe the Russian, and the Sun, are serious. If it weren't worth a 9 or 10 I wouldn't use it!*

NAZI U-BOAT CAPTURED BY U.S. NAVY SHIP

***Weekly World News,* Nov. 26, 1991**

by Roger Treadway

German sailors think Hitler is alive and Roosevelt is President!

A Nazi U-boat that sailed out of Hamburg in 1942 was captured by a Navy destroyer after it surfaced in the North Atlantic just three weeks ago — on October 17, 1991!

Nobody knows for sure how the vintage World War II submarine sailed from the past to the present but sources say it is almost certainly linked to a second, sunken U-boat that made international headlines when it was found less than 100 miles off the coast of New Jersey a month earlier, on September 2.

Equally as strange, the captain and crew of the captured U-boat insist that Adolf Hitler and President Franklin Delano Roosevelt are alive, call themselves "prisoners of war" and apparently haven't aged a day since 1942.

"This is like something out of the Twilight Zone," said the Washington-based Navy officer who leaked the report a few days after the sub was captured.

"First we find a sunken U-boat in mint condition off the Jersey coast and then we find an armed and manned U-boat cruising the North Atlantic less than 150 miles from the spot where the first vessel was found.

"The crew itself thinks the year is 1942 and their uniforms are not only new, they're authentic. Both the U-boats are 50-year-old ships but from what I understand, they look like they were manufactured yesterday.

"The craziest thing about all this is that the crewmen have identified themselves as sailors whose names have been verified in war records. And because they're all young men in prime physical condition, it is believed that they haven't aged a day since 1942.

"I don't know all that much about time warps," he continued, "but that seems to be the only explanation for this whole situation.

"What else can I say? Something's

going on in the North Atlantic that doesn't make any sense at all."

The capture of the vintage German U-boat reportedly unfolded while the destroyer was on maneuvers a few hundred miles east of New Jersey on October 17.

According to the officer's report, the unidentified Navy vessel picked up the sub on sonar at 5:10 p.m. and less than a minute later, spotters saw it surface off the ship's starboard bow.

The U-boat bore Nazi insignias. But even though it looked like it might attack, the crew quickly raised a white flag.

The Washington-based officer said the U-boat's crew of 63 was in good health but extremely disoriented when they were taken aboard the U.S. ship.

The only English-speaking Nazi on the U-boat, German S.S. officer Heinrich Martin, insisted that the date was August 24, 1942, while he was being interrogated on the destroyer. He then pledged his allegiance to Adolf Hitler and demanded to see President Roosevelt — who died in 1945.

The source refused to say what the Navy has done with U-boat and crew.

Navy spokesmen declined repeated requests to be interviewed and threatened to "damage" one TV newsman who accused the Navy of a cover-up.

Paranormal researcher Art Garrett is one of several experts who have offered to help the Navy in its investigation.

He said: "If we really are dealing with a time warp then the portal from past to present must have opened twice — once to let the live submarine and crew into 1991 and again to let in the sunken U-boat.

"This is a most troubling development," he added. "If time has become so unstable as to let two submarines travel 49 years into the future, who's to say that other vehicles of mass destruction — such as the American warplane that dropped an atomic bomb on Hiroshima — won't follow as well?" ●

☐ *I have my own "time warp" stories and I can't resist ending my book with this one!*

No one can convince me the Weekly World News *is consistently making up this information, even for love or money! This is just one of many which eventually will prove to the world that life and its reality just ain't what you think it is! It's a 10+ to me and I wish to congratulate the* Weekly World *tabloid.*

ALIEN COUSINS?

I called Dr. Salter in North Dakota,
Who claims to have been in a UFO.
He and his son were escorted in,
And then examined from toe to chin!

Most of the Aliens were four feet tall,
They're a whiz at reading minds —
They seem to know just what you think,
Language won't matter — they use all kinds!

The Dr. knows that he feels great,
He's as healthy as a kid.
His hair and nails grow like young weeds,
It's not only minds they seem to feed!

The Salters know they've been programmed,
To remember, at the Aliens' command.
Their missing time was just a blank —
They couldn't recall at their demand.

If you think this unusual,
Don't kid yourself my dear —
Dr. Salter and his son John III
Feel there isn't too much to fear!

The Aliens have assured them
That they'll return some day.
That thought is glued right in their minds,
If you do research, it's what you'll find!

I had a case in Circleville, Ohio —
It happened in February, 1948.
Bruce Stevenson was fifty feet away,
When Aliens hovered over his driveway!

He was mentally told not to approach,
But they'd be back someday.
He knew when they came, he'd go with them,
Regardless of what might happen to him!

When I heard Dr. Salter's story,
I knew I'd heard it before —
I'm sure there are many people
Who've had Aliens by their door!

References

The following are a few of the books which have helped form my opinions on UFOs.

Adamski, George and Leslie, Desmond, *Flying Saucers Have Landed*
——— *Inside the Space Ships*
Allingham, Cedric, *Flying Saucers From Mars*
Anderson, Carl, *Two Nights to Remember*
Angelucci, Orfio, *The Secret of the Saucers*
Arnold, Kenneth, *The Coming of the Saucers*
Barker, Gray, *They Knew Too Much About Flying Saucers*
Beckley, Timothy, *MJ-12 and the Riddle of Hangar 18*
Bethurum, Truman, *Aboard a Flying Saucer*
Cerminera, Dr. Gina, *Many Lives Many Loves*
Citadel Press, Flying Saucer Review - World Round Up
Condon, Edward V., *Scientific Study of Unidentified Flying Objects*
Constance, Arthur, *The Inexplicable Sky*
von Daniken, Erich, *Gods From Outer Space*
——— *Chariots of the Gods*
Davis, Roy E., *This is Reality*
Drake, W. Raymond, *Gods and Spacemen of the Ancient West*
——— *Gods and Spacemen of the Ancient East*
——— *Gods and Spacemen of the Ancient Past*
Edwards, Frank, *Flying Saucers Serious Business*
Fawcett and Greenwood, *Clear Intent*
Fort, Charles, *Wild Talents*
——— *The Complete Works of Fort*
Fowler, Ramond E., *The Andreason Affair*
Fuller, Curtis G., *Proceedings of the First International Congress*
Fry, Dan, *The White Sands Incident*
——— *Alan's Message to Men*
Gibbons, Gavin, *The Coming of the Space Ships*
Girvan, Wavenery, *Flying Saucers and Common Sense*
Grewal, Badhu Balwart, *Reincarnation*
Hansen, L. Taylor, *He Walked the Americas*
Head and Cranston, *Reincarnation*
Herd, Gerald, *Is Another World Watching?*
Hind, Cynthia, *African Encounters*
Howe, Linda, *An Alien Harvest*
Hodson, Geoffrey, *Theosophy Answers Some Problems of Life*
Howard, Dana, *Over the Threshold*
Hopkins, Budd, *Intruders*
——— *Missing Time*
Hynek, Dr. Allen J. *The Hynek UFO Report*
——— *The UFO Experience*
Hynek and Vallee, *The Invisible College*
Jung, Carl G., *Man and His Symbols*
——— *Memories Dreams and Reflections*
——— *The Structure and Dynamics of the Psyche*
Jessup, M.K., *The Case for the UFO*
——— *UFO and the Bible*
——— *The UFO Annual*
——— *The Expanding Case for the UFO*

Keel, John A., *The Mothman Prophecies*
——— *Why UFOs*
——— *UFOs Operation Trojan Horse*
——— *Disneyland of the Gods*
Keyhoe, Donald E., *Flying Saucers are Real*
——— *Flying Saucers From Outer Space*
——— *The Flying Saucer Conspiracy*
——— *Aliens From Space*
——— *Flying Saucers Top Secret*
Kraspedon, Dino, *My Contact With Flying Saucers*
Layne, Meade, *The Ether Ship Mystery and Its Solution*
——— *The Coming of the Guardians*
Leek, Sybel, *The Second Chance Reincarnation*
Lorenzen, Coral and Jim, *Abducted*
——— *The Great Flying Saucer Hoax*
Lorenzen, Coral E., *Flying Saucers — Startling Evidence of the Invasions from Outer Space*
James, Trevor, *They Live in the Sky*
Matthews, Paul, *Beyond This Day*
Menzel, Donald, *Flying Saucers*
Meier, Eduard, Stevens, Elders and Welch, *Message from the Pleiades*
Meier, Eduard, and Stevens, *UFO Contact from the Pleiades, Vol. 1 and Vol. 2*
Michell, Aime, *The Truth about Flying Saucers*
——— *Flying Saucers and the Straight Line Mystery*
Mundo, Laura, *The Mundo UFO Report*
Probert, Mark, *The Magic Bag*
Roberts, Jane, *The Seth Material*
Ruppelt, Edward J., *The Report on Unidentified Flying Objects*
Reeves, Bryant and Helen, *The Flying Saucer Pilgrimage*
Reeves, Bryant, *The Advent of the Cosmic Viewpoint*
Sagnier, Thierry J., *The IFO Report*
Saturday Evening Post, *Adventures of the Mind*
Saunders, David R. and Roger Harkins, *UFOs Yes*
Scully, Frank, *Behind the Flying Saucers*
Shroeder and Ostrander, *Psychic Discoveries Behind the Iron Curtain*
Spencer, John W., *Limbo of the Lost*
——— *No Earthly Explanation*
——— *The UFO Year Book*
Spielberg, Steven S., *Close Encounters of the Third Kind*
Steiger, Brad, *Worlds Before Our Own*
——— *Gods of Acquarius*
Steiger, Francie, *Reflections from an Angel's Eye*
Stevens and Pallman, *UFO Contact From Planet Itibi-Ra*
Stevens and Denaerde, *UFO Contact From Planet Iarga*
Stevens and Sanchez, *UFO Contact From Reticulum*
——— *UFO Contact From Undersea*
Streiber, Whitley, *Communion*
——— *Transformation*
Van Tassel, George W., *I Rhode a Flying Saucer*
Vallee, Jacques and Janine, *Challenge to Science*
Williamson, George, *Other Tongues and Other Flesh*
Williamson, George and Bailey, *The Saucers Speak*
Wilkins, Harold T., *Flying Saucers Uncensored*
——— *Flying Saucers on the Attack*

Alphabetical Index

6-Year-Old Boy has 2 Hearts — *Sun* 168
11 Girls Give Birth to UFO Aliens — *Sun* 85
200-year-old Bullet Found in Baby's Chest — *Weekly World News* 139
600 Missing Kidnap Victims — *Weekly World News* 155
1956 Sighting on Sunbury Road — *Public Opinion* 27
2,000-year-old Mummy has Artificial Hip — *Sun* 110
5,000-year-old UFO Found in Red Sea — *Weekly World News* 100
10,000-year-old UFO Found in Jungle — *Weekly World News* 124

A 1962 Sighting in Columbus, Ohio 43
A Dream Come True 130
A UFO Sucked Us into the Sky — *Weekly World News* 151
A Visit with Rev. M.J. Miller 3
Abducted by Blue-Goggled Space Aliens — *National Examiner* 162
Alien Captured in Russia — *Sun* 174
Alien Found Alive in UFO Wreckage — *Sun* 84
Alien Repairs Crippled Balloon — *Weekly World News* 100
Aliens are Guests of US Government — *National Examiner* 86
Aliens Cured AIDS Case — *Weekly World News* 215
Aliens From Space 52
Aliens Plan to Take Over — *National Examiner* 63
Aliens Seek Human Blood and Body Parts — *Weekly World News* 153
Aliens Who Can Go Through Walls 10
Amazing UFO Photo — *Weekly World News* 234
An Introduction to Time Travel with Sally, Ray, Gidaon and Hodan 70
Ancient Video Set Used for Communication — *Weekly World News* 98
Angelhair at Marysville 26
Another Local Sighting in the '50s 30
Astrology Rules Our Lives — *Sun* 114
Astronomy and the Intergalactic Looking Society 20
Atlantis Found — *Weekly World News* 222
Atlantis Found 80 Miles From U.S. — *Sun* 221

Baby Bigfoot — *Sun* 197
Baby Born Speaking in Dead Dad's Voice — *Sun* 142
Baby Born Talking — *Sun* 136
Baby Born Talking, Describes Heaven — *Sun* 185
Baby Born Wearing Dead Dad's Ring — *Sun* 136
Baby Born With Artificial Heart — *Weekly World News* 147
Baby Boy Born With Wooden Leg — *Weekly World News* 135
Baby Girl Locates Fortune — *National Examiner* 144
Baby Glows in the Dark — *Weekly World News* 159
Baby's Father From Outer Space Says Scientist — *Weekly World News* 166
Beam From UFO Revives Dead Man — *National Examiner* 214
Beamed up by Giant UFO — *Weekly World News* 175
Bigfoot City — *Weekly World News* 204
Bigfoot Cured My Arthritis — *Sun* 207
Bigfoot Family Found — *Sun* 196
Bigfoot From Outer Space — *Weekly World News* 201
Bigfoot is My Buddy, Swears Hermit Trapper — *Sun* 202
Bigfoot Lives — *Sun* 194
Bigfoot Lives in China — *Weekly World News* 206
Bigfoot Rescues Boy From Alligator's Mouth — *Sun* 207
Bigfoot Saved Me From Being Buried Alive — *Sun* 205
Bigfoot Saved My Life — *Weekly World News* 200
Bigfoot Spooks Loggers — *National Examiner* 194
Bigfoot to the Rescue — *Weekly World News* 204
Bigfoot Tribe Kidnaps Five Kids — *Sun* 203

Bizarre Beings Lurk in New England Triangle — *Sun* 195
Bizarre Tales of 200 UFO Kidnap Victims — *National Examiner* 154
Bizarre Voices From Outer Space 64
Born Again — *Weekly World* 139
Born Wearing 3,000-year-old Anklet — *Weekly World News* 138
Born With Ring — *Weekly World News* 136
Boy Grows New Arm — *Sun* 115
Boy Thug Returns as Dog — *Weekly World News* 140
Bride and Groom Spend Honeymoon in UFO — *Sun* 162
Bruce Stevenson Learns about "Flying Saucers" 2
Buried at Sea in 1926 — *Weekly World News* 219

Call For Halt to Radio and TV Signals 64
Canals on Mars are Full of Fish — *Weekly World News* 192
Charlotte Moberly and Eleanor Jourdain 72
Chased by a UFO 40
Chariots of the Gods 45
Children Abducted by UFO — *Weekly World News* 151
Chinese Team Closing in on Bigfoot — *Weekly World News* 194
Christmas Message — *Weekly World News* 123
Civil Rights Leaders Reincarnated as Holocaust Victims? — *National Examiner* 133
Claims African Tribe Came From Mars — *Weekly World News* 192
Claims to Have Seen Bigfoot Skiing — *Sun* 206
Close Encounter That Changed a Man's Life — *Sun* 150
Coma Man Wakes Speaking Ancient Greek — *Weekly World News* 135
Cop Shoots Space Alien — *Weekly World News* 92
Cop Vanishes After Taking Alien's Picture — *National Examiner* 164
Cops Baffled by a Flying Banana — *Sun* 102
Couple Encounter UFO Alien Beings — *Sun* 153
Courageous Bigfoot Rescues Family — *National Examiner* 198
Crash Survivors Rescued by Bigfoot — *Weekly World News* 201
Crew Survives Fiery UFO Crash — *Weekly World News* 81
Crippled Starship Sends SOS to Earth — *Weekly World News* 62
Cross-Breeding 29

Dan Fry's Two-Way Trip to N.Y. 14
Dead Dad Reborn as Own Son — *Sun* 141
Dead Girl Reborn as Younger Sister — *National Examiner* 145
Dead Passengers and Crew Land in Brazil — *Weekly World News* 219
Death of a Soldier — *Weekly World News* 141
Detailed Account of Sighting 37
Devil's Triangle Shocker — *Weekly World News* 218
Did UFO Give Woman Cancer? — *National Examiner* 82
Doc Says Teen is Child of Space Aliens — *Sun* 237
Documentaries such as *Outer Space Connection* and *Chariots of the Gods* 48
Dr. J.B. Rhine — Mind Over Matter — *Public Opinion* 109
Drawing of UFO Found in Pyramid — *Weekly World News* 90

Elephants Snatched by UFO — *Weekly World News* 160
Enormous Crystal Blamed For Devil's Triangle — *National Examiner* 68
Era of Flying Saucers Started 40 Years Ago — *National Examiner* 81
ET Posse Corrals Bank Robbers — *National Examiner* 119
ET's Brought Bigfoot to Earth — *National Examiner* 116
Examiner World Exclusive — *National Examiner* 223
Excerpts From Cynthia's Letter 173

Fact, Not Fiction, Says of UFO — *New York Times* 103
Family Abducted by UFO — *Weekly World News* 159
Family Plucked Off Earth by UFO — *Weekly World News* 164
First Scientific Proof Astrology is For Real — *National Examiner* 111

Fishing Trawler Nets UFO — *Weekly World News* . . . 108
Frank Edwards and the News . . . 53
Furry Green Aliens Panic Golfers — *National Examiner* . . . 122
Furry Space Aliens Mated With Earth Women — *Weekly World News* . . . 194

George Van Tassel and the Spaceman . . . 10
Getting Down to Brass Tacks . . . 58
Ghastly Irish Triangle — *National Examiner* . . . 116
Giant Bigfoot Captured Alive — *Sun* . . . 199
Giant Bigfoot Sightings Alarm Indian Village — *National Examiner* . . . 200
Girl is Reincarnation of Movie Star — *Weekly World News* . . . 134
Girls Give Birth to UFO Babies — *Sun* . . . 176
Glowing Space Alien in His Bedroom — *National Examiner* . . . 113
Government Captures UFOs — *National Examiner* . . . 122
Government Blasted for Failure to Probe UFO Kidnappings — *National Examiner* . . . 150
Grandmother Made Blind by Aliens — *Weekly World News* . . . 173
Green Aliens in Spaceship Sucked Me Up — *National Examiner* . . . 158

Hairy Spacemen Kidnap Cop — *Weekly World News* . . . 198
Ham Radio Operators Hear Secret Calls to Mission Control — *Sun* . . . 93
Homeless Boy is a Space Alien — *Weekly World News* . . . 83
Hot News From TASS: Tourists in Space — *New York Times* . . . 103
Housewife Videotapes Outer-Space Show — *Weekly World News* . . . 117
Hubble Telescope Shows UFO Fleet — *Sun* . . . 235
Hubby Fined $110 For Killing Wife — *Weekly World News* . . . 172
Huge Angels Seen in Space — *Weekly World News* . . . 91
Human Skeleton on the Moon — *Weekly World News* . . . 121
Hynek and His Debunking Service . . . 52
Hypnosis . . . 28
Hypnotized Time Travelers Discover Future Paradise — *Weekly World News* . . . 76

I Believe . . . 60
I Came Face to Face With Bigfoot — *Weekly World News* . . . 203
I Found Four Bodies After UFO Crash — *Sun* . . . 101
I Killed a Bigfoot — *Weekly World News* . . . 197
I Talked, Ate and Slept With Bigfoot — *Sun* . . . 202
I Took a Ride on a Starship — *Weekly World News* . . . 168
I was Billy the Kid — *Sun* . . . 137
I was Taken to Heaven in a UFO — *Weekly World News* . . . 182
In Defense of the Grocery Store Tabloid . . . 80
In Defense of George . . . 16
Incredible Powers From Aliens — *National Examiner* . . . 120
Is Boy Reincarnation of Robert E. Lee? — *Weekly World News* . . . 137

Jack W. Grant and "The Saucers" . . . 13
Jack and George . . . 4
John and the UFO . . . 33
John's Dream — Rescuing Souls — *Public Opinion* . . . 183
Jungle Tribe Worships Face on Mars — *Weekly World News* . . . 190

Kentucky's Little Green Men . . . 20
Killer Cloud Melts City — *Weekly World News* . . . 235

Leading Scientists Raised 25 People From the Dead — *Weekly World News* . . . 213
Letter From Mabel Trautman . . . 112
Letter From Russia Confirms Discovery — *Weekly World News* . . . 94
Libyan Targets Buzzed by UFO — *Weekly World News* . . . 98
Life After Death Proof — *Weekly World News* . . . 185
Living Two Lives — *Weekly World News* . . . 140
Loses Face — *Weekly World News* . . . 175

Lost City Powered by Crystals? — *National Examiner* . . . 118
Loving Old Couple Experience Paradise — *Weekly World News* . . . 184

Machine to Recall Past Lives — *Weekly World News* . . . 146
Magic Ray Cures 22 People — *Weekly World News* . . . 106
Major Ruppelt — "Blue Book" and the Scoutmaster . . . 53
Man Burned by UFO — *National Examiner* . . . 120
Man Snatched From Cabin by Space Aliens — *National Examiner* . . . 161
Mark Probert and the "Inner Circle" . . . 6
Maybe You Were There in a Previous Life . . . 59
Meeting Edna . . . 3
Memories of Zachary Stoddard — *Sun* . . . 145
Minister Ties UFOs to Bible — *Columbus Dispatch* . . . 109
Moon Craters and the Moon Bridge . . . 20
More Speakers and More Ideas . . . 59
Mother Seduced by Alien Toy Boys — *National Examiner* . . . 87
Mr. X and the Captain of a Spaceship . . . 12
Murdered Child Reborn — *National Examiner* . . . 143
My Interview with Henry — *Public Opinion* . . . 110
My Introduction to UFOs . . . 2
My Views in 1962 . . . 43
Mysteries on Bigfoot — *Weekly World News* . . . 195
Mysterious City Found Near Face on Mars — *National Examiner* . . . 193
Mystery Crystal Baffles Scientists — *Sun* . . . 67

Nazi Astronauts Return to Earth — *Weekly World News* . . . 126
Nazi U-Boat Captured by U.S. Navy Ship — *Weekly World News* . . . 238
New Arm and Leg — *Weekly World News* . . . 114
New Galaxy Shaped Like Fetus — *Weekly World News* . . . 36
NICAP . . . 15
Noah's Ark Did Not Land on Mount Ararat — *National Examiner* . . . 108
Noah's Ark Found? — *Weekly World News* . . . 87
November, 1896 Sightings — *Public Opinion* . . . 8

Ohio Woman Reborn After 76-Year Interval — *Weekly World News* . . . 132
Olan Moore — Leta Koon . . . 29
One Way Trip? . . . 14
Only the Pentagon Knows . . . 26
Out of Body Traveler Visits 5 Cities Within Seconds — *Weekly World News* . . . 113

Pacochea . . . 132
Passenger Train Vanishes in Tunnel — *Weekly World News* . . . 76
Pattern of Rebirth Shown . . . 7
Peter Hurkos and the UFO . . . 17
Phantom Squadron Prowls Sky Over Devil's Triangle — *Weekly World News* . . . 220
Phone Line to Heaven — *Sun* . . . 180
Pigs in Space? — *Weekly World News* . . . 101
Pilot Enters Heaven During Devil's Triangle Flight — *Weekly World News* . . . 182
President to Meet with UFO Abduction Victim — *Sun* . . . 236
Probe Finds Face on Venus — *Weekly World News* . . . 188
Probe Finds Face on Mars — *Weekly World News* . . . 188
Proof ETs Making Test-Tube Half-Breed Babies — *National Examiner* . . . 84

Ranchers Kill Monster From Prehistoric Past — *National Examiner* . . . 208
Ray from UFO Cures 22 — *Weekly World News* . . . 223
Reincarnation of Chieftain's Son — *Weekly World News* . . . 134
Reincarnation Nightmare — *Weekly World News* . . . 144
Reincarnation or the Recycling of Souls . . . 130
Reincarnation Shocker — *Weekly World News* . . . 59
Religion . . . 44

Reporter Believes Saucers Were Nearby — *Public Opinion* . . . 69
Rescued by Supermen — *Weekly World News* . . . 216
Russian Cosmonauts Return to Earth Years Younger — *Weekly World News* . . . 221
Russian Doctors Deliver Alien Baby — *Weekly World News* . . . 118

Sally — Reborn as Ruth . . . 143
Satellite Orbiting Earth — *Weekly World News* . . . 65
Savage Tribe Ate 6 Space Aliens — *Weekly World News* . . . 92
Schoolboy Claims UFO Aliens Cured Acne — *National Examiner* . . . 217
Scientist Finds Evidence of Visitor From 2081 AD — *Weekly World News* . . . 66
Scientists Can Hardly Believe Their Eyes — *Weekly World News* . . . 95
Scientists Examine Bigfoot Baby — *Weekly World News* . . . 117
Scientists Were Wrong . . . 63
Screaming Christians — *Weekly World News* . . . 73
Seeing Through Metal Etc. — *Public Opinion* . . . 212
Shipwrecked Fisherman Gets Younger Since Rescue in Devil's Triangle — *Weekly World* . . . 220
Shipwrecked with an Alien UFO Pilot — *Sun* . . . 115
Six Oaks and the UFOs . . . 21
Skydivers Disappear into Thin Air — *Sun* . . . 156
Slave Traders From Outer Space — *Weekly World News* . . . 157
Small Town Named UFO Capital — *National Examiner* . . . 102
Soldiers Discover Living Breathing Baby Bigfoot — *Weekly World News* . . . 196
SOS From Dying Planet — *Weekly World News* . . . 61
Soviets Blast Spaceship — *Weekly World News* . . . 65
Soviets Capture UFO Captain — *Weekly World News* . . . 104
Space Alien Cures Dying Child — *Weekly World News* . . . 218
Space Aliens Cure Teen's Muscular Dystrophy — *Weekly World News* . . . 215
Space Alien Docs Healed My Cancer — *Weekly World News* . . . 220
Space Aliens Examine Kids — *Weekly World News* . . . 168
Space Aliens Fed Farmer — *Weekly World News* . . . 91
Space Aliens Use Spheres of Light to Spy on Us — *Weekly World News* . . . 96
Space Creatures Seen on Earth — *Weekly World News* . . . 36
Space Mummies Found — *Weekly World News* . . . 94
Space Music Draws UFOs — *National Examiner* . . . 55
Space Probe Records God's Voice — *Weekly World News* . . . 180
Space Probe Sends Photos of Messages Carved on Martian Surface — *Weekly World* . . . 189
Space Probes Take Photos of Heaven — *Sun* . . . 181
Space Rainbows May Be Source Of UFOs — *Sun* . . . 96
Space Shuttle Attacked By 200 Ft. UFO — *Weekly World News* . . . 89
Spacemen Kidnapped My Science Teacher — *Weekly World News* . . . 155
Starship's SOS Stuns Scientists — *Weekly World News* . . . 62
Starving Hunters Rescued by Gentle Giants — *Weekly World News* . . . 199
Stone Face Found in Antarctica — *Weekly World News* . . . 191
Super Jets Travel Back in History — *Weekly World News* . . . 73
Swiss Astronomer Claims to Have Received Moon Message . . . 64

Thanks to W. Raymond Drake . . . 45
The 1950 Ohio State–Michigan Game . . . 9
The Alien at Saranac Lake . . . 48
The Andreason Affair . . . 10
The Anglican Priest From New Guinea . . . 29
The Army Chaplin . . . 27
The Betty and Barney Hill Movie . . . 42
The Bumblebee Can Fly . . . 47
The Children at Johnstown . . . 32
The Condon Report . . . 38
The Devil's Triangle — *Weekly World News* . . . 222
The Dublin Episode . . . 34
The Grain Buyer from California . . . 18
The Jimmy Flynn Story . . . 49

The Little People . . . 39
The Lunatic Fringe . . . 40
The Message From Bala Krishnan . . . 44
The Mexican and the Spaceman . . . 5
The Missing Professor . . . 46
The Mundo UFO Report . . . 41
The Pilot of a Spaceship — 1958 . . . 28
The Reeves Come to Columbus . . . 5
The Reincarnation of Natalie Wood — *Sun* . . . 146
The Truman Bethurum Story . . . 13
The UFO and the Computer . . . 39
The World is a Gigantic Crystal . . . 68
The Vanishing ETs — *Weekly World News* . . . 89
Third Face in Space Found on the Moon — *Weekly World News* . . . 189
Those Gulf Breeze Sightings — *National Examiner* . . . 105
Those Trinidad UFO Pictures . . . 47
Time Warp Plane Baffles Scientists — *Weekly World News* . . . 75
Time Warp Story to Dumfound — *Weekly World News* . . . 75
Top Scientist Finds Proof of Time Travel — *Weekly World News* . . . 69
Tossed Back for Being Too Fat — *Sun* . . . 156
Town Found on Venus — *Weekly World News* . . . 193
Travis Walton and the Woodcutters . . . 46
Tribe Eats Spaceman — *Weekly World News* . . . 98
Two Fishermen From Mississippi . . . 158
Two-Headed Bigfoot Terrifies Town — *Sun* . . . 194
Two "Lost" Hours Found Four Years Later — *National Examiner* . . . 165
Two Men Who Sailed into the Past — *Weekly World News* . . . 74
Two-month-old Baby Speaks 8 Languages — *Weekly World News* . . . 133
Two UFOs and a Headache . . . 12

U.S. Invaded by UFOs 100 Years Ago — *National Examiner* . . . 8
U.S. Pilots Flying Captured UFOs — *National Examiner* . . . 125
UFO Aliens Rape Our Women — *National Examiner* . . . 88
UFO Aliens are Living Under Pacific Ocean — *National Examiner* . . . 83
UFO Aliens Saved Burning Barn — *Sun* . . . 90
UFO Aliens Kidnap 1,400 Farmers — *National Examiner* . . . 152
UFO Aliens Kidnap Bride — *Sun* . . . 161
UFO Aliens Kidnap Couple — *National Examiner* . . . 167
UFO Aliens Kidnap Farmer's Sheepdog — *National Examiner* . . . 157
UFO Aliens Steal 4-1/2 Hours of Teens' Lives — *National Examiner* . . . 163
UFOs Aliens Taught Indian Medicine Woman — *National Examiner* . . . 67
UFOs Are Really Time Travelers — *Sun* . . . 72
UFO at Lockbourne Airbase? . . . 31
UFO Baby Reads Mom's Mind — *National Examiner* . . . 125
UFO Baby Speaks at 3 Months — *Sun* . . . 99
UFO Bases in the Rocky Mountains — *National Examiner* . . . 86
UFO Beams Corpse into Sky — *Weekly World News* . . . 214
UFO Buzzes Jet — *Weekly World News* . . . 166
UFO Contact from the Pleiades . . . 51
UFO Dentists Fixed Our Teeth — *Sun* . . . 99
UFO Docs Save Girl's Leg Aboard Spaceship — *Sun* . . . 107
UFO Dogfight — *Weekly World News* . . . 123
UFO Expert Says Mass Sightings Were Genuine — *National Examiner* . . . 233
UFO Flies Out of the Ocean — *Weekly World News* . . . 51
UFO Found on Playground — *Weekly World News* . . . 93
UFOs in Time of Catastrophe . . . 41
UFO Invasions . . . 64
UFO Kidnap — *Weekly World News* . . . 154
UFO Landing Bases Discovered Worldwide — *National Examiner* . . . 113
UFO Led Moses and His People Out of Egypt — *Sun* . . . 88
UFO Returns Coeds Kidnapped in 1966 — *Sun* . . . 237

UFO Ride at Carnival — *Weekly World News* 169
UFO Scuttlebutt 22
UFO Seen Hovering in Scene From 1928 Movie — *Weekly World News* 86
UFO Ship Saves Climbers — *Sun* 213
UFO Wreck in 1947 — *Weekly World News* 97
UFO Veggies — *Sun* 126
UFO Rescues Girl — *National Examiner* 216
UFO Snatches Plane, Then Disappears — *Sun* 170
UFOs and Dr. M.K. Jessup 19
UFOs and the Ostrich People — *Sun* 172
UFOs are Bugging My Brain — *Sun* 11
UFOs are Not From Other Planets — *Sun* 238
UFOs are Raping Earth Girls — *Sun* 171
UFOs Come From Heaven — *Sun* 183
UFOs Have Abducted at Least 2,300 People — *Sun* 158
UFOs Helped Rescue 3 Trapped Whales — *Sun* 217
UFOs Kidnap Earth Women to Breed Half-alien Children — *National Examiner* 170
UFOs Killed All the Dinosaurs — *National Examiner* 208
UFOs Stealing Islands? — *Weekly World News* 124
UFOs Terrorize Russian Town — *Sun* 106
UFOs Watched Japs Bomb Pearl Harbor — *Sun* 233
Uncanny Happenings 34
Underwater UFO Base Found in Pacific — *Weekly World News* 127
Unidentified Flying Objects 31
Unusual Life Forms 35
US Air Force Test-Flying Captured UFO — *National Examiner* 82

Vampires From Space Drank Our Blood — *Weekly World News* 121
Voyager 2 Photographs "Identical" Face on Neptune — *Weekly World News* 190

World Wave of Sightings Sparks Secret Superpower Treaty — *Weekly World News* 60
We Entertain Desmond Leslie 5
What Happened to Dr. Hynek? 19
Woman Believes She Receives Alien Messages 64
Woman 'Dies' and Goes to Heaven — *National Examiner* 184
Woman Kidnapped by Alien — *National Examiner* 152
Woman Recalls UFO Abduction — *National Examiner* 163
World's First Space Alien Interview — *Weekly World News* 95
Writer Believes She Saw Her First Saucer — *Public Opinion* 11

You be the Judge 22

Poems
- Alien Cousins? 240
- Angels 186
- Crystals 128
- John and the Oxen 148
- Kidnapping 177
- Looking Back 56
- The Custodian at Tokyo Computek 225
- Those Carved Faces 209
- Time Warps 77
- UFOs 24

THE LIFE HUNTERS

They sail our skys,

They probe the depths,

Our oceans open doors to craft

Which disappear within a bosom so foreign

Man cannot understand how this can be.

He's forgotten life must adjust

To that which he's created.

And as the search goes on and on

Life after life,

Body after body,

No matter how many times,

Or what those forms may be —

Eventually man will sail the skys

And understand the ocean depths,

And finally find those many mansions

Which have been created by

The God who lives within us all.

Lillian Crowner Desguin
February, 1992